Arthur Miller

D0305833

Arthur Miller

1962–2005

CHRISTOPHER BIGSBY

Weidenfeld & Nicolson
LONDON

First published in Great Britain in 2011
by Weidenfeld & Nicolson

1 3 5 7 9 10 8 6 4 2

© Christopher Bigsby 2011

All rights reserved. No part of this publication may be
reproduced, stored in a retrieval system, or transmitted,
in any form or by any means, electronic, mechanical,
photocopying, recording or otherwise, without the prior
permission of both the copyright owner and the above publisher.

The right of Christopher Bigsby to be identified as the author
of this work has been asserted in accordance with the
Copyright, Designs and Patents Act 1988.

A CIP catalogue record for this book
is available from the British Library.

ISBN-13 978 0 297 86315 1

Typeset by Input Data Services Ltd,
Bridgwater, Somerset

Printed and bound in the UK by
CPI Mackays, Chatham, Kent

The Orion Publishing Group's policy is to use papers that
are natural, renewable and recyclable products and made
from wood grown in sustainable forests. The logging and
manufacturing processes are expected to conform to
the environmental regulations of the country of origin.

Weidenfeld & Nicolson

The Orion Publishing Group Ltd
Orion House
5 Upper Saint Martin's Lane
London, WC2H 9EA

An Hachette UK Company

LIBRARIES NI	
C700561347	
RONDO	16/02/2011
812.52	£ 30.00
OREACH	

As ever, for Pam

CONTENTS

PREFACE

The first volume of this biography ended in 1962. Some reviewers were baffled. Why end halfway through Arthur Miller's life? Was it not a way of evading difficult questions about his Down's syndrome son, Daniel, born five years later? Did I not feel that his work for International PEN was worth exploring? Others thought it a sensible point to end. After all, were his major plays not now behind him? Was his relationship with Marilyn Monroe, which in the eyes of one or two was his principal claim to fame, not now at an end? The answer was more banal. The book was a third of a million words long. If I had tried to extend it to 2005 it would have stood at some risk of damaging those who tried to lift it.

In fact, the second half of Miller's life was packed with interest, and a second volume already existed in draft. In 1962, a further eighteen plays lay ahead (including his third-longest-running – *The Price* – his fourth-longest running – *After the Fall* – and the Olivier-award-winning *Broken Glass*), as did five films, a novella and a cluster of short stories. Alongside these were collections of essays and the books he produced with his wife, the Magnum photographer Inge Morath.

As the House Un-American Activities Committee pointed out in 1956, Arthur Miller had been an inveterate signer of petitions and letters of protest, but with the 1960s he moved more directly into the political arena. The Vietnam War became a central concern – a crusade, even. He flew to Paris to negotiate with the North Vietnamese, attended one of the first teach-ins on the war, became a regular figure on the public platform at protest rallies. He campaigned for Senator Eugene McCarthy. In 1968 he went to the infamous National Democratic Convention in Chicago as a delegate and witnessed the fallibility of the democratic process. Beyond that, he became President of International PEN, in which role he would work for the release of imprisoned writers around the world, even as the CIA attempted to penetrate the organization, almost certainly having a hand in his election.

He fought against censorship, lobbied on behalf of writers. He met the leading political figures of the time, including Mikhail Gorbachev, Nelson

Mandela and Fidel Castro. Awarded international prizes, he seized the opportunity to make contentious public statements. In Spain, he spoke of the evils of the Spanish Civil War. In accepting the Jerusalem Prize, he attacked aspects of Israeli policy. Invited to Washington to deliver the Jefferson Lecture, he mocked politicians, many of whom were in the audience.

If Arthur Miller was shaped by his times, then he equally set himself to shape them, frequently leaving his desk to take up the issues of the day. Until 1962 he had seldom been abroad. Now, married to Inge Morath, he became a world traveller and his work reflected this fact. He set plays in France, Czechoslovakia and South America. He published books with Inge as they explored Russia and China together. He directed plays in Europe and Asia. He also became one of the first American dramatists to engage with the Holocaust, an implacable fact which he saw as raising questions not only about the country that initiated, planned and enacted it (and he remained suspicious of a united Germany) but also about human nature. His notes are scattered with references to Cain and Abel, to the first murder as brother turned against brother, creating a template. An atheist, he remained fascinated with the evident need to create a God as moral sanction, even though religion lay at the heart of so many conflicts. This, in turn, took him back to his Jewish identity, always problematic and always there.

Broken marriages always offer their fascinations, less because truth emerges at the breaking point than because they expose emotions normally kept under cover or control. In Miller's case there was another reason, as his story, for a while, became entangled with that of the most famous woman in America. Although his marriage to Marilyn Monroe lasted not much more than four years, and their relationship a decade, inevitably it draws the eye. What to make, then, of a happy marriage that lasted forty years?

There is a reason for the last chapter of Volume One ending with Inge Morath and the first chapter of this book beginning with her. I deliberately rewind the narrative to the beginning of that new story in his life. Inge was his lodestone. She was an independent person with a career of her own, but, unlike Marilyn, without a sense of dependency, a fact that she thought central to the success of their relationship. She transformed Miller, opening doors that had been closed, embodying as she did a European history that could not be wished away by American pragmatism. She was a partner in every sense. When she died, he was distraught. Intensely lonely, at the end of his life he found a young companion, a June and January romance that potentially leaves the outsider and the family alike uneasy, though for different reasons. She was, after all, young enough to be his granddaughter. There is no doubt, though, that he found consolation and companionship with her, and, when he fell ill, support, though in his last days he made his way back to his family and to the house in rural Connecticut he had left only a few weeks earlier when his deteriorating health made hospital a necessity. This was where he had been happy and where he had written all the plays, films and stories discussed here.

A major theme of this volume is the critical disdain with which he was increasingly treated in his own country. For some thirty years he suffered attacks from those who chose to see him as a relic of another age, some critics even returning to his plays of the 1940s and 50s to find there less classics of the American theatre than flawed efforts by a man whose reputation had outstripped his abilities. His plays of the 1970s, 80s and 90s had short runs, closing after a handful of performances. As a consequence Miller suffered from depressions, not clinical or lasting but a response to the virulence of the attacks.

Balancing this, however, was an international enthusiasm for his work that, far from slackening over the years, intensified. Awards proliferated. An unproduced work from the 1930s (*The Golden Years*) was rescued from oblivion and performed for radio, television and the stage. Other older plays were revived, including his first, failed, work, *The Man Who Had All the Luck*. His new works were embraced and celebrated. Alongside Samuel Beckett, he was seen as the most significant playwright of the twentieth century. In Germany, productions multiplied. In Eastern and Central Europe he seemed an accurate reader of the modern sensibility. In Israel he held the record for the longest-running play. In China he seemed to speak to their own situation.

Why should this be? Is it a matter of productions, fashion, taste, national predilections? Does theatre, perhaps, play a different role in different cultures? Miller had his own theories. He felt the lack, in his own country, of a theatre he could call his own, the kind of subsidized theatre that was the backbone of European drama. He had had high hopes for Lincoln Center but they had been quickly dispelled. In fact, for rather too long he clung to his belief that Broadway was the ultimate test, even as he denounced Broadway producers, the economics of the Great White Way and the peremptory power of the *New York Times*, cultural gatekeeper, in a position to determine whether a play ran or closed, whether an out-of-town production would move to New York or not. He was not alone in this. Edward Albee persevered too long in believing that Broadway was his natural home, eventually reconquering it by way of European, regional and Off Broadway theatres. Sam Shepard, by contrast, kept his distance.

In the end, perhaps, it is impossible to be sure. But by the end of his life Miller saw things begin to change. The film of *The Crucible*, starring his son-in-law to be Daniel Day-Lewis, was a significant success, the best film of any of his plays. *Focus*, the novel he had written when he despaired of making it as a playwright, now found its way to the screen. In its 1997–8 season the small Off Broadway Signature Theatre, under its director James Houghton, devoted a year to his work, including both an early radio play and the premiere of *Mr Peters' Connections*. There were major revivals of his earlier work (Brian Dennehy in *Death of a Salesman*, Liam Neeson in *The Crucible*). His final two plays (*Resurrection Blues* and *Finishing the Picture*) both opened in regional theatres.

Once Miller wrote, somewhat petulantly, to the editor of the *New York Times*, complaining that its second-string reviewer had been assigned to review his new play. When he died, the same paper assigned his obituary to a second-string reviewer along with a staff writer. While outlining his career, they suggested that his reputation would hang on a handful of plays, that he had not had a solid critical and commercial success in nearly forty years, that he was 'probably the least subtle' of America's major playwrights and that his moral conclusions often 'glare from his plays like neon signs in a diner window'.[1] His successes outside America had evidently passed them by.

As I write this, it is sixty-six years since the failure of *The Man Who Had All the Luck* on Broadway. As the second decade of the twenty-first century begins, Miller's plays are being staged everywhere from Broadway to theatres around the world. When they were first performed they had often seemed tied to the moment, responding to the pressures of the times. He, however, always insisted that he wrote metaphors rather than plays, and that is why they continue to live on the pulse, constantly reinvented, earthed in new realities. At a time of economic collapse and corporate corruption *All My Sons*, and *The American Clock*, seemed new-minted. But it is not a case of fortuitous echoes. The relevance of Arthur Miller's plays derives from the fact that fathers continue to wish to live through their sons, that individuals are still invited to bow to arbitrary orthodoxies, that we all recognize and share the desire to leave some trace of our passing and are tempted to declare our own innocence even if it be at the price of declaring the guilt of others. In the last decades of Miller's life his plays explored the nature of reality, the degree to which performance becomes a substitute for being, the extent to which what was once apparently so fixed has turned out to be arbitrary and evanescent.

In his last plays he looked back through his life, trying to make sense of it. A biography does no less, except that it is the nature of a life that it can never be contained within the covers of a book. If it could, it would not be worth writing about. In his review of a biography of August Strindberg Miller praised it for its refusal 'to regard the writer's novels, poems, essays and plays as "nothing but" some kind of barely disguised reportage of his life experiences … Everyone knew who his characters "really were", but the gossip is gone and his art, in the end, is what endures.'[2] At the same time he endorsed Ibsen's claim that his true autobiography was to be found in his plays. It is inevitable, perhaps, to see the traces of Miller's life in his work. In the end, though, he who in truth regarded all biography as a species of gossip, is immune. It is indeed the work that endures.

1

NEW BEGINNINGS

I feel strongly that Oliver Wendell Holmes was right. Not to share in the activity and passion of your time is to count as not having lived ... St Augustine said ... 'Never fight evil as if it were something that arose totally outside of yourself. *Revd William Sloane Coffin*[1]

The plays are my autobiography. I can't write plays that don't sum up where I am. I'm in all of them. I don't know how else to go about writing. *Arthur Miller*[2]

On a hot 1st of July in 1960 a thirty-seven-year-old Austrian woman set out from New York on her first trip across the United States. She was heading for Reno, Nevada, but followed a red crayon line drawn on her map by a friend that would take her on a southern route via Memphis and Albuquerque. With eighteen days to go before her assignment was due to begin she and her companion decided to take their time and see something of the country. They were both photographers. Her name was Ingeborg Morath (pronounced Mor-at), while her companion was her long-term lover, the fifty-one-year-old French photographer Henri Cartier-Bresson. She had worked as his assistant in the early 1950s before, in 1955, becoming a full member of the Magnum photographic agency. He had proposed marriage to her, despite himself being married. Inge declined. 'Darling,' she later told a friend, the writer Honor Moore, 'some people are lovers and some people are husbands. Don't marry anyone unless you want to live with them.' She had had both, a passionate lover in Spain, who had also proposed marriage, and a less than passionate husband in England.

Cartier-Bresson had begun as a painter, a friend of the Surrealists, but had turned to photography in the early 1930s. He subsequently met and worked with a Hungarian photographer called André Friedmann, who changed his name to Robert Capa. Later the two of them, together with others, co-founded Magnum, the photographic agency (named after the bottle of champagne kept in their office). Also in the thirties Cartier-Bresson, a one-time enthusiast for the Communist Party, co-directed an anti-fascist film called *Victoire de la vie*, to raise funds for the Republican medical services in the Spanish Civil War. During the Second World War he spent three years in a prisoner-of-war camp, finally escaping and working for the underground, retrieving the Leica camera he had buried and photographing events in the last years of the war.

In Paris in the late 1940s, Inge had spent evenings with Capa and Cartier-Bresson when they met Sartre and Simone de Beauvoir. She found herself part of the intellectual world, going to galleries and the theatre, seeing a production of *The Crucible* by a man who was no more than a name to her and who lived on a distant continent. Then, as a photographer, she visited a country that had always fascinated her – Spain. The result was a book, *Guerre à la Tristesse*, published in 1955 (the English-language edition appeared the following year under the title *Festival in Pamplona*). She photographed the bullfighter Antonio Ordoñez, celebrated by Hemingway, as he prepared for a fight – intensely masculine but in his ornate clothes and with an attentive dresser, touched with the feminine, like many of the best actors from Olivier to Brando to Malkovich.

She went to Spain first in 1953, with Cartier-Bresson, and then in 1954 on her own. There she took a picture of Picasso's sister and her family and in return was given a Picasso drawing that a decade later would hang in her new home in Roxbury, Connecticut. Susequently she would work in Iran, Mexico, South America and South Africa, but confessed that certain countries always exerted a particular fascination: Spain, Russia, China – all countries, she explained, whose influence extended beyond their borders, mother countries. And it was writers and artists, dancers, sculptors and actors, who eased her into these cultures.

From the end of the 1950s, she found herself working more often in the United States. The first photographs she took there have something of that awe which struck many European visitors. They feature not simply skyscrapers, but the different architectures juxtaposed seemingly randomly, Gothic church spires seen against angular office buildings. There is often a surreal quality to her images, the most striking example her picture of a llama, its head sticking out of the rear window of a car in Times Square. A photograph of a woman in a beauty parlour with a man, the fingers of one hand on her forehead and the other a blur, is called Perfect Eyebrow but is disturbingly reminiscent of Buñuel's *Un Chien Andalou* in which a woman's eyeball is slit with a cut-throat razor. In another picture women in fur-lined, figure-hugging costumes skate on the ice inside a bank on Madison Avenue.

Inge spoke of the advantage of having begun her career when she did, of inhabiting a less photographed world in which the image had not become as dominant as it later would. There were few photographic archives then, little sense that photographs belonged in books or on gallery walls. Their claim on attention was as a bringer of news, and the photo story dominated magazines which offered to put the world, suitably burnished on high gloss paper, in the hands of an awed and space-bound reader.

She was, she said, usually labelled a photojournalist. In many ways it is a misleading description, but one accepted by all members of Magnum. She recalled Cartier-Bresson's explanation for this:

> May I tell you the reason for this label? As well as the name of the inventor? It was Robert Capa. When I had my first show in the Museum of Modern Art in New York in 1948 he warned me: 'Watch out what label they put on you. If you become known as a surrealist (surrealism is after all the concept of life that probably influenced me the most – much less so than surrealist painting) then you will be considered precious and confidential. Just go on doing what you want to do anyway but call yourself a photojournalist, which puts you into direct contact with everything that is going on in the world. So let it be, Henri.'

Cartier-Bresson and Inge travelled as photojournalists in 1960 on assignment to photograph a film then being shot in the Nevada desert. Having seen nothing beyond New York and Los Angeles, for Inge the journey was her first venture into the heart of America. Together they travelled to Gettysburg and Harper's Ferry and on via the Blue Ridge Mountains to the small town of Asheville, North Carolina, where Thomas Wolfe had been born, an author whose work she knew and admired. Then it was on to Oak Ridge, and its Atomic Energy Museum, to Memphis and Little Rock, where American troops had had to defend the right of black children to attend a formerly all-white school. Inge noted: 'The guide says it is called the city of roses and that there are a couple of things to see but in our minds this is the symbol of racial hatred ... Do they dislike our cameras? Maybe they pay no attention, but their town is stamped and they too and one cannot like Little Rock anymore and just visit it and forget it.'[3]

For Inge the trip was her first experience of hamburgers. She had never before encountered drive-ins, motels, slot machines, Main Street America, in-room coffee machines, shoulder pads, the open road where cars

> run like hurried beetles, stuffed with their passengers, men and women and children, with suitcases and paper bags, with beds and blankets. Sometimes a couple of naked feet stick out of a window to cool off, sometimes a tired arm stretches against the cool wind. There are the carelessly strung villages, the lonely trade posts announcing gasoline and Indian curios and coffee and hamburgers ... The car makes its way past Española into the forests west of

Taos [New Mexico] ... There is a loneliness now in front of us, dust weaves a trail behind the car as we wind our way ... Beyond Albuquerque, going west, signposts start to announce the last place to get gasoline before the desert starts, the last place to buy Indian headdresses and Squaw moccasins, the last place to see live snakes for free ... The noises of men die slowly but as our car rolls over the continental division we know that the waters we will drink from now on will belong to rivers that in their turn belong to the Pacific and not anymore to our grey Atlantic and the noises of animals have taken over. The night is theirs.[4]

Inge wrote this just three years after Jack Kerouac's *On the Road* appeared and it is a reminder that before she was a photographer she was a writer, and alongside the photographs she took on this journey she kept a journal that is a record of her induction into a country that would become her own. Sometimes she is in awe of what she sees, sometimes disapproving. Las Vegas, which 'receives you, wearing stage make-up in full daylight and with the sophistication of a ham actor in an ambulant road show', is a 'perishable world', which she characterizes as having 'grown out of barbaric desires to gamble and gain and forget'.[5]

They arrived in Reno on the evening of 17 July into 'a world so different from the loneliness of the trip, the world of a movie being started'.[6] At this point Inge Morath's journal ends. It would not be published until after her death, when it appeared with an afterword by her husband, Arthur Miller, who had first glimpsed her in the coffee shop of the Mapes Hotel, where most people involved in the film *The Misfits* were based. Having by now seen both *Death of a Salesman* and *The Crucible* she expected a solemn man. Instead she encountered him as he swam in a pool, telling what she described as 'a very funny story, and very long',[7] a story that would later be published as *Fame*. Beyond that, he made little impact. 'Arthur was always busy trying to get Marilyn to the set or from the set, so he was very remote. He came to dinner with a group of us – once. Otherwise he had to wait in the hotel. So I didn't really get an impression of him as a person. Everybody was working quite hard. We were working from morning to night, for ten days or so.' She was busy taking photographs, unfazed by the celebrity status of those she met, though Clark Gable did inscribe the back of her collar: 'Clark Gable, Reno, Nevada, July 21st, 1960'.[8] On his advice she later had it embroidered, for fear it would wash out.

Though she seems not to have noticed, it was in the heat of the Nevada desert that Arthur Miller's second marriage, to Marilyn Monroe, was turning to ice. It was a film whose climax envisaged the possibility of an older man and a younger woman finding happiness together. The very title, however, had proved ironic as actors and crew watched the dissolution of a relationship that had always seemed unlikely and that would finally prove unsustainable. For the most part, though, this was lost on Inge Morath, whose present commission gave her the opportunity not only to see more of her adopted country but to meet and photograph some of America's leading actors, including the most iconic, Marilyn Monroe. She photographed Miller but found it difficult to persuade them to pose together. The playwright-turned-screenwriter was amusing but she had no thoughts of a new relationship. Besides, Miller was married, if only just.

She already knew the film's director, John Huston, from working on the set of *Moulin Rouge* in London and on *The Unforgiven*, filmed in Durango, New Mexico. It was on this shoot that she had rescued Audie Murphy, not only a movie star but the most decorated American of the Second World War. As she explained:

> They went duck hunting. John Huston was there and José Ferrer. Huston was shooting duck so I went off on my own. I had a new telephoto lens and as I was looking through it I saw two heads in the water, way out, where there had been a boat. So I thought, somebody is in trouble. Someone was there so I gave them my camera and stripped down except for my bra, because I figured maybe someone could hold onto it. So I swam out and, indeed, Audie Murphy had fallen into the water wearing these western boots, so that he could hardly swim. The other guy had already been holding him for quite a while. By this time he was too tired to struggle very much. So we put him on my back, holding onto my bra strap, and the other man swam along beside. I would think twice about doing it again, though, because it was an awful long way to get back. All the others had just watched us. None of the big guys had come out to help us. They took us back in a Land Rover and someone from *Time* magazine got the story.[9]

By way of thanks Murphy gave Inge the watch he had worn during the war. Years later it stopped working and her then husband, Arthur Miller, gave it to a man who claimed he could mend it. He promptly disappeared.

Having finished her work, Inge returned to New York. Miller would follow some time later in a state of emotional disarray. It was November 1960. Clark Gable, with whom he had got on so well, now died of a heart attack. Here was one more reason for depression, though on 2 December the Magnum photographer Eve Arnold wrote to him saying that she had photographed Gable the week before his death and that he had told her he had loved the part and insisted that not a word should be changed.

The film was completed but a second marriage had ended in failure (his first, to Mary Slattery, finally concluding with his relationship to Marilyn), this one lasting only four and a half years. He and Marilyn were no longer speaking. He flew back alone, unsure what lay ahead. *The Misfits* had been the only piece of sustained writing he had done in seven years. He consulted his psychiatrist, Rudolph Loewenstein, and made a brief contact with Marilyn, retrieving photographs from her apartment and later meeting her at his mother's funeral in March 1961.

The *Misfits* shoot had been a humiliation. Marilyn had treated him with open contempt and her affair with Yves Montand during the shooting of *Let's Make Love* had been common knowledge. A relationship that was to have redeemed them both had ended in bitterness and recrimination. He took a certain pride in the film itself, though Bosley Crowther's review in the *New York Times* had been dismissive. He found the characters shallow and inconsequential, as he did the film which, he asserted, 'just doesn't come off'.[10] *Time* magazine described it as a dozen pictures all rolled into one and offered the opinion that 'most of them, unfortunately, are terrible'. It was 'an obtuse attempt to write sophisticated comedy, a woolly lament for the loss of innocence in American life and, above all, a glum, long, fatuously embarrassing psychoanalysis of Marilyn Monroe and what went wrong with their marriage'.[11]

Miller was conscious that the momentum of his career had stopped. In the brief eight years between 1947 and 1955 he had seen four of his plays produced, plays that would come to be seen as highpoints of American theatrical history. Since then he had lost his sense of direction and purpose, distracted by the demands of a wife he had hoped might liberate and support him, but also suffering from the aftermath of his involvement with the House Un-American Activities Committee. He was free now to return to his study, but was uncertain if he should do so. America was changing. A writer who had derived energy from resisting the mood of the times, questioning his country's myths, he now felt he had little purchase on events or attitudes. Asked later why he had stopped writing for so many years, he said that he had become disillusioned with the theatre:

> The production of *A View from the Bridge* clinched a growing feeling that the work I was doing was unimportant ... I felt I was a kind of entertainer, succeeding in drawing a tear or a laugh, but it seemed to me that what was behind my plays remained a secret ... I decided that either the audience was out of step or I was. There seemed to be no resolution – and yet there must have been one. I began to write more and more for myself.[12]

In truth, for much of the rest of his career he would suffer from momentary depressions, never amounting to a clinical condition but prompted by serious self-doubts as critical responses to his work eroded the confidence that had carried him through the 1940s and into the 50s. He would shake these off. Indeed, in some ways his periods of depression seem to have acted as a stimulus. But in the years that followed he would frequently abandon projects, losing his way or his self-belief, only to return to his desk the next day to start a new project, jot down his thoughts in a diary, engage with political issues. It is tempting to believe that the various causes he embraced were displacement activities, a reason to leave his desk and the difficult business of writing in what he felt was an increasingly hostile critical environment – except that he never did stop writing. Indeed, he was about to enter one of the most productive periods of his career, staging three plays in the four years between 1964 and 1968, even as he threw himself into opposition to the Vietnam War, became President of International PEN and travelled widely in Europe.

These last activities guaranteed a continued concern on the part of the FBI, which had not lost interest in him simply because he had survived his battle with the House Un-American Activities Committee, though as ever the content of the files it maintained hardly generates much confidence in its investigative capacities. In 1953, for example, HUAC had been desperate to establish the communist activities of those in the entertainment business. It had already summoned two of those involved in the production of *Death of a Salesman* (Elia Kazan and Lee J. Cobb), and Arthur Miller had been in their sights for many years. Then, *Time* magazine reported on a court case that cast an ironic light on the FBI's attempt to prove that Miller had been a card-carrying member of the Communist Party.[13] While it had been pursuing one Arthur Miller as a supposed subversive another Arthur Miller was a genuine spy.

It was suddenly revealed that in 1937 the Communist Party had planted spies in the New York Police Department. One of the most successful of their plants stayed in place for sixteen years, rising to the rank of lieutenant, and was on the verge of becoming captain when he was unmasked. In that time he had been so successful that when the department established Special Squad No. 1, designed to infiltrate the Party during the Second World War, four of its members were communist informants; as a result a number of the squad's spies were unmasked. In 1944, twenty-eight detectives and police women had been Party members, supplying regular reports to Party HQ, one of them reportedly acting as a courier between the American Communist Party and Portugal. Finally the lieutenant was exposed and cited for trial, but then disappeared and was dismissed from the force in his absence. His name was Arthur Miller. So, as the FBI looked for evidence that a playwright called Arthur Miller had been a member of the Party and thus constituted a threat to America, another Arthur Miller was indeed a member and was busy subverting an investigatory unit. But then, while the playwright Miller was attending Communist Party meetings, he was also working in the Brooklyn Navy Yard, a high-security facility, repairing frontline warships, a fact that seems not to have troubled the Bureau.

In 1961, and in the wake of the spiritual debacle in Reno, retreat to his home in rural Connecticut seemed to have its attractions, retreat even from the business of writing. And when Miller did begin to write, the play he produced was not entirely new because he had been working on what was a blend of *After the Fall* and *The Price* for many years. It expressed his sense of false loyalties and lost certainties. The world had changed and so had he. As the central character in *After the Fall* laments, 'I had a dinner-table and a wife, a child, and the world so wonderfully threatened by injustices I was born to correct! ... Remember – when there were good people and bad people? And how easy it was to tell! The worst son of a bitch, if he loved Jews and hated Hitler, he was a buddy. Like some kind of paradise compared to this. Until I begin to look at it. God, when I think of what I believed I want to hide.'[14]

Speaking of her generation, Mary McCarthy once remarked that they were perforce believing socialists but also practising members of capitalist society. It was a contradiction that few negotiated with any grace. This was true of Miller. Old convictions were no longer sustainable, but nothing had replaced them beyond a general commitment to the idea of personal responsibility. Society, after all, which he had once seen as an expression of mutuality, had in his experience been transformed into a coercive force, deeply conservative and vindictive. There were, however, positive signs. A month after his return to Connecticut, John F. Kennedy was elected, a man seventeen months younger than himself; and in January Miller went to Washington, this time not summoned by a Congressional committee but to attend one of the many inauguration balls. His private life was also, and much to his surprise, about to be transformed.

In *After the Fall* the central character, Quentin, at one point confesses to his state of mind: 'It all lost any point. Although I do wonder sometimes if I am simply trying to destroy myself ... I have walked away from what passes as an important career ... I still live in the hotel, see a few people, read a good deal, stare out of the window.' In New York, Miller too lived in a hotel – the Chelsea – and had a similar sense of treading water. For all this, within two months of his return to New York he was involved with Inge. In a mere eight weeks he went from despair at the collapse of one relationship to the eager pursuit of another. He had met Inge again at the Magnum Agency, where he had gone to inspect photographs, and later hosted her in Connecticut when she and Cartier-Bresson went there to photograph him as part of a series on American intellectuals. He was not, it seems, a man who could be without female companionship for long. He needed emotional stability – something, of course, that had been lacking in his relationship with Marilyn.

At first, he and Inge were nervous about committing themselves. Both bore the scars of previous failed relationships, while Inge suspected she might be no more than a port in a storm for someone so recently divorced. He invited her to lunch and dinner. They were awkward occasions. Neither was any longer young. They felt an attraction but were at first both wary of commitments. Recently divorced, Quentin in *After the Fall* is unsure of his right to begin a new relationship: 'I'm not sure, you see, if I want to lose her [Holga], and yet it's outrageous to think of committing myself again ... I have two divorces in my safe-deposit box. I tell you frankly, I'm a little afraid ... of who and what I'm bringing to her ... doubt ties my tongue when I think of promising anything again.'[15] However, he also confesses that he cannot bear to be a separate person.

Inge said later, 'We came to rely on each other and understand each other. Then we worked together on the movie version of *A View from the Bridge*. I started to photograph that so that we started to work together. Then he came after me to Paris', on the way buying a Land Rover that would still be in his front drive forty-four years later, when he died. He was courting a woman he did not know whether he should marry. She was equally uncertain. In *After the Fall* Holga, the character modelled on her, remarks, 'I am not helpless alone. I love my work. It's simply that from the moment you spoke to me I felt somehow familiar, and it was never so before ... It isn't a question of getting married; I am not ashamed this way. But I must have *something*.' In contrast to Quentin's wife Louise, however, she tells him: 'I am not a woman who must be reassured every minute, those women are stupid to me.'[16] If Miller liked his privacy – something that had baffled and irritated his first two wives – then so did Inge: 'He doesn't like being disturbed when he's working, but neither do I. He has a few bad habits like picking his teeth with a matchbox ... But he's so kind and relaxed. ... He also has a very strong practical side. Up to now, I've always changed my own wheels. Now he does it.'[17]

For his part, Miller was torn. In *After the Fall* he captures the feeling. In reply to Holga's insistence that he is not obliged to be with her Quentin replies, 'Holga, I would go. But I know I'd be looking for you tomorrow.'[18] For all their doubts about marrying again, Inge explained, 'I guess we finally decided we had fallen in love and might as well.'[19] There is a curious dying fall to the sentence and in the end it was perhaps her pregnancy that forced the issue. These were not days of casual abortions, nor of having children without the sanction of marriage. Besides, the fact of pregnancy focused their minds. The question of their future together was firmly on the table. With whatever doubts, they decided to give it a try – like her own parents, however, believing that their decision might yet prove revocable.

Miller's relationship with Inge marked the beginning of a new phase in his life. The tensions of his marriage to Marilyn were behind him. Ahead lay a new child, unplanned but welcome. Ahead, too, lay an invitation to write for a new theatre, and if the first play he wrote for it looked backwards, that was because there were ghosts he needed to lay before moving on. For a man who had undergone Freudian analysis, the idea that the path to the future might lie through an exploration of the past was second nature. That play, *After the Fall*, would be an attempt to explore his own life but also that of the wider world. Like the sociologist C. Wright Mills, he remained convinced that 'Neither the life of an individual nor the history of a society can be understood without understanding both',[20] and in a way Miller's was what Mills called a 'sociological imagination'. What was lacking in the sensibility of modern men and women, it seemed to him, as to Mills, was an awareness of 'the intricate connexion between the patterns of their own lives and the course of world history ... the interplay of man and society, of biography and history, of self and the world'.[21]

He rejected de Tocqueville's definition of individualism as the 'considered feeling which disposes each citizen to isolate himself from the mass of his fellows and withdraw into the circle of family and friends' leaving 'the greater society to look after itself'.[22] It was not that his characters, for the most part, consciously enrol in the joint stock company of society but that they have internalized what they perceive as its values, even as they are motivated by personal necessities they can barely acknowledge. They contain the yes and no of their society. They call out their own names because they feel their identities under pressure, aware, if only vaguely, that there is a gap between their own self-image and the life they lead – a gap that Miller, in his early work, was inclined to see as generative of tragedy: 'I think in the plays of mine that I felt were of tragic dimensions, the characters are obsessed with retrieving a lost identity, meaning that they were displaced by the social pressure, the social mask, and no longer could find themselves, or are on the verge of not being able to.'[23] Of the protagonist of his first, failed, play, *The Man Who Had All the Luck*, he says, 'He wants to know ... where he leaves off [and] the world begins. He's trying really to separate himself and to control his destiny.'[24] At the same time there is a permeable membrane between the self and society which makes that tension unresolvable.

That sense of the tragic would now largely disappear from his work, though not the existential anxiety nor his exploration of the conditions under which the private and the public would interact. That would be evident in *After the Fall*, and *The American Clock*, in *The Ride down Mount Morgan* and *Broken Glass*. He would, however, now broaden his canvas, and not only in terms of a new epic form (*The American Clock*). To the Ohio of *All My Sons*, the Brooklyn of *Death of a Salesman* (where he confided it was set) and of *A View from the Bridge*, the Salem of *The Crucible*, he now added a European dimension, and it was Inge who opened the door to that wider world, to the opacities of the Holocaust and the surrealities of life in the totalitarian states of Central and Eastern Europe, as she lured him out of the America whose values he simultaneously embraced and challenged.

Writing in 1959, Mills had asked, 'What fiction, what journalism, what artistic endeavour can compete with the historical reality and potential facts of our time? What dramatic vision of hell can compete with the events of twentieth-century war? What moral denunciations can measure up to the moral insensibility of men in the agonies of primary accumulation?'[25] Writing in 1966, Philip Roth doubted literature's capacity to capture American reality, quoting, approvingly, the critic Benjamin DeMott's observation that there seemed to be a 'universal descent into unreality'.[26] What Miller thought to be lacking was precisely an account that could address the need of individuals to understand themselves within the wider context. Mills wrote as a sociologist making the case for sociology, but the need he registered was one that Miller understood and sought to address – not in the belief that we are pure products of social process but in the conviction that the self cannot be abstracted from society nor society understood outside the parameters of human behaviour. He was not offering himself as a sociologist. He did, though, see his function as a playwright as lying in the need to situate his characters in a world that was both an expression and a shaper of human desire.

History, for Miller, was not what it was for Descartes as described by Isaiah Berlin, a tissue of gossip and travellers' tales. Nor was it some implacable fact. It was a consequence of willed decisions by people whose cruelties, betrayals aspirations were equally displayed in their private lives. A natural existentialist, Miller did not believe that responsibility ended where social action began, and that conviction led him into a darkness he now felt the need to address. Like so many others at this time he began to acknowledge the significance of the Holocaust, the shock of which had led to a two-decade-long silence. When he had briefly seen a group of survivors on his 1947 trip to Italy they had meant nothing to him. They were so much 'burnt wood'. Now, and precisely because of his relationship with Inge, he sought to penetrate what otherwise could seem a mystery without solution. But he did so not as if the Holocaust were some event entirely separate from his American concerns, his exploration of the sensibility of individuals bewildered as to their own motives and actions, but as of a piece with them. He had always, of course, located his characters in history, acknowledged the distorting pressures of social values and political fiats. Now, he began to probe deeper, not least because he was willing to acknowledge his own complicity in the moral failings he dramatized.

None of this, of course, says anything about the quality of work he was to produce. Nor is it to suggest that his earlier plays lacked profundity, had any less engagement with history (he later wrote an essay called '*The Crucible* in History') or leverage on present concerns. Indeed, his had always been an art that registered contemporary anxieties, a modern sense of alienation and moral equivocation for which he recognized historical parallels (as in his early radio play, *Thunder from the Hills*, which related Montezuma's capitulation to Cortés to the European appeasement of the 1930s). It is simply to observe that in his work of the 1960s and after there was a broadening of his concerns and an intensified determination to track social and historic facts to their origins in a flawed human nature, if also a gradually growing doubt about the substantiality of identity and the history he wanted to inhabit and claim.

Miller now wrote in a very different environment from that in which he had scored his major successes. His most recent play, *A View from the Bridge*, had been staged in 1955 at a time of political reaction when, if dissent was suspect, so, too, was unsanctioned sexuality. The 1960s, it was already clear, were to be different. In 1962 Daniel Bell, another sociologist, published *The End of Ideology*, whose subtitle was *On the Exhaustion of Political Ideas in the Fifties*. Miller was instinctively hostile, though the fifties had marked his own defection from Marxism and, interestingly, Bell devotes space to an account of the Brooklyn waterfront and the murder of Pete Panto, which had inspired *A View from the Bridge*. In part, his suspicion of Bell may have been because, a one-time member of the Young People's Socialist League, he had drifted to the right, and in part because he seemed to be suggesting a new age of conformity, the abandonment of a resistant spirit. Miller retained his passion, even if it had lost its ideological context.

In fact, he should have found Bell's analysis disturbingly apt. Bell wrote: 'In the West, among the intellectuals, the old passions are spent. The new generation, with no meaningful memory of these old debates, and no secure tradition to build upon, finds itself seeking new purposes within a framework of political society that has rejected, intellectually speaking, the old apocalyptic and chiliastic visions ... At the same time, American culture has almost completely accepted the avant-garde.' Ideology, he insisted, 'is intellectually devitalized' even as the 'emotional energies – and needs – exist'.[27]

Miller was, indeed, confronted with an avant-garde for whom his commitments seemed, at first, an irrelevance, though as the decade advanced, so Vietnam and a revisionist version of Marxism gained traction on the arts. Bell recognized the emergence of a 'new Left' which evidenced passion and energy but, he complained, 'little definition of the future', projecting a utopia void of content and justifying, along with previous utopias, the moral primacy of that future over the present. Miller was to feel the same impatience with the new radicals and what seemed to him their disregard of history and, indeed, of present paradigms, except when their interests coincided with his own on the issue of Vietnam. In terms of his own plays, whatever his commitments, he had never been an ideological writer (except in his first college plays). They can, however, be read as in part a critique of prevailing political and cultural assumptions. In the plays he would write in the second half of his career he continued that critique and those explorations, but registered more profound tremors in the moral world; and later he questioned the status of the real, the extent to which lives are performed rather than lived. The desire for an authentic identity remained a primary subject (*The Ride Down Mount Morgan, Broken Glass, Mr Peters' Connections, Finishing the Picture*), but this was seen now in the context of a deeply problematic reality (as in *Two-Way Mirror*). Increasingly, his characters seemed to lose confidence in their own substantiality.

Once, in the 1930s, he had embraced a chiliastic view, looking for an immediate transformation of society, a redemptive revolution of thought and action such as that advocated by Norman Thomas, six times socialist candidate for the presidency of the United States, whose cry was 'Socialism in our time'. Now, he had moved to what Max Weber called an ethic of responsibility. This remained his position, but in the context of the Holocaust (as reflected in *After the Fall, Incident at Vichy, Playing for Time* and *Broken Glass*) he was prepared to grant its moral complexity. As the twentieth century ended and the twenty-first began, his perception would be that America and the world were winding down, in parallel with his own life. The progressive vision that had driven him through the 1930s, 40s and 50s, had seemingly foundered. One of his last stories, 'The Turpentine Still', published after his death, featured the ruins of a once idealistic venture – to install a turpentine still on a hill in Haiti, now presided over by a bent-backed, silver-haired old man. As the protagonist muses, 'Now it will all slide into oblivion, all that life and all that caring, and all that hope, as incoherent as it was.' Who, he asks himself, 'could feel the quality of that hope anymore?'[28] Socialism had foundered on 'the Russians ... The camps ... And American prosperity.'[29] What would be left, though, was the still itself, 'like a kind of work of art that transcended the pettiness of its maker, even his egotism and foolishness'.[30] This would be Miller's last word on his career. His art would survive. For the moment, though, he took a breath and began the business of reconstructing his life after Marilyn, and his career as a playwright, following so many years of silence.

Something else had changed. When he had considered Aaron Copland as a possible composer for one of his plays, he was embracing a man who shared his values. Copland's *Fanfare for the Common Man* had taken its title from a speech by Henry Wallace, whom Miller had supported when he ran for the presidency in 1948. Like Miller, Copland had attended the Waldorf Conference (the supposed peace conference effectively sponsored by the communists at which the CIA began its policy of intervening in the cultural life of the country) and suffered accordingly. He, too, was tracked by the FBI and had been refused renewal of his passport. The title of Miller's first success,

All My Sons, had been an expression of this social ethic. When he wrote an essay called 'Tragedy and the Common Man', then, like Copland he was asserting a social and not only an aesthetic value. The plays he had written before the break necessitated by his marriage to Marilyn – and which featured a salesman, a farmer and a dock worker as well as a suspect capitalist – were an assertion of a value. Now he found himself in a new world.

It was not that Miller abandoned his earlier stance when he returned to New York and embarked on this new phase of his life. Speaking at Yale University in 1998, he would affirm that in creating a character his aim remained the need to 'create somebody who would be seen as a creature of society as well as a spirit all of his own, a self-generating person at the same time equally formed by social forces'. That, he asserted, 'has been the only consistent thing from the beginning'.[31] He remained equally convinced that 'ultimately everything is political. Everything finally ends up being part of the way we govern ourselves ... I want the play to reflect the fullness of life, so that ultimately whatever I am doing, I think has some resonance politically', at the same time insisting: 'I don't write political plays.'[32] What changed was his definition of the political, the breadth of his canvas, his concern to press beyond the social.

Where he remained consistent was in the value he gave to the past, his continuing fascination with memory: we are 'ninety per cent memory, after all, from the language we carry with us to the actual images that we have, and these plays are refracting the past all the time, because I don't really know how you understand anybody only from his present actions. We need the past to comprehend anything.'[33] So he would reach back to the 1930s of his youth in *After the Fall* (also, to the 50s) and *The American Clock*, to wartime France in *Incident at Vichy*, Kristallnacht in *Broken Glass*, the Holocaust in *Playing for Time*, and to 1960 in his final play *Finishing the Picture*, as if there were issues there never entirely resolved. Yet the past he would now engage with would take him into deeper water than before, as he would also come to question the nature of memory and reality itself in such plays as *The Archbishop's Ceiling*, *Two-Way Mirror* and *Mr Peters' Connections*.

On his return from California, Miller had set himself to work, living now for part of the time in a sixth-floor apartment in the Chelsea Hotel at 23rd Street between 7th and 8th Avenues, then and later a hang-out for writers. He was broke and struggled financially for a number of years, paying alimony to Mary and taxes on his own and Marilyn's income. It was at this moment that he deposited many of his papers at the Harry Ransom Center at the University of Texas, a tax write-off. On one of the pages of typescript can still be seen the imprint, in lipstick, of Marilyn's lips, stored away now in the climate-controlled files of a research library.

The Chelsea Hotel opened in 1884 in what was then the heart of the theatre district. It became home to an astonishing number of writers, artists, actors, musicians and film directors, ranging from Mark Twain and William Sydney Porter (O. Henry) to William Burroughs, Jack Kerouac, Janis Joplin, Willem de Kooning, Jasper Johns and Stanley Kubrick.

Miller moved into what he described as 'a lovely two-bedroom apartment with a big living room and a separate kitchen', at Inge's suggestion (she had been introduced to it by Mary McCarthy in the 1950s). He did so in part to escape the attentions of the press. He was assured by the owner that no one would know he was there. With a straight face, 'he claimed total innocence a few weeks later when the news began popping up in papers here and abroad'.[34] Curiously, Miller knew little of the Chelsea's reputation though he had been there in the early fifties when Dylan Thomas was edging towards death. In October 1953 he even appeared with him in a symposium about poetry and film in which Miller suggested that the introduction of words into film was 'an aesthetic impurity' and Thomas recalled a visit to an avant-garde play with Miller: 'The only avant garde play I saw was in a cellar, or a sewer, or somewhere. I happened to be with Mr Miller ... We saw this play going on ... I'm sure it was fine. And in the middle, he said, "Good God, this is avant garde." He said, "In a moment, the hero's going to take his clothes off" ... He did.'[35]

Thomas died in the nearby St Vincent's Hospital, taken there from the Chelsea by ambulance. Others, including Nancy Spungen, Syd Vicious's girlfriend, and Charles R. Jackson, author of *The Lost Weekend*, died in the hotel. But Miller and Inge quickly adjusted to its air of what he called 'uncontrollable decay', though in some ways it was an unlikely home for them since neither could be said to share the Chelsea's bohemian air. In his time there he got to know Brendan Behan, who sometimes showed evidence of having recently vomited. He shared breakfast at a 7th Avenue automat with Arthur C. Clarke – he wrote *2001: A Space Odyssey* in the Chelsea – who alerted him to the risk of global warming long before it became a subject of general concern, and he was there when Andy Warhol was shot as he entered the lobby, though by then the Millers had moved out, simply using the hotel for overnight stays.

His New York home between 1961 and 1967, the Chelsea was somewhere between shabby and seedy but it was quiet, and when they married Miller and Inge lived there in suite 614 with their new daughter, Rebecca. If there was always the faint, and sometimes not so faint, smell of marijuana (still evident today in a building which continues to be frequented by writers and artists), and the hotel detective was systematically stealing the guests' property, there were also advantages, even if these did not extend to maids familiar with the mysteries of vacuum cleaners. There was a protective atmosphere (though one day someone shattered the front doors with gunfire). Virgil Thomson was on hand with what Miller characterized as 'lethal martinis', and a drunk George Kleinsinger, composer of 'Tubby the Tuba', would jog past him in the lobby. Larry Rivers's paintings hung on the walls. He and Inge would move out when it was time for Rebecca to go to school. He explained, 'The 60s were very rough in New York. The Chelsea especially had a lot of dope. It was not a good place to bring up a kid. They were lying in the halls. It was a terrible atmosphere and we decided to get out. We moved to Roxbury. I would use hotels when I came to New York, naturally the Chelsea. Then it got very difficult. You often couldn't get a hotel. So we decided to buy an apartment on East 68th Street.'[36]

Back in May 1961, though, Miller turned his hand to fiction, in three weeks writing 'The Prophecy' a twenty-thousand-word story that seems partly to reflect his sense of disorientation. One of the characters is a left-wing Jewish writer who has suffered for his views and, like another couple in the story, is now divorcing. It is less that, though, which signals Miller's state of mind than the writer's observation that 'I guess it's that there is no longer any aim in life any more. Everything has become personal relations and nothing more.'[37] For over four years Miller had been involved in a psychodrama of his own. The question was what any longer mattered to him, mattered enough, that is, for him to wish to write? Beyond that, would audiences be interested in what he had to say? A short story enabled him to sidestep the problem. As he later suggested in the introduction to a short-story collection, a story opened up a space between the writer and the 'monster' that was the audience to a play, 'the terrible heat at the center of the stage'.[38] It was an interesting choice of words. He wrote this, after all, after the violent reaction to *After the Fall*, the play with which he would re-enter the American theatre.

For the moment, though, as he would explain in his autobiography *Timebends: A Life*, he tried out another play, one that might register current anxieties while, as ever, reaching back into the past. He decided to write about the atom bomb. In *Timebends* he dates the play to 1960 but in fact this is uncertain as it bears no date and was later filed with another 'bomb' play dated 14 December 1969.

It begins with a scientist standing alongside an actor before striding towards a lectern. A conference is plainly going on throughout the building, with other lectures in other spaces, including one to which a Russian delegate hurries, having confused the rooms. The lecturer, a man named Vessel, recalls the morning's lecture in which he had spoken of the need to visualize an object before making it, so that the object becomes a concrete version of a pre-existing vision or dream. He then breaks off to introduce an actor who, he explains, is also his patient. He has been institutionalized for three years with schizophrenia. The patient, named Krakauer, has an unlikely CV, having a Bachelor's degree in psychology and a Master's in history, with two years in law. He has a Purple Heart, a soldier's medal and a seaman's certificate. He has served two years for grand larceny and has acted in four movies as well as coming second in a race at Indianapolis and writing a book on medieval adaptations of Roman band instruments. He has also been a member of the Communist Party, while presently being a director of the Oil Importers Association.

The patient now steps forward and attests to the truth of Vessel's statements because, he says, people agree to them since a thing becomes real only when more than one person believes it. As Vessel leaves the room to fetch an attendant from the mental hospital, Krakauer reveals a gun which he fires in the air as Donald, the attendant, enters, phlegmatically accepting what has happened – a character note, since he is someone who accepts the reality presented to him without question.

The lecturer now brings in another patient, a forty-year-old woman, Lilly, who has been hospitalized for twenty years and who always believes what people tell her. She animates only when people look at or speak to her. She is followed in by Dr Battle, a Nobel Prize-winning astrophysicist of twenty-three, who announces that space is curved. There is a drum roll and the play moves into verse. The conversation continues to the beat of music as Battle explains that what we see is not what is, that the light from the stars comes from the past just as Lilly's past can now be verified by no one. So, too, a space opens up between people, a space of time which we long to close. There is no reality. For Krakauer, the real horror is that scientists command a reality which others cannot possess and that their reality requires no confirmation. It subsists in the fact of the bomb. By the same token, scientists give no credence to social visions of what the world might be, because it is not subject to confirmation.

At this point, aside from a momentary and disturbing shift of names, we are told that we will now examine the life of an individual. Krakauer takes off his jacket, tie and shirt and is left in a T-shirt and trousers, stepping back in time, he explains, to the day before history began. And that world is Miller's own, for we are back when he was playing basketball with a friend, the day a young Miller had bought a bicycle for twelve dollars only to see it stolen. Like Miller, he is struggling with algebra, has a race with his brother, that brother falling, as Miller's had done, to enable him to win. And so the play continues, with the story of Isidore Miller's arrival in New York as a boy of six and all the details of the Miller family during the Depression, the closing of the banks and the collapse of a marriage, as the reality of their lives seems to dissolve.

The play never returns to the lecture theatre or to the original characters. It has become something else. Primarily what it has become is the outline for

After the Fall, the play he now began to write, in which, despite his contemporary denials, he sought to explain himself to himself, to explore the nature of his relationship with Marilyn and, eventually, to justify beginning a new relationship when he had so manifestly failed in two previous ones. That new relationship was with Inge, who would emerge in the play as a redemptive figure, a woman who, in Europe, had seen the worst of human nature, who had herself experienced marital failure but who represented the possibility of new beginnings.

On 17 February 1962 Arthur Miller, then forty-six, married thirty-nine-year-old Ingeborg Morath. There is a photograph of the two of them in the snow of Roxbury, he in a sheepskin coat, she in a leopard-skin one. There is no doubting their happiness. She was already two months pregnant with Rebecca. Vital, talented, self-confident, Inge had swept into his life. Their relationship would prove the most important of both their lives, while the marriage they contracted with such caution and uncertainty would last for the rest of their lives. It was a marriage that changed both of them and that certainly altered the direction of Miller's career. Part of his attraction from Inge's point of view lay in the fact that 'he also had a very European awareness. It wasn't in his work at that moment. In his work it was totally American traumas. Mine was a European trauma. Also a European refinement. In a lot of things we were very different. But at the same time Arthur immediately had a very great awareness of all these problems, and that must have been from his being Jewish.'[39]

They now retreated to Roxbury, the rural idyll he had planned and rebuilt with Marilyn Monroe and with which he had originally tempted Inge. Here they set about planting six thousand evergreen trees on the hills around their Connecticut home, using nothing more than a trenching tool, Miller still thinking of creating a tree farm to produce timber. They also planted nine varieties of ornamental trees, for landscaping. Indeed, part of him wanted to withdraw from the public world and turn farmer. For her part, Inge slowly began to master a domestic world she had once despised, though in contrast to her first marriage there was never any question that this would define the limits of her possibilities. She became a fine cook, though at first cooking was something of a mystery to her. Years later, asked to supply a recipe for a writers' cookbook, Miller replied:

> When we married my wife could just about (nervously) boil an egg, so I did the cooking and as a result she very shortly learned how to cook and became one of the world's best. So anyone who asks me for my recipes has got a very short reply coming. My repertoire veers toward broiling butterflied legs of lamb, after my wife has marinated them for a day or two (in what, God knows) and chicken after she has similarly massaged the halves in marinated

stuff. My only talent is to sense when something's done – and it is not merely when everybody's drunk. I did once broil some chicken halves after tossing some salt and pepper, butter, paprika, and oregano on them. And we're still married so I guess it turned out pretty good. Also fried eggs with a little garlic.[40]

Inge established a vegetable garden and grew apples (five kinds), pears, plums, cherries and quinces, along with varieties of soft fruit. She would serve homemade borscht, marinate wild rabbit, cook Spanish omelette from a recipe given to her by Picasso. She cooked her own French baguettes in tins made by her husband.[41] As Miller would comment: 'In due time she became the great mother, the mistress of a very busy house, and one morning, about a year after we married, she suddenly exclaimed "My God, we've been married all year!" Periodically this went on for forty years.'[42]

At this time they still maintained their apartment in the Chelsea Hotel, the converted farmhouse in Roxbury being a place of retreat, an equivalent of the cottage in Far Rockaway where the Miller family had spent summers in the 1920s. In time, though, their Connecticut home became the place where Miller would write all his plays. For a man who had lived in no fewer than ten different houses or apartments, this was finally somewhere to sink his roots and, once they had settled there, he took to the rural life. In subsequent years he would drive a tractor, cutting the grass around his house but also in the field across the road, using the hay as a mulch on his garden and shunning the use of sprays. He helped in the vegetable plot, fifty feet by seventy, not least because Inge had a liking for salads which, he once remarked, only existed because of women. Inge's mother, known as Titti, a botanist, would look sceptically at his efforts, accusing him of planting the wrong vegetables in the wrong place (years later, the actress Prunella Scales pointed out that the flowers referred to in *Death of a Salesman* appear in the wrong order, to which he replied, 'I didn't know anything about flowers'). He grew them, in part, he explained, because he could not bear walking past an unplanted fenced garden. Without a garden to till and plant, he said, he would not know what April was for, even though he knew that the order he worked for would be undone by weeds, flood, drought or his own dereliction.

Meanwhile, he would venture into his own woods – wearing a luminescent orange jacket as a defence against poachers with rifles – to drag fallen trees to his barn, where he fashioned furniture. He was a natural fixer of broken things, from cars to household fittings. The house was soon decorated with memories of their separate lives. Inge hung works by Saul Steinberg, whom she had photographed in New York and who created an elaborate unofficial marriage certificate for the couple. She made her own cushions, two of them fashioned from the saddlebags of a camel she had ridden in Iran. He hung posters from some of his plays, in 1968 adding an engraver's plate marking the one-millionth copy of the paperback edition of *Death of a Salesman*. He also built a granite fireplace.

There were, though, occasional echoes of the past. In 1990 he would publish a short story in the *Michigan Quarterly Review* called 'Bees' (later rewritten as a television play which earned him a quarter of a million dollars). It carried the subtitle 'A Story to Be Spoken', not least because he took pleasure in reading it aloud. It was a story that took him back to his early days in Roxbury and the house where he wrote *Death of a Salesman*, while still married to Mary. It recounts his battle with the bees that colonize his property. The protagonist mounts a campaign using chemicals, plaster, cement, anything that comes to hand. Defeat follows defeat. Eventually, he seems to win, collecting the pile of dead bodies, though not without a certain regret. He then recalls selling the house and separating from his wife. Later, now living with someone else, he is approached by the current owner of his first property. The bees have returned. Some battles, it seems, can never be won. The dead bees and a dead marriage are left behind but not, apparently, entirely. Wall them up, attempt to kill them, and they still return. The story was accompanied by Inge's photograph of Miller looking not so much a writer as a gentleman farmer.

Each morning Inge would rise at six to do yoga exercises, a discipline she maintained throughout her life. He would walk up the slope to a spare wooden studio where he would write every morning, a room with no telephone but with an intercom he installed so that he could be summoned back to the house for meals or urgent calls. For relaxation, they would play tennis, using courts in the grounds of their neighbours, the writers William Styron and Francine du Plessix Gray. Or, in the years that followed, they would stage picnics. There is a photograph of one such, a decade later, in which they are pictured playing host to Andrei Voznesensky, along with his translator Olga Carlisle and their Roxbury neighbour Harrison Salisbury. As Rebecca grew up they would also stage puppet shows in the barn. Rebecca named the family dachshund 'Becky Too'.

It was a place, too, where Inge could photograph this world she had chosen to enter. Miller turned the barn silo into two rooms in which she could work and she continued to pursue her own career, uninhibited by her new child. Sitting in her Connecticut house, she told me:

> I always took her with me, everywhere. She was on my back. I first started here [in Roxbury], though I can work anywhere. So I did the Connecticut book [*In the Country*] based on the stories Arthur told me when he first tried to intrigue me to come to Connecticut. He told these wonderful stories about the old settlers. It was like a fairy tale. It was marvellous. So when I came up

here they were still here, these guys. And so I took Rebecca. We were haunting Connecticut. She was strapped in the car, then she was strapped on my back. So I never left her. Arthur was always here or we were in the Chelsea Hotel. She was always with us. The first time we left her, for ten days, it nearly broke my heart. That was when we went to Russia [in 1965]. But I took her to Japan. [At home] I used to let her sleep under the dining room table. In all the parties she was there. I just took her up when she was fast asleep. So she had all these languages. I had a brother whose children were always sent away but with one I found it very hard to do.[43]

One of the stories Miller told her he claimed to have heard from a local Roxbury man who had lived there before, he said, land became real estate. He recalled two unmarried brothers who had lived in the farmhouse Miller had converted when he married Marilyn Monroe and in which he and Inge now lived:

They were real churchgoers, don't y'know, went down there every Sunday. And around January or so they didn't show up. Then next Sunday come and they're not there either. Finally, after they hadn't been there for three Sundays, a committee was appointed to go up and see if there's anything wrong. Well, they come up the house and knock, and the door opens, and there's one of them, and they goes inside and asks why they hadn't been to church all month. And he says his brother's died and he didn't feel he ought to leave him. 'Ought to leave him! Why, where is he?' 'In the front room,' he says. And sure enough, they go over to the parlor, and there he's got him laid out on two sawhorses and a board. 'I'm waitin' for the thaw,' he says. That'll give you an idea how cold those houses were.[44]

Roxbury, which runs through the watershed of the Shepaug River (Shepaug, a Mohegan name for rocky water, being the town's original name), today has a population of 2,340. When Miller moved there the number was 750. It was settled in 1713 and incorporated as a town in 1796. A local tribe, the Pootatooks, sold their last land to the whites and moved to the reservation at Scatacook. Originally a farming community, its granite provided building material for both Grand Central Station and the Brooklyn Bridge, from which it was possible to look down on Red Hook, the setting for *A View from the Bridge*.

This part of Connecticut is a place of sweetcorn and potatoes, of apples, pears and cherries. This is where, in the fall, pumpkins are piled on tables set at the side of the road. When Miller first lived in Roxbury there were barns not yet made into homes, though over the years the original inhabitants began to make way for incomers from the city. Houses on the hillside where he lived for the next forty-five years have spring-fed ponds, held in place by small dams erected by the Corps of Engineers to prevent a repetition of the lethal floods that once swept several people to their deaths.

This is a town full of eighteenth-century buildings: American clapboard classicism. There are family names here that have sounded down the centuries. This is what Miller referred to as 'the other time'.[45] In more recent years, the town had changed. In one sense a process of decay had been halted. Roofs had been repaired, clapboard regularly painted, gates set back on hinges, but those who restored the order were no longer those whose families lay beneath the slanting gravestones in the churchyard. They were the new rich in search of a second home only two hours from New York City, or who, like Miller and his wife, wanted to step off what he called the 'Great American Train',[46] as if that were possible.

It was his stories of Roxbury's past, of the men and women he had met there and who provided a sense of continuity, that inspired his wife to discover pleasure in photographing her immediate locality. To be sure, at first it had that strangeness that had always enabled her to encourage the viewers of her photographs to see the familiar through fresh eyes, but she also found herself content, for a while, with capturing the immediate world that surrounded her. And there is a powerful sense in which Miller's work attests to values lost somewhere back there, before a man's worth was judged by his price, an issue he was to dramatize in *The Last Yankee*, based on one of his Roxbury neighbours. It is hard to think of any of his works in which that is not an underlying concern. It is more difficult, though, to say when those values last thrived. In Roxbury the very buildings seem to hint at a lost world:

> The stark wooden churches with their discrete ornamentation are like shards of a lost comet whose meaning is now read through the mists of nostalgia – a yearning for a vanished individualism – when they signify, in truth, the direct opposite. This pristine architecture celebrates not the loner freed of communal obligation, not man in a state of unacknowledged war with his fellows, but the ideal of mutuality and its suspicion of worldliness. The buildings are now seen most commonly with sentimentality, although they were designed like arrows pointed toward the rocky road littered with the baggage of the world and its illusions.[47]

He was fully aware, though, that the other side of this coin was the American gravitational pull towards the tyranny of the majority, identified early by de Tocqueville. It was, he admitted, harder to stand apart in the country than in the city, in which anonymity had its virtues. During the Vietnam War the dissenter was liable to have a hard time and Miller himself experienced hostility. Nonetheless a man on his own land still seemed to him to have resources denied someone who works for wages, and there is, in Miller's work, a tendency to value the individual who labours with his hands and has a relationship to the land, which is equally reflected in Inge Morath's images in *In the Country*, the book they would publish in 1977 but whose pictures reflect these first years together at Roxbury.

For Miller, the idea of the countryside 'was oddly like that of the theatre, an arena in which one's presence could change and shape, while the city was concrete and repelled the touch of the hand with its indifference. Others made the city; a place of one's own waited on its creator.'[48] Miller came to Roxbury a city boy who thought that people were born to live in houses, with the distant sound of subway trains, or in apartments, with other people sandwiched above and below, the sound of their living blending in with his own. Country, to him, had meant Central Park, where New Yorkers took their sleds in winter and lay on the grass in the summer, pretending it was the frontier territory Roxbury was, or had been once. There had been Indians there, as there had, of course, in Central Park, and this New England town was still cross-hatched with dry-stone walls created, originally, by settlers clearing the land for planting once the Indians had gone. These farms had long since failed, given way to woodland or sculpted lawns that now fronted the winding roads and back lanes.

The Connecticut townships Inge photographed were a compromise between past and present. In her photographs centuries-old houses turned supply stores, antique shops, boutiques, are shown linked by looping telegraph wires and alongside tarmacked roads, marked out with white lines, cracked open by the winter frost. Back in New York, the past was regularly erased (Miller would make this a key image in *Mr Peters' Connections*). It was the source of its defining energy. In Roxbury, in Southbury and Waterbury, past and present coexisted, stories within stories.

The photographs Inge took, and which she would later publish alongside Miller's text, show men at work with cows, cords of wood stacked against the winter, drugstore counters cluttered with food, the carpenter alongside his planed planks. Interspersed with these are pictures of buildings with the patina of age, isolated houses, unpeopled as though deserted, set against a countryside tangled, wild, undemarcated, undomesticated.

The camera looks out of and into windows, at deserted bars, vacant staircases. *In the Country* becomes a study of the terms under which men and women relate to the world and to themselves. It is full of the stories of those who once farmed the land, tended the stock, worked the wood, hunted the deer, in one way or another sustained themselves and the community or simply lived out the generations – resisting laws, refusing conformity, turning their backs on jobs they suspected might demean them or deny them the respect that was their purchase on life. Miller writes of a woman, 'rooted in a place, a community, and hence in herself', who would lack this if she lived 'in an anonymous crowd'. Elsewhere, he speaks of farmers bidding up the prices at a forced auction in a 'gesture of solidarity, mute and unconfessed'[49] in the 'workless suburb of strangers that the country has become'. A similar scene would go directly into *The American Clock*, the play in which he would look back to the Depression and acts of solidarity in the face of suffering.

Miller's retreat to Roxbury was always something more than a desire for a quiet environment, a temporary relief from the pressures of urban living (at first, he and Inge would return to New York when the weather did its worst; later, though, they would settle into this place that would become a genuine home). To him it was a model of what America had been, a natural democracy, a place where people worked with their hands, as did he in his great barn where he shaped wood from the surrounding hills into the objects that defined his everyday world. He took pleasure in attending town meetings in which people came together to make decisions, to battle against public utility companies or to choose delegates.

Inge's photographs dwell on the striations of wood grain on a heavy timbered door, a gate in need of repair which implies a man who is likewise, neglect being at odds with the necessity he might be taken to serve. It is a compromised community that she pictures and that Miller describes, but it is a community. Marilyn Monroe came to Roxbury and decided that her house lacked a swimming pool. Inge Morath chose instead to swim in the spring-fed pond with its fish, frogs and, for a time – until chased away by the various dogs they would own – snapping turtles. Over the years she would fall into a routine of visiting the pond each day, swimming in summer and walking across the cataracted ice in winter. For Marilyn, it was to be a kind of movie set; for Inge, a natural resource.

In time there would be famous people in Roxbury, people who made their names acting or writing: William Styron, Richard Widmark, Tom Cole a fellow playwright (who lived in Miller's old house where he wrote *Death of a Salesman*), Dustin Hoffman (who moved there in 1984 when he was playing Willy Loman in the Broadway production of *Death of a Salesman*). Already there when Miller arrived was the sculptor Alexander Calder, known as Sandy, who with his wife would inspire *I Can't Remember Anything*, Miller's 1987 one-act play. When Calder had finished a piece he would call Inge to come and photograph it. She took the last photograph of him, summoned by his wife to capture him in a sweater she regarded as so old that he had to be shocked into abandoning it by seeing it on film. Nearby in Sherman, Connecticut, like Roxbury in Litchfield County, lived the choreographer Martha Clarke, who became a close family friend and who, like Miller, seemed as happy with a chain-saw as working in the theatre.

Retreat to Roxbury, however, was never going to represent retreat from the world for either of them. Inge's commissions would continue to take her around the world, sometimes with her husband, sometimes not. In the years that followed Rebecca's and Daniel's births (Daniel, their second child, born five years after his sister), Inge continued to travel, less now to feed magazines than to create her own books. Before settling in America she had already had three exhibitions of her work but after 1969 the pace would quicken, with five major exhibitions in the 1970s, eleven in the 80s and thirty in the 90s. She would go on to be awarded the Grand Austrian State Award for Photography and the Honorary Gold Medal of the federal capital Vienna, along with honorary degrees, returning to a place with bad memories as well as good.

Her restless travelling reflected a fascination with other cultures but equally a desire to act, as she had in the immediate postwar world, as an interpreter. Her pleasure lay, she explained, in 'meeting people in many countries, recording their lives with my camera, with my particular vision and intentions, so that there might be better understanding in the world.'[50] Miller's earlier rejection of Communist Party literature, even at a time when he was drawn to the Party, had been formulated in terms of its failure to 'stand as witness to reality and life', its failure to generate 'those images of life that art can most vividly create, and which at their profound best toughen a nation's spirit against self-pity and self-delusion and may . . . cry up warnings against calamity in good time'.[51] That was plainly what both he and Inge saw their work as doing.

Inge travelled alone when she visited places of no particular interest to her husband, sometimes sleeping rough in the jungle or on the deck of a ship when she wanted to share the experience of those whose lives she set out to capture. But she was involved in his work. There was, she said later, 'nothing quite like the excitement of the beginning when the voice of the playwright could be heard from outside the studio reading a scene to himself; one assumes that he found his way into the inner life of a new play. There are no pictures for this, just the outside of the little wooden building, and later the actors on stages around the world.'[52] She would, though, become the official photographer for all his plays, taking pictures of rehearsals and portraits of actors.

Her photographs of actors in rehearsal would be designed to capture not the actors themselves but the way in which they became someone else, and that, too, brought playwright and photographer together. For Miller, part of her quality as a photographer would be her 'recognition that human beings are forever impersonating', that our 'defenses are as true of us and perhaps more socially revealing than the more embarrassing private characteristics that the candid photographer is always trying to flush out'. It is not that her subjects were simultaneously themselves and the image they wished to project, though she herself spoke of her subjects 'being seen as they wish to be seen, almost as one makes that critical assessment of oneself in a mirror, alone'. It is that both she and her husband saw lives as performed, and performance as potentially something other than deceit, though he was increasingly aware of that capacity. When he says of her collection of portraits that they 'are extraordinarily civilized portraits in that people are seen to be worthy of their impersonations rather than ludicrous for having imagined themselves in one or another disguise', this is the condition that his characters seek as they struggle to bring their lives into alignment with their concept of themselves. There is connection between the actor reinventing himself on stage, and the actor, or anyone else, reinventing himself off stage. 'Why are we forever recreating ourselves?'[53] he asks. Because, he replies, we are a social animal. Miller would comment on the fact that his wife had a tendency to photograph her subjects 'front-face' as if they were happy to reveal themselves as they wished to be. His characters, like Eddie Carbone in *A View from the Bridge*, likewise allow themselves to be fully known.

The marriage into which Miller and Inge entered so tentatively, and with such self-doubt, in 1962, would prove not only durable but transforming. Coming as they did from different worlds, they nevertheless complemented one another emotionally and professionally. Her European scepticism about aspects of American society was echoed by his own liberal critique of a culture suspicious of history, so assured of its own accomplishments. Her internationalism was bred in the bone. His, at first, had been a product of ideology but would now be encouraged by his wife and enter his work. They would be committed not only to their separate careers but to one another's. Their series of joint books was something more than a commercial venture: they were what *The Misfits* had been intended to be but never quite became, a place where private and public lives could coincide, a narrative they could inhabit together. They were both lovers of literature, art and music, both private people who contrived to live public lives, entertaining the stream of writers, actors, directors, academics and journalists who would make their way to Roxbury. Inge would cook (her shopping lists were often written in different languages), picking from a range of national dishes she had mastered on her travels.

In later years interviewers would obsessively ask Miller and, on the rare occasions when they got the chance, Inge, about the shadow of Marilyn, which they evidently presumed must be a dominant presence in their lives. For obvious reasons it irritated both of them, but talking to her friend the writer Honor Moore, Inge explained that when she first married Miller she had a dream. As Honor would later recall, 'We were talking about the whole thing of Marilyn and I said, "How is this for you to talk about?" and she said, "Well, I had a dream soon after I married Arthur. I was in a bar and Mary and Marilyn and I were all sitting on tall bar stools and some music started.

Marilyn got off her stool and started to dance and I got up and danced with her and after that everything was all right." So Inge!'[54]

As for Miller himself, he was soon drawn back to the theatre, though a month after Rebecca's birth it was public events that commanded everyone's attention when, in October, the Soviets were discovered to have placed missiles in Cuba, a fact quickly detected by American reconnaissance aircraft. For a few days it appeared as if the future of something more than American–Soviet relations was in the balance. World war seemed a distinct possibility as President Kennedy and his advisers debated the appropriate action. Invasion, which had failed so spectacularly at the Bay of Pigs, was clearly one option, if not, as it happened, one favoured by the White House. Miller fired off a cable to Kennedy, supporting his demand that missiles be removed but praising his restraint, adding his own warning against invasion. The real issue in Latin America, he added, was poverty. The cable ended with Miller offering his sympathies to Kennedy in his struggle.

The Miller who returned to the theatre in the mid-1960s was a different man from the one who had written the essay 'On Social Plays', and staged dramas that turned on the individual's responsibility to society and society's to the individual, and different even from the author of tragedies of the common man. There were, it now seemed to him, more profound questions to do with human nature itself.

Many would view *After the Fall* as an account of his marriage to Marilyn, and it was, doubtless, an act of self-analysis, a painful survey of a series of failed relationships, but what gave it its direction was his decision to marry a woman who had come out of a different world. The nature of that world was underlined for him when she took him to Mauthausen concentration camp near her home city of Graz, confronting him and herself with a history that should have divided them, she being the daughter of a man who, for pragmatic reasons, had been a member of the Nazi Party, and he a Jew who had lived out the war in America.

Though Inge took him there to confess to what, no matter how irrationally, she felt as her complicity, at least as important was the fact that it was this visit that reminded him of his Jewishness and placed the Holocaust at the centre of his concerns. He was – he realized, now more acutely – a survivor, if only by virtue of the fact that his family had chosen to leave when others stayed. Standing in Mauthausen, he could all too clearly imagine himself in this place. Earlier in his career he had both written about anti-Semitism and declared his intention not to be bound by claims that he had a special responsibility as a Jewish writer. He had enthusiastically welcomed the establishment of the state of Israel, while refusing to accept the obligation to write about Jewish characters. Like so many other Jewish intellectuals, he had embraced internationalism, finding in socialism a more plausible connective tissue than that offered by what had long since seemed to him the alien and alienating rituals of faith. Standing here, in a place where so many had died, to separate himself seemed like a form of treachery. In the decades to come he would be drawn to address that threatened identity and existence even as he became ever less tolerant of an Israeli state that seemed to him to betray the promise he had seen in it when, one snowy day, he had attended a meeting to hail its beginnings.

For many, the full implications of the Holocaust had not struck home. For the writer and art critic Harold Rosenberg it would be the Eichmann trial that represented what he called 'a recovery of the Jews from the shock of the death camps, a recovery that took fifteen years and which is still not complete' (he was writing in November 1961). It was not, he explained, that the information had not been available but that it was questionable whether the growing body of knowledge had 'entered the general consciousness or even that of many Jews ... For most who lived through this period, the Nuremberg Laws, asphyxiation buses, atrocities, gas chambers, are all jumbled together in a vague hurt as of a bruise received in the dark.'[55] In 2009, Hasia Diner (in *We Remember with Reverence and Love: American Jews and the Myth of Silence after the Holocaust*) would challenge this idea of a delayed response, arguing that there was ample evidence of engagement. For many, though, it was a fact whose full significance had not registered.

Miller was not alone in his renegotiation of his Jewish identity. The critic Irving Howe confessed that 'Jews who did not believe in Judaism as a traditional faith had serious problems: they were left with a residual "Jewishness" increasingly hard to specify, a blurred complex of habits, beliefs, and feelings. This "Jewishness" might have no fixed religious or national content, it might be helpless before the assault of believers. But there it was, that was what we had – and had to live with.' He observed, with a certain wryness, what he called the various 'vicarious pilgrimages to Hasidism' of several Jewish intellectuals. Leslie Fiedler (Hebrew name, used for religious purposes, Eliezar Aaron), the critic and enthusiastic member of the CIA-funded Congress for Cultural Freedom, was one of them. *Commentary* magazine even held a Seder one Passover evening, inviting the writer Edmund Wilson along. The sociologist Paul Goodman, Harold Rosenberg and Clement Greenberg, he noted, all attempted to redefine their relationship to Judaism, anxious nonetheless not to return to the parochialism they feared. Goodman, in particular, chose to embrace the stories at the heart of a faith he was doubtful of embracing in its full rigour. In Howe's words, they 'wanted a Jewishness of question and risk, while the American Jewish community, at least most of it, was settling into good works and self-satisfaction'.[56]

For his part, Howe turned to the editing and translation of Yiddish poetry and prose, opening a door that was surely about to close despite the Polish-born writer Isaac Bashevis Singer's Nobel Prize in 1978. His work was apparently so aberrant to the American literary tradition that the *Los Angeles Times* greeted the news with the headline: 'Pole Wins Nobel', though Saul Bellow's translation of Singer's short story 'Gimpel the Fool' (Bellow spoke Yiddish) in *Partisan Review*, in 1953, had caused a flurry. As to the Holocaust, the twenty-year silence had been a product of tact, bewilderment, incapacity, shock. Howe remarked:

> If you ask what a sufficiently strong or quick response to the Holocaust would have been, I can hardly answer. Some friends did make halting efforts to cope with the enormity of the gas chambers, and from them I gradually learned that I had to give up the pretense that any world view could really explain what had happened ... What most people felt was sheer bewilderment and fright. No one knew what to say, no one could decide whether to cry out to the heavens or mourn in silence. We had no language. 'The great psychological fact of our time which we all observe with baffled wonder and shame,' wrote Lionel Trilling, 'is that there is no possible way of responding to Belsen and Buchenwald. The activity of the mind fails before the incommunicability of man's suffering.'[57]

To this Howe added, 'Many of us were still reeling from the delayed impact of the Holocaust. The more we tried to think about it, the less we could make of it.'[58] He argued that one reason for his own, and others', delay in addressing it was the modes of thought established through their commitment to Marxism. They had believed history to be rationally explicable in terms of class and the inner dynamic of capitalism. The rise of Hitler had seemed easily assimilable to such an approach. Mass murder, however, was something different. Even Claude Lanzmann (whose monumental and disturbing film *Shoah* would confront viewers with victims and persecutors), he noted, saw it as a product of Western history. The writer and radical Dwight Macdonald, as early as 1945, had argued that what was new was that the Holocaust served no purpose. It was an end in itself and, as Hannah Arendt had insisted, systematic mass murder strained the very categories of political thought. In that sense, understanding was an affront in that it offered to pull this phenomenon into the very rational world it threatened to annihilate.

There was, perhaps, another reason, one that worried Miller and which Clement Greenberg expressed in 1950:

> Not only is the mind unable to come to terms with the dimension [of the Holocaust] and so resolve some of its oppressiveness, and not only does it prefer to remain numbed in order to spare itself the pain ... the mind has a tendency, deep down, to look on a calamity of that order as a punishment

that must have been deserved ... For what? The mind doesn't know, but it fears – fears in an utterly irrational and amoral, if not immoral, way that we were being punished for being unable to take the risk of defending our-selves ... we were not punished by God for having transgressed ... We were punished by history.[59]

The question of a supposed Jewish passivity lay at the heart of the controversy over Hannah Arendt's book on Eichmann, and had been invoked by Bruno Bettelheim, but it was an issue that had already disturbed Miller. As to the role of God, that too was a subject with which he would engage in *After the Fall* and to which he would return in *The Creation of the World and Other Business.*

He was not tempted to flirt with a religiosity for which he had some contempt, but he too was drawn to the founding stories (rediscovering the Bible and turning to it as a source), while the affront of the Holocaust now had a special edge, even if he was no clearer than others yet as to how to address it. In common with those others, he had abandoned Marxism and felt the loss of transcendence it had offered, so much so that a sense of loss would become a central theme. What he derived from his Jewish upbringing was the pressure of the past (though his concern had other, theatrical origins, too), an ethical imperative, the pull of community and an awareness of vulnerability. There might, to be sure, be a secular basis for his sense of the fragility of civilization. After all, the Depression had taught him that nothing was secure. On a deeper level, however, he had learned from his father the menace that could underpin the quotidian. Willy Loman in *Death of a Salesman* feels temporary because he is wedded to an American myth which projects meaning into the future; but Jews, too, live in expectation of an event that will retrospectively flood life and history with meaning, with the risk that the present moment will, if not be drained of meaning, then defer it: the Jews, Harold Rosenberg remarked, are held together by 'a net of memory and expectation'.[60] The Holocaust, however, seemed to break a covenant, to disrupt the residual assurance even of a secular Jew. For Miller, the mystery would be not how God could permit such an affront to humanity but that people should feel the need to invent a God whose betrayal they would be forced to account for.

After the Fall would explore his own life, and the life of his society, for evidence of betrayal and a justification for living. He had been working on it in one form or another for many years. What his visit to Mauthausen did, it seems, was to place an obligation on him he had not felt before, and to offer a connection between the failed hopes, duplicities, denials and cruelties of private life, of social interactions, and those of the Holocaust whose meta-physics were, in truth, still beyond him, as they were beyond so many. Twenty years after the war's end, everybody was a survivor. The question was, what gave them the right to be such – not so much to live when others had died as to live when the justification for life had been so radically challenged? A concentration camp tower, a correlative of the genocide, would thus become a dominant image in the play, though its integration with other aspects of the drama would, perhaps, remain problematic. Miller's sense of shock at seeing in person what he had previously registered as historic fact necessitated its presence, but that same sense of shock made it difficult for him convincingly to locate the connection that would make it the logical image for something beyond its own numbing mysteries. In the end, though, few noted this dimension of the play, distracted as they were by what seemed the spilling of private information into the public realm.

And there was another question, one raised by a writer whom Miller would later admire and whose sudden death would come as a shock to him, W.G. Sebald. He had said that 'the construction of aesthetic or pseudo-aesthetic effects from the ruins of an annihilated world is a process depriving literature of its right to exist'.[61] The Holocaust, in other words, was not available for fictive use. If he was aware of the warning signs, Miller failed to recognize them. Indeed, he felt a new necessity that neutralized such concerns. Denial was a central theme of this play and of his work. *After the Fall* was to be about the return of the repressed in private and public life.

I quote above from a number of those thought of as New York Intellectuals. Miller was not of their company. Theirs was an incestuous world. They reviewed one another's books, praised or denounced one another in *Commentary* or *Partisan Review*. In their various autobiographies they describe their sometimes Byzantine relationships to one another. Miller is hardly mentioned. He was simply not seen by them as one of their number, or even as contributing to the debates that so preoccupied them. Yet he engaged with the same dilemmas, explored the same paradoxes. In many ways his early commitments had mirrored theirs, though his continued loyalty, until 1950, to the lost cause of communism had opened a gulf. The fact was that he had no wish to join their fraternity, become part of this postwar, largely Jewish, intellectual dance. He was, of course, part of the debate through his work. *The Crucible* had said as much about McCarthyism as any number of essays. He was also, like them, a secular Jew in search not of faith but of meaning. In the face of the Holocaust, however, all differences and distinctions dissolved. Those who died in the camps, believers or sceptics, died as Jews. And that was a fact he struggled with from this moment in his career onwards, trying to negotiate a path between the particularity and resistant opacity of the event and his desire to render it as exemplary fact. As Howe remarked, the Holocaust resisted political or social analysis and sent the observer back to an inquiry into human nature. But there was another argument: for Miller it was a metaphor while, for many others, to see it as such was a betrayal of its sheer facticity.

In October 1963, perhaps newly sensitized to the plight of Jews, Miller took part in a conference on the status of Soviet Jews, only to find his attendance questioned by the cultural section of the Soviet Embassy. He responded by asking why Jews were being persecuted in the USSR. As Nathan Abrams has noted, he was then attacked by the *Morning Freiheit*, a Jewish newspaper affiliated with the Communist Party of the USA, for whose *Jewish Life* he had once written. Far from backing off, Miller subsequently wrote a piece for the anti-communist *New Leader* attacking Soviet anti-Semitism.

After the Fall took the form of a confession; it was a confession in that Miller had reached a stage in his life when he needed to come to terms with his past before he felt justified in moving forwards. It was a work in which he tried to confront those aspects of his sensibility, those experiences, those events, that had left him bemused, guilty, self-doubting. What he wanted was to write his way out of his confusion, to reconcile himself with his own life and engage with those moral and political realities that had caused him such anguish from 1945 onwards. The play, then, featured his parents, with whom he had had a difficult relationship, and his failed marriages, but he also looked back to the House Un-American Activities Committee and, beyond that, to the concentration camp, that last standing as an image of the ultimate human betrayal.

To achieve his aim he returned to the work he had begun in 1950, when he had first met Marilyn, and to a character called Lorraine, plainly based on her. Working now both in Connecticut and the Chelsea Hotel, he wrote a play that paralleled his life in great detail. It was to be about a man 'desperate for a clear view of his own responsibility for his life, and this because he has recently found a woman he feels he can love, and who loves him; he cannot take another life into his hands hounded as he is by self-doubt'.[62] The woman, of course, was Inge Morath. For the director Harold Clurman, '*After the Fall* is a turning point ... a signal step in the evolution of Arthur Miller as man and artist. The play's auto-criticism exposes him to us; it also liberates him so that he can go on free of false legend and heavy halo. Had he not written this play he might never have been able to write another.'[63] The drama critic Martin Gottfried quotes from a brown spiral notebook kept by Elia Kazan in which he asks, 'What is more heroic, more deeply *human* than the spectacle of man looking into himself ... without deception ... to judge himself?'[64]

The play was to be produced at a theatre located at the new Lincoln Center for the Performing Arts. At least in the eyes of those who initially undertook its artistic direction, this was to be an answer to Europe's subsidized theatres, an alternative to the commercial imperatives of Broadway and the small-scale, exuberant but still, seemingly, marginal Off and Off Off Broadway. It was designed as a national theatre, a pretension largely without meaning in a country the size of the United States. Lincoln Center, established with Rockefeller money, was to bring together the New York Philharmonic, the Metropolitan Opera, the New York City Ballet and a repertory company. The Board invited Elia Kazan to serve on an advisory committee while the producer Robert Whitehead was put in charge of establishing the company. He persuaded Kazan to join him as an equal partner. Together with the designer Jo Mielziner, they planned the interior.

To be sure, this was a theatre created, in part, by individuals forged by another time. Robert Whitehead, a Canadian, had begun his producing career in 1947 and was forty-eight when the Center opened. Kazan, who had been a Group Theatre member and had directed *Death of a Salesman*, was fifty-five. Miller himself was forty-nine. Nonetheless, this seemed to many to be a venture with genuine promise and Miller threw his energies into it as, more formally, did Whitehead and Kazan.

But from the beginning there was a fundamental flaw in its conception in that the Board was dominated by those whose primary experience was of business and who believed that the theatre should be a paying concern. This, it seemed, was to be Broadway shifted twenty blocks north and gilded with the moral respectability of art. Both Whitehead and Kazan, after all, had Broadway successes to their name and it was these, rather than Kazan's Group Theatre affiliations, that seemed the guarantee of their utility. The glitter was to be an assurance of social cachet; the co-directors, of theatrical professionalism and assured success. That it did not work out that way surprised no one, in retrospect. Nor did the fault lie purely on one side. Kazan later admitted to his own culpability in a poor choice of plays and inadequate direction. His commitment to theatre, in fact, was now giving ground to an interest in the movies and the novel. The only genuine early successes of this theatre would be two new plays by Arthur Miller, the first directed by Kazan and the second, on his departure, by Harold Clurman – both plays, though, treated with a blend of suspicion and contempt by a number of key critics even as they were embraced by audiences.

Miller wrote with enthusiasm for the new theatre. It was, he thought, to be an escape from commercialism. Rehearsals would no longer be restricted to a few weeks [rehearsals for *After the Fall* in fact lasted for twelve weeks]. Tickets would not price out audiences. He noted that his play was already sold out until July and that tickets would soon be available into the fall. In May, Kenneth Tynan wrote from the National Theatre in England saying that he and Laurence Olivier were waiting 'on tenterhooks' for the first full

draft of *After the Fall*, hoping that the National might work out a deal similar
to that which Miller had with Lincoln Center. In the end, it would not be
the National that first staged it in Britain but the Belgrade Theatre in
Coventry, and not in 1963 or 64 but 1967.

The idea of a repertory company, however, did not sit easily with the
businessmen who dominated the Lincoln Center Board, not least because it
meant that the venture would be loss-making. If the product was to be so
good, why would it not make money like any other Broadway hit? Speaking
in 1972, Miller remarked:

> I'll say something I've never said before: the Lincoln Center board *never*
> intended to have a repertory theater ... when the point arrived at which the
> operational budget began to come up, it turned out that they had never
> established a budget on how much money would be allotted to the building,
> and how much was to be reserved for paying salaries for actors ... They were
> building a twelve-million-dollar monument, period ... it may be as stupid as
> this: donors like to have their names on the back of a seat. When you pay an
> actor's salary your name doesn't get engraved on the back of his head.[65]

Miller recalled that the smallest repertory company he knew of in Europe
comprised seventy-five people. Lincoln Center managed twenty-three. In the
end, he noted, apart from a few weeks in the 1968–9 season, it never operated
as a repertory theatre. When the Vivian Beaumont Theater was ready, three
months early, unbeknown to Kazan and Whitehead the Board were in negotiations with the producer Alexander H. Cohen to open it with Rex Harrison
in a British comedy.

Repertory theatre, by its nature, is likely to prove a costly approach to
production. The old Federal Theatre, which Miller had never quite forgotten,
had been financed by government money, as were most of those European
models he so admired and hoped to emulate. But it would be several years
before the federal government and city agencies, and then grudgingly, would
see the subsidizing of theatre as a legitimate if not essential endeavour. Thus
Lincoln Center was launched with much hope but little agreement as to its
precise nature. Whitehead, Kazan and Miller may have believed that they
had a new freedom, even a freedom to fail. They may have dreamed of
experiment, liberated from the tyranny of *New York Times* reviews and the
bottom line, but they would soon discover otherwise. Nonetheless, for the
moment, there was a genuine sense of excitement, a feeling that a new age
was dawning.

Kazan, however, found himself under fire from Lee Strasberg, who believed
that the Actors Studio should provide the actors for the new company –
his long-term relationship with Kazan, through the old Group Theatre,
convincing him that this was a natural extension of their work. The venture

thus found itself attacked from two different directions long before its first production was staged.

That production was to be Miller's new play. The problem was that playwright and director had not spoken, beyond a brief acknowledgement at Marilyn's behest, since Kazan had appeared before HUAC and named names. Accordingly, Whitehead was deputed to meet Miller in the Chelsea Hotel, where he was still working on the unruly manuscript. The theatre itself would not be ready for some time. To fill the gap a temporary building was constructed on West 4th Street on land leased from New York University for a peppercorn rent, the price of peppercorns being $1 a year. The building was to consist of a geodesic dome containing the auditorium and a stage that left no room for flying scenery. As it happened, this suited the style of the first production.

Miller responded positively. He had long wanted to be able to write for a specific theatre, to have a continuing relationship with a company. With Harold Clurman as dramaturge and the Actors Studio founder Bobby Lewis as head of the attached acting school, this seemed close to reinventing the Group Theatre that had inspired him as a student. As to Kazan, time had passed and to refuse to work with him would be to replicate the idea of a blacklist against which he had himself reacted so vehemently. Nonetheless, he had his doubts. He still despised Kazan's decision. What it came down to, he said, was

> whether his political stance and even moral defection, if one liked, should permanently bar him from working in the theatre, especially this kind of publicly supported theatre. As for morals, perhaps it was just as well not to cast too wide a net; for one thing, how many who knew by now that they had been supporting a paranoid and murderous Stalinist regime had really confronted their abetting of it? If I felt a certain distaste for Kazan's renouncing his past under duress, I was not at all sure that he should be excluded from a position for which he was superbly qualified by his talent and his invaluable experience with the Group. Nor could I be sure that I was not merely rationalizing my belief that he was the best director for this complex play; but to reject him, I thought, was to reject the hope for a national theatre in this time.[66]

One of those who had supported a paranoid and murderous Stalinist regime longer than he might, of course, had been Miller himself, so that there was, perhaps, more than a trace of guilt at the heart of his generosity of spirit.

Some of these arguments made their way into the play's text, as a character squarely based on Kazan is allowed his own rationalizations. This character, indeed, added one more twist to the relationship between the two men. It was unequivocally a portrait of Kazan and was seen by him as such. Somewhat astonishingly, though, it did not deter him from directing the play or even claiming identification with that character, so that if the playwright had stepped into his own work, so too did the director. There was to be a certain looking-glass quality to this production. Throughout, Kazan frequently asked the producer Robert Whitehead what he had thought of his collaborating with HUAC. Whitehead was unforgiving. Plainly, Kazan was never entirely at peace with his earlier decision even though he continued to justify it. Martin Gottfried recalls Miller's son Robert being asked about his father working with Kazan by the daughter of a couple who had suffered under McCarthy: Madeline and Jack Gilford, both summoned before HUAC. Robert reported back the next day: 'My father says that Elia Kazan has changed. He's sorry.' Jack Gilford then told his daughter: 'You tell Bobby Miller to tell his father that if Mr Kazan takes a half page advertisement apologizing, like he did explaining why he finked, then we'll believe him.'[67]

In his autobiography, Kazan asks: 'Was I really a leftist? Had I ever been? ... Wasn't what I'd been defending up until now by my silence a conspiracy working for another country? ... Why were my old softhearted "progressive friends" ... stonewalling? Answer: they were protecting the Party. Did I really believe in the noble motives they professed? Weren't they also protecting, as I had for so many years, their own pasts?'[68] The passage mirrors a speech in *After the Fall* in which Mickey, summoned before the House Un-American Activities Committee, says: 'The Party? But I despise the Party, and have for many years ... What am I defending? It's a dream now, a dream of solidarity. But the fact is, I have no solidarity with the people I could name ... the truth is ... my truth is, that I think the Party *is* a conspiracy ... they took our lust for the right and used it for Russian purposes.'[69] Mickey proposes that he and Lou, also subpoenaed, should name one another, as Kazan and the playwright Clifford Odets had proposed they should jointly do. Unlike Odets, Lou refuses.

For Miller, such protestations rang hollow. They may have been defending their own pasts but to his mind Kazan, for one, did not act out of patriotic motives. He had declared his loyalty to the new imperative because it served his purpose to do so. All the same, Kazan seemed oddly content with the portrait of himself, although he found Miller's self-portrait 'turgid'. He commented, 'There is a character based on me and my testimony, and although that character is not how I thought of myself, Art must have considered it reasonable, even generous, and I was ready to accept it as how, looking back, he saw the events.'[70] This is in part, no doubt, because Miller does allow him to justify his betrayals, to give voice to views that hovered uncertainly between honest disaffection with his own past and specious self-justification. Indeed, Miller allows Mickey/Kazan an extended speech (slightly shorter in the final version than the one with which the cast entered rehearsals) in which he justifies his actions in precisely the terms Kazan had done in the advertisement, drafted by his wife, that he published in the *New York Times* immediately after his appearance before the Committee in 1952. The idea of Kazan directing an actor playing the part of himself, and offering the very rationalizations that had brought such obloquy upon him, was, at the very least, bizarre.

When he and Miller met again, after a tense separation of more than a decade, no mention was made of their past and they quickly fell into their old professional and personal relationship. As it happened, Kazan did not like the first act, in which he made his appearance as a character, but did admire the second, while urging Miller to be even more forthright in mining his own life. There had, he knew, been certain exchanges between the playwright and Marilyn (here called Maggie) which, if transposed into the play, could invest it with a powerful if disturbing energy. He had seen something of that relationship and its bitterness and had spoken to Monroe after the breakup. She had, he recalled, 'revealed her anger at Art and a degree of scorn ... She'd expressed revulsion at his moral superiority toward her.' It seemed to Kazan that 'there were scenes between her and Miller that were a lot more dramatic than those he's let us see'.[71] He instanced the fight that the two had had on the set of *Some Like It Hot* (in 2009, Tony Curtis implausibly claimed that this was a result of the revelation that Marilyn was carrying his baby, a supposed fact curiously withheld for over forty years until there was nobody left alive to contradict him). It was the first act, now rewritten, that finally seemed to him to be 'strong and true'.[72] It was the more bewildering, therefore, that Miller subsequently 'denied, foolishly, that the story of that relationship in the play was based on his personal history, denied that his character, Maggie, was based on Marilyn. But he put into the mouth of Maggie precisely what Marilyn had thought of him, and particularly her scorn for him at the end of their marriage. This character is true ... Art is rough on himself, giving us all that Marilyn said in her disappointment and resentment.'[73]

As Kazan remarked, 'I'd seen how she'd humiliated him with the Frenchman [Yves Montand], and I was sympathetic to Art, not to her ... I also knew the degree of anger and vengeance she'd felt.' The sniping, he insisted, had been 'unremitting and without pity, and now it was all in the play. I admired Art for being so candid about their relationship, and I did not think him, as some people in our circle did, self-serving. I believe Marilyn came off better in the play than he did.'[74]

For his part, though, Miller professed total surprise when Robert Whitehead remarked that Maggie would be seen as a portrait, 'purely and simply', of Marilyn and when this proved to be how critics and audiences responded, blamed this on the blond wig Kazan had persuaded Barbara Loden, playing

Maggie, to wear. Speaking in 2008, Miller's sister Joan remarked on his refusal to acknowledge the portrait of Marilyn: 'He was able to do that. He was able to shut out very real events in his life and minimize things at the very least. He could do that ... I think that happens to a lot of creative people. It happens a lot to actors. The original event or relationship transmutes into something new and different.' But his denial 'was so silly. How could he possibly think that people would not recognize her? How could he have kidded himself to think that nobody was going to call him on it?'[75] Writing later, Miller conceded that he had protested too much, explaining that 'in disconnecting the fictional from any real person I was blinding myself to the obvious'.[76] However, in his mind the play was not about blame or self-justification but the degree to which people, all people, are ultimately responsible for their own lives, their own actions, and thereby for the lives of others. Finally, in 1987, he was ready to acknowledge that 'it's the most personal statement that I've made'.[77]

When he had first been approached by Whitehead and Kazan, Miller was far from ready. The play, consisting of several hundred pages, was still lacking the inner coherence for which he was reaching. Despite his enthusiasm for the new theatre, he was also reluctant to offer his play to a repertory company that would stage it for a limited season, alternating, as it would, with a number of other productions, but in the end the excitement of the project was enough for him to sign up.

For the moment though, he was struggling with his manuscript, interrupted as it was by news of the sudden death of his former wife in August 1962. It was not a surprise to him; he had long since registered what seemed to him her death wish. By then, he had been married to Inge for six months, but it was nonetheless an intrusion of a painful reality into the fictive world he and Kazan were constructing.

Kazan had now disappeared to Turkey to shoot a film, and wrote to inquire about progress: the last time he had heard the rough first act, he assured Miller, it had seemed 'enormous' to him. Miller, meanwhile, had urgencies of his own. In September Inge gave birth to Rebecca – 'a little prematurely,' Inge explained, 'because I was hanging from a crane earlier that morning. I still had what I thought was ten days.'[78] Kazan read the news in *Time* magazine and sent his congratulations, though still with his mind on the play, asking whether Miller had ever met George C. Scott.

Miller records that he had been writing *After the Fall* for two and a half years when he was approached by Whitehead and Kazan. In fact, he had been working on it for rather longer. What particularly appealed was the fact that there seemed to be a connection between the philosophy of the proposed new theatre and the emerging theme of his play, which was, he remarked, in its very form and essential idea, an attempt to bridge the gap between personal psychology and those other areas of life with which it is hard to establish a link. It was a play designed to enable audiences to acknowledge their responsibility for the world they had conspired in creating. It was a public play for a public theatre.

In the summer of 1963 Robert Whitehead, Elia Kazan and the playwright met at Miller's Roxbury studio. As Kazan put it, 'Our theatre was hanging from a rope that we were braiding together ... The Repertory Theater's fate was being decided in that cabin back of Miller's home in Roxbury and we knew it .'[79] At least for a time, Miller was protected from knowledge of the tensions between the businessmen running the project and those responsible for its artistic strategy. The chairman of the Board was a director of the Campbell's soup company, with interests in steel, oil, glass and investments. His knowledge of theatre was minimal at best. He and others opposed the temporary building that was to stage *After the Fall*. Nonetheless, for a time, Whitehead was successful in getting his way, but it was not a success that was to be repeated. Lincoln Center was fated to become a continuing disappointment, as a succession of directors were hired and fired.

In July Kazan wrote outlining his production ideas and recording the essence of a conversation he and Miller had had a few days before. From the list of scenes it is clear that the play had yet to settle into its final form. It is, however, fascinating in that Kazan insists on locating every scene, as it then existed, in terms of precise dates, dates that match up with Miller's life. It is a list that includes a graduation ceremony in 1938 (the year of Miller's graduation), Quentin's childhood home in 1930, Quentin's New York hotel (Miller was living at the Chelsea), Maggie's first New York apartment in 1955 (the year Marilyn acquired hers), Maggie and Quentin's place in Long Island (Miller and Marilyn rented a Long Island house), a café in Salzburg (Inge's home town). So it continues. His concern with dates, Kazan said, was prompted by a need to dress the characters appropriately. In fact he was fitting the action into the known details of Miller's life.

Miller, meanwhile, was searching for a way of staging a play that was essentially to take place within the mind of the central character, Quentin. In a letter, Kazan suggested that he should enter the stage accompanied by the other actors, who would represent the memories he carries with him, the people with whom he would speak and who mark key moments in his life. They were to remain on stage throughout the play, stepping forward as Quentin summoned them as though they constituted what he called the geography of Quentin's mind. In the eventual production Kazan found other ways of staging this internal drama but the essence of these plans was carried forward. From late July onwards, he began the business of casting, already pressing the claims of his mistress Barbara Loden, despite others suggested by Miller's agent Kay Brown and, indeed, by Miller himself. In a letter on 29 July Kazan explained to him that he thought Barbara had Maggie's first scene well within her grasp. As for the part of Quentin, he urged the casting of George C. Scott. The name of Jason Robards came up, but at first Kazan resisted an actor who, he declared, looked like someone who had been in bars a lot – not unreasonably, as it turned out, since he did indeed go on a somewhat spectacular bender during rehearsals.

Those rehearsals began, according to the actor Paul Mann, with Kazan announcing to the gathered actors, 'Hello, my name is Elia Kazan, and some of you know this play is about an informer; and some of you know that I am an informer. Those of you who didn't know, know it now.'[80] He then added, 'This is the first rehearsal of the Repertory of Lincoln Center. In a moment Arthur Miller will read you his play.'[81] He duly did, having told the actors, 'This is a happy play, the happiest work I've ever written.'[82] For Kazan, the response of the actors was disappointing, while Jason Robards (who regarded Miller as 'a terrible reader'), as Quentin, was alarmed that his role seemed to be that of commentator rather than full participant. In public, Kazan was enthusiastic, though in a way that betrays his approach to the play. In a television interview he remarked: 'The guy writes better than he ever did. He writes more eloquently, more movingly. In fact a whole emotional thing has opened up in that man that wasn't there before. You feel that what's happened to the hero of the play has happened to him. This whole emotional release that's happened to Miller these last years has made him a much deeper writer, a better writer.' On the other hand, he was prepared to concede: 'It's far more daring. It's far more unusual. It's generally experimental. It's difficult to do. There's no precedent for it. There's never been a play like it. I think it cuts very deep. It says a lot. I'm scared of it and I'm exhilarated by it.'[83] Beneath the praise it is possible to hear the doubts.

The result was a deal of rewriting, especially of the second act, in which Kazan came to have increasing confidence, especially since he felt he had found in Barbara Loden an actress who would sympathetically portray a character based on Monroe: 'I hadn't needed anyone to tell me she fitted the role. I knew her past in detail and knew Marilyn's personal history as well. They'd both been "floaters" and come out of almost identical childhood experiences, which had left them neurotic, often desperate, and in passion difficult to control.' She might have a range that went from A to B, but within that range, he claimed, she went deep. She was 'able to go from the kind of innocence we used to believe fifteen-year-old girls possessed to a pitch of rage that actually frightened Jason Robards'.[84] He had earlier suggested Madeleine Sherwood, who had played Abigail in the original production of *The Crucible* and had been blacklisted, but the idea was abandoned. The minor role of a nurse was played by Faye Dunaway, who would later star as Maggie in a film version.

Jason Robards was not happy either with his role or the atmosphere in rehearsals: 'I certainly did think it was a little odd that [Miller] was working with Kazan. Especially since Gadg [Kazan] had been mixed up with Monroe. And in those first weeks of rehearsal, I thought that Gadg was shutting down. In fact, I almost quit the show. The atmosphere was so bad. I'd go off and get drunk. I said to Whitehead, "Get Miller out of the rehearsal." And they did. There was this thing underneath, he and Gadg, even though they'd said they had settled their differences.' According to Martin Gottfried, Robards told his wife (Lauren Bacall): 'It's a whole snake pit. I'm in a nest of *snakes* here. I don't know what's going on at rehearsal ... I started misbehaving.'[85]

Robards returned on 22 November 1963, as news came through of the assassination of John Kennedy. The cast were sent home. Miller was in a hardware store when he heard the announcement. Like many, he found it difficult to believe. 'A radio was playing. "The President has been shot," came the voice through the shine and glitter of housewares ... I felt an urge to laugh, maybe at the absurdity. The two clerks continued waiting on people. ... For about a minute I couldn't locate the radio in all the clutter of mixers, irons, appliances. My mind kept saying, No, it's going to change, it's a mistake.' To Miller it was reminiscent of Roosevelt's unexpected death in April 1945 when even reporters had broken down in tears, describing the cortège as it passed down Pennsylvania Avenue. A finger, he remarked, had been pushed 'through the delicate web of the future'. Even in the thirties, it seemed to him, 'as bad as things got, there was always the future; certainly in all my work was an implicit reliance on some redemptive time to come, a feeling that the cosmos cared about man, if only to mock him. With Kennedy's assassination the cosmos had simply hung up the phone.'[86] He was not alone in thinking so. For Edward Albee it 'changed the course of the United States',[87] while for Don DeLillo it 'broke the back of the American century' and 'injected a sense of randomness and ambiguity'.[88]

The assassination was a defining moment for Miller, as for so many others. He had attended an inauguration ball with Joe Rauh, his old lawyer from the HUAC hearings, and felt more attracted to this president than any since Roosevelt. At the same time, this man had been responsible for the Bay of Pigs and for laying the groundwork for Vietnam. Robert Lowell, invited to the White House in May 1962, subsequently wrote to Edmund Wilson: 'Then the next morning you read that the Seventh Fleet had been sent somewhere in Asia and you had the funny feeling of how unimportant the artist really was, that this was sort of window dressing and that the real government was somewhere else, and that something much closer to the

Pentagon was really running the country ... we should be windows, not window dressing.'[89]

For the moment, though, Kennedy's death seemed to expose a fault line in the American psyche, to mark the end of what appeared to be a new commitment to liberal values at home and abroad. A 'strange futility,' Miller explained, 'crept into the very idea of writing a play.'[90] Death was also closer to home: during rehearsals, Kazan's wife Molly died – it was she who had favoured a more realist version of *Death of a Salesman* and who had rejected the analogy at the heart of *The Crucible*. Martin Gottfried observes that the moment was registered in a hastily scrawled and strangely formal note in Kazan's notebook: 'Molly Kazan had a stroke at about seven PM on December 13, 1963. She died in the emergency ward at Bellevue at 5:37 PM on December 14th.'[91]

After the Fall finally opened on 23 January 1964. The temporary theatre was barely finished in time. Miller and Whitehead bought screwdrivers and personally fixed six rows of seats on their brackets as water dripped through the roof. In fact, the theatre proved remarkably appropriate for a play whose set was deliberately spartan. There was no furniture in a conventional sense. Instead there were three levels, with the characters sitting on ledges or in crevices. Rising above this and, as Miller required, dominating it was the stone watch-tower of a concentration camp, its 'wide lookout windows ... like eyes which at the moment seem blind and dark'. Bent reinforcing rods were to 'stick out of it like broken tentacles'.[92]

The play begins as the lights rise and the characters move down from the rear of the stage. Their whispers are directed at Quentin, a man in his forties. These figures from his life crowd into his mind, demanding space, requiring attention, as he begins to talk, apparently to someone just beyond the stage but effectively to himself, seeking justification if not absolution.

Quentin is a kind of dangling man, like Saul Bellow's character poised in hesitation. He had, he explains, abandoned his job some three or four months before, following the death of Maggie, a name which means nothing to us except that in uttering her name he effectively animates a memory made concrete in the form of Maggie herself who 'stirs' on the platform above him. And this is to become the method of the play as characters, conversations, places, materialise in his mind, which is the site of this drama. The effect, Miller suggested, was to be 'the struggling, flitting, instantaneousness of a mind questing over its own surfaces and into its depths.'

Stripped of those ideas and values which once motivated and justified him – 'Socialism once, then love' – Quentin is surviving without purpose and living without meaning. Once, he had felt the world threatened by injustices he had been born to correct, a Manichean world in which to live was to battle for a self-evident right. Once, history, or an agreed set of values, might have served to render some verdict on his life, a verdict the world would have condemned or justified but which at least offered a structure of meaning. But now he feels that 'the bench' is 'empty'. A visit to a concentration camp reinforces this idea. So absolute a denial of transcendence, or even of a common humanity, leaves him aghast, his own lack of faith merely rendering him powerless before the rational processes and irrational faith of those who constructed such temples to death, since 'Believers built this, maybe that's the fright – and I, without belief, stand here disarmed.' And though he confesses to having discovered love, in the person of Holga, the woman who has entered his life, his history of failure and betrayal, resonated on a public level, seems to earn him no right to it.

The play, in effect, is his attempt to discover a reason to go on, to embrace his newly discovered love, and therefore faith, in the face of this private and public history of failure. He thus scans the past in order to accuse so that, at the end, he can absolve, and not himself alone. And, as a consequence, he seeks to discover and reveal the connections between his own betrayals and those which seem, to him, to have threatened meaning itself for only then will redemption seem a possibility.

Beyond the personal failures lie two facts which seem to threaten any conception of order, any notion of shared values: the concentration camp and the House Un-American Activities Committee. And if these seem disproportionate in their substance and effects, as is the connection between them and the private denials and betrayals he recapitulates and re-experiences, then a central function of the play is to establish those links. For behind the play is a conception of history that proposes it as a product of human actions and not a force of nature defying understanding and unrelated to daily experience.

The concentration camp tower looms over the stage and, therefore, over Quentin's consciousness. It constitutes the context within which he struggles to understand the entropic nature of his experience. It stands as an expression of an absolute denial of human connectiveness, an image of human abandonment and the nullification of values whose echoes he hears in his own life and that of his nation, for the assumption of the play, and the justification for its method, lies in the belief, expressed by Quentin, that 'Everything is one thing.' Thus, when he speaks of the isolation he feels when offering to defend a friend, Lou, summoned to appear before HUAC, he could equally be talking of a truth discovered at the camp: 'It's like some unseen web of connexion between people is simply not there. And I always relied on it, somehow.

The truth towards which Quentin makes his way is that the camp does not stand as some alternative reality, some caesura in human affairs, but that it is of a piece with entirely recognizable human characteristics.

There can be something portentously solemn about Quentin's philosophical journey and the language with which he expresses it. It was certainly something that Kazan felt as, in another sense, did Jason Robards who, reportedly, saw his role as pivotal without being dramatically compelling. The action turns around him as if he were no more than the axle that drives the wheel of the play. It would be reassuring to feel that his linguistic pretentiousness was wholly an aspect of character but there are moments when it seems to be generated by a certain solemnity of purpose on the part of the author.

The text abounds in question marks as Quentin tries to understand his life, to synthesize his experiences. The play may recapitulate the processes of the human mind but Quentin is required to distil the meaning of each scene, to become a critic analyzing his own text. That synthesis can occur in his mind rather than in that of an audience. In his earlier plays Miller had often dealt with characters incapable, for one reason or another, of analyzing or expressing their situation. The audience was placed in the position of judge. Here, Quentin is the judge as he is also the penitent. He arrogates to himself responsibility for discovering and elucidating meaning.

With Quentin, Miller chooses for his protagonist a man who deals in words, whose job, as a lawyer, is to analyze and deploy evidence either to defend or prosecute. Yet that is precisely Quentin's dilemma. The linguistic probing is both an expression of his search for truth and of his evasion of it. He is the accuser and the accused and language is the agency of his being. Professionally, he works through questions, each one designed to build a case, uncover a truth. And, as with any lawyer, that truth lies in the past which must be explored for the light it throws on present justice.

Miller was more than content with the production. Kazan, he thought, had 'created a production of great control and truthful feeling, surely one of the best things he had ever done'.[93] The audiences responded positively, and by most standards the play was a success. Indeed, Whitehead and Clurman would soon be asking Miller for another play, which he would duly complete in record time, *Incident at Vichy*. For Miller, though, it was less the reviews, which were mixed, than the extra-theatrical attacks which shocked and dismayed him. He was accused of cerebral pornography, of exhibitionism, of the betrayal of a woman no longer able to speak back.

As its title implies, *After the Fall* concerns itself with how it is possible to live with a knowledge of human failure, on a personal or a public level. Its principal proposition is that we all live after the fall, with full knowledge of the fact that we serve our own interests, and are prepared to sacrifice others to do so, intent always on declaring our own innocence at the price of affirming others' guilt. He found evidence for this in his own life.

After the Fall, though, initially had a literary rather than a personal source, a fact that seemed to pass reviewers by. It is this literary origin that underscores the degree to which Miller saw the play as a philosophical speculation rather than primarily an act of exorcism or a therapeutic gesture, though it plainly also functioned in that way. It was in part inspired by Camus's *La Chute* (*The Fall*), first published in 1956, a book he had once been asked to adapt and whose implications had continued to concern him. Camus was a writer Miller admired and with whom he felt affinity. The Spanish Civil War had been as central to him as it had to Miller. Indeed, he joined the Communist Party as a result. He too had been married to a woman addicted to drugs. Where they differed was over Camus's absurdist convictions. Camus proposes universal guilt as a condition of being. As throughout his work, Miller's only interest here lay in the transformation of guilt into responsibility. Lost in the scandal of a play that featured America's recently dead screen icon was a work of genuine complexity – Miller's attempt not merely to debate with Camus but to create a counterpart to his philosophical inquiry.

At the centre of *The Fall*, as of Miller's play, is a successful barrister who suffers a sudden sense of existential doubt. The book carries an epigraph from the Russian poet and novelist Mikhail Lermontov that has immediate relevance to *After the Fall*. He describes his novel *A Hero of Our Times* as 'a portrait but not of an individual; it is the aggregate of the vices of a whole generation in their fullest expression'. It is also a novel, he admits, in which 'the author had portrayed himself and his acquaintances'.

Camus's central character, Clamence, watches a woman throw herself into the Seine and does nothing to intervene. He has failed in love and come to feel that he is motivated only by self-concern: 'That's the way man is ... he can't feel without self-love.'[94] His only connection with others, he suspects, is guilt. The novel, like *After the Fall*, takes the form of a confession to an invisible listener. The anxiety Clamence feels, though, is not restricted to himself. He lives in the Jewish quarter of Amsterdam from which seventy-five thousand Jews, he observes, were 'deported or assassinated' in 'one of the greatest crimes in human history'.[95] But he did not serve in the Resistance. He had watched from a distance, in safety, secure not merely from danger but from examining his own responsibility towards others. 'People,' he observes, 'hasten to judge in order not to be judged themselves', since the 'idea that comes most naturally to a man, as if from his very nature, is the idea of his innocence ... each of us insists on being innocent at all costs, even if he has to accuse the whole human race and heaven itself.'[96] Just how closely Miller, who had himself sat out the war in the security of America as his brother served in the Battle of the Bulge, engaged with Camus's work is evident in his remark that, 'the basic thrust of the play is that the enemy is innocence ... That is, until you give up your innocence, you are very open to crime.'[97]

Clamence's confession, 'I don't believe there is a single person I loved that I didn't eventually betray',[98] is precisely echoed by Quentin's acceptance of his own culpability in that same regard. So, too, Clamence's observation, with respect to the Holocaust, that 'crime consists less in making others die than in not dying oneself'[99] would find an echo in *After the Fall*, when Quentin observes that no one would not rather have sanctioned deaths in the camps, no matter how indirectly, than himself die in one.

The Fall is in effect a monologue addressed to a stranger – and since the speaker is a lawyer, perhaps to a judge, except that the judge turns out to be himself. In a sense that would prove equally true of Miller's play. Where Clamence finally relieves himself of responsibility through asserting that his is a shared condition, Miller wishes to edge beyond Camus's position in claiming that judgement remains a necessity. Human contradiction, to his mind, does not dissolve moral distinctions. What it does is to lay down a challenge to discover the basis on which life can continue in full knowledge of imperfection but without, as he would be accused of doing, homogenizing guilt. While accepting that 'everything is one thing',[100] that there is a connection between private acts of betrayal and a national abandonment of mutuality, unlike Camus he wishes to discover the basis on which it would be possible to move forward. For Camus's ironies he wishes to substitute a belief in the future – possibly an American, possibly a Jewish, faith in futurity. This was one reason Miller found the theatre of the absurd unacceptable, hermetic in its circularities. Whenever people played with the notion of an amoral existence, it seemed to him, the Jew was always the one likely to suffer. Aware that 'some unseen web of connection between people is simply not there' – HUAC and the camps providing public evidence – a connection on which he has always relied, Miller's protagonist, Quentin, discovers the necessity of living with imperfection, taking a wager on the future.

The component elements of Miller's play, in other words, were all in place, from its dramatic strategy, which has a man summon up figures from his life, confessing to his own guilt, through to his elision of personal failures with the fact of the Holocaust. Even the setting derives from Camus. Miller calls for his set to be 'neolithic, lava-like ... distinguished by the greyness of its landscape',[101] as Camus describes 'a pile of ashes'.

At the same time, Camus's invoking of the Holocaust had now gained a new reality for Miller that can be traced to his visit to Mauthausen and to Inge's decision to take him there (she was, he said, 'sifting through a past with which she wished to make peace').[102] It also served as a reminder of his own immunity and the residue of guilt that left, an issue he had explored in the fable that was *The Man Who Had All the Luck*. John Updike once remarked: 'If you haven't fought in a war, as I have not, or had any real disaster visit your body, there is a nagging feeling that there is something tinny and unfelt about your inner self.'[103]

Primo Levi asked, 'Are you ashamed because you are alive in place of another?' adding, 'It is no more than a supposition, indeed the shadow of a supposition: that each man is his brother's Cain, that each of us ... has usurped his neighbor's place and lived in his stead.'[104] He wrote as a literal survivor, but there were others, who never experienced the camps, who felt that same sense of shame. References to Cain, indeed, are to be found everywhere in Arthur Miller's work (the original title of *All My Sons* was *And Cain Went Forth*), including in the essay he would write about the Auschwitz trials he attended in 1964 alongside Inge.

The reason such a seemingly aberrant event as the Holocaust compels attention is not its remoteness from ourselves but, Miller observes, our complicity with it, murders from which we all profit if only by virtue of having survived. In *After the Fall*, part of the acknowledged guilt is of not having died. On the other hand, and disturbingly, he also confessed to that frisson which comes with the death of others, the unworthy afterthought, even at the graveside, that I am alive, that someone else was ahead of me in the queue for death. As the camp chaplain remarks in Armand Gatti's *L'Enfant-rat*, 'Survivors of a war never stop killing the dead. How else can they prove that they themselves have survived?'[105] The temptation is to presume that survival is to be equated with innocence. Inge recalled classmates disappearing from her school. They were Jews, but she believed they must have been guilty of some offence, or why would they be thus punished? This was the world of Franz Kafka, whose own sister would tread the path towards the camps. For Arthur Miller, Kafka represented the paradigm, understanding that 'everything is permitted',[106] a frightening truth echoed by the figure of Caligula in Camus's play of that name. There had been a joke current in Buchenwald that the letter 'U' some were required to wear did not mean *Ungar*, 'Hungarian', but *unschuldig*, 'innocent'.

Understandably, writers approach the Holocaust with some uncertainty. Even those who experienced it and who wrote directly of their experiences had their doubts. 'Try to look. Try to see,'[107] Charlotte Delbo, a concentration camp inmate though not a Jew, instructs herself, repeating the phrase three times, almost immediately adding, 'Do not look ... Do not look at yourself.'[108] 'All words,' she says, 'have wilted long ago',[109] and besides, 'I am no longer sure that what I have written is true', even if 'I am sure it happened'.[110] Then there were those who chose not to remember. In Aharon Appelfeld's *The Immortal Bartfuss* (1988) a character remarks, 'Memories don't interest me. I live in the present, the present tense.'[111] But as Irma Kurtz has said, 'Jews did not die in those infernal camps because they failed to flee or could not fight, they did not suffer and die through choosing the martyr's way, they did not die because they were good or bad, Orthodox or lapsed, rich or poor, even if they had forgotten the faith of their ancestors, they died because they had been born Jews.'[112]

Miller was one of the first playwrights to engage with the Holocaust. But at this early point, in what was to become a fierce debate about the nature of the experience, its meaning, its expressibility, he was unaware of the passions that attached themselves to the idea of staging, even at the level of metaphor – or perhaps especially at the level of metaphor – an event that seemed to exist outside the parameters of art and perhaps of language itself, that defied the power, indeed the right, of theatre to engage with it. His visit to Mauthausen, though, 'made me certain that I had to write about it. However, the use of those images [of the camp and the House Un-American Activities Committee, which stood as the other public evidence of betrayal] in themselves were not of interest to me.' What was of interest was that they described the death of love, people incapable any more of a human connection, not just with their victims but probably with each other or anybody at all, something that Miller had experienced on a personal level: 'I had lived through that.' It was, he said, 'a very difficult play to write'.[113]

For all this, the primary emphasis of the play undoubtedly lay on his private life and, despite his curious denials, on his relationship with the woman from whom he had so recently parted, a figure he was still, in early drafts, calling Lorraine, a woman 'trusting in her candor ... non-judgemental ... whose very candor brought her little but disguised contempt in the serious opinion of the world ... bewildered and overwhelmed, she secretly came to side against herself ... until denial finally began its work, leaving her all but totally innocent of her own collaboration as well as her blind blows of retaliation. She felt besieged, could trust nothing anymore.'[114]

Quentin revisits the failure of his relationship with Maggie, first his mistress and then his wife. Meanwhile, other dramas are being acted out. A friend and colleague is summoned before the House Un-American Activities Committee precipitating a moment of crisis. Will Quentin the barrister defend him and bring danger to himself and his firm? He is relieved of the burden when that man commits suicide. In the background, still, is the concentration camp tower, a symbol of some ultimate betrayal whose seeds lie in a flawed human nature for which betrayal seems an ever-present possibility. When Quentin remarks, 'I never quite believed that people could be so easily disposed of',[115] he is referring equally to personal relationships, to the abandonment of others in naming names, and to the ultimate disposals enacted in the camps.

The central character is patently Arthur Miller, who had emerged from the 1930s so sure of his mission, so content with his good fortune, that in *The Man Who Had All the Luck* he created a play in which the protagonist feels a mixture of alarm and guilt at his success. Miller's paradise was lost, regained, and then lost again. *After the Fall* is his attempt to understand why, and he wrote it with an unblushing honesty. In 'The Last Comedians', the unpublished story in which, appearing as a man called Rufus Solomon, he struggles to make sense of two broken marriages, he remarks on the joy he had derived from being able to confront the disasters in his life, from being judged not only by his own government, as well as by two wives, but by himself. Beyond that, he observes, lies only God.

Miller's own experience was to be offered as exemplary in that the play was 'primarily to me almost totally a work in which I was trying to discover by what means, by what cathexis, anybody could seize the reality of his life, which can only be the question of how responsible he is for his life. That's what this play is about, and it's utilizing this experience for that end.'[116] At the same time there is no doubt that the immediate function of *After the Fall* was to allow Miller to seize the reality of his life, then to acknowledge responsibility, and hence to move on.

Just as Maggie was patently Marilyn, so all the other characters were portraits of people in his own life – from his parents, to his first wife Mary, to Elia Kazan. Maggie is 'a beautiful piece trying to take herself seriously',[117] who has been 'chewed and spat out by a long line of grinning men',[118] and whom Quentin sets out to save, as Miller had convinced himself he could save Marilyn. His relationship with her is traced out in detail and not without sympathy. If Maggie is self-regarding, hysterically demanding, Quentin accuses himself of failing her. When Louise, his first wife, remarks, 'You want a woman to provide an atmosphere, in which there are never any issues, and you'll fly around in a constant bath of praise,'[119] Miller is reproducing Mary Miller's complaint against him, which he was inclined to accept as valid. The parallels are many and precise, but to Miller's mind this had deflected attention from what seemed to him to be the essential themes of the play.

Quentin effectively summons a series of witnesses in a trial of his own conscience which is simultaneously a trial of human nature. A failure of human connectiveness seems apparent on all levels and betrayal emerges as a social instinct. So, individual failures of conscience are juxtaposed with more public instances – the House Un-American Activities Committee, for which betrayal was a modus operandi, and the concentration camp, a symbol of the nullification of any sense of shared obligations, of a shared humanity.

One logical, and indeed moral, objection to the play is that in relating individual acts of betrayal – a child is deceived by his parents as they take a brother to the seaside and leave him alone, as Miller's parents similarly deceived him – to the horrors of the camps he is at risk of making everything equivalent. Miller's answer when I questioned him on this was to say that everything has to begin somewhere. The other risk is that if everyone is indeed born after the fall, then everyone is guilty and therefore everyone is innocent. Oddly, this was a point put to Adolf Eichmann by his Israeli judges: 'You ... said that your role in the Final Solution was an accident and that almost anybody could have taken your place, so that potentially almost all Germans are equally guilty. What you meant to say was that where all, or almost all, are guilty, nobody is.'[120] For Miller, that was indubitably true, not just of the Germans, to whom he was disinclined to grant absolution (though the Israeli judges would have nothing to do with the idea of collective guilt, insisting that in the judicial context guilt and innocence were objective terms), but in that the desire to insist on innocence is itself at the very root of human cruelty. Quentin remarks, looking up at the concentration camp tower, 'Who can be innocent again on this mountain of skulls? I tell you what I know! My brothers died here but my brothers built this place.'[121]

Hannah Arendt, accused, because of her references to Jewish guilt, of eroding the difference between victim and guard, explained: 'The distinction between victims and persecutors was blurred in the concentration camps, deliberately and with calculation.' It was 'an aspect of totalitarian methods'[122] and not evidence of shared culpability. Miller, accused of the same offence, was inclined to retort that far more disturbing than the contrast between those who suffered and those who inflicted the suffering, plain though that was, was the unpalatable truth that, as Quentin points out, 'this is not some crazy aberration of human nature to me. I can easily see the perfectly normal contractors and their cigars, the carpenters, plumbers, sitting at their ease over lunch pails; I can see them laying the pipes to run the blood out ... good fathers, devoted sons, grateful that someone else will die, not they, and how can one understand that, if one is innocent? If somewhere in one's soul there is no accomplice of that joy ... when a burden dies ... and leaves you safe?'[123]

Arendt came close to a similar conviction. In an essay on 'Organized Guilt and Universal Responsibility' she remarked, 'For many years now we have met Germans who declare that they are ashamed of being Germans. I have often felt tempted to answer that I am ashamed of being human. This elemental shame, which many people of the most various nationalities share with one another today, is what finally is left of our sense of international solidarity.' It is tempting to feel that this was true of Miller, whose sense of solidarity had once turned on a belief in the triumph of a reformed society achieved by an enlightened humanity but who had then come to believe that what we share is less a millenarian fate than a flawed nature. 'Our fathers' enchantment with humanity,' Arendt had continued,

> was of a sort which ... did not conceive of the terror of the idea of humanity and the Judeo-Christian faith in the unitary origin of the human race ... For the idea of humanity, when purged of all sentimentality, has the very serious consequence that in one form or another men must assume responsibility for

all crimes committed by men and that all nations share the onus of evil committed by all others. Shame at being a human being is the purely individual and still non-political expression of this insight. Perhaps those Jews, to whose forefathers we owe the first conception of the idea of humanity, knew something about that burden when each year they used to say 'Our Father and King, we have sinned before you', taking not only the sins of their own community but all human offences upon themselves. Those who today are ready to follow this road in a modern version do not content themselves with the hypocritical confession 'God be thanked, I am not like that,' in horror at the undreamed-of potentialities of the German national character. Rather, in fear and trembling, have they finally realized of what man is capable ... This, however, is certain: Upon them and only upon them, who are filled with a genuine fear of the inescapable guilt of the human race, can there be any reliance when it comes to fighting fearlessly, uncompromisingly, everywhere against the incalculable evil that men are capable of bringing about.

For Miller, Arendt's observations would have seemed entirely germane. Her existential stance was an echo of his own. Yet what was to be done in the face of this? For Arendt, the obligation that she identifies may be one that people 'do not wish to assume';[124] but a new politics was necessary, for if a common guilt was denied it left the route open for one race, one group, one nation to believe that its own assumed superiority, its innocence, justified the extermination of those deemed inferior, alone guilty of presumed crimes. For Miller in *After the Fall* the knowledge that 'we are very dangerous ... that we meet unblessed; not in some garden of wax fruit and painted trees, that lie of Eden, but after, after the Fall, after many deaths', necessitates not so much a new politics as a new commitment. Was it enough, though, to acknowledge that 'the wish to kill is never killed'? For Miller, it is necessary, if not sufficient, to confront and embrace the truth of human fallibility in an unending battle to transcend that heritage. As an individual, Quentin's love for Holga, a renewed declaration of faith by two damaged people, stands for a similar necessity for humanity at large: 'No, it's not a certainty, I don't feel that. But it does seem feasible ... not to be afraid. Perhaps it's all one has.'[125]

For Quentin, and beyond him for Miller, the truth towards which he works his way is that humankind is, indeed, born after the fall and that this is a truth finally to be embraced. The camps, though, did not stop history or invalidate those who sought to reconstruct a moral world. HUAC, with its casual cruelties, did not render idealism defunct or commitment a dangerous irrelevance. Nor did failed relationships negate the possibility of new relationships. One of the play's central images is of life as an idiot child that must be embraced despite, if not because of, its imperfections, a metaphor that was to become disturbingly real when Inge herself gave birth to a Down's syndrome child.

Neither Quentin nor Miller was present when Maggie and Marilyn died, yet both feel responsibility, both seek some kind of permission to continue their lives. When Quentin says, defensively, 'It's not that I think I killed her',[126] he echoes Miller's own insistence, but behind such statements lies at least a sense of unease. The writer W.J. Weatherby says that he 'had heard from mutual friends that [Miller] had the feeling, amounting often to tearing guilt, that the divorce had helped her [Marilyn] toward her death and that he should have been able to do something to save her ... but had been persuaded that he was no longer part of her life. A friend told me of his anguish and said that his new wife persuaded him to write *After the Fall* to lay the ghost to rest and so set their own marriage free.'[127]

The British premiere took place at the Belgrade Theatre in Coventry, a city largely destroyed in a Baedeker raid during the war. Outside the theatre were the gaunt ruins of the bombed cathedral, a reminder of another raid – that on Dresden, which itself had a concentration camp. Seen in such a context, the outline of the camp tower assumed a centrality it had not in the American production. It was not that the figure of Monroe became irrelevant or that personal betrayals deferred to public ones, but that the balance of the play seemed different. It had become another play. Today, no one walks out affronted on grounds of taste or reads *After the Fall* through the prism of private anguish. The personal has become the exemplary, while social imme-diacies have deferred to metaphor.

There is a photograph of Miller and his wife on opening night, perched on the parallel metal bars that guard a backstage staircase. He is in a tuxedo, she in a strapless gown. He is staring at his feet, seemingly deep in thought. She looks at him, apparently anxiously. There was good cause for anxiety. The novelist James Baldwin walked out, supposedly shocked by its portrait of Marilyn, though his own connection with her was tenuous. Simone Signoret regretted that he should have chosen to write about Marilyn. Noël Coward dismissed the play as 'a three-and-a-half-hour wail about how cruel life has been to Arthur Miller'. His philosophy, Coward complained, 'is adolescent and sodden with self-pity. His taste is non-existent.' The Marilyn Monroe part he found 'vulgar beyond belief'. Though 'hailed as a masterpiece and treated with the greatest possible reverence', it was, he declared, the product of 'a mediocre mind'.[128] Susan Sontag attacked Miller's 'staggering imper-tinence' in equating personal problems with public issues as if they were 'on the same level'. The 'shapely corpse of Marilyn Monroe', she asserted, sprawled on the stage in a way that could only elevate personal tragedy and demean public ones. It was a play that evidenced bad faith and was 'sadly wanting, in both intelligence and moral honesty'.[129] In proposing that we are all both innocent and guilty, responsible and not, victims and victimizers, he was offering an unearned exoneration. It failed as a play because of what Sontag called its intellectual softness, as Rolf Hochhuth's then current play *The Deputy* (which indicted Pope Pius XII for his failure to challenge the Holocaust) failed because of its intellectual simplicity and artistic naivety. Jacqueline Kennedy would soon refuse to attend a performance of *Incident at Vichy* because, in her view, Miller had been 'horrid to Marilyn'.[130]

For his part, Miller expressed shock that concern over a possible portrait of his former wife should reveal so limited a critical awareness of the play's broader themes. Torn between berating such critics for ignoring the under-lying theme in favour of scandal, and pointing out that the play contained, in confessional form, the very self-accusations with whose supposed absence they now wished to belabour him, he found himself resisting too precise a parallel between events in his own life and those on the stage. Accusing others of denial, he was far from free of it himself. He was, he remarked, 'soon widely hated but the play had spoken its truth as, after all, it was obliged to do, and if the truth was clothed in pain, perhaps it was important for the audience to confront it uncomfortably and even in the anger of denial. In time, and with difficulty, I saw the justification of the hostility toward me, for I had indeed brought very bad news.'[131]

In the 7 February issue of *Life* magazine Miller published an article under the title, 'With Respect for Her Agony – But with Love'. The character of Maggie, he insisted, 'is not in fact Marilyn Monroe'. Maggie 'is a character in a play about the human animal's unwillingness or inability to discover in himself the seeds of his own destruction'.[132] She is an exemplification of 'the self-destructiveness which finally comes when one views oneself as pure victim'. Besides, those who now sought to defend his former wife against the dramatic uses to which Miller put her were, he noted, frequently those who had abused the real Marilyn Monroe when she was alive. The hypocrisy, in other words, was theirs and not his. But the fact is that these events were so recent, his private life so much part of public record, that to hope that American critics would retain a sense of detachment was perhaps to hope too much. He conceded that 'elements of my life have been publicized to the point where, in some minds, fiction and design seem to have given way to reportage'. Himself accused of bad faith, he had in fact written a play in which that was a principal concern. The problem was that he was so stung by the response that his own reply was less than convincing: he continued to insist that the play was no more autobiographical than his other work.

Miller was especially indignant that the play should have been seen as Quentin's – and hence his – attempt to exculpate himself, since, as he rightly pointed out, it was precisely concerned not to permit its central character exculpation. In his words; 'There is not, and cannot truly be, a divestment of guilt [but] a recognition of the individual's part in the evil he sees and abhors.' This was to be the link between *After the Fall* and the second play he wrote for Lincoln Center, *Incident at Vichy*. It is, as he says in his *Life* magazine article, 'always and forever the same struggle: to perceive somehow our own complicity with evil ... Much more reassuring to see the world in terms of totally innocent victims and totally evil instigators of the monstrous violence we see all about us. At all costs, never disturb our innocence.'

As to those who attacked him, 'all those who in real life laugh at the Maggies of the world, who mock their hopes and take advantage of their ignorance, their vulnerability, their terrible loneliness and need – all those cannot, with a tear or two, "decently" pay their "respects" to the victims of their hypocrisy. All this the play, thank God, prohibits.'[133]

There had always been critics who had dismissed his work. The Non-Communist Left had found his earlier plays ideologically suspect. Robert Warshow, Eric Bentley, Mary McCarthy, Eleanor Clarke had all taken issue with him. *After the Fall* and *Incident at Vichy* provoked further hostility; *The Price* largely aside, ahead lay thirty years of critical rejection in America as his new plays were dismissed and earlier successes devalued.

A key figure in this dismissal would be Robert Brustein, a critic for the *New Republic* who went on to become a professor first at Yale and then Harvard. His response to *After the Fall* was to see it as a 'spiritual striptease'. The opening line of his review asserted that there was already a 'notoriety connected with [Miller's] name'. The new play was 'a three-and-one-half hour breach of taste'. It was an 'invasion of privacy'. Miller had produced a 'shameless piece of tabloid gossip, an act of exhibitionism that makes us all voyeurs'. Beyond that, though, it was 'a wretched piece of dramatic writing, shapeless, tedious, overwritten, and confused'. It 'lacked forward movement'. Jo Mielziner's design, meanwhile, was rendered 'completely useless', while he might have suspected Kazan of deliberately undermining the production, were the material not so 'intractable'. Beyond that, the play was politically suspect. For Brustein, Miller 'still conceives of politics in the simple-minded language of the thirties'. All the ex-communists in the play, for example, are merely 'fighting injustice', while the friend who committed suicide is 'a decent broken man that never wanted anything more but the good of the world ... After all these terrible years, is Miller still defining Stalinism as if it were a sentiment without any reference to ideas, ideology, or power?' Miller's talent, to his mind, had always been minor, and Lincoln Center nothing more than a 'fashionable culture emporium'.[134]

Philip Rahv, an old antagonist from *Commentary*, and *Partisan Review*, echoed Brustein's sentiments in a piece significantly called 'Arthur Miller and the Fallacy of Profundity'. Most of his ire was reserved for *Incident at Vichy* but in passing he dismissed *After the Fall* as 'a disaster, a piece so pretentious and defensive that virtually nothing good can be said about it'.[135] Richard Gilman, who wrote primarily for *Commonweal* magazine and the *New Republic*, like Brustein inveighed against Lincoln Center as well as Miller. He described the former as 'a nightmare ... a corpse that thinks itself to be ... a vigorous living organism'. In a piece entitled 'Still Falling' he then dismissed *After the Fall* as 'not even the simulacrum of a drama'. It involved, he said, 'a process of self-justification which at any times is repellent but which becomes truly monstrous in the absence of any intelligence, craft or art'. The play contained 'no drama at all, no true confrontation and no movement from confrontation to understanding'. It consisted of 'adolescent mutterings'. Furthermore, Kazan had made bad material 'even more atrocious'. In a later piece on Lincoln Center he described the play as 'disgraceful ... morally and technically'.[136] He noted, nonetheless, and with some bemusement, that the play was sold out for its entire run.

For Stanley Kauffmann the play was 'tainted with a wriggly feeling of exculpation', but this did not surprise from a playwright 'not talented enough to keep free of dubious artistic means'. It was an attack he would sustain in the coming years.[137] Eric Bentley suggested that the play was, like John Osborne's *Look Back in Anger*, 'one long adolescent tantrum ... What *After the Fall* is really about,' he suggested, 'is the adolescent male discovering sex: at first it is absolutely yummy but a little later on, girls turn out to be awful bitches, and one needs to let the world know it – loudly."[138] Martin Gottfried, who was later to write Miller's biography, thought it 'pompous and pretend-intellectual'. A further viewing convinced him of its excellence but, oddly, also renewed his sense of its meretriciousness. He, at least, admitted to ambivalence. Others were implacable, and for the most part not only with respect to *After the Fall*.

The controversy did not die down and nor did Miller's anger. In an interview he observed: 'The critics have not judged my work severely. They have judged me.' They had not discussed what he had written: 'They spoke about me and my right to write on a certain subject.' The real subject was 'the story of a man trying to find out why he is alive'. But this, everyone ignored. He had not expected 'such a narrow-minded reaction, so cruelly and miserably mean'; he had not thought to encounter such incredible and degrading short-sightedness. Insisting that it was the best play he had written, experimental in form and containing 'an aesthetic experience my other plays lacked', he found it explored only for its ostensible biographical subject. 'It is clear,' he wrote to Kazan, 'the Marilyn business has effectively overwhelmed the play for almost all the "critics".'[139]

Once again he tried to identify what appeared to him to be the principal theme. Most people, he suggested, 'never get around to wondering why they are alive. They think maybe it is because they are breathing, because they wake up in the morning and another day has begun. We live for something more than this, something that we can only discover by baring our soul completely. Is a man who bares his soul "disgusting"?' His reply to his own question was, 'Certainly he is if, when he exposes his own nakedness, he strips the others around him, too, without their leave.' This was not, though, what he regarded himself as having done: 'You ask why so many people bear a grudge against me; they resent it because I remind them that for thirty, forty, perhaps sixty years of their lives, they have never once stopped to wonder why they were alive. Well, I have stopped to wonder.' As to the personal dimensions: 'If I can't refer to my own life in my own work then I might as well give up.'[140]

If *The Misfits* had been the work in which he offered a benign portrait of Marilyn, a piece of fiction that acknowledged her bruised innocence and his hopes for a restored relationship, *After the Fall* is a requiem for a woman whose capacity for self-destruction was finally beyond his ability to limit. In the former, she is an embodiment of life, reanimating those she encounters and in particular a man older than herself who sees a chance to start over again. In the latter she is a woman whose self-doubt is such that she tries to find the limits of her husband's love, seeking final confirmation of the judgement made by so many others throughout her life. She discovers those limits.

For all the heat of the controversy, the play was a success. By 8 February, the *New York Times* was reporting that the rights had been sold to seventeen countries, including South Africa, where, at Miller's insistence, it was performed only before non-segregated audiences. In the *New York Times* Howard Taubman not only praised it but defended Miller against accusations of bad taste:

> It is nonsense to deprecate 'After the Fall' on the ground that it is often transparently autobiographical. All drama worthy of the name is flesh of the playwright's flesh and blood of his blood. Writers resort to fiction because it enables them more freely to pierce to the bone ... Whether or not Maggie in her warm simplicity and demonic fury is Marilyn Monroe to the life I do not know. Nor do I care. Maggie emerges as a touching, pathetic human being – lovable and hateful, vulnerable and wounding. I do not feel that she is in the play merely as the author's means of purging himself in a kind of public self-analysis. She serves an important dramatic purpose. Mr Miller has been at pains to show that the conflict between Quentin and Louise, his first wife, grew out of her desperate battle to assert her own separateness. In Quentin's relations with Maggie the roles are reversed; it is Quentin who struggles in his separateness.

Taubman ended his article with a ringing endorsement: 'Welcome to the Repertory Theater. And welcome back to Mr Miller, who courageously has ripped the veil from his own life to tell us something about our world and a questing man's search to understand his place in it.'[141] For Miller, though, the play had, in his own words, blown his image away. He felt that he was hated by a number of people.

The public, if not critical, success of *After the Fall* brought Robert Whitehead back to Miller, this time with the director Harold Clurman. Other plays in the new repertory had not proved as popular and they looked to him to rescue a venture that was showing signs of strain before it had even made its way to its new theatre. The problem was, in part, as Kazan was to acknowledge, that this was a theatre without a clear mission. Was it to produce the best of world drama, to look to American writers, to concentrate on the contemporary, to provide an upmarket version of Broadway, or was it to innovate?

Miller's response to a request for a new play was *Incident at Vichy*, which he wrote as Laurence Olivier was rehearsing *The Crucible* in London. He felt, Olivier explained in a letter in August 1964, 'like a young chap in love for the first time'. The following month he wrote again explaining that he was to stage the play in a 'strictly realistic' manner, 'very, very, very early American with nothing particularly Breughel about it'. Meanwhile, he was awaiting 'the new back-scratching line for Abigail'[142] a reference to the forest scene which he was thinking of including and whose sexuality he had asked Miller to consider sharpening.

Incident at Vichy was in part influenced by Miller's attendance at the trial in Frankfurt of a number of guards from Auschwitz, but there was another reason for his return to the Holocaust. It was now firmly on the agenda, indeed the subject of fierce controversy. Between February and March of 1963, Hannah Arendt had published a series of reports in the *New Yorker* on the trial of Adolf Eichmann. Arendt's articles subsequently formed part of a book, called *Eichmann in Jersusalem*, published later that year to a series of hostile reviews.

What was objected to was partly her tone, which struck some as inappropriately frivolous as she responded to the absurdities of Eichmann's arguments, and partly her coined term 'banality of evil' by which she meant both the bureaucratization of mass killing and the fact that evil lacks dimension, only the good having true depth. Eichmann, she suggested, had no imagination. Irving Howe, though rejecting the idea, nonetheless recalled that Simone de Beauvoir had described the Vichy French Prime Minister, Pierre Laval, convicted of treason, as 'commonplace ... an unimaginative and inconsequential little fellow'.[143] Saul Bellow also rejected the idea: 'The banality of evil ... just blames evil on modern mass civilization and on technological society and says that there is no *true* evil any more ... To me this is nonsense. I think that when human beings murder they know what they're doing ...

this is to remove the guilt from [Eichmann] and place it upon society as a whole and upon the rest of us.'[144] Banality, he suggested, was 'the adopted disguise of a very powerful will to abolish conscience'.[145]

Arendt had described Eichmann as terribly and terrifyingly normal, a phrase which many regarded as an affront. But that was precisely what Miller would observe when he attended the Frankfurt trials in 1964. It was a characterization, though, which some saw as an invitation to generalize guilt beyond the accused, to rob the crime of its particular horror. Nor were Arendt and Miller alone in this. Harold Rosenberg, in an article in *Commentary* magazine, recalled a report of a trial in 1946 of a major general of police named Otto Ohlendorf, which describes him as talking 'in a matter-of-fact tone, admitting each mass killing as calmly as if the victims had been cattle or sheep'. In appearance he was 'not particularly brutal or inhuman, looking more like a somewhat humourless shoe salesman one might meet anywhere'. Ohlendorf, the report continued, 'described the manner in which Jews were rounded up and killed as a man might describe an ordinary business trans-action'.[146]

Though he did not contribute to the debate over Arendt's book, which became extraordinarily vitriolic – Mary McCarthy writing to Arendt to say that attacks on her amounted to a pogrom – Miller did stray into this contested area. In fact, an article he wrote on the Frankfurt trials became one of the weapons deployed by McCarthy in her battles with Lionel Abel, himself a playwright, and others in the pages of *Partisan Review*.

On one side were those who thought that Arendt had accused the Jews of complicity in their own fate and turned Eichmann into a simple bureaucrat of death. Along with Abel were Norman Podhoretz, writing in *Commentary*; Judge Michael Musmanno (who had been involved in the Eichmann trial and whose review of the book prompted over a hundred letters, mostly in support of Arendt), in the *New York Times*; and Marie Syrkin – staunch Zionist and, from 1965, on the executive of the Jewish Agency – in *Partisan Review*. On the other side were Mary McCarthy, Robert Lowell, Stephen Spender, Bruno Bettelheim, Daniel Bell and Dwight Macdonald, himself a former editor of *Partisan Review*. William Phillips, its then editor, tried to hold the middle ground, sending a copy of Abel's attack to Arendt with a letter that expressed his personal embarrassment. This was the New York Intellectuals doing battle and, according to Phillips, taking altogether too much pleasure in doing so.

Nor was the debate limited to the East Coast. Macdonald drew attention to a headline in an issue of the *Intermountain Jewish News* (admittedly hardly a major publication, being a weekly paper published in Denver) which announced of Arendt, 'SELF-HATING JEWESS WRITES PRO-EICHMANN SERIES'. A French review asked, 'Hannah Arendt, est-elle une Nazi?' Musmanno suggested that *Eichmann in Jerusalem* would comfort Eichmann's family and be well received in Germany, the latter an accusation equally levelled at *Incident at Vichy*. Arendt's friend Gershom Scholem claimed that he could find no evidence in her book of the Jewish concept, *Ahabath Israel*, 'love of the Jewish people'. McCarthy suggested that responses to the book had divided Jew from non-Jew as if what was at stake was less the truth or otherwise of the book than responsibility to a tribe.

In a summary of these events in 2007 Michael Ezra recalled a comment by Norm Fruchter, editor of *Studies on the Left*, which not only addresses this issue but also makes a distinction of relevance to Miller:

> The attempt to see the controversy as a simply Jew versus non-Jew split is inaccurate. One of the crucial divisions may be between those Jews whose ethnicity is part of their identity, but whose concerns, work, direction and commitment transcend their Jewishness and relate them to a wider community of purpose and value, and those Jews who tend to maintain the traditional myths of Jewish identity, and are more closely connected to Jewish organizations, and seem more rooted in Jewish ambiance.[147]

The truth is that Miller, Jewish though he was, always looked beyond his Jewishness precisely towards that wider community of purpose, and that this attracted a certain suspicion, because in the eyes of some it made it impossible for him to acknowledge the offence he caused in treating the Holocaust as an example of inhumanity, a springboard for other concerns, and not an implacable, accusatory fact.

In trying Eichmann in Jerusalem, the Israelis wished to place not simply one man in the dock. According to the then Prime Minister of Israel, David Ben Gurion, it was not the Nazis alone who were on trial but anti-Semitism through the ages. In other words, they themselves were broadening the emphasis. To broaden it further, however, seemed an affront. A debate in a midtown New York hotel attracted five hundred people, with a Holocaust historian speaking for Arendt, who herself declined an invitation. He was not, he later complained, allowed to finish his speech, Lionel Abel pounding on a table with his fist in protest. When the critic Alfred Kazin tried to speak, Abel shouted him down. The American Jewish Congress published a pamphlet entitled *Arendt Nonsense*.

For Podhoretz, as quoted by Macdonald, 'In place of the monstrous Nazi, she gives us the "banal" Nazi; in place of the Jew as virtuous martyr, she gives us the Jew as accomplice in evil; and in place of the confrontation of guilt and innocence, she gives us the "collaboration" of criminal and victim.'[148] For Macdonald, however, there was nothing objectionable about Arendt's concept of the banality of evil: 'I see nothing shocking here: the discrepancy between the personal mediocrity of Stalin and Hitler, the banality of their ideas, and the vastness of the evil they inflicted – is she really the first to notice this?'[149] Macdonald drew attention to the fact that Arendt had not blamed the Jews, or even, strictly speaking, the Jewish councils – which had drawn up lists of their fellow Jews at the instruction of the Nazis – for their actions. Her objection was to their very existence. There was, she had admitted, 'no possibility of resistance, but there existed the possibility of *doing nothing*'.[150] This, Macdonald implied, might be a subtle distinction, but it was a crucial one. There is a difference, he said, between doing nothing and refusing to do anything. It was a distinction that Miller, who readily embraced the concept of the banality of evil, was not ready to make.

Mary McCarthy, once critical of Miller's drama but about to become an ally in her response to the war in Vietnam, replied to Lionel Abel's attack on her, as a defender of Arendt, by asking, 'What is a Nazi?' and replying, 'The German Everyman, it would seem, during the Hitler years. This is becoming evident again,' she added, 'in the Auschwitz trial; Arthur Miller has made the point very well in his *Herald Tribune* report. What did it take to be a Nazi, an SS man, an Eichmann? Very little, evidently. This is what is so terrible.'[151] She ended by suggesting that since one of the functions of art is to give sense to suffering, Arendt had performed that function for the Jews. For some, however, that was the problem. To give shape to the shapeless, coherence to contingency, a face to inchoate evil, was to deny the essence of the Holocaust.

That, of course, was the challenge for anyone approaching this experience, a problem for Miller no less than for anyone else. His own liberal rationalism, his instinctive desire to universalize, his existential insistence on personal and public responsibility, were potentially at odds with his wish to come to terms with an experience he had circled for so long without fully engaging, precisely because it failed to offer itself easily to such an approach. He had maintained a kind of discretion because, for the Jews – and, beyond them, for all those who chose to contemplate it – the Holocaust 'represents a defeat. It was as though there were a war and you had lost. It was a defeat, too, for all the values. There was nothing any more between the individual and total destruction and therefore there was a silence which was evidence of an inability to digest the depth and breadth of this defeat.' That it took so long was in part a consequence 'of guilt, the guilt of the survivor. People had no objective reason to feel guilty but they did feel that.' The silence was also in part due to a lack of explanation beyond the proposition that 'human nature was by definition evil'.[152]

He had another explanation for his own delayed response, for his own and others' failure to press the Jewish cause during the war and for the feeling of helplessness that left him and others bystanders to genocide. It seemed to him that Hitler had detected that the world was ready for it, that he had induced a feeling of helplessness and that what he proposed and enacted was in essence literally unthinkable.

For Philip Rahv, Miller, in proposing that we are all Cain, all capable of the violations epitomized by the Holocaust, was in danger of reducing it to a mere example of man's inhumanity to man, a metaphor rather than the thing itself, a black hole from which no light could escape. He suspected Miller of suggesting that there is a gene for barbarity and that we are all carriers. Gone, then, he fears, is any distinction. For Miller, there was indeed such a gene. It was original sin. In *Incident at Vichy*, he would ask himself whether a neutralizing selflessness might also form part of a fundamentally divided sensibility.

Miller's motive for going to Frankfurt was oddly reductive. He had never knowingly laid eyes on a Nazi and thought it worth a few hours' drive to do so. He also thought that it might provide him with useful material. As he wrote to Kazan on 31 March 1964. 'I am going back tomorrow to Frankfurt, Germany. I may be wasting my time, but partly as a result of attending the Auschwitz trials there, and partly from my age-old fascination with Naziism as a human phenomenon, I have the feeling there is something there I can use … I will stay a few days talking to prosecutors, lawyers and others who have been up to their necks in some sinister stuff for years now.'[53]

The trial was of twenty-two former Auschwitz administrators and guards. Before 1959 such trials had been the province of international prosecutors. The Frankfurt trial was the first conducted by the West Germans themselves. The problem was that though the lead prosecutor, Fritz Bauer – who had once been the youngest Supreme Court justice in the state of Hesse, a man who had fled to Sweden during the war – saw the trial as an object lesson for the German people, testimony tended to concentrate on the more sadistic defendants.

The trial took place, Miller recalled, in a 'new and impressively sedate tan marble courtroom'.[54] It was sparsely attended. Miller was approached by a reporter from one of the wire services who urged him to write about it, explaining that he and others had been having difficulty placing stories. The German press, on the other hand, reported it extensively. The writer W.G. Sebald later remembered the impact the coverage in the *Frankfurter Allgemeine Zeitung* had on him, part of a process that would lead him to focus with ever greater intensity on the Holocaust. The trials were also attended by the German dramatist Peter Weiss, who drew on the evidence in his play *The Investigation* which opened in October 1965, and by the Austrian-born Jean Améry, who had suffered at Auschwitz-Birkenau and now wrote *At the Mind's Limits*, originally entitled 'Beyond Guilt and Atonement'. In the United

States the trials prompted some hundred stories in major newspapers, though seldom on the front page and seldom with any depth.[155] Miller duly wrote a piece which appeared in several newspapers.

The principal defendants were Wilhelm Boger and Josef Klehr, both SS staff sergeants, and Oswald Kaduk, a former SS corporal and block officer. They were defended by Hans Laternser, who had refused to join the Nazi Party and defended a member of a Catholic nursing home when the Church opposed the state's euthanasia policy. After the war, however, he defended those who had practised it. He now challenged the Court's right to hold the trial. He told Miller and Inge over lunch one day: 'As Americans are the first to point out, there can't be a just trial when the prosecution's witnesses are all dead or so old they can hardly recall anything.'[156] Miller was, indeed, struck by the fact that the witnesses had difficulty remembering some of the details of their time in Auschwitz-Birkenau, a point seized on by the defence. Arendt preferred to put it down to self-deception as a moral prerequisite for survival, and a mendacity that had become an integral part of the German character. Given the fact of German 'forgetfulness', it seemed to Miller more important than ever to retrieve truths that bore on the present. He was also acutely conscious that the women jury members 'were of an age which indicates they lived in Nazi Germany while this was happening: they were shopping, putting their children to bed, going on picnics on sunny days . . . while other mothers like themselves and children no different from their own were forced to undress, to walk into a barren hall, and breathe the gas which some of the defendants now sitting here carefully administered'.[157] For a man who had always believed, and who made it a principle of his theatrical approach, that the past inheres in the present, that past acts have present consequences, the trials underlined a fundamental truth.

Miller had gone to Frankfurt (according to his FBI file from Vienna, en route to Paris, and now weighing 185 pounds and standing 6 feet 2 inches tall) 'to see the horns on their heads'. But there were none. They were 'just insignificant little jerks, such as we have everywhere, except that they were killing. They had the power of life and death over people. That was the strength of National Socialism.'[158] He left Frankfurt, therefore, aware of the particularities of Nazi crimes but also with a sense of how thin the membrane between what we take as normality and the aberrant, the friendly neighbour and the monster. The camps had been an assault not just on the Jews, on gypsies and homosexuals, but on the idea of human autonomy. The defendants at the Auschwitz trials were largely middle to low-ranking figures. They included a cabinet-maker, a butcher, a teacher, an accountant. They also included manifest sadists. They were not so much following orders, though that was their defence, as seizing the occasion to indulge in their own fantasies of power. Indeed, that was the basis on which they were being tried since, bizarrely the courts recognized the legality of Nazi laws. Merely presiding over mass murder was insufficient so long as they had not broken the law as defined by the Third Reich. It had to be shown that those on trial were aficionados of the perverse.

Arendt once said that in the works of great writers there is usually a dominant metaphor, peculiar to them, which seems to act as a focus for their whole work. For Miller, it was not so much a metaphor as an animating idea. That idea had to do with the necessity to create the values by which one lives and therefore to accept responsibility for one's life. That was the basis of his liberalism and his resistance to the totalitarian. For him, acts have consequences, the acknowledgement of which is the basis of a moral existence and, not incidentally, of his dramatic strategy. The Holocaust thus represented a challenge. Where was the space for free decision when men themselves became the agents of absurdity, and when others were mocked for their incapacity to deflect their fate? Committed as he had been to the idea of tragedy, which itself was an expression of resistance to an acknowledged determinism, what was he to make of those in some cases quite literally born astride the grave?

This paradox, as absurdity was acted out by those who believed themselves immune because the will-less agents of an abstract power, or by others who walked to extinction only belatedly understanding the terms of their contract with existence, left him at times stunned. It left him, too, levelling accusations at those he felt should have refused their fate or, at the least, should not have gone gentle into that dark night. This was not a comfortable position and he had difficulty articulating it, or doing so with any real conviction. *Incident at Vichy* was born out of a desperate wager on a residual autonomy. He needed a hero, one who acted in full knowledge of the fate that awaited him but who, in embracing it, transcended his circumstances. He needed someone who could resist rather than deny absoluteness, change the ending of a story which only *appeared* implacable. Ironically, and for some unforgivably, he chose a non-Jew as his protagonist. He had known the story on which he based *Incident at Vichy* for some fifteen years but had been unable to see how it could be made to work on stage. Anyway, he had had other priorities, which in retrospect seemed solipsistic. Now, his priorities had changed.

There was one other observation of Arendt's that he had never embraced. She pointed out that you can defend yourself only as the person you are attacked for being. If you are attacked as a Jew it is not sufficient to say, but I am an individual or a Frenchman or an upholder of the rights of man. One consequence of this truth is that often diaries and memoirs that emerged after the war and which seemed not to acknowledge the importance of Jewishness, and more particularly of faith, were attacked. Anne Frank's diaries caused discomfort to those who found an absence at their heart, an absence that turned not on the Frank family's failure to fight (Bruno Bettelheim's bizarre accusation) but on the lack of a redemptive insistence on belief, tradition, a supportive history. For Miller, however, in the play he was writing, and which seemed all the more urgent after his brief visit to Frankfurt, religion and ideology, redemptive or destructive, were beside the point. Yes, the Jews were persecuted and killed as Jews, but to resist as such was already to cede territory to the enemy, and the enemy was not only the Germans (and he never believed that German guilt stopped at the barbed wire of Auschwitz-Birkenau) but the idea of human insignificance, of men and women as no more than products of the pressures exerted on them. Hemingway, in *A Farewell to Arms*, has Frederic Henry reject abstractions – freedom, dignity and much more – in a novel in which an army turns on itself and spring brings a dead child strangled by its umbilical cord. With the Spanish Civil War, however, of central importance to Hemingway as to Miller, those abstractions were embraced again and a man sacrifices himself for others partly to keep the idea of sacrifice alive. In *Incident at Vichy* Miller was to do no less and his visit to Frankfurt gave a face to those who until then had been no more than an expression of abstract terror.

Miller's article on the trials, which appeared in March 1964 (and which was noted in his FBI file, along with a note about his having donated royalties to the Polish League of Women in 1947), was one of the few that sought to broaden the issues before the court to apply to others than the Nazis, though he, too, was appalled by the evidence he heard. He was struck in particular by the case of Kaduk, who had fired his pistol at random when he walked around the barracks, shooting anyone on a whim. After the war he had become a hospital nurse and earned himself the title 'Papa Kaduk'. What seems to have concerned Miller was the possibility of its happening again, afraid as he was of the German 'capacity for moral and psychological collapse in the face of a higher command'. [159] What was at stake in the trial was that six million Jews died because those required to kill them never questioned their orders or their duty to carry them out. Of the 'six thousand SS men who did duty in Auschwitz during its four years of operation', he observes, 'not one is known to have refused to do what he was told'.[160]

The issue, for Miller, was one of individual conscience and personal responsibility in a country whose citizens, it appeared to him, had a preference for identifying with disciplined killers rather than their victims. German responses to his article (he received a deluge of hostile letters) were, understandably, resentful. They wished to distinguish between the Nazis and themselves. To Miller, though, their primary desire was to forget. Yet at the same time he acknowledged the inutility of a generalized sense of guilt, not least because he feared it would prompt a renewed nationalism.

Interestingly, in an article he wrote for the *New York Herald Tribune* the first paragraph emphasized not so much the past as the future, not simply yesterday's Germany but tomorrow's: 'There is an unanswerable question hovering over the courtroom at Frankfurt ... Can this kind of movement [National Socialism] which gave life-and-death power to such men ever rise again in Germany?'[161] There certainly seemed no appetite among Germans for trials such as this. He suspected that the lawyers 'know their people and they know that even if every last SS man were convicted for this particular crime, it would not in itself prevent a new recrudescence of brutal nationalism which could once again confront the world with a German problem'.[162] For Miller, dominated in his twenties by an opposition to fascism, the 'German problem' was rooted in national character. He quotes a judge, with no connection to the Frankfurt trial, as confessing 'that his fears for Germany stemmed from precisely this profound tendency to abjure freedom of choice, to fall into line on orders from above'.[163] The problem, he reported a court official as telling him, perhaps lay in the authoritarian nature of the German father, a microcosm of the German state. For Miller, it was the Jew who had tempered this with scepticism. It followed that in driving Jews out, or annihilating them, the Germans had removed that resistant element.

Staring, he said, into the German heart, he asked, 'Does the rule of law reach into that heart, or the rule of conformity and absolute obedience?' The difficulty for the Germans, he suggested, 'is that they are being called upon to identify themselves with the victims when their every instinct would lead them to identify with the uniformed, disciplined killers'.[164]

This makes for strange reading, and though prompted by his visit to Frankfurt it was a conviction that stayed with him. Germany had been the great menace of his youth and it remained such now. He never seems to have bought into the idea of Germany as a new model democracy. Even now, in trying to reach for some cause for hope, he suggests that Germany's desire for conquest may be restrained not by any change of policy or mitigation of instinctive aggression, but by the fact that it was no longer flanked by what he called 'peasant countries', unable to defend themselves, but by industrialized countries with military strength – in other words, members of the Warsaw Pact. Ideologically, that put him in an odd position, still inclined to grant revanchist motives to a country now seen as the front line against potential Soviet aggression and the showcase of democracy and capitalism.

Whatever had been laid down years before had plainly not been purged in the two decades since the war in which his brother had fought with such gallantry and integrity, nor in the three since German fascism had dominated his imagination, the anti-matter to his admiration for Russia. With a new father-in-law who had been a member of the Nazi Party and a wife from a country that had gifted to the world Adolf Hitler and Adolf Eichmann, perhaps he had reason enough to ask himself questions about the past. What is surprising is the persistence for another twenty-five years and more, beyond his visit to Frankfurt, of his suspicions of a resurgent Germany ready – if circumstances permitted – to revert to what he seems to have convinced himself was its natural default position as aggressor nation, ready to obey authority and perhaps once more to threaten Jews.

His visit to Mauthausen, followed by his brief time at the Auschwitz trials, seems to have moved the question of the Holocaust into the forefront of his mind as the Eichmann trial had not done. Nonetheless, the concluding part of his article in *Partisan Review* focused not on Germany but on the wider implications. For, as he commented, 'the question in the Frankfurt courtroom spreads out beyond the defendants and spirals around the world and into the heart of every man. It is his own complicity with murder, even the murders he did not perform himself with his own hands. The murders, however, from which he profited if only by having survived.'[165] This was a sentiment that lay at the heart of his new play *Incident at Vichy*, as it had of *After the Fall*.

Miller finished the final draft in three weeks in May 1964. It came, he remarked, 'fully formed'. No more than twenty or thirty lines were changed. He did no research, which perhaps explains the historical flaws detected by some. He admitted that the racial laws had not in fact been enforced by Pétain in Vichy France, even though that appears to be the play's proposition. *Incident at Vichy* was anyway not about the Nazi occupation of France, nor the destruction of the Jews, he said. It was about the human capacity to put oneself in the position of another person, to feel his pain and to address that pain through self-sacrifice.

He had heard the story, some years before, of a man who sacrificed himself to save another. Only now did it cohere in his mind. Miller derived the plot partly from his psychoanalyst, Dr Rudolph Loewenstein, and partly from Inge. From Loewenstein he took the account of an analyst who had been detained in Vichy France with a group of others. They were held in order to determine which of them were Jewish. Those identified as such faced probable death. Those declared 'innocent' would be given a pass which secured their exit from detention. Among those to receive a pass was one who handed it to a Jew, sacrificing himself for another. For the character of this person Miller turned to the figure of Prince Joseph von Schwarzenberg, an Austrian friend of his wife, a man who had resisted the Nazis and served out the war doing menial labour.

Discussions between the play's director Harold Clurman, Miller and the designer Boris Aronson began in August, and it was produced in December 1964, just eleven months on from *After the Fall*. Like that play, it required a larger cast than would have been sustainable on Broadway (fifteen in the case of *Incident at Vichy*, over twenty for *After the Fall*), this being one of the advantages of a repertory company. Clurman's production struck him as 'quite beautiful', but its reception seemed to him to have become confused with the arguments over Lincoln Center itself and Kazan's artistic policy. Kazan was later to confess to a feeling of inadequacy, undertaking plays to which he was not well attuned. His career had been based on what he saw as social realism (a surprising remark, given both *Death of a Salesman* and *After the Fall*), and the failure of a number of his productions was, he thought, a product of over-ambition.

A year later the British production of *Incident at Vichy*, directed by Peter Wood and with Alec Guinness, was well received. In the late 1960s it was banned in the Soviet Union – then, as Miller pointed out, in an anti-Semitic period. Following six nights of previews it was closed down the night before its opening but, then, it included a less than favourable portrait of a communist. It was not, Miller stressed, until 1987, following Gorbachev's liberalization, that the play was produced in the Soviet Union. It also failed to receive a production in France, 'for fear of resentment at the implication of French collaboration with Nazi anti-Semitism.'[166]

Following *After the Fall*, in which he had focused on the centrality of self-interest, an isolating self-concern, as a key to human behaviour, he set himself to explore a selfless act. Camus's protagonist in *The Fall* had failed to save another. In *Incident at Vichy* Miller staged a drama in which a man does. It is his attempt to locate meaning at the very heart of the absurd. He had himself stood in a concentration camp, but was not prepared to accept this as the final word on human nature or the human plight. As ever, he wished to see history as a human product, a construction, and not as an expression of an unfolding fate.

As a child Thomas Buergenthal, born in 1934, survived concentration camps and a death march, an experience that he described in his autobiography *A Lucky Child*. Years later, looking back, he asked a question that Miller had posed in *The Man Who Had All the Luck* and that lies behind both *After the Fall* and *Incident at Vichy*. Why do some survive and others not, and how to justify such survival? More specifically, like Miller in *Incident at Vichy* he asks, 'What is it in the human character that gives some individuals the moral strength not to sacrifice their decency and dignity, regardless of the cost to themselves, whereas others become murderously ruthless in the hope of ensuring their survival?'[167]

The characters in *Incident at Vichy* are confronted with a situation that defies reason but spend much of their time trying to impose reason upon it. They have all been brought to a place of detention with no explanation. They attempt to understand their plight, deploying ideas and values they had thought central, only to discover that they have no relevance. Even as they struggle there is a sense of resignation, a resignation that had disturbed Miller ever since the 1930s. Just as once he had asked why America had not intervened in Spain or resisted Hitler when it could, why Jews did not leave when they might have done or resist when they could, so he was now inclined to ask why racial injustice was tolerated (suggesting that this was in the back of his mind while writing the play) and why people so often refused to intervene in their own lives, as if powerless in the face of an inevitability they conspired in sanctioning. The challenge in *Incident at Vichy* was to create a man who not only acts, but does so at the price of his own extinction.

Miller does so in part by taking as his subject Prince Von Berg, a man in search of his own justifications and redemption who comes to realize his complicity as a consequence of his love for his Nazi cousin. According to Miller, the play's central question is not Cain's 'Am I my brother's keeper?' but 'Am I my own keeper?' Brotherhood with those threatened with death is one thing, but at the heart of his gesture in handing his pass, his exit from detention, to a condemned man is a more refined sense of self-regard. He simply cannot live with the idea of himself that would be the product of betrayal. In a gathering of people concerned with only one thing, survival, he, too, looks to survive, but in his case it is his survival as a moral self that matters. Von Berg goes to his almost certain death not simply to preserve the idea of a moral world in which sacrifice is still possible – too abstract a notion to be sustained – but because that path offers him a possibility of redemption denied by a life which he realizes has not been lived without equivocation. He can do no less than stare into his own confused motives in a search for understanding and peace.

The Nazis are not to be understood. They may pursue the irrational by rational means but they are the product and embodiment of the perverse. There is nothing to be learned from them, locked as they are inside their own echoing justifications. There is, however, something to be learned from his own failures and from the desperate rationalizations of those among whom he finds himself. The irony is that Von Berg can only save an equivocator, the Jew prepared to pass as a gentile. The gypsy and the old Jew who are among their number are simply what they appear, as they wait in the antechamber to hell. He can only save one who has the fortune to be able to deny himself into life, carrying the pass that declares him to be what he is not and thus liberating himself by betraying the very self that seeks liberation.

Harold Clurman, years earlier angry at being denied the right to direct *All My Sons*, was the director. His skills had always been those of the critical analyst rather than of the conductor of actors and it is hardly surprising that his director's notes should prove so informative about a play that is necessarily static, as the people at its heart have their lives placed on hold in this 'place of detention'. These notes were never designed for the actors. They represent a discussion with himself as he attempted to understand the play and its dynamics. His first note goes to the heart of the play, with its almost absurdist sense of stasis, of deferred meaning: 'General action: to wait, to know – in motionless anxiety'.[168] Clurman's original intention was to freeze the action for thirty seconds, but what struck him as the inadequate lighting of the Washington Square Theatre led him to abandon the idea, though he retained a pause before the first speech as the characters look around, no less concerned to make sense of things than the audience exposed to this scene.

The figure characterized only as the old Jew never speaks. He is, Clurman suggests, the Chorus. He is also, though, the solution to the question they implicitly and then explicitly ask: Why are they there? It is a solution they cannot accept. The gypsy functions in the same way. These two are the paradigms against which the others are to be judged. They are already condemned, though this knowledge, in the audience's possession, only slowly becomes apparent to those who puzzle over their fate.

In a conversation with the designer Boris Aronson on 12 August 1964 Miller asked for an unspecific setting, 'Kafka-like', and there are indeed overtones of *The Trial* in a play in which the characters assume the legitimacy of arrest, seek to understand the nature of their supposed 'crime', and plead their innocence. Like Kafka's Joseph K, they are driven by a central question: what have they done? The audience view the scene through a history to which they have already been exposed. They know the depth of an irony the characters can only suspect. Different in their ideologies, their social circumstances, their nature, these people who await their fate are homogenized by their situation. Some will live and some will die, but the taxonomy that decides the issue is no more than the order of an antinomian world. The prince responds with an arbitrary gesture. He is, in a sense, testing a proposition. If it is possible to harden your heart to stone (as Camus's Caligula does in the play of that name), is the opposite possible? Are selflessness, sacrifice, love still possible? Yet it all comes from the same source. It is irrational, instinctive. If all things are possible, then so too is love. In a context in which there is no choice, he chooses. In a world of pseudoscience, in which 'experts' operate as they did in Salem during the witch trials to identify the supposed devil, he asserts the significance of instinct. He becomes the embodiment of refusal.

This is not a world in which some are free and others are not, though some of the prisoners will be released, and those who guard them and seemingly decide their fate presume their own autonomy. In fact, they are all subject to the same fiat, all exist within the same universe in which the real is defined somewhere beyond the walls of this limbo. There is a script to be followed and any deviation is likely to be punished. This is a world apparently drained of ambivalence. Gathered together are a communist, an actor, a psychiatrist and a businessman. Their very heterogeneity is a source of puzzlement to them. What can they have in common? Why are they here? And when they discover the probable truth each in turn invokes as protection the very ways

in which they have attempted to address the greater question, the element of
contingency implied in a life anyway doomed to end in death. Art, working-
class revolution, religion, material progress become shields against a disturbing truth.

The play is full of questions to which there appears only one answer, an
answer which for some is unbearable. In truth, though, as Clurman wrote in
his notebook, 'They are waiting for an answer to a question to which there is
no answer.'[169] His notes about the individual characters are as useful an
approach to the play as any. Thus, of Von Berg, the prince, he says, 'He wants
to believe the best – he hopes for amelioration. That is why it takes him so
long to realize the worst. He asks the cardinal question of our time: "But
what is left if one gives up one's ideals?" Of Leduc, the psychiatrist, he
observes, "He is inclined to 'pessimism', through a scientific or objective
recognition of the facts." But, less consciously, he desires a "mitigation" of the
facts ... When Leduc tells Von Berg that man is full of hate of the other, this
"dreadful truth" is a form of self-crucifixion ... a desire to put some terrible
blame on himself.'[170] Lebeau, a painter, is a man who feels guilty yet clings to
hope. Bayard, an electrician, is a socialist sustained by his political beliefs
even if here they seem to break on the rocks of the implacable. The actor,
Monceau, places his trust in his art. The businessman simply presumes his
immunity.

Those who are to interview, condemn or release them are not all wholly
assured. A major, invalided from the Front, has been given a repugnant job
and tries to deflect his own sense of guilt on to those he is obliged to sacrifice
to their fate. A professor, however, like other professionals under the Third
Reich, performs his function of identifying Jews with enthusiasm. He is,
Clurman notes, 'absolute' – and that, of course, is the source of the power of
those he serves. A Vichy policeman, meanwhile, relishes the prospect of
unfettered power.

The drama acted out by this cast, suddenly snatched out of their daily lives
and placed on an anonymous stage, is one in which the meaning of suffering
is debated, the justice of a precarious life, the absence of transcendent values.
Incident at Vichy is a response to Miller's new-found interest in the Holocaust
but it is plainly a great deal more than that. He spelled out how much more
in an article in the *New York Times Magazine* on 3 January 1965.

In Miller's eyes it was a contemporary play about a contemporary situation
simply displaced in time, in that it addressed a violence in which all become
complicit so long as it seems remote from themselves. Without, he insisted,
wishing to lift the weight of condemnation of Nazism, he asked whether its
power did not become more comprehensible 'when we see our own helplessness toward the violence in our own streets? How many of us,' he asked,
'have looked into ourselves for even a grain of its cause? Is it not for us – as

it is for the Germans – the others who are doing evil?'[171] He pointedly saw this story, set in wartime Vichy France, as commenting on contemporary American realities, in particular, perhaps, on a racial situation in which some rested content in their supposed remoteness from the problem. Who among us, he inquired, 'has asked himself how much of his own sense of personal value, how much of his pride in himself is there by virtue of his not being black? And how much of our fear of the Negro comes from the subterranean knowledge that his lowliness has found our consent?'[172] The play's action takes place two decades earlier, in Europe. Its implications, it seemed to him, were relevant to 1960s America.

The self-sacrifice at the heart of the play, based on a man whose name was never known, came to mind, he explained,

> when I read about the people in Queens refusing to call the police while a woman was being stabbed to death on the street outside their windows ... Whenever I felt the seemingly implacable tide of human drift and the withering of will in myself and in others, this faceless person came to mind. And he appears most clearly and imperatively amidst the jumble of emotions surrounding the Negro in this country and the whole unsettled moral problem of the destruction of the Jews in Europe.[173]

German denial was connected with American denial. In the context of a society that seemed to him to be becoming increasingly relativistic, ethically permissive, ready to validate all experience as a lifestyle choice, he was aware of, and wished to explore, those acts of selflessness that asserted the survival of moral concern. In a year in which civil rights legislation finally made its way on to the statute books, it nonetheless seemed to him that most people were prepared to tolerate injustice and suffering provided they were remote from themselves: 'Is it too much to say that those who do not suffer injustice have a vested interest in injustice?'[174]

In an article in the *New York Times* Miller wrote, 'Everyone believes that there are some few heroes among us at all times. In the words of Hermann Broch [the Jewish Austrian novelist, who later converted to Catholicism], "Even if all that is created in this world were to be annihilated, if all aesthetic values were abolished ... dissolved in scepticism of the law ... there would survive untouched the unity of thought, the ethical postulate." In short, the birth of each man is the rebirth of the claim to justice and requires neither drama nor proof to make it known to us.' However, beyond that Miller was aware of the degree to which 'those who side with justice' are implicated 'in the evils they oppose'.[175] In Germany and America alike, he suggested, those who stand by aghast are complicit, but even those who intervene may be blind to what they share with those they condemn. Compromises begin early, and slowly atrophy the will. The desire not to know is a familiar one, as is the unspoken satisfaction in the consent we offer to a social order from which we benefit at the price of others. What, he asked, was the lesson he drew? 'It is immensely difficult to be human precisely because we cannot detect our own hostility in our own actions.'[176]

Beyond his concern with race lay another issue, one that was becoming increasingly vital to him. Who, he asked, 'knew enough to be shocked, let alone to protest, at the photographs of the [South] Vietnamese torturing Vietcong prisoners, which our press has published? The Vietnamese are wearing United States equipment, are paid by us, and could not torture without us.'[177] He was confident that 'most people, seeing this play [not quite all, since he excepted a number of critics] are quite aware it is not "about Nazism", or a wartime horror tale'.[178] But once again Miller found himself under attack. For Robert Brustein it contained 'the same noisy virtue and moral flatulence' as *After the Fall*. It was, he suggested, a moral sermon, 'tedious, glum, and badly written'.[179] Martin Gottfried found it 'awful'.[180] And whereas Howard Taubman had announced that the play returned the theatre to greatness, for Brustein it 'returns the theatre, more accurately, to the thirties, a period the author never seems to have left'. As to Miller's suggestions of a wider significance to the events in Vichy France, Brustein, in a now familiar argument, found this merely a means of letting the Germans off the hook, because if 'everybody is guilty, then nobody is guilty, and the extermination of six million can be attributed merely to the universality of human evil'.[181]

There were also those who challenged the historical accuracy of a play set in Vichy France at a time when Jews were as yet not under the kind of risk he dramatizes. One of those who attacked him on these lines was the actor-director turned academic Edward Isser. He argued, 'The scenario of *Incident at Vichy* is built upon a fallacious understanding of the historical situation ... The events represented in the drama never occurred, and never could have occurred. The only Jew at risk in the play, from a historical perspective, would have been the bearded Hasid because presumably he was not a French citizen. All the others, and particularly the protagonist Leduc – a war veteran – would have been protected by Vichy/Nazi agreements.' More significantly, Isser took exception to the fact that the Jews are blamed for their own plight, for being paralysed by fear and self-delusion, with 'no recourse to tradition, ritual, prayer or community'. They 'meekly await their fate ... The Jews in *Incident at Vichy* are assimilated to the point that they have no Jewish identity what-soever.' It was not surprising, he suggested, that the play would prove so popular in Germany, since it 'universalizes the predicament of the Jews and asserts that the terror of Nazism is not unique to the German nation'.[182]

An attack in a similar vein was launched by Leslie Epstein, the Jewish novelist (and son of one of the twins who wrote the screenplay of the film *Casablanca*). For him, *After the Fall* had expanded Miller's own bad conscience until it became lost in the guilt of the world around him. Quentin's crimes, he said, 'were dissolved into the sins of the world, so the guilt of the Nazis fades away in the general culpability of mankind'. In *Incident at Vichy*, he argued, guilt becomes classless, nationless and independent of race: 'So everyone, the French policemen, the frightened waiters, the vulgar masses, the refined patrons of art, everyone from the SS thug who cracks the heads of the Jews who are half convinced of their inferiority anyway – they are all collaborators, all the willing mechanics of the machine.' Like Isser, he claims that the play will be popular in Germany because it will offer a form of absolution. He accepts the concept of a shared guilt but says it is a matter of degree. Throwing Jews into ovens is not the same as being *tempted* to commit a crime. To suppose otherwise is to embrace moral nihilism. To invoke an exception – and a gentile one at that – is a 'high school gesture, not an act . . . Unable to judge men, Miller offers his handkerchief.'[183]

Richard Gilman now returned to the attack. After once more invoking *After the Fall*, 'which could not have been a more disgraceful work' – despite or perhaps because of its manifest success at the box office (itself, for Gilman as for Brustein, evidence that the new Lincoln Center theatre was indeed ruled by a Broadway ethos) – he dismissed *Incident at Vichy* as 'a windy, dated sermon about guilt and responsibility'.[184] It was, he said, in a review in *Newsweek*, like watching 'a second-rate but superficially engrossing movie about the Nazis . . . Melodramatic, tendentious, dated . . . Miller's poverty of ideas is naked . . . [he tries to] implicate us unfairly in his personal problem of inarticulateness and philosophical confusion.'[185] This was the man who had spoken of Miller's 'intellectual deficiencies', of his 'limited perspectives', and who had said of *A View from the Bridge*, revived in March 1965 with Robert Duvall and Jon Voight, that it was 'anything but a masterpiece'. It aspired to tragedy 'without the equipment to achieve it, since it suffers from a basic failure of vision, a muddled grasp of how psychic action relates to existential truth, and an insufficiency of language rich enough to support its theme'. *Time* magazine suggested that while aiming for the playgoer's conscience, *Incident at Vichy* had only grabbed his lapels. The critic John Simon saw it – curiously, along with Tennessee Williams's *Cat on a Hot Tin Roof* – as 'striking most discriminating viewers as bundles of attitudes: mere posturings conforming to the current expectations of middlebrow theatregoers'.[186] John Lahr, speaking more generally, spoke of Miller's 'turgid naturalism'.[187]

The most direct, and intellectually shaped, attack was launched by Philip Rahv. Granting that *Incident at Vichy* was a recovery, 'if only to a limited extent, from the disaster of *After the Fall*', he objected in particular to its ending, which he thought 'a sheer *coup de théâtre*'. The author, he remarked, condemns human nature and then exonerates it. Granting that Miller was an authentic playwright, he accused him of intellectual confusion, a confusion rooted in his politics, and here, once again, Miller's Marxism is invoked against him fifteen years after he had abandoned it.

To Rahv, Miller was one of those intellectuals left 'high and dry' by the collapse of Marxism who, as a result, was 'looking for "profundities" from whatever source, to cover their nakedness'. The profundities they had gone in for were attempts to explain totalitarianism. In place of 'the concrete analysis of historical forces in their specific social and political manifestations', however, such intellectuals had 'settled for moralistic attitudinizing'. Hannah Arendt was one such. Miller was another. Nazism, Rahv said, was no mystery. It had simply commanded technological means to effect its atrocities. The interesting question was not what the Nazis did (others, he pointed out, had slaughtered large numbers) but how they did it. The real villains were businessmen, intellectuals, the military and the working class, manipulated by Stalin. In place of such an analysis, Miller offered only a fashionable existentialism that saw everyone as responsible for their own actions and for the society they conspire in creating. Such an idea he found 'scarcely convincing ... a Christian idea put to false uses'.[188]

For Miller, though, the play was neither an attempt to examine the nature of Nazi genocide nor a fig-leaf to cover abandoned ideals. It was concerned with exploring the human capacity to condemn the other. Even the Jews, he insisted, have their Jews. 'How many of us,' he asked, 'have looked into ourselves for even a grain of its cause? Is it not for us – as it is for the Germans – the others who are doing the evil?'[189] Hence his citing Vietnam, which even now had barely made its way into the American theatre, and in his 1965 *New York Times Magazine* article Miller stressed the extent to which he saw Vietnam as relevant. 'There is no way around this,' he said, 'the prisoner crying out in agony is *our prisoner*.'[190] Guilt, he insisted, is not 'a featureless mist but the soul's remorse for its own hostility'.[191] It is a form of self-punishment for what, subconsciously, we know to be a failure of charity, and in the racist violence of the South, in the casual brutalities of daily life in northern ghettos and in Vietnam he saw a connection with those who believed themselves relieved of responsibility for a violence that was unreal because it had seemingly not touched them.

It was a theme Miller would take up again on the occasion of the assassination of Robert Kennedy in 1968. Writing in the *New York Times*, he would ask, 'Is it not time to take a long look at ourselves, at the way we live and the way we think, and to face the fact that violence in our streets is the violence in our hearts, that ... we are what we were – a people of violence.'[192] Listing the individuals and groups who had suffered from violence in America, and identifying popular culture's dissemination of its images, he saw America as disregarding its poor and contemptuous of its minorities.

There is another dimension to *Incident at Vichy* that is not without its disturbing aspect. The Jews in this play fail to act. They remain passive in the face of their fate. It is a non-Jew, the Prince, who acts and who emerges as the moral talisman. Just as Miller had wondered at his own Jewish relatives who, confronted by pogroms in Poland, failed to leave as his grandparents had done, so now he contemplated the Jews who had surrendered themselves as ordered and walked to their fate, and asked how they could so readily have cooperated in their own destruction. It is a pitiless question, but one also asked by Raul Hilberg, historian of the Holocaust, and by Bruno Bettelheim. As early as 1933, with the burning of the Reichstag, Hannah Arendt, who at that moment had decided she could no longer be a bystander but must act, nonetheless 'thought immediately that Jews could not stay'.[193]

Hilberg observed: 'If . . . we look at the whole Jewish reaction pattern, we notice that in its salient features it is an attempt to avert action and, failing that, automatic compliance with orders. Why is this so? Why did the Jews act in this way?' Over two millennia, Jews had learned that 'in order to survive they had to refrain from resistance',[194] The fact that they did survive, he argued, bred a passivity that they believed was the source of redemption. Bettelheim identified what he called a ghetto mentality which predisposed Jews to comply, thereby seeming to justify the acuity of Hitler's remark, 'One must not have mercy with people who are destined by fate to perish' – though Bettelheim stated that it could be no one's fate to be annihilated, provided they understood their situation and planned their resistance. There, though, from his point of view, was the problem. He quoted approvingly a letter he had received from the widow of a rabbi who said: 'I could not understand that the Jews offered so little resistance, and I remember blushing with shame about the passivity of my fellow Jews who accepted so submissively what the Nazis did to them.'[195]

Like Miller, Bettelheim spoke of Jews walking into the gas chambers, a curious way of putting it given the extremes to which the Germans went in order to conceal the truth of the imminent destruction. He offers a number of examples, however, of those who forbore to escape even when offered the opportunity, some of whose situations closely resembled that staged by Miller in *Incident at Vichy*. He recalls a story told by Jean-François Steiner in a book on the revolt in Treblinka, about a Jewish officer of the Red Army who finds himself on a death march with fellow Jews. He attacks a guard and calls on the others to join him. They refuse, murmuring the Sh'ma Yisroel: 'For if God exists nothing can happen that he has not willed.' They are killed. He recalls, too, several thousand Jewish women rounded up in France before being handed over to the Germans. Members of the French Resistance manage to see them, offering forged papers and escape. Fewer than 5 per cent accepted the offer, among them Hannah Arendt. Arendt, however, told a rather different story. She escaped, she explained, because she made friends with the man who arrested her in Berlin, not France, a man who had been promoted from the criminal police to the political division and who now helped her. This was not her only disagreement with Bettelheim.

What was at stake was not merely acquiescence but denial. Bettelheim asserted that too many Jews refused to eat from the tree of knowledge, a formulation that would have appealed to Miller, for whom expulsion from Eden had always proved a potent image of flawed humanity. For Bettelheim, Jews were succumbing to the death instinct or to a principle of inertia: 'The first step was taken long before anyone entered the death camps. It was inertia that led millions of Jews into the ghettos that the SS created for them. It was inertia that made hundreds of thousands of Jews sit home, waiting for their executioners, when they were restricted to their homes.'[196] Those who resisted, he said, went underground, joined resistance movements and mostly survived. Others had failed to act on their own behalf. Arendt was concerned with the collaboration of Jewish leaders, without whom, she felt, the killing of Jews could not have gone on with the same efficiency (a charge that was the source of further attacks on her), not least because the Israeli judges at the Eichmann trial constantly asked witnesses, 'Why did you not rebel?' But it was a question that struck her as 'silly and cruel', especially when Bettelheim developed his theories and, indeed, accusations, from it:

> The well-known historico-sociological construct of a 'ghetto mentality' (which in Israel has taken its place in history textbooks and in this country [the USA] has been espoused chiefly by the psychologist Bruno Bettelheim – against the furious protest of official American Judaism) has been repeatedly dragged in to explain behavior which was not at all confined to Jewish people and which therefore cannot be explained by specifically Jewish factors. The suggestions proliferated until someone who evidently found the whole discussion too dull had the brilliant idea of evoking Freudian theories and attributing to the whole Jewish people a 'death wish' ... This was the unexpected conclusion certain reviewers chose to draw from the 'image' of a book ... in which I allegedly had claimed that the Jews had murdered themselves. And why had I told such a monstrously implausible lie? Out of 'self-hatred', of course.[197]

Miller was less absolute, more inclined, like Arendt, to generalize that sense of passivity (even as he ignored the uprising of Jews in Warsaw and Treblinka, those who escaped to the partisans and fought), but it is not hard to see why he was drawn to the story he had been told. Beyond his insistence that sacrifice could still be chosen, his determination to counter what he saw as Camus's absurdity, denial had always been a central concern. The concentration camp, or even the limbo in which he pictures his characters in *Incident at Vichy*, might represent a special case, but it was one in which he could dramatize basic themes. He would therefore have embraced Bettelheim's regret that so many Jews chose to see the Holocaust 'only from the perspective of their own history and not from that of world history, to which it belongs'.[198] It was a broadening of perspective that many resisted, as if the very particularity of the Holocaust was definitional and to be protected. For Bettelheim, the Jewish response during the Holocaust was available as an urgent lesson: 'As we Jews succeed in freeing ourselves of whatever remnants of ghetto thinking we still harbor, it may fall on us to teach the Western world that it must, as we all must, enlarge the feeling of community beyond our own group . . . not because all men are basically good, but because violence is as natural to man as the tendency toward order.'[199] For Miller, though, writing in 1984, what in fact lay ahead, in Israel, where there was no trace of ghetto thinking, was 'a bellicose armed camp whose adamant tribal defensiveness has inevitably hardened against neighboring peoples to the point of fanaticism. Jewish aloneness is back, but it is now armed.'[200]

Incident at Vichy, which ran for just thirty-two performances, was an uncomfortable play, unlike anything Miller had written before. If its themes were familiar – denial, guilt, responsibility, betrayal, paralysis – they were now cast in a context about which he had previously known little or had been unable to dramatize. His own Jewishness leaves him problematically positioned in a play in which a gentile alone seems capable of acting and in which religion and ideology are presented as the source less of consolation than of deceit and evasion.

Lincoln Center, meanwhile, launched with such energy and hope, quickly foundered, and with it Miller's hopes for a theatre of his own. An article in *Time* magazine noted: 'News pictures of Miller and Kazan sweating out the "death watch" for daily reviews after an opening illustrated how far they never got from Broadway.'[201] When *Incident at Vichy* was followed by one of Eugene O'Neill's less engaging plays, *Marco Millions*, and S.N. Behrman's *But for Whom Charlie*, described by *Time* as an old man's play, a drawing-room harangue, it seemed to underscore a lack of direction, a failure to identify a function. Kazan later admitted that he was ill equipped to handle either. *Newsweek* responded by saying that when an audience cringes in embarrassment and can barely bring itself to applaud, the result is a cultural disaster. Season ticket sales had dropped by a third; now they dropped even further. Having announced in 1961 that he was quitting Broadway, Kazan now left Lincoln Center, Robert Whitehead was fired and Miller gave up his association with the theatre, which passed to Jules Irving and Herb Blau who had successfully run a West Coast experimental theatre but would be merely the second duo in a long line of those to fail at Lincoln Center.

When Whitehead was fired, Miller was the only one to make a statement in the *New York Times*. He castigated the critics for attacking actors and directors while paying no attention to the Board, which he saw as at the root of the theatre's problems. It was not only that the abandonment of repertory was a blow to the American theatre, as it seemed to him, but that he had lost what he had always wanted, a theatre that would stage his plays outside the hit-or-miss world of Broadway.

As Miller remarked, 'It all collapsed. I didn't write. I was terribly discouraged, partly because of the collapse of that theatre, partly because I sensed before the theatre opened that there was a hostility, a negative cynicism.'[202]

2

PEN

... everything ultimately is political. Everything finally ends up being part of the way we govern ourselves ... But I don't write political plays in the sense that I'm writing some kind of argument. I'm interested in the results of life as they affect individuals ... they are about people seen, I hope, in a totality of which the society is a part.[1] *Arthur Miller*

The year 1965 began with a death threat. Miller had been receiving anonymous letters since 1954. This one was rather more specific, though from the same correspondent. It insisted that José Quintero, who had directed Eugene O'Neill's *Marco Millions* at Lincoln Center, should be fired. If he was not, Harold Clurman would have ten days to get his affairs in order before committing suicide. If he failed to do this, then 'I hereby swear on the graves of my mother and father that I will murder Arthur Miller'. It was signed 'Alter Ego or The Establishment'. For once, the FBI became openly involved in Miller's affairs. The Secret Service was informed.

Usually the letters, over that eleven-year period, had been scatological rather than threatening. The writer specialized in obscene Christmas cards. In the course of the last twenty months Miller had received forty-three letters, all written in the regulation psychopath green ink. The matter was handed back to the Post Office and the New York police. A photostat of the 1965 envelope shows it as posted in New York City. Ironically, it is overstamped with a reminder that aliens should report their addresses that January. Perversely, the letter seems to have renewed the FBI's enthusiasm for keeping on eye on Miller. An 18 June entry in the file rehearses old information dating back nearly twenty years.

In February, Miller and his wife undertook their first trip to the Soviet Union. They paid their own way, travelling by train from Düsseldorf to Moscow, two days through winter snow. They were met at the station by a delegation from the Soviet Writers' Union, their arrival duly noted in a cable from the US Embassy to Washington. Nearly a decade after Miller's appearance before HUAC there were still those who felt it right to keep a watch on him. In fact, his FBI file suggests that the couple had arrived by air but, as so often with such reports, this information had been derived not from agents but the press, in this case the *New York Herald Tribune*. It noted that they were on a private visit to meet writers there and in Leningrad, though the trip was to begin with their attending the funeral of the former Deputy Premier, Frol Romanovich Kozlov.

The Millers' was not a political gesture. It was a journey of discovery. Their itinerary sidestepped the familiar iconography of the Soviet state. They were interested in cultural consciousness, images generated by, or associated with, artists and writers. Inge had long been fascinated by the country, perhaps in part because her friend Robert Capa of Magnum had been the first photojournalist to visit it, along with John Steinbeck, on what he called his 'vodka tour'. The trip had resulted in a famous series of photographs, some of which appeared in *Ladies' Home Journal*. It also resulted in the cancellation of his American passport. Thirty years earlier a young Arthur Miller had read Russian novels on the subway rides from Brooklyn to Manhattan, and recommended Russian films to his tolerant mother living out the Depression in Brooklyn while he was at college describing himself as a communist. Now, he was visiting a country he had previously entered only through its fiction, and which he had once elevated to an exemplary socialist state with a unique grasp on the future.

In going to Russia Miller was conscious of visiting a country that in some respects seemed to mirror his own. America might have chosen to apotheosize the individual but it had begun as a communal venture. Both societies embraced progress as a secular faith, were fascinated by the mechanical, by process, were millennial. Nonetheless, even while asking himself if the tragic sensibility could operate in a country in which people had apparently signed up to the inevitability of their future, it seemed to him that things were changing, that the young now felt they had some kind of choice, at least in terms of employment and personal style. As he would in his and Inge's book *In the Country*, published in 1977, he compared the mutuality of rural life with the city, to which people were drawn as the source of economic power and personal transformation, albeit at the price of alienation. Though focusing on Russia, he invoked a pre-First World War America 'where the cities were filling with country people who had to learn to be up-to-date – to forget the idea of mutual help'.[2] He seems to search here, much as he did in America, for something missing, for a lost sense of genuinely shared values, for some purchase on experience that offered a confident possession of the world.

And there *were* aspects of the Soviet Union that were reminiscent of home. Conversations with apparatchiks in the Writers' Union reminded him of nothing so much as talking with members of HUAC. In both he found incredulity at the notion that writers should be allowed to publish whatever they wished. From both he received instruction in the patriotic duty of the author in an embattled world. Both looked for power over writers, but he was aware that in the Soviet Union that power could be absolute, and that writers could be confronted with worse fates than appearing in Washington before self-seeking politicians.

In Moscow he met Ekaterina Furtseva, Minister of Culture, and as such in charge of all translators and, implicitly, of censorship. She made a good impression and it seemed to him that writers rather liked her, though in fact that was not generally the case. Inge's photograph of her, frowning, was later seen as the reason that their 1969 book, *In Russia*, was withdrawn from sale.

When Miller complained about the performance of *A View from the Bridge*, then being staged in Moscow – edited, he discovered, and crudely directed to make explicit the very feelings that the protagonist Eddie Carbone necessarily suppresses – he received an apology from Furtseva. He was subsequently presented with an envelope containing cash – royalties, he was told, in an odd echo of the 1930s when American writers on tours of the Soviet Union would find cash pressed into their hands. Sometimes it was for works not yet written, as if in a parody of expectations about capitalist authors, if also in an attempt to buy silence and acquiescence.

While there he followed up on an article he had written denouncing Soviet anti-Semitism. In March 1964 he had published a somewhat curious piece in the *New Leader*, originally founded by the American Socialist Party but which became a liberal anti-communist magazine, almost certainly receiving funds from the CIA during the 1950s. It had published Khrushchev's 1956 speech denouncing Stalin and went on to publish the work of East European dissidents, including the Yugoslav writer and university professor Mihajlo Mihajlov, with whom Miller would soon be involved; later it would publish the work of Joseph Brodsky and Solzhenitsyn. Its March 1964 issue reproduced a series of grotesque anti-Semitic caricatures (very like those deployed in Nazi Germany) from a new book, *Judaism without Embellishment*, published by the Ukrainian Academy of Sciences, in the very year, an editorial noted, that Rolf Hochhuth's *The Deputy* accused the Pope of bowing to Nazi power. Included in the issue was Miller's essay 'On Obliterating the Jews', written before the publication of the Ukrainian book but which took up the question of Soviet anti-Semitism.

It was in some ways an odd essay in that it began with his admission that he had never visited Russia or any of the communist countries, that he knew no Soviet Jews, and that he was in no position to confirm or deny the truth of charges against individual Jews. Even as he was prepared to accuse the Soviet press, at least, of racism, he confessed to not having read much of it. Nonetheless, on the basis of Western reports, he complained both about

Soviet actions and press coverage: 'You say that in fact a large proportion of the criminals you have caught happen to be Jews. I am not prepared to deny or affirm this, but I do affirm that you have made a point that they are Jews and that this is anti-Semitism.'[3] He acknowledged that Jews held high positions in the Soviet Union and that they might be felt to have greater loyalty to Israel than to their own country, and that his own country had 'yet to prove its acceptance of equality and freedom for all'. He was aware, too, that the Soviet Union was heir to a tradition that rejected racism and anti-Semitism as reactionary, but was, he said, unsure whether such feeling presently existed or was widely shared. However, he noted that Yevgeny Yevtushenko's poem *Babi Yar* had been condemned and that various restrictions had been placed on the production and sale of matzo bread. He hoped, he wrote, that his remarks would reach the desks and hearts of those who dealt with the question of Jews in Russia.

There is something almost touchingly naive about the tone of this piece, but it is interesting to note that he who was so equivocal at times about his Jewishness, spoke here as a Jew: 'I am not religious. I do not believe in Jehova or any being in the sky. I believe, nonetheless, that I am a Jew.' He acknowledged that 'it is not only you the Russian who must free yourself of ancient and archaic fears, however rationalized they may be, it is we who must move with you'. Nonetheless, he regretted the Soviet failure to publish Jewish literature, to support a Jewish theatre or Jewish press. He was unhappy, he explained, to make such remarks when he had been such an admirer of the sacrifices made in the war by Russian troops which had permitted the survival of many Jews. What was at stake, he insisted, in a somewhat equivocal statement, was 'not a religion but the good name of a people, a people that has in fact suffered beyond all measure of its possible failings'.[4]

The *New Leader* had a circulation, at best, of thirty thousand, though there is little doubt that there were those in Moscow and other capitals in Central and Eastern Europe who received reports on it because it had become a publication of choice for dissidents (the journal closed in 2006, seventeen years after the end of the Cold War that had given it special relevance).

In Moscow Miller met Aaron Vergelis, editor of *Soviet Homeland*, the only Yiddish periodical in Russia. Vergelis was an ambiguous figure. He had visited New York as part of a Soviet delegation in 1963 and warnings were issued by a number of people that he did the bidding of his Soviet masters, who had delegated certain powers to him in relation to Jewish culture. When he returned to America Miller was surprised to discover that an account of their meeting had been released by the Soviet Embassy in Washington. Miller's worries had been set at rest, it said. In fact, Vergelis knew of his earlier article and Miller had repeated the points he had made there. Why had *Judaism without Embellishment* been issued? Why were Jews not allowed to bake matzo? Why were they not allowed their own theatres? He was told that the book had been withdrawn, but not that another had replaced it. Jews could now obtain matzo, he was assured, and a Jewish theatre might be set up. When he complained that Jews whose families had been broken up by the war were not allowed to leave the Soviet Union, he was told that some were and more might be. The idea that the number of Jewish economic criminals was being exaggerated was denied. Miller summed up the response as an assertion that there are no problems, but we have solved them. He, meanwhile, was accused of being used by warmongers. It was not a fruitful encounter.

Together, Miller and Inge took in rather more theatre than the unsatisfactory production of his own play. In particular they visited the Sovremennik Contemporary Theatre, under the direction of Oleg Efremov, then staging Yevgeny Schwartz's *The Emperor's Clothes*, and Yuri Lyubimov's production of John Reed's *Ten Days That Shook the World* at the Taganka Theatre. It seemed to Miller that the Russian theatre still had what he had hoped the American theatre would have, a centrality, a compelling quality. He observed:

> No one who goes to the theatre in Russia can fail to be struck by the audience. It is not bored and it is not uncritical, but it is passionately open to what it has come to see. ... It is as though there were still a sort of community in this country, for the feeling transcends mere admiration for professionals doing their work well. It is as though art were a communal utterance, a kind of speech which everyone present is delivering together.[5]

Andrei Voznesensky, a poet who, Miller noted, received his first encouragement from Boris Pasternak, together with Yevtushenko, popular in both East and West, were at that time trying to establish a poets theatre, just as several of Miller's contemporaries were in America.

No fan of ballet, Miller also visited the Bolshoi, in the company of Voznesensky and his wife, the writer Zoya Boguslavskaya. The prima ballerina Maya Plisetskaya was a friend of Voznesensky. Despite her dancing a special cadenza for Miller, he and Inge left at the end of the first act for the journey back to Paris and New York.

If Miller had been feeling at odds with his anonymous correspondent at the beginning of the year – plainly a man with an interest in the theatrical world, if also in need of secure accommodation – he also felt at odds with a theatre that was itself undergoing a fundamental reappraisal. Off and Off Off Broadway were spawning a different breed of writers and performers. Distrust of authoritarianism extended to authors. The spontaneous gesture seemed to carry more authenticity than the structured text, which now existed only to justify the improvisation it provoked.

This was the time of flower power (a term coined by Allen Ginsberg in

1965), of the rock band the Doors with their coded reference to William Blake. Ahead lay Woodstock and the Age of Aquarius. America's youth clothed itself in Afghan jackets and psychedelic shirts, or stripped naked in the belief that the body was the source of truth, an antidote to a destructive technology. Love, both sexual and platonic, it was proposed, had the ability to disarm power. In the green of a San Francisco park or the mud of a farmer's field, to the sound of rock music and the smell of marijuana, young Americans were transforming not so much America itself as the way in which they chose to see it, stepping out of urban urgencies into a timeless world of desire unrestrained by rationality. They did, that is, unless they were among the many more millions who did not. Decades are not always defined by the experiences of the majority.

Capitalism was momentarily wrong-footed, until it adjusted to the new market and learned to service the needs of those who assumed themselves to be turning on, tuning in and dropping out – Timothy Leary's formulation, first pronounced in 1966. Here was a generation that seemed to believe that intractable problems could be addressed by walking away, stepping into a liberated imagination, constructing a chemical landscape – but only until the demands of Vietnam exerted their authority. Even then, many American servicemen experienced that war high on drugs and risked their lives and those of others to the throb of rock music as well as that of helicopters. Francis Ford Coppola's *Apocalypse Now* in 1979 would capture some of the moral anarchy of the war. All of which might seem so at odds with Miller's own commitments as to make it seem an irrelevance, were it not for the fact that he has described an abandoned film script called 'The Love Drug', written more than a decade later, in which he struggled to come to terms with this aspect of the sixties. It concerns a young man at Columbia University, a musician, who discovers a chemical compound with the power to remove all aggressive tendencies, a love drug that inspires not so much sex as affection. The chemical ends up in the hands of a pharmaceutical company who market it as 'Love'. At first it is a success but it rapidly emerges that aggression has a positive as well as a negative use. The military may abandon all thoughts of war, but professional football comes to an end and the drive necessary to everyday life dissipates.

America bombs Russia not with high explosives but with this drug, and eventually the world is reduced to a soporific existence, with the exception of adherents of orthodox religions who have been banned from taking it. Ironically, they combine in an alliance to stamp out love, perhaps evidence of Miller's prescience, since religious fundamentalism would be at the root of much late twentieth-century and early twenty-first-century violence, trampling not only love but much else under foot. He abandoned the script, as well he might, but it can stand as his comment on the age of flower power. Surprisingly, in 2005 news leaked out that the Pentagon had explored the possibility of developing an aphrodisiac bomb. The six-year project cost $5 million, invested in the hope of creating chemicals that might 'cause' homosexuality or make its victims sexually attractive to what it identified as annoying or injurious animals. These plans were dated 1994, but there was another project dating back to 1945 called the 'Who Me?' bomb, which would produce odours that suggested that other soldiers were farting. It was abandoned when it was discovered that in certain parts of the world faecal odour was too familiar to be offensive.[6] Miller's imagination, it seemed, stopped somewhere short of the wilder shores of military planning.

Even political revolt in the theatre would seem to him less an appeal to the intellect than a visceral ritual. *Hair*, for example, which opened at Joseph Papp's Public Theater in 1967 before moving to Broadway the following year, he found a psychedelic celebration of the body that sidestepped rather than addressed the issue of the war that allegedly provoked it. Indeed, he was surprised to discover that it was supposedly designed as a protest against the war, so concerned was it with a generalized sense of liberation. He was not alone in this. The word with which the British-born theatre critic Clive Barnes summed it up on its first outing was 'charm'. Leonard Bernstein, who walked out of the production, found the songs no better than laundry lists. The carnivalesque was pitched against the coldly rational, the body against the machine. Its anarchistic spirit was oppositional, but not in any way, it seemed to Miller, that could hope to understand, let alone deflect, the processes at work in a society ever more completely dedicated to illusion. In the end the homeopathic pitching of a psychedelic imagination against a surreal world in which helicopter gunships were called Jolly Green Giants and chemical defoliants were described as Agent Orange, seemed less than effective. It was not the sensual body that would interdict the military machine, but bodies united in demonstrations blocking railroad tracks, Buddhist monks sitting cross-legged, incandescent with gasoline rather than ecstasy.

The ceremonies, rites, incantations of theatrical performances proposed a solidarity whose political implications were often echoed by vaguely worded manifestos and statements. To Miller, though, such groups and performances offered to substitute myths for history, brief epiphanies for broad understanding. These were gestures that exhausted themselves in their own presentation, leaving little residue in the form of thought. The writer, meanwhile, was subsumed in work which foregrounded the actor as a sign of the resistant self.

This was a physical theatre designed to assault the sensibility, and occasionally the person, of the audience in an effort both to disturb and to establish direct contact. It was suspicious of texts which could not be broken open by actors, who became collaborators, co-inventors, whose improvisations were themselves gestures towards the freedom claimed and represented figures whose supposed authenticity was the ultimate defence against social and political manipulation. Words were in part a mantra, a spell to cast out demons; but they were to be subordinated, finally, because language had itself been compromised in a society in which politicians and advertising copywriters corrupted it in the name of their own advantage. Miller responded to the energy of this work but found that it lacked an awareness of history, the mechanisms at work, the power of words not only to deceive but also to enlighten. He wrote, but never published or produced, a parody in which the actors on stage begin the performance naked and slowly dress while audience members alternately enthuse at what they see and make sexual advances to one another – something, incidentally, not unknown among audiences of the Living Theatre.

For someone like Miller who had been the victim of a repressive government in the 1950s, his youthful Marxism a response to a genuine crisis of capitalism, the idea that the artist might have an oppositional role was scarcely new. What did seem different about the new radical theatre was that its revolt was more generalized. Its targets were not at first Vietnam or capitalism but authority, rationality, language. Its proponents were the new romantics, but their romanticism was in danger of seeing history, politics and individual ethics as secondary to a celebratory physicality. The drugs that some groups took were the symbol of an evasion at the heart of their enterprise. Miller felt distinctly at odds with a rebellion that seemed to him to lack substance or direction, but when it took a more familiar form, reshaping itself into a revolt against the Vietnam War, he felt altogether more secure. In fact he threw himself much deeper than many others into the politics of the decade, both in his work and in his public life. He was, after all, clear that the writer was now confronted with a direct challenge posed by domestic and foreign politics. While he had felt curiously abstracted from the civil rights movement, oddly insisting to me that it was a matter for the young – he was thirty-nine when the 1954 school desegregation decision was made by the Supreme Court and only ten years older when the Civil Rights Act was passed – at the age of fifty he became a major player in the anti-war movement.

Civil disturbances at home and in Vietnam began to change the nature of the artist's relationship to society, and to radicalize many of these theatre groups. In June 1965, Lyndon Johnson attempted to woo American intellectuals with a White House Festival of the Arts, specifically designed to allay opposition to the war. The project rapidly fell apart when not only did Robert Lowell refuse his invitation, but a petition denouncing America's policy in Vietnam was circulated at the dinner table by Dwight Macdonald, of whom Leon Trotsky had once reputedly said that while every man had the right to

be stupid Comrade Macdonald abused that right. He had once been considered by the CIA-influenced Congress for Cultural Freedom (CCF) as a
potential editor of *Encounter* magazine, but his ideological position was
seldom consistent. When others had attacked Hannah Arendt's *Eichmann in
Jerusalem*, he defended it.

The petition already had a host of signatures when the writers arrived at
the White House, including those of Hannah Arendt, Lillian Hellman,
Alfred Kazin, William Styron and Mary McCarthy; nine more signed at the
dinner, precipitating a fight between Charlton Heston and Philip Roth.
Lowell admitted that he had at first accepted the invitation 'greedily'. After
a week's consideration, however, he decided that to do so could be read as
making a public commitment. His public letter to the President read:

> Although I am very enthusiastic about most of your domestic legislation and
> intentions, I nevertheless can only follow our present foreign policy with the
> greatest dismay and distrust. What we will do and what we ought to do as a
> sovereign nation facing other sovereign nations needs now to hang in the
> balance between the better and worse possibilities. We are in danger of
> imperceptibly becoming an explosive and suddenly chauvinistic nation, and
> may even be drifting on our way to the last nuclear ruin. I know it is hard for
> a responsible man to act; it is also painful for the private and irresolute
> man to dare criticism. At this anguished, delicate and perhaps determining
> moment, I feel I am serving you and our country best by not taking part in
> the White House Festival of the Arts.[7]

This was not Lowell's first letter to a President. In 1943 he had written to
Roosevelt refusing 'the opportunity you offer me in your communication of
August 6, 1943, for service in the Armed Forces'[8] He had actually volunteered
for both the Navy and the Army a year earlier, but was repelled by reports of
mass civilian deaths in the bombing campaign in Europe and by demands for
unconditional surrender. There was therefore a certain consistency in his
stance over Vietnam. If he were still eighteen and liable for the draft, he said,
'I pray that I'd take the position of the draft evader, not leave the country but
go into jail.'[9] Speaking in 1971 of his declining the White House invitation,
Lowell remarked that it had brought him more publicity than his poems, and
that he felt miscast, burdened with the need to address public issues.[10] He
was not alone in experiencing a tension between his role as a citizen and his
function as a poet.

It became increasingly clear that the administration and the intellectuals
were in opposite camps. Miller subsequently invoked Lowell's action as
evidence of the increasing importance of the writer, repeating his praise for the
poet that same year at the International PEN Congress in Bled, Yugoslavia,
though, in truth, he found his political views hard to take. Lowell regarded

Roosevelt with contempt while to Miller he remained a model of liberal virtues.

After the Fall and *Incident at Vichy*, like his commitment to the anti-war movement, reflected a renewed interest on Miller's part in a world beyond the boundaries of a self-referring United States. In part, his changed perspective can be traced to Inge Morath. She would later say that her husband would happily have stayed at home, had she not taken him along on a number of her trips. There was also, though, another reason for his engagement with the wider world. In 1965 he undertook the presidency of the writers' organization International PEN. Twenty years on from the war, he was still interested in opening up channels to the Soviet Union, this time, though, in cultural terms.

The approach from PEN was apparently no more than an inquiry from an organization looking for new leadership. In fact, it seems Miller may have fallen into a CIA trap, part of its plan for America to dominate and lead Western culture. 'I had no idea,' he later explained, 'until one day, toward the end of my term, I was having a drink with David Carver, who ran the whole thing from London. We were talking about the quasi-scandal about *Encounter* magazine [later revealed to have been secretly funded by the CIA] when David said, in a curiously pointed way, "Well, I wish they would give us some money, wouldn't you?" It occurred to me later that they had already taken some.'[11] In fact the Agency seems to have worked to place people close to the centre of PEN: CIA money, laundered through obliging front organizations, most notably the Congress for Cultural Freedom, funded travel expenses for those attending PEN's 1965 Bled conference. It also did its best to ensure Miller's election.[12]

Miller was then, according to Frances Stonor Saunders, author of *Who Paid the Piper? The CIA and the Cultural Cold War*, being enrolled in a CIA plan, unfolding since the time of the Waldorf Conference and its immediate aftermath, to use the Non-Communist Left (NCL) as a Cold War weapon. This was a world as full of hidden powers as Puritan New England, and equally manipulative of the individual conscience.

Those who joined the Communist Party, or were held in its gravitational pull, and those who opposed it only to find themselves unwitting dupes of those for whom culture was a battleground, often failed to realize the extent of their manipulation. If the Comintern had its agents and front organizations, so too did the CIA, which when it was not, like its Soviet counterpart, overthrowing democratic governments, was enrolling magazines, editors and writers in its cause – sometimes wittingly, more often not. Miller, who had found himself enrolled by one such in 1949 at the Waldorf Conference, plainly a communist-inspired occasion, was, it seems probable, ensnared by another as he agreed to accept a job for which, unbeknown to him, the NCL – with its links to the CIA – had apparently already earmarked him, even taking the precaution of neutralizing a potential rival run by the French.

The Congress for Cultural Freedom was founded in 1950. Michael Josselson, chief of the Agency's Berlin Office for Covert Action, was appointed as executive director of its Paris secretariat. The CCF was designed to be the CIA's key weapon in the culture wars of the 1950s and 60s. The distinguished sociologist Edward Shils, former member of the Office of Strategic Services (OSS) and member of the Congress, described its formation as 'an act of solidarity with the intellectual victims of the repressive imposition of Communism ... It was also an address to the intellectuals of Western countries to remove the blinkers from their eyes and to see the Communist societies as they really were.' The CCF, he maintained, stood 'in a tradition of intellectuals of a common outlook joined together in a common task – it is a product of the eighteenth-century Enlightenment'. It was 'anti-Communist because the Communists and their accomplices and their dupes were infecting the intellectual and public life of their societies, misleading them by their false accounts of both Communist societies and liberal democratic societies'.[13] Whatever the source of its funding, Shils said, it determined its own policies. The difficulty with this was that its CIA links were kept secret and that it sought to influence a wide range of organizations and individuals covertly.

The CCF's strategy reflected the aims of the CIA but, since these involved demonstrating the primacy of American culture, its funding often underwrote the work of major figures, financing their travel and the magazines that published them. Its aim was to secure a hearing for the American point of view, to open channels. In the process, it often proved a valuable sponsor for emerging literatures – in Africa, the Caribbean, Latin America.

Among the publications established by the CCF was the German magazine *Der Monat*, whose funding subsequently passed to the Ford Foundation, which contained an administrative unit to coordinate with the CIA. It was the Ford Foundation that sponsored the East European Fund, a CIA front linked with the Chekhov Publishing House, which bought proscribed Russian works. In Africa, the Congress sponsored the first African Writers' Conference. It also funded the Transcription Service, designed to oppose left-wing political writing but which nonetheless, and thanks to its director Dennis Duerden, played an important role in fostering African and Caribbean literature, including the work of Wole Soyinka – whose release from prison, and from possible execution, by the Nigerian government headed by General Gowon, was later secured by Miller, by now President of International PEN. That release was secured when Gowon was told that Miller had been married to Marilyn Monroe. A request from a playwright was one thing. A request from a man linked to a Hollywood star was another.

Miller's involvement with PEN began, in 1965, with a telephone call to Inge's apartment on rue de la Chaise in Paris, the apartment in a sixteenth-century house that she had sublet to Mary McCarthy. They had come to see Luchino Visconti's production of *After the Fall*. The call, from London, was from Keith Botsford, a novelist and teacher whom Miller knew only as editor, with Saul Bellow and Aaron Asher (subsequently Miller's editor at Viking), of the *Noble Savage*, a literary magazine. Along with the novelist Ralph Ellison and others Miller had attended its launch at the Algonquin Hotel and had submitted two stories to it.

Botsford was born in Brussels in 1928. His mother went under the disconcerting name of Carolina Elena Rangoni-Machiavelli-Publicola-Santacroce and was, he claimed, descended from Niccolò Machiavelli himself. Perhaps the Machiavelli genes were still active, though in 2002 Botsford would deny aspects of the story as outlined by Frances Stonor Saunders. Immediately after the Second World War, he served briefly in military intelligence. Writer and academic, he published under a number of different names and would later work on a study of the Non-Communist Left, including several of those employed, directly or indirectly, by the CIA.

The next day Botsford arrived in Paris with David Carver, whom Miller described as Sydney Greenstreet without the asthma. Carver had been the Duke of Windsor's aide in the Bahamas during the war, the duke having effectively been exiled, partly because of British doubts about his contacts with Nazi Germany. He went on to be Secretary General of PEN for many years, and it was he who proceeded to outline its history to Miller, who had only the vaguest notion of its function. Established after the First World War, it was, Carver explained, an international organization designed to help prevent war, fight censorship and support writers in their battles with power. It had been dominated by the English Centre, John Galsworthy having been its first international president. In 1933 it had denounced the Nazis for expelling communists from the Berlin Centre and for their racism. In 1956 it had succeeded in securing the release of Hungarian writers, but now it was in trouble because it had failed to make a real connection with younger writers and also because the Cold War had damaged its credibility with those countries not necessarily pro-Western. What was needed was some kind of détente with the East. The pitch was calculated to appeal to Miller, the more so when it was further explained that PEN had had some success in saving the lives of writers and that Miller would have no administrative or organizational duties.

Twenty-two years after this meeting, Miller remarked: 'I had a suspicion of being used and wondered suddenly whether our State Department or CIA or equivalent British hands might be stirring this particular stew.' To 'flush them out', he asked what the reaction would be to inviting Soviet writers to join. As he recalled it, 'Carver's mouth dropped open, "Why, that would be wonderful."' Two days later Miller agreed to take the job on, but, he later commented, 'I was left with the mystery of why I had been chosen.'

Later, when he secured his dossier from the FBI under the Freedom of Information Act, Miller's suspicions belatedly deepened, but only because a cable from the US Embassy in Moscow, which he had visited just before his trip to Paris, had commented on the warmth of his reception there. It now seemed to him that perhaps knowledge that he would prove acceptable in Russia had led to the invitation to join PEN, and that this information might have reached Carver from sources other than the newspapers, which had also reported his favourable reception.

Writing in 1987, he was ready to acknowledge that PEN 'stood stuck in the concrete of what I would soon learn were its traditional Cold War anti-Soviet positions', but he still felt that it was trying to 'bend, and acknowledge Eastern Europe as a stable group of societies whose writers might well be permitted new contacts with the West'.[14] In fact, his suspicions fell a good way short of what seems to have been the truth, though truth is a rare commodity where intelligence agencies are concerned.

He had, it appears, been selected by the CIA as part of its strategy of using culture as a bridgehead and establishing the United States as a leader of Western civilization. Those who directed the cultural dimension of the Cold War had judged that now was the time to open up channels to Soviet intellectuals and artists. Indeed, in 1956 Ignazio Silone, a stalwart of the CCF, arranged a conference in Zurich in which East was supposed to meet West. Nothing came of it. In the mid-1950s the Congress attempted some kind of arrangement with the Polish Writers' Union, *Encounter*, *Preuves* and *Tempo Presente*, all Congress front magazines, sending greetings to its annual gathering. *Preuves* even published a special Polish issue. The Congress also sent books and magazines to Hungary, Rumania and Lithuania, which, as Peter Coleman in his book *The Liberal Conspiracy* has pointed out, was 'the Congress's regular method of entry into the dictatorships around the world'.[15] In addition, it secretly funded individuals and secured publication in the West of banned writers. The Soviet Union, however, was proving a harder target.

In 1959 Melvin Lasky, on the staff of the anti-Stalinist *New Leader* and a correspondent for *Partisan Review* before editing the CIA-financed *Der Monat* and *Encounter* magazines, had proposed a series of East–West meetings which had also come to nothing, though the Congress did arrange one meeting of scholars. Nicolas Nabokov suggested a conference on a Venetian island in honour of Tolstoy, as a counterweight to one in Moscow in which the writer would be presented as part of a Bolshevik tradition. Sixteen Russians were invited; none of them appeared. In their place the Soviets sent four apparatchiks, including the police informer Vladimir Yermilov and

Georgi Markov, secretary of the executive committee of the Union of Soviet Writers. A proposed exchange of articles between *Encounter* and *Novy Mir* in 1960 failed to happen. Briefly, things seemed to open up in the Soviet Union in 1961, but by 1963 the door had slammed shut with some finality as *Encounter* was denounced by *Pravda*.

Plainly, there had to be a change of tack. Arthur Miller, with a reputation at home for being at odds with the right wing and a reputation in Eastern Europe as a progressive, seemed to fit the bill. It was a wise move, and not before time. Two years later, the left-wing magazine *Ramparts* would reveal that the CIA, under the direction of Cord Meyer, had been funding student groups, while the *New York Times* would expose the CIA's role in the Congress for Cultural Freedom and its funding of *Encounter*. One of those named was the feminist Gloria Steinem (*New York Times*, 21 February 1967) who had worked for the CIA-funded Independent Research Service. But she was one of many. The whole complex of CIA-funded magazines and organizations began to fall apart. The Irish writer and politician Conor Cruise O'Brien would even deliver a lecture, distributed to delegates at the 1966 PEN Congress, presided over by Miller, attacking *Encounter* as a tool of the Washington power structure – a gesture not without its irony, since that Congress itself had a strong CIA presence.

Things were not improved when in the *Saturday Evening Post* Thomas Wardell Braden, of the CIA's International Organization Division, attempted to defend its manipulation of the Non-Communist Left, though an article by Andrew Kopkind was called 'CIA: The Great Corrupter'.[16] Ironically, Miller's old *bête noire*, *Partisan Review*, itself in receipt of Congress funds, chose this moment to condem secret subsidies to magazines. Philip Rahv denounced those who had collaborated with the Congress for Cultural Freedom and accepted CIA subsidies 'without being clear in their minds as to what was involved [as] in many ways to be compared to the "fellow-travelers" and "stooges" of the 1930s, who supported Stalin's reading of Marxism and his murderous policies even as they spoke of the Russia he despotically ruled as a "workers' paradise" and "classless society". But in contrast to the "stooge" of yesterday,' he maintained, 'the "stooges" of today are paid cash on the line for their various declarations.'[17]

Decades later, Miller remarked: 'It passed through my mind – that the government might have wanted me to be president of PEN because they couldn't otherwise penetrate the Soviet Union, and they figured that traveling behind me could be their own people. They wouldn't expect me to do it, I don't think. One of the early people who approached me about PEN – I can't remember his name now – but people would later say about him, "Why, that guy was an agent all the time." Now I have no evidence of that – it was gossip.'[18] The man he refers to here was Keith Botsford. As to his status with the Agency, however, that was by no means clear, and he denied being part of it.

Botsford had also attended two CCF-sponsored conferences in Berlin, the first in 1962, where Willy Brandt, then Mayor of West Berlin, collaborated with Nicolas Nabokov (on a salary from the CCF), who thirteen years before had been part of the opposition to Miller at the Waldorf Conference. The second, in 1964, was the Berlin Festwochen, on which the CCF spent large sums to fly writers to the city. Among their number were Botsford, Robbie Macauley (CIA) and John Hunt (CIA and a case officer for the CCF). Speaking in 2002 Botsford remarked,

> Had I known of the CCF's CIA funding I would have gone without demur ... Once into my twenties I lost all sympathy for the socialist 'cause', having seen it first hand in operation in Germany in the immediate post-war. So just was the CCF's own cause, that of combating anti-democratic movements and ideologies, that I felt deeply committed to that cause. And remain so ... though many people spoke to me of their 'suspicions' I found the facts, when revealed, not surprising. I have been told since, by unimpeachable sources, that the Agency had indeed considered recruiting me, but had rightly decided I was too non-conformist for the job. No approach was ever made and the only person about whom I had my doubts was Michael Josselson.[19]

He was, of course, not wrong about Josselson, who had appeared on the final day of the Waldorf Conference in 1949 and was for a time to be a key link between the CIA and what had once been the Trotskyite Left but was now closer to Arthur Schlesinger's 'Vital Center'.

Botsford, a permanent roving ambassador of the Congress for Cultural Freedom, had been invited to join by John Hunt, whom he had known since 1949 but whose CIA affiliation Botsford claims not to have known until 2001. Botsford had spent three years in Latin America as a representative of the Congress and had overseen Robert Lowell's disastrous visit to Brazil and Argentina. Before he left, Elizabeth Hardwick wrote to Lowell asking, 'Who pays for the Congress for Cultural Freedom, anyway?'[20] It was a good question, but not one that Lowell (known to his friends as Cal), for all his fear of political manipulation, was interested in pursuing. As Botsford later explained:

> In preparation for [Lowell's] trip, which the CCF paid for (with the accompanying retinue of Elizabeth Hardwick, who played the blowsy southern lady for some weeks, perspiring and fanning, until she went home, and their singular, spoiled, whiney daughter Harriet), I had translated and published a little pamphlet on Cal for Brazilians, including four poems I translated into Portuguese. It was evident to me from the very first night that Cal was not

well. I knew vaguely that he went through cyclical manic-depressive phases. He arrived already well along the rising curve and was to go back home from Argentina, after confinement under restraint in a private clinic, heavily sedated on Thorazine and with many picaresque incidents and offended people in his wake.

The picaresque incidents consequent on Lowell abandoning his medication and sinking rather too many vodka martinis (six doubles before lunch) included speeches praising Hitler, stripping naked in the middle of the city and climbing every equestrian statue he could locate, before being restrained in a straitjacket by six strong men in the corridor of his hotel. He was taken back to America by Blair Clark, who would later be Eugene McCarthy's campaign manager, a campaign in which Lowell, like Miller, would play an enthusiastic part.

Lowell, under whom Botsford had studied at the University of Iowa, had been picked out by the Congress as an outstanding literary figure to counteract the left-wing Pablo Neruda (then being touted for a Nobel Prize), though Botsford claims not to have known of any such plan ('Recipients of the Stalin Prize were unusual choices. A bon vivant of the "gauche sympathizante", [Nerada] was not my cup of tea'). As he said, 'If I were Cal's leash, as against his guide, translator, fetcher-and-carrier and general fix-it (I knew those literatures in which he moved infinitely better than he did), then who held the reins? Whither was he being led?' In Botsford's view, 'the whole trip was a hopeless enterprise, due to Cal's mental state, which deteriorated stop by stop.' He remarked in 2002:

> Had the Agency sent Cal down to South America, then the Agency would have been as mad as he; but at the time I knew nothing about the Agency and knew far more about the estimable Jack Thompson at the Farfield Foundation, and McNeill Lowry at the Ford, who were my ostensible spon-sors. I was not able to confirm (as opposed to suspect) that the Agency had a hand in my sojourn in Latin America until much later and John Hunt, by then a close friend, continued to deny his connection to me until last summer.[21]

Since Farfield was a pure CIA product, however, and the Ford Foundation a conduit for CIA money (Ford would give money for PEN's Bled Congress), there seems little doubt that the Congress did have a political agenda in Latin America, though whether Lowell was a wise choice is another matter.

Lowell wrote to Botsford, a man he described as quite attractive in slightly too sharp a way, apologizing for his behaviour. It is not clear how sincere he was, given that he wrote to the poet Elizabeth Bishop saying: 'I enjoyed your limerick on Keith. I finally wrote him a sort of apology and bread and butter letter. Poor thing, all ticks and angles.'[22] Though he knew Botsford worked for the Congress it is clear he knew nothing of its purpose any more than he did of the true nature of the Farfield Foundation, suggesting to Elizabeth Bishop that it might finance a translation of her work.

As Frances Stonor Saunders has observed, 'The truth is that the CIA made every effort to turn PEN into a vehicle for American government interests and the Congress for Cultural Freedom was the designated tool.' Originally, the CCF had been concerned to keep the Soviets out, and put pressure on David Carver, PEN's secretary, to oppose Soviet entry. It deployed for the purpose former communists who were happy to assist, including those who had worked for or with the Congress before, including Arthur Koestler and Stephen Spender as well as Ignazio Silone. In the 1920s Silone had been a communist agent in Italy but was expelled when he opposed the Party's policies. In the 1930s he wrote *Fontamara* and *Bread and Wine*, two anti-fascist works which were distributed to the Italians by the US Army after the liberation in 1943. He was a contributor to *The God that Failed*, a book in which former communists explained their reason for defecting from the cause. During the war he became an agent of the Office of Strategic Services. His codename was Len, but it was not, it later turned out, his first codename. Towards the end of the millennium it would be revealed that he had been an informer for the Italian secret police between 1919 and 1930, under the name of Silvestri, though in 1928 his brother was arrested as a terrorist and tortured – an event that seems to have been a key reason for his discontinuing his activities. These revelations, however, lay far ahead. For the moment, with Nicola Chiaromonte, who had flown in André Malraux's squadron fighting the fascists in the Spanish Civil War but who later became an anti-Stalinist and wrote for *Partisan Review*, Silone was editor of the CCF's magazine *Tempo Presente*.[23] Spender became editor of *Encounter*, of which, according to Saunders, David Carver acted as an unofficial agent, distributing it at PEN meetings.[24] Both Silone and Spender would insist that they were kept in the dark as to the funding of these magazines. Spender told Mary McCarthy that he had been told of the CIA's role by Nicolas Nabokov in 1966, but then denied it in his autobiography.

The sociologist Paul Goodman had revealed the CIA's involvement with the CCF in the winter 1962 issue of the leftist journal *Dissent*, only to have Nabokov deny it. Mary McCarthy, at least, was convinced that Silone knew of the source of the funding, even though she absolved her friend Chiaromonte. The fact that, unlike *Encounter*, *Tempo Presente* had published anti-American articles she put down to the fact that the CIA people involved could not read Italian. McCarthy's biographer Carol Brightman, however, also relates those articles to the strategy of the CIA's International Organization Division, which she quotes as being: '"Limit the money to amounts organizations can credibly spend ... Use legitimate, existing organizations;

disguise the extent of American interest; protect the integrity of the organization by not requiring it to support every aspect of official American policy."[25]

McCarthy herself was far from unaware of the games being played. The achievement of the CIA was to have recognized that in certain respects their best allies were those on the left. As Carol Brightman observed, 'For intellectuals, the Cold War consensus was born with the CIA's historic perception that "socialists who called themselves 'left' – people whom many Americans thought were no better than Communists – were the only people who gave a damn about fighting Communism."[26] As Norman Podhoretz observed, the fact that the Agency was interested in deploying the Non-Communist Left underlined how far they had travelled in their beliefs, but also gave them access to funds that no other branch of government would offer.

The complexities of such cultural politics, the labyrinthine workings of the CIA and the CCF, seem, however, to have passed Miller by. To his mind he was riding to the rescue of a near-defunct organization he believed he might redeem. In opening up contacts with the Soviet Union, he felt he was doing something to address a Cold War politics that alarmed him even as, unbeknown to him, he was being enrolled to play his part in just such politics. The irony is that CIA policies and the inclinations of people such as Arthur Miller could often overlap, not least because there were those in the CIA whose sentiments were at odds with those of the politicians they ostensibly served. The CIA had been as opposed to Joseph McCarthy as those on the left, though for different reasons.

It was, in fact, the CCF that decided that Keith Botsford should be an assistant and deputy to Carver at PEN, much to the anger of the French section which seems to have been aware of the CIA link and saw this as part of a plan to take over the organization – not, as it turned out, simply a piece of Gallic anti-Americanism. Certainly Botsford has suggested that Carver was 'a thoroughly decent man but one with no great vision or knowledge of the complex cultural politics involved in international relations', and that 'it was intimated that David being of mature years, I might succeed him'.[27] Botsford's salary came from the CCF.

Carver had originally had his eye on John Steinbeck as President of PEN. Miller was second choice. The French proposed the Guatemalan poet and novelist Miguel Ángel Asturias, who had been twice exiled, once from his own country and subsequently from Argentina. He had been at odds with the CCF, which made him the wrong choice for those anxious to exert influence on PEN. Indeed, a year later he would win the Lenin Peace Prize, thus confirming their suspicions. Ironically, in 1967 he followed this with the Nobel Prize for Literature, so that PEN passed up the opportunity to be led by a recipient of the highest international award – a man, incidentally, who might more easily have opened up channels to the Soviet Union. He would not, however, have been the CCF's (and therefore the CIA's) man.

Michael Josselson, a primary figure in the CIA's efforts to conduct a cultural Cold War, called Asturias 'that old Nicaraguan fellow-travelling war-horse'[28] and attempted to persuade André Malraux, also associated with the Congress, to block Asturias's nomination, suggesting that it would undermine Carver, who, on 21 April 1965 himself wrote a lengthy letter (eight closely typed pages) to PEN members attacking the French for nominating and lobbying for a candidate when they knew that someone else – Miller – had already been proposed by the Congress and sponsored by the host PEN Centre in Yugoslavia. In the past, Carver notes in his letter, the French had been led by distinguished writers and had been fully cooperative. Now, protocols, courtesies and traditions had been flouted. The French Centre had been asked to withdraw its candidate but had refused. Carver accordingly set out the requirements for an international president. These included represent-ing a 'great literature', being a writer of international stature, backed by a PEN Centre in his own country and writing in the language of that Centre (or one of the two approved languages – i.e. English or French). This person must also have shown an interest in PEN for some time and be free of national or political bias. Asturias, Carver claims, qualified under none of these headings (nor, in truth, did Miller, with respect to long-term interest). Asturias, Carver wrote, nominated by the French Centre, was a Guatemalan living in Italy who wrote in Spanish. At the top of his typewritten letter is a handwritten note: 'This is the first counter-attack!'

When he received the letter Lewis Galantière, president of the American Centre, wrote to fellow members of the PEN executive warning that what he called the French offensive was 'designed not only to thwart the election of an American international president, but also to capture the International Secretariat'. He considered the French move to be 'one more example of the overweening hubris that has seized French officialdom (for I do not doubt this has the approval of the Quai d'Orsay).'[29]

Carver then wrote to Miller explaining that he intended to see the president and secretary of the French Centre to 'press the matter of the withdrawal of Asturias vigorously'.[30] In April, he wrote to Miller expressing the hope that he would allow his name to be circulated as a candidate along with the agenda for the Bled conference, assuring him that, should it come to an election, he could be assured of 'an overwhelming vote'.

Two days later, Botsford wrote to Miller offering to tell him 'what's underneath it all, off the record, it goes without saying'. What he called 'the French plot' concerned:

(a) true literary mediocrity in its most virulent form. The Fr. Centre is a collection of misérables. [Yves] Gandon crams bosoms on to the page like some shove cream puffs into their mouths. One of those Frenchmen who are sure that just because they write in French they are making a contribution to civilization. He is the President [of the French Centre]. The Secretary is a tub-of-lard called de Beer ... They have none of the good writers in France (if such there be) in their Centre, actively ... (b) ... de Beer is close to the extreme Left of the Royal Party ... our Fr. Friends think that PEN is a great instrument for crawling on all fours (with their own trips paid) to Moscow, Peking and beyond ... (c) Underlying the *politique* to which the Fr. Court aspires is a deep-rooted anti US (and anti USSR) prejudice – but more anti US than anti USSR (some pigs being more piggish than others) ... they cannot have the Hqs in London, nor Carver as Sec'y, nor myself as Ast. This is Anglo-Saxon hegemony, intolerable to the Fr., who can only understand Fr. Hegemony. Thus they have spent all the time since I came into this bloody business, in attacking me, poor David, our plans, our magazine, you, US Congress, and anything else to hand. (e) You fall across this because you present them with ... an American president, an American asst Sec'y – a takeover bid ... For all these purposes, Asturias is a candidate for the French. He is old; he lusts after the approval of France; and he's in heat about the Nobel Prize. He belongs in the Fr. Centre's pocket and is to be trusted, as some proverb says, like a Rumanian and/or Lithuanian (depends where you come from). He was deep in the Deep-Left ... but for his own purposes ... and what is worse, backed out of it when the going got rough in Guatemala. However, as a Guatemalan, he does have one thing: he is profoundly, rabidly, unreservedly anti-American, and hence an ideal candidate from the Fr. point of view. As he is a dummy, the centre of influence (according to the Fr. Plans) will then shift to Paris, and PEN, which never has been political, into politics, and of the most unpleasant sort ... That's the picture. There's absolutely no need for *you* to fight Asturias. We'll do that for you. He has practically no support, and he'll have even less once we get through with the French ... It may not be pleasant, but it has to be done, and if you don't back us up now, the whole edifice will go to pot.[31]

Quite what Miller was supposed to make of this is not clear. He had been invited to head an international organization in which writers would work together for the common good, only to find himself in the eye of a storm. Botsford's complaint about a leftist writer must have struck him as decidedly odd, though he was not in a position to appreciate the irony of his lamenting that the French might politicize an organization that he was himself, it seems, there to politicize, the only difference being the nature of the ideology in play. And Yves Gandon, far from being pro-Soviet, had written enthusiastically of

Arthur Koestler's *Darkness at Noon*. For his part, Miller knew nothing of Asturias, though Botsford's systematic trashing of a fellow writer must surely have disconcerted.

As it happened, Asturias turned out to be a great deal more gracious and less self-serving than Botsford had suggested. In June, he wrote to 'the great writer Arthur Miller' in order, he explained, to avoid any misunderstanding or the suspicion that either of them might 'have sought something for someone, who ever that may be'. It was a strange remark. He had been made aware, he told Miller, of 'some difficulties' that had arisen and was writing to assure his American colleague that he would not have allowed his name to go forward had he known that such a man as Miller was willing to accept nomination. He wished to 'show where responsibilities lie'. It was an accommodating letter, but also heavily coded. He was not withdrawing from the contest but, no doubt advised by the French Centre that had put him forward, was indicating his awareness of those who were working behind the scenes.[32]

Botsford commented: 'Coming after the Hungarian Revolution and taking place in a country which was explicitly against Soviet hegemony and Soviet culture, the election of a communist/Stalinist to the presidency would have been an affront to most PEN members. The farthest one could go [is] to say that a powerful candidate was needed and that Arthur very much fitted the bill and proved a distinguished president.' As it happened, steps were taken that ensured that PEN members would not have the opportunity to be affronted.

Frances Stonor Saunders has explained the next move. The American PEN Centre sent Robbie Macauley to London. He was editor of *Kenyon Review* (an excellent magazine whose distribution was aided by the Congress and which, like many other such magazines, received Farfield money), as well as a senior editor at Harcourt Bracc. His literary career, he later admitted, was a cover for his CIA activity. 'With Macauley, the CIA had a man with executive power in American PEN. This meant that Cord Meyer decided to send him to London as the IOD's case officer for PEN.' The IOD, the International Organizations Division, was a propaganda unit set up under National Security directive NSC-68, designed to unite intellectuals against Soviet cultural influence. Cord Meyer worked under Frank Wisner, director of the Office of Policy Coordination, the espionage and counter-espionage wing of the CIA, and became part of Operation Mockingbird, aimed at influencing the American media. He was involved in funding the CCF and the National Student Association. In 1964 his wife, who had been having an affair with President Kennedy, was found murdered in Georgetown. The motive behind the murder, like the murderer, remained unknown.

As Saunders observes, 'With Botsford and Macauley in London, and Carver a recipient of Congress funds (and, more directly, of Farfield funds), the CIA had achieved excellent penetration of PEN.'[33] Farfield, in order to cover its tracks, would later make grants to the Living Theatre, the ACLS and the MLA, as well as to Mary McCarthy and Lionel Trilling.

In 2002 Botsford, who on 3 March 1965 wrote to Miller regretting the 'emotional blackmail' he had used to persuade him to take the presidency, was not so much inclined to deny these suggestions as to see them in a different context. Meyer and Macauley were, admittedly, CIA (Macauley had been at the Iowa Writers' Workshop with Botsford), and PEN, through the Farfield and other sources, partly CIA-funded, but this 'overlooks the fact that most of us who participated didn't think of PEN, or for that matter the CCF, as any sort of "instrument". We thought, and I still do, that it did excellent and valuable work in combating the very kind of mentality that F[rances] S[tonor] S[aunders] displays in "instrumentalizing" an intellectual process by which most participants had come to see communist penetration of the intelligentsia for what it was.'

This, then, is what lay behind Botsford's ostensibly innocent telephone call to Arthur Miller in the Paris apartment. As with so many caught up in the grand conspiracy that had seen US government funds pour into the arts in an attempt to exploit the Non-Communist Left, he knew nothing of this. The Agency might operate behind the scenes, but for the most part it was careful not to seem too interventionist in the activities of the organizations it indirectly funded and quietly suborned.

For his own reasons, Miller wanted to open up contacts with the Soviet Union. So too did the CIA, and PEN seemed a natural route provided that it spoke with an American accent. If channels were opened up to the East, well and good. If they were not, at least what they wished to make a key organization would be seen as part of an American initiative, and where better to rehearse complaints against the repressive tactics of Soviet authorities towards their own citizens? Indeed, perhaps it was not irrelevant that the CIA chose a Jewish writer, author of a novel about anti-Semitism, to engage a Soviet Union whose own anti-Semitism, as Miller's article in the *New Leader* had indicated, was increasingly clear.

Within weeks of accepting nomination for the presidency Arthur Miller received a supportive cable addressed to him at Inge's apartment in the rue de la Chaise and sent by the Yugoslav organizer, the Slovene poet and former partisan Matej Bor (real name Vladimir Pavšič) who had himself protested against the imprisonment of Mihajlo Mihajlov. By then, Miller was feeling a real enthusiasm for PEN. He was persuaded to take on the presidency of an organization of which he knew very little and which was in a state of some disarray. He did so with a degree of suspicion and apprehension, but also with broad hopes for what it might signify, though on the aircraft to Bled for the Congress at which he would be nominated he found himself in the company of a man who represented a magazine that had hardly reflected his own views in the past, and who was one of the many delegates, paid for by the CCF, who had been on a list drawn up by Keith Botsford and John Hunt:

> The man who took the seat next to mine that June afternoon in 1965 looked familiar, although I knew we had never actually met. 'Norman Podhoretz,' he said, offering a handshake. I was surprised that the editor of *Commentary* magazine should dignify enemy territory by his presence in Yugoslavia, but in a few moments I was finding him warm and rather funny about literary people and the New York scene. Still, if he was going to Bled to see what this PEN thing was all about, I had to assume it was with some scepticism if not outright suspicion. As for myself, I hadn't the slightest idea what to expect of this, my first congress, whose president I incredibly was. I was glad that Podhoretz, a broadly educated essayist, thought there was some point in the organization, but at the same time his presence beside me clarified at least one of my reasons for having accepted the presidency. PEN seemed to promise an awakening of humanist solidarity at the time when the opposing creed of untrammelled individualism and private success was beginning its most recent sweep of the American landscape.[34]

It might be thought that the presence of Podhoretz (who would be mocked in Joseph Heller's 1979 novel *Good as Gold*) would have led to suspicion on Miller's part. After all, he was on the board of the CCF and had denounced those who opposed the Vietnam War, though the Committee for the Free World that he would subsequently lead and that would one day applaud American policy in El Salvador lay many years ahead, as did his advocacy of the bombing of Iran. Even then, however, before his attacks on homosexuals and his dismissal of critics of the mass killings at the Chatila and Sabra Palestinian refugee camps as anti-Semites, he was of the Right. The fact was, however, that the Right had reasons of its own for rapprochement.

Nor, in truth, was Miller yet the President of PEN. That would depend on the election to be held in Bled, where critics had dubbed that body a mysterious, semi-clandestine, Freemasons' organization. At the same time, in so far as the CCF and CIA were involved in the event, directly or indirectly funding both men, untrammelled individualism and private success almost certainly came higher up their list of priorities than humanist solidarity, even though for many of those involved that may, indeed, have been the subtext of the occasion. The CCF made it clear that if any delegate on the list could not attend, any substitute must seek the approval of the CCF, based in Paris.

This was the first time PEN had returned to Yugoslavia since 1933, when it had met in Dubrovnik. Then, in the year of the Nuremberg Laws, a number of writers including Sholem Asch, Ernst Toiler and H.G. Wells had attacked the new Germany. As a result the German delegation walked out and PEN excluded Nazi Germany from its ranks. Thirty-two years later they were meeting in a country which uniquely reflected the changes that had swept over Europe after 1945, a country with internal ethnic and ideological divides but which was perhaps a useful halfway house between West and East.

Miller went to Bled by way of Zagreb, where he gave an interview to a Belgrade newspaper in which he stressed the need for writers to resist political interference. It was a hopeful thought, given the forces active both within PEN and without. The FBI, meanwhile, transcribed a Serbian-language broadcast from Belgrade in which, on 3 July, Miller remarked on Yugoslav gallantry in the Second World War – something that had moved both himself and his first wife, Mary: 'I began to follow the events of Yugoslavia with special attention at the beginning of World War Two. I heard a lot about the misdeeds of the occupying forces in this country. When I heard for the first time about the Yugoslav resistance I was deeply moved.' From this he went on to praise Yugoslav political strategy: 'You Yugoslavs have the opportunity to work in a stimulating way ... I can say with certainty that your self-management constitutes a significant achievement in the development of social ideas. What is more interesting is that this idea has an expressly original Yugoslav imprint and leads to true socialist forms of life.' This was dangerous territory since, despite the heroic efforts of the partisans, internal divisions had at times been vicious. As to welcoming a true socialist form of life, this tribute must have stirred a few minds in Washington; the FBI report 100–333 798–76 is dated 16 July 1965.

Bled is a beautiful resort town on the edge of a lake in the Slovenian mountains. It was, Miller thought, a fairy-tale place, with an island in the lake on which a small castle had been built 'for some forgotten prince's children to play in', he recalled in a piece written in November 1993:

> Marxist intellectuals in Yugoslavia were remarkably open in their criticisms of the economy and politics of the country ... Yugoslavia was prodding the limits of socialism; and to come there from the dictatorships of Hungary, Czechoslovakia, East Germany, not to mention Russia, was to experience the shock of fresh air ... There was one taboo, unmentioned but obvious: the ethnic nationalism that Tito had ruthlessly suppressed.[35]

In 1965 such tensions were officially denied. Miller wrote about them in 1993 precisely because they had erupted into the present as the innovative future he had once hailed collapsed in a spasm of 'ethnic cleansing', the 1990s euphemism for atavistic slaughter. Even at the time, though, he had noticed a certain nervousness when the question of ethnicity was raised, and in retrospect recalled an evening spent at a local strip club in which his Serb, Croatian, Montenegrin and Slovenian colleagues all assumed that the girl entertaining them must come from a different ethnic group. It turned out she was from West Germany.

What followed, for Miller, was a crash course not only in world literature – he had never heard of many of the writers he was now expected to embrace in the name of literary solidarity – but in Central and East European cultural politics. Opening up the organization to the Soviet Union would require more than a few glasses of vodka and anodyne speeches about the international brotherhood of writers. Realpolitik was as real and as politic as ever.

The CCF provided much of the funding for the delegates. If Miller had doubts about its source, though, he did not voice them at the time – at least not to Botsford, who saw a different kind of politics at work, with the Russians favouring Miller as much as their American counterparts:

> I strongly suspect that Leonid Leonov [Soviet novelist and playwright] ... would (if unleashed from the KGB man in the delegation [Giorgio Breitburd, a minder often assigned to writers though described as a translator]) have voted for Arthur. They got on well. And if Arthur had suspicions, he could have acted on them; and he might well have asked how to account for Leonov's moving defense of his own relations to the USSR apparat and his hope to write as a free man. (He handed me the mss of his speech, which I had urged out of him, and it was stolen from my briefcase by Breitburd, a man whose gold teeth told you a lot about why he had come to work for the KGB.)[36]

The irony was, Miller suspected, that many delegates from Central and Eastern Europe responded to him because they assumed that his American nationality would act as a counterweight to pressures from the East. In fact, he had undertaken the job in part to find a basis on which the Soviet Union could become a full participant in PEN, and in no way regarded himself as representing those whose values and politics he had frequently found himself opposing.

The day before the Congress began, and despite Carver's efforts, elections took place for the presidency. The French persisted in nominating Asturias. Yves Gandon proposed a special committee to discuss the rival candidacies. A vote of the executive committee, however, rejected the proposal by 26 to 14, at which point Gandon finally conceded defeat and withdrew Asturias's name.

In his speech to the Congress Miller began by thanking Asturias. He had accepted the presidency, he explained, because it provided an opportunity for people from different countries, and with different ideologies, to meet. Conceding a prevailing intellectual provincialism, he welcomed the chance to encounter other writers face to face, insisting that whoever made him inspect his own position, challenge his own assumptions, opened a door to insight. PEN provided an opportunity, he went on, to examine what he called the human content of their convictions. He ended with a few words in French, hastily handwritten, declaring that everything he said in English he also said in his heart in French.

Beneath the bureaucratic manoeuvring by a Soviet delegation, headed by Ilya Ehrenburg, which wished to join at the price of PEN abandoning part of its constitution, he found himself beginning to believe in the organization, made aware in greater detail of the dilemma of writers around the world. In his closing speech he said: 'You never do any good ... unless you get into some trouble. I am not sure people who write will not be getting into trouble in America again, and we may need your assistance. We must look at every culture with the same eyes.'[37]

For all the discouraging political game-playing of the Bled Congress (Russian and Yugoslav writers might sing partisan songs together, the smell of Balkan cigarettes in the air and slivovitz to hand, but they were there to represent their opposing governments) Miller began to respond to the possibilities of an organization that could use its potential communal strength to support writers, to free them from imprisonment and persecution. He claimed it was as a result of the Congress that Mihajlo Mihajlov, then an assistant professor at Zadai University and author of *Moscow Summer* (1964), was granted his freedom, having been released from jail just before the meeting even though he had originally been arrested at the behest of President Tito.

Mihajlov had been arrested for suggesting that Lenin had organized political labour camps before Hitler. His release, after nine months in prison, was secured, Miller later suggested, by David Carver. The story, though, was more complex than that. The District Court of Zadar had condemned Mihajlov to prison but the Republican Court of Zagreb had cleared him. He was released just in time, as it turned out, for the Bled conference, but was re-arrested the following year, and after three and a half years in prison once again released, only to be arrested a third time. He did not receive an amnesty until 1977, and that following a campaign in the West and a hunger strike. Events, in other words, were not quite as simple as Miller imagined at the time and recounted in his autobiography in 1987. Nonetheless, after the Bled conference he began writing a series of appeals for the release of Russian dissidents. The man who a lifetime before had seen the Soviet Union as a beacon of freedom and justice now devoted increasing efforts to freeing its victims.

A feature of the Congress was the round tables, at which writers would discuss, supposedly openly, with one another rather than merely listen to lectures. They had been devised by Botsford, who, after the conference, published a story in the *Paris Review* (co-founded by the novelist Peter Matthiessen while he was a CIA agent, and used by him as cover). It was called 'A Member of the Delegation', and offered a fictional insight into the

Soviet delegation and the round tables. The discussion on the second day was entitled 'The Artist and His Responsibility': 'Twenty-two of us seated before pads and pencils, glasses at each place, painted earthenware carafes of white wine with beads of moisture up to their tall, slender necks and bottles of once-icy, soon warm brandy.' The alcohol was doubtless designed to loosen tongues. For the most part, to judge by this story, it achieved little in that direction.

Susan Sontag, who decades later would become President of American PEN, wrote an account of the Bled Congress for *Partisan Review*. She was not unimpressed. American PEN, she conceded, had been something of a joke, an excuse for vaguely literary cocktail parties. Not unreasonably, she asked where the organization had been when Miller was denied a passport, when Lillian Hellman had been threatened with jail and Dashiell Hammett actually imprisoned. Why had PEN not stood up for Anna Akhmatova? Sontag did, however, sense that the organization now had a chance of reinvigoration, with Miller's election after the absentee presidency of Alberto Moravia and the caretaker presidency of the Dutch critic Victor van Vriesland.

Her comment about Akhmatova was strange. She had been expelled from the Writers' Union in 1946, which effectively deprived her of a living, but following Stalin's death had been largely rehabilitated and had even visited Italy the year before the Bled Congress and received an honorary degree from Oxford. (She died a year after Bled.) Nonetheless, Sontag was accurate enough in suggesting that PEN had not been active with respect to writers suffering censorship and imprisonment in Eastern Europe.

Sontag presumed that Miller's two primary goals were to revive American PEN and to increase representation from Asia and Africa. She seems not to have suspected that his actual aim was to open it up to Eastern Europe, though since the editors of the CIA-funded *Preuves* and *Encounter* were present, along with the editor of *Commentary*, who sat on the board of the CCF, there were likely to be those who understood more clearly what the agenda was from their point of view. The CIA, however, in so far as it was indirectly behind Miller's candidacy, must have had pause for thought when he chose the occasion to praise Robert Lowell's refusal to attend the White House Arts Festival as a gesture against the Vietnam War.

Another account of the PEN Congress was offered in the *New York Times Book Review* by Robbie Macauley. This detailed the case of Mihajlo Mihajlov and recalled that he had written about Soviet 'concentration camps'. Macauley welcomed the 'astonishing' election of Miller to the presidency in the face of 'a left-wing Guatemalan exile', though quite why he should have found it astonishing is hard to say, since he would have been fully aware of the machinations that had brought it about.

The FBI now added to Miller's file, though by way of items that had appeared in newspapers, the Swiss German-language *Der Bund* and the *New York Herald Tribune*. The latter reported his condemnation of Spain and Portugal for their restrictions on the freedom of writers but noted his failure to mention the case of Joseph Brodsky – for fear of offending Soviet writers, it presumed, who were expected to join the organization. The report was inaccurate. The first plenary session, on 3 July, discussed 'The Writer in Prison'. Mihajlov's case was invoked but so was Brodsky's. Two weeks later more clippings were added, this time from the West German newspaper *Die Welt*, one quoting from an interview Miller had given to the Russian news agency Tass, in which he had urged closer contact between American and Russian authors. Tass, however, noted that Alexei Surkov, Secretary of the Soviet Writers' Union, had criticized the West for its interest in such figures as Pasternak and Brodsky, the latter 'too insignificant an author' to warrant international disagreements.

One thing that did emerge from Bled was a feeling that something was amiss with Keith Botsford. In July, David Carver wrote to Miller to say that he no longer thought he could work with him. He had, at the least, upset a considerable number of people and his 'temperamental displays' had made management of the Congress more difficult than it need have been. He noted that since Botsford's arrival nine months earlier he had had more difficulties with those in PEN Centres and his own office than ever before. In particular Botsford had seemingly been at odds with Matej Bor, head of the PEN Slovene Centre, who had facilitated the Congress. Botsford, Carver had decided, was 'too much of a liability', and wrong for PEN. Neither he nor Miller could put their finger on what his agenda was or the reason for his behaviour, but Carver had decided to tell him that he should go. In reply to Carver's letter, Miller wrote that he did not know what to say about Botsford and was confused as to his motives.

In August, Botsford himself wrote to Miller admitting that he had left many of his friends in the lurch and that he was perhaps not made out for this particular work. He regretted what he characterized as a 'stupid business', claiming that he had previously tried to resign. But Miller had more urgent matters to address than that of Keith Botsford. Vietnam now, and for years to come, became the focus of his attention.

3

VIETNAM

I've given up the idea objectively that anything I write was going to get anyone elected. But I do think that in a very small way, probably historically of no importance, what one writes can change people in the sense that it gives them a new idea of themselves ... You will shift the consciousness of a certain number of people.   *Arthur Miller*

For much of 1964 the war in Vietnam had taken second place to that other piece of unfinished business from the Kennedy years, civil rights. But then, on 2 and 3 August things took a new turn, when North Vietnamese PT boats in the Tonkin Gulf were reported to have attacked the American destroyers *Turner Joy* and *Maddox*. In fact, on 2 August the *Maddox* had fired warning shots, receiving in return a single machine-gun bullet. On the 4th the *Maddox* opened fire, responding to what seemed to be radar traces. The captain quickly sent a cable withdrawing the claim, but US Defense Secretary Robert McNamara later denied having read it until he returned from briefing President Johnson, who ordered retaliatory air strikes, going on television to announce his decision. Three days later, Congress passed a joint resolution authorizing the President to 'take all necessary measures to repel any armed attack against forces of the United States and to prevent further aggression'. Senator William Fulbright was not the only one to feel bitter at his own naivety in voting for the resolution.

Once Barry Goldwater had been defeated in the 1964 elections, the pace of the war hotted up. On 27 January 1965 National Security Advisor McGeorge Bundy and Robert McNamara sent a memo to President Johnson saying that the US should either escalate the war or withdraw. At the turn of the year two South Vietnamese battalions had been virtually wiped out, while on 6 February the Vietcong attacked a US base at Pleiku. Eight Americans were killed. The next day Johnson ordered a limited bombing of North Vietnam. The first combat troops were sent on the 9th. As a result of the bombing, the Soviet Union agreed to supply ground-to-air missiles to the North Vietnamese. On 18 February there was a coup in South Vietnam. In a matter of a few days Lyndon Johnson had committed America to a war that would take nearly a decade to conclude. A programme of carpet-bombing by B52s, under the codename Rolling Thunder, began on 2 March. The second strike followed on the 13th. It was this escalation that triggered revolts on America's campuses. At the time, however, opinion polls showed 85 per cent support for the President's actions. It was a figure that would consistently decline thereafter.

On his return from the Bled Congress, Miller drafted a letter to President Johnson. He explained that as the new President of International PEN he had had discussions with a large number of writers and scholars from a range of countries, and that he had found almost total agreement that the Vietnam War could only strengthen what he called 'Stalinist forces' throughout the East. It would, he insisted, end whatever rapprochement there was with China (though in fact China had its own interest in supporting the war). Even those from communist countries, he said, saw the war as destabilizing, while it seemed evident to him that the Vietnamese governments represented anything but progressive forces. There is no evidence that he sent the letter and no record of a reply, but it does underline the extent to which he was already committing himself to the anti-war cause.

The teach-ins in America's universities, which became a focus for opposition to the Vietnam War, began at Miller's alma mater, the University of Michigan, on 24 March 1965. Originally planned as a one-day strike, a tactic that brought its organizers into conflict with the Governor's office and the state legislature, this transmuted into a teach-in supported by over two hundred faculty members. Beginning at eight at night, it continued until eight the following morning, despite a series of bomb scares. The three speakers that first night had all spent time in Vietnam. In his autobiography, Miller recalls being present with Tom Hayden, a former Michigan student and once editor of the *Michigan Daily*, who had worked for the civil rights movement in the South and written most of the SDS (Students for a Democratic Society) Port Huron statement, the activists' manifesto. In 1965 Hayden had also visited Hanoi in the company of the peace activist Staughton Lynd and the Marxist historian Herbert Aptheker. In fact, though, Miller seems not to have been present at that teach-in. He was thinking of an occasion later that year.

The teach-ins spread rapidly around the country, from Columbia on one coast to Berkeley on the other. In April, fifteen thousand students picketed the White House. On 15 May, a teach-in in Washington was even attended by members of Congress. For all Miller's suspicion that this new generation was fated to experience the same swing from idealism to disillusionment, Vietnam was an issue that engaged him for the second half of the 1960s.

America was by now bombing both North and South Vietnam, the latter assault continuing daily (on one day there were 532 missions). Miller was no longer content with making speeches. He wrote a satirical piece about those South Vietnamese forced out of their villages for denying shelter to the Vietcong, images of which he had seen in a CBS news report. Why, he wondered, did the peasants not realize that the burning of their homes was for their own benefit? Why did they not embrace their fate? Victory, it seemed, would only be declared once there were no longer any Vietnamese in the countryside to liberate.

Behind the satire was a genuine anger mixed with a sense of unease, deepening to guilt. His visit to Frankfurt to attend the Auschwitz trials and his reading of Hannah Arendt's study of Eichmann had raised the question of a people's acquiescence in, and hence responsibility for, the crimes committed in their name. He scrawled a poem in his notebook, a poem never published but which he would recite at a Poets for Peace event in New York's Town Hall in November 1967. It was a poem, he explained, to save his soul, as he outlined the lies Americans told themselves, the indifference that had facilitated violence, the shame at too ready an acquiescence. It was a poem in which he made explicit the connection with what he called the German crime.

Whatever options Miller might have had, silence was clearly no longer one of them. While *Commentary*, *New Leader* and *Reporter* magazines were preoccupied with the emergence of a new anarchic Left in the form of the Berkeley Free Speech Movement, he was acknowledging the primacy of Vietnam. The fact that 'the German crime' suddenly became 'understandable' underscored the connection between *Incident at Vichy* and Vietnam.

In September 1965 he went to Ann Arbor for an international conference on 'Alternative Perspectives on Vietnam', convened by the Inter-University Committee for Debate on Foreign Policy (an organization of the University of Michigan Office of Religious Affairs and the Faculty and Student Committee to Stop the War in Vietnam). This was the occasion he recalled in *Timebends*. The best record of the event, Miller's transcript aside, lies in the FBI's files, documents clearly having emanated from more than one informant.

Among those present were Linus Pauling, a Nobel Laureate in chemistry, the sociologist David Riesman, the poets Robert Lowell, W.D. Snodgrass, Denise Levertov, Louis Simpson and Louis Untermeyer, along with a rabbi and suffragan bishop from Chicago as well as representatives from the United Automobile Workers (UAW) and the Students for a Democratic Society. From Europe came Fenner Brockway, the British socialist politician, and Jean Lacouture, the French biographer and journalist who worked for *Le Monde*. A declaration of support was received from Martin Luther King.

The event followed a demonstration on campus by the Student Non-Violent Coordinating Committee (SNCC) against the presence of a Marine and Navy recruiting booth. There was concern that Michigan could go the way of Berkeley where there had been mass arrests. The conference, it was hoped, would be a more sedate affair. Teaching was suspended for three days in favour of what amounted to a continuous discussion, beginning at ten in the morning and going on into the night. As he witnessed a younger generation convinced that it could change history, stop a war, it all seemed reminiscent, to Miller, of the fervent debates about Spain in 1936 in which he had himself taken part on that same campus. Sleeping in the Michigan Union, it was impossible not to recall that younger self, not to remember both how right he and others had been about Spain and how wrong about the Soviet Union. Walking across the campus he met a young soldier who told him that he believed the war was winnable, but only if America committed a million men. In fact, by the end of 1965 the number would be 200,000 and by the end of the war more than half a million men would be serving.

Miller warned the students that there were doubtless FBI agents in their meeting. He was not wrong. He spoke to a reported four thousand people in the Hill Auditorium on the evening of 17 September. He was on a panel with Fenner Brockway and representatives from the UAW and the SDS. His speech was duly reported in his old paper, the *Michigan Daily*, in the *Ann Arbor News* and in his FBI file. It was as though he were back in the 1930s calling for brotherhood. The auditorium, he said, 'is full of ghosts to me. I attended many meetings here when I was a student.' He recalled Chinese students walking out when a Japanese had come to lecture and he remembered meetings at which he and others had tried to raise money for the Spanish Loyalists. Now he declared:

> I think we are in a wrong war, not because I read political articles, but because I listen carefully to what my leaders tell me, and it just doesn't ring true. The President says he is for negotiation. I believe he is for negotiation. But the opposite side have set forth four precise points on which they say they are willing to negotiate. This occurred, I believe, in August. I don't know how many civilians have been torn apart by American made shells and bombs or burned by napalm. Presumably, if we can believe the Air Force, there have been many. What is our answer to these four points? I haven't heard an answer.
>
> I am not ready to convict the man of absolute duplicity – I prefer to say he is at the mercy of forces he cannot control ... It has been reported ... or rather taken for granted (and for good reason) that we are inevitably doomed in this war, that we don't possess those numbers in the field at the moment ... and for this reason we ought to not continue the war. What I am worried

about is that we may win and that we may win a graveyard ...

I said there were ghosts in this auditorium. Well, there are also ghosts who never came into this auditorium when they should have, for example, during the McCarthy time, when the intellectual community of this country laid over on its back like a sick bug. This time will be a dress rehearsal for the future if this war goes on for two, three, four, five or ten years. The intellectual freedom which we have today, however much it has been struggled for, will be eroded and forbidden on patriotic grounds ... are we to become the new Rome of this age?

People forget that we didn't lose China – it didn't belong to us ... Are the Vietnam people expendable? Or are we to feel ultimately responsible for the destruction of their country? I think we do feel responsible for it or we wouldn't be here ...

I hope, in coming here, that I give you no false idea that anyone else but you can change the world. Nobody really listens to me. But I am responsible for myself and you are responsible for yourselves; and no President can ever reduce that responsibility by one ounce. [FBI file 62–11–39–183]

Fourteen copies of the documents that FBI agents had secured, along with a transcript of Miller's speech, were forwarded to Washington, along with eleven copies (one for the Secret Service) of a declaration issued by the meeting calling for what was described as a 'Mobilization in Washington', to take place on 27 November. It was sponsored by Miller, along with the childcare writer Dr Benjamin Spock and Martin Luther King. Others listed included Miller's Roxbury neighbour Alexander Calder, Jules Feiffer, the psychoanalyst and social theorist Erich Fromm and the actor-playwright Ossie Davis and his wife, the actress Ruby Dee. It read:

We see no gain coming from the war in Vietnam. We see only the victimization of the Vietnamese people, the erosion of a better society at home, and the clear possibility of world conflict. Caught between terror, torture, and the senseless use of force, the Vietnamese people have seen their land turned into a bloody testing ground by the Vietcong, the Saigon government, by the North Vietnamese and the United States.

Caught in a competition for the loyalties of the poorest nations, the Soviet Union and China will seek to prove their militancy by aiding North Vietnam, thus increasing the chance of a direct clash with the United States.

The statement called for a ceasefire, an end to the bombing of North Vietnam and American acceptance of the need for negotiations.[1] The declaration, though, reveals something of the naivety of a movement that had itself not yet taken on board the objectives of the North Vietnamese. It announced that its signatories were for 'U.S. support for U.N. or other international machinery and guarantees to supervise the ceasefire, provide for peaceful establishment of a new government in South Vietnam, protect the rights of minority groups and protect the neutrality of North and South Vietnam'.[2] The demonstration was to take place in front of the White House. In fact a demonstration of a hundred thousand was staged a month earlier than this – the march on the Pentagon in which the activist Abbie Hoffman announced that he would levitate the building. In the event, it remained resolutely in place.

Miller was, then, there at the beginning of the anti-war movement, and that fact is significant. There was no question this time that the issue was 'for another generation'. Indeed, he was at a student teach-in at the very moment that *Partisan Review* was announcing:

> We do not think that the present or past policies of the United States in Vietnam are good ones, and we lament the increasing and often self-defeating military involvements which these policies require. We have not heard of any alternative policy, however, which would actually lead to a negotiated peace in Vietnam. This is not to say that the critics of American actions in Vietnam are therefore required to propose a specific policy. But it is not unfair to ask that their criticism be based on more than a political assumption that power politics, the Cold War, and Communists are merely American inventions. Most of the criticism of Administration policy at teach-ins and in the various petitions we have been asked to sign, has simply taken for granted that everything would be fine if only the Yanks would go home.[3]

The signatories included Eleanor Clarke (the Trotskyist who had written a waspish rejection of *Death of a Salesman* sixteen years earlier), Alfred Kazin, Irving Howe, Bernard Malamud, the historian Martin Duberman, Norman Podhoretz and the critic Richard Poirier. It was not well received. Indeed, in the fall issue of the magazine even one of the signatories expressed some doubts. Thus, Irving Howe observed that:

> Though I signed the statement ... I felt uneasy about it once the issue came out. [However] apart from a few minor exaggerations (e.g. I doubt that '*most* of the criticism of Administration policy at the teach-ins ... has simply taken for granted that everything would be fine if only the Yanks would go home'), the thrust of the statement against the kind of campus pietism which revels in the worst about U.S. policy while turning mush-headed about the Vietcong seems to me justified.[4]

He could not, though, he confessed, 'discount the possibility of drifting into a war that would be politically and militarily frustrating, as well as humanly appalling'. In these circumstances, he added, 'I feel the pontifical foolishness that has fringed the otherwise excellent teach-ins is not nearly so important as the need to struggle for changes in U.S. policy.'[5]

Other respondents were altogether less forgiving, Norman Mailer, in particular, offering a heavily ironic dissection of the original statement and a statement of his own: 'The editors call for a counter policy. I offer it. It is to get out of Asia.'[6] Herbert Marcuse, Susan Sontag, David Riesman and Dwight Macdonald all piled in.

While *Partisan Review* was trying to sort out where it stood and the New York Intellectuals were engaging in polemics, and while *Commentary, New Leader* and *Reporter* magazines were preoccupied with the emergence of the Free Speech Movement in Berkeley, Miller had stood up in front of a student audience in Hill Auditorium to challenge American foreign policy, along with the head of the United Automobile Workers, the union whose strike he had reported on in 1937, and which had gone on to be stalwarts of the anticommunist Americans for Democratic Action (ADA).

Miller had only just returned from Michigan when, on 25 September 1965, he received a cable from the White House:

THE PRESIDENT HAS ASKED ME TO EXTEND TO YOU AN INVITATION TO ATTEND THE SIGNING OF THE ARTS AND HUMANITIES BILL ON WEDNESDAY, SEPTEMBER 29, AT 9:45 A.M. YOU SHOULD PRESENT YOURSELF AT THE NORTHWEST GATE NO LATER THAN 9.30 A.M. PLEASE ADVISE ME BY RETURN TELEGRAM IF YOUR SCHEDULE WILL PERMIT YOU TO ATTEND.

It was signed by Lawrence O'Brien, Special Assistant to the President. Miller immediately sent a reply, turning a simple invitation into the occasion for a public protest when he published it in the *New York Herald Tribune:*

The President's signing of the Arts and Humanities Bill surely begins a new and fruitful relationship between American artists and their government. But the occasion is so darkened for me by the Viet Nam tragedy that I could not join it with clear conscience. Specifically it is five and a half months since Hanoi radio broadcast four conditions on which they would be willing to negotiate a ceasefire. No concrete response has yet come from the President. Meanwhile American casualties are mounting daily. Our air force is carrying out gigantic bombardments through thick cloud cover which can only mean immense civilian suffering in Viet Nam and death for innocent women and children. Please be assured I am not alone in my inability to understand our war aims. Our actions appear to indicate we want a total victory and unconditional surrender. In that case we will win a graveyard. A lasting work of art is the work of love and sincerity. I beseech the President to most

fittingly mark the signing of the Arts and Humanities Bill by responding to
the Hanoi four points offer with a definite American proposal for ceasefire
and standfast negotiations. When the guns boom the arts die and this law of
life is far stronger than any law man may devise.[7]

The four points required that the rights of the Vietnamese be recognized
on the basis of the 1954 Geneva Agreement on Indochina; that the division
of Vietnam continue pending peaceful reunification, with no foreign troops
in either zone; that the internal affairs of South Vietnam be determined by
the South Vietnamese in accordance with the National Liberation Front
programme; and that reunification be accomplished without foreign interference. Miller acknowledged potential flaws in these proposals but simply
wished, he explained, to know the US response.

When his answer to the White House invitation was published it prompted
a series of attacks. WLBW-TV in Florida denounced his 'fuzzy thinking',
dismissing him, ironically, as a 'great international affairs expert and watchdog
of American morals' who was calling for capitulation; he had no interest in
'American boys who have made [the] supreme sacrifice'. Marguerite Higgins,
in an article headed 'Miller's Level of Ignorance' which appeared in *Newsday*,
and with a similar penchant for irony, suggested: 'It would be asking too
much of even so theatrically versatile a man as playwright Arthur Miller to
be an authority on the stuff of human drama and the war in Vietnam too ...
The escape from make-believe,' she argued, 'seems more than the eminent
dramatist can manage.' Whereas most people would have said that the bloodi-
est revolt of 1956 had been the Hungarian uprising, she insisted that in fact it
had been the uprising in North Vietnam of peasants protesting against
collectivization. The outcome had been 75,000 peasants wrongly jailed, while
even the Communist Party admitted to at least 15,000 people wrongfully
executed. In particular, though, she was incensed that Miller should have
invoked the arts as part of his argument over Vietnam. His assertion that
'when the guns boom the arts die' struck her as 'palpable nonsense'. By way
of evidence she invoked *All Quiet on the Western Front*, Lillian Hellman's
Watch on the Rhine and *Bridge on the River Kwai*, along with George M.
Cohan's First World War song 'Over There' and Tchaikovsky's 1812 Overture.
Besides, like many anti-Vietnam 'intellectuals' (the quotation marks were
hers), Miller had, she claimed, evinced no concern for the arts when the Nazi
guns were sounding. She then cited the bloody history of the Vietnamese
communists.[8]

Marguerite Higgins, who was married to a lieutenant general in the Marine
Corps, was a distinguished war correspondent and Pulitzer Prize winner. Nor
was she ignorant of Vietnam – indeed, she nearly died there on 25 May 1954
when Robert Capa, standing beside her, trod on a landmine and was killed.

In 1965 Higgins published a book on Vietnam, *Our American Nightmare*, criticizing the American overthrow of Ngo Dinh Diem, President of South Vietnam. In the year she wrote this article she contracted a tropical disease in Vietnam from which she would die on 3 January 1966: as a tribute to her war reporting, she was buried in Arlington Cemetery. Robert Capa was not, his mother preferring the quiet serenity of a Quaker cemetery.

It is not clear how much of this Miller knew. For him, Vietnam was an issue, a moral battleground. For Higgins, it was a place she knew well, visiting it on many occasions. On 16 November he sent a reply to the *Newsday* article. Interestingly, he began by addressing not her substantive points about Vietnam but her list of artistic works prompted by war. *All Quiet on the Western Front*, he conceded, was born out of war but was a violent protest against it. *Watch on the Rhine* had been an attack on fascism, and *Bridge on the River Kwai* had underscored the insanity of war. Since Tchaikovsky had been born twenty-eight years after the event his overture commemorated, it could hardly, Miller remarked, be said to have been an immediate product of the battlefield. In fact, with the exception of 'Over There' none of the works cited had been written during wartime. More serious, though, he suggested, was her assault on intellectuals. The placing of the word in quotation marks was an indication of her position while her comparison of the two wars seemed to him inappropriate; he recalled in particular the fact that the Axis had declared war on America. He had, he reminded the magazine, simply been imploring the President to engage in serious negotiations with Hanoi. Marguerite Higgins seemed to him to be more concerned to score points against 'intellectuals' than to acknowledge the need for peace.

Others, however, were also stung by his reply to Lyndon Johnson's cable. Both the theatrical producer David Merrick and the author Paddy Chayefsky rejected his stance. Merrick was quoted in *Time* magazine as saying: 'We finally get a subsidy in the theater, and we have an Administration that is in favor of the arts, and then Mr Miller has to make his statement. All the children who work in the theater and films should stay out of politics. They are always completely naïve about it.'[9] *Show Business* magazine attacked Miller for choosing to link his attack on American foreign policy to a celebration of the signing of an important arts initiative, noting that its readership represented 82,000 people in the theatre, 90 per cent of whom were unemployed. Miller replied that if employment in show business depended on bombing civilians in Vietnam, then the theatre deserved to die. In St Louis the *Globe-Democrat* referred to him as a 'pinko playwright'.

In October, the Senate Internal Security Subcommittee released a study dealing with communist exploitation and infiltration of peace movements, communist policy in Vietnam, the anti-Vietnam agitation, the origins of the teach-in movement, the national teach-in in Washington of 15 May together

with teach-ins planned for later in the year. It cited Miller's refusal to attend
the signing of the new Arts and Humanities bill, and the subsequent attack
on him by David Merrick. The document was hardly balanced. It quoted
from a *New York Herald Tribune* essay:

> When playwright Arthur Miller refused to attend the signing of the new Arts
> and Humanities Act in protest against the Government policy in Vietnam, he
> stated that 'When the guns go boom-boom, the arts die.' But Mr Miller did
> not get away that easily. David Merrick, one of Broadway's busiest producers,
> pointed out that: ' . . . This is not what he said when he was all for the guns
> going boom-boom a few years ago against Nazi aggression. I find it puzzling
> he doesn't want the guns to go boom-boom to stop the Red Chinese
> aggression.'[10]

'The fact is clear,' the study concluded, 'that many of the most vociferous of
the Government's critics do not oppose the use of force. They simply oppose
the use of force against Communists.'[11]

Alexander H. Cohen, in supporting Miller, deplored those who attacked
the political motives and loyalties of a fellow countryman for believing that
little could be accomplished in the second half of the twentieth century with
guns. The television writer Howard Fast, on 29 September, wrote praising
his stance and suggested he had signed his name 'for mankind'.

Miller prepared, but did not dispatch, a lengthy article responding to those
who criticized him. He noted that the letters he had received were running
forty to eight in favour of his stance. Conceding that this in itself meant little,
he noted that he had been accused as much of bad taste as anything but
that the issue was too serious for his response to be so casually dismissed.
Nevertheless, he would not, he wrote, have taken the action he did had not
the bombing of Vietnam, through cloud cover – and hence, in his view,
indiscriminately – begun. Merrick, he pointed out, had suggested that artists
had no business meddling in public affairs, then had himself called a press
conference before flying off to Vietnam, where one of his shows was being
presented for the military. The duty to protest, Miller observed, might be no
greater for artists than for anyone else, but by the same token it was no less.
The *Show Business* attack seemed to amount to little more than the suggestion
that people should keep their mouths shut if they wished to be paid.

He pointed out that he had always advocated federal aid to the arts, even
when people called him a Red for doing so. He had felt unable to go to
Washington, he explained, because certain images had flooded his mind. One
was Guernica, not least because a week earlier he had seen the French
documentary film *To Die in Madrid*. It was not, however, just the fact of
Guernica that returned to him – though it was a traumatic memory from his
youth – but Picasso's painting, a reminder of the nexus between politics and

art. He recalled, too, the cellist Pablo Casals who had exiled himself from Spain. In making a connection between the arts and war he was not, he stated, breaking new ground. Beyond all this, though, was his fear that he would meet a Vietnamese man injured by American bombing on the very day that he himself was in Washington being photographed with the President.

Included in the putative article is the text of a letter from a serving soldier in Vietnam, writing to his sister. The letter recounts the story of a patrol that pursued five Vietcong in and through a village. On suspicion that the villagers must be Vietcong sympathizers, a paratrooper had thrown a grenade into a bomb shelter. The author of the letter had rescued a young girl, who died in his arms. All the dead and wounded were reported as suspected Vietcong: 'I doubt if you will read this in the news, but don't let this letter get away from you. They might court-martial for the truth.'

Miller refused to attend the signing of the bill, he explained, because if he did, it would be evidence of a failure of will on his part. America, it seemed to him, had run out of options. His response to President Johnson had been no more than a request that the government should set out its terms for peace. The article breaks off in mid-sentence. In another draft he wondered why he was judged of sufficient importance to be invited to the signing, given that his views were seen as beside the point. The irony was that Miller believed it to be entirely possible for America to win the war, in military terms. He simply thought it immoral and unwinnable in political terms. He wrote a long letter to Carroll Kilpatrick of the *Washington Post*, in response to a cable from him, in which he laid out the history of Vietnam since the early 1950s, explaining that the problem was that the Americans seemed incapable of believing that a Marxist state could also be nationalistic. The bombing struck him as counterproductive and incompatible with negotiations. The letter was not written for publication.

In November, the *Washington Post* took exception not merely to his declining the presidential invitation but to his sponsorship, along with Benjamin Spock and others, of the peace march on Washington scheduled for the 27th. The author of the piece, John Chamberlain, attacked him, in doing so reminding his readers that Miller was President of PEN. Reverting to the question of whether his views on communism differed from his views on fascism, Chamberlain noted that while 'Miller has, on occasion, set himself up as his brother's keeper . . . he is manifestly selective about his brothers. If they are victims of Fascism, he wants the guns to go boom-boom and celebrates it in his art. If they are victims of Communism, he averts his eyes.'[12] What, he demanded to know, was Miller doing, as President of PEN, about the plight of his fellow artists in Moscow and Peking? This, of course, had been the line developed in 1956 when Miller had appeared before HUAC. Then he had been vulnerable. He was so no longer, since he was already engaged in addressing the plight of such writers. Chamberlain identified Andrei Sinyavsky in particular as a victim of persecution.

Three days later Lewis Galantière, President of US PEN, sent a reply. Galantière had worked behind the scenes to head off the French nomination of Miguel Asturias as President of PEN and secure it instead for an American. He was, as Frances Stonor Saunders has remarked, something of a Cold War warrior. Certainly, he began his letter to the *Washington Post* by dissociating himself from Miller's views. How anybody could fail to see the hand of Communist China in the Vietnam War, he said, 'passes my understanding'. What he was primarily concerned to do was defend PEN. He pointed out that the Bled Congress had rejected a draft resolution calling for a cessation of hostilities as an intrusion of politics into the affairs of a literary organization. He outlined PEN's record of working on behalf of persecuted writers in Eastern and Central Europe. With respect to Sinyavsky, he explained that the case was complicated by the fact that he was suspected of being the Abram Tertz who had smuggled works to the West (he was, indeed, Tertz, named after a Jewish outlaw from Odessa, though it was later that year before the KGB established the connection) and was sensitive to the possibility of being lured into being identified as such. Nonetheless, PEN was working on his behalf. He rejected Chamberlain's comments about Miller and the organization.

In fact, on 28 October, after their meeting at a conference in Avignon, David Carver had written to Miller precisely about the Sinyavsky case: 'Whether he is Abram Tertz or not, he is certainly a very good writer ... But whatever is the real situation, the arrest of Sinyavsky is a curious commentary on the Soviets' declared wish to join PEN. This may be a move by the political police and the Writers' Union may have made ineffectual protests. Would you consider writing to the First Secretary of the Writers' Union – Konstantin Fedin – expressing your concern and asking for information?'[13]

On 6 November Miller duly wrote to Fedin, noting the arrests of Sinyavsky, Valery Tarsis and Yuli Daniel at the very moment attempts were being made to break down the barriers between writers from West and East. As President of PEN, he explained, he was requesting that the arrests should be rescinded if relations were not to be endangered. He asked for information, noting that he would be in rehearsals for one of his plays that December. Sinyavsky and Daniel had been arrested – according to Yevgeny Yevtushenko, at the instigation of the CIA, though this is disputed – and tried. In February 1966, Sinyavsky was sentenced to seven years (later reduced to six) and Daniel to five. Miller's protest evidently carried no weight.

In April 1966, Carver would go to Moscow for talks with representatives from the Writers' Union. They defended the treatment of the two dissident writers, one describing them as riff-raff who should not jeopardize East–

West relations, another identifying them as liars who had received lighter sentences than many believed justified. Nonetheless, they looked forward to the possibility of attending the next PEN Congress in New York.

For Miller, Vietnam represented a form of neocolonialism. He detected a desire for world dominance on the part of a democracy for which such an ambition should be unacceptable. Power, it seemed to him, had become not merely a mechanism but an objective. The peace movement was the source of hope, but as yet it lacked popular support. When the commander of an American Legion post marched with demonstrators in the small Connecticut town of Simsbury, fifteen miles west of Hartford, on 10 November, he was denounced by a large crowd. Miller, too, ran into trouble in his home state when the teachers in a high school in Torrington, a town neighbouring Roxbury, invited him to speak to the students. The local American Legion threatened recriminations. Nonetheless, he spoke about the war, as several people took notes – doubtless, he assumed, to forward them to the authorities 'because they were very right wing there. It was a very Catholic area. This was before there was any disillusionment with the war, which was supposed to be over in a few months, and then everybody would be coming home. This was supposed to be good against evil. There was total ignorance. They didn't know where Vietnam was.'[14]

Looking back nearly two decades later, he remembered a young local man called Howie whom he had known from the age of six and who lived a bare half-mile from Miller's Roxbury home. One day Miller met him in New York and offered him a lift home. On the way they talked about the war, until, alarmingly, Howie suddenly asked why anyone should want to live any more. Miller had helped to secure him a place at the Neighborhood Playhouse, where he had studied for two years and excelled. Six months later, Howie sat down cross-legged on the grass behind his house, poured gasoline over his head and lit a match. Another boy had blown his face off with a shotgun that same year. In both cases, the cause was Vietnam. Yet another, Dan Kerner, son of the Roxbury hardware store owner, faced with being sent to the war, turned to drugs. One midnight he knocked on the sliding glass door of Miller's sitting room, offering to write a poem on any subject. He was drugged. Less than nine months later, he was dead from an overdose. These incidents made such an impact on Miller that he recounted them in a 1983 speech at the University of Southern California.

Asked in 2001 how he felt about appearing on public platforms, as he now increasingly did, he replied:

I hate it. I have always hated it. The alternative, though, was to sit there silently when you knew that there were certain things that could be said. It seemed to me an imperative. I suppose I have always had it in the back of my mind that some kind of real, blanket fascistic repression was always possible, in any society, and that if that ever happened and I thought back to what I could have said and didn't say, it would be hard to live with myself. I often wished that I could have put a different name on my plays so that I could have lived anonymously and answered the mail of the guy who wrote the plays. I would have lived a much more placid and much more productive life. Because you take a lot of crap from people if you get out there in front and it takes a lot of psychic time. You don't just stand up and make a speech. It reverberates for days afterwards. On the other hand it is a kind of engagement that is productive in its own way. A writer here is probably just an entertainer. People don't think of him as being some kind of a moral conscience. He is just an actor who writes. There is an Anglo-Saxon aversion to connecting art with anything else but art.[15]

With the 1966 PEN Congress in view that April, David Carver, writing from London, reported on an executive meeting in which a Bulgarian delegate, 'that old trout Dora Gabe, intervened with a long read statement on the Sinyavsky/Daniel case'. Carver explained that the 'prospects of a Soviet Centre are, of course, nil unless S[inyavsky] and D[aniel] are released, but we are inviting Soviet observers to New York officially'.[16] In the same letter he announced that he had secured funding to bring a number of European writers to New York. The source of that funding was ambiguous. In June 1965 the CCF had given Carver £1,000 to begin planning the 1966 meeting. As Frances Stonor Saunders has pointed out, this was followed by a lunch with John Hunt, while the Ford Foundation, a conduit for the CIA, made a grant of $75,000, to which the Rockefeller Foundation added a further $25,000. Other money came from the CIA-funded Free Europe Committee.

In preparation for the Congress, over which he would preside, Miller sent a circular to a number of American writers inviting them, stressing in particular the need to involve the Soviet Union, writers from smaller countries and those of different races. But America remained central, if only because of the dominance of the United States. It was time, he told them, 'that the writers of two of the most powerful countries in the world learned how to talk to one another', time, too, to abandon parochialism: 'Few of us can even name accomplished artists in small countries, to say nothing of those in Russia. Beyond the borders of France lies terra incognita.' It was, in truth, a confession of his own ignorance. He drew attention to the fact that PEN was substantially a white organization, and that problems of translation established barriers that had to come down. America, he declared, had a central role to play.

Willy-nilly, for much of the world the American style sets the style of the age. We have arrived first at the moment toward which every other industrial society is heading. Whether it be the vulgarity we lament or celebrate, the destruction of old forms, the mindless conservatism or the vague radical protest, more often than not the form of these reactions is initially American. Our kind of energy and address, our kind of failure and success, the very idea of contemporaneity is linked to the idea of America. And this is a kind of power.[17]

So it is, and this was what interested the CIA and the CCF. The same circular suggested the need for American and Russian writers to meet outside the bounds of ideology. The New York PEN Congress would be highly successful in bringing Latin American writers to the United States, but it was the opening of doors to Russia that remained his principal objective.

Miller was President of PEN for four years. The second Congress over which he presided took place in New York, in June 1966. It advertised itself as the broadest forum of American and foreign writers ever assembled, with some five hundred delegates. Its various round-table panels were to discuss 'The Writer as Public Figure', 'Literature and the Social Sciences', 'The Writer in the Electronic Age'. Miller published an article in the 4 June issue of the *Saturday Review* outlining his ideas for the role of PEN, in which he identified what seemed to him the demoralization of the writer in the face of what he called 'scientism'. The writer's function, he believed, was to 'create a synthesis of meanings for life' at a time when that life was being reduced to experiment and statistics, when theory appeared to prevail over experience and imagination, an imagination that was itself 'a political and social force'.[18] This last phrase was, of course, offered as underlining the writer's role as resister. And he was not the only person aware that the writer was potentially a political force.

Once again, unknown to Miller, the CIA through its various other front organizations and foundations put up much of the money for the PEN conference (the Farfield Foundation had made its first grant to the American Center in 1963). In 1967, on the revelation of the Foundation's status as a CIA front, the Board of American PEN would sever all relationship with it. Meanwhile John Hunt (who claimed descent from Davy Crockett) sought to place Marion Bieber, who had been Deputy Executive Secretary of the CCF and in charge of organizing many of the Congress's activities, either in Carver's office or in the New York office of the Congress itself.[19] He also, as Frances Stoner Saunders has pointed out, placed the CIA agent Robbie Macauley at the disposal of American PEN. This was the first time the American Center had hosted an International PEN Congress and the CIA, through its various operatives, was determined that the stage would be properly set.

In seeking US government help over visas, stress was laid on the extent to which, beyond its internationalism, the organization was serving American interests. A confidential internal memorandum, prepared for a visit to a State Department official, explains that at Bled they had secured 'the unanimous election ... of the first American International President ... and this over the organized opposition of the French PEN Center, which had put up a candidate whose own attitude was inimical to the United States and whose friendly relations with communist circles were well known. There could hardly be better evidence of the respect in which the American literary community was universally held and the service which, by its very existence, it rendered the American national interest.'[20]

A PEN report written after the Congress has a triumphalist tone that would have fully justified the CIA's investment, though Miller had succeeded in bringing Pablo Neruda from Chile, scarcely the Agency's favourite author. The invitation had necessitated the waiving of key clauses in the Immigration Act of 1952. In a letter to Neruda, whom he had met briefly in Avignon, Miller quoted from a speech by President Johnson in which he had instructed the Secretary of State and the Attorney General to find ways of removing such hindrances in granting visas. Miller was, it seems, quickly learning the diplomatic game. At the Congress the American Center, confronted with visa problems, sponsored a resolution disapproving of 'measures taken by any government which has the effect of preventing PEN members from leaving their own country or entering a foreign country'.

Miller invited Neruda to stay with him for a weekend and catch trout. In reply, all too conscious of the fragility of the Chilean currency and the adverse exchange rate (6,000 pesos to the dollar), Neruda asked Miller whether he could legitimately cash in his first-class air ticket for two economy ones so that his wife could accompany him.

Neruda was only one of several South American writers to travel to New York, and the occasion proved a vital one in enabling them to break out of an isolation which extended beyond an American ignorance of their accomplishments. In truth, national barriers had to a remarkable degree kept them in ignorance of one another. In July, following the Congress, Carlos Fuentes wrote from on board the *Statendam*, a Holland-America line ship, offering thanks for Miller's hospitality and stressing the importance of the meeting:

> Most of us had never met before. We had never discussed our common problems – from the most concrete to the most, well, metaphysical. We knew we were part of a common tradition yet had never put it to the test, had always felt captured in extreme provincialism. The meeting permitted us to break these very old and terrible barriers. And also to see ourselves within a new context ... [he welcomed] the real, warm human presence of Communists and liberals, conservatives and anarchists, Jews and Catholics, [the fact] that literature is still the great means of <u>reaching out</u>, of addressing

oneself and others, of maintaining that irreducible craving for understanding, communication, doubt ... sharing, that comes from the depth of every man who sincerely takes up a pen and becomes, in the same act, HE and OTHERS. We can still say what the TV screen or the electronic computer or the news flash cannot say: we can still bring the news of that which, without the writer, would be forever unsaid.[21]

In fact, the CIA was not unhappy to see South American writers invited, provided only that this served to reinforce the central role of the United States in PEN. It had, indeed, worked hard through the CCF (the lead being taken by Michael Josselson and John Hunt, and with Keith Botsford as a key player) to influence them, establishing one of its many magazines, the Paris-based *Mundo Nuevo* (funded by the Ford Foundation), a successor to *Cuadernos del Congreso por la Libertad de la Cultura* (financed by the CIA's Farfield Foundation). Its aim was to undermine the idea of the writer as a political revolutionary, even while opening its pages to those who might not seem to support its political agenda. Fuentes was one of the major writers published by the magazine which, in all its issues, carried the statement, 'The Congress for Cultural Freedom is an international association of writers, professors, scholars and artists. It does not depend on any government or any political group, and intends only to defend freedom of creativity.' As Dwight Macdonald remarked, the Cold War mentality was that it was sometimes necessary to lie for the truth.

Because *Mundo Nuevo* was part of the CIA's network of publications, each could reprint material from the others, so that Arthur Miller could appear alongside the new writers from Latin America. When the CIA connection became known in 1967, Gabriel García Márquez was one of those who felt betrayed, launching a vigorous attack.[22] In 1966, however, a year before the shoe dropped, the presence of Latin American authors at the PEN Congress was entirely consonant with CIA policy, a number of its operatives taking an interest in the political as well as the aesthetic significance of an emerging literature, one such being Melvin Lasky, editor of *Encounter*, who looked to encourage Cuban writers willing to break with the regime. The CCF also funded a number of magazines for Spanish émigrés. In its post-conference report PEN declared that 'the pre-eminence of the U.S. as the pace-setter of contemporary civilization was triumphantly confirmed by the [fact] that the congress took place in New York City', while the 'concentration on the writer's role in society, and his concerns as artist, was something that redounded to the credit of our country'.[23]

The CIA's hand in the New York Congress, though, should not detract from the event's very considerable success. Fuentes's comments were indicative of how valuable PEN could be, beyond its mission to support threatened writers. As he went on to remark: 'I wanted to say how much meeting and hearing men like Miller and Neruda means to me, how it stiffens the literary and human backbone of a relatively "younger" scribbler to feel, through you, that one can and should be faithful to one's vision, profoundly affected by the world but never drowned in worldliness, in fads and distractions'.[24] Miller's address to the Congress lamented continuing divisions in the world – and there were abrasive clashes, for example, between Ignazio Silone and the sociologist Daniel Bell on the one hand and Pablo Neruda on the other – and in doing so set out his literary philosophy:

> Only from the point of view of another planet is it enough to know that a human being has managed to walk in space; on the earth, the imporant question is whether he is Russian or American. A feeling of sadness miraculously caught in a poem is not merely sadness now; disenchantment is not merely disenchantment. If it is a Russian poem, these emotions are implicitly political, and in an American poem, hardly less so. At least the world is inclined to think so. In short, the integral beauty of a thing in itself, its degree of perfection as a created complex of inner tensions and resolution, is subordinate to its relevance – its relevance to the survival and prestige of the social presumptions in which it was brought forth.

PEN existed not only to support writers around the world – and he recalled his own treatment at the hands of HUAC – but to support the idea of literature as independent of the forces exerted on it.

> Because PEN is not engaged in political warfare, it ought to make more possible a view of literature as literature, as an expression of universal human conditions and feelings, universal human ideals. It is important that we meet not only in order to shake hands but to revitalize our awareness of something that is as real, as palpable, and as decisive as the conflicts between our nations.[25]

He had himself, he declared, 'always been committed', and thought his work none the worse for that. He also believed that readers and audiences were more likely to be moved by what they saw as impinging on their own social problems, but acknowledged that a 'writer can be as foolish as anyone else about politics and forecasting the future'.

Just how foolish was underlined at the time of the PEN Congress when Conor Cruise O'Brien, who held the Albert Schweitzer Chair at New York University but who had joined student demonstrations against the Vietnam War, delivered a lecture in which he denounced *Encounter* as an agent of foreign American policy. *Encounter* responded with an anonymous article, in fact written by the journalist and academic Goronwy Rees, later accused of being a communist spy by the KGB defector Vasili Mitrokhin. As a result,

O'Brien sued and *Encounter* settled. The covert activities of the CIA were beginning to break surface.

Once again, though, Miller knew nothing of this and, like many in the years in which government money made its way by circuitous routes into genuinely worthwhile causes, could hardly be said to have been tainted. In the immediate postwar world in which Europe, in particular, was bankrupt – through, indeed, to the 1960s – without such funding intellectuals of one kind or another would hardly have been able to travel and meet one another. On some level most assumed that America was trying to buy favour. They simply failed to understand to what degree and by what mechanisms.

Around the world the Agency, working through the CCF, endeavoured covertly to further government policy. In Australia, the CCF-funded *Quadrant* magazine ran supportive articles in its 'Reports on Vietnam' feature, even printing a piece supplied by a CIA agent. The Agency also funded a seminar at Melbourne University endorsing American involvement in Vietnam and paid for a book that did likewise. It underwrote a conference held in Kuala Lumpur. Behind the scenes was the same Michael Josselson who had turned up at the 1949 Waldorf Conference. By early 1967, however, the game was all but over. Josselson and John Hunt resigned from the now discredited Congress for Cultural Freedom in May.

In truth, for some people the link between the CIA and the CCF had been an open secret for years, though it was steadfastly denied by those at the heart of the conspiracy. Writing in *Encounter* in 1990,[26] Edward Shils, active in Congress affairs, recalled being approached by a Mr Gorwala in Bombay in 1959. He had heard that the CIA had a hand in the CCF; he had been told, he said, by the novelist James T. Farrell. Shils wrote to Nicolas Nabokov, seeking confirmation or denial. In return he received an accountant's report on the Farfield Foundation, an implicit denial which struck him later as a deliberate attempt to deceive and deeply cynical. In the 1960s he heard that an employee of the United States Embassy in Paris had seen a file, prepared by John Hunt, which revealed that the Congress had reported directly to the CIA. Shils wrote to Michael Josselson, asking if this were true and insisting that, were it to be, links with the CIA should be severed immediately. He received no reply from Josselson beyond a telegram stating that Shils's informant should cease spreading gossip.

For many, the intelligence community's flirtation with the Non-Communist Left had been a mistake from the beginning, despite what might seem its evident successes. James Burnham, a one-time Trotskyite who became a key figure in intelligence circles and in the success of the CCF, summed up his perception of the CIA involvement in culture and its decision to use the Non-Communist Left thus:

The CIA estimated the NCL as a reliably anti-Communist force which in
action would be, if not pro-Western and pro-American, at any rate not anti-
Western, anti-American. This political estimate is mistaken. The NCL is
not reliable. Under the pressure of critical events the NCL loosened. A large
proportion – in this country as in others – swung toward an anti-American
position, and nearly all the NCL softened its attitude toward Communism
and the Communist nations. Thus the organizational collapse is derivative
from the political error. This political error is the doctrine that the global
struggle against Communism must be based on the NCL – a doctrine
fastened on the CIA by Allen Dulles. Cuba, the Dominican Republic, and
above all Vietnam have put the NCL doctrine and practice to a decisive test.
A large part of the organizations and individuals nurtured by the CIA under
the NCL prescription end up undermining the nation's will and hampering
or sabotaging the nation's security.[27]

Miller, who, unknown to himself, had been so nurtured, had challenged
American policy in Vietnam, though in doing so had hardly undermined the
nation's will or sabotaged its security.

In 1966, however, now as President of International PEN, his job was to
offer the opening address at the New York Congress. But before he could do
so, a private event intervened. On the day he was to deliver the speech, his
father, Isidore, died. This was the man who had travelled from Poland to
America with a label around his neck at the age of six. Now his son was about
to preside over a meeting at which Polish delegates had come to hear him
talk. Suddenly, with his death, an undeclared competition came to an end.
For Miller it was a relationship which, despite its moments of family solidarity,
had always been touched with a sense of guilt because he knew that his success
had been seen as a reproach by a man who, himself illiterate, could not read
the words his son wrote.

He and his brother Kermit had visited their father a year before his death,
when he was no longer able to think with any clarity. He recognized neither
of them. Now this man, with whom Miller had wrestled, whose ideas and
values he had contested and yet whom he could never drive from his heart
and mind, was gone. It was just five years since his mother's death. For her,
he realized, he had been an expression of her own frustrated hopes. She had
tried to live through him but he had resisted her embrace. Now, with both
parents dead a kind of biological protection was stripped away. He was the
leading edge. Their death was a reminder of the inevitability of his own.

In 1966, he published a story in the *Saturday Evening Post* called 'A Search
for a Future'. It concerned an actor whose father is approaching death and
who grudgingly, and not without a certain trepidation, appears at an anti-war
rally. Beyond the theatre, the Vietnam War is raging. His dresser's nephew

has been blinded there. The actor's mind, though, is preoccupied with the man who, like Miller's own father, is ending his life in a rest home. Though the protagonist shares Miller's birthplace, Harlem, he is unlike him in that he has not previously put his name to protests. Nonetheless there are plainly points of contact. He fears he could lose his audience and be called to account by an investigating committee asking why he had attended the meeting. Although he doubts that his appearance could make much difference, the enthusiasm of a younger generation, particularly the dilemma of a young man who may face the draft, encourages him to appear.

He visits his father, whose language is slipping away from him because he has suffered a stroke and whose wife, like Isidore Miller's, is dead, along with his brothers and sisters. As he walks away and takes a bus to Harlem, his memories are clearly Miller's. He recalls the Minervas and Locomobiles that used to cruise by and the cop on 114th Street who threw the ball back when he and his friends, like Miller and his friends, played baseball.

What strikes the protagonist, suddenly, is that his father is the only person not acting. In theatre, everything is performance. It seems to him that the protest meeting, too, was performance, that politics is performance, indeed that everything but a man reduced by infirmity and illness is performance. He feels the lack of necessity in his own life. Acting may simulate the real but the thing itself seems out of reach. He receives a call to tell him that his father has walked out of the rest home. They find him in Harlem. He was trying to go home, to the home he remembered, to the time when things appeared to make sense. His future is his past. Now the son waits for the call that he knows will come that will tell him his father has died. Meanwhile, however, these events have made this man of the theatre feel the need to move in a new direction, to rediscover something he too has lost.

It is tempting to hear something of Miller in the last words of the story when his protagonist says of acting what *he* might say of playwriting – that for moments, 'just for moments, he makes me feel as I used to when I started, when I thought that being a great actor was like making some kind of gift to the people'.[28]

Despite the shock of his father's death, Miller went ahead with his address to the PEN Congress. He had begun to invest his hopes in an organization that offered a new version of the solidarity he had once sought in Marxism. Here, after all, gathered from around the world, were writers united not by ideology but by a belief in the significance of writing itself and therefore in the need to protect the writer, whose censorship, imprisonment and some-times death were the early warning of a more widespread oppression.

The Congress was a considerable success, but was not without its conflicts. Ignazio Silone, speaking in French, delivered an impassioned speech de-nouncing totalitarianism in all its forms, including fascism and communism.

Pablo Neruda then attacked him for speaking favourably of *Dr Zhivago*, which he suggested was being used as a Cold War weapon. Silone replied that Neruda was the one caught in a Cold War mentality. Valery Tarsis then attacked Neruda, the Soviet government and the Nobel Prize committee, which that year had awarded its literature prize to Mikhail Sholokhov. He called for a war on communist ideology, at which point communist delegates rose and demanded that he should be silenced. For his part, Miller rejected the rhetoric of war. Controversy did not end there, however: a Vietnamese delegate suggested that protesting Buddhists in South Vietnam were in fact communists in disguise. This prompted an East German protest, which David Carver cut short.

The Congress, then, as Fuentes acknowledged, brought together writers of different and even opposing ideological convictions, PEN offering them a context in which such differences played a secondary role. Despite the various arguments that broke out, it seemed to both Miller and Carver that they were making some progress with their project to involve Soviet writers. Already Carver was using the Congress's success to encourage Miller to serve a second two-year stint as President, urging him to do so in a letter (dated 26 October 1966) in which he also describes attending a party, thrown by John Hunt of the CIA, at which he had met members of the CCF. It is not clear whether he knew the precise nature of the company he was keeping. In late December, Miller was still trying to make up his mind: he had now had considerable contact with Yevtushenko and had been invited to a Soviet writers' congress scheduled for the following year. Finally, he accepted the invitation to serve two more years as President, and with Carver discussed the possibility of holding a Congress in Havana, despite the difficulties it would obviously raise.

At the same time, he was beginning to test PEN's power by securing the release of Wole Soyinka in Nigeria and Fernando Arrabal in Spain. Thereafter, in country after country, he deployed whatever credit the organization or he himself might have acquired to protect those whose writing had provoked oppressive action.

Vietnam, though, remained a priority. In June 1966, he attended a meeting entitled 'Vietnam and the American Conscience' held in New York Town Hall as a tribute to Thich Nhat Hanh, founder of the Buddhist University in Saigon and editor of *Thien My*, a leading Buddhist weekly. Miller introduced the event. He was joined by Robert Lowell and Daniel Berrigan, SJ (a Catholic priest, poet and peace activist). An FBI agent recorded his comments, as he did those of Hanh, who wanted the United States to stop the bombing and believed that US troops would be able to leave within eight or ten months. Meanwhile, he added, too many Vietnamese peasants were being killed by troops who could not distinguish them from the Vietcong.

The purpose of the evening, Miller explained, was to hear what a Vietnamese had to say about the war. At the same time, he wished to set out why he personally was opposed to it. America, he pointed out, had refused to acknowledge the fact that a civil war was being waged, or to accept the corrupt nature of the South Vietnamese government. America was in an undeclared war without the consent of the people it was allegedly there to defend. Marshal Ky, the South Vietnamese leader, was manifestly an American creation who promised to destroy anybody who advocated a negotiated peace. Political intelligence, he concluded, had disappeared.

The FBI agent who attended the meeting noted Miller's participation. Once again, file 100–154784, going back to the 1940s and his attendance at Communist Party meetings, recapitulated his record.

4

DANIEL

The doctor told me, 'There's nothing you can do.' He told me, 'Don't take him home or otherwise you will never be able to make the decision. It's the right decision.' We decided to place him in a home where he would be better off.

Inge Morath[1]

For all Miller's concern with public events, a private one proved infinitely more disturbing. In April 1966, Inge became pregnant again. It was not a planned pregnancy, any more than the first had been. Nonetheless, they both had high hopes for this addition to their family, a brother or sister for Rebecca. Inge was just short of her forty-third birthday; he was fifty-one. There were risks, but the pregnancy seemed to progress normally. They made the usual preparations, explaining to Rebecca about the imminent arrival.

The baby was born in a New York hospital. The delivery itself was straightforward. These were the days before *in utero* testing and sonograms – there had been no means even to tell the gender. When the baby finally arrived on the morning of 7 January 1967, it was immediately apparent to Miller, who attended the delivery, that something was wrong. The child suffered from what we now call Down's syndrome, though then it was called mongolism. As Miller explained, talking to me in 2001, 'I knew immediately. The doctor kept denying it. I knew it from his hands. They have one crease across the palms'[2] – the crease first noted in the son of the man who gave the condition its name.

Inge recalled that straight after the birth nobody mentioned anything untoward. 'They brought him in, but he was comatose. I had him in my arms. I immediately knew that something was wrong but they didn't tell me right away.'[3] It was her husband who identified the problem. The shock, she confessed, was almost like losing a child.

Joan Copeland, Miller's sister, was with her brother the night before the baby was born. 'We went to dinner in a Chinese restaurant when Inge went to the hospital and I called the next day to find out how she was, and the baby, as I would like to go to the hospital. He said there seems to be something wrong with the child. He didn't go into it. He said it wasn't a good time to visit her.' For Miller it immediately brought to mind a cousin, Carl, who had suffered from the same condition: 'I had a cousin who was similarly afflicted and he had two sisters who were older than him. One never got married. She was perfectly lovely. The other did and spent half of her life taking care of him. She never had any children of her own. I was brought up in the next street and so I knew how they reacted to him.' In *Timebends*, published twenty years after Daniel's birth, in which he makes no reference to his son, he offers a description of his aunt Betty, a good-looking woman, a one-time burlesque dancer:

> When she realized, twenty years ago, that her baby son was what was then called mongoloid, she turned to religion and expectantly watched for spooks out of the corners of her eyes as she wiped poor Carl's chin, by turns flying at him in a rage, mocking his fluffy speech to his face, and dressing him up in expensive suits and ties to proudly walk with him, teaching him how to take her arm like a real gentleman.[4]

In 2001 Miller recalled Carl: '[He] was miserable, because we could all play ball but he could do nothing. He wanted to do it. He wanted to be like everybody else. It was simply impossible. He didn't have the coordination. He couldn't see that well. He was my age.'[5]

It was these memories that led him to decide to follow medical advice and hand their son over to specialists: 'As soon as I saw him I thought of my cousin ... so I thought that the best thing would be if we could find a way of bringing him up among people who he could possibly not compete with but not feel overwhelmed by. And, indeed, it ended up quite well. He works. He has a job. He's a very sweet, hard-working guy.'[6] Joan Copeland thought that her brother's response might also have been due to seeing the impact on her and her husband of her own son, who had cerebral palsy, as he saw their lives constrained. Whatever the truth of it the hospital doctor advised the Millers that their new child should be raised with others like himself. Accordingly, they decided, virtually immediately, that he should be placed in an appropriate home and not brought back to Roxbury which would, Miller said, have been to nobody's advantage.

They named the child Daniel Eugene, the second being a traditional name in Inge's family, and with the help of the doctor's wife Miller set about the business of locating a suitable place for him to live. At the time, he and Inge's doctor were both afraid she would form an attachment that would make it difficult for her to act. Inge explained:

> Arthur had had a mongoloid cousin so we decided to put him in a home where he would be better off. My doctor talked to me. The doctor said, don't

take him home otherwise you won't be able to make the decision. He said, it is the right decision for this kind of mongoloid because he will never be able to learn. This doctor was wonderful. He said, look, make this decision now because otherwise you will just be dragging. The doctor told me that there was nothing I could do. It was very hard but you have to make that decision. And I knew it would be worse [to bring him home].[7]

Daniel was never taken home. It was not that the family intended to sever all links with him but that they believed at the time, and reiterated that belief thirty-five years later, that his future would be more assured and less confusing if he had one home and not two, convinced, as they were, of his need for continuing specialized care. Even so, and despite the speed with which they moved, they were not without regrets; Miller later recalled the tears they had both shed.

He recalled, too, the odd foreshadowing of this event in his own work, wondering where that might have come from. He was conscious, for example, of the odd coincidence that Holga, in *After the Fall*, had spoken of the need to embrace your life 'like an idiot child . . . I dreamed I had a child, and even in the dream I saw it was my life, and it was an idiot, and I ran away. But it always crept on my lap again, clutched at my clothes. Until I thought, if I could kiss it, whatever in it was my own, perhaps I could sleep. And I bent to its broken face, and it was horrible . . . but I kissed it. I think one must finally take one's life in one's arms.'[8] Struggling to make sense of the flaws in human life, the protagonist of that play remarks, 'With some gift of courage one may look into its face when it appears, and with a stroke of love – as to an idiot in the house – forgive it; again and again . . . for ever?'[9] Miller recalled, too, the fact that the protagonist of *The Man Who Had All the Luck* had been afraid that his wife would give birth to a defective child.

Years later, talking to the family friend Honor Moore early in their long friendship, he remembered another coincidence. After Daniel's birth, the doctor had given him the address of a home and he went there to see if it would be acceptable. While there, he saw another couple plainly in the same situation. He called his composer friend David Amram to come and have dinner. They went to Chinatown, sat down in the restaurant, and there was the same couple. Looking back, it seemed to Honor that this anecdote was Miller's way of telling her of Daniel's existence.

The decision to place the baby in a home was painful and decades later, when it became public knowledge, Miller would be denounced for doing so. The fact is, though, that this was entirely consonant with medical advice in the 1960s. Speaking in 2002, an official of Britain's Down's Syndrome Association remarked that back then it was not uncommon for mothers to be told, 'Leave that one here and go and have another.' In October 2007 the

Guardian newspaper made similar inquiries, interviewing Stuart Mills of the Down's Syndrome Association: 'here, the standard advice was to leave the child in hospital from where it would be consigned to an institution ... Parents were told there was little chance of their child talking, walking or being toilet-trained, that if they were lucky they might expect them to live into their 20s.'[10] Parents were often informed that such children would never learn to read or write and never be able to function without specialist care. There was relatively little medical understanding of the condition. As Jon Henley pointed out in his *Guardian* article, 'These were the dark ages; there was no understanding of the heart problems that 50% of people with Down's syndrome are born with, or how to treat them. Children with Down's were considered ineducable.'[11] As late as the 1970s, one in four Down's adults in the United Kingdom were still living in long-term institutions. Carol Boys, Chief Executive of the Down's Syndrome Association, remarked in 2007, 'There are still issues ... But it is true to say the situation's improved beyond all recognition since the 1980s.'[12]

In 1961, a number of geneticists wrote to the *Lancet* suggesting that the term 'mongoloid idiocy' should be abandoned. In 1965 the World Health Organization also abandoned the term though, bizarrely, not on health grounds but following a complaint from a Mongolian delegate. The term 'Down's syndrome' was adopted in recognition of the work of the one-time superintendent of what was then called the Royal Earlswood Asylum for Idiots, John Langdon Down, who, in the nineteenth century had first identified the condition, which he observed in his own son as well as in those for whom he had responsibility. He did so in a paper entitled, 'Observations on an Ethnic Classification of Idiots'. In the 1970s an American revision of scientific terms abandoned the possessive form so that it is called 'Down syndrome' in the United States and 'Down's syndrome' in the UK. It took some time, however, for the new term to be adopted and the attitudes of doctors and members of the public – in part, perhaps, shaped by the previous nomenclature – to change.

Down's syndrome's genetic basis was not identified until 1959, following work by Jérôme Lejeune and Patricia Jacobs who located a third chromosome 21 (trisomy 21). The first World Down Syndrome Day was held on 21 March 2006, the day and month chosen to reflect trisomy 21. In 1980, life expectancy for a Down's child was twenty-five years; by 2002, it had risen to forty-nine.

In 2009, Anne Crosby published *Matthew*, a book about her own Down's syndrome son, born a year after Daniel. Like the Millers, she had another child, a six-year-old daughter (Rebecca Miller was four). In her book she recalls the eminent child psychiatrist Dr Donald Winnicott saying to her, after Matthew's birth, 'Here is the important child [indicating her daughter],

the bright and whole one. We can safely say the other is the throwaway child.'
He advised that Matthew should be placed in a residential home to 'protect'
his sister. Anne Crosby subsequently said that she thought her daughter had
suffered as much from his absence as she would have done from his presence,
but at the time she thought she was doing the best for everybody, including
for her marriage since her husband found it difficult to envisage any other
course of action. She said of him, 'He was a good man, an honorable man,
and he tried to do the right thing.' It was, though, impossible for him to
imagine what their new son thought or meant.

In the end that son died at the age of twenty-five, desperately trying to get
well to please his absent father. His mother, meanwhile, found herself attacked
by a new generation for, as they saw it, abandoning her child; her daughter
later revealed that she herself had 'had an amnio when I was pregnant ...
I wouldn't have been a good parent to someone like Matthew. I only had one
child. Perhaps I felt, well, I've got one healthy one, I won't risk any more.'[13]

Every story is unique. Every story contains its own tangle of pain and guilt.
As the sister of the throwaway child indicates, questions are still there to be
answered and even now people answer them in different ways. Nor has guilt
entirely disappeared – it has simply changed its nature.

Daniel spent many of his early years in the Southbury Training School ten
minutes' drive from the Miller house in Roxbury. The school, established in
the 1930s, consisted of 125 buildings on a 1,600-acre site. Admissions closed
in 1986 at a time when 1,111 people lived there; nearly seven hundred still lived
there in 2000, on average having done so for forty years. In 1984, the school
was required to ensure that there were sufficient staff to protect and enhance
the life of residents and to create more community-based opportunities for
them. In 1994, the Justice Department concluded that residents were not
being properly cared for; in 2006, federal monitoring ended.

When Daniel first went to Southbury it had a good reputation. Its prox-
imity to Roxbury was another recommendation, enabling Inge to make regular
visits. Over time, however, that reputation began to fade. It was seen as failing
those who lived there in certain key areas. By the early 1980s attitudes had
changed, and it was thought advisable to encourage a move out into the
community. Jean Bowen, a disability rights advocate, recalls Miller and his
wife attending a meeting and endorsing the idea with respect to Daniel, at a
time when many parents opposed such a move.[14] Thirty years later, Daniel,
now living in the community with a fellow Down's syndrome man, worked
in a number of jobs. The two men were visited every day to check on their
needs. 'The State has a programme,' Miller observed, 'that is terrific. We visit
him frequently.' Daniel could not, Miller noted, read, write or count, but 'he
gets on with people beautifully. All kinds of people.' In fact, Daniel's talents

went far beyond this. He enjoyed sport, attended public events, and was extremely sociable. He would speak out at advocacy groups. Indeed, when Miller was speaking on behalf of a learning-disabled man convicted of murder, Danny, who was there with a self-advocacy group, embraced him. The fact that he had flourished seemed, to Miller, to justify the decision they had made so many years earlier.

Neither parent ever regretted their decision: 'On the contrary,' Miller said, while admitting that 'there is no satisfactory conclusion since you are dealing with a consciousness'.[15] Inge, too, remained convinced that they had made the only possible decision: 'It would have ruined our entire life, and for him, too. What would he have done here? I still think it was the right decision because it would have been impossible to give him the life that he has now.'[16]

But children see the world differently. Unsurprisingly, Rebecca wished to know where her new sibling was: 'It took a lot of explaining . . . It was never really dealt with early on, why he didn't come home.' For a while, she seemed to become the baby they had not brought home, suddenly infantilized. Looking back, however, her memory is that, not fully understanding what had happened, she drew the conclusion that there were good babies and bad babies and that bad babies did not come home. What offence Daniel might have committed, she did not understand. Accordingly, she set herself to be a good baby. Thirty years on, she saw this event as offering an explanation of her desire to please, to achieve, both at school and university.

For Rebecca, speaking to me in 2001, on the same day that I had discussed the issue with her parents, Daniel 'was a huge presence in my life', though not in a literal sense:

> I was very confused as to why he didn't come home. They chose not to make him a part of our lives and that, to me, was very strange. It was odd. It's still odd, in a way. It's a mystery. They know the answer. I *don't* know the answer. I didn't see him too much when I was growing up. My mum saw him the most. My mum carried the burden of the whole thing. Looking back, I don't know what was going on in their heads. I don't think I will ever know. No one ever told me why they did what they did. I think it has to do with not being able to deal with it, to look things in the face.[17]

In the years after her father's death, and herself married with children, she has welcomed Daniel into her home.

When Inge died in 2002, none of the obituaries listed Daniel, who remained not so much a secret as a private fact, shared with a limited number of friends and acquaintances. He was put aside because that seemed the necessary and perhaps even the right thing to do, but necessity can breed something more painful than regret. They took pride in his accomplishments, in his limited but proud independence. Yet paths not taken are not paths forgotten, and his living presence just a few miles away was, if not a reproach, then at least a reminder of hopes betrayed, possibilities unrealized, and a decision whose consequences could not have been known when they made it. Years afterwards Miller admitted feeling a residual guilt at what might seem their desertion of their son, but there had been no right answer to their dilemma – only an effort to do the right thing while never fully sure what the right thing might be. Today, with prenatal testing, parents are offered a choice of a different kind. In Britain and the United States some 92 per cent of Down's syndrome babies are aborted. It is not altogether clear whether that could be said to be a better solution than that adopted by the parents of a child who today, by general consent, is a happy and engaging man in his forties.

In an episode in 1982 of the popular hospital drama St Elsewhere called 'Down's Syndrome', written by the dramatist turned television writer Tom Fontana, a couple are told that their new baby will have Down's syndrome, will be what the husband calls 'mongoloid'. In the screened version (though not in the online text) they are advised that some Down's children will live into their twenties but that the average mental age is seven. After a tortured discussion between the parents, the child is aborted. It was not an episode that went down well with NBC. Fifteen years on from Daniel's birth the choices were different, the anguish the same.

In his biography of Miller, published in 2003, Martin Gottfried accuses him of never visiting his son. Speaking to me, Miller suggested otherwise. (Gottfried, incidentally, was also wrong with respect to another of Miller's children. His daughter Jane did not, as Gottfried asserts, suffer the cot death of a child. She has never had children.) If Miller did so, though, it was seldom, and that does pose a significant question. Joan Copeland, speaking to me in 2008, remarked of her brother, 'He was able to shut off very real events in his life or to minimize things at the very least.' Inge, though, did visit Daniel regularly, sometimes taking Rebecca with her.

In its September 2007 edition, Vanity Fair published an article under the heading 'Investigation', which purported to reveal a truth known only to a few. Miller, the article said, had 'erased his son [whose birth it 'corrected' from Gottfried's suggested 1962, repeated by Jeffrey Myers in his 2009 book The Genius and the Goddess, to the equally erroneous 1966] from the public record ... cut him out of his public life, institutionalizing him at birth, refusing to see him or speak about him, virtually abandoning him'.[18] In 2008, Rebecca Miller would say of the article: 'I just think ... that it was undertaken in the spirit of irresponsibility and actually, finally, a kind of malevolent spirit ... to take someone down without looking at [the issue] with any subtlety or having really spoken to the people that they needed to speak to, to really get a sense of what it all meant. So I find it very disappointing.'[19]

Though some of those interviewed for the article were named, others were identified as 'close friends'. One 'friend' was quoted as saying that Inge had wished to keep the baby while her husband would not let her, denied by Inge herself. Another 'friend' insisted that it was 'a decision that had Rebecca at the center'. Another recalled that 'Inge tried to bring him home, but Arthur would not have it'. 'Some say' that Daniel Day-Lewis had been 'distressed at his father-in-law's attitude'. The anonymous informants give the piece a dubious tone. The article then outlined the history of the Southbury Training School and the poor treatment it came to offer. The novelist and biographer Francine du Plessix Gray is quoted as recalling Inge saying that it was 'like a Hieronymous Bosch painting' there. The article did, however, acknowledge that Daniel had left the institution and that Miller and Inge had favoured this at a special meeting, and reported Daniel's subsequent semi-independent life, along with Miller's decision to write him into his will as an equal beneficiary with his siblings.

It concluded, however, by saying that 'Miller excised a central character who didn't fit the plot of his life as he wanted it to be'. He had been motivated, it suggested, 'by shame, selfishness, or fear – or, more likely, all three', and 'he never wrote anything approaching greatness after Daniel's birth'[20] as if that birth and his response to it were aspects of a general decline. In fact, ahead lay his third-most successful play, *The Price*, produced a year later, along with the Olivier Award-winning *Broken Glass* and many other accomplished works. Nor is there any evidence for Miller having felt fear (for what?) or shame. Was it selfishness? Perhaps. Was he anxious about the impact on four-year-old Rebecca? Almost certainly. Did he dread the idea of a family that would have to focus on the needs of a Down's child? Quite possibly. Under-standing our own motives is hard enough; understanding other people's, harder still.

The *New York Times* picked up the story, describing Daniel's existence as 'an open secret' – as well it might, since I had known of his existence for many years, as had his British director David Thacker, perhaps because both of us have learning-disabled children too. Rather oddly, the *New York Times* article quoted Martin Gottfried as saying that 'Miller had been built up as a moral conscience ... But by the time of "After the Fall" ... was laboring under the weight of godliness'.[21] Miller's long-term adversary, *Commentary* magazine, weighed in with a blog which, while granting that the insti-tutionalizing of a child with Down's syndrome was not an uncommon practice at the time, regretted Miller's action, while, incidentally, seizing on the occasion to castigate *The Crucible*, thereby echoing its position of fifty years earlier.

In the end, the mystery is not why Daniel was placed in an institution, but that Miller did plainly find it difficult to visit him, usually relying on Inge to do so. It is tempting to say that a man who wrote so frequently about denial was himself in denial. This is certainly the explanation offered to me by his actress sister Joan.

> It was an ugly truth. It was a fact. And he managed somehow to involve himself in other aspects of his life so that he could live without going crazy, but he managed to suppress it enough, I think, so that he could function without publicly recognizing this child. I must say I never heard anybody discuss it in the house and I was constrained when asking about it. They never mentioned it and I wondered if Rebecca even knew about this child, because she was a little girl. And I only recently discovered how much she knew and how attentive she is to this child. I was up there making a movie that she directed and Daniel came and watched Rebecca shooting the film. He came with the person who looks after him. They are very close. And he felt very at home. He came to visit me in the house I was given to change my clothes in and get made up, and I didn't know who he was. This young man was brought to me and I was told, this is Daniel. I had seen him once. Inge took me. She told me, I am going to visit Danny and I wasn't quite sure who this was. I said who? She said our son. I said I've never seen him. And she said, well, do you want to come with me? So I said I would love to. So we went to visit him where he was staying and met him. He would have been about fourteen. And he was very dear, a nice guy. He was very personable and chatted a little bit. Since then his speech has improved from those many years back. And he is very friendly. When I saw him recently I said, do you remember me? I met you a long time ago. He said, I think I do. Then he said, yes, I do. I remember you now. He hugged me. He was not as badly afflicted with Down's as our cousin was. He was sweet and affectionate. Carl lived until about sixty-five years old. His mother devoted her life to him but it was his two sisters, younger than him, whose lives were compromised.

In a public conversation conducted in 1998, Miller remarked, 'It's the nature of human beings to deny. Denial is one of the structures of our character. Possibly because it's impossible not to deny certain things that are simply unacceptable to our consciences.'[22] He spoke in the context of a discussion of public events that included Germany's responsibility for the Holocaust and America's actions in Vietnam and Cambodia. The statement, though, by a man who always insisted on the connection between the private and public worlds, was perhaps no less relevant to certain denials in his own life. Was Daniel one of them? To a degree the answer would seem to be yes, if we mean by that not his capacity to set him aside, but his evident hesitancy to embrace him with the love he felt but found difficult to express.

Many of the blogs that blossomed on the Web following the *Vanity Fair* article were heavy with *Schadenfreude*. They attacked Miller as one who had set himself up as a moralist but was now revealed to have feet of clay. Others revelled in the fact that a left-wing writer was being publicly exposed. Still others assured readers that they would have made different decisions or, indeed, had done so. Relatively few showed much awareness of the changing attitudes to Down's syndrome in the forty years since Daniel's birth. In the end, those confronted with a learning-disabled child set themselves to do the best they can for that child and today, the roughly 8 per cent who do not abort Down's children are still confronted by the choice that faced Miller and his wife in that hospital ward in 1967. In 2008, Joan remarked:

How dare anybody criticize what a parent of a child should do, must do, must not do, has to do? It really resides in the conscience ... of the parent. And he did it one way ... Somebody else would have done it a different way. That's the way he did it. And I'm sure there was pain there. Lots of pain ... It's hard to conjecture ... when you say to somebody, 'What would you do if you were in my position?' You know that wonderful John Kander and Fred Ebb song, 'What Would You Do If You Were in My Position?' Yes, what would you do? ... Some people might believe in God. And a lot believe that certain things were predestined and had to be. Others might say, 'Well, you just go with it.' Other people might say, 'Well, this might damage the remaining child. You have to protect [against] damage.' There's no way to say how you would do it until you face it. Nobody can explain anybody. Nobody dares blame this man![23]

5

1968

It's the nature of human beings to deny. Denial is one of the structures of our character ... we were moved into the Vietnam War by a trick, basically a lie, went and pursued that war long past any excuse for it. Killed a lot of people, fundamentally destroyed a country ... But you don't find us walking around thinking about that stuff. It's too painful.[1]

Arthur Miller

Perhaps one reason for Miller throwing himself so wholeheartedly into public events thereafter was precisely the emotional turmoil that accompanied Daniel's birth, though a month later he was absent from a peace rally in New York at which he had been scheduled to appear. The truth was that, however confident he and Inge were that they had taken the right step, theirs was a home defined by an absence, and it took time for them to begin to adjust to what had happened.

In June 1967, though, he attended a rally of men and women in the arts concerned with Vietnam, held at the Ambassador Hotel in Los Angeles. Fellow sponsors were the novelist Alvah Bessie (one of the Hollywood Ten, about whom he had been questioned at his appearance before HUAC), Ray Bradbury and Jessica Mitford. The FBI duly noted an article announcing the event which appeared in the communist *People's World*.

Nor was Vietnam the only issue confronting Arthur Miller. In August that year he received a letter from the Minerva Players, a non-white group of amateur actors in Cape Town who were requesting permission to mount a production of *A View from the Bridge*. Since he was a signatory of a declaration prohibiting the performance of his plays before segregated audiences, they felt the need to approach him. Their preference was to perform before mixed audiences, but this was plainly impossible. They therefore asked him to break his own embargo by serving its spirit rather than the letter. The law, they explained, 'is very powerful. If it cannot be opposed by other means, theatrical activity may well serve to bridge the ever-widening gap which tends to place us in a mental void. We must reiterate that we in no way condone segregation by asking your permission in this way.'² Miller agreed to the production, replying that he regarded this as an act of protest since it seemed to him that apartheid was less about banning mixed audiences than excluding blacks from South African life. He also waived his royalties.

In 1967 the Millers returned to the Soviet Union. They were met at the station in Moscow by a man who turned out to be a somewhat shady figure, at one moment suggesting that he was a journalist, at the next offering to arrange a hunting trip on which Miller and Inge could shoot bears from a helicopter with machine guns.

Miller was now once again charged to explore the possibility of Soviet writers joining International PEN, three or four unofficial emissaries having turned up at a PEN Congress in Abidjan, Ivory Coast, which he had also attended. Following a hint from Alexei Surkov, head of the Writers' Union, and with Carver's support, he went to see him, having sent a stream of letters and telegrams protesting the arrest of writers. Surkov, a white-haired man in his sixties, was accompanied by a professor of linguistics whose feet, Miller noted, pointed outwards like a penguin's. At a meeting lubricated, as back in Bled, with vodka, Surkov again expressed interest in joining. As before, though, it would first be necessary to change PEN's constitution. Confronted with such a bizarre request – that PEN, established to ensure the freedom of the writer, should sign up to an abrogation of that freedom – Miller rediscovered the 'miraculous rationalism of the American Bill of Rights' which 'suddenly seemed incredible, coming as it did from man's mendacious mind. America moved me all over again – it was an amazing place, the idea of it astounding.'³

In Russia, jointly produced by Miller and his wife, and which draws on both his 1965 and 1967 visits, places considerable emphasis on writers – those who were driven to their deaths by the regime, those who accommodated, those who embraced its values – as if they were not just a barometer but a moral test of the country. In one sense it was a country that retained its mysteries. Indeed Miller saw in Inge's photographs a muteness that was an expression of the fact that no one knew what Russia was saying, since silence was the recommended strategy and truth a subject best avoided. On the other hand it was a country in which literature, theatre, art seemed to have a power they lacked in the West.

Writing of Tolstoy, he remarks that 'shorn of his moral passions' he 'would be a mere story teller'. Much the same could be said of Miller himself. It was not that he was a moralist, a writer of didactic tales, any more than was Tolstoy, but that he wrote out of a conviction that there is an exemplary force in literature. For all the impoverishment of the life he found in Russia, its history of extreme cruelty, its callous disregard for the needs of the individual, there was still a hunger for literature as a source of values. He found a moral coherence lacking in his own country where the word 'freedom', it seemed to him, had lost its true meaning. As he observed, 'The poor man's freedom consists of not being poor any longer; for the middle class freedom consists of being necessary, at best, and at worst of being undisturbed in the quest of enjoyment and pointlessness.'[4] The final ironic words of *Death of a Salesman* are 'We're free'. Willy had desperately wanted to be necessary and had ended up irrelevant.

Nadezhda Yakovlevna Mandelstam, he noted, had learned her husband's poems by heart so they would survive. The past, as Miller has a character in *After the Fall* remark, is holy, and that is a bridge between his work and Inge Morath's. Her craft, too, lay in memorializing. Her photograph of Nadezhda, smiling like a Shawnee princess, captured the image of a woman who herself contained the past. As Andrei Voznesensky, once denounced by Khrushchev for slandering socialism and threatened with 'the harsh frost', was to say of the photographs Inge collected for her 1991 book *Russian Journal*, 'I don't know what will have happened to Russia by the time this book is published. Perhaps ... it will no longer exist, and with it the world will have lost its poetic principle – terrible, ungainly, beautiful, ugly, ours is perhaps the last poetic country.' Nonetheless, he remarked, Inge Morath's photographs would 'remain as a testimony to what the country was', as though she had 'taken photographs of Pompeii before its destruction'.[5] The visual twenty-first century, he suggested, would read her photographs in place of words.

Voznesensky visited the United States that same year and stayed with the Millers, a stay which he commemorated in a poem celebrating their dog Hugo, who would sit on his master's foot, like an oversize slipper, as he shuffled across the room. Miller responded by writing an introduction to the American edition of his poems, praising his ability to forge a private speech for public occasions. Robert Lowell in welcoming him to America praised him for being in trouble with his own country, adding that it was a hard time to be a poet in either.[6]

Inge's was a craft of preserving what otherwise vanishes on the wind. Like Miller's plays, her work brings the past into the present moment. She took photographs of those hidden by the state or chased into what it hoped would prove obscurity, as he was to write of their plight and, through the work he did for PEN, challenge the state to release them back into time. They had travelled to see the grave of Boris Pasternak, a man harassed and driven, as the state wished to believe, out of mind. Decades later, in February 1990, they would fly in from Berlin where, six months earlier, Miller had told a crowd that Hitler would have killed that writer twice over, once as an intellectual and once as a Jew. In doing so he perhaps echoed Marina Tsvetaeva's remark that all poets are Jews, in the sense that they are all persecuted as such.

According to Nadezhda Mandelstam, who quoted that remark in a 1968 letter to Miller, being a poet is being a Jew raised to the second power. The Millers would be there, then, in 1990, in the snow of Peredelkino, for the inauguration of the Pasternak Museum on the hundredth anniversary of his birth, his house now restored to its original state and with his possessions back in place. The past had not, after all, proved so easy to inter.

Inge Morath's attraction to Russia, whose language she learned as she would later learn Chinese before going to China, was long-standing and deep:

> I was after Russia for years and years and years, because there is something to me mysterious and attractive and it is almost always linked to literature in my case, because I read the writers, I read the poets and they really express the essence of a country. It would, for me, have been criminal not to have learned Russian and not to be able to read this literature. And from Russian you can go into other languages, Slav languages. I feel the same for Spain and South America and China.[7]

She would be drawn to China by its painting and its poetry. 'There is a mystery in the painting and the poetry, particularly the short poems, but now I know because I can write it. I thought, a people who have created such an immensely refined art and culture and yet could be so brutal are fascinating. The same is true of Russia and, in a way, of Germany, though I like Germany less.'[8]

Photographs, or sequences of photographs, she believed to be capable of capturing the essence of a country, especially when gathered into books, hence the series of such books that she produced throughout her life. It is, perhaps, she conceded, the fact of being a foreigner that makes it possible to see what the inhabitants of the country do not, until presented with such images.

For Yevgeny Yevtushenko, she pictured Russia with an understanding purged of sentimentality. She saw what it had been, and buildings from the past provide the backdrop to her scenes of daily life, but she also pictured a society that was changing, albeit slowly and with desperate repressions. In Leningrad in 1967 she visited the poet Joseph Brodsky, recently released from prison, discussing poetry with him in an apartment no doubt observed and possibly bugged. Brodsky had been convicted of being a 'social parasite' and sent to a mental institution. Among those who spoke up in his defence was Dmitri Shostakovich, whom Miller had met at the Waldorf Conference in 1949 when the Soviet composer was sent by Stalin to denounce himself on foreign soil. Brodsky was sentenced to five years' hard labour but his sentence was commuted in 1965 following protests from the West, as well as from Anna Akhmatova. Two days after their conversation, Inge climbed with him on to the roof of the Fortress of Peter and Paul, past the official No Entry signs and carrying a camera, itself often a forbidden instrument.

There is a photograph, taken that day, of Brodsky treading the edge of the roof, outlined against a flat sky – an echo of his situation in a no man's land in which to stay is to accept persecution and suffocation and to leave is to abandon the known and the loved. It was a dilemma that Miller would come to understand when he visited Czechoslovakia and from which would come *The Archbishop's Ceiling*. The image in Inge's photograph is framed on one side by the domes and spires of yesterday's city and on the other by a man, seen from behind, looking at another figure further along the roof, also seen from the rear, an echo of himself. The Peter and Paul Fortress, where revolutionaries had once been imprisoned, was now a symbol for another repression, from which Brodsky had so recently been released. Brodsky's dilemma was to be resolved when he was forced into exile in 1972, working for a while at Miller's old university, at Michigan. In 1987 he won the Nobel Prize. In his speech he explored the relationship between the writer and the state in a way that would precisely echo Miller's own:

> To say the least, as long as the state permits itself to interfere with the affairs of literature, literature has the right to interfere with the affairs of the state. A political system, a form of social organization, as any system in general, is by definition a form of the past tense that aspires to impose itself upon the present (and often on the future as well); and a man whose profession is language is the last one who can afford to forget this. The real danger for a writer is not so much the possibility (and often the certainty) of persecution on the part of the state, as it is the possibility of finding oneself mesmerized by the state's features, which, whether monstrous or undergoing changes for the better, are always temporary.[9]

Russia, as Miller and his wife discovered, was a nation of images, framed photographs of writers, political figures, the dead. They were on display in parks, on huge hoardings, on graves, in homes. The jumble of such images on an apartment wall in one of Inge's photographs mirrors that of icons crowding one another on the walls of a basilica. Here, then, is Morath taking pictures of pictures, one moment containing another, one timescale another, like a Russian doll, like a Miller play. And this was a place where past and present coincided. Tchaikovsky's breakfast room, which Inge photographed, has a cup and saucer still ready for morning tea. The lamp suspended over Chekhov's table at Yalta is the one that once lit the room of the doctor-playwright. In her photographs the eleventh, nineteenth and twentieth centuries seemingly coexist, as people live out their lives apparently oblivious to the layered history that provides the architecture of Russian experience. This was the sense in which Miller had seen time in *Death of a Salesman*, past and present coterminous, like sedimentary layers suddenly exposed.

There is a suggestion, in her photographs, that the Revolution is older than the remnants of Tzarist Russia against which it acted out its own drama. The energy has long since leached away and been replaced by a bureaucratic orthodoxy, or simply the improvisations of ordinary experience. She began taking photographs in Russia when Brezhnev was in power and repression was a natural instinct. She was still taking them when Gorbachev opened up the Soviet Union, far more quickly and completely than he would once have wished or even imagined. The tonal change is there in the photographs but throughout there are older traditions, like a counter-current to the deadening inertia of government. There are pictures of the instinctual hospitality that links this with earlier periods, gatherings of artists and writers of a kind that would have characterized the nineteenth century, and with the same subversive overtones.

In Morath's photographs, people predominate. For her, as she explained, man was always the measure. Even in her landscape pictures she would often try to capture the human figure. 'I want to affirm the importance of the individual.'[10] In her portrait photographs she endeavoured to locate people in their home surroundings. 'I will always remain curious about people. I like to photograph them in the places where they live or where they spend much of their time, places that have absorbed something of their person. Naturally I prepare myself by reading the books they have written, looking at their paintings or sculptures, or seeing their performances. Sometimes the best preparation is simply watching someone who has aroused my curiosity or what Goethe called "elective affinity". No encounter is the same as another. The final, wonderful surprise is always the person itself.'[11] She took her pictures discreetly, with her small Leica camera, while talking to her subject so that the photographs become part of that conversation.

Russia offered conundrums. Reality was never quite what it appeared. A lifetime of necessary dissembling, of practising survival mechanisms, made it difficult to know the truth about anyone or anything. On a day of heavy snow they visited Ilya Ehrenburg, shortly before his death (he died on 31 August 1967), a man whom Stephen Spender had found uncommunicative when he met him at the International Congress of Writers (a communist-front organization) in Valencia and Madrid in 1937, at the height of the Spanish Civil War.

At that time André Gide had just published his *Retour de l'URSS*, based on his visit to the Soviet Union the previous year. While praising much that went on there, he attacked Stalin's dictatorship and the conditions of the poor. More damagingly, he affected to discover an echo of fascist injunctions to faith and obedience in a country he had believed to be dedicated to freedom and which, of course, was fighting against fascism in Spain. Overnight, he became the enemy. From being hailed as the world's greatest writer, he was, unsurprisingly, suddenly a fascist and a traitor. Ehrenburg, Spender recalled, said nothing as the communist delegates attacked Gide and Trotsky and praised Stalin. It is hard to see, of course, what he expected him to say. Back in Russia and, indeed, in Spain, liquidations were the order of the day.

Ehrenburg had gone to the Spanish Civil War as a journalist, as Miller might have done, and he witnessed the sufferings of those who returned, only to be regarded as traitors. Speaking to Miller in 1967 he recalled those days and the Twentieth Party Congress that had revealed a portion of Stalin's crimes. He claimed that Khrushchev's revelations, however, had underlined not the weakness of the Soviet state but its sense of its own strength. Such revelations, he believed, could only be made by those assured of their own ideas and position. Far from rendering him free to speak, they convinced Ehrenburg that he dared share his mind with no one. The silence that Spender recalled was a survival mechanism long after the 1930s. As Miller admitted, however, it was equally possible to read such silence as evidence of a bad conscience. In not speaking, he did not speak out. A duty was refused. Or perhaps, Miller thought, it was the silence of a man betrayed. Interestingly, in reaching for an analogue to Ehrenburg's stunned response, Miller proposed the idea of a man who falls in love with a seemingly perfect woman who turns insane, a woman to whom he has dedicated his works, his idealistic feelings. The shadow of Monroe had yet to leave him.

There was another, dark, side to Ehrenburg, who wrote a vitriolic wartime pamphlet calling on Russians to kill Germans wherever and whenever they could, deploying a rhetoric so extreme that there were those who would accuse him of inciting the murders and rapes perpetrated by Soviet soldiers as they advanced into Germany.

For Alfred Kazin, who also visited him in Russia, Ehrenburg was more boastful than any other Soviet writer, and had 'played a role (what role? – nobody will say exactly what) when Stalin openly turned on Jews, framed and shot twenty-four of the most prominent Jews in the Soviet Union'. He was a man who had 'not changed anyone's mind about anything. Perhaps,' he added, 'he will be remembered only as one who had the ability to survive.'[12] Howard Fast recalled Ehrenburg's response to an appeal from the Russian poet Itzik Feffer who had stood up for the Jewish-Soviet writer David Bergelson. Ehrenburg refused to join him. 'Then I'll do it alone – and when they arrest me and kill me, my death will be upon your soul for as long as you live!'[13] Feffer, like Bergelson, was killed. Ehrenburg survived. On the other hand, when Pasternak was awarded the Nobel Prize, he refused to join in denunciations. Twenty years after his death, it was revealed that he had willed his archives to Jerusalem's Yad Vashem Library.

For Miller, his visit to Ehrenburg was a reminder of how difficult it was to define the real in a world in which language and silence alike were so deeply compromised. Ehrenburg sat smoking Gauloises, surrounded by paintings, including Picassos. He was free, as other writers were not, to visit foreign countries, and he became something of an intermediary. It is tempting to see in him one source for the figure of Marcus in Miller's 1977 play *The Archbishop's Ceiling*. Set in what is plainly Czechoslovakia, it in part explored the dilemma of the writer in a repressive regime.

By contrast, what Miller found in talking to the widow of Osip Mandelstam – who had once been told by Alexei Surkov, in control of Soviet literature, that 'Pasternak's novel is no good because its hero, Dr Zhivago, has no right to make any judgements about our way of life – "we" had not given him this right'[14] – was a powerful sense of the past, of a Russia for which communism was merely a momentary phenomenon, and one not entirely unfamiliar with authoritarian power. A society that had presented itself as leaning into the future, and which Miller had responded to in part because of that prophetic dimension, was, she explained, rooted in its own history. The irony was that both America and Russia had proposed themselves as exemplary, future-oriented states, but that while America swept the ground behind it as if to insist that it was its own Platonic creation, the Soviets left the evidence of the past and never succeeded in obliterating it from the consciousness of its citizens.

Inge Morath's photographs linger on buildings from another age, on writers' houses, museums, churches, the latter anathematized but still rooted in the mind and spirit no less than in the Russian soil. Though Miller does not say so in the book that resulted from his several trips, during the war the churches had suddenly moved to the centre of people's lives, as German forces moved in on what was then Stalingrad. And the memory of that had not yet faded. For a moment Stalingrad was Petersburg and would become so again by the century's end. Beyond that, and beyond the pictures of the contemporary writers they sought out, Morath's were photographs of what had been lost. Besides a scatter of images of street scenes, in contrast to America largely stripped of traffic and of people going about their daily business, she photographed memories. She turned her lens on stuccoed buildings, on the preserved treasures of another age.

Hers was less the Soviet Union than Russia, and this was the name of the book that came out of these trips: *In Russia*. She and her husband even visited a state horse farm because it was there that she could photograph troikas, driving across the unchanged landscape of a Russian winter, which they associated not with collective farms but nineteenth-century novels. She photographed the palaces and art of earlier centuries, but mostly she focused on the homes of those who had shaped another Russia: Pushkin, Tolstoy, Dostoevsky, Tchaikovsky. In one ironic picture she captures a bust of Gogol, with two dabs of snow where his eyes should be, staring blankly out over the

Workers' Gardens in Leningrad. There is a series of pictures of places associated with Raskolnikov, as if fictive figures had marked the Russian consciousness more completely than the whole panoply of Soviet heroes and
heroines, all absent from her portfolio.

Everyone constructs the countries they visit, finds what they seek,
sometimes even inferring its existence from its very absence. That had
certainly been true of those who visited Russia in the early days of the
Soviet state and returned proclaiming they had seen the future. What
Miller found now was a blend of idealism, a deadening and insensitive
bureaucracy, cynicism, indifference and a qualified hope. He seems to have
embraced those elements that echoed his own predilections. There were
aspects of this Russian visit that echoed the mood back in America when
he returned to battles over Vietnam and Cambodia. Russian distrust of
the autonomy of art, he acknowledged, derived from a sense of present
danger. He found much the same in America in the person of LeRoi Jones
(later Amiri Baraka), for whom literature existed to serve the cause, at that
time black liberation, and later, ironically, Marxist-Leninism. For Miller,
Hollywood's sturdy acquiescence in American pieties was a mirror image
of Soviet cultural conservatism.

Miller and Inge were always conscious of the microphones that must be
presumed to be concealed in the walls and ceilings of the hotels in which they
stayed, the houses they visited. They became used to their hosts turning tape-
recorded music on when they wished to have serious discussions. The result,
Miller found, was surreal, especially if there was a disjunction between the
mood of the music and that of the conversations, which might last two hours
and were conducted in whispers. On one occasion, a man he did not know
entered his hotel room, asking after a daughter he had never met while
handing the startled guest a sheet of paper that asked him to maintain the
conversation while writing out his responses. They continued to talk, handing
pieces of paper back and forth. A decade later, reinforced by a reminder of
such surveillance during a 1969 visit to Vaclav Hável in Czechoslovakia, this
would form another component of *The Archbishop's Ceiling*, in which concealed
microphones would form a key element.

They flew back from their second visit to Russia, Miller noted in the final
paragraphs of the book, to a land of plenty uncertain of its moral direction
and into riots and student protests: 'the blacks and the students hoisting
strange flags on the statues, the magazines announcing revolution in five-
color photos, cities on fire beside the green golf course, more bombs dropping
on one Vietnam than on the whole earth in World War II'. Meanwhile,
'Somewhere in Moscow that writer is standing in a hallway, wondering if he
dare go home.' [15] Beneath their aircraft had lain the dead of wars and revolution, layered history. Treblinka and Auschwitz. Violence suddenly seemed

the common currency of a world that appeared serene only from thirty-five thousand feet.

The visits to Russia in 1965 and 1967 were to prove crucial. Miller immediately began to work to free those imprisoned and ease the situation of those who were oppressed. Writing from Moscow in 1967, Voznesensky thanked Arthur and Inge for the letters and cables they had sent on his behalf: a year later, in writing of the success of *The Price* in Moscow, he confided that he remained metaphorically in chains.

In the 1930s Miller's internationalism had been little more than a romantic association with the cause of the Spanish Loyalists, with the proletariat and then with wartime allies seen at a distance. He had visited France and Italy after the war, partly in a spirit of adventure, partly conducting research. Beyond that, his trips were usually tied to productions of his plays. The 1960s saw a different kind of commitment. If it derived, in some part, from his marriage to Inge Morath, as European history was suddenly earthed in the experiences of this individual, it derived, too, from a new awareness of obligations that transcended those of a country wrapped in its own necessities. PEN opened new doors of consciousness.

The ideological divide between East and West was real enough but so, too, were the shared anxieties and desires. It seemed to him that some terrible balance was being maintained, a balance, though, easily overthrown. In Russia he witnessed repression, but also a sense of resistance; in America a foreign war was beginning to corrode the spirit, to generate demands for a commitment of a kind he had not felt for twenty years. The difference was that where the future had once seemed assured, a utopian vision bright with promise, now there was the smell of apocalypse. As he asked himself, flying west from Russia on his way back to America, 'Is there still, beneath the polemics and the threats, an admitted commerce of a human kind? Or is there truly no fresh wind in any corner of the sky to blow away the fumes of fear we all breathe now, this terror of each other that will finally murder us all?' Recalling Nina's lines from Chekhov's *The Seagull* – "... to endure. To be able to bear one's cross and have faith. I have faith. I'm not afraid of life"' – he added, 'How terrible that seventy years later, seventy years of the most astonishing acquisition of knowledge in man's history, it is so very much harder to speak these lines without fatuousness on this planet.'[16]

In Russia was not well received in the Soviet Union, which immediately banned all his works, partly, perhaps, because a year earlier he had called for the Soviet Union to lift its ban on the works of Aleksandr Solzhenitsyn, though the immediate reason for the ban of *In Russia* itself was, several thought, a photograph of Ekaterina Furtseva, the Minister of Culture whom Miller had taxed with the changes made to the text of the Russian version of *A View from the Bridge*. It was Furtseva who had once told Sviatoslav Richter that he should obey her and represent the Soviet Union abroad. To Yevgeny Yevtushenko the photograph revealed 'the suffering confusion of a woman facing the incompatibility of talent and fate, the constant fear that tormented her soul'.[17] Voznesensky believed the book was banned because it 'revealed a terrible state secret – the number of wrinkles on the face of Minister of Culture Ekaterina Furtseva. The state took offence.'[18] In truth, the meaning comes from the context. Furtseva looks worried and bemused. Perhaps this was, indeed, the reason for the book's banning, though the inclusion of suspect writers would have been enough without that. As it was, the Millers were not the only ones to lose. Later, Furtseva lost her job and reportedly attempted suicide in her bath. Even the most secure could see their power disappear on the wind.

For its part, the US-funded Radio Liberty, as Nathan Abrams has pointed out, broadcast the entire text of *In Russia* in the USSR, sparking official anger, especially at what was seen by officials as its anti-Soviet preface. *Literaturnaya Gazeta* published an article in which Soviet writers denounced Miller, recalling that they had supported him during the McCarthy years.

On his return to the United States in November 1967, Miller wrote to the Soviet premier Aleksei Kosygin explaining his desire for Soviet writers to play a part in PEN. He acknowledged that in the Soviet Union writers tended to be judged in terms of their contribution to the government and to society, and he was not challenging that, but he warned against the damage to the reputation of the state if it took action against them. At the same time he sent a letter to David Carver in which he confessed that his talks with two representatives of the Soviet Writers' Union – B. Rurikof, one-time editor of *Literaturnaya Gazeta*, and Alexei Surkov – had convinced him that nothing could be done, since both favoured censorship and feared the consequences of freedom. He was anxious, though, not to lose whatever leverage PEN might have to protect dissident authors. The question was, what *could* be done? Voznesensky, for example, he noted, was staying out of Moscow for fear of arrest or expulsion from the Writers' Union; deliberately planted rumours of collaboration with the CIA appeared in the provincial press.

Back in America, Vietnam remained at the centre of his attention. When a 10 per cent income tax surcharge was proposed to cover the cost of the Vietnamese conflict, an organization called Writers' and Editors' War Tax Protest sought support from those who would agree not to pay it. One reluctant signer was Norman Mailer, who now wrote to his fellow Brooklynite Arthur Miller in search of 'rich company for my misery'. Writing on 23 October 1967, he pointed out that a signature might lead to real problems: 'It is possible,' he observed, that 'those who take the pledge will have to pay at some indefinite hour in silent steamy sessions with Internal Revenue agents going over one's returns on items that have nothing to do with this. It is yet to be demonstrated,' he added, 'that the Internal Revenue Service is not vindictive.' It was, he conceded, 'an unpleasant test of conscience', not least because its effects might be felt long after the war was over. Yet while 'its fruits suggest chill pleasure', after 'looking for every good, decent, honorable, even specious argument I could find in defense of not joining this tax protest, I succumbed I suspect because of some deep-seated appreciation of the liver that to give an extra 10% to Lyndon Johnson and his fine company of Snopes [a reference to William Faulkner's amoral characters] would prove a penalty greater in its damage to any vested admiration for myself than some haggling sessions with the IRS in years to come."[19]

The letter reached Miller as he prepared to go into rehearsals for *The Price*. He had, he claimed, thought up the notion of withholding the tax himself, but had changed his mind. He was, he explained, generally unembarrassed by gestures but felt that this one was flawed, since the government would surely seize the money anyway, along with 6 per cent interest. There had to be something wrong with this because they would then have *more* money with which to finance the war. He was tempted to suggest that they burn all their money, as the only way to be sure that the government would be frustrated, but such an act would not only be unAmerican, it would be unpolitical – which meant without persuasive force, reeking as it would of plain insanity. It was an elaborate justification for not joining the protest, but his fundamental reason for declining was that he now believed that the time for such oblique gestures had gone. The moment had come for him to leave his desk, following the production of *The Price*, to turn aside from theatre for a while, and enter the political system in some other way than merely putting his cross on a ballot paper or signing yet more protests. Certainly, as judged by an unpublished poem, the war was something more than a political issue to him.

The poem was prompted by a speech by General Westmoreland, who had commanded US troops in Vietnam since replacing General Paul Harkins in 1964. In April 1967 he had addressed Congress, offering a confident account of the war and asking for the commitment of 200,000 men. That November, he declared the end in sight and in an end-of-year report saw a brighter future for the following year. Twenty-nine days later (a week before Miller's *The Price* opened at the Morosco Theater), the Tet Offensive exposed such bland assurances for what they were, as the Vietcong not only staged attacks in Saigon but also penetrated the US Embassy compound. The poem spoke of the need for the poet to say no to the universal yes.

On 12 November Miller joined some of America's leading poets at New York's Town Hall in a capacity event called 'Poets for Peace', sponsored by the Compassionate Arts of the Fellowship of Reconciliation, an international organization founded fifty years earlier. Part of the proceeds was to be used to buy medical supplies for both North and South Vietnamese. Later, a record of the event was released by Spoken Arts. The poets formed a semicircle on stage, stepping forward in turn. Among those appearing were Richard Eberhart, Richard Wilbur, Anaïs Nin, W.D. Snodgrass and Robert Lowell, along with Paul Goodman and Daniel Berrigan. Miller read his poem called 'What Blood-Red Law'. It was inspired, he said, by his reading of Jules Roy's *The Battle of Dienbienphu*, and the poem did indeed trace America's war back to France's colonial battles. Once again, he was intent to show that to understand the present it was necessary to understand history.

After the Fall and *Incident at Vichy* were both written in the shadow of Vietnam. So too was *The Price*. Though looking back to the 1930s, it was nonetheless relevant, Miller said, precisely because of its assertion that the present is explicable only in terms of the past and that the past is easily reinvented to serve present need. It was also about the obligation to assume responsibility for one's actions. To him, America, in Vietnam, was in the business of inventing a history that would justify its actions even as it betrayed its integrity. Denial – as so often in his work – remained a key to private and public action. He later commented:

> You know you have reached a certain age when irony dominates whatever you see. When I spoke and wrote against the Vietnam War, it felt like a rerun of the Spanish Civil War with new actors, a movie of defeat that I'd seen before. In the militancy of the sixties, the black awakening, the thrilling alienation of the times, I saw the seeds of a coming disillusionment. Once again we were looking almost completely outside ourselves for salvation from ourselves; in the absolute right and necessary rebellion was only a speck of room for worrying about personal ethics and our own egoism. At fifty and counting, I tried to block out the echoes of past crusades, but it was impossible. *The Price* was in part an exorcism of this paralyzing vision of repetition.[20]

Miller had been working on *The Price* for many years. Its origins can be traced to a poem in which he assembles some of the constituent parts of the play without as yet seeing what they amount to. The poem refers to a man and his two sons in a room full of furniture, along with the wife of one of them. What, he asks himself, are they doing there, where have they come from and what will they say in this room full of the detritus of the past? Beyond the poem, the Miller papers contain drafts of a work that would eventually split into two different plays: *The Price* and *After the Fall*. In an early version, the character he was then calling Quentin contained elements of both himself and his brother Kermit. It was, he noted, an attempt to end their struggle. Kermit had opted for security but was aware of a deficiency, a lack of drive, which was supplied instead by his wife. He himself had represented something altogether more aggressive, regarding his brother's loyalty to his father as a sign of naivety, even as he was grateful to be relieved of the responsibility himself. The theme of the play, he then thought, was the legitimacy or impracticality of conscience. In other words, it was to be a gesture towards the brother he had left in his wake as he drove towards success. This early in the play's gestation, he was tempted to bring the two figures together into one. In *The Price* they spun off into separate identities.

The play concerns two brothers who meet after a long separation to dispose of the furniture left by their father. Once again there are echoes of the Depression. It was then that the two men had decided to go in different directions, one leaving for university, and an eventual career as a surgeon, the other staying behind to look after their father, later becoming a policeman. Their meeting is a confrontation with the past but it is also a debate about those qualities necessary for their own and their society's survival in the present. And there is an embodiment of that principle of survival in the form of a secondhand furniture dealer brought out of retirement at the age of ninety in order to buy the items piled high in the apartment, the physical expression of a life now lost.

The building in which the play is set is about to be demolished. Along with it will go not just the accumulated furniture of a man now sixteen years dead but also memories that may, we discover, be contested but which contain a key to present discontents. Buildings are easily torn down but the past exerts its presumptive rights.

One of the two brothers who meet to agree on the sale of this compacted history, the policeman, Victor, is a man, we slowly discover, who has lived a life of regret. He apparently abandoned thoughts of his own career in the belief that his father, ruined (as he thought) by the Depression, needed him. He settled for the security of a job with a pension and appears to have spent his life causing as few waves as possible. He has never been promoted and has done nothing to warrant promotion. Like Willy Loman in *Death of a Salesman*, he has lived a temporary life, looking forward to retirement when, he assumes, he will be able to become himself. His one consolation is that he has done his duty, not so much in his profession as towards his father who had, he insists, relied on him.

His brother Walter seems the polar opposite. He is the successful surgeon who has succeeded in cutting money out of people. He exudes condescension, while having an eye to the main chance. The furniture dealer, Solomon, is regarded by him as a potential shyster, an old Jew intent, he believes, on capitalizing on their ignorance. The audience, in other words, seems to be invited to choose between a man who has stood by his father, sacrificing ambition to filial responsibility, and his brother who has made a success out of other people's pain and who seems to have allowed material gain to substitute for the humanity his profession should imply.

By degrees, however, this simple model begins to seem less sustainable. The surgeon has evidently undergone a crisis of conscience and confidence, sensitive to the very charges his brother might be tempted to bring. He makes a clumsy gesture at restitution by suggesting that Victor might work for him, an offer that merely serves to underline the incapacity of a man who had abandoned his formal education. On the other hand, Victor's motives are hardly more secure. He has mythicized the past, reinvented it as a justification for his own failure of will and imagination. The father, we learn, had not been as close to ruin as had appeared and as Victor claims to have believed. He had resources of his own. The furniture, Walter insists, is in itself evidence enough of this. He had been happy to accept his son's sacrifice, but scarcely needed it. On some level it becomes increasingly clear that Victor had been aware of this; he has chosen to dignify his father's failure as an act of fate and his own as a heroic sacrifice to necessity. It is his protection against reality. His wife has chosen alcohol.

The past, in other words, is not as solid and implacable as the pile of furniture suggests. For Victor, it is too painful to be confronted without being retrospectively re-imagined. For Walter, it is the root of a sense of guilt he has been unable to discharge. The two brothers come together in the present but the context for their encounter is the past, which is the true source of their anxiety and meaning.

They encounter one another at a moment of pause. They are paralysed by their own sense of failure, one financial, the other, he suspects, moral. The trauma of thirty years before has left them living lives without real substance. Victor has made himself a victim, exerting no agency in his own life. Walter sees nothing in his success but a reflexive self-concern of a kind that once led him to turn his back on moral demands, which may have been equivocal but which he dealt with by walking away.

The catalyst in their confrontation is the Jewish furniture dealer Solomon. He is summoned back by a telephone call and must now decide whether his life is over or not. That life has been marked by pain. Marriages have come and gone. A daughter has committed suicide. He emerges, though, ironic, detached at first, but finally committed. He is not inclined to deny his life nor, in the end, to regard its meaning as complete. In some ways he is a vaudevillian, a ragged-trousered philosopher viewing the world from the perspective of his ninety years. An immigrant, he has struggled all his life but never surrendered to self-pity. Even now he is not ready to close down on life. He does not deny the past, even though it contains pain enough – he embraces it. That it contains failure, betrayal, denial is a sad truth, but not one that invalidates each day's struggle, each new commitment.

Neither brother is quite what the other assumes. There is guilt on both sides, a feeling of obligation never quite earthed in truth or self-knowledge. Walter denied Victor a loan to enable him to finish college, but did so knowing that his brother was financially supporting a man with four thousand dollars of his own. Victor has come to this encounter not simply to agree on the sale of the furniture but to lay before his brother a sense of grievance that he hopes will prompt an acknowledgement of obligation.

The irony is that the father respected not the son who stayed but the one who left. He admired success even as he was happy to see one of his sons sacrifice it to secure his own comfort. The real pain in their house, all those years before, they finally see, is that there was never any love in it. They were held together by nothing but a kind of mutual need which devolved into moral blackmail. The two brothers are incomplete. They are, Walter realizes, like two halves of the same person and Miller insisted that the world needs the qualities of both men. The selfish, ambitious individual fuels advance, generates progress. The domestic individual consolidates the social world, but challenges nothing. It is as if Ahab and Starbuck were contrastive brothers, as in fact they are in spirit. Miller took pleasure in the audience's oscillating sympathies in a play that he described as being 'without candy'.

The private drama at the heart of *The Price* was initiated by a seismic shift in the social world. It was the collapse of the economic and social system in the 1930s that precipitated the tensions which deformed the lives of the brothers for years to come. For Miller, the 1960s were hardly different. Once again there was a dramatic shift in values. If he was arguing that the roots of Vietnam lay in an unexamined past, he was also conscious that the war was providing the context for private lives that would bear its marks for decades. At a time when the past was declared irrelevant and the moment celebrated, he felt obliged to insist on causality, the logical and moral consequences of past actions. It was in this sense that he claimed *The Price* had an immediate relevance to a war never mentioned by any of its characters.

Writing thirty years later, Miller said that the play was a reaction to two things: 'One was the seemingly permanent and morally agonizing Vietnam War, the other a surge of avant-garde plays that to one or another degree fit the absurd styles. I was moved to write a play that might confront and confound both.'

[The 1960s were] a time when a play with recognizable characters, a beginning, middle and end was routinely condemned as well made or ludicrously old-fashioned ... That beginnings, middles and ends might not be mere rules but a replication of the rise and fall of human life did not frequently come up ... But as the dying continued in Vietnam with no adequate resistance to it in the country, the theater, so it seemed to me, risked trivialization by failure to confront the bleeding, at least in a way that could reach most people.

Conceding now that *Hair* might have done so in offering a laid-back lifestyle as opposed to the aggressive military-corporate one, he nonetheless suggested that

one had to feel the absence – not only in the theater but everywhere – of any interest in what had surely given birth to Vietnam, namely its roots in the past. Indeed, the very idea of an operating continuity between past and present in any human behavior was démodé and close to a laughably old-fashioned irrelevancy. My impression, in fact, was that playwrights were either uninterested in or incapable of presenting antecedent material altogether. Like the movies, plays seemed to exist entirely in the now; characters had either no past or none that could somehow be directing present actions. It was as though the culture had decreed amnesia as the ultimate mark of reality. As the corpses piled up, it became cruelly impolite if not unpatriotic to suggest the obvious, that we were fighting the past.

This piece, written so long after the play's first performance, for all its assertiveness suggests the extent to which both at the time, and thirty years on, he had felt himself at odds with aspects of the American theatre. The word 'old-fashioned' is repeated, less as an acknowledgement of facets of his own work than as a confession of his feeling of rejection. His comments about Vietnam are apt enough, but far sharper than anyone seeing the play would have felt. All the same, still dwelling on his reason for writing the play, he added:

We were fighting in a state of forgetfulness, quite as though we had not aborted a national election in Vietnam and divided the country into two separate halves when it became clear that Ho Chi Minh would be the overwhelming favorite for the presidency ... As always, it was the young who paid. I was 53 in 1968, and if the war would cost me nothing materially, it wore away at the confidence that in the end Reason had to return lest all be lost. I was not sure of that anymore. Reason itself had become unaesthetic, something art must at any cost avoid. *The Price* grew out of a need to reconfirm the power of the past, the seedbed of current reality, and the way to possibly reaffirm cause and effect in an insane world ... If the play did not speak the word Vietnam, it speaks to a spirit of unearthing the real that seemed to have very nearly gone from our lives. Which is not to deny that the primary force driving *The Price* was a tangle of memories of people. Still, these things move together, idea feeding characters and characters deepening idea.[21]

That he should assume that audiences would make the leap between this drama and the war then claiming so many lives perhaps offers more evidence of the fierceness of his political commitments at that moment than of any obvious connection between the two. He certainly felt obliged to gloss the play in articles published both at the time and later. The absurd, in collapsing past and present, except in the ironic *Krapp's Last Tape*, was rejected because it denied causality and hence, along with that, a moral imperative. It is not hard to see, though, why he was conscious that his drama might itself seem to speak of another time.

The past in *The Price*, however, is not some irreducible fact but a territory to be disputed. Despite revelations, confessions, attempts at absolution, neither is there an end to it. For Solomon, it is a refusal of endings that marks him out, while for Esther, Victor's wife, forgiveness still lies ahead, as hoped for and as unrealizable as the green light across the bay seen by Jay Gatsby. *The Price*, in other words, is so much more than Miller's defence would make it seem and so much less than an allegory for the war that he wished to present it as being. He had, after all, been working on it long before the war became an issue.

Like so many of Miller's plays, it had its roots in his personal life. The New York policeman and his elder brother were, he admitted, 'not precise portraits of people I knew long, long ago, but, close enough',[22] (the former was based on his schoolfriend Sidney Franks, himself a policeman) while Gregory Solomon's Yiddish-Russian accent was that of a dealer he had known. He was inclined to deny that the brothers were also modelled on himself and Kermit, but Kermit, and his wife Frances, thought otherwise, as did Miller's sister Joan:

> I remember I was asked if I wanted to understudy. It was late at night and the script had been delivered here [at her Central Park West address] and I sat down to read it at about midnight. It was a thick volume and very verbose, dense ... I was up until about three or four o'clock in the morning reading it and I was so wiped out by it because it was so real for me. The tension between these two characters was so honest and so true and so Arthur and Kermit I didn't dare suggest to him that he really had that relationship because I knew that he would not accept that this had anything to do with him. I guess he had to distance himself from his reality in order to be able to write the play about two brothers. And he was able to that and do it successfully. He seemed to be so honest in this piece and he was brutal with his own character. Kermit was his hero, from the very early years. That he managed [to stand back from this] ... there's something very mystical about that, to put what was a very close relationship – and they really cared for each other – to be able to put that away and somehow transmogrify it ... is very mysterious. He was willing to say that an uncle was his model for Willy Loman – and my uncle's family never really forgave Arthur for writing that

because they never saw their father as he saw him ... and yet he was willing to deny [of *The Price* and *After the Fall*] that this was his life.

Speaking of her brother but also of Eugene O'Neill, she added: 'Writers are very brave to be able to do that. They're not changing [these figures] beyond recognition. People who know them know that these are figures in the writer's life. I don't know how they do that. They were so close.'[23] Like the father in the play, Isidore Miller had had resources of his own, something Kermit claimed to have discovered only several decades later, calling his brother to inform him. When I asked Kermit, in Miller's presence, whether the play reflected their relationship Miller shook his head, but Kermit's wife Frances said, 'Sure.'

The production was not without its problems. The actors – Arthur Kennedy, Kate Reid, Pat Hingle – were frequently at odds with the director, Ulu Grosbard. Indeed, so bad did relations become that in the Philadelphia try-out Miller was forced to take over the direction two days before opening night. He was still rehearsing the company as the preview audience assembled in the lobby when news arrived that David Burns, playing the key role of Gregory Solomon, had been taken to hospital. The understudy stepped in. Twenty years later, Pat Hingle recalled the occasion:

I can't remember (or probably never knew) why the original director was dismissed. I do clearly remember that until Arthur took over I did not feel I knew what the play was about or where my character, Victor Franz, was coming from. If the original director knew, he was not able to communicate it to me; and I was unable to figure it out for myself. I am reasonably sure the other actors were in the same boat. (Maybe not David Burns, who I feel had a special genius for playing Solomon.) Arthur did not restage anything. He did not re-do the show in any way. For me he answered two questions I asked him.

1. What is 'the price'? He believes there is a price you pay for everything you get in life. The 'price' and 'what you get' varies greatly in each individual. And each person has to honestly look into his own soul to know 'the price' and 'what you got'. He alone really knows.

2. What is Victor looking for? Victor knows the price he paid taking care of his father, but he doesn't know what he got from it. And that's his main problem in the play. It took him almost the entire play for him to find out. Once Arthur answered these questions, I could do the rest. I assume he did the same for the other actors. At any rate, when he took the helm, the ship righted itself and we had a hit. *The Price* is the only play of the twenty-two I've done on Broadway where I've communicated directly with the playwright.[24]

The Price ran for 429 performances.[25] It was a major success, but not in the eyes of some of the critics. *Time* magazine dismissed it as 'a museum piece' which, like the sound of the harp played by Victor, was 'slack, jangled and flat'.[26] Three months later, in an article pointing out that no play had been judged worthy of a Pulitzer Prize in the 1967–8 season, the same magazine described it as 'a problem drama calcified in the technique and mentality of the late 1930s'. Miller, its reviewer suggested, had been 'rendered . . . obsolete'.[27] More significantly, he received an ambivalent review in the usually crucial *New York Times*. Clive Barnes, while acknowledging that it was 'superbly, even flamboyantly theatrical', thought it not quite credible, dubiously motivated and contrived. The confrontation between the two brothers was, he thought, 'too rigged, too pat. We are asked to believe too much, and the characters are paper thin. Even the motivation of the story is flimsy, and will bear little surveillance. The details of the story are extraordinarily clumsy.' He had, he said, 'been treated to an extraordinarily diverting show, which was excellent of its kind, but a kind that is itself of less than first importance'. However, he had nothing but praise for the cast and conceded that it was 'a great evening in the theatre'.[28]

The critic Walter Kerr suggested that, at a time when theatre was celebratory, Miller's focus on the over-serious potentially threatened the future of that theatre. It was a strange observation in that *The Price* is one of the funniest of his plays, a work ultimately about survival and reconciliation, both qualities that seemed problematic in 1968. Martin Gottfried dismissed it as 'old-fashioned drama', a melodrama, and Miller himself as a 'slackening artist'. The play was not a story, he objected, but a discussion. The comedy was a 'self-indulgence' and the twists and turns of the plot 'ludicrous and complicated'. It may be, he concluded, 'that the playwright has had his day'.[29] For John Simon the problem was that 'it addresses itself to social problems of the Depression thirty or forty years too late, and in a language that (as usual with Miller) is either trying too hard to be poetry or finding it too easy to be prose'.[30]

Miller summarized his response to the critics in a letter to his old Michigan professor Kenneth Rowe, in which he confessed to confusion over the contradictions inherent in their remarks. It would, he noted, probably take European productions to establish the play. That last comment was a prescient one, in that from this point onwards his career and reputation in America would decline while he would increasingly rely on European productions to validate his work. For the moment, though, he took pride in *The Price* and, despite his forebodings and the negative reviews, it was an undoubted success.

In January 1969 the play was staged in Leningrad, translated by Konstantin Simonov who wrote to Miller enclosing photographs of the production, expressing his admiration and looking forward to welcoming him. Shortly afterwards, Miller's work was banned. Ten years later, on 20 March 1979, as a revival of *The Price* was in rehearsal at the Harold Clurman Theater, Miller once again wrote to Rowe, observing that he remained out of fashion with American critics, who offered him nothing beyond condescension.

In 1968 Miller was aware that the theatre, no less than the society with which it engaged, was in transition. Broadway, in particular, which he had always regarded as the principal venue for his work, was changing, and by 1968 had changed. Despite the success of *The Price*, he felt that his old audience had moved to the suburbs. From the mid-to-late 1960s, it seemed to him,

> you no longer had a coherent middle-class audience ... There were a lot of visitors from out of town ... who were getting cheaper tickets because they were buying them en masse, and there were a lot of business people who were given tickets or who had bought tickets who were in town for two days. Those people are not your audience. They are not interested in life. They want to escape. They are busy making money all day. In the evening they want a good time ... that is not the audience I had known.[31]

New York in the previous decade had seen the rise of Off and Off Off Broadway. Chicago had its equivalent – Off Loop – and in the following decade theatre would decentralize, with new buildings opening in cities across the country. Audiences began to fragment along the lines of gender, nationality, sexual preference and race. The emphasis shifted from the writer to the performer. Indeed, performance became a central trope of society, a fact signalled in 1959 by Erving Goffman's *The Presentation of Self in Everyday Life*. As Miller observed,

> It was hard to understand why, but a strange futility had crept into the very idea of writing a play. I am not sure whether it was the age we were entering or my own evolution, but wherever I looked there seemed to be nothing but theatre rather than authentic, invigorating experience. Practically everything – plays, department stores, restaurants, a line of shoes, a car, a hair salon – was being reviewed as though it had become a self-conscious form of art; and as in art, style was the thing, not content ... In the theatre, it was said, we were in the age of the director, with the playwright his assistant, in effect – but didn't this flow from the fascination not with what was being said but how? The very existence of the playwright was under challenge now ... Only in spontaneity could truth be found, the mind being a congenital liar, and words but persuasive deceits. Gesture, preferably mute, was truth's last refuge, and even there it could only be a suggestion open to all kinds of interpretation, the more the better.[32]

The most influential theatre theoretician of the time was Antonin Artaud, whose *The Theatre and Its Double*, published in America in 1958, had called for a theatre less dependent on language and questions of a social or psychological kind – in other words, Miller's kind of theatre. Another was Jerzy Grotowski. His book *Towards a Poor Theatre*, published in 1968, placed emphasis on the actor, negotiating a unity between the individual and the collective. Peter Brook's *The Empty Space*, also published in 1968, called for 'a language of actions, a language of sound – a language of word-as-part-of-movement, of word as lie, of word as parody, of word as rubbish, of word-as-contradiction, or word-shock or word-cry'.[33]

The state of the theatre, now so at odds with Miller's conception of its role and procedures, seemed to him a reflection of a deeper malaise that had come with violence at home and abroad.

> I was never a Kennedy partisan but it seems more and more possible that the American soul was shot down in those assassinations, and that of Martin Luther King. The unconscious never sleeps, and speaks only rarely, but it governs from its silence. The Vietnam War has hollowed us out far more thoroughly than perhaps we are prepared to acknowledge, and the implacability of the race conflict too. We have been defrauded and defrauded ourselves, to a point, maybe, where art can no longer make believable claims for us. Implicit in any high theatre is a high claim for man, his importance and capacity to renew himself.
>
> The abdication of so many playwrights in deference to directors seems connected with this. The playwright traditionally sought to protect the play's hidden but decisive conception, its thematic coherency; directors and actors were necessarily caught up in sheer behavior, acting rhythm, stage effects – the play's skin. Like so much of social science plays devolute to behaviorism where assertions of value are embarrassing. It is not altogether astonishing when in the larger arena of the world common sense knows that everything exists in order to be contradicted. Thematic coherency is, after all, a species of prediction, regularity, even symmetry.[34]

For Miller, raised on Ibsen, from the beginning placing language at the centre of his work, this was all suspect, as was what he regarded as the romanticism of those who believed they could transform society with theatrical gestures. The Living Theatre, for example, had returned from Paris in 1968, where Jean-Louis Barrault's Odéon theatre had been at the centre of the student rebellion, the participants believing themselves to be leaders of a revolution and the theatre to be its natural expression. Miller, who by chance had himself been briefly in Paris and watched as students threw stones at the police, recognized something of their spirit of rebellion. What this new generation seemed to lack, though, it appeared to him, was a clear politics, while their notion of theatre tended to make the writer redundant and to replace human understanding with gestures.

At the same time, he did see a parallel between the 1930s, the era that had in many ways defined him, and the 60s:

> The Thirties and Sixties 'revolutions', for want of a better word, show certain stylistic similarities and differences. The earlier radical took on a new – for the middle class – proletarian speech, often stopped shaving and wore the worker's brogans and the lumberjack's mackinaw: his tailor, too, was the Army-Navy surplus store. He found black jazz more real than the big band's arranged sentimentality, found Woody Guthrie and Ledbetter and folk music authentic because they were not creations of the merchandizer but a cry of pain. He turned his back, or tried to, on the bounds of family, to embrace instead all humankind ... The goal was the unillusioned life, the opposite of the American Way in nearly all respects. The people were under a pall of materialism, whipped on unto death in a pursuit of rust.[35]

There were differences, too. The thirties radical, faced with a system that had simply stopped, metal grinding on metal, wanted to give power to the masses, restart the machine along the lines exemplified in Soviet Russia or, as he said, 'the pork-chop union leaders and their cigars'. In the 1960s:

> Dope stops time. More accurately, money time and production time and social time. In the head is created a more-or-less amiable society, with one member – and a religion, with a single believer. The pulsing of your heart is the clock and the future is measured by prospective trips, or interior discoveries yet to come. Kesey, who found his voice in the Sixties, once saw America saved by LSD, the chemical exploding the future forever and opening the mind and heart to the now, to the precious life being traded away for a handful of dust ... What had to be projected instead was a human now-ness, Leary's turning on and dropping out, lest the whole dark quackery of political side-taking burn us all in our noble motives. The very notion of thinking, conceptualizing, theorizing – the mind itself – went up the flue.[36]

Miller saw no more hope in this than he did, in retrospect, in the revolution of the 1930s.

> Because a man cries 'Brother!' doesn't make him one, any more than when his father muttered 'Comrade' ... the religious accents of Sixties radicalism were not entirely apart from those of Thirties radicalism ... If the last thing Jesus or Marx had in mind was a new fatalism that was nevertheless what most human beings made of the stringent and muscular admonitions these prophets pronounced and what most of the voyagers into the Age of Aquarius were making ... The latter-day Edenism of the Sixties had a sour flavor, for

me at least: it was repeating another first act of another disillusioned play. I saw the love-girls, free at last, but what would happen when the babies came?[37]

'Scorched by an earlier Inevitable, I shy away from this one,' Miller said.[38] What was missing from this world, it seemed to him, was moral discrimination: 'By means of drugs or prayer or sex, we'll merge all impulses into a morally undifferentiated receptivity to life, and evil will shrivel once exposed to the sun. It is as though evil were merely fear, fear of what we conceal within, and by letting it all hang out we leap across the categories of good and bad.'[39] If he despaired of nihilism he despaired, too, of what seemed the antinomianism of those who met on some spiritual plain on which distinctions had been declared void, and goodness reigned because evil could be wished away with romantic gestures.

Nonetheless, looking back on this time decades later, he acknowledged a miracle in the fact that America did withdraw from Vietnam and Richard Nixon did meet his nemesis, even if 1960s radicalism was simply absorbed into capitalist enterprise, with rock stars worth millions, commerce capitalizing on style while the products of free love were being left parentless and alienated. This, though, lay ahead. For the moment he felt estranged, increasingly aware of repressions abroad which placed those of his own society in perspective, while as the war drew on so flower power gave way to a harder-edged radicalism and he found his own interests intersecting with those from whom he had initially felt alienated.

As the decade progressed and the Vietnam War became a dominant fact, many theatre groups were radicalized, some of them a presence on Vietnam marches, at a time when presence itself became a sign of authenticity. Miller was at odds with some aspects of this but was in tune with those who were challenging the presumptions of a ruling elite on matters of personal freedom, individual rights, political commitments and race. But he also found himself at odds with a new militant generation of black activists who took issue with a work by his neighbour, William Styron, whose novel *The Confessions of Nat Turner* caused considerable offence.

A fictionalized account of the nineteenth-century black slave rebel, it fell foul of a number of black writers who published a counter-attack deploring what seemed to them the distortion of a black cultural hero by a white Southern novelist. When a film was proposed, they managed to block it, and an organization calling itself the Association to End Defamation of Black People wrote to Norman Jewison at United Artists accusing Styron and the film's potential producers of murdering the spirit of Nat Turner by turning a black rebel into 'just another black boy itching to fornicate with white women'. The book was also attacked by the Marxist historian Herbert Aptheker.

Miller felt obliged to respond, wandering into the same racial minefield as his neighbour, in an article he drafted but never published.

The issue turned in part on the fact that Styron had created a Nat Turner who lusted after a white woman, the only person, as it happened, whom he killed. The demand, it seemed to Miller, was that this black hero should be untouched by troubling ambiguities. What it brought to mind was the 1930s and the insistence that art should serve the cause. He recalled, in particular, Communist Party assaults on Richard Wright's *Native Son*, whose central character Bigger Thomas had also felt attracted to a white woman and who was presented as intellectually inadequate. What was required then, and it seemed to him was being required again, was an art whose form and content were to be determined by social and political necessities.

He recalled, too, the attacks on Ernest Hemingway for his portrait, in *For Whom the Bell Tolls*, of the cruelties perpetrated by those on the Republican side during the Spanish Civil War. The truth of art, Miller insisted, could never be the mere product of ideology. It was, after all, why he had ended his own flirtation with the Party. Assaults on *Nat Turner* seemed to be of a piece with these earlier examples, not least because this was once again a revolutionary period, even if this one lacked a coherent and sustaining philosophy. But in a sense he was missing the point. The attacks on Styron had less to do with the figure of Nat Turner, about whom relatively little was known – and that, largely through the original 'Confessions', themselves refracted through a white Southern author. They were more to do with who had the right to tell the story of black Americans. It was of a piece with changes in the struggle for black rights which had seen a shift from interracial organizations to those dominated by black leaders, from demands for integration to assertions of racial consciousness and the consolidating of the ghetto.

Miller, though, was resisting what seemed to him to be demands for inspiriting melodramas, an exemplary art sacrificing truth to desire. He praised Mikhail Sholokhov for his efforts to infuse humanity even into those who appeared to block the path to what was presented as progress, no matter how ambiguous that notion itself would turn out to be. To Miller, the attacks on Styron were also reminiscent of the furore consequent upon what seemed to him to be Hannah Arendt's suggestion that in one sense the Jews in Nazi Germany had been accomplices in their own deaths, despite his own anxieties in this regard. Those who attacked her, he felt, did so because they had no conception of what it meant to live under a totalitarian government, with its pressure towards quietism and adaptation. There had, he acknowledged, been Jewish rebellions, but for the most part it was the erosion of hope that distorted the sensibility. Thus Styron's Turner was not only a rebel but also a man whose psychology had been deformed by the pressures brought to bear, by the hopelessness of the rebellion on which he was nonetheless embarked. Now, living in a time in which rebellion seemingly had its force, it was difficult to conceive of a time when things were otherwise. Solidarity is an appealing slogan. But potentially it does violence to that human distinctiveness it is supposedly designed to protect.

Miller evidently decided not to publish the article, though it ran to many pages. He anyway had other commitments in this *annus mirabilis* that would take him away from his desk. In a remarkable year, art and politics seemed to come into alignment to a degree that had not been achieved since the 1930s, and it is hardly surprising to find him making a connection with that earlier period. Once again he found himself working with others to change the direction of his society, and the question of art's role was squarely on the agenda. *The Confessions of Nat Turner* won the Pulitzer Prize and became a bestseller.

The Price now a Broadway hit, he turned aside from theatre and followed the logic of his convictions, committing himself not merely to protests against the war but to political action, visiting Paris – where peace talks were under way – and appearing as a delegate at the Democratic National Convention, an event shaped by Vietnam where 25,000 American lives had already been lost. The war, clearly, was doing something more than sap morale; it was eroding the country's moral values. In February 1968, television stations aired film of a South Vietnamese police chief shooting a Vietcong suspect in the head. In March, Walter Cronkite, the CBS news anchorman, denounced the war on air in his report, while in Vietnam itself Charlie Company of Task Force Baker entered the hamlet of My Lai and slaughtered an estimated two hundred people, mostly old men, women and children. Ahead lay assassinations and widespread domestic violence.

Despite his opposition to the war, Miller, though, refused to compromise PEN by agreeing to accept a resolution, dated March 1968, from the East German Centre, which had stated:

> For years US troops have been destroying palaces and pagodas, museums and libraries in Vietnam. However, they destroy more than shrines and treasures of an ancient culture. They who pretend to save civilization are about to eliminate the present and future of this culture. Their targets are not individual artists and writers. They are about to eradicate an entire nation with all its talents of today and tomorrow. Anyone who remains silent, shares the guilt. We appeal to all PEN societies and International PEN to call a halt. We request them to lodge protests with the President and the Government of the United States.[40]

Among the signatories was the German writer Christa Wolf who, after the fall of the Wall in 1989, was found like many others to have been an informer for the Stasi. The document was accompanied by a wide-ranging critique of PEN's actions, and complaints about travel restrictions placed on East German writers by NATO countries. Miller sent a reply, regretting that he would be unable to attend the PEN executive committee meeting to be held in London but outlining his objections. On 24 March he wrote to Professor Heinz Kamnitzer, Vice-President of the East German Centre, pointing out that he had opposed the war from the beginning and accepted that it was clearly the most significant issue then confronting the world. He also acknowledged that most PEN members were opposed to it. However, he insisted that were the motion to be accepted, it could threaten the existence of PEN by politicizing it. The result, he added, could only be the kind of stalemate that then characterized the United Nations.

As an example, he suggested that the West German Centre might condemn some action of the DDR on the grounds that it affected writers, along with others. He noted that the East German Centre had also complained, in a message directed to the International Executive Committee of PEN, about what it saw as an undue emphasis on the treatment of writers in the Soviet Union, especially when such writers had been subject to legal proceedings. Miller was unequivocal in his reply, pointing out that PEN was at that time also protesting about the imprisonment of Greek writers. He also denounced the self-evident inadequacies and political corruptions of Soviet justice, most particularly in the case of Sinyavsky and Daniel. Adroitly, he regretted the failure of the DDR Centre to identify those South Vietnamese writers who, he felt sure, must be suffering. In fact, in May 1969 PEN would send a telegram to the South Vietnamese Prime Minister Tran Van Huong Nguyen, protesting against the imprisonment of Pham Viet Tuyen, a professor and journalist (who, after the fall of Saigon, moved to France, where he died in 2009).

It was a shrewd response to a patently political document. He had plainly learned much about dealing with the East in those three years. The DDR resolution was rejected by the executive committee, prompting a further response from Heinz Kamnitzer in which he objected to the cases of Greek and Soviet writers being linked together; a pamphlet issued by PEN had given greater prominence to photographs of the Soviets. At the same time he agreed to undertake further investigation of the plight of South Vietnamese writers which, he suggested, had not been addressed by PEN.

David Carver dismissed the East German claims, more especially because of the role he saw the DDR playing with respect to Czechoslovakia, which he described as 'particularly foul'. Expressing the hope that the Czechs would 'get away' with their revolution, he recognized that the British government 'is being attacked for being so spineless. We have a rather dreadful record on Czechoslovakia, which many of us contemplate with considerable distress.'[41]

Plainly Miller and, indeed, Carver (who wrote to Miller on 22 July conveying his sense of what he called the tragedy of Robert Kennedy's death and expressing his hope that Eugene McCarthy would be elected) had their own views of the situation in Vietnam, but they were agreed that to allow PEN to be used in this context would destroy it.

Miller continued to be extremely active in PEN, particularly with respect to imprisoned writers. In November 1968, on receiving news that he might be in imminent danger, he would call on writers to send birthday greeting to Aleksandr Solzhenitsyn. The same year he also received a telephone call from Mexico City, asking him to intervene in the case of José Revueltas, a Marxist writer arrested following demonstrations. Inge, who spoke fluent Spanish, took the call, having been warned that the line was probably tapped. The Mexican police, Miller knew, had killed a number of people. With the Olympics due to start on 10 October, a student movement had planned the demonstrations. Secret cables were sent from the US Embassy and the CIA to a nervous White House. The Mexican government, under Díaz Ordaz, saw the hand of the Soviet Union and Cuba at work. A telegram from the Embassy to the Department of State seemed to endorse this.

In August the CIA reported a possible attempt by the Cuban government to smuggle arms to the students. Following the killings, however – the government put the number of dead at twenty-seven; Robert Service, then a diplomat at the Embassy, at two hundred – these reports were discounted in a further cable from the Embassy. Revueltas was accused of being the author of the student movement. In December, Miller wrote to the President of Mexico objecting to his arrest and detention, and later called for a worldwide protest. For his part, while in jail Revueltas wrote his popular book, *El Apando* ('The Thief'), published the following year.

In the October–December issue of *La Pajarita de Papel* Miller published his letter to Ordaz, stating:

> The work and name of Revueltas are widely known and it is quite evident that his arrest has drawn deeply concerned attention from many quarters. I wish to ask, Mr President, for your personal intercession so that he may be liberated as quickly as possible ... The continued imprisonment of Señor Revueltas, according to the many communications I have been receiving, appears to contradict and nullify your Government's stated commitment to dialogue and a reasonable solution ... I ask you to do all in your power to terminate the detention of José Revueltas.[42]

On 7 January 1969 he would write to his old friend Harrison Salisbury asking him to contact any friends he might have in Mexico City to establish the current situation, while noting that that morning he had himself received a call informing him that Revueltas had now been deprived of books and that the screws seemed to be tightening on him.

It was in 1968 that Miller approached the Mexican novelist and playwright Carlos Fuentes in the hope that he might take over as President of International PEN. In some ways it was a curious invitation, given that Fuentes was denied access to the United States. Invited by NBC in 1962 to debate with Richard Goodwin, then Under-Secretary of State for Latin America, he accepted, only to be denied a visa by the American Embassy. Asked why, its officials refused to answer. Four years later PEN had succeeded in gaining entry for him on the occasion of their New York Congress, but when he tried to enter Puerto Rico in 1967 he was again refused (under the McCarran-Walter Act of 1952, which denies visas to 'unwanted persons'), securing entry only when Senator Fulbright intervened. When Miller invited him, therefore, Fuentes declined, explaining that he was in contention with his own government, was persona non grata in the United States, at odds with the Soviet Union after the invasion of Czechoslovakia (and hence persona non grata there as well) and opposed to the Cuban government. In the circumstances, he suggested, he would probably not make a good choice (and not least because of his dislike of air travel). A decade later he was made Mexican Ambassador to France, resigning when Díaz Ordaz was made Mexican Ambassador to Spain.

To succeed him as President of International PEN Miller then suggested another Mexican writer, Octavio Paz, who that same year resigned from the diplomatic service when the Mexican Army opened fire on the demonstrators in the Plaza de las Tres Culturas in Mexico City. Miller was anxious to choose a Latin American. In the end, however, he was prepared to back Ignazio Silone, an excellent writer who opposed the Vietnam War but who had been a member of the CCF, creating the magazine *Tempo Presente* under their auspices. Edward Shils described him as a man who 'almost single-handedly' had been conducting 'courageous and lonely battles for a liberal and humane standpoint against the solid mass of rancorous and unsparing enemies – Communists, fellow travellers, *naïfs*, and *badhats*'.[43]

Miller, though, was worried what the East German response might be. In fact the new President turned out to be not Silone but the French poet, Pierre Emmanuel (real name Noël Mathieu), who would serve until 1971 and who was also a member of the CCF, staying on after the revelations of CIA funding, though angry at his own manipulation.

When Miller was approached, three years later, for his view on the two candidates then standing for the presidency, the choice lay between a second term for Emmanuel, a member of the Académie Française, unsurprisingly backed by the French, and Heinrich Böll. Miller favoured the latter, but in a letter to David Carver dated 4 August 1971 he asked that his support be kept secret. In the end on a mail vote the national Centres split 16 votes to 16. The decision was left to the Dublin Congress, at which the French repeatedly challenged the vote, staging a vociferous protest when Böll was elected by 24 votes to 20. They were unhappy that David Carver had counted the ballots, but when they were recounted, the result was the same. According to Thomas Fleming, then President of American PEN, the French then sent a delegate from the Ivory Coast to the platform. He seized the ballots, only to have Carver snatch them back. Emmanuel then called for a further recount.

Whatever the circumstances of Miller's own election in 1965, he had undoubtedly taken a largely moribund organization and made it not only a vibrant and effective forum for writers from around the world, including those previously excluded, but also an effective voice on behalf of imprisoned writers. The rapprochement with Russian authors, for which he had hoped, had not come about; indeed, their invitations to the Geneva Congress had been revoked. Censorship was intensifying, something of which he was aware in terms of his own work. The Leningrad production of *The Price* was having trouble with the censor, in part, he guessed, because the figure of Solomon, the old Jew, was too favourably drawn. Nevertheless, he had managed, in the most troubled decade, to prevent PEN being directly embroiled in the political issues then splitting the world. Despite his own fierce opposition to the Vietnam War, he had refused to allow it to become an instrument of political resistance.

If those who had covertly funded PEN had hoped that American leadership would enhance national cultural prestige, they too must have felt satisfied, until Miller became the focus of opposition to the war. By 1969, though, they seem no longer to have felt the need to boost PEN's funds. Certainly, when Böll took over it was already in financial difficulties.

In his autobiography *Timebends*, Miller claims to have received a call in 1970 from the Revd Sloane Coffin, Chaplain to Yale University, whom Norman Mailer once described as equal parts union organizer and Ivy League crew coach, and who described himself as a 'yellow dog Democrat'. As he recalled, it was then that Coffin, who was to become a key friend over the following decades, urged him to speak against the war in a demonstration to be held at the university. It seems likely, however, that Miller was confusing this with a call he received at the end of February 1968 which had led to his appearance, with Coffin, at a rally on the New Haven Green on 2 March that year. In front of a crowd of five thousand, he attacked American policy in Vietnam and endorsed the candidacy of Eugene McCarthy. Coffin was already famous for taking part in the freedom rides to Montgomery, Alabama, in 1961. He was to be at the heart of the resistance to Vietnam, urging students to burn their draft cards.

Coffin had served under Patton in the Second World War, having, he later recalled, convinced a drunken commandant that he had a facility with languages on the basis of his ability to sing two Russian songs in the original. One of his jobs at the end of the war, for which he subsequently felt considerable guilt, was repatriating Russian soldiers in the knowledge that their fate was likely, at the very least, to be deeply unpleasant. It was this guilt and the hatred he had learned for the Soviet system that in 1949 took him to the Waldorf Conference, at which Miller delivered his swansong as a Stalinist, and that in 1950 led him to join the CIA. He was stationed in West Germany. His work for the Agency involved attempts to encourage and ferment a political underground in Russia, a project that proved an almost total failure. Hundreds of CIA agents were sent to their deaths. Nonetheless, he had seen the Agency as winning a considerable victory, using the Non-Communist Left to beat the communist Left – in other words to beat the likes of Miller. Vietnam, however, along with American interventions in Africa and Latin America, had changed his mind (though as early as 1953 he had left the CIA).

Thereafter, he dedicated himself to the civil rights movement. In 1961 he had gone to Mississippi with the Freedom Riders and had been arrested and convicted for violating local Jim Crow laws, before being cleared by the US Supreme Court. Now Vietnam had become his principal cause. In 1968 he was indicted before a federal grand jury, charged with conspiracy to counsel and abet draft resistance. He was found guilty, but in 1969 the conviction was reversed on appeal. He was fond of reminding hostile audiences that Abraham Lincoln had opposed the war in Mexico in 1847, then asking whether he had been unpatriotic to do so. In the end, Coffin would serve eighteen years as chaplain at Yale. Subsequently, he would appeal for the release of Soviet writers and be a leader of the anti-nuclear movement.

He was, in short, a 'turbulent priest' and a natural friend for a turbulent playwright. Asked to define his philosophy, he quoted Oliver Wendell Holmes's observation that not to share in the activity and passion of your time is not to have lived. His friendship with Miller would last nearly four decades. Later he would officiate at the wedding of Rebecca and Daniel Day-Lewis. For the moment, though, he was the inspiration for Gary Trudeau's cartoon figure in his strip 'Doonsbury', the 'counter-culture priest', the Revd Scot Sloane.

Shortly after his appearance at Yale, Miller wrote to the Anglo-Irish writer James Stern expressing his belief that the war lay at the heart of a wider corruption: 'The war is a cancer ... eating us alive ... You can't open a paper anymore without reading about some big executive or other turning out to be a Mafia member or a crook. The young people are almost entirely alienated and the smell of marijuana is all over. I spoke at Yale last week about the war but nobody upstairs is listening to anything but the generals' demands for still more troops. It's all a dream – nobody believes in the war and nobody can stop it!'[44]

On the evening of 31 March 1968, President Johnson in a television address had announced, 'I shall not seek, and I will not accept, the nomination of my party for another term as president.'[45] It was the second of two alternative endings to his speech, the first committing him to seek a second term. Vice-President Humphrey had been called with the news that it was to be the second version he would deliver. His decision seems to have been triggered partly by exhaustion, but partly by an awareness that he might well lose. Signs from Wisconsin, where the next primary was to be held, were not good. In the end, on 2 April Senator Eugene McCarthy scored 412,160 votes against the President's 253,696.[46] Either way, Johnson was out of the race, leaving the peace candidates, McCarthy and, soon, Bobby Kennedy, battling against the Vice-President. When Bobby entered the race, his brother Edward was opposed to it, remarking that 'Bobby's therapy is going to cost the family $8,000,000'.[47]

In New York on his first visit to America, for the opening of his play *The Memorandum*, Václav Havel went to see Miller's *All My Sons* then delayed his departure to take part in a demonstration of over a hundred thousand people in Central Park protesting against the assassination of Martin Luther King and in support of civil rights. In May, Havel returned to Czechoslovakia and the Prague Spring that would be snuffed out on 21 August when Soviet troops invaded. Miller would meet him the following year and in 1977 base a character on him in *The Archbishop's Ceiling*.

The anti-war movement, meanwhile, was breaking old allegiances and forming others. Such significant figures as Arthur Schlesinger Jr, John Kenneth Galbraith and Richard Goodwin, all members of Americans for Democratic Action (ADA), had met in 1966 and decided to work together to try to end the war. The events of 1965 had changed their sense of the nature of the conflict. In June 1966, a peace candidate had received 45 per cent of the vote in a Democratic primary in the Seventh Congressional District in California.[48] Students were by now in open revolt. In 1967 Joe Rauh, of the ADA, and Miller's lawyer when he appeared before HUAC, wrote a paper calling for an end to the war.

Mary McCarthy flew to Hanoi, arriving in a Chanel suit and carrying many suitcases. When she published an account of her visit, the book opened with letters between herself and the critic Diana Trilling which revealed that even now old battles had not been forgotten but had simply found a new arena. McCarthy had proposed a unilateral withdrawal by America. Trilling, though herself against the war, objected that she would be abandoning America's loyal friends and leaving South Vietnam to the communists. In reply, McCarthy invoked the arguments that had divided the Left in the 1940s and 50s and which had ensnared Miller, damaging his reputation. Mary McCarthy, along with others, had attacked those like Miller at the Waldorf Conference for being fellow travellers. Now, effectively accused of the same offence, she responded not simply by defending her stance over Vietnam but, oddly, by attacking the very New York Intellectuals with whom she had once made common cause, even summoning into her argument Soviet dissidents. 'The imminent danger for America,' she declared,

> is not being 'taken in' by Communism (which is what [Diana Trilling] is really accusing me of – that I have forgotten the old lessons, gone soft), but being taken in by itself ... if as a result of my ill-considered actions, world Communism comes to power, it will be too late then, I shall be told, to be sorry. Never mind. Some sort of life will continue, as Pasternak, Solzhenitsyn, Sinyavsky, Daniel have discovered, and I would rather be on their letterhead, if they would allow me, than on that of the American Committee for Cultural Freedom, which in its days of glory, as Mrs Trilling will recall, was eager to exercise its right of protest on such initiatives as the issue of a US visa to Graham Greene and was actually divided within its ranks on the question of whether Senator Joseph McCarthy was a friend or enemy of domestic liberty.[49]

The war, meanwhile, seemed to have an impetus of its own and so long as Johnson was prosecuting it with vigour, if not conviction, there seemed no way in which the political ship could be turned around. Robert Kennedy had kept his distance. George McGovern had shown no interest. Only Eugene McCarthy had picked up the banner. Now, though, things were different.

McCarthy, too, was different. He was a politician who wrote and quoted poetry. For Robert Lowell, he was 'a lost-cause man' not 'much interested in the vote-getting boasts, which probably someone else had written for him'.[50] Lowell nevertheless supported him, campaigning in New Hampshire. Kennedy thought McCarthy lazy and vain. When the latter announced his candidacy for the presidency at the beginning of December 1967, though, he genuinely seems to have been motivated by a moral imperative. 'There comes a time,' he said, 'when an honorable man simply has to raise a flag.'[51] His daughter was already working for the peace movement. In the end he opted to go with her version of politics.

At first, it seemed a maverick move. The President was the incumbent, with the power of the party machine behind him. McCarthy was even disinclined to take part in the New Hampshire primary, planning to reserve his efforts for more significant states; but the party machine was less commanding there and he was persuaded to run, though privately Robert Kennedy told him that he was himself considering running in the spring primaries. Somewhat surprisingly, McCarthy replied that he was seeking only one term and that Kennedy could be next in line, a reply which baffled Kennedy, who indicated to friends that he would step forward if McCarthy could be persuaded to withdraw. On 12 March 1968 came the result of this, the first primary. Johnson had won with 49 per cent but just behind him on 42 per cent was McCarthy. Republican write-in votes reduced the margin to under 1 per cent. Ahead lay a series of primaries in which suddenly the President seemed vulnerable: hence his withdrawal, which left everything to play for.

It is true that he was swiftly replaced by his Vice-President, the liberal and ADA member Hubert Humphrey (enthusiastically supported by James T. Farrell, former chairman of the CCF), who was nonetheless ostensibly as much in favour of the war as Johnson. The certainties, however, had dissolved. Everything seemed possible. It certainly appeared so to Robert Kennedy who, four days after the New Hampshire poll, announced his own candidacy – it seemed to many, capitalizing on McCarthy's success. There was a scramble to get him on to the ballot in the remaining primaries.

The tide began to turn in early May with Indiana, where Kennedy secured 42.3 per cent to McCarthy's 27 per cent, and Nebraska, where Kennedy scored 51.7 per cent, to McCarthy's 31.2. Oregon, though, was natural McCarthy territory. He won by 46 per cent to Kennedy's 36. Next came California. As Robert Lowell, who travelled with him for a month and a half, observed, 'It didn't strike me that McCarthy could be President. I was surprised when he carried Oregon and northern California against Bobby Kennedy. I could feel the excitement of that, and maybe thought we were riding a high tide. I wrote a poem to him that midsummer ... "Coldly willing to smash the ball past those in the park". There was allure in having a friend whose shadow had fallen like a hand on the handle of the grindstone.'[52]

As far as Arthur Miller was concerned, though, the story had begun in Connecticut, a state with a powerful Democratic machine which by 1968 had been in the hands of the same man, a Hartford-Irish lawyer, John Morgan Bailey, for twenty years. The process whereby the McCarthy forces came to challenge this system was lucidly explained by a team of British journalists writing for the *Sunday Times* who went on to produce a major study of the 1968 elections: *An American Melodrama*.

In December 1967 a group had met at Yale University to discuss a possible McCarthy campaign. They discovered that a new system for choosing convention delegates had been introduced thirteen years earlier, but never used. Under this, the 169 towns of Connecticut could select delegates to the state convention, where final decisions about representation at the Democratic National Convention in Chicago would be made. As the authors of *An American Melodrama* explain, in towns of under five thousand, such as Roxbury, delegates would be chosen by a caucus. To general astonishment, on 10 April 1968 'more than forty-four per cent of the Democrats who voted in primary elections in thirty-one large Connecticut towns – primaries that most residents of the state had never realized they could have – were for McCarthy'.[53] Not that that meant they would necessarily secure significant representation in Chicago – that would depend on the bargaining to be done at the state convention in Hartford.

To his surprise Miller was nominated as a delegate by the Roxbury Democrats. As he recalled,

> The Roxbury Democrats, fifty or so people of whom only a handful were known to me, sat listening expressionlessly in the tiny wooden town hall as I explained that since I had no parliamentary experience they would be much better served by electing my neighbor, a dairy farmer named Birchall, a party regular with whom I was in a dead tie. I did not think by this time that my participation was really going to slow the war, but they had another ballot and I won by one vote. It pleased me to think I had bred such confidence in the town, for I rarely left my land to mix in its affairs.[54]

He and his fellow candidate had been called on to set out their positions on major issues. Miller later described the occasion:

> My opponent ... said very little, since all present were aware he would follow the Johnson–Humphrey leadership. In my turn I said what they also knew, that I was for McCarthy and a pullout from Vietnam, notwithstanding which I was prepared to stand down in favor of my friend, who, apart from keeping the roads clean, had worked his head off over the years for any and all Democrats. Privately, I had no hope whatever that the McCarthy delegates could make a dent in the party's coming decisions, so that my election, apart from as a minute effect as propaganda against the war, seemed an injustice, however remote, to this long-time laborer in the party vineyards ... I won the honor by two votes [his winning margin had doubled in his memory between 1967 and 1987]. Dazzled by this unexpected dawning of a political career into which I had entered by attempting to exit, the embarrassing truth finally struck me. I had all but forgotten that actual living individuals are supposed to decide the fate of this country, and with enough determination might, from time to time, even manage to do so. Deferring to my friend was irresponsible and maybe worse, a surrender to cynicism about the democratic process itself.[55]

It was not a position he had sought and not one he would have been too anxious to embrace, had it not been for the fact that the American attitude to Vietnam might well be decided at the Democratic National Convention in Chicago. The Tet Offensive had finally exposed the truth of affairs. It was clear that the war was being lost, and a large numbers of lives with it. In the draft of an article called 'Are Facts the Same as Truth?' he noted that, following the Tet Offensive, in which thirty-five Vietnamese cities had been attacked simultaneously, the so-called Pacification Programme had, in the Administration's view, been 'set back'. In other words, control of much of the countryside had been lost. Tet showed that the cities themselves were no longer secure. Miller had not doubted that the war was militarily winnable. Now he was inclined to believe he had been wrong. He had watched television pictures of helicopter gunships firing down into Saigon's streets. Those supposedly being liberated were now in the line of fire and had presumably colluded with the Vietcong forces that had infiltrated the city. For Miller, it brought to mind his trip to Bled where he had visited a museum in which German wartime notices had shifted from announcing their friendship for the people of Yugoslavia through to warnings that intensified with the passing months until reprisal shootings were detailed. The German public, he recalled, had been baffled by attacks on their troops, having themselves accepted the propaganda fed to them that they were in Yugoslavia as liberators.

McCarthy made his first visit to Connecticut in February 1968, drawing more people to his rally than John Bailey did to a fund-raiser. On 3 April he returned. That January, Bailey had insisted that the National Convention was effectively over. Lyndon Johnson would have the nomination. McCarthy now announced: 'You only need a strong organization when you don't have people who can make independent judgments.' A week later, the Connecticut primaries revealed his widespread support.

On 15 May Miller attended a meeting of Democratic delegates in Woodbury, a few miles from Roxbury. In his notes he commented on the theatricality of the occasion – the chairman, a man who had been defeated in an election for chief dog-catcher, sitting under a reflector light in a manner that struck Miller as very Brechtian. In his speech supporting a peace resolution Miller stated that, quite apart from the innate evil of the war, it was a distraction from necessary social reforms within the country, reforms having to do, in particular, with the plight of black Americans.

He pointed out that McCarthy, with little money and without the backing of the Democratic machine, had won considerable support in the country, as evidenced most recently by his victory in New York. If the Democratic Party did not change its policies, he insisted, then it could not hope to win a national election. The war was a cancer. He recalled Dwight Eisenhower's victory over Adlai Stevenson, won with a promise to end the Korean War. While declaring that he was not a political person (an odd remark given his history), he had agreed to become a delegate because no one seemed to be listening. He was offering a resolution, he went on, because he did not want the young to see politics as a kind of game played by professionals who closed their eyes to realities. It was for the Democratic Party, the party of Roosevelt, to commit itself to securing peace, which would in turn enable it to rebuild America.

On 19 May, Miller appeared at a rally for McCarthy at Madison Square Gardens, an event, the *Nation* observed, which was largely ignored by the press. Each speaker was allotted four minutes – two more, Miller told the crowd, than he needed. The speech he gave was perhaps beyond the ability of the press to précis as he presented resistance to the Vietnam War as one aspect of a worldwide revolution. It is hard to imagine what the gathered crowds thought – perhaps it was the tone, the feeling of solidarity with a generalized rebellion that appealed. In any event, it was hardly a conventional rallying cry for his chosen candidate. The *Nation* reprinted part of it in its June issue. He supported McCarthy, Miller said,

> because I am sure that without him there would be no talks in Paris now [Averell Harriman and Cyrus Vance were negotiating with the North Vietnamese] ... without him, Hubert Humphrey would still be reminding us of the fine things Johnson was doing for the country, and Senator Kennedy's opposition to the war would still not have prevented him from urging everyone to support Johnson ...
>
> From Moscow to Warsaw to Prague to Paris to Rio to Berkeley and New York, there is a deep and boiling rebellion against institutions and institutionalized feeling. Be it a government, a university, a moral code or a way of life, the institution as king is naked now. The mere fact that it exists is no longer proof of its value. In the past four years the war in Vietnam has become an institution, an institution with high, private sacred ceremonies of death and sacrifice, and all the sanctification of a holy crusade. Now, you can criticize an institution, you can suggest improvements and even point out its failings, but there is one thing you dare not do excepting at the risk of your public life, and that is to ask why it should exist at all ... The next President is going to face a revolutionary country and a world in revolution, and he will need a lot more than gallantry. He will need the habit of mind to perceive in the institutions he leads what is dead and inhuman and must be dismantled. The next President will not be able to lead by consensus, by the expert manipulation of opinion, or by calls for unity, however passionate. For our disunity has been institutionalized into this country and this world by virtue of the rule of the contented over the desperate. A unity based on injustice cannot last and it ought not to last.
>
> The next President will have to weigh every action for what it will do to people. Every one of the candidates in this campaign knew perfectly well what the Vietnam War was doing not only to the Vietnamese but the American people. Why did they not speak directly to this issue? Because the institution of war in Vietnam was sacrosanct, it was forbidden territory.

Forbidden to all but one who dared to stand and face that frightful juggernaut
while the others were on their knees thinking their private thoughts.[56]

It is hard to see how McCarthy recommended himself as a leader of a
revolutionary country. His skills lay in the quiet statement of moral principles.
The cause gave him a fiercely loyal and enthusiastic following, but he was
hardly offering himself as a challenge to all forms of government or institutionalized values.

Robert Lowell, one of a number of writers who put their energy behind
his campaign, sent a cable to his fellow poet Richard Wilbur, urging his
support:

EUGENE MCCARTHY CAN AND MUST WIN IN CALIFORNIA. WE
URGENTLY APPEAL TO YOU TO SPEAK THERE ON HIS BEHALF. THE
VOICE OF THE EASTERN INTELLECTUAL COMMUNITY CAN INFLUENCE
MORE VOTES AND IMPEL MORE POLITICAL ACTION IN CALIFORNIA
THAN THE APPEARANCE OF A MOVIE STAR. AT NO OTHER TIME AND
IN NO OTHER PLACE IN THE CAMPAIGN HAVE YOU BEEN SO NEEDED.
BILL STYRON, ARTHUR MILLER, JULES FEIFFER AND I ARE GOING TO
OREGON THIS WEEKEND AND THEN ON TO CALIFORNIA. WILL YOU
JOIN US?[57]

Whether California was eagerly awaiting the arrival of the eastern intellectual
community must be in doubt, but Miller followed the McCarthy campaign
there in May 1968, and on his return to the East Coast, two days before the
televised debate between McCarthy and Kennedy, jotted down his thoughts
about the candidates. Humphrey, it seemed to him, was intellectually compromised and bankrupt. His claim for support lay in his stress on continuity,
on his inheritance of the trappings of power. He was undignified. Kennedy
also depended on a sense of continuity, in his case dynastic. His virtues were
that he seemed willing to engage with those problems ignored by Humphrey,
to do with race and poverty. Personally attractive and passionate, he had a
vision for America which went beyond that offered by McCarthy. His vacil-
lation, however, as demonstrated by his precipitate entry into the race after
the New Hampshire primary, having previously supported the administration,
had left a taint of opportunism. It was McCarthy who had moral primacy.
At the same time there was something patrician about McCarthy. He seemed,
at times, more concerned with the single issue of Vietnam than with being
elected, though his seeming conservatism of manner appeared to offer his
primary hope of wider appeal.

The California primary was plainly going to be crucial. Kennedy and
McCarthy appeared to be dead-heating. Having resisted proposals for a head-
to-head debate, Kennedy now changed his mind, and on 1 June they duly

met, though the ABC *Issues and Answers* programme offered less a chance to debate than to engage in what McCarthy called 'a kind of joint press conference'.[58] Characteristically, while Kennedy actively prepared for it, even cancelling a breakfast meeting with union leaders, McCarthy, though he had done some homework, in fact came to the programme directly from a meeting with Robert Lowell.

McCarthy was infuriated when his opponent accused him of planning to move large numbers of blacks into the highly conservative Orange County and of being willing to negotiate with communists. For his part, Kennedy indicated his willingness to export jet fighters to Israel. As McCarthy later pointed out, he had no such plans with respect to Orange County, would necessarily have to negotiate with communists if the war was to end, while Israel had not even asked for jets. On the other hand, McCarthy's supporters had tried to implicate Kennedy not only in early decisions about Vietnam, under his brother's administration, but also in involvement in the Dominican Republic, invaded by US forces in 1965 on the instruction of President Johnson.

The debate was, perhaps, best seen as a tie, though McCarthy signed off with a not untypical piece of obfuscation. Real leadership, he stated, was not a case of someone saying, '"You have got to follow me", but at least to be prepared to move out ahead somewhat so that people of the country can follow'.[59] From McCarthy's point of view, Kennedy's performance had seemed merely cynical. He concluded that it would be impossible for him to support his rival for the presidency, should he secure the nomination.

On the eve of the California vote on 3 June 1968, Miller wrote to David Carver in London explaining that he had just spent ten days campaigning for McCarthy in Oregon and California in the belief that the election represented a last chance to stop what he called the war machine. He still believed, he told him, that McCarthy had an outside chance and that Humphrey could lose his advantage once he was required to clarify his position on the war. In passing, he noted that *The Price* had opened to considerable success in Israel, Zurich, Berlin, Vienna and Buenos Aires.

The result of the California primary gave the forty-four-year-old Kennedy 1,445,880 votes and McCarthy, 1,305,728. Kennedy had won by 140,000 votes, securing 174 delegate votes. 'It's on to Chicago and let's win there,' he announced. He never made it to Chicago. Immediately following his victory speech, at fifteen minutes past midnight on 5 June in the Ambassador Hotel, he was assassinated by twenty-four-year-old Sirhan Sirhan, using a .22 calibre Iver-Johnson Cadet revolver. It was, seemingly, in revenge for Kennedy's support of Israel in the Six-Day War a year earlier. One of those who struggled with the assassin was a friend of Miller's, George Plimpton, editor of the

Inge Morath and
Arthur Miller
in February
1962. Roxbury,
Connecticut
(Inge Morath/
Magnum)

Henri Cartier-Bresson,
1972 – the father of
photojournalism
(Martine Franck-
Magnum)

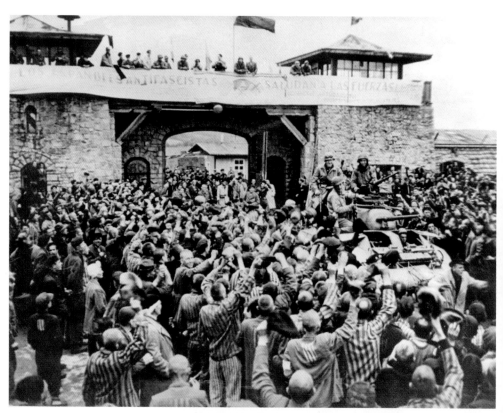

Prisoners of the
concentration camp
Mauthausen celebrate
their US liberators
in Mauthausen,
Germany, 5 May 1945.
(Press Association)

Wilhelm Boger, the
concentration guard known
as 'the devil of Auschwitz, on
trial in Frankfurt, April 1964.
(Press Association)

Arthur Miller and Inge
Morath leaving the
Frankfurt trials, 3 April 1964.
(Press Assocation)

Jason Robards as Quentin
and Barbara Loden as Maggie
wearing the notorious blonde
wig in *After the Fall*, 1964,
based on Arthur Miller's
marriage to Marilyn Monroe.
(*Getty*)

(top left) With fellow playwright Tennessee
Williams (left), and director Elia Kazan, 1967
(Press Association)

(bottom left) Nadezhda Mandelstam
in her apartment, Moscow 1967
(Inge Morath/Magnum)

(above) Joseph Brodsky on the roof of the
Fortress of Peter and Paul, Leningrad 1967
(Inge Morath/Magnum)

A jubilant Peter Reilly talks to reporters after charges against him for the murder of his mother were dropped. 24 November 1976 (Corbis)

Arthur Miller, Peter Reilly and Reilly's attorney, T.F. Gilroy Daly (Press Assocation)

Paul Clemens, Joan Bartel and Peter Reilly, 12 February 1978. Paul played the part of Peter Reilly in the television film *A Death in Canaan* directed by Tony Richardson and featuring Brian Dennehy and Stephanie Powers. (Corbis)

Arthur Miller and interpreter Su Guang in front of a Yuan dynasty sculpture, 1978
(Inge Morath/Magnum)

William Hinton,
author of *Fanshen*
(Inge Morath/Magnum)

Fania Fénelon, member
of the Auschwitz-
Birkenau women's
orchestra and author
of *Playing for Time*,
17 September 1980
(Press Association)

Paris Review (and whose bust was a feature of Miller's favourite restaurant, Elaine's). Kennedy died at 1.44 a.m. the following day.

Robert Lowell sent a letter to Jacqueline Kennedy, enclosing a poem. Miller immediately wrote a piece for the *New York Times*, 'On the Shooting of Robert Kennedy'. It was published two days after Kennedy's death, but with cuts. It was an angry article. He listed those leaders who had been assassinated and added to them the anonymous black men who had been enslaved and lynched, the Indians who had been killed, those beaten to death in police cells. His, he observed, was a society stained with violence and blind to social needs. At home there was wilful neglect, abroad American troops were required 'to take the side of proven grafters, morally bankrupt mercenaries who had already lost the support of their own people' (one of the passages cut by the *New York Times*). There was violence on the streets and on television. There was deprivation at home and abroad. Left in was his call to end the war: 'We are at war not only with the Vietnamese but with Americans. Stop both. We are rich enough to wipe out every slum and to open a world of hope to the poor. What keeps us? Do we want peace in Vietnam? Then make peace. Do we want hope in our cities and towns? Then stop denying any man his birthright.'[60]

He had, he explained in the original draft (another passage not included in the article), spoken only the night before at a local town meeting of the Democratic Resolutions Committee to determine the state Democratic platform. There, he had pointed out that with money going on the war other problems would be left unattended. Money, he had said, had simply gone down what he called the Viet Nam rat hole. A country in which people could not walk in safety on their own streets had 'not earned the right to tell another people how to govern itself, let alone to bomb and burn that people'.[61] America, he suggested, was marked by fear because of its failure to address the real problems of the poor, the marginalized, the victims of social injustice, at home and abroad.

It is hard to avoid the conviction that Miller was something of an innocent abroad as he left his study for the public platform, the convention floor, the backroom world of domestic politics. He was no less so when he chose direct intervention in international politics. Convinced that the impasse in the Paris negotiations might be resolved by a proposal that two thousand mothers and children should travel from the United States to North Vietnam, and vice versa, where they would live until negotiations were complete (a guarantee, it seemed to him, against ceasefire violations), he flew to Paris, as part of a group led by the peace campaigner Cora Weiss. Weiss would later be an organizer of the 15 Novernber 1969 anti-war demonstration in Washington DC, and appear as a witness at the Chicago Seven trial in which Tom Hayden and others were charged with incitement to riot. Later still, she would be active in SANE, the anti-nuclear movement that Miller too would support.

Miller's proposal may have been naive, but he was not unique in this. In 1972, during the bombing of North Vietnam, Mary McCarthy, Dwight Macdonald and others proposed that a group of prominent Americans should travel to Hanoi to prevent the attack. No more came of this than had of Miller's earlier plans, though perhaps the greatest surprise was that in Paris in 1968 the North Vietnamese were willing to listen to him.

It was now fourteen weeks since talks between Ambassador Averell Harriman and the chief of the Hanoi delegation, Hanoi's Xuan Thuy, had started. There was nothing to show for it, not least because Thuy insisted that he was there to talk about a cessation in the bombing rather than peace. The one could only follow the other. Miller thought that he might be able to break the stalemate. He spoke first to the delegation from Hanoi, in a conversation lasting three hours, in a small apartment in a Paris suburb, driven there by an expatriate Vietnamese who, like his fellow expatriates, insisted that this was a war of independence. While in Paris Miller also spoke to various American, French and British experts along with an American Quaker who had recently returned from Vietnam. Ambassador Harriman refused to meet with him, citing what he called 'delicate negotiations'. Initially believing himself something of an expert, Miller was quickly disabused and even began to have some sympathy for President Johnson, if only in so far as he gradually realized the complexity of the issues at stake. Most of all, he came up against people who believed that the war had already been won politically.

Xuan Thuy had been minister without portfolio appointed to head Hanoi's negotiating team in April 1968. He was also a member of the Communist Party Central Committee and head of its foreign relations section as well as a close confidante of Ho Chi Minh. The French had imprisoned him on a penal colony in the South China Sea as a young man. He was fluent in French and Chinese and had travelled widely.

Miller met Xuan Thuy, whom he described as a soft-spoken middle-aged man in a double-breasted suit, in a house owned by the French Communist Party, one of a group of buildings set around an earth-floored court with a high concrete wall on one side. Outside in the compound, in a desultory rain, were four sleek Citroëns and their chauffeurs, watching a young man playing shuttlecock without a net, something of a metaphor for the aimless negotiations going on inside. Another man was hitting a swing ball on a length of rubber. As a white-coated waiter poured yellow tea, and nuts and pastries were offered, Miller sat on a blue couch and outlined his ideas. Six Americans and seven or eight Vietnamese sat on upholstered or folding chairs to hear an American playwright offer his plan, if not to end the war, then to bring about a ceasefire. These conversations lasted for five hours.

Miller began by asking what had been happening in the regular Wednesday discussions with Harriman. Thuy replied, 'Absolutely nothing.' The negotiations between Harriman and Thuy were translated by two women from Vietnamese into French and then into English, since the Americans included no Vietnamese speakers in their party – or, Miller presumed, French speakers. For his part, Miller presented his proposal. Evidently suppressing a degree of amusement, Thuy asked whether it might not be simpler for America to cease its bombing campaign. The pointlessness of the plan Miller was outlining suddenly stood exposed. As he noted at the time in an aide-mémoire, back in America it had seemed simple. The problem was that he had forgotten something: that he had been seeing the war from an American perspective. It was a disgrace from which he hoped to redeem America. It was a tactical blunder by Johnson, based on an arrogance of power. In America, Vietnam was an issue; in Vietnam it was a daily reality. His proposal, he now saw, was nonsensical and he was suddenly struck by Thuy's patience. The talk continued. More tea was poured. Familiar points were made. Then the meeting broke up, Thuy assuring him that the day would come when Vietnam and America would once again be at peace and trading with one another. The delegates got into their Citroëns and left this suburban meeting place for central Paris.

In a note written immediately afterwards, Miller observed that before Johnson's withdrawal from the presidential race there had been half a million US troops in Vietnam. That number had already grown by forty thousand. Though the number of provinces being bombed had been reduced, the tonnage had increased. He also noted Thuy's insistence that even to have come to Paris while the bombing continued was a concession. He recalled Thuy's final remark, that it required more than a little self-control to be polite to Americans while women and children were dying.

The following day Miller met a delegation from the National Liberation Front, an encounter from which he emerged convinced that the North Vietnamese believed they were winning the war. He had assumed he might have a role in moving things forward. Now, he realized that they were simply awaiting what they assumed would be their victory. He flew back from Paris chastened, with a new awareness of the complexity of the negotiations and a conviction that the only way to end the war was to end the war. It needed a leader with a sense of the moral necessity to act, less concerned with saving face than saving lives.

He could also see that the Tet Offensive of January 1968 had marked not a setback for the so-called Pacification Programme, but its wholesale failure. The disturbing thought was that if he, who had been opposed to the war, had assumed that America was winning, why should Lyndon Johnson have thought otherwise? In a draft article entitled 'If It Is True', written four weeks after his Paris trip, he asked himself what the so-called pacification meant if not that once the South Vietnamese were in charge of a village or town, they would arrest or kill National Liberation Front sympathizers and level suspect settlements. That, it seemed to him, was what passed for peace in South Vietnam.

To look back on this period of Miller's life is to encounter a man more passionately committed to a cause than he had been in the 1930s. There is no suggestion that he could feel content to sit on the sidelines. He wrote articles, publishing some and abandoning others, whose language betrays something more than political disquiet. He was angry, ready to travel to Michigan, Chicago, San Francisco, Washington, Paris, wherever was necessary, to confront the administration and end the war. Hence, perhaps, his conviction of the relevance of his plays to these events. So *Incident at Vichy*, prompted by events in Europe, was to be seen as a comment on Vietnam. *The Price*, begun many years before, was likewise to be presented as addressing the contemporary political situation and its historical roots. Vietnam was a vacuum at the heart of the body politic sucking everything else into it, and his work was subject to that same centripetal pull.

The Connecticut state convention was to take place on 22 June. The night before it began John Bailey, chairman of both the Connecticut and the national party, determined to maximize the number of Humphrey delegates, joined the McCarthy people in the Hotel America in Hartford. There he met Miller and his next door neighbour William Styron, both of whom had agreed to be sponsors for the campaign back at the beginning of the year. It was not a particularly profitable encounter. As Chester, Hodgson and Page point out in *An American Melodrama*, Bailey had always previously selected those to attend the National Convention. McCarthy had likened him to the Wizard of Oz: 'When you pull the curtain back, there is only a voice.'[62] But it was not that simple. Miller was surprised that the McCarthy people were allowed as much leeway as they were. The assassination seemed to have discouraged too open an expression of dissent.

McCarthy's people had entered the hall with 224 of the 911 delegates but a first vote had raised the number to 281 – still not enough, though, to give them any real leverage. There was a feeling among them that it might be necessary to opt out of the Democratic Party, not a view that Miller was ready to endorse. For his part he offered a resolution, asking the convention to support the proposal of U Thant, Secretary General of the UN, to stop the bombing, negotiate with all parties, including the North Vietnamese National Liberation Front, and declare a ceasefire. To his surprise, rather than simply vote it down, the Humphrey delegation called on Senator William Benton to urge everyone to place his or her faith in the President.

When it became evident that Bailey would resist efforts to give the McCarthyites a proportionate number of delegates, the Revd Joseph Duffey, member of the Americans for Democratic Action (once Miller's *bête noire*) and leader of the McCarthy delegates, announced a walk-out. Miller was doubtful, aware that there were those who might be moved to violence at what they assumed to be a lack of patriotism. Nonetheless, he joined his fellow delegates. About a third of them left. Initially, Bailey had offered to accept five McCarthy delegates to go to Chicago. In the end he settled for nine. But there were thirty-five Humphrey delegates, despite the McCarthyites winning 44 per cent of the votes in the primaries.

The process was a revelation to Miller. Democracy, it seemed, was required to defer to machine politics. He began to see that in a number of states there was no necessary connection between votes cast in a state's preferential primary and the delegates sent to the National Convention. As Chester, Hodgson and Page point out, 'Of the 3099 delegates in Chicago (wielding a voting strength of 2622) ... no fewer than 600 were selected by state party organizations, and another 600 were elected, by various procedures, before the first campaign shots were fired in New Hampshire.'[63] Such delegates were likely to favour the Democratic machine and thus vote for Humphrey.

Looking back in 1973, Theodore H. White identified what seemed to him to be wrong with the Democratic Party system in 1968, attempts to reform which would cause problems in the 1972 elections:

> It was wrong, for example, flatly wrong, that a single Governor and state chairman could, as they did in two Southern states, name the entire state delegation to the national convention. It was wrong, flatly wrong, that the delegation-selection process should begin in the ward politics of some states – as in Massachusetts – fully three years before the Presidential campaign, before anyone knew what the issues (and who the candidates) might be. Proxy voting was always wrong – a system under which, when a caucus was called, some local baron might pull out a list of absentees and slap down a paper majority which would outweigh the presence of concerned citizens gathered to vote. And wrong that a state committee, as in New York or Pennsylvania, could name one third of its state's entire delegation and in Illinois more than half.[64]

After the Connecticut convention, Miller could no longer imagine himself voting for Humphrey, a man who had justified the killing of innocent people. To him, Humphrey was an unreconstructed liberal of the anti-communist fifties. He lacked any conscience. At least McCarthy, whatever his other faults, had that. He could not understand why Humphrey had not resigned at the same time as Johnson, who had withdrawn, in part, because his presence on the Democratic ticket would have been divisive.

Humphrey represented not simply those who had sustained the war but those who a quarter of a century and more before had set themselves to attack what they regarded as the Stalinist Left and fellow travellers such as Miller. The reason for their sustaining the war, to Miller, seemed to lie in that same political Manicheanism that had underlain the Cold War and so divided America in the 1950s. His own private fear was that since politics entails the pursuit and exercise of power, this very process is incompatible with morality. And was he himself not associating himself with someone who pursued power, no matter how pure his motives? To become effective, McCarthy would have to become the thing he despised.

Miller's reaction seems to have been a mix of fascination and moral revulsion, at least as judged by an unfinished story he wrote at this time. It is called 'The Delegate: A Story of a Political Man',[65] and it expresses something of his disillusionment with the political process that he felt as a result of his brush with state politics. It centres on an honest man, Frank Unwin, who for most of his life has taken pride in his work and offered help to others when needed. In the war he had served as an officer in an all-black unit and saved the lives of three men (a story that recurs in Miller's unpublished work). Afterwards, he had brought his skills to a number of professions, never really being rewarded for his efforts, a quiet man alive to the decline of standards.

He had joined the local Democratic club more out of a desire to recreate that sense of comradeship he had once felt in wartime than because of fierce conviction. Sensitive to the needs and fears of others, he proved helpful to a machine that needed to keep in touch with the voters, while he himself found the sense of solidarity he sought. He quickly discovered the limitations of his new position, however, when, during the McCarthy period, he made a speech at a state convention condemning the firing of teachers. The machine, it was clear, disapproved.

His son had been fourteen when the Vietnam War became serious. Frank himself served on the draft board and was afraid of what was coming. The emergence of Barry Goldwater as a contender for the presidential nomination sharpened his alarm and brought his interests back into line with those of the machine, pushing, as it was, for the election of Johnson. Suddenly, he is in demand again from the party bosses and finds himself seduced by their willingness to embrace him. Offered advance information about a highway development, he buys land, not so much for the financial gain as to feel part of the process from which he had become abstracted. Johnson, anyway, he was sure, would stop the escalation in Vietnam. The story breaks off as his son comes of age for the draft, pumping iron on the beach, ready for a life which implicitly is now menaced by a process in which his father has become complicit.

It is no more than a sketch, but it seems to register something of the shock that Miller was feeling, his awareness of the cynicism of those who ran state politics and his growing awareness of the moral contamination seemingly implicit in the pursuit of power, albeit a power sought in the name of an ideal.

In July, McCarthy wrote to Miller: 'I did not want to let the campaign go much longer without thanking you for your effort on behalf of my campaign for the Presidency. If I lose, it will not be because I lacked the support of the nation's best talent.'[66] That same month, polls showed McCarthy leading Humphrey, but in August a new candidate appeared: George McGovern, whom Robert Kennedy had once described as the most decent man in the Senate, a man with a PhD in American history. He had been urged to run by a number of Kennedy's erstwhile supporters. There was thus another potential split in the peace camp, but, more importantly, Humphrey had slowly been building up his delegate numbers and was in reach of locking up the impending convention in Chicago. For his part, and with an increasing sense of urgency, Miller began to throw himself into the national as well as the local campaign. He was present at an anti-war rally in Times Square on 3 August. A report duly appeared in his FBI file. Those attending were urged to go to the Democratic National Convention in order to further the anti-war cause. The rally, the agent noted, ended with a march from Times Square down Broadway to 34th Street and the 71st Regiment Armory at Park Avenue.

The Republican Convention opened on 5 August in Miami. Nelson Rockefeller had launched a campaign, claiming: 'The war has been conducted without a coherent strategy or programme for peace.'[67] Now he threw money around in the hope of winning there what he had plainly not won through the primaries. It was a lost cause. Nixon won the nomination with 692 votes to Rockefeller's 277 and Ronald Reagan's 182. His first decision was to put forward Spiro Agnew as his running mate. With Watergate four years in the future, that would make two unexploded bombs waiting their moment to detonate – Agnew being deeply corrupt.

As a prelude to the Convention George Plimpton, with William Styron, organized what they called a 'Mini-Gala for McCarthy' at the Cheetah discotheque on Broadway and 53rd Street. Allen Ginsberg wandered around with what Joe Flaherty called 'a knapsack affair over his shoulder, sowing his seeds of love'. The composer David Amram delivered 'roundhouse endorsements for two of his loves—Gene McCarthy and prizefighting' while Miller read his anti-war script 'The Reason Why'. Asked why he supported McCarthy when, as a Senator he had voted for the motion condemning him for contempt of Congress, he indicated that, 'That was just a bad time for the country', insisting that 'He's an honest man and unbelievably honest for a politician. He just makes the most fucking sense.'

Meanwhile, Chicago prepared for the Democratic National Convention to be opened on 26 August, six days after Soviet troops entered Czechoslovakia, an event that gave substance to those who had been speaking of a communist menace in Vietnam and strengthened the hands of those drafting the party platform. McCarthy sought to present it as simply a further example of great powers intervening in the affairs of other countries and insisted that he did not see the invasion as a major world crisis. It was yet more evidence of what many thought of as his disdain for the business of politics, which had resulted in his securing so little support from fellow legislators and in his listing a series of potential nominees for cabinet posts which included a number of millionaires and Republicans. On 27 August, he publicly accepted that Humphrey already had the nomination in his pocket. It was true enough, but hardly the note on which to enter a convention. Johnson had withdrawn as a candidate but had not lost his power and influence, which was why Humphrey could not denounce the war. The platform was 65 to 35 for Humphrey's position. McCarthy had arrived in Chicago on 25 August on a chartered airliner, accompanied by Robert Lowell and William Styron. It was hard to imagine Humphrey arriving with a poet and a novelist.

Mayor Daley, who was himself privately against the war, was expecting trouble. The Yippee movement (Youth International Party), born at the turn of the year, had announced its intention to stage major demonstrations. Daley also feared the arrival of other war protesters and, only four months on from the riots that had followed Martin Luther King's death, was fearful that the ghetto might erupt again. Accordingly, the police (twelve thousand strong) were put on twelve-hour shifts while six thousand National Guardsmen were on call. The ghetto did not erupt, but Yippies and protesters did find themselves doing battle with the police as inside the convention hall the curious business of American democracy worked itself out. There were moments when the smell of tear gas reached those debating the question of who was to be the next President of the United States, as it would also make its way into Hubert Humphrey's hotel room courtesy of the air-conditioning system. Indeed, violence penetrated the International Amphitheatre itself, as delegates were arrested and newsmen were beaten to the floor.

On his arrival, Miller noted the barbed wire that topped the cyclone fence around the parking lot of the Amphitheatre. Norman Mailer, there to observe proceedings for *Harper's* magazine and what would become *Miami and the Siege of Chicago*, confessed that he had not seen such enthusiasm for a candidate since Henry Wallace. Five thousand turned out for McCarthy's arrival at Midway Airport.

Miller was struck, during the first two days, by what he called 'speeches of a skull-flattening boredom'.[68] Like Mario Vargas Llosa, who would run unsuccessfully for the presidency of Peru in 1990, he was dismayed by the reductive language that passed as political coinage. Vargas Llosa commented, 'I think that probably the most difficult obstacle for a writer when he enters politics is the language problem. The kind of relationship with the language that a politician has is completely different from the relationship that the writer has. Political language is made of clichés, stereotypes, banalities. In a political campaign you have endlessly to repeat very simple ideas if you want to reach big audiences and all this, for a writer, can be very embarrassing and destructive.'[69]

Miller, too, had had to make adjustments, but he found the ritual speeches in the convention all but unbearable: '"Vision" is always "forward", "freedom" is always a "burning flame" and "our inheritance", "freedom", "progress", "sacrifices", "long line of Democratic presidents", fall like drops of water on the head of a tortured Chinese.' For most delegates, however, just being there 'is the high point, the honor their fealty has earned them. They are among the chosen, and the boredom of the speeches is in itself a reassurance.'[70] It was none the easier for knowing that 80 per cent of the Democrats who had voted in the primaries had supported the positions of Kennedy and McCarthy but that the convention was all but sewn up.

In a speech supporting the peace resolution before the convention Miller outlined his position. The Vietnam War, he maintained, was the primary cause of disaffection among the youth of America. It was siphoning money away from the major social issues confronting the country: housing, jobs, education. The price of waging war abroad was the decay of cities at home. The war was a cancer and the party owed no allegiance to the leaders who had taken them into it. He had accepted election as a delegate because the Democratic Party was no longer listening. The primaries had proved that the people wanted peace, which could only be assured once the bombing had stopped. He called on the Democratic Party of Connecticut to take the lead.

The Connecticut delegation was divided. Bailey, as the Democratic national chairman as well as the state chairman, sat on the platform. He was the head of a machine presumed to be loyal. As a result his delegates attracted little attention from the police, though Miller did find his credentials being checked. The New York delegation – including, as it did, many McCarthyites – was hemmed in by Chicago plainclothes men, who arrested a number of them. The McCarthy supporters, sitting on grey steel chairs, had been warned not to bring posters into the hall, but when Humphrey's name was mentioned the convention floor suddenly bloomed with colour photographs of the Vice-President. The McCarthyites were told they could not distribute any printed material while the administration's recent Vietnam report was to be found on every seat. Someone's thumb was securely on the scales. Yet at the same time Miller claimed not to have met any Humphrey supporter who believed he could beat Nixon. They were simply, it seemed to him, people who needed to belong, in this case in the camp of a man who appeared to represent the legitimate party as defined by its functionaries. He conceded, though, that he felt something similar about McCarthy. If Humphrey had changed his policy on Vietnam, however, and despite his already impressive liberal credentials on social issues, Miller would still have found it difficult to support him. He simply belonged with McCarthy.

When the Connecticut delegation of forty-four gathered in caucus, they were addressed by Senator Benton, who endorsed the administration and therefore the American bombing of Vietnam. Spokesman for the McCarthy cause was Paul Newman, a long-term inhabitant of Connecticut who had campaigned across the country and, when Kennedy became involved, criticized those who had 'cashed in' on McCarthy's courage, held their finger up to see which way the wind was blowing, putting career before the cause. The key figure, though, remained John Bailey, the Connecticut party boss. As Miller remarked, 'The delegates would commit suicide if John Bailey told them to.'[71] One McCarthyite, a teacher, stood up and announced that the war was immoral and that there would be a revolution on campuses across America. The pro-administration majority sat impassive. When the roll was called on the minority plank, Miller recalled, one machine man switched sides. On the central issue of which candidate to support, ten voted for McCarthy and thirty-four for Humphrey. Just one man had changed sides. He reversed his position when the vote on the majority plank – President Johnson's position and now Humphrey's – was held.

Writing in 2009, the British politician Shirley Williams recalled being present in Chicago and playing a role with respect to the Connecticut delegation, though her memory seems not entirely accurate:

> I managed, through a little selective string-pulling among my American friends, to get myself appointed as page, the person who arranged meetings and interviews, to the Connecticut delegation ... [which] had not been mandated to vote for any particular person by its state caucus, and therefore offered a tempting field for candidates keen to pick up votes ... The delegation was minded to vote for Senator McCarthy, but felt that they should hear from him first. I was sent off to invite him. The senator kept me waiting a long time while he finished an interview with the editor of a high-school magazine. He showed little interest in meeting with the delegates from Connecticut. I too admired him but I was driven to the unwelcome conclusion that he was not serious, although so much was at stake. He was indulging himself in being the centre of attention.[72]

The delegation was seated beside that of Illinois, dominated by Daley's supporters. When Daley was denounced from the platform for the actions of his police by former Governor of Connecticut, now Senator, Abraham Ribicoff, who insisted that with George McGovern as president there would be an end to Gestapo tactics, the Mayor, Miller later recalled, taunted him by shouting, 'Jew! Jew!'[73] and drawing a finger across his throat. Ribicoff replied: 'How hard it is to accept the truth. How hard it is.'[74] Mailer's version was that Daley had invited Ribicoff to have carnal knowledge of himself. One by-product of this moment was that Ribicoff, who was up for re-election that year, secured the enthusiastic support of previously sceptical McCarthy supporters.

Among those working on the McCarthy strategy at Chicago was Joe Rauh – who years earlier had been Miller's lawyer when he appeared before HUAC. His chief tactic was to challenge the credentials of some of those representing Southern states, using as justification a decision taken at the 1964 convention (which had seated a largely segregationist delegation from Mississippi) that there should be a racial balance at subsequent conventions. This failed when McCarthy's supporters tried to broaden the challenge to northern states.

As it became clear that McCarthy was not going to be able to carry the day, Miller drafted a statement freeing delegates to vote for whomever they wished. This was vetoed. McCarthy was willing to see votes go to George McGovern, who was equally keen to conclude the war in Vietnam, but not to Teddy Kennedy, now being floated by some as the natural inheritor of his dead brother's support, though Theodore White later suggested that McCarthy did indicate that if he failed he would personally be willing to support him if it came to it, as he would not have been willing to support Robert Kennedy. In the end such manoeuvring meant nothing, since the nomination had been decided months before. The convention was simply a celebratory floorshow, to be accompanied by well stocked hospitality suites to which, Miller bitterly complained, he had been required to donate $100.

The real battle, though, was not on the convention floor. It was on the streets. 'I'll never forget the look on those Chicago cops,' Miller remarked. 'I think they were on the verge of attacking us, the delegates, and it was very frightening.'[75] Here was state violence, perpetrated at the very heart of the democratic process. The largely student crowd chanted, 'Pigs, pigs, oink, oink', while the police yelled, 'Kill 'em!' Seven hundred protesters were hurt and six hundred and fifty arrested. Eighty police were injured. The worst violence came as demonstrators tried to march south from Grant Park to the Amphitheatre. Walter Cronkite of CBS News called the guards 'thugs'. CBS newsman Mike Wallace was struck on the jaw while his colleague Dan Rather was punched in the stomach, both on the convention floor. McCarthy, who saw the police violence from the window of his twenty-third-floor suite in the Hilton Hotel, remarked, 'It's incredible ... like a Breughel.'[76] His headquarters became a first-aid room.

In *Miami and the Siege of Chicago*, Mailer quotes a *Village Voice* reporter:

'A few feet away a phalanx of police charged into a group of women, reporters, and young McCarthy activists standing idly against the window of the Hilton Hotel's Haymarket Inn. The terrified people began to go down under the unexpected police charge when the plate glass window shattered, and the people tumbled backward through the glass. The police then climbed through the broken window and began to beat people, some of whom had been drinking quietly in the hotel bar ... Demonstrators, reporters, McCarthy workers, doctors, all began to stagger into the Hilton lobby, blood streaming from head and face wounds.'[77]

It was in this lobby that Miller met his old friend Rauh, though there had been no time to talk politics or anything else. With tear gas in the air all they could do was cough.

There were other writers present: Allen Ginsberg, William Burroughs, Jean Genet (originally denied a visa to enter America), Terry Southern. Genet, predictably, had his own particular take on events, drawn to describe the enticing sexuality of a policeman whose thighs 'extend on up into an imposing member and a muscled torso, made even firmer every day by his police training in the cops' gymnasium ... America,' he opined, 'has a magnificent, divine, athletic police force, often photographed and seen in dirty books.'[78] But while swooning at the blue of their uniforms he found himself running away from them, blinded by tear gas from which he recovered in Ginsberg's hotel: then a policeman, 'holding his billy club in his hand the way, exactly the way, I hold a black American's member – escorts us to our car and opens the door for us'. Allowed into the press section of the convention, he finds the process bewildering and has 'an urge to go outside and touch a tree, graze in the grass, screw a goat, in short do what I'm used to doing'.[79] His final thought was contained in an address to hippies: 'In order to fuck all the old bastards who are giving you a hard time, unite, go underground if necessary in order to join the burned children of Vietnam.'[80]

Chicago turned out to be a writers' convention, some there to soak up experience as much as to protest, a blend of party and apocalypse. William Burroughs set off on a non-violent march, 'feeling rather out of place since non-violence is not exactly my programme'.[81] In the convention hall (he, too, had press credentials) he booed Humphrey, he explained, to while away the time. Ginsberg invited those being beaten to respond by chanting 'OM', a suggestion that, astonishingly, some accepted. Mailer himself missed several of the key moments on the street because he was in a bar with Styron and Lowell on one occasion and in his hotel room on another, before ending up in the Playboy Club. He did, though, make a somewhat self-regarding speech in which he reminded his listeners that he was the author of *The Naked and the Dead*. Though caught up in the same events, Miller and Mailer seem not only not to have met but also to have existed in different worlds. For the most part, Miller was inside the Amphitheatre watching the bad theatre of the convention play itself out. Mailer was staging his own drama as actor/observer.

The convention went its preordained way. The balloting began at eleven-twenty. Humphrey was elected with 1,759 votes to McCarthy's 601 and McGovern's 146. A bid to insert a plank calling for an end to the bombing of Vietnam was defeated by the platform committee, and McCarthy and Ted Kennedy both refused to join Humphrey at the podium. America was beginning to come apart and the liberal Left seemed to have no response.

At two in the morning, when the fighting had largely quietened down, Miller joined some five hundred delegates in a candle-lit march past the scene of what had in effect been open battle. To the sound of 'We Shall Overcome' they marched up to the soldiers who were holding rifles to bar access to the convention hotel. In a last speech to supporters McCarthy, typically, quoted from a Robert Lowell poem:

> Only man thinning out his kind
> sounds through the Sabbath noon, the blind
> swipe of the pruner and his knife
> busy about the tree of life ... [82]

Miller was still there at four in the morning, 'with the arc lights blasting the street, and no one knowing when the police and the troops would again go beserk'.[83] The irony was that Johnson had refused to run again on the grounds that his candidacy would be divisive, while in Chicago that division was being acted out on the streets as a new generation, themselves in line for the draft, no longer saw any purpose in a political system so unresponsive to the electorate. In one of the corridors of the convention centre he had been accosted by a student from the University of Chicago radio station, who asked him how he could have agreed to be part of a supposedly democratic process that had resulted in an endorsement of the administration and the violence on the streets: 'My answer, which I found embarrassing at that moment, was that I had hoped to change it and that it might be changed if people like me tried to move into the party in a serious way rather than only during presidential campaigns.'[84] The source of the embarrassment was clear. He had no intention of throwing himself into party politics. He had also learned that town meeting politics could not be extended to a national level. Yet, as he asked the student, what else was there?

The following afternoon, Miller was scheduled to take part in a television programme to be transmitted to England via the new Telstar satellite. But the satellite, he was told, had been pre-empted by the US government because of the crisis in Czechoslovakia. Such was the paranoia of the moment that more than one of the participants thought that the loss of the satellite link might have been a deliberate attempt to prevent wider publicity for the chaos of Chicago. In fact, it later emerged, the satellite had not been pre-empted.

Miller offered his analysis of the violence in Chicago:

> There had to be violence for many reasons, but one fundamental cause was the two opposite ideas of politics in the Democratic Party. The professionals – the ordinary Senator, Congressman, State Committeeman, Mayor, office-holder – see politics as a sort of game in which you win sometimes and sometimes you lose. Issues are not something you feel, like morality, like good and evil, but something you succeed or fail to make use of. To these men an issue is a segment of public opinion which you either capitalize on or attempt to assuage according to the present interests of the party. To the amateurs – the McCarthy people and some of the Kennedy adherents – an issue is first of all moral, and embodies a vision of the country, even of man, and is not a counter in a game. The great majority of the men and women at the convention were delegates from the party to the party.[85]

At four in the morning a group of police raided the Hilton Hotel, riding elevators to the fifteenth floor where McCarthy's young supporters were staying. They beat them and told them to leave town. McCarthy himself was summoned down to the lobby. Eventually the police left and a notorious convention came to an end. Humphrey, now planning the next stage of his campaign, seems to have been unaware of these developments. George McGovern left the convention convinced that if Humphrey was not elected President that November, he himself could be in 1972.

Miller would never again seek to play a direct role in the American political system, instead retreating to his old tactic, signing petitions, making speeches, embracing causes, but not involving himself in local or national politics. He left town before the final speech, the candidate himself having decided that it was too dangerous to appear. As Miller left O'Hare Airport he was passed by a group of draftees, one of whom, black, shouted out, 'We're off to defend your country.'[86] In a post-convention poll the majority sympathized with the police. Back in Connecticut, Miller was asked to organize a protest about the jailing of Czech writers by the invading Russians. Having just witnessed assassinations, burning cities and political violence, he was not unaware of the irony.

On 29 October Senator McCarthy, while stressing that Hubert Humphrey's position on Vietnam 'falls far short of what I think it should be', nonetheless endorsed him for President, while maintaining that the endorsement was 'in no way intended to reinstate me in the good graces of the Democratic Party leaders, nor in any way to suggest my having forgotten or condoned the things that happened both before Chicago and at Chicago'.[87]

On 1 November President Johnson halted the bombing and on the 5th

Richard Nixon was elected, with the assistance of George Wallace of Alabama, whose ten million votes sealed the fate of the Democrats. His Vice-President, Spiro Agnew, former Governor of Maryland, who would resign in December 1973, after pleading no contest to a charge of income tax evasion, denounced the 'anarchists and ideological eunuchs' who protested against the war and the 'effete corps of impudent snobs who characterize themselves as intellectuals'.[88] Arthur Miller, presumably, was one of them.

The election of Richard Nixon, who years before had made his reputation with Miller's old nemesis HUAC, left him feeling despair and artistically frustrated. Asked how he felt at that time, he replied, 'Hopeless. Anger. How can you write in anger like that? It was just like being caught on flypaper. You went from LBJ to Richard Nixon ... There is a democratic instinct here that is powerful, if you can call it up, but it gets betrayed all the time ... and they lose their sons that way. They lose their peace. Oh, dear God.'[89] At least with Kennedy and Johnson, he noted, he had been dealing with conflicted people whose domestic interest in protecting the weak and the victims of prejudice had left them with doubts when they went into Vietnam. With Nixon, it seemed to him, the country had a wholly different animal.

In a speech delivered in the Battell Chapel at Yale in November 1968, Miller began with the announcement that the war was apparently coming to an end, with 28,000 empty beds in 28,000 homes where young American men had once lived. It was the first war America had not won. A little old man with a stringy beard, he noted, who presided over a country whose population was only twice that of metropolitan New York, had effectively brought down a President. Speaking immediately before William Sloane Coffin, he suggested that the country would 'bend lower to the god of violence if it did not examine the failures of its might against such a small foe as North Vietnam'.[90] God, he observed, no longer marched with the big battalions. His announcement of the war's imminent conclusion, though, was more than a little premature. It still had several years to run, and another 28,000 Americans would die before it came to an end.

6

CZECHOSLOVAKIA AND CAMBODIA

... they kill you. They can really destroy you ... I remember Chekhov
writing somebody a letter saying that if he had listened to the critics he
would have died drunk in the gutter ... I was just reading a biography
of Ibsen, in which he was inveighing against critics in the same way ...
I don't think twelve people in this country could name the Norwegian
critics at the time of Ibsen, and yet they were the real bane of his life.[1]

Arthur Miller

In 1969 Miller decided to use his art as a weapon, with an anti-war allegory
called *The Reason Why*, filmed at his Roxbury home for $14,000, with Eli
Wallach and Robert Ryan. Ryan was then starring in a Broadway production
of *The Front Page*, and travelled up the day before the shoot. The actors were
all paid $120 plus a percentage of the nothing the film might receive, since it
had not been pre-sold. Inge provided a lunch of cold roast beef sandwiches
for the actors and the ten-man crew.

Ostensibly about the killing of a woodchuck, it was offered as a comment
on violence and, by implication, Vietnam. It had begun partly as a short
story and partly a reminiscence, though seemingly without any political
implications. Miller then wrote it as a play before getting the idea of using it,
as he explained, as 'a sort of metaphor. What I wanted to put down were the
facts, the way we're made, the impulses of the human animal toward war,
violence and murder. We have to be aware of what's inside of us, otherwise
we'll destroy ourselves and the world.'[2] He also felt that writing still had a
role to play. 'Despite everything,' he said, 'I still thought writing had to try
to save America, and that meant grabbing people and shaking them by the
back of the neck.'[3] Such shaking clearly had little effect, though Ryan too
expressed his sense that a 'scene of this nature can say more than all the
speeches in the world.'[4]

Two men sit on the grass admiring the natural world until they spot a
woodchuck some three hundred yards away. For no particular reason, one

wonders whether he could shoot it at such a distance and fetches a rifle. They discuss what it is to kill in war, as one of them recalls a day on which he had shot several dozen woodchucks:

> Honestly, I began to feel a real hatred. I'd get up in the morning and there they were, a field full of the bastards again. And it was getting expensive. One of those bullets cost fifteen cents, and you don't always hit with one shot … And the truth is, for what it cost to kill them we could have bought all the tomatoes we'd eat in a year. Seriously, it began to remind me of Vietnam. For what it cost to kill them we could have given every one of them a tractor and sent their kids to the University of Texas.

He squeezes a bullet off and kills the woodchuck. 'What the hell'd you do that for?' his friend asks. 'I don't know,' his friend replies.[5]

In fact, the play turned film was based on an incident when Miller and Robert Whitehead had tried out a rifle with telescopic sights. Miller was not a hunter and the animal he aimed at – according to Whitehead a groundhog rather than a woodchuck – was a quarter of a mile away. They were both surprised and distressed when the bullet struck home, and the two of them went on a long walk through the woods, guilty at the casual cruelty. For Miller the writer, Whitehead later observed, nothing went unnoticed.

Also in 1969, he began a play called 'Who Killed Tommy Hamilton?' in which three sets of parents receive back their sons' flag-draped coffins and meet the President. One family takes pride in their son's sacrifice, as they do in their own achievements. Another does not. The mother is inclined to be philosophical: the father, though proud of his son's bravery, is not, explaining that he sees no purpose in his loss. The third father rejects even this well mannered protest, insisting that his son had not wanted to go to war and that there is nothing to be thankful for. The text breaks off. Miller's anger over the war had not dissipated. The indirectness of *The Price* was evidently no longer sufficient.

Even when Americans landed on the moon, on 20 July 1969, a triumph in the very middle of the war, Miller marked the occasion with an article in the *New York Times* in which he urged a rediscovery of planet earth and in particular a transfer of the money used to wage war to rebuild American society. He looked forward, he said, to a time when a scientific expedition would land on 125th Street or the North Side of Waterbury, Connecticut, but doubted that Congress would authorize something that would explore the ecology of a place that evidenced the debris of past explosions. It was by now a familiar Miller refrain, as he called for a sense of social responsibility that would redeem the plight of the black American and the poor on planet earth.

For all his political activities, however, and his attempt to use his art to effect a change in national priorities, for Miller the sixties were 'a time of stalemate'. He had 'lost the last belief in any social prophecy, whether the common expectation that America was being revolutionized by the youth and black movements or the pretensions of the orthodox to a democratic crusade in Vietnam. I could find no refreshing current such as I had imagined touching in the thirties and forties, only a moral stagnation that mocked creation itself.'[6]

To read Miller's published and unpublished pieces is to realize how deeply he felt about the war. In an article for the *New York Times*, in June 1969, under the title 'Are We Interested in Stopping the Killing?' he expressed incredulity that no one appeared to notice that, in a television discussion, Averell Harriman had suggested that it was the United States and not the Vietcong who were on the offensive. The article ended:

> If he is right and the offensive is basically American, then it is we who are escalating the war at a time when the whole public stance of the Administration implies that it wishes to end the war. Now the Congress and many State Legislatures are busy dreaming up ways to suppress campus unrest, and there is no lack of consternation about the refusal of youth to believe anything any more. As a non-youth, I hereby declare I would like to believe something, so will the Administration address itself to this question and settle it? If this is not answerable, if it is an uncouth question, then down we go again into the Blanding Machine and, as our former President said, only violence will force change.[7]

In a draft article at the end of Nixon's first year in office he even suggested ironically that dropping the atom bomb might have proved less damaging than the poisoning of the environment with Agent Orange and the bombing of both North and South Vietnam.

Later revelations of Lyndon Johnson's deceptions came as a shock, but not a surprise, to Miller. It had seemed to him from the beginning that the war belonged alongside America's slaughter of the Indians and its Philippine campaign. The Vietnamese were simply resisting a familiar American colonial drive. The question, it now seemed to him, was why he and those like him had understood this while others were duped. In his own case the scepticism had been born long before, since he saw the war as a product of the Cold War whose roots lay in the 1930s. This, in turn, had roots going further back, to the initial days of the Russian Revolution when American troops had fought alongside the Whites in Siberia. If that involvement had shown bad faith, the opposite did likewise when, in the 1930s, Roosevelt, declaring neutrality, had blocked sixty million dollars' worth of gold which the Madrid government needed in order to buy arms to resist Franco, a fact which Roosevelt had lived to regret. And so it had continued. The communist victory in China, as a new Republican administration found itself in power, led to the myth of a monolithic communism with its agents in the American government, its universities, its arts.

He was not denying the imperialist pretensions of the Soviet Union. However, the idea of a huge underground plot in America, its tentacles spreading out into all areas of American life and with the power to undermine the state, had always been absurd. But such a notion had fed a paranoia that was liable to see every instance of communist subversion overseas as part of a coordinated strategy ultimately threatening the home front. The fall of China to communism was thus seen as having no connection with the then existing state of China. The war in Vietnam was seen as detached from history – the history of Vietnam, that is, as opposed to that of a global Cold War – from any local realities, any nationalist pretensions, any sense of an existing corrupt system.

The Cold War, however, was not only invoked in relation to Vietnam. In August 1969, Miller had a telephone conversation with Henry Raymont of the *New York Times* on the subject of the dissident author Anatoly Kuznetsov, who earlier that year had defected to the United Kingdom carrying with him film of the uncensored version of his documentary novel *Babi Yar*, which described the slaughter of over thirty-three thousand Jews in a ravine in Kiev. That original version had been critical of the Soviet Union, and the Soviet government demanded Kuznetsov's return. The British refused. The Soviets demanded access. Kuznetsov refused. Raymont now published an article based on his conversation with Miller, without his permission and in a way that reflected precisely the Cold War mentality that Miller opposed. Beyond that, Miller had his doubts about Kuznetsov, never fully accepting his story and doubtful about his character. As it happens, he was not alone in this. William Styron thought Kuznetsov should have remained silent after leaving the Soviet Union, while Lillian Hellman accused him of cowardice for failing to protest against Soviet censorship while in his own country. Their views, however, were less significant than those of a writer who remained in Russia.

Time magazine, in December 1969, printed a statement by Andrei Amalric, himself a dissident writer, who that year predicted the dissolution of the Soviet empire. He accused Kuznetsov of being a KGB informer as a means both of getting his work published and of escaping to the West. He had even fed a false story to his controllers implicating fellow writers, including Yevgeny Yevtushenko. Amalric wrote:

> You speak of freedom, but only of external freedom. You say nothing of internal freedom. To struggle against the KGB is a terrible thing, but what, in effect, threatened a Russian writer if, before his first visit abroad, he had refused to collaborate with the KGB? That writer would not have gone abroad but he would have remained an honest man. In refusing to collaborate,

he would have lost a part, perhaps a considerable part, of his external freedom, but he would have achieved greater inner freedom.

He had himself, he went on, been invited to inform, first in 1961 and then in 1963, when he was taken to the Lubyanka prison. Again in 1965 he had refused to talk with them and had been exiled to Siberia – which was what, he said, gave him the right to attack Kuznetsov: 'It seems to me that no oppression can be effective without those who are willing to submit to it. It sometimes appears to me that the Soviet "creative intelligentsia" – that is, people accustomed to thinking one thing, saying another, and doing a third – is, as a whole, an even more unpleasant phenomenon than the regime that formed it.'[8]

What is significant about this is not whether Miller was right or wrong in his suspicions, but that he had them at all. In a situation in which vice and virtue, right and wrong, seemed clear, as writers found themselves up against the state and he, from the standpoint of PEN, was invited to align himself with the writer, he had learned a thing or two about the moral complexity of the world and the suspect nature of an apparent reality, a subject that would soon move to the centre of his work. Totalitarian governments provoked a form of theatre in which individuals were required to perform their lives. What was said in public, even what was said in private (since in such a world what is ever truly private?), was a necessary deceit. But in such circumstances where was the self located? How operative could private reservations be if they could never make their way into action or even language? In such a world compromise can seem both necessary and justified, but what is offered in return? The gap that Amalric identified, between thought, word and action, which in Miller's early plays had been the source of irony and at times of tragedy, would become the basis for later works – *The Archbishop's Ceiling, Two-Way Mirror, The Ride down Mount Morgan, Mr Peters' Connections, Finishing the Picture* – in which he explored the construction of meaning. From sociology he moved towards ontology.

There was, or had been, something Manichean about Miller's sensibility. The world had often seemed to present itself to him in clear terms. First had come the battle against fascism and capitalism, against anti-Semitism and racism. Then he had unequivocally opposed the repressive forces in his own society. Even now he tended to make references to his own experiences before HUAC when speaking of the plight of writers around the world. He had never registered any ambiguity with respect to the Vietnam War or nuclear weapons. His experience with PEN, however, and in particular his time in Russia and later in Czechoslovakia, introduced him to a more nuanced world in which things were not always what they seemed nor people what they represented themselves as being. Writers were sent abroad to watch other writers. He himself had been invited to play out necessary charades as those paid to follow and eavesdrop tracked the steps of those he would talk to.

He had also become more aware of the factitious nature of his own society in which politicians were manifest performers and rituals were played out as if they had some basis in human need. In the 1970s and thereafter he would write plays in which reality was suspect and identity under threat, and he owed this in part to these earlier years when he learned to pass his fingers over the suspect Braille of late twentieth-century life.

Kuznetsov wrote nothing for the next ten years, and died in 1979. Amalric protested against the trial of Andrei Sinyavsky and Yuli Daniel and was arrested in 1970, spending three years in prison. On his release he was sentenced to another three years, commuted to one after international protests. Offered a visa to Israel (though he was not Jewish), he turned it down, but was forced to emigrate in 1976. He spent time in the Netherlands, the USA and finally France. He died in a traffic accident in 1980 on his way to a conference to review the Helsinki Accords of 1975, whose seventh point had been a call for freedom of thought.

In October 1969, an estimated two million Americans marched in support of the Moratorium to End the War in Vietnam. Peace demonstrators gathered on the steps of the Capitol in Washington. General Wheeler, chairman of the Joint Chiefs of Staff, called them young people who were strangers to soap and reason alike. In New York the Mayor, John Lindsay, ordered the American flag to be flown at half-mast while policemen and fire-fighters drove with their headlights on to protest against Moratorium Day.

Miller drafted an open letter to the President explaining that students at the nearby Torrington, Connecticut, high school had asked him to speak on Moratorium Day but that, having nothing new to say, he had suggested that instead they should plant a tree for peace. He did so, he told the President, because he ran a small nursery and felt that planting trees was better than blowing them up. By the same token, the young protesters were voting for life rather than the deaths they saw being inflicted by their country in Vietnam.

The tree was never planted. The American Legion objected, and since they 'and other patriots' had cut down a similar tree on a church lawn a compromise was agreed. Miller was invited to talk to an English class about *The Crucible*. He described the event:

> The room was packed when I arrived. Faculty sat in a clump to one side. I had already learned that in inviting me to speak the students had struck terror in some faculty hearts, and the fear in the place was thick enough to grease a pan with. I thought I saw encouragement in a few faculty faces, but

none of them joined the pounding applause of the students, all of whom knew about the cancelled tree planting. Their questions, clearly pre-arranged among them, were variations of the same one – whether I saw any connection between the hunting of witches and conditions in the present time.[9]

America, though, was not the only country whose government was at odds with its people. That same year Miller and Inge went to Czechoslovakia, where one hundred and fifty-two writers were blacklisted. In January, he had added his name to a letter to the *New York Review of Books* – also signed by John Cheever, Robert Lowell, William Styron, Maxwell Geismar and I.F. Stone – denouncing the Soviet invasion as 'a brutal crime and act of aggression'. The letter praised the resistance of the Czechs and their refusal to be seen as 'a colony of the Soviet leadership' and stated that, as people who had always opposed imperialism, they viewed the invasion and its aftermath 'with utter abhorrence', condemning it 'without reservation'. Declaring themselves equally opposed to the war in Vietnam, they suggested that the Soviet invasion was 'a severe setback for world socialism', impeding as it did 'the anti-imperialist struggle'. They called for an end to 'acts which dishonour the Soviet Union'[10] and pledged their political resistance to the assault on the Czech people, declaring solidarity with them. They collectively demanded the immediate withdrawal of all Soviet troops and the restoration of Czech authority.

The letter's reference to the risk of a setback for world socialism and of a threat to the anti-imperialist movement was clearly calculated to appeal to the Soviet Union, but the Soviet leaders plainly regarded the Prague Spring as the real threat to socialism, a counter-revolutionary movement that could destabilize other socialist countries, while they would no more describe their own policies as imperialistic than America had traditionally described its own. For the readers of the *New York Review of Books*, meanwhile, the language must have been a reminder of earlier days and of the radical loyalties of the signatories – in Miller's case, at least, a reputation that had done him harm and continued to do so.

His response to the Soviet invasion was odd in another way. In a draft for an article entitled, 'American-Soviet Cooperation – Should There Be Any?', he seemed favourably disposed to the Soviet argument that they had acted to block the German road to the East. While he challenged the right of any state to invade another, the Soviets, he thought, had been justified not in their actions but in their fear and distrust of the Germans, not least because Germany was currently ruled by many ex-Nazis, while big business remained in the hands of those who had designed the Nazi industrial state. What was vital, he argued, was that some kind of détente be arrived at between the United States and the Soviet Union, precisely because this would prevent

Germany 'blackmailing' either party. He noted with pride that no major Russian writer had supported the invasion, but thought that those who feared Germany were justified even though their motives were more complex than that would suggest. What was important was to support those within the Soviet Union who argued for détente and who distrusted its hardline policies. Finally, he drew a parallel between the Soviet action in Czechoslovakia and the American action in Vietnam. Neither revolution nor counter-revolution, he suggested, could justifiably be exported.

He and Inge made their way to Czechoslovakia by car from Austria. Just a year after Warsaw Pact forces had invaded, the mood was tense. Hundreds of Soviet tanks were still parked in the countryside. In a Prague where he could taste the brown coal burned in the city and a brownish dust blew across the sidewalks, he was shown around by two playwrights, Pavel Kohout and Václav Havel. Kohout, in his youth a fervent Stalinist, then a dissident, was subsequently driven out of the country, escaping to Vienna. Havel was to spend time in prison and under house arrest before the collapse of communism elevated him to the presidency.

They were under surveillance throughout their stay, a surveillance conducted openly as a form of intimidation. When they went for a walk amongst Christmas shoppers hunting amongst the well stocked stores, they were tailed. At dinner in a novelist's house his host's child drew attention to a car parked across the street. This was a man whose manuscript had been seized by the authorities, a subject to which Miller would return in 1977 when he set his play *The Archbishop's Ceiling* in Prague (though the city is not directly identified). A seventy-year-old philosophy professor Miller met had been barred from teaching for all but eleven of his thirty-six-year career.

Immediately after Miller's death, in 2005, Havel recalled their meeting with some embarrassment, and rather differently from Miller.

> At the time I was so utterly taken up with local events that I failed to realise something of great importance. At that time I met him in the apartment of my friends, the artist Libor Fára and the photography theorist Aneta Fáreva, who happened also to be a friend of Miller's wife and later organised an exhibition of her photographs in Prague. I think we lunched together at the Fáras'. And right after lunch I excused myself because I had to collect my car from the auto-repair centre, and left, as if unaware that I had a chance to speak with this visitor from the heavens and that I was leaving for reasons that must appear trivial or even absurd to him. But I really did urgently need my car for some patriotic task, and the repair centre closed early and it was not possible for them to deliver it to my home – as in capitalism; I had no one to pick it up for me, the weekend was coming and I just had to go for the car. My departure was extremely inappropriate, of course, and I agonised

over it afterwards – particularly in jail, when I discovered how actively Miller was working for my release. That discomfiture lasted at least twenty-one years, i.e. until I started meeting Miller more and more frequently after our revolution, and I discovered that not only had he not been annoyed with me, but that he had no memory at all of my hasty and somewhat shameful departure .... I have used this occasion ... simply to admit for the first time how stupidly I behaved all those years ago, when he descended from the literary and civic heavens before my very eyes and how that recollection tormented me for so long. I am sending this message to him in the real heaven to which he departed not long ago.[11]

The Czech writers, as opposed to their Soviet counterparts, were not expressly forbidden to publish abroad. Thus, as Miller later wrote in a draft article he was calling 'The Hole in Europe', a playwright like Kohout could read press notices from nearly every European country and America, while he could not visit his own theatre, read his plays in his own language or leave the country lest he be refused re-entry. His work could not be produced in Czechoslovakia, so that he was, in effect, Miller observed, the author less of plays than of translations. Writers in Czechoslovakia were not shot but were described as having emigrated even as they walked along the streets of Prague.

In 1974, Miller would receive a New Year's card from Czechoslovakia. It arrived several months late. On its front was a photograph of a man in a suit, with a spotted bow-tie and hat. He is carrying an umbrella. Alongside him is a woman in a flowered dress. She is also wearing a hat. They are both resting their hands on a lifebuoy, which contains a small black dog. The two people are up to their waists in water. She is smiling: he is more serious. It was Pavel Kohout who, in 1967, had read Solzhenitsyn's protest letter to the Congress of Czech and Slovak Writers. The following year he became one of the 152 Czech writers forbidden to publish in their own country or, in his case, to have his plays produced. Officially, he had left the country but, as the photograph indicates, was unaccountably still there. The photograph of the couple half submerged therefore had a certain accuracy. They were simultaneously in and out.

The Czech novelist Ludvik Vaculik, in *The Guinea-Pigs*, offered an allegory of life in a totalitarian world which featured a guinea-pig tortured by an obsessive bank clerk, as polite as Vaculik's communist interrogator had been. He places the guinea-pig in water: 'As the water rose, the guinea-pig rose too, although it ordinarily doesn't stand around on its hind legs, but rather squats like a hare or a rabbit. Now it stood on its hind legs, though, and raised its body above water level. "Well, how are things going?" I said gently. "Not so hot," it replied.'[12] Miller's surreal New Year card, no less than Vaculik's novel, seems to have captured the mood in late-sixties, early-seventies Czecho-slovakia as accurately as Kafka's 1925 novel *The Trial*, the former featuring a bank clerk, the latter a bank manager.

Miller met with thirty writers in the office of *Listy*, the Prague literary magazine. They included Ludvik Vaculik, Jiri Mucha, Ivan Klima and Lubos Dobrovsky. The Writers' Union, Miller noted, had issued a declaration of support for the Soviet invasion. Missing, however, were the names of all the country's major writers. Four hundred and seventy-five of the 590 members of the Writers' Union had been removed and 130, including Václav Havel, were blacklisted.[13] Milos Forman emigrated. The assembled writers wanted Miller to know that they were about to be jailed by those acting for the occupying forces: 'I could smell the apprehension among them.'[14] The surprise to Miller was that with Vietnam still raging, and images of America's burning cities having been transmitted around the world, they should be turning to the United States. Yet, as was evident in the various statements he made in the mid-1950s when seeking renewal of his passport or defending himself against HUAC, his arguments with America had always been born out of the conviction that it did, indeed, represent a set of possibilities, a mindset, not always observable elsewhere. As he was to say in an article in 1973, 'No listing of hopeful improvements can really alter the despair with modern life which is heard everywhere; the difference, if there is one, is a residual eagerness in Americans to believe despair is not life's fixed condition but only another frontier to be crossed.'[15]

The Czech writers may have contacted him because his voice, as that of an American, would speak louder than others, but Miller was still the son of an immigrant father. Somewhere beyond the tainted politics, the persistent racism, the evidence of social decay, was a conviction that America did, indeed, have a manifest destiny which was not the nineteenth-century imperial drive but a vision, clouded at times, of something more than mere material improve-ment. What the Czechs seemed to long for were precisely the freedoms enshrined in America's constitutional documents, and he had begun to wonder whether America might yet have a role to play, though he was acutely conscious of a history of betrayals which he tracked backwards through the decades:

> Johnson fabricated the Tonkin Gulf hysteria. Kennedy set the country on the rails into Vietnam even as he espoused humanistic idealism. Eisenhower lacked the stomach to scuttle Nixon despite his distaste, if not contempt, for Nixon's unprincipled behavior. Roosevelt tried to pack the Supreme Court when it opposed him and stood by watching the destruction of the Spanish Republic by fascism because he feared the outrage of the Catholic hierarchy if he supported a sister democracy.[16]

Yet for all that, he still looked out at the world from a moral vantage point which owed something to the country with which he had spent his life wrestling, a country that, despite its frequent lapses into political opportunism and cynicism at home and abroad, still seemed to be betraying values which were nonetheless real for being set aside so casually.

The conversation during the meeting was stilted, for the most part steering clear of dangerous topics. Miller had been in the country for only twenty-four hours. He spoke of the need for détente, confessed to America's problems with race and crime and the destabilizing fact of Vietnam. Asked about the American theatre, he said he felt the lack of a psychological drama of cause and effect, an intellectual force – a theatre, in other words, such as his own. He had, he explained, no sympathy for a theatre that tried to shock with nudity or proposed eroding the barrier between performer and audience. He was equally repelled by what seemed to him to be the nihilism of the absurd, which to his mind excluded the human element.

He asked what the Czech attitude was towards the United States, what the impact of American popular music and the hippie movement had been. For the most part it was not a conversation that touched on the exposed nerves of those present, at least not until the end when he was asked what he thought of the death of Jan Palach, the Czech student who had taken part in the November 1968 strikes against the invasion and occupation, and who on 16 January 1969, at the ramp of the National Museum at the top of Wenceslas Square, had set fire to himself with gasoline in protest. Miller replied that his death was like a work of art in that it provoked and challenged. The hero, he said, sheds light on the truth, which is why Palach had sacrificed himself to the fire. It was at this point that the meeting concluded.

Shortly afterwards *Listy* was closed down, a reminder that, a year on from the Soviet invasion, international condemnation meant little. For the moment, though, what had struck Miller, both in the Soviet Union and now in Czechoslovakia, was his kinship not simply with oppressed writers but with those who had themselves once, like him, looked to the East for redemption only to find a false messiah. He had grown up identifying repression with fascism. This had been the embodiment of an implacable power, distorting human relations. Marxism had represented liberation, scientific in its methods, transcendent in its vision. Now the tanks had rolled into Prague, supposedly offering to liberate from counter-revolutionaries those who would soon find themselves imprisoned. Looking back later, he recalled meeting a Soviet political scientist not long after his return from Czechoslovakia. The occasion was a conference where Miller was to speak on the impediments to better cultural relations between the Soviet Union and the United States. 'I found myself,' Miller related, 'facing this ... Soviet whose anger was unconcealed. "It is amazing," he said, "that you – especially you as a Jew –

should attack our action in Czechoslovakia."' Confused, Miller asked him to explain: '"But obviously," he said (and his face had gone quite red and he was furious now), "we have gone in there to protect them from the West German Fascists."' The idea of Warsaw Pact forces marching to the rescue of the few Jews left in Czechoslovakia struck Miller as wonderfully bizarre, but evidence of a kind of self-deceit that he himself recognized.

The closest analogy he could think of was with the apologists for the Vietnam War. While acknowledging that he and others were free to attack US policy, he noted that many had paid a price for doing so. The parallel, though, had more to do with the pressure, 'by those holding political power, to distort and falsify the structures of reality ... The sin of power,' he insisted in an article in the *Index on Censorship*, 'is not only to distort reality but to convince people that the false is true.' Lies might be told about Czech writers but so, too, had they about him, though he was keenly aware that he had access to freedoms denied to them:

> I have been lied about in America by both private and public liars, by the press and the government, but a road – sometimes merely a narrow path – always remained open ... I know what it is to be denied the right to travel outside my country, having been denied my passport for some five years by our Department of State. And I know a little about the inviting temptation to simply get out at any cost, to quit my country in disgust and disillusion, as no small number of people did in the McCarthy fifties and as a long line of Czechs and Slovaks have in these recent years. I also know the empty feeling in the belly at the prospect of trying to learn another nation's secret language, its gestures and body communications without which a writer is only half-seeing and half-hearing.[17]

If we are to take this seriously, here is Miller confessing to a temptation to abandon America during the McCarthy years. It may be no more than a rhetorical gesture of solidarity with those now faced with just such a choice, but it sounds rather more than that. Certainly the British, anxious to avoid political embarrassment, had feared he might stay in 1956 when he came with his new wife Marilyn Monroe and, as he says, a number of Americans did, including Carl Foreman, Sam Wanamaker, Ring Lardner Jr and Larry Adler. The temptation would have been considerable. England never succumbed to McCarthy-style witch-hunts, despite having produced a disturbing number of Soviet agents with impeccable Oxbridge credentials. On the other hand, Miller wrote the above remarks not in 1969, on his return from Czechoslovakia, but in the summer of 1978 in the aftermath of his play *The Archbishop's Ceiling*, in which he explored both the temptation and the price of expatriation and the distorting nature of power.

But for all his rejection of the Marxist model that had dazzled him for so long, he still felt uncomfortable with a capitalist system that seemed to him no more than a pointless cycle of production and consumption. He trusted that the battle for rights on the part of East and Central European dissidents was predicated on the value of freedoms that would not simply be exchanged for corporate scrip. When Soviet troops invaded Czechoslovakia Miller had been focusing on the Democratic Convention. Now he appeared to be making amends and would later become directly involved in supporting the Czech writers who signed Charter 77, a document accusing the Czech government of failing to implement the human rights provisions of the Final Act of the 1975 Conference on Security and Cooperation in Europe – the Helsinki Accords. Among the signatories were Václav Havel and the man who had once sent Miller a photograph of himself up to the waist in water. The process of drawing up the Charter would not be without some degree of farce. Having spent much of the day writing addresses on the envelopes that were to contain the petition, Havel, his fellow writer Ludvik Vaculik and the actor Pavel Landovsky set off pursued by a cavalcade of police cars, six of which crashed on the ice before the conspirators were taken in for questioning. Havel was arrested on 7 January 1977. Tom Stoppard marked the occasion by writing a television play – *Professional Foul* – dedicated to Havel. Like *The Archbishop's Ceiling*, it concerns the fate of what the authorities regard as a subversive typescript.

Where once Miller had been hesitant about travelling, he had now accustomed himself to transatlantic flights. The year 1969 saw visits not only to Czechoslovakia and the Soviet Union but also to France, Spain and Holland. A brief stay in Amsterdam brought back memories of Camus's *The Fall*, when he saw a young woman crossing a bridge, as another once had in fiction. Camus, he reminded himself, had died in 1960, smashing his car into a tree as if in evidence of the truth of his absurdist beliefs.

The year ended when on 14 December he finished a partial draft of a work later filed under the heading 'Bomb play'. Its subject he noted was the several faces of fear which he defined as communisim, the Depression, race riots and colonial liberation, though none of these is directly addressed. It is a verse play in which President Truman defends his decision to drop the bomb. In common with many others he had rejoiced at the dropping of the bombs on Hiroshima and Nagasaki, which had ended a war that had seemed likely to take many more lives before it was over. With time, however, the anxieties of those involved in the project had come to light; the refusal, in particular, of the US administration first to drop a demonstration bomb. In common with others he now felt shocked by, if not guilty about, his own earlier response.

Behind the public issue in this play was another that bore more directly on his own dilemma, in that he was concerned with the personal impact of public issues. How had those involved lived with the inevitable ambivalence? The question boiled down to 'Why was one responsible if one had no evil intentions?' – and, beyond that, more disturbingly, 'Where was the heart of evil if not within us?'[18]

Such questions were not particular to him. They had lain at the heart of the liberal debates of the early 1950s. Lionel Trilling, Arthur Schlesinger Jr, Reinhold Niebuhr, all members of the Americans for Democratic Action, had reacted against the utopian politics of the 1930s by stressing man's fallen nature and urge to power. For a time Miller had found himself at odds with their fierce anti-communism. He did not, though, demur from their analysis of the human condition, which proposed a fundamental flaw. Indeed, it was precisely such a conviction that had drawn him to a concern for modern tragedy. He had no interest in simply renovating an exhausted form. He was responding to what seemed to him to be a tragic sense of life.

To research the material for his play, he had conducted interviews with Hans Bethe, designer of a key component of the bomb, who had tried to persuade Truman not to drop it on people, and with the nuclear physicist J. Robert Oppenheimer, himself subsequently pursued by the security forces. What he was looking for is not entirely clear. It was, he later said, 'emphatically not mere blame or guilt', but, rather, the connection between the professional work of these scientists and their private lives, not least because it was that nexus that perplexed him about his own life, his drive 'to find an absolute truth while blinding myself to facts'.[19]

> I had changed the lives of others, my wives and children certainly, and maybe even people across the world in the audiences of my plays, and yet I could only dimly glimpse myself in my work, as the physicists might be denying themselves in theirs. It seemed impossible to evolve at all without a more complete, more living vision of one's responsibility for oneself, a surgically painful investigation.[20]

This was plainly a man interested in something more than the moral dilemma of scientists creating weapons of enormous power while trying to reconcile their work with their moral beings. This was Arthur Miller, at a moment of self-doubt, trying to understand the gulf that had opened up between his ethical and aesthetic commitments and his manifest personal failures. The writer who had created Willy Loman – a man whose social vision was at odds with the human necessities of his family – who in *The Crucible* had created, in the figure of John Proctor, someone whose personal betrayal had come close to making him confederate with the forces he would challenge, was all too aware that he himself had failed to reconcile his public and private selves.

It seemed to him that, in terms of theatre, *Hamlet, Othello, Oedipus Rex* defined the effort to give reality to life by acknowledging denial. Now, he found himself confronting essentially the same dilemma. Was he not responsible for the wreckage he had left in the wake of his life, with two divorces and disillusioned children? How could this be related to the moral commitment he wished to believe had driven him in his life and his work? How, too, could what seems to have been a brief affair that he conducted with the artist Edith Isaac-Rose? For an exhibition of her work in 2009, she outlined her background:

> I'm a first generation Jewish American. My mother's parents and most of her family never left Hungary. From when I was 9 during the war and through the 1950s, it was my job as the one who spoke and read English, to fill out the forms to substantiate the fate of our family following the Holocaust. I could not imagine a world without justice or that power would not make sense but it would be believed. Over the years, slowly and reluctantly, I have learned to express the inexorable fears that now underline my work.[21]

She grew up in a Jewish neighbourhood in Chicago and in 1951 graduated from the Art Institute there, moving to New York in 1959. While willing to confirm that her relationship with Miller had, indeed, been 'intimate' and that it lasted a year – 1969 – she did not wish to revisit those times. Reminded that in 1969 Miller was married, she replied, 'Yes, I know.'[22] Edith Isaac-Rose would come out as a lesbian and establish a personal and professional relationship with Bea Kreloff, a child of socialist parents, raised, like Miller, in Brooklyn and dedicated to various liberal and radical causes, including gay rights and feminism.

They met in 1979. Kreloff was a former head of the art department at Fieldston School, New York, and had taught painting and lectured on art. For thirty years she and Edith Isaac-Rose have run Art Workshop International in Assisi based in a hotel that still looks out over the Umbrian plateau.

The theme of betrayal runs throughout Miller's work. He focused particularly on sexual betrayal, as in *Death of a Salesman, The Crucible, A View from the Bridge, After the Fall* and *Some Kind of Love Story.* It lies at the heart of his unpublished novel 'The Best Comedians' and of his novella *Homely Girl,* while his play *The Ride down Mount Morgan* features a man who maintains two separate homes with two different women. In each case Miller is making a more general point having to do with a breach in the social contract no less than in private affairs, but he was aware of the extent to which these works reflected aspects of his own sensibility.

It was during the concluding months of 1969, from August to November, that Miller wrote a one-act play, never published or performed, about a woman apparently abandoned by her lover. The woman, the four-times married Caroline Heffner, plainly in the middle of a nervous breakdown, is overseen by an older woman, Mrs Rogers. Caroline, we learn, was discovered naked under a mink coat and brought home under the guidance of a doctor (who makes a brief appearance). The action takes place in the early hours of the morning. The title, *Behind the Times*, refers to Caroline's obsession with time, even as fragmentary memories tumble into her mind. Somewhere in the background a war is being waged but news of it is little more than a rumour. With a record of failed marriages, she claims to be 'partly' a lesbian. By degrees we learn, or appear to, that she has seen a doctor in Coney Island to rid herself of a baby. Convinced that she is still pregnant, it seems that she has already lost it. Her life, like the watch of her minder, has effectively stopped. The action ends as Mrs Rogers knocks the watch repeatedly on the table.

Miller began the play on 20 October and finished the first draft in five days, then revised and finished it on 7 November. There is no evidence that he ever tried to place it, but he once confessed that 90 per cent of what he wrote was abandoned. *Behind the Times* was simply one more for the filing cabinet.

Miller should have felt considerable affinity with Oppenheimer when he interviewed him some decade earlier, a man who, like him, had attended Communist Party meetings without, it seems, ever signing a Party card, and who had, again like Miller with Mary, married a convinced Marxist. Oppenheimer, like Miller, had had an affair while married (even making advances to fellow scientist Linus Pauling's wife) and had been called before the House Un-American Activities Committee, where he refused to name names (though he did so later in a Senate investigation). He had also, like Miller, approved of dropping the bomb, stressing the human cost of failing to do so and the price already paid by so many as a result of supposedly conventional armaments, only to become opposed to the use of nuclear weapons. Oppenheimer, it seemed to Miller, was a flawed man, given to depressions, whose work took primacy and whose greatest successes lay in the past. Miller's interest, then, was perhaps less in the question of Truman's decision to drop the bomb than in the complexities of those who put the weapon in his hand and, in the case of Oppenheimer, in the parallel between his equivocal personal history and his own.

He found Oppenheimer diffident and noncommittal. He had, after all, been pursued by government agencies and had his security credentials withdrawn. However, on one question he was responsive. Miller asked whether everyone deadens their connections, and their psyches, in the face of actions they find it difficult to justify. 'Plainly moved, his eyes filled with what I took for vulnerability, he looked into my eyes and said with quiet emphasis that this was not always true. In other words, he was indeed suffering, was not merely a man who had known power and was able to distract himself by recollecting his unique accomplishment.'[23] It is easy to see why this question should not only have been the one to which Oppenheimer was most responsive, but the one that was most central to Miller, middle-aged, aware of his own contradictions and unable to convince himself that past accomplishments were sufficient to sustain him.

Miller would also have felt a certain affinity to Hans Bethe, though for different reasons. A German Jew, he had fled the Nazis in 1933, and first opposed and then worked on the hydrogen bomb. When Miller met him, he was campaigning for the Partial Test Ban Treaty, which would be agreed in 1963. Later, he would oppose Ronald Reagan's Star Wars anti-ballistic missile system, and in 1995 urge fellow scientists to refuse to work on atomic weapons projects. Miller himself would become an active anti-nuclear campaigner. The problem for these physicists was that they had unleashed a power that was not theirs to control, and the truth that Miller carried away was that they were of necessity in denial – that, indeed, 'Men had to deny.'[24]

He wrote the beginnings of the play in Roxbury, working in blank verse. In the end, though, he thought it too observed rather than felt. He broke off. It was plainly going nowhere. The bomb play was, he said, interesting rather than horrifying. It was another failed work and, as such, disturbing: 'I did not know how long I would live, and I longed to leave something absolutely truthful; this play might well illuminate the dilemma of science, but it failed to embarrass me with what it revealed, and I had never written a good thing that had not made me blush.'[25]

In March 1970 Miller and his family flew from Hong Kong to Cambodia, where Inge wanted to photograph. At that moment, 'because I had arrived',[26] President Nixon and Kissinger decided to bomb eastern Cambodia, the Ho Chi Minh trail down which men and munitions were moving. The decision, made in a meeting attended by National Security Advisor Henry Kissinger, Secretary of Defense Melvin Lair and the head of the CIA, William Rogers, was shared with only a select number of Congressional leaders. The Foreign Relations Committees of House and Senate were deliberately misled. News of the bombing was kept from the public and it would be 1973 before the Congressional leaders discovered that the bombing campaign had initially started without their permission. In June that year both houses passed legislation to halt it, but Nixon responded with a veto, which prompted Congress to override the veto and pass the War Powers Resolution limiting presidential freedom to act. The campaign was called Operation Breakfast, the meal eventually consisting of three times the ordnance dropped on Japan in the Second World War, killing an estimated hundred thousand Cambodians and destroying 20 per cent of the country's property. The Cambodian Prime

Minister, Prince Sihanouk, endorsed the decision to bomb.

The Millers were staying in a hotel, built by Prince Sihanouk, opposite the twelfth-century temple of Angkor Wat. They only began to suspect that something might be wrong when they noticed that the lunch tables were unoccupied and their daughter Rebecca reported on what she had heard from a friend. As she explained to me in 2001, 'I remember the hotel closing. I had made a friendship with a little girl called Penny who one day in the pool told me that there were no more planes leaving and that her parents were very worried. I remember going back to my dad and saying, "Penny says there are no more planes leaving." I didn't know what it all meant. Her father was a British diplomat. Then suddenly we noticed that they were draining the swimming pool. Everyone was just getting out, but nobody said anything.'[27] Then two station wagons of tourists arrived at their hotel, announcing that the airport had been closed.

An Englishman named Foxton, who had been head of Shell Oil in the Philippines and with whom they were lunching that day, began to suspect something significant was happening. The manager of the hotel denied anything was amiss, but the French guests continued to leave. Miller called the American Embassy, where the Cultural Affairs Officer assured him that there had been no coup, denying that anything untoward was happening. The airport, they assumed, would reopen soon, though in fact Prince Sihanouk, then on a trip to Moscow and Beijing, was being overthrown, and the bombing had begun. Marshal Lon Nol deposed Sihanouk on 18 March. He established the Khmer Republic seven months later, which was superseded by the genocidal Khmer Rouge, the US having bribed Nol with $1 million to leave. Sihanouk broadcast an appeal from Beijing, calling on the people to resist the coup. The South Vietnamese Air Force began air strikes on 20 March.

The French tourists, meanwhile, apparently already knew what was happening, even as the Cultural Affairs Officer was denying it. 'This son of a bitch was telling us to stay there, because they wouldn't admit that Mr Kissinger had done what he was doing.'[28] Foxton, however, had contacts in Phnom Penh and decided that they needed to leave, but by then the French had commandeered all the vehicles except one twelve-passenger Mercedes bus, which they bought from the owners for a few hundred dollars ('an enormous amount of money,' Rebecca remembered thinking). The owner was to drive them to the border, some four and a half hours away. There were no real roads, only desolate, rocky terrain. Rebecca later recalled that her main concern was to hold on to her friend's Winnie the Pooh.

The next morning, at four thirty, they set off, joined now by one of Foxton's British friends. Ten miles out of town they were stopped by troops and searched until Foxton's friend intervened: 'One guy on the bus we thought was a spy. He was English but spoke fluent Cambodian. He got us across.' Rebecca recalls an explosion nearby. At the Thai border, carrying their children and luggage, they crossed a gorge on a rickety bridge with loose wooden boards. At the Thai army post they caught up with the French and once again had to compete with them for transport to Bangkok. Foxton began to haggle with a Thai army captain, hoping to obtain an army vehicle, a deal that fell through when they were overheard by a French civilian. The captain was afraid of being compromised. Later, Foxton 'produced this small Fiat' into which six people, a driver and their baggage were piled. When they were about to leave a woman approached them, claiming that she and her sick husband should have the car in their place. When Miller, faced with trying to get his family to safety, refused, she replied, 'And you call yourself a humanitarian?' to which he replied, 'Not today.' They reached Bangkok and safety on 23 March.

On his return from Cambodia, Miller wrote a piece for *Harper's* magazine, which appeared in their July issue. It features a Bangkok prince and princess, in which the former justifies the taking of opium and the legitimacy of prostitutes while she enthuses about elephants. Written wholly in dialogue as they both address an unknown listener, it largely ignores the political situation, except that the princess insists that the guerrillas in northern Thailand are native to the country and not Vietcong; the prince is more interested in bombings in America than events in his own country.

Miller addressed the issue of Vietnam and Cambodia more directly when, shortly after his return from the latter, he went to West Point where, as a young boy, it had been his ambition to study, and where he now expected a hostile response. It was a speaking engagement he undertook with some trepidation:

> I was trembling a little. There was this whole class of cadets and their officers, a lot of medals all over the place, and most of these officers had served in Vietnam. What I was going to tell them was that the war was absolutely hopeless and pointless, and that the sacrifices being made were too horrifying to contemplate, because they were not in a good cause. So I got up there and said, 'I've just come back from Cambodia and all I'm going to tell you is, you can't win. We're on the wrong side and, if you did win, it would be sand that would simply pour through your fingers.'[29]

'I figured,' he explained, 'that I might as well be eaten whole as in pieces.' At first, the response was much as he had predicted: 'A cadet with a size seventeen neck – I later learned he was the son of the Teamster boss in Chicago – was the first to raise his hand in the question period. He said he was outraged that I should be allowed to make this kind of defeatist propaganda at the Military Academy.'[30] To Miller's surprise, though, a colonel who had served as military attaché in Phnom Penh for twelve years confirmed his diagnosis. Later, at dinner, he was told that the Army had always regarded the war as unwinnable and that hostility towards those in uniform on the part of the civilian population now meant that they were liable to be attacked in the streets of their own cities. America was at war with itself.

As he was about to leave, his host took a book down from a shelf and read Eisenhower's speech to the troops on the eve of D Day, as they were readying to leave for Normandy. In a talk to University of Southern California students in 1983 on 'Denial and Vietnam', Miller recalled this moment. The speech had been about the justness of the cause and the struggle against tyranny. There was, he remembered, a moment of silence and then the host had asked whether any commander would be able to make such a speech again.[31] Thirty years later, Miller was asked to contribute an essay, in which he recalled this visit, to a book celebrating the two-hundredth anniversary of West Point.

On 30 April 1970 President Nixon addressed the nation on television to announce that he was sending troops to Cambodia. 'We live,' he said, 'in an age of anarchy, both abroad and at home ... We see mindless attacks on all the great institutions which have created free civilizations in the last 500 years. Here in the United States great universities have been systematically destroyed.'[32] After the speech demonstrations took place on over five hundred campuses across the country. Nixon referred to campus radicals as 'bums'. 'You see those bums, you know, blowing up the campuses. Listen, the boys that are on college campuses today are the luckiest people in the world and here they are burning up the books, storming around on this issue. You name it. Get rid of the war and there will be another one.'[33]

For all the teach-ins, marches and petitions, one event in particular under-lined the internal tensions over Vietnam. In May 1970, four unarmed students at Kent State University, protesting against the bombing of Cambodia (now public knowledge), were shot dead by National Guardsmen. William K. Schroeder from Lorain, Ohio (birthplace of Toni Morrison), was nineteen years old and a member of the Reserve Officers Training Corps (ROTC). He had been a bystander. Sandra Lee Scheuer, also from Ohio, was on her way to a speech therapy class. Jeffrey Glenn Miller, who had transferred from Michigan State University, was shot in the mouth on an access road to the parking lot. Allison Krause, who had put a flower in a guardsman's rifle barrel saying 'Flowers are better than bullets', was shot on her way to class. They were all killed when Sylvester Del Corso, Adjutant General of the Ohio National Guard, claimed that a sniper had opened fire. *New York Times* reporter John Kifner denied the claim. A further six students were treated for gunshot wounds. On 5 May, presidents of thirty-seven colleges and uni-versities urged Nixon to demonstrate 'unequivocally' that he intended to end American military involvement in South-east Asia. Protests shut down or curtailed activities in an estimated four hundred and fifty colleges and universities. Miller published an article in the July issue of *McCall's* magazine. The war, he claimed in his draft (much of which never made its way into the published piece), had finally come home when American soldiers killed American children on their school grounds. It had been happening with blacks for a long time, he noted. Maybe now that white was killing white it would finally strike home.

It was frightening, he went on, not merely because National Guardsmen had faced students with loaded rifles but because those guns had effectively been directed by the President himself when he called the students 'bums' and got away with it. The 'bums', he maintained, were afraid of being murdered either by the war itself or by police and the National Guard. They were determined to express and demonstrate their moral disgust for a war that Nixon had expanded even while having sought election with the promise of ending it.

There was, he thought, a gulf between the generations. If everyone over thirty disappeared he was confident that peace would be within their grasp. Nor was this entirely a new thought. He invoked *Death of a Salesman* to make his point about a shift in values: when Biff Loman had tried to convince his father that he had a right to an ordinary life, the life of a simple worker, it had been like a man spitting on the Bible. Nixon and Agnew, he suggested, were no Willy Lomans. Willy, at least, had a sense of the insufficiency of the values to which he had committed himself. They were 'like Uncle Ben ... who went into the jungle and came out rich', never questioning the pursuit of success, the value of materialism or an instinctive distrust of the stranger.

At New Haven, by contrast, the Yale President, Kingman Brewster, and Chaplain William Coffin had attended a demonstration called to protest against the Panther trial then under way. In May 1969 a Black Panther member had been tortured and murdered by a fellow Panther. The organization's leader, Bobby Seale, had spoken at Yale the previous day and unaccountably was charged along with others. In May 1970 the pre-trial proceedings began and twelve thousand Black Panther supporters arrived in New Haven. The university made classes voluntary and Brewster, who had appointed Coffin, declared his scepticism that a fair trial would be possible. Coffin himself expressed shame at the silence of so many in the face of the injustice being perpetrated. For Nixon and Agnew, it seemed to Miller, any bridging of the generations was impossible, along with the right to dissent. 'Nobody died at Yale,' he observed, while 'four died at Kent. The legitimacy of radicalism was recognized at Yale. It was abhorred and fired at in Ohio. Which way, America?'[34]

In April 1971, Miller once again found himself among the military, though this time he joined a gathering of Vietnam veterans preparing for a large rally due to take place in Washington. This was the so-called Dewey Canyon III, named after two military incursions into Laos by US and Vietnamese forces. One decorated veteran appeared on 22 April in a televised Senate hearing to voice his own feelings. His name was John Kerry. He spoke of the stories told by his fellow veterans. They had confessed that 'they had personally raped, cut off ears, cut off heads, taped wires from portable telephones to human genitals and turned up the power, cut off limbs, blown up bodies, randomly shot at civilians, razed villages in a fashion reminiscent of Genghis Khan, shot cattle and dogs for fun, poisoned food stocks, and generally ravaged the countryside of South Vietnam'. He recalled that Vice-President Agnew, speaking at West Point the previous year, had remarked that 'some glamorize the criminal misfits of society while our best men die in Asian rice paddies to preserve the freedom which most of those misfits abuse'. This statement, Kerry asserted, was a distortion that explained their presence in Washington 'because we in no way consider ourselves the best men in this country, because those he calls misfits were standing up for us in a way that nobody else in this country dared to, because so many who have died would have returned to this country to join the misfits in their efforts to ask for an immediate withdrawal from Vietnam'.[35]

Thirty-three years later, Kerry would be the Democratic candidate for the presidency. In 2004 it was revealed, unsurprisingly, that his 1971 appearance had earned him the attention of the FBI, which duly opened a file on him. For the moment, though, his was one voice among many former veterans who now converged on the capital.

The group of 'misfit' veterans that Miller encountered was modest in size. There were no more than twelve hundred, he estimated, though the administration had nevertheless sought injunctions. Many of them were long-haired, but they wore battle ribbons. They were, Miller noticed as he walked among them, the grandsons of the world war veterans known as the Bonus Army who had been driven out of Washington in 1931 when Douglas MacArthur, with his aide Major Eisenhower, had led a charge on his white horse, burning the shacks in which the men had been camping. When he told those gathered for the march of this event, he discovered that they knew nothing of it – further evidence, he thought, of America's disregard of history.

At the end of the year, along with Noam Chomsky, Faye Dunaway, Jane Fonda, Dick Gregory and others, he protested against an event that took place in a small country town. GIs had converted an old theatre into the Covered Wagon Coffeehouse, in Mountain Home, Idaho (population in the 2000 census, 11,143). It was established by those who opposed the war, to offer counselling to members of the military, but it also housed women's meetings. It was not popular with the local community. On 18 November a member of the project was beaten up. Two nights later the words, 'This is just a warning' were painted on its walls. The following night it was burned to the ground. The protesters called for funds to build a new centre. It was rebuilt, but two years later burned down again.

7

THE OBLONG BLUR

You went from LBJ to Richard Nixon ... I suppose the country gets
the leadership it deserves.[1]   *Arthur Miller*

Looking back on the 1970s, Miller referred to them as 'an oblong blur'.
'I have no memory of [the decade] at all. I sometimes doubt whether it
really happened! I could not tell you what was going on in the seventies. It
was a terrible waste of time ... If we can we should send them in and exchange
them for something good! The Vietnam War was over and Carter was coming
in. So that was nothing happening in a big way.'[2] Václav Havel remarked:
'John Lennon once said that the 1970s weren't worth a damn. And, indeed,
when we look back on them today ... they seem, compared with the rich and
productive 1960s, to be lacking in significance, style, atmosphere, with no
vivid spiritual and cultural movements. The seventies were bland, boring, and
bleak.'[3] Certainly, for Miller they did not begin auspiciously, despite the award
of several honours, including membership of the American Academy of Arts
and Letters. In fact, this was the beginning of what would prove to be a long
period of disaffection with Miller's new plays in America. Increasingly, he
would be honoured only as the author who had created a series of classics in
the 1940s and 50s. *After the Fall, Incident at Vichy* and *The Price* would soon
fade in the public memory and new works be treated with a degree of
disregard.

Rebecca later recalled this period. Speaking in 2001, she admitted: 'I was
very emotionally invested and very worried about the response. Very often
reviews were bad and I hated, I dreaded reviews. I always felt very protective
of my father. Even when we crossed the street I would make sure I was on
the traffic side. I always felt very worried. I sensed his vulnerability. I knew a
time in the 70s when he had doubts about himself as a writer. I remember
him talking about it.' She recalled the sinking feeling in her stomach when
they waited for reviews that were increasingly negative.

She grew up with a sense of her father as a failure – which, paradoxically, gave her a freedom to develop that might not have been the case if, like her half-brother and sister (Jane and Robert, Miller's children by his first wife, Mary), she had grown up when he was at the height of his public success:

> I think that saved me. That's the difference between myself and my brother. He grew up with him when he was rocketing up with the kind of self-absorption that he would have had for that which was much more than it is now. That must have been difficult for a son. I grew up with a father who was failing all the time. Every time he put something up, people knocked it down. That's why I felt protective of him because my experience of him was not of him being the most successful man in the world. My experience of him was of someone who was continually working so hard and they would just brush it away. I felt terribly bad for him. Since then everything has picked up but there was a very dark period and that was exactly the 70s and the 80s when I was growing up.

In 1971 Miller announced a new play to be set in the 1930s:

> AM is writing a play drawing in part on some of the material in Studs Terkel's 'Hard Times', a collection of interviews with people who lived through the period of the thirties. Miller's play, tentatively titled 'The American Clock', will deal with the period as the matrix of the present in what he sees as a race between a developing sense of the American self and certain fundamentals of democratic life. The play will have a large cast and music.

He set himself to reading newspaper accounts of the mid-1930s, looking for some central motif. For him, it had been the fight against fascism, but it had plainly also been a time when basic American values and assumptions were being challenged by the Depression. In the end, the play would take the best part of a decade to write, while its emphasis would shift. For the moment, he abandoned it.

His first completed works of the 1970s were two one-acts – *Fame* and *The Reason Why* – at New York's New Theater Workshop. They ran for twenty performances. His next was no more successful.

The Creation of the World and Other Business, which opened on 30 November 1972, is in a sense a continuation, in a different mode, of a fundamental issue raised in *After the Fall*, a play in which the implications of the Holocaust were seen to underlie what he might previously have seen as social or political questions. As he noted a year after *Creation*, what the Holocaust posited was a new enemy: man.

The play begins in the Garden of Eden, before the Fall. In what amounts to a vaudeville routine, God and Adam set out to name God's creations. Into this idyll comes Eve, who adds to the comic misunderstandings that characterize Adam's relationship to the world. At Lucifer's urging, she eats the apple and persuades Adam to do likewise, and the clock begins to tick. With awareness comes knowledge and death, hardly the bargain they thought on offer. And death, born out of the conflict between brothers, is engendered by pride and a desire for power.

From Miller's point of view the play was about the need for a story that would account for human fallibility and yet offer the possibility of transcendence. It is not man who is created in God's image, but God in man's. He is an externalized conscience. His vengeance becomes the apparent root of justice and a seeming limit on an unremitting and unpitying licence. And when some absolute act – murder, or, in the case of the Holocaust, mass murder – seems to destroy the credibility of such a compassionate, even impartial judge, then faith lies less in continuing belief than in an understanding that He has to be recreated from the very need He had failed to satisfy. The creation, Miller noted,

> was really the first tragedy in our religious mythology, a fratricide, but I treated it comedically, as man's groping his way to his own human nature with no instructions ... The fluctuating moral consequences of a given human nature are really what all my plays are about in a way ... man is thrashing around blindly, yet in a kind of touching and moving way, toward some tolerable civilized form for his alienated feelings, which, he instinctively senses, are murderous.[4]

The Creation of the World and Other Business, however, was a rather too self-conscious fable. The humour can seem too adolescent, at times, to bear the weight of the philosophical speculation on which it rests.

On 15 August 1972, Miller had written to the play's director Harold Clurman offering answers to questions raised by the actress Barbara Harris, who was to play the part of Eve. What the play asked, he explained, was whether there was such a thing as right and wrong and why mankind felt the need to insist on its reality. When Eve conceived, what instinct led her to sustain the child, to welcome life rather than destroy it? Were ethics, then, rooted in biology, a product of psychology rather than edicts to be obeyed because they derived from the idea of ultimate authority? This, in other words, was a play that reiterated a familiar Miller motif. An atheist, he had always been fascinated by the human need to invoke the existence of God, the instinct to create the values by which we live.

It is hard to know what Clurman was supposed to make of this four-page letter and still harder to know what Barbara Harris could have been expected to do with it as an actress. Miller seems, more than anything, to be having a conversation with himself. The closest he gets to offering usable advice is to suggest that Harris should, in terms of her voice and acting, be seen to move from adolescence to young womanhood to mature woman. Adam and Eve, he said, should begin to behave as a married couple.

Once again, as with *Incident at Vichy* and *The Price*, he claimed that Vietnam was an off-stage presence in the play, just as a country which dealt in images of itself as a new Eden, a City on the Hill, sought to reconcile a sense of its own particular innocence with acts of violence. Like *After the Fall* and *Incident at Vichy*, therefore, it engaged with the question of the human capacity for violence, those contending forces in the human psyche that enable creativity and destruction to coexist. It offered the spectacle of 'the purely loving and practical Adam and Eve, looking down in disbelief at the murdered Abel and the unrepentant Cain', two progenitors who 'can only fear for their lives under a God who not only permits such monstrous acts but has apparently designed mankind so as to perpetuate them. In this play the catastrophe is built into man's primal nature; in his very brotherhood he first tastes the murder of his own kind.'[5]

That Miller chooses to shape his drama as a comedy hardly conceals his continuing debate over human nature and the human capacity to betray, deny, destroy. In Eden, there is no guilt because no sense of sin. To survive as something more than a fact of nature, and hence of God, it is necessary to step outside the Garden, but there is a price to be paid for that. Miller, the man who had signed up to the Oxford Movement's peace pledge back in college, never ceased to be disturbed by evidence of the regressive instincts not least of those who declare their own innocence, personal and national, as if unaware of the contradiction at the heart of their claim. Cain kills to secure primacy in God's love. He does so, therefore, out of passion rather than the cold indifference advanced by Lucifer. No wonder Miller saw the play as a 'catastrophic comedy'. It proved, he suggested, that there was no rational ground for hope and that it was necessary, therefore, to live happily, constructing meaning and accepting the price of freedom.

The play ends with the familiar Miller existential statement as Adam declares, 'God's not coming anymore – we are all that's left responsible!' Mercy, if it is to prevail, can only be a human gift, not a proffered grace. The need for transcendence may account for the desire to invoke a God, but that need is born out of a human dissatisfaction with the given, which itself is the generator of meaning. This is the source of creativity. God is the Godot who is always about to appear, the origin alike of a kinetic energy and of a moral imperative. *The Creation of the World and Other Business*, Miller continued, was 'a play that asks, among other questions, what sort of psychological situation must have given rise to the creation of God in the first place'.[6] One reason for his continued fascination if not with religion then with a human need to believe was precisely this sense of a loss of purpose and direction. Politics no longer served the common weal. Art seemed to have lost its nerve.

For Pascal, God was a wager worth making. What did anyone have to lose by believing? If God existed, you gained eternal life. If He did not you were no worse off than if you had never believed in the first place. There might be some loss, in terms of forgone satisfactions, but these were minor. It was a view that the philosopher William James, for one, found 'simply silly', its subjectivism an affront to science which serves truth rather than opinion, a truth that did not transcend the physical world but codified it and in so doing acknowledged a responsibility to mankind. Fascinated by the desire to believe, Miller felt its gravitational pull. He might declare himself an atheist but he recognized the need for some context to life, some source of adjudication for right behaviour, a structure of being that would render life as something more than mere contingency.

In his published and unpublished work he repeatedly returned to the story of Genesis, to the Book of Job, as if the fables there contained offered a clue, irrespective of their context in a book whose authority he was no longer prepared to concede. The deconsecrated state of the archbishop's palace in *The Archbishop's Ceiling*, his 1977 play, suggests that he had no belief that we exist within God's eye, having replaced the idea, under Marxism, with an equally omniscient state. There was, however, a space in Miller's soul that God had occupied, if only for a moment, and which Lenin had filled for rather longer, aware as Miller was of what William James called 'the contradiction between the phenomena of nature and the craving of the heart to believe that behind nature there is a spirit whose expression nature is'.[7] But what could that be? As James observed, 'Goodness, badness, and obligation must be *realized* somewhere in order really to exist; and the first step in ethical philosophy is to see that no merely inorganic "nature of things" can realize them.'[8] But if not the nature of things, or obedience to arbitrary injunctions religious or secular, in the name of what was a moral world to be constituted? The contradiction of which James spoke could, after all, be generative alike of religion or secular humanism.

Now Miller spoke out in the name of what he liked to call human charity, a sense of right behaviour, which he found ever less in evidence. He stood for justice, as if its nature were self-evident and not contingent – hence his involvement in campaigns to right injustices. But was this the transcendence he sought or simply a well regulated space to occupy pending the grace of a more convincing account of human affairs, a compelling master story? He was tempted to feel that the failure of his own stories, his sense of being cut off from audiences to which he had once felt himself umbilically connected, reflected a more profound dislocation.

In the notes he wrote to himself at this time, these uncertainties are registered both in his sense of his own alienation and failure and in his consciousness that he inhabited a society that continued to announce its self-evident virtues while jumping the rails of its presumed values. The fact that he signed petitions, aligned himself with liberal politicians, repeatedly took a principled stand, led many to assume that he was confident in himself and his sense of the world. Increasingly, this was no longer true. He was certainly resilient, never deflected by negative responses even as he resented them, but he felt ever less certain about his ability to address a society that seemed to him to have lost its sense of direction. His depressions were not clinical, but they were frequent. His years in analysis had prompted an internal dialogue in which he frequently sought to explore his motives, doubts and ambitions along with his increasing sense of failure. Yet a solution was always to hand in the form of his writing, published and unpublished, and he would frequently seek to understand himself not only by keeping notes but by generating fictions that delved into his psyche, sometimes in consequence refusing to allow them to be either completed or offered for publication. They were a way of maintaining equanimity.

In 1996, he would contribute to a volume about the Book of Genesis. In this he recalled his first encounter with the story at the age of six or seven as he worked his way through it in Hebrew with an old man with a long yellowed beard who smelled of snuff tobacco. It was, he recalled, 'heavy duty' simultaneously learning a language and how the world was made. *The Creation of the World and Other Business*, he now stated, had in part been inspired by the revolts of the 1960s in so far as they echoed his experience in the 1930s. The 'high tide of idealism and outrage' would inevitably be followed by disillusionment, as it had for him. 'The Fall had to follow the Creation.' It was in this oblique way, he suggested, that the 'story resumed its life in my mind. But now it appeared to me as myth generated by strictly human dilemmas that no human logic was able to rationalize. It became the story of how man created God, but a god and a cosmology that so beautifully answered to human needs that he ended up being worshipped.'

Without the murder of Cain, however, 'the Bible is but one more clan history, a curio. It is this fratricide that anchors the Jewish religion in human life ... For if a brother could murder a brother, nobody is safe, all bets are off, and there is no future.' God 'may not exist in Heaven but he surely does in the mind of man ... whether God came from man or man from God; an appeal to an ultimate sanction above and beyond our wits' end is part of the essence of our human nature ... If there is a hostile force in all this, it is indifference, the sealing up of the heart ... In his terrible way Cain too has served; he has filled out our definition of the real nature of man.'[9]

In *Timebends* Miller emphasizes the moral seriousness of the play. In contemporary interviews he stressed the comedy, citing his enjoyment of the great comedians. Written in six weeks, it was the play he liked to read aloud to friends even as he was working on another 'serious' play. And there, perhaps, is the problem of a play whose humour and simplicity can seem less underpinnings of philosophic inquiry than at odds with it.

The Creation of the World and Other Business had a troubled history on its way to Broadway. In 1971, casting proved difficult and it was deferred for a season. The director, Harold Clurman, was fired, while both Hal Holbrook and Barbara Harris left during try-outs in Boston. The final act was reportedly rewritten fourteen times, though according to Mark Lamos, who played Abel, in rehearsals Miller had slapped Boris Aronson's fibreglass set with a rolled-up copy of the script and said, 'This is the best goddamned play I've ever written. It's better than *Salesman!*'[10]

Gerald Freedman later explained something of the problem:

Creation of the World was in trouble in Boston. Robert Whitehead, with the blessing of Harold Clurman ... asked me to take over the direction ... He confessed they probably had gone into production prematurely. Arthur had written some wonderful scenes with wit, wisdom and humour, retelling the Genesis story. But had he written a play? It was a father-and-son conflict without a resolution. The cast was demoralized as a result of cast changes out of town and there was more to come. There was a feeling that there was no clear sense of what Arthur had to say. The production moved to the Kennedy Center in Washington and we continued to work on the play. We agreed that Arthur had addressed some important questions in three episodes of Genesis but some larger issue had not emerged.[11]

For Harold Clurman, writing to Boris Aronson on 11 October 1971, it was a 'philosophic comedy' about power, with God and Lucifer representing contending forces here externalized but present in humanity. It was concerned with a battle between reason and love. Miller accounted for the play's failure, as he had of his first Broadway play, *The Man Who Had All the Luck*, by suggesting that the production had never found its feet: 'They never found the style of the play ... we didn't have the luck or perspicacity to create the style the play needs.'[12] It was not, however, a comedy that seems to have appealed; and *Creation* is indeed a slight work, playful, almost as if Miller wanted to mimic something of the naive enthusiasm of his characters. Its failure, then, was hardly a blow, except that it proved one in a sequence of such failures. Reviews were now inclined to offer an obituary not for a single play but for a career.

Clive Barnes in the *New York Times*, with a backward glance at *The Price* – which, he suggested, fell 'short of the radiance of his early promise' – struggled to like it and acknowledged that he had been disappointed but in the end was inclined to regard it as a comic-strip version of Genesis to which people should give a 'fair shake'[13] because of the importance of its author. However, it gripped him neither intellectually nor dramatically. Equivocal reviews in the *New York Times* have never saved a show, and did not on this occasion. Looking back in 1983, the critic Frank Rich began his review with the words, 'In the beginning – or, to be precise, in 1972 – Arthur Miller created *The Creation of the World and Other Business*, and Broadway saw that it was not good.'[14] Richard Watts in the *New York Post* found it confused and confusing. Douglas Watt in the *New York Daily News* thought it devoid of wonder, mystery or fancy. It was, he observed, flat and mechanical. *Time* magazine's review described it as 'a feeble, pointless play'. A 'feeling of sadness', it added, 'clings to the event'. Miller 'has come a cropper'. It was an unequivocal disaster.

Perhaps the most devastating review – though there were plenty to choose from – came from Stanley Kauffmann. 'Going to Arthur Miller's new play,' he reported, 'is like going to the funeral of a man you wish you could have liked more. The occasion seals your opinion because there is no hope for change.' His weaknesses were evident to what he called 'the best critics', but apparently not to those abroad whose respect for him he thought possibly a result of the fact that 'his language improves with translation', which, of course, left the British curiously placed. Otherwise he ascribed his success with audiences to the fact that he gave what Kauffmann called 'the illusion of depth', whereas in fact his plays 'suffer from fuzzy concepts, transparent mechanics, superficial probes, and pedestrian diction'; though doubtless, he mused, 'he has done the best he could'. Nor did condescension end there. Miller's problem, he explained, was that he evidenced 'the peculiar falseness of honest writers who are not talented enough to keep free of dubious artistic means ... I got nothing more from this play than that it was by a writer starving for subject matter, anxious to keep busy, who grabbed at an available classic subject and, to mask his desperation, treated it comically.' What was on offer was 'a rehash of homiletics, inconsistent and stale ... muddle, aching along from one glib irony to another'. Beyond that lay another familiar accusation. Suggesting that the play consisted of a blend of the Bible and the borscht circuit, he saw this as evidence of 'one more evasion with which Miller might be indicted, his evasion of Jewishness in his career'.[15] In this respect he recalled *Death of a Salesman*.

That same year, Kauffmann reviewed a revival of *The Crucible*, which he found 'thematically schizoid'. The first three acts struck him as 'too plotty to be deep', while observing that 'the plotting sometimes creaks'. All the same, he thought it his best play, though its popularity, like Miller's, derived from the fact that he 'deals almost exclusively with received liberal ideas'. He 'makes enlightened folks feel even better about themselves'.[16] A year earlier, in the context of a review of Edward Albee's *All Over*, he had added to his opinion that Albee was a 'weakening mediocrity' (ahead lay a further two Pulitzer Prizes) the observation that Miller was 'all munched out'.[17] In 1975 he reviewed a Circle in the Square revival of *Death of a Salesman* directed by George C. Scott, who played Willy Loman. To see it again, however, was not to warm to its virtues but to realize with greater clarity that Miller 'lacked the control and vision to fulfil his own idea', and that its language was 'slightly ludicrous'. Beyond that, thematically the play was 'cloudy', while Miller was 'anti-business, anti-technology', and Willy Loman a 'mentally unstable man'. *Death of a Salesman* was 'a flabby, occasionally false work'.[18]

What is striking about Kauffmann is that he was a reviewer for the *New Republic* and the *New York Times*, that he served as a visiting professor of drama at Yale and taught at the City University of New York. Like Robert Brustein, however, who also worked for the *New Republic* and played a significant role at both Yale and Harvard, he had a general dislike for the classic American dramatists. *The Creation of the World and Other Business* is admittedly not a good battleground on which to defend Miller. It is indeed a minor work, a strained fable, but what is striking about its reviews is that it was seen as an occasion to dismiss Miller's earlier achievements.

In 1972 Miller continued to protest against the Vietnam War. Asked to write a piece for the *Chicago Sun-Times* about *Death of a Salesman* on the occasion of a new production starring Jack Warden, he explained that 'it is a difficult thing to do on a morning when Navy planes are dropping mines in the harbors of North Vietnam'.[19] Two months later he returned to the world of political conventions, this time in Miami, where George McGovern was looking for the Democratic Party nomination. One rival had already removed himself when, on 19 July 1969, Teddy Kennedy drove off a bridge at Chappaquiddick and drowned more than his companion of the evening: this bizarre incident marked the end of his presidential ambitions at the time, though in 1980 he would run in the Democratic primaries against Jimmy Carter.

There was the same sense of theatre as in 1968, though this time the pressure was lower. Chicago, he recalled, had been as theatrical as *Follies*, Stephen Sondheim's musical, with everyone performing according to the script. Those who gathered in Miami were performers too, but more conscious of the fact, more ironic about the form of the drama in which they were appearing. McGovern himself had chaired a committee that brought about wholesale changes in the system, designed to eliminate many of the anti-democratic procedures of the previous election. As a result, there were more black faces, more women. The average age had dropped. The mood, too, had changed. The convention, it seemed to Miller, had the highest IQ level of any in history. Though he went there sure that McGovern would be robbed of the nomination, as McCarthy had been, what was most striking was the absence of the power players, the party men, so that his fear that McGovern would not win the nomination quickly gave way to a fear that it would not be worth winning, as those with the real power walked away, ready to wait for their moment to come again. John Bailey of Connecticut, however, was there with his delegates and supporters, including two sheriffs bemoaning the fact that as a Ukrainian and a Pole they did not merit representation in the same way as black Americans. They had little time for McGovern – South Dakota, they explained to Miller, had no ethnics.[20]

This time the streets were not a battleground. The hippies were present but now just lay in the shade of the palm trees in Flamingo Park 'like the cast of an abandoned show',[21] not far from a group of elderly Jews playing shuffleboard in the sun. There was a sense, as the 1960s finally ended two years later than decade's end, that the party was over. The national mood had changed. To Miller's surprise, some supporters and delegates he spoke to showed little interest in the war as an issue.

McGovern attracted the votes of individuals who believed there were those who seek power solely in order to surrender it, not in the rhetorical way that the Right announces its intention of returning America to the Americans, cutting taxes, removing the constraints on big business, but because they seem suspicious of the power they seek. He was, apparently, a decent man with honest convictions. His doctoral thesis had been on the massacre of the coalminers in the Colorado fuel and iron strike of 1913–14. In his declaration speech on 18 January 1971 he had suggested that citizens had lost their confidence in the truthfulness and common sense of their leaders and rejected those who governed by expediency. The *Nation* responded by asking: 'Can a good man win?' The answer quickly became clear. Certainly, there were those dedicated to stopping him. As Max M. Kampelman, adviser to Hubert Humphrey, observed, 'By the time of the convention there was indeed a strong feeling on the part of the other candidates that it was in the best interests of the Democratic Party to stop McGovern getting the nomination.'[22] Gary Hart, McGovern's National Campaign Director, agreed: 'I do believe there were statements made by representatives of one or more candidates that they would sink the party rather than see McGovern get the nomination.'[23] Norman Podhoretz, recalling that as a student McGovern had backed Henry Wallace for the presidency, and given his opposition to the Vietnam War, attacked him in *Commentary*, ultimately voting for Nixon, his first ever Republican vote.

At the convention the hardened party men had not really disappeared, but they were scarcely united in their support of their nominee. Ben J. Wattenberg, adviser to Henry (Scoop) Jackson, a rival candidate, summed up the situation:

> There were two definite camps that had polarized; and whichever side won, the other side was going to go away mad. But in terms of the perception of the potential voters watching us on television, if somebody other than

McGovern had won this terrible brutal fight, the results in terms of November would have been far, far less damaging. The perception that the American voters had of who and what McGovern was representing at that convention was nothing short of catastrophic; and once they felt that the McGovern element had taken over the party, it was all over.[24]

The war might still be a concern, but it was not at the heart of the convention's debates. Issues were no longer an issue. Style was beginning to replace substance. The crowd was no longer a threat or a promised redemption; this was a celebration of sharing without a clear sense of what might thereby be achieved. Senator Humphrey was still running, but this time without the imprimatur of the President. For his part McGovern had to deal with some of his own supporters who wished to grandstand for the television cameras. These individuals wanted to call him to account for a remark about not over-taxing Wall Street and leaving troops in Thailand.

Nonetheless, witnessing their brief sit-down strike at the Doral Hotel Miller went back, in his mind, to the sit-down strike at the Fisher body plant in 1936, thirty-six years earlier, when as a young Marxist he had thrilled to the sight of communal action in the name of workers' rights. This time, though, he witnessed a strange alliance of people, some chanting 'Fuck McGovern' and believing – a young man who had appeared in *The Crucible* at college told Miller – that the Vietcong were bourgeois, some attempting a Dadaist intervention, while others awaited reassurance from their candidate, plainly having nowhere else to turn in a convention void of real alternatives.

Preparing issues with which to confront McGovern, his young supporters had difficulty identifying any. When he appeared, he ignored the clamour and reiterated his assurance that the war would end on Inauguration Day and that troops would be recalled within ninety days. When people shouted out key phrases – abortion, legalization of pot, a guaranteed annual wage – he explained that they would never agree about everything. He returned to his suite, the cameras were turned off and another individual stepped up to Miller to tell him that he had appeared in *The Crucible*, this time at Louisiana State University. This man, an associate professor, bearded, naked to the waist and wearing shorts, explained that he was dressed that way because 'This is theatre ... you don't go on stage in your ordinary clothes ... Come over to Flamingo Park in the morning. I'll show you our plans to trash the Republicans in August.' 'It was,' Miller noted, 'precisely the same tone a director might use toward his next production, that suppressed brag about a coming masterpiece, that basic joyfulness in being an artist at all.'[25] At one point police were called to the lobby, but Chicago was not to be repeated in Miami.

There this time as an observer rather than a delegate, Miller was plainly charmed by McGovern, despite his apparent shortcomings. As at Chicago he was a believer not in the process but in the integrity of his chosen candidate. Yet at the same time there is an acknowledgement of the game-playing involved, and surely a sense that those who share his politics have had their hands on power only once in his lifetime, when the aristocratic Roosevelt slipped socialism past the guard of a bewildered people as if it were the logic of history. John Kennedy, gracious to writers, was in Miller's view already compromised when elected and more so when he died.

In a piece about the convention that he published in *Esquire*, Miller remarked: '[The] truth is that the legitimizing weight of the working class was not there to make it the real reflection of America it wanted to be ... [If] only for this absence it can be but a stage along the way.'[26] No one had used such language in America in thirty years and really meant it. The fact is that Miller had never abandoned his attachment if not to Marxism then to the language of socialism, or at least an inclusive liberalism. It was simply that few others were fluent in this language in a decade of increasing disengagement.

There was, to be sure, a hint of nostalgia in his remarks. In a way he was responding to what seemed to him to be the lack of an ideology in American political rhetoric. McGovern, with his heterogeneous supporters drawn from all parts of the American spectrum, albeit not enough to effect or achieve real political power, anticipated the direction that politics would go in the succeeding decade. The terms 'Left' and 'Right', it seemed to Miller, no longer carried persuasive power. In their place he found only 'mood', and this may explain the gap that was in the process of opening up between him and the culture and therefore between him and the theatre, though his *Esquire* article constantly reverts to theatre as a metaphor both for its processes and for its authenticity, or lack of it. A play, he remarked, must forge an audience out of disparate people and a politician must do likewise. A politician, 'like a playwright, has to work with his viscera as well as his head or he's no good',[27] something McGovern seemed not to have understood.

The lack of passion at the convention was a product of the absence of any sense that power would ever attach itself to this man. A minor player in the 1968 convention, he had moved to a more significant role but only as best supporting actor. And the means whereby he triumphed in Miami (using the very procedural devices he affected to despise), and still more the graceless and less than heroic way he mishandled first the question of who was to be the next Democratic National Chairman, and then who was to serve as Vice-President, revealed a man both less than competent and, to many, not fully to be trusted. He seems to have promised the National Chairman's role to several people, while his one thousand per cent support for Tom Eagleton as Vice-President shrivelled to nothing virtually overnight when it was revealed that he had been hospitalized for stress on several occasions. Senator Abe Ribicoff, McGovern's great supporter in the Senate, ruled himself out

ostensibly because (he told Miller) he had other things to do with his life –
'other', presumably, being a substitute for 'better', though he insisted that
those who thought McGovern unambitious were wrong, his stance on the
war misleading people who thought doves by nature soft.

Miller recalled meeting McGovern back in Roxbury when he attended a
party in support of Joe Duffey, an anti-war candidate for the Senate (he lost
to Republican Lowell Weicker who, despite his party loyalties, would be one
of those who hounded Nixon over Watergate). McGovern had struck him
then as 'a beautifully tailored, middle-aged cowboy with that long blue gaze
and thick thumbs'.[28] Far from soft, he was an operator in the Kennedy class.

In 1968, there had been an edge to Miller's comments about the convention,
a passion about his denunciation of a system so unresponsive to urgent moral
necessities. In Miami his tone was different. Though he was a McGovern
man, the candidate himself did not encourage passionate attachment. His
very moderation tended to dissipate the kinetic energy discharged so dis-
astrously four years before. In Chicago, America had watched as if the future
of the country was genuinely in the balance. Now, in a sultry Florida, there
was very little sense that anybody believed the future was being decided. Nixon
hardly merited a mention. To Miller, McGovern embodied not radicalism but
righteousness. Righteousness, however, had been in short supply for some
time, and even as he was being endorsed as the Democratic candidate, men
in the White House were beginning to wonder how they could escape the
consequences of their own actions as the first intimation of the Watergate
plot began to appear.

The Republican Party Convention, meanwhile, appalled Miller with its
blend of smugness and hypocrisy. He was struck in particular by the fact that
Nixon's wife was claiming that he had brought peace despite the fact that the
Vietnamese were still being bombed. At the same time as America was being
told that Nixon had crime under control, Miller complained that he was
having discussions as to how the actors in *The Creation of the World and Other
Business* could safely be conveyed from the theatres in Boston and Washington
back to their hotels because of violence on the streets.

Miller was even more perplexed, though, at having been told that a sizeable
number of Jews were intending to vote for Nixon because they believed
McGovern to be unreliable when it came to Israel. In a draft article he
simultaneously embraced and distanced himself from his Jewish identity,
defining that experience, embracing his membership of a persecuted people,
and yet offering a critique of a human disregard that seemed to him to have
come to typify some Jews. A Jewish turn to the right, Miller declared, would
not only be a political mistake, it would be a denial of Jewish identity itself.
The Jew had always been at the heart of change and the embodiment of
justice and respect for the individual. Political reaction, he insisted, was never

good for the Jews. A case in point seemed to him to be the Greek regime, which had opened its territory for use by the US military but which regarded the Jew as the enemy of the Greek spirit. American and Israeli security forces were implicated in a regime condemned for its torture and repressions, while Spiro Agnew was congratulating members of what Miller called a fascist junta who were hunting down communists. The very confusions of the Democratic Convention as opposed to the 'dead note' of the Republican were to him an earnest of the fact that whereas the former had been alive with debate, albeit not passionate, the latter had been rigid in its misdirections.

The article exists in several drafts. Its bitterness attests to what seemed to him the importance of the issues at stake. He accuses some Jews of voting with their bellies, of being the immigrants who wish above all to hold on to what they have, a flight from idealism that was also destroying the soul of Israel. A diatribe originally directed at Nixon showed signs of broadening into an attack on conservatism at home and abroad. Describing himself as a pro-Israeli Jew, he nonetheless insisted that if the existence of Israel depended on undermining democracy in other countries, then there was something wrong with both Israeli and American policy.

In yet another draft article he contemplates the victory of a party that had no need to pretend that it had any interest in the poor. The tax system, after all, favoured the rich, as he admitted it did him. The text, like several others, breaks off, not least because they all turn on what plainly seemed to him the inevitability of a Republican victory. Nor was he wrong.

Vietnam, as ever, remained an issue. Nixon's attempt to Vietnamize the war in Laos had been exposed in spring 1971 when an invasion of that country proved abortive. At the same time the details of Lieutenant Calley's crimes at My Lai had became public property when, years after the event, he was brought to trial. Nixon's popularity rating was on the slide. But presidents always hold cards that mere candidates do not. He moved to address a deepening economic crisis and made a breakthrough in foreign policy by visiting China. The economy turned around and began to boom, and with it his popularity. By the time of the election, despite Nixon's own doubts, which would lead him to approve, at least in retrospect, the plan for 'plumbers' to raid the Democratic headquarters in the Watergate building – an event that would eventually destroy him – he was seemingly unbeatable.

As most had suspected, in November Richard Milhous Nixon won a landslide victory, only Massachusetts bucking the trend. Even Miller's own Connecticut voted for a man who, unknown to its citizens, indeed unknown to everyone, had so enmired himself in crime in the effort to be re-elected that he would leave office in disgrace. There was, however, one more irony. A month after Nixon's inauguration the Vietnam War did come to an end and the draft was abolished as McGovern had wished. But in less than a year

the Vice-President resigned in disgrace and the President was announcing,
'I'm not a crook.' Twenty months after taking office, rather than face impeachment, he left the White House.

The year 1972, then, marked the true end of the 1960s. It was a decade, it
seemed to Miller, in which politics had had less to do with rationality or
morality, or an awareness of the ambiguous inheritance of a suspect past, than
with a desire to live in the moment. To be sure, there were major issues that
seemed to galvanize the culture, but these were in some sense isolated from
their causes. The rhetoric of morality was deployed, but in the name of
expediency. There was a sense, he explained in an article in *Esquire*, that what
had to be projected 'was a human nowness, Leary's turning on and dropping
out, lest the whole dark quackery of political side-taking burn us all in our
noble motives. The very notion of thinking, conceptualizing, theorizing – the
mind itself – went up the flue.'[29]

For much of the decade Miller had chosen to be in the eye of the storm,
on public platforms, on convention floors, yet he had been aware that it was
a form of theatre, and not always the kind of theatre he was ready to embrace.
Opposition to Vietnam was principled but it was also pragmatic. Once it was
cleared out of the way, what exactly would be resumed, what version of
the American way? There was no space for such discussions. Vietnam had
apparently come from nowhere and would disappear to nowhere because the
price was no longer worth paying. In the end, he suspected, it was the army
that decided the war was unwinnable as it was politicians who decided that a
war supposedly fought in the name of principle could be terminated for
reasons not of principle but expediency. The apparent yet momentary cama-
raderie of protest, like the seeming epiphanies offered by theatre groups
celebrating a supposed spiritual and physical togetherness, was already beginning to feel factitious.

There was, though, a reminder of the culture wars that had supposedly
ended with the revelations in 1967 of the CIA's involvement in many areas of
American life, but especially its cultural activities. On 25 January 1973, Miller
joined a large group of writers and editors (seventy-three in all) who wrote to
the *New York Review of Books* protesting against the Ford Foundation's grant
of $50,000 to the International Association for Cultural Freedom in Paris,
the successor to the Congress for Cultural Freedom, now run by 'Shep' Stone,
who had served in military intelligence and had himself worked for the Ford
Foundation. The grant was for *Encounter* magazine. The point of the
letter, though, seemed not to be political. It expressed indignation that
Ford should be supporting a foreign publication that wished to extend its
influence into the United States, while pleading poverty when approached by
American publications. At the same time, this was only six years on from the

revelations about *Encounter*, and the change of name of the Congress for Cultural Freedom was less than convincing for some. Ironically, one of the signatories of the letter was Frank Kermode, once editor of *Encounter*; while, still more ironically, another was the ex-CCF member Leslie Fiedler, one of whose articles for the magazine had come close to exposing its and his sponsorship.

For all his concern for the financial well-being of American magazines, however, Miller's real commitments lay further afield. A year later, he would join with others (including the novelist Jerzy Kosinski, John Hersey and the President of Random House, Robert L. Bernstein), to protest against the treatment of Vladimir Bukovsky, who had exposed the Soviet use of psychiatric hospitals for political reasons. In 1972 Bukovsky was sentenced to seven years' imprisonment for 'slandering psychiatry' and distributing samizdat material. As the joint letter asserted, 'Now [Bukovsky] is confined in a punishment barracks, on greatly reduced rations, deprived of the right to have visits, mail, legal counsel, and medical treatment essential to his survival.'[30] The signatories appealed for his freedom and the right to emigrate. In November 1976, Bukovsky was exchanged for the Chilean communist leader Luis Corvalán, not returning until 1991.

Did such letters achieve anything? It is clear from comments by Sinyavsky and others that they regarded them as vital. Dissident writers assumed a special role in Soviet society. They were a focus for resistance. As a result they were persecuted and imprisoned. International publicity ensured that this happened in the public eye. It is doubtful whether the moral arguments sometimes advanced by American protesters had any impact. Constant publicity did. It was not difficult for Miller to add his name to others, but in his case it was a logical extension of the work he had been doing for over a decade to secure the release of writers, and a number of them thanked him personally for his efforts.

In February Miller sent a telegram and a letter of a different kind to Premier Chou En-lai of China. In the telegram he stressed his friendship with Edgar Snow, author of *Red Star over China*. He and Inge were planning a book to be published by Viking. He would like, he said, to meet with Chou and other revolutionary leaders and working people. He sought aid in obtaining a visa. He introduced himself as a dramatist, listing his plays, and Inge as a Magnum photographer. Their purpose in visiting, he noted, was simply to familiarize themselves with China and, if blessed with the inspiration, write about it. His London agent, meanwhile, made inquiries as to whether any articles written by Miller would be welcome in British or American publications. The response was positive. The response from Chou En-lai was silence. Evidently the idea of a writer and photographer wandering around his country failed to appeal. Miller tried again in 1976. He, Inge and

Rebecca had been entertained by the Chinese Ambassador, and in his letter of thanks Miller asked for help in obtaining visas, pointing out that his letter of 1973 had yet to be answered. This time the answer was not silence but refusal.

The unfinished business of the 1972 elections was Watergate. Desperate for re-election, Nixon had authorized the burgling of the Democratic national headquarters in the Watergate building in Washington. In one way it struck Miller as being of a piece with the political deceits of the Democratic Party in enmiring the country in Vietnam. It was also, he thought, the pay-off for underwriting the CIA, whose manipulations of foreign elections and corruption of foreign political systems in the name of national security had eroded the country's moral standing and provided a justification for questionable actions that now spilled over into domestic politics. The truth was, he suggested in an article on 'Watergate and the Imperial', that the only novelty about Watergate was that this time the enemy was the Democratic Party rather than Chile, Guatemala or Iran. Ironically, though, it was to be the CIA that refused to help Nixon frustrate the Watergate inquiry. As a result its director, Richard Helms, was fired.

It seemed to Miller, as it had to Representative John Brademas, that Watergate was in effect a *coup d'état* planned by the President and his coterie, a *coup d'état* foiled not by the agencies of government but by pure chance, a guard having noticed a piece of tape on an office door. But for that, Nixon and his co-conspirators would no doubt have continued to pontificate about morality and law and order. What Miller saw in Watergate was loyalty to authority of a kind he had witnessed before at the Frankfurt trials. What he saw in Nixon was something that would surface in *The Ride down Mount Morgan*, a play on which he would later work for a decade – a self-destructive instinct, the desire, born out of guilt, to be discovered and destroyed.

In September 1973 he tried his hand at writing a play about Watergate. This was to be based on *Julius Caesar*, with everyone dressed in togas. At the centre of the action is Hickey, 'an innocent' who has failed his FBI exams and is now set to watch the outside door of the Watergate building and warn the conspirators of any problems. The scheme quickly unwinds as a guard discovers the taped door. Miller breaks off. Satirizing the Watergate plumbers was evidently harder than he had anticipated and the Shakespearean conceit difficult to sustain.

In an article in *Harper's* magazine, in September 1974, he wrote about what struck him as the absurd and damaging drama of Watergate and its aftermath. Richard Nixon, he pointed out, was the chief law officer of the United States. At the time of writing, more than forty of his 'appointed cohorts' were either in jail, under indictment or on the threshold of jail for crimes which the

President had done his best to conceal. Quoting from transcripts eventually prised from the White House, he described what seemed to him a presidency that was ending in farce. Here was a man who had arranged for the bugging of his own office, debating strategies that were not merely illegal but bizarre and expressed in a self-annihilating language. In this excerpt (quoted in the article) John Dean, White House Counsel to the President, and John Haldeman, Chief of Staff, discuss with Nixon whether John Mitchell (who became the only Attorney General to serve a prison sentence) should testify in front of the Ervin Committee, set up by the Senate:

NIXON: Do you think you want to go this route now? Let it hang out so to speak?

DEAN: Well, it isn't really that . . .

HALDEMAN: It's a limited hang-out.

DEAN: It is a limited hang-out. It's not an absolute hang-out publicly or privately.[31]

Why, Miller asks himself, did Nixon arrange for the recordings to be made and why did he not turn off the machines at the point they became dangerous? Part of the time, he observes, Nixon had clearly forgotten the tapes. At other moments he implicitly addressed them. Plainly, in 1974, Miller was already laying down the material for what, three years later, would turn into his play *The Archbishop's Ceiling*, set in Eastern Europe but bearing on American reality and unreality.

In retrospect, what is surprising is the sheer time and energy Miller devoted to the public world. The man who had once worked obsessively at his plays had, since 1965, thrown himself into the major political issues of the day. His private papers are full of articles – some published, many not – that worry at the implications of America's foreign and domestic policies. There are multiple drafts of polemical pieces designed not only to comment on but also to intervene in the politics of the period. Some are overheated in their passion. There was, it seemed to him, an observable continuity between the repressions of the late 1940s and 50s and what he repeatedly characterized as the criminalities of public policy. Perhaps it was in part that, indeed, that would lead him to involve himself in an actual criminal case, a case which exposed the corruption of justice as if it were of a piece with what he had observed and deplored in American society.

There is a reason why his plays are full of policemen, lawyers and judges: the question of justice was central to his concerns both as a playwright and as a citizen. But it was seldom a matter of mere legality that interested him. Justice was a matter of morality, social values and, ultimately, metaphysics.

8

PETER REILLY

We are ninety percent memory ... from the language we carry with us to the actual images that we have, and these plays are refracting the past all the time, because I don't really know how to understand anybody only from his present actions. We need the past to comprehend anything.[1]

Arthur Miller

Fifty-one-year-old Barbara Gibbons lived with her eighteen-year-old son Peter in a small house on Route 63, Falls Village, five miles from Canaan, Connecticut, and forty-eight miles from Arthur Miller's home in Roxbury. In truth, the house was little more than a shed, with a single bedroom ten feet by twelve and a small living room. She and her son slept on bunk beds. The rent was $55 a month and the building was warmed by a kerosene heater. She had explained to Peter that he was the result of rape and that she had arbitrarily given him the name Peter Reilly. He was still at school; she was unemployed and spent her day reading and drinking. She was regarded as somewhat eccentric. Born in Berlin and raised in England, she had lived in New York City before the family moved to New England.

On Friday 28 September 1973 she drove into town, withdrew some money from the bank and bought herself a new leather wallet, her old one having been stolen two weeks earlier and the theft reported to the police. That afternoon, when Peter returned from school, mother and son played cards before Peter went off with friends. He and fellow pupil Geoffrey Madow returned briefly, then left again, each driving his own car, to go to a meeting at the Methodist church Youth Centre in Canaan; it was twenty minutes past seven. Geoffrey had just returned to his home after the meeting when the telephone rang. It was Peter. Something had happened to his mother, he said.[2] The Madows were responsible for driving the local ambulance, currently parked at a nearby nursing home. A back-up ambulance was soon on its way, along with a police car.

Joan Barthel, who later wrote a study of the crime, explained what they found:

> Barbara lay sprawled on the floor, a pool of blood around her neck. Her short black curly hair was soggy with blood. Her throat had been slashed and her vocal cords hung out. She was nearly beheaded ... There were gaping cuts in her stomach. Three of her ribs were broken, and both her thighbones were broken too. Her legs were spread apart; she was nude. Her blue jeans and underpants lay beside her body, soaking wet. Barbara's left arm was lying flat, but her right arm was bent at the elbow, in an upraised position. Her right fist was clenched. Her nose was broken. Her eyes were blackened and staring open.[3]

As the person who had discovered the body, suspicion immediately fell on Peter, though at five feet seven and weighing 121 pounds he seemed an unlikely assailant. A local sergeant checked his hands and chest and then called his supervisor, Lieutenant James Shay. Peter was put in a patrol car by Trooper Bruce McCafferty and read his rights before giving a statement. He was kept in the car for three hours. What followed over the next hours at the Connecticut State Police Barracks headquarters was prolonged questioning, without benefit of a lawyer, in which Peter was slowly convinced of his guilt and asked to imagine why and how he might have committed the crime.

At Peter's request a polygraph test was carried out. He showed a naive faith in its ability to confirm what initially he claimed was the truth of his innocence. The test was conducted by Sergeant Timothy Kelly, whom Miller described as a fatherly, portly man within weeks of retirement to his houseboat in Florida. He began by explaining that the polygraph could read Peter's brain:

> P: Does that actually read my brain?
> K: Definitely. Definitely. And if you've told me the truth, this is what your brain is going to tell me.
> P: Will this stand up to protect me?
> K: Right. Right.
> P: Good. That's the reason I came to take it. For protection.

Kelly then began to feed suggestions to Peter, a process that would continue through subsequent interrogations:

> K: Let me say something, Pete. I've had people here who have committed serious things. As serious as this. They needed help. It wasn't a vicious thing they did. They just couldn't help themselves. I've had people actually come in here and take this test because they knew they were guilty but

they didn't know how to tell somebody. They were looking for help. Maybe you're looking for somebody to help you.

P: What do you mean?

K: Say you did this thing last night. Say you hurt your mother. Maybe you want the polygraph to help you.

P: If I had any doubts, I would see a doctor.

K: Well, if I feel there is something wrong, this is what we would do for you. Get a doctor. A lot of times people don't know they need help. It's amazing but true.

P: Right.[4]

After initial questioning on the machine, which Kelly described as 'a warm-up', the exchange continued:

P: Does it look like I was lying to you?

K: That wouldn't be fair for me to say. You're nervous. Do any of these questions bother you?

P: Well, whether I harmed my mother or not.

K: Why?

P: Well, that question ... they told me at the barracks yesterday that – how some people don't realize – all of a sudden [they] fly off the handle for a split second ...

K: Right.

P: ... and it leaves a blank spot in their memory.

K: Right. This will help bring it out.

P: Well, I thought about that last night, and I thought and I thought and I thought, and I said no, I couldn't have done it, I couldn't have done it, you know. And now, when you ask me the question ...

K: Peter, let me say this one thing.

P: ... that's what I think of.

K: If you did this, this is probably how it could have happened ... It could have been an accident with her last night, right?

P: Right.

With the machine now on, Kelly asked a series of questions to which Peter replied, consistently denying any involvement. On one question, however, he hesitated:

K: Do you have a clear recollection of what happened last night?

P: Yes.

K: Is there any doubt in your mind, Pete?

P: Can you stop the test?

K: OK.

P: I don't understand that last question.

K: I think we've got a little problem here, Peter.

P: That last question . . .

K: I was just trying to probe your subconscious.

P: But I wasn't sure whether you meant what happened to her, or whether I knew who did it to her and everything.[5]

That stumble seems to have been identified as indicating a vulnerability. Certainly, when they began again, Kelly suggested that the machine had reacted to several of Peter's answers, including that last one, which he now interpreted not as an uncertainty over the meaning of the question, but an uncertainty as to the events and his own role in them:

K: You are unsure as to what happened in that house last night, aren't you? You're unsure as to what——

P: What I did?

K: Yes.

P: I'm sure what I did.

K: Then why did you say here a moment ago you're not sure if you hurt your mother last night?

P: Wait a second, you've got me confused now.

K: No. I'm not trying to, Pete. But you said a moment ago that you had doubt in your mind if you flew off the handle last night and you don't recollect.

P: It doesn't seem like me. I've never flown off the handle.

K: . . . From what I'm seeing here, I think you've got doubts as to what happened last night. Don't you?

P: I've got doubt because I don't understand what happened.

K: Are you afraid that you did this thing?

P: Well, yes, of course I am. That's natural.

K: . . . You're not sure, are you?

P: What do you mean?

K: In your mind, if you hurt your mother last night.

P: I'm not sure. It scares me a little bit. You know what I mean?

K: . . . What I'm talking about Pete, is, do you have any recollection as to how she got hurt?

P: No. I absolutely do not.

K: Are there any blank areas? Could you have had an argument with your mother last night and not realized it?

P: No. I don't know. I'm not the one to say.

K: You were there, Peter. I see things here that I don't like. On the question about hurting your mother, you gave me quite a reaction to that.

P: I know it . . . But if I did it, and I didn't realize it, there's got to be some clue in the house.

K: I've got this clue here. This is a recording of your mind ... the polygraph
can never be wrong, because it's only a recording instrument, recording
from you.[6]

Peter Reilly had had only a few hours' sleep and was still without legal
representation. When the interrogation continued, suggestions had become
facts. Kelly now insisted that Peter would have been at home at the time his
mother died. The polygraph, he explained, 'shows me from your heart that
you hurt your mother last night. How, I don't know' – to which Peter replied,
'I don't know either.' Kelly then offered an explanation as to how this slight
young man could have broken both his mother's legs.

K: If you came roaring into the yard, a Corvette is a car you go like hell with.
My brother-in-law has one, and I know how he drives it. You come flying
in with the damned thing, and you went over her with the car, and you
panicked.
P: I didn't, though. I don't remember it.
K: Then why does the chart say you did?
P: I don't know. I can't give you a definite answer.
K: You don't know for sure if you did this thing, do you?
P: I don't. No, I don't.
K: Why?
P: Well, your chart says I did. I still say I didn't ... Would it definitely be
me? Could it have been someone else?
K: No way. From these reactions.
P: Now I'm afraid, because I was so sure I didn't do it ...
K: This isn't the end of the world. As long as you don't get it straightened
out in your mind, you'll never have a day of peace.
P: I gotta get it straightened out right now.
K: Right. Once we do that, we're halfway home. There's no doubt in my
mind from these charts you did it. But why and how?
P: That's what I don't know ... I'm not purposely denying it. If I did it,
I wish I knew I'd done it ... I don't want to go into a mental hospital.
I don't mind a session with a psychiatrist once a week ... but I'm hung up.
I don't remember.
K: My charts say you remember this right now.
P: ... I don't remember doing the things that happened. I believe I did it
now.
K: I know that you know that you did it, but I feel you're afraid to come out
and say it. I have no reason to hurt you, but I have reason to help you.[7]

And so it continued, hour after hour, and still with no legal representation.
Peter's denials were refuted by what he was assured were the scientific precision

and accuracy of the polygraph, which had an uncanny ability to read his heart. He was offered plausible stories about his behaviour. It was an accident, a moment of rage, an act of violence suppressed by his conscious mind. He had broken her legs with his car or, alternatively, jumped up and down on them. He had killed her with a knife, though he volunteered the information that there was a straight razor on the premises. He and his mother, he confessed, had had arguments in the past. This, the officers suggested, would have been the case again, and if he could not remember it, and if his story changed as they suggested alternative scenarios, this was because the trauma of the event had blotted out the truth, a truth that could now be exposed. Peter was even reduced to making suggestions as to how this concealed truth could be exposed.

K: You know what I think, Pete? You're afraid we're going to lock you up someplace and throw away the key. This isn't going to happen ... You're such a decent guy ...
P: Could it be that I've totally put it out of my memory?
K: RIGHT! This is our problem. Once we get this out into the open and get you the proper help, it will all be over with.
P: Would truth serum help? Sodium pentothal?[8]

Slowly, and without benefit of pentothal, Peter himself began to try out possible scenarios, things he might have done, what Kelly called 'visions'. He even reminded Kelly that though he had no marks on his body from apparently slashing someone with a knife or razor he did have a red knuckle. When he had concerns they were obligingly addressed.

P: The whole thing I'm worrying about is jail.
K: Peter, don't worry about things like that.
P: That's not going to help, throwing me in jail.
K: Damn right it's not going to help, throwing you in jail. I've said that for many years. I'm the guy that says, 'This guy needs some help from a doctor.' And they'll take my word for this.[9]

Peter was now questioned by Lieutenant Shay, but finally asked whether he could have someone present. Anxious to keep lawyers at bay, Shay offered the state police: 'We on the State Police are not your enemies ... We don't find happiness in other people's misfortune. If we can help you, and I know we can help you, we will help you.' When Peter insisted that he had 'to have someone to turn to', they suggested Trooper Mulhern, who was known to Peter. 'Now why don't you just try this? Try and believe in somebody. Believe that we're not out to hurt you ... if you don't try to trust somebody, somewhere along the way, there's no hope here.'[10]

So the questioning resumed, Peter now accepting most of the suggestions put to him, even as he continued to insist that he was not sure of his guilt. 'Peter, I think you're sure,' Kelly said, Shay adding, 'You've got to trust someone. I think you ought to trust me ... Pete, you're sure.' Peter remained confused: 'No, I'm not. I mean I'm sure of what you've shown me, that I did it, but what I'm not sure of is how I did it'[11]

When the time came to write a statement, however, Peter seemed to have regained something of his equanimity. When asked if he recalled cutting his mother's throat with a razor he said, 'I imagine myself doing it. It's coming out of the back of my head. But I'm not absolutely positive of anything.' Shay, despairingly, now accused him of playing 'head games', somewhat ironically, given the fact that he and Kelly had been feeding him with numerous possible scenarios. Peter's reply was accurate enough: 'I've been drilled so much that it seems like I did do it. And the chances are that I did do it. That's what it is boiling down to. But, I'm not positive.' He then asked if the statement could be used against him. Told that it could, he asked, 'Then why should I say something that I'm not sure of ... ?[12] Nonetheless, the session went ahead, Peter sometimes denying details and at other times seemingly recalling cutting his mother's throat with a razor. He signed the statement and then, bewilderingly, asked Shay if he could come and live with him and his family: 'I've taken a liking to you, a kind of father image, and I trust you.'[13]

Kelly, after a brief absence, returned. He had learned a further detail about the murder and was anxious for Peter to confirm it. Asked to think what other terrible thing he might have done, he volunteered rape. But there was no sign of rape. He suggested that he might have had oral sex, but again there was no evidence of this. It became a bizarre guessing game, Kelly throwing out hints without specifying. Maybe he had strangled her, offered Peter. There was no evidence for this, either. He tried hysterectomy. He was plainly getting warmer – Kelly sounded encouraging. Mutilate her? offered Peter. He had finally, after trial and error, confirmed the detail. 'Right ... right,' replied Kelly, who now asked him why he had thought of that. 'That's all I could think of left,' he replied.[14]

The interrogation took twenty-five hours. Peter was taken to jail and charged with murder. He was arraigned on 1 October, three days after his mother's death. At his request he was represented by Catherine Roraback, founder of the New Haven chapter of the Civil Liberties Union. Bail was reduced from $100,000 to $50,000, but since this could not be raised he was returned to jail.

The following week, local people began to rally to Peter's aid. A defence committee was formed. On 7 November, Peter Reilly was indicted by a grand jury. A pre-trial hearing followed in December, conducted by Judge Anthony Armentano, a former lieutenant-governor of Connecticut. Catherine Roraback sought to have Peter's confessions ruled inadmissible, including:

Any and all statements, confessions or admissions, oral, written or recorded, taken from him, on the grounds that the same were involuntary, coerced, taken during and after the defendant had been in custody and isolated for a substantial period of time, and without having counsel present during his interrogation, and in violation of his rights to privacy, to be secure in his person, to due process of law, not to be compelled to be a witness against himself, and to counsel, all as guaranteed him by the First, Fourth, Fifth, Sixth, Ninth and Fourteenth Amendments to the Constitution.[15]

On 13 February Judge Armentano refused a motion to suppress. It was announced six days later and jury selection began the following day. When Joan Barthel's article on the case appeared in a magazine, *New Times*, it printed extracts from Peter Reilly's interrogation. As a result a woman in Manhattan, who had no connection with the case but had been appalled by the story, offered a loan of $44,000 towards the bail bond. This secured a bank loan, but interest would be payable. On 21 February, nearly five months after his arrest, Peter was released, with his schoolfriend's mother Marion Madow signing as surety. Peter moved in with the Madows, with whom he would continue to live.

At the trial, which began on 1 March 1974, Peter's attorney called for the presiding judge, Judge Speziale, to rule Peter's confessions inadmissible. He refused. He also restricted coverage of the trial. As a result, CBS abandoned plans for a network feature. Only Connecticut newspapers covered the occasion. The *Hartford Times* protested against the restrictions: 'The charges of a coerced confession, whether ultimately sustained or not, should not be hidden from the public.'[16]

A nurse who testified that she had received an emergency call from Peter Reilly at 9.40 on the evening in question, thus placing him at the scene of the crime at the estimated time of death, supplied the first evidence. Only much later did it become clear that this timing was erroneous and that the prosecutor, John Bianchi, was suppressing evidence that would demonstrate this to be so. Furthermore, at the trial a contrary time was given by a state trooper, who noted that the hospital had contacted him a crucial eighteen minutes later. For some reason, Catherine Roraback seemed not to register the significance of the discrepancy. She also, as Donald S. Connery pointed out in his book on the case, lacked the funds to pay for daily transcripts of the testimony. A fingerprint had been found on the back door of the house, but when asked about it a Sergeant Pennington explained that it had proved impossible to identify, not least because 'It's a time-consuming job. I mean, it takes years to go through all of them.'[17]

A shoeprint had been found on the bloody carpet but no blood was on Peter's shoes – indeed no blood was found on his clothes, even though when taken into police custody he was still wearing the same outfit that he had earlier in the evening. In his interrogation Peter had mentioned using a razor. Testimony was offered that no blood had been found on the one in the house. A knife was introduced and flourished in court, even though no evidence was offered that it was the murder weapon. It was a less than impressive example of Connecticut justice. In her summation, Catherine Roraback, somewhat unexpectedly, expressed regret that the Scottish verdict of not proven was not available to them. 'I think,' she said, 'that's really what we are talking about here. We are not talking about a verdict of innocent but a verdict of not proven'[18] – and this despite having just reminded the jury that the accused was to be regarded as innocent unless proved guilty beyond a reasonable doubt. The fact that she did not challenge the contradictory timings on which the trial effectively turned would prove crucial later in the Peter Reilly story. She did remind the jury that the newly purchased wallet was missing and that the back door had been found open.

The jurors retired and a first poll showed five who thought Reilly guilty, four who believed him not guilty and three who were undecided. They began their deliberations at 12.56 p.m. on Thursday 11 Apirl 1974 and returned to court with their verdict the following day at 3.04 p.m. It was Good Friday. Peter Reilly was convicted of manslaughter. On 24 May he was sentenced to six to sixteen years. Bianchi had asked for seven to sixteen. Catherine Roraback had asked for a suspended sentence. Bail was raised to $60,000 pending a decision about the proper place for Peter to serve his sentence. Most of the local press were hostile to the verdict and the police methods that had led to it.

Joan Barthel had become interested in the case as a journalist, but in time became part of the support apparatus. To raise money she wrote to prominent Connecticut residents, including Philip Roth, Paul Newman and Joanne Woodward, Martin Segal, William Buckley, William Styron and Mike Nichols, the last of whom himself began writing letters. She also approached Arthur Miller, recalling the line from *Death of a Salesman:* 'Attention must be paid.' It was. It was a small-town case that would become a source of national concern, spawning two books and a film starring Stefanie Powers and Brian Dennehy, who would later appear as Willy Loman in the fiftieth-anniversary production of *Death of a Salesman.*

On the afternoon of the sentencing, Miller called Barthel. He had followed the case and read the *New Times* article she had sent him, with its selection from the lie-detector test. This seemed to him to be reminiscent of a scene from Arthur Koestler's *Darkness at Noon.* He was uncertain as to Reilly's guilt but convinced that the police sergeant conducting the polygraph test had planted ideas in the boy's head. Even so, he could hardly understand how anyone could be persuaded to confess to cutting his own mother's throat. He invited Barthel to his studio.

At first he was not impressed. Evidently misunderstanding the extent of her commitment, it seemed to him that she lacked the objectivity he had expected of a reporter. In a note he wrote about the meeting, Miller admitted he knew little about courts, but his own experience with HUAC, and the subsequent legal case, had taught him that the law and justice were not always in alignment. Here was perhaps one reason for his interest in the case. He, a prominent figure, had found himself harassed and misrepresented. But here was a young man much less able to defend himself, also a possible victim of injustice. The fact that he lived in the same county was an added incentive for Miller to take action.

The immediate issue had to do with the money needed to cover the monthly interest on the bail bond, now mounting at the rate of $400 a month. Miller suggested the names of people who might donate. Barthel now revealed that she was not necessarily convinced of Reilly's innocence; it was merely that procedures had been faulty, she said, and that various leads had not been followed up. She clearly expected Miller to become involved in the case, though when they parted that afternoon it had not yet occurred to him that he would. Nonetheless, by degrees, and despite his own doubts, he found himself increasingly committed.

A week after meeting Barthel, he drove to Canaan and met Peter along with some of his supporters. They were sitting on the front lawn of the parish house when the state attorney John Bianchi passed by. Miller then arranged a meeting at William Styron's Roxbury home. Among those attending were Mike Nichols, Jean Widmark (wife of Richard Widmark), the producer Lewis Allen and the writer Renata Adler (whose Jewish parents had fled Nazi Germany in 1933). When it was suggested that Roraback, whose father had recently died, was exhausted, Miller told them that he was already looking into the possibility of a replacement. Several of those present agreed to contribute money for the interest payments on the bail bond.

In her account of these events Joan Barthel was anxious to stress that without the support of the people of Canaan Peter would have been alone. Despite her own articles, the trial had not attracted much media interest. Support came from celebrities including Elizabeth Taylor, Candice Bergen, Art Garfunkel, Jack Nicholson and Dustin Hoffman, but it was those who knew Peter who provided much of the energy for the campaign, which now urged a reopening of the case.

On 15 June 1974 Miller wrote an account, apparently for himself, in which he described what seemed to him to be the principal issues. Quite rightly, as it turned out, the first he focused on was the one of timing. It was surely impossible for Peter to have committed the murder given the time available.

It took place between 9.30 and 10 p.m. Peter had left the youth centre between 9.30 and 9.40, together with a friend whom he dropped off at 9.45. He then continued to his own home, a further six miles distant. Even if he had driven at sixty miles an hour, Miller calculated, he would have walked through the doorway of his mother's home six minutes later at the earliest. When he discovered her body he had telephoned the Madows, the family doctor, an ambulance and the local hospital, who in turn called the police. This would have left him three or four minutes to kill his mother, cutting through her collar bone, slashing her and breaking both her thighs, before – since the police found no trace of blood on him – changing into a duplicate set of clothes, concealing what must have been the heavily bloodstained originals and then washing himself thoroughly without leaving evidence of having done so.

This had indeed been John Bianchi's contention. Since the room was splashed with blood, up the walls and over the curtains, there was no other explanation, it seemed. Either that, Miller noted, or Reilly had undressed and killed his mother in the nude, which had a certain Freudian appeal, but was otherwise somewhat bizarre. The police explanation for the breaking of the victim's thighs was that Reilly had run her over before dragging her into the house, an account later contradicted by the medical examiner's finding that the thighs had been broken after death.

The second issue was the confession, which seemed to Miller a consequence of relentless questioning without counsel during which Reilly was asked to put his trust in the authority and experience of his questioners. The third issue was a central contradiction in the prosecution case. Peter had apparently planned the murder – or why else would he have secreted his clothes? – while at the same time supposedly committing it in a sudden state of fury. He noted too that there had been no attempt to explore the possibility of another person having committed the crime. Where, after all, was the new wallet and the money that had been in it? He was also struck by Peter's refusal of a plea-bargain offer. On 11 July, in an attempt to explain the confession and understand Peter's psychology, he jotted down a series of questions in a spiral-bound notebook. It amounted to a list of forty-eight points.

Catherine Roraback now began to doubt the wisdom of an appeal, not least because she was uncertain whether Peter was up to it. Miller consulted the then Dean of the Harvard Law School, who suggested that either a team of students might help (a course which alarmed Miller, who saw Reilly becoming mere raw material) or a criminal lawyer should be employed, the prospective bill likely to be in the range of $20,000 to $100,000. As Miller explained:

I was getting nowhere ... so I called my law firm in New York and told them that I was getting upset about this because it seemed to me that there had to be some kind of responsibility somewhere ... They went to work on it and finally told me that Roy Daly in Fairfield would be somebody who would respond to this. I contacted Daly. We had lunch. I explained the whole case to him and said there would be no money, but maybe, some way or other, it could be raised. But he didn't say much about a fee. He was interested in the case and finally agreed to take it on. Why did he do it? Whatever the reasons, I wouldn't for one moment underestimate his idealism.[19]

Miller did have certain doubts. He had thought Catherine Roraback too high-minded, a civil liberties type who lacked the instincts of a criminal lawyer. On the other hand, Daly, who had experience of the New York Federal Prosecutor's office, was 'a fashionable, very tall, blue-eyed horseman in a tweed jacket, a suburban lawyer ... he struck me as an unlikely gutter fighter – and I sensed that the gutter was where this case was going to be fought out in the end'.

T.F. Gilroy Daly from Fairfield, Connecticut, had been an assistant district attorney under Robert Kennedy and had unsuccessfully run for Congress. The Reilly case, he said later, would turn out to be the most satisfying of his career. Miller watched him as he set to work on this long and largely unpaid case. 'His patina of horsey-set sophistication fell away; there built up in him a cold personal outrage at what had been done to justice in his state.'[20] In the end, Miller conceded, for all the time he personally spent on the case it was Daly – and a private detective who now entered the scene – who slowly began to put the pieces together. Daly decided on a two-pronged approach: to appeal against the verdict and seek a new trial. With no full transcript yet available he had to work from Barthel's notes.

The private detective, James Conway, had written to Catherine Roraback during the trial, offering his help. Though his assistance had been rejected at the time, when Daly took over Conway drove to see him. Having researched his background, Daly hired him, warning him that there was little money around. Though he now lived in Connecticut, Conway – described by Donald S. Connery in *Guilty until Proven Innocent* as a stocky man with an open Irish face and dark bushy eyebrows, who often wore a dirty white trench-coat and rain-hat – had been a policeman in New York and a bail bondsman. He had been born half a dozen blocks from the Miller home on 111th Street. As Connery put it, 'Peter's future would be determined by the actions of three remarkably dissimilar individuals who came to his defense after he was convicted and sentenced. Arthur Miller, T.F. Gilroy Daly and James G. Conway. Each played a special role in seeking Peter Reilly's vindication: Conway found new evidence and fresh witnesses; Daly assembled the information and presented it in the courtroom; and Miller, the catalyst, used his influence to secure press coverage and public support.'[21] And press coverage was not easily obtained when the media were full of the story of the kidnapped heiress Patty Hearst, who had turned terrorist and was now on the FBI's most-wanted list.

Barthel described Miller's relationship with Peter, with the Madow family (with whom he was staying while on bail) and with Conway:

> Arthur Miller had stayed in close touch with Peter and the Madows, and he was a regular visitor in Canaan. The boys were accustomed to having him at the table now. That first night he'd come, not long after Peter was sentenced, they'd felt shy. Nan served fried chicken, and the boys weren't sure whether, with Arthur Miller there, they should pick it up with their hands. Then Arthur Miller picked up a piece of chicken, and the boys grinned. 'O-*kay*,' Geoffrey said and everybody picked up a piece of chicken, too. Jim Conway and Arthur Miller hit it off right away. Miller liked the earthiness of the ex-flatfoot, and they spent a lot of time in the low-ceilinged living room of Miller's elegant old farmhouse, trying to figure it out.[22]

Miller, though, did not 'hit it off right away'. In unpublished notes he admitted that Conway's appearance put him off at first. A nearly bald man with a large stomach and a penchant for narrow-brimmed hats, he had what Miller called a Harlem way of speaking such as he had not heard since his days at a 112th Street school. He was suspicious, too, of his talk of justice, presuming that eighteen years as a New York City patrolman would have beaten such notions out of him and that he was merely trying to appeal to what he must have assumed was a liberal intellectual. But Conway committed himself to the case, sometimes at potential risk to himself. When he had just begun work he received a telephone call from a detective warning him off. Later, he would be arrested for carrying an unlicensed weapon (the licence, it turned out, applied only within the township that issued it; the prosecutor was to be Bianchi).

Where Miller and Conway agreed was in their surprise at Peter's apparent ingratitude. For Miller, though, 'Peter Reilly can't say, "I thank you" because there is no "I" to say "I thank you".'[23] He lacked both self-worth and a sense of identity. Miller continued his struggle to understand Reilly, a man who under duress had admitted to his mother's murder. He must, he thought, as a child, have witnessed his mother's sexual encounters. Indeed, there was evidence that he had thrown one man out of the house. Perhaps, Miller surmised, guilt at his own inaction, feelings that he might have been a voyeur of his mother's humiliation, and a desire to think of himself as a man capable of action, might have led Reilly to confess. Perhaps he was deliberately sacrificing himself.

Miller was not alone in looking for a sexual explanation. The police too had seen that as a motive, questioning Reilly as to whether he had ever had sexual relations with his mother. For a writer whose notebooks are full of references to incestuous feelings there was plainly a fascination to the case that went beyond the simple, or not so simple, matter of securing justice. Indeed, he was already seeing the murder in terms of a drama, staging the scene in his mind. It is not that, in his notes, he is regarding the case as the potential source for a play, but that his analysis draws on his sense of an internal dramatic logic. Arthur Miller detective was close kin to Arthur Miller playwright.

There was another possible suspect, a man with a history of theft and drink, but no one seemed to be interested in widening the investigation. As Miller noted in a later memo that he headed 'Lessons of the Reilly Case', Lieutenant Shay, then in charge of the investigation, had simply arrested the wrong man and nobody above him had the courage or will to stop it. Both the police and the state attorney's office seemed to have a vested interest in Reilly's guilt. What was at stake, in other words, was no longer the identity of the murderer but the reputation of those who investigated and prosecuted Reilly.

In the fall of 1975 Miller went to the *New York Times* and asked the reporter John Corry to write about the case. Corry enlisted the help of some New York City detectives, who were shocked by the polygraph transcript, and himself went to Canaan. As Conway recalled, one day, out of the blue, Daly said, '"I heard from Arthur Miller and they're going to send a guy up from the *Times*." We had been talking about it. Now we were getting somewhere.'[24] Miller remarked, 'The press in Connecticut just wasn't doing the job. There were exceptions like the *Lakeville Journal*, but the story still wasn't getting out. It was time to break out of this cosy little Litchfield County courthouse and let the world at large hear about this. If this trial could have happened in the first place, and they convicted this boy without a case, then why couldn't they do it again? In fact, the second time might be easier if you had the same kind of silence.'[25] (In fact there *was* a later case, in which Miller would involve himself.) Public interest was picking up. CBS filmed a segment for *Sixty Minutes*, with the newsman Mike Wallace. *Time* and *Newsweek* sent reporters. In mid-December, the *New York Times* published a two-part front-page article.

The petition for a new trial cited three factors: the withholding of evidence, new evidence, and a new time sequence for the events that had taken place three years earlier. Witnesses now placed Peter's arrival home later than had been suggested, and a CBS executive confirmed the precise timing of a television programme erroneously used by a witness to substantiate her evidence. The fingerprint found on the back door of the house had now been identified. It belonged to one Tim Parmalee. It was not on file at the time of the crime but had been taken following his theft of a car in 1974. He had been a frequent visitor to the house and claimed an alibi, supported by his sister. He did, however, have a brother, Michael, whose wife now withdrew her earlier evidence that he had been with her on the night in question. He had not, she now claimed, and had been visibly disturbed that night and for some weeks thereafter. He had also previously asked Peter Reilly to lie about a supposed homosexual relationship between the two of them, invented so that he could be dismissed from the Army. As a result, Peter's mother had taunted him. Peter now claimed that Michael had stolen money from her. Called to the stand, Michael Parmalee protested his innocence and challenged his now estranged wife's testimony.

Miller had arranged for two New York doctors to appear, one, Dr Spiegel, a psychiatrist. Connery noted Daly's remark: 'I called Arthur Miller ... and told him that Spiegel was the man we wanted. I asked him to get him for me even if we didn't have any money for him. Arthur is a persuasive man. He arranged an appointment for us.'[26] Barthel explained his involvement:

> Arthur Miller called Dr Spiegel. 'If Peter has amnesia, can you get it out under hypnosis?' Miller asked, and the doctor said yes, he could. On January 6, 1976 Roy Daly and Arthur Miller drove Peter to Dr Spiegel's office in New York. The doctor tested Peter using a method called Hypnotic Induction Profile ... he found Peter had 'a break in his concentration' and couldn't be hypnotized. Still, he told Peter that he was in a trance and that he should keep his eyes closed. Dr Spiegel told Peter to imagine a movie screen and then describe what was happening on it. Peter accounted for every fifteen-second interval, from the time he walked into the little house. There was no amnesia, no lapse of memory, no 'gray area'.[27]

In the hearing Spiegel would testify that Peter suffered from low self-esteem, and was likely to concur with suggestions put to him in the context of an interrogation, particularly if told that he must have suffered from amnesia and that a scientific instrument, the polygraph, could supply the truth he was suppressing.

The second medical expert was Dr Milton Helpern, whom Miller had approached in February 1975, the same month that a new lie-detector test was to be carried out at the Madows' house. Dr Helpern, a former Chief Medical Examiner for New York City, was also, at seventy-five, the world's leading forensic pathologist. He affirmed that in his view it would have been impossible for Peter to commit the crime. Given the short time he had had in which to commit it and the fact that there was no blood on his clothes or his person, it was simply not feasible. Daly submitted papers to Litchfield's Superior Court at the beginning of April, calling for a new trial. It was another nine months before the hearing was held.

That hearing, before Judge Speziale, began on 15 January 1976 and lasted five weeks. On the final day, the prosecutor John Bianchi asked to continue his examination of Spiegel, whose opinions he felt could not be introduced as new evidence. That night, Miller invited Spiegel and his son back to Roxbury. As Spiegel later recalled:

> We were sitting around talking about the hearing . . . and Miller was telling us about the importance of coming up with new data in the hearing if there was to be another trial. Well, I had been living with my Induction Profile Test for eight or ten years – it's part of a long research project – but it's only recently been described as something new in the field in an article published only a year ago, well after Peter's trial. Miller got really excited about this because it looked like it might qualify as newly discovered evidence. We telephoned Daly. He loved it.[28]

The next day Daly argued that the test Spiegel had conducted, and on which he based his opinions, did indeed constitute new evidence. The judge summoned Daly and Bianchi to the bench and said, 'While I am not going to prejudice what weight I am going to give to your testimony I wish to say that you are the most credible expert witness that I have ever heard in my years on the bench and as a private attorney.'[29]

The judge's memorandum ran to thirty-four pages. Its conclusion was that an injustice had been done and that the result of a new trial would probably be different. It was an implicit suggestion that Bianchi should drop the case. Among those Peter telephoned on hearing the news was Arthur Miller. Speaking to a *New York Times* reporter he said, 'Do you know what this shows? . . . It shows that if people don't simply accept what's handed down from above, and if they don't surrender to despair, they can change things. They can get justice.'[30] Bianchi, however, was not ready to give up. He announced his intention to proceed with a new trial; but then died suddenly, at the age of fifty-four, on the Canaan golf course.

The trial never took place. When Bianchi's replacement, state attorney Dennis A. Santore, was going through the files he came across a piece of evidence that had been suppressed. Frank E. Finney, an auxiliary state trooper, and his wife Wanda had given statements placing Peter Reilly in Canaan – that is, five miles from his home – at 9.40 on the evening of the murder. This evidence, which effectively exonerated Reilly, had not been passed to the defence. On 24 November at a sixteen-minute hearing Santore told Judge Cohen that he had discovered the two statements in the file and that these were consistent with the argument put forward by the defence. Daly called on the judge to drop the manslaughter charge. When Santore stated that the state would have no objection the judge, sitting without a jury, dismissed the charges, ruling that Reilly had not been at the scene of the crime when it was committed and ordered a special investigation of Reilly's arrest and prosecution to be conducted by Superior Court Judge Maurice Sponzo. He was released from custody.

Miller remarked: 'This wasn't just a miscarriage of justice . . . This was the prosecution of a man whom they knew from the outset was innocent. A few hundred thousand words later and a few million dollars later and we're still back where we started: Who killed Barbara Gibbons?'[31] A scathing piece in the *New York Times* asked why Bianchi had prosecuted a man when he had in his own hands convincing evidence to refute the state's case. On 1 June 1977 Sponzo revealed the findings of his grand jury investigation – while ordering that an addendum to his report be kept secret because it contained a list of people he thought might have committed the murder. He did, however, say that mistakes had been made by both the police and the prosecution, and that Reilly should never have been arrested. He praised the work of James G. Conway. The police, however, were not convinced, and continued their efforts to find evidence against Reilly. In 2001, in the television programme *American Justice*, it was claimed that the police still regarded him as guilty.

Miller was involved in the case for some five years, in that time locating a crucial private investigator, a new lawyer and key medical experts. The obvious question is why such a dramatic story never found its way directly into his work:

> I found it impossible to write about despite having been closer to its center than anyone except Conway and Daly. I was uneasy with the idea of using this attempt to right a wrong to my own advantage and possibly adding to Peter's suffering. But in time I sensed another reason for my absence of creative enthusiasm ... I think I was oppressed by a certain brute repetitiveness in the spectacle of the Reilly prosecution .... it offered a vision of man so appallingly unredeemable as to dry up the pen. Except for the intervention of private citizens, a young man, physically slight and in many ways still psychologically a boy, would have been tossed to the wolves in the state penitentiary and eaten alive ... It all seemed to bespeak an evil transcending any commensurate gain or motive, as one understands gain and motive, and I could not escape the feeling that I was watching a shadow play of mindless men dumbly miming roles of very ancient authorship.[32]

In fact, he did try out several pages of dialogue, though this may have been his attempt to understand the case, putting it into a clearer form. Later, aspects of the case were to surface in *Some Kind of Love Story*, one half of the double bill *Two by A.M.* which became *Two-Way Mirror* and subsequently *Everybody Wins* (before that, *Almost Everybody Wins*).

Peter Reilly had eventually been released, but Miller felt that the authorities would have been perfectly content to see him rot in prison and the real murderer go free. What appeared to him to be the utter indifference of those supposedly committed to principles of justice and order was further evidence not simply of the decay of values in America but of that antinomianism he had always feared as a primary enemy. Unmotivated evil or, in this case, simply a fathomless indifference, implied precisely that absurdist stance he had always struggled to resist. At its heart he saw 'the mystery of all the senseless and profitless conflicts I have known, and to write yet another [play reflecting this theme] was beyond me'.[33]

His experience with Peter Reilly reinforced his opposition to the death penalty. In the typewritten draft of an article he noted that if Connecticut had had a death penalty Reilly would probably have been executed, the death penalty making no allowance for inept, cowardly or corrupt police officers or for prosecutors more concerned to protect themselves and their reputations than to secure justice. Reilly was set free only because of the fortuitous death of a prosecutor and because there were those who cared enough to support him despite the state's insistence on his guilt.

Thirty years after the Barbara Gibbons murder, an application was made for the release of police files relating to the case. The police opposed this on two grounds. The first was that the case was 'ongoing'; the second, that the files had been erased. A state freedom of information commissioner likened this response to something from *Alice in Wonderland*.

The Reilly case, though, was not to be the only case in which Miller would involve himself. In March 1987, another caught Miller's attention, when Bernice Martin, an eighty-eight-year-old woman in Manchester, Connecticut, was raped, stabbed and strangled, then left to die inside her apartment in a senior citizens' complex as the building was set on fire. The fire was reported by Richard Lapointe, a man of five feet four with learning difficulties. He was married to a woman with cerebral palsy. He had no criminal record. Two years later he was arrested and interrogated, without legal counsel, for nine and a half hours, at the end of which he signed a confession, or rather a series of confessions. He could neither read nor write. There was no recording of the interrogation. There *was* a recording of his wife's confirmation that he had been with her at the time of the crime, but this was not introduced at the subsequent trial.

Lapointe waited two and a half years in jail before being sentenced to life imprisonment – rather than the execution called for by the prosecution at his trial. In 1993 *The Hartford Courant*'s Sunday magazine, *Northeast*, published an investigative article concluding that he was innocent. The following year Miller became involved, and in an address to the Connecticut Bar Association described the case as a miscarriage of justice. Despite the campaign and further local and national television programmes declaring Lapointe's innocence, it was not until 2009 that appellate judges sent the case back to court.

In September 1995, however, it was at a conference on false confessions at the Atna Center for Families in Hartford, that Miller, who was there to deliver a speech on Richard Lapointe, spotted his son Daniel in the audience. The two embraced and had their picture taken.

In 2008 Peter Reilly was a salesman living in Tolland, Connecticut, and the prime caregiver to Marion Madow. He continued to campaign on behalf of those wrongly convicted, including Richard Lapointe.[34] In August 2010 the habeas hearings of Lapointe ended. His lawyers were to submit post-trial briefs by the end of the year with Superior Court Judge John J. Nazzaro due to decide in 2011 whether to vacate his conviction and order a new trial, twenty-four years after his conviction for murder.

9

THE ARCHBISHOP'S CEILING TO THE AMERICAN CLOCK

It seemed to me that we had completely lost any historical sense . . .
continually seem to devour or wipe out our past.[1]   *Arthur Miller*

For all his involvement in public affairs, Miller continued with his creative work. In April 1974 after rehearsals in New York, he went to his old university in Ann Arbor for a production of *Up from Paradise*, a musical version of *The Creation of the World and Other Business*, staged in the Power Center. There was perhaps something appropriate about this since it was at Michigan, he claimed in his autobiography, 'that I discovered the Bible for the first time', a dubious claim given the requirements of his bar mitzvah at the age of thirteen. What he seems to mean is that then he encountered it 'as a man-made collection of fascinating literatures by different authors'.[2] The production featured professional actors from the New York theatre, though with students designing the costumes, lighting and sets. Seth Allen, who had been an original member of the La Mama Troupe and the Open Theatre, played the part of Cain. An Obie Award winner, he had also appeared in *Hair*, as had Bob Bingham, who played God while also appearing in *Jesus Christ Superstar*. Perhaps appropriately, Bingham was also a leader of a Buddhist organization dedicated to the achievement of world peace. Kimberly Fan, whose career included a production at Joe Papp's Public Theater, played the part of Eve.

The music was by Stanley Silverman, who had written music for the original production of *The Creation of the World and Other Business* and was also an Obie winner. The orchestra consisted of a sextet, mostly woodwind, while Miller himself narrated and directed. It replaced the advertised production of *The American Clock*, which remained unfinished. Miller had been lured there by Richard D. Meyer, director of the University of Michigan Theater Programs, who had worked at Lincoln Center when Miller's plays were staged there. It was a relief, Miller said, to be presenting a new work away from the febrile atmosphere of Broadway, and he indicated as much in a programme note in which he welcomed the chance to stage a play in front of an audience that was neither 'jaded' nor nostalgic for the 'comfortably known'. Here, he added, he could receive from the audience 'that support for his adventure which has been all but crushed in the New York situation'. It was plainly somewhere he could lick his wounds.

In a friendly account of the forthcoming production, Mel Gussow in the *New York Times* recalled the flop of *The Creation of the World and Other Business*. Miller, he reported, had initially turned back to the play he had begun writing on the Depression – *The American Clock*. It was Silverman who sold him on the idea of a musical version of *Creation*. Miller now admitted that the original production had been 'too heavy', with 'no stylistic unity'. He celebrated the fact that the musical version lacked 'any deadly realistic attitude' and that he did not 'have to prove anything on Broadway'.³ The production was scheduled to last only six days. It was a brief respite.

Back in New York, he continued working on *The Archbishop's Ceiling* while remaining committed to supporting a campaign for freedom of expression at home and abroad, and much of his time was taken up with writing articles and joining other campaigns. In a decade in which he wrote little in the way of plays, he devoted considerable energy on behalf of others. This did little to endear him to those who persisted in regarding him as a relic of the ideological struggles of the past, though his attacks were now directed as much at the Soviet Union as at America's client states.

In July 1974 he wrote an article complaining of the treatment of Andrei Sakharov, the Soviet nuclear physicist who had worked on both the atomic and hydrogen bombs but who in 1968 had written a paper on peaceful coexistence, which he published outside the country. As a result he was banned from military-related research. In 1970 he had been a co-founder of the Moscow Human Rights Committee. The following year he wrote to Leonid Brezhnev, General Secretary of the Communist Party of the Soviet Union, asserting that the Party was indifferent to violations of human rights and to the future of mankind. In 1973 a newspaper campaign was launched against both him and Aleksandr Solzhenitsyn. When the writer Lydia Chukovskaya, one of whose books (*Sofia Petrovna*) had been about Stalinist oppression, wrote and circulated a piece in his support she was expelled from the Soviet Writers' Union.

Sakharov went on hunger strike, even as Nixon and Brezhnev were meeting to discuss economic cooperation, without a mention of the plight of dissidents. Miller wrote:

> By refusing to so much as register American awareness of the Soviet persecutions, let alone express his distaste, Mr Nixon is effectively strengthening

the most illiberal elements in the Soviet Government ... By standing silent, Mr Nixon is not doing nothing; he is doing something. The message will go down into the prisons, and up to the highest reaches of the regime, that the United States is a moral nullity.[4]

In his last months in power, however, Nixon was too concerned with what he saw as his own persecution to have time for the persecution of others.

In 1975, which saw the first New York revival in twenty-six years of *Death of a Salesman* (at the Circle in the Square rather than on Broadway), Miller protested against the imprisonment of writers in Iran, denounced actions that isolated Israel, and appeared before the Senate Subcommittee on Investigations to support the freedom of writers around the world. American foreign policy, he told the Committee, was worthy of a moral eunuch. He urged an end to the American support of dictatorships, no matter how anti-communist they presented themselves as being. He insisted that Congress should require from other countries a respect for human rights (citing Czechoslovakia, Chile and South Korea) and refuse to be blind to repressions abroad as to injustices at home.[5]

In 1976 Miller took part in a symposium on Jewish culture, warning of the apocalyptic situation that still threatened the Jewish writer, and protested (along with Philip Roth, Gore Vidal, Noam Chomsky, Woody Allen and others) against the violent takeover, with government help, of the foremost daily in Mexico, *Excelsior*. The letter they wrote noted that Octavio Paz, editor of *Plural*, the paper's literary section, had resigned. Readers of the *New York Review of Books*, to which the letter was addressed, were invited to write in protest to the President of Mexico. Six months later, in February 1977, Miller joined with fifty-three other literary figures protesting to the head of state of the Czechoslovak Republic, Gustav Husak, about the arrest of dissidents.

Not that Miller had forgotten old political resentments. In 1976, he published *The Poosidin's Resignation*, a bitter piece about Johnson, Nixon and Vietnam. He explained its origins in a note:

> The Poosidin fragment was the work of a couple of late afternoons – playing around in that helpless anger so many of us knew at the time. The principals were so outrageous, it was impossible to feel much more than contempt at their endless lying, self-praise, lugubrious insensitivity to the monstrousness of their deformities. They lodged in my mind, finally, as merely impersonators doing a bloody takeoff on something called greatness. They were fakes, genuine only in their bad acting, so bad as to evoke a certain sympathy for their struggle to seem authentic. They were W.C. Fields playing F.D. Roosevelt in whose shadow they grew up and whose royal self-assurance they felt forced to invoke. I apologise that it isn't better on the page, but I can read it aloud

and, in the right mood, can make it sound almost – not quite – as stultifying as the models who inspired it.[6]

What would later become his familiar comparison of presidents to actors aside, this is a comment that conveys his continuing anger even as its apology strikes what seems at first an odd note. The play is written in an idiosyncratic language, in part designed to represent what is offered as an alien and quasi-religious ceremony and in part to convey a political rhetoric void of meaning. The action presents the sacrifice of young men who are fed into a furnace, in a rite presided over by priests. A chorus chants nationalistic platitudes:

> Forever! Freedom! Nyla dadoola, dadooli, dadoolum!
> Security! ... The country, the god, the name'
> Mothers wave their sons on their way:
> I know as my boy burns that my womb
> Has been Presidentially blessed ... Why would these things happen
> If this had not been glorious?[7]

Fathers manfully shake the President's hand, until one resists, in the name of love asking 'Why?' The Poosidin [President Johnson] explains:

> By repulsion of attack on our Navel off Indochinery
> Thus and thus alone, pre-eminently thus
> The fire got lighted up. And thus and thus alone
> The God began incidnerin' our neares' and deares' ...
> ... every great Poosidin
> Has his crosspatch to bear, his war. No
> great Poosidin can be great without great unimies.

The Poosidin-Elect (President Nixon), acknowledging that he was elected to bring about 'an honoral Peace', asks, 'Why must Billy go blowing up the flue?' The answer is: 'He has that right, sacredly and unemotionally.' Meanwhile, 'I premise you once again, the very first moment / When we can find our honor, the fire goes out.'[8]

In the draft of an article called 'On Sublimation' Miller makes a distinction between Nixon and other presidents. Unlike them, he argues, he did what he wished without sublimating it. Just as Hitler had unashamedly explained his attitude to the Jews – and Miller invokes that parallel while acknowledging that it is not wholly appropriate – so Nixon asserts his objectives, reportedly telling Eisenhower, hesitant to nominate him as Vice-President, to 'piss or get off the pot'. Where other presidents dreamed of destroying people, Nixon did. It is not the plausibility of this argument that is striking but that he makes it, even in a draft. Elsewhere in the same article, he compares Nixon to Mao in his ruthless pursuit of power. He recalls a meeting that he himself had with Billy Graham in which he had asked the preacher what his central message was. When he replied 'Love', Miller chose to interpret that as 'Love me', suggesting that no one has confused love and power so completely as Graham, who thus became an entirely apt chaplain for Nixon.

Written in the aftermath of the fall of Saigon at the end of April 1975, *The Poosidin's Resignation* is perhaps a suitably surreal footnote to an issue that had dominated Miller's time and imagination for a decade. More than fifty-eight thousand young Americans had died in Vietnam, committed to a war whose purpose and conduct had been understood by few and defended by a succession of presidents whose rhetoric of honour and sacrifice had always seemed to him at odds with the values of the society they led. Today, what remains of that war, besides the wounds, physical and mental, carried by those who served, is a beautiful and simple memorial in the Washington Mall, designed by a Yale undergraduate, Maya Ying Lin, and dedicated in November 1982. It lists the 58,260 who died. Forty years on people still trace out those names with paper and pencil, carrying the tracings away with them as if they were something more than the record of family members, friends or comrades. Cap badges, scrawled messages, the occasional flower, are left where Lincoln's statue looks out over what was during his time a divided nation and which from 1965 to 1975 was divided again. Vietnamese casualties are believed to be approximately one million combatants and four million civilians.

In 1976, along with Heinrich Böll, Philip Roth, Jean-Paul Sartre and Tom Stoppard, Miller was the recipient of a letter from thirteen Czech writers including Václav Havel and Pavel Kohout, which called on them to protest against the sentences pronounced on those who had sent their work abroad for publication. It also asked that the addressees should work to ensure that the paragraph on free exchange of information contained in the Helsinki Accords be defined more precisely at the forthcoming Belgrade conference on security and collaboration in Europe.

In the March/April issue of the magazine *Society*, alongside pieces on censorship by Harrison Salisbury and William Styron, Miller responded to speeches delivered before the Senate Permanent Subcommittee on Investigations on 18 November 1975. One of these had referred to the notion that Americans should do business with whomever they could without interfering in the affairs of other countries. Miller pointed out that, fine as this was, it bore no relation to the truth of the situation, since America had helped to establish numerous South American dictatorships while overthrowing democratic governments, such as that in Chile, that did not serve its purposes. The challenge, he insisted, was 'how to place our weight on the side of human rights and the sanctity of the individual'. Détente was no more than a word for maintaining the status quo – which meant that 'in Czechoslovakia a whole generation of writers is still blacklisted, still forbidden to publish its works, its unfinished manuscripts seized by the secret police. American and Soviet astronauts,' he observed, 'can transfer from one spaceship to another; but applause comes hard when, as Ludvik Vakulik has recently written, he and other Czech writers cannot transfer a thought from the right to the left sides of their brains without fear of retribution.' The Helsinki Accords, he noted, 'bind both sides to respect elementary human rights' – so:

> Why are we so powerless to speak to this issue? Do we fear that the other side will make noises about the race situation in Boston, the tortures of our client-state Chile, the re-arrest on fake charges of the South Korean poet Kim Chi Ha? ... The plight of the Czech writers and intellectuals is not unique in a world of repression, jailing, and the outright murder of writers by their governments is ordinary news. But their plight is special in one respect: they have nowhere to appeal for relief. As citizens of a socialist country it is futile to look to other socialist states for support; and their case is ambiguous in the eyes of the European Left whose rabid anticapitalist stance mutes its indignation against repression in the East. The prospect, therefore, is that they will continue to be sacrificed on the altar of peace ... Congress has the obligation to decide whether Czech repression is in contravention of the Helsinki Accords. If it is, the State Department should be instructed to ask the Soviet government what it intends to do about the matter as a signatory of the agreement.[9]

The conclusion he drew from the rationalizations of the Warsaw Pact invasion of Czechoslovakia was that power constructs its own realities, as the United States had done in Vietnam. In face of this, he suggested, 'all culture seems to crack and collapse; there is no longer a frame of reference'.[10] In that sense, Salem in 1692 and Czechoslovakia in 1977 evidenced the same imploding sense of the real. It was this feeling that made its way into his most European of plays, *The Archbishop's Ceiling*.

This is a play that asks what happens when the individual is reduced to playing the role of performer in a drama devised by the state. It raises the question of authenticity when words are liable to be monitored. It explores the nature of identity and integrity under pressure. These had been living issues in the America of McCarthyism. They were living issues now in those states in which every utterance, every thought, was potentially available for inspection, as they were in an America in which even the President tape-recorded conversations – including, it turned out, his own. Of the Czechoslovakia on which the play was based, Miller said:

> You never knew who the hell you were talking to, what side he was on, whether he was your friend or your enemy, whether you were digging your

own grave by raising certain issues in certain environments. So the whole question used to occur to me: how do we define ourselves ... The nature of human reality began to come into play, what it was, what it entailed, and whether, indeed, you could even speak of sincerity any more, since everybody had to engineer his speech in one way or another, even with the best of motives.[11]

In an article published in 2009 Brian Moynahan quotes Václav Havel's remark, 'We are all morally sick, because we all got used to saying one thing and thinking another', and recalls a sign above an East European altar that read: 'I am Cain *and* Abel.'[12] This, of course, would have resonated with Miller, who found in the story of Cain and Abel a clue not just to nearly half a century of Cold War politics but also, as we have seen, to human behaviour.

Miller had now finished *The Archbishop's Ceiling* but was far from confident it could succeed or that he could find anyone interested in producing it. Milos Foreman expressed an interest, but quickly dropped out. He had family in Czechoslovakia. No one else stepped forward. It was now eight years since he had scored a Broadway success. He felt increasingly adrift, with no one in the theatre to whom he could turn, and no belief in his own skills. He was suffering, he thought, from a blend of despair and passivity provoked by a lack of contact with like-minded people. He no longer believed, as once he had, that he had news to rush out to the world. He was no longer even confident about his earlier work. He felt marginalized as far as critics and public were concerned. His was no longer deemed a necessary voice. He decided to withdraw the play because it seemed to appeal to no one. His time, he had come to feel, was over.

Indeed, in a letter dated 16 September 1976, he wrote to a friend that he had been feeling more depressed about his work than ever before. Nobody was listening, and he doubted if he had anything to say. He felt out of step with his own country, out of touch too with the passions that once stirred him and generated his work. Nor was his mood improved by the death on 11 November that year of the sculptor Alexander 'Sandy' Calder, his friend of many years. He and his wife Louisa had bought their house in Roxbury in 1933, converting an icehouse into a studio; there he had made the first of his mobiles, a name given to them by Marcel Duchamp. Sartre wrote an essay for an exhibition of his work in 1946. The Millers were regular guests at their house. One drunken evening Calder drew a 'Portrait of Arthur Miller' on a barn wall in felt-tip pen on a painted gypsum board. It was later removed and hung in the Miller home. In a eulogy at Calder's memorial service at the Whitney Museum of American Art, Miller spoke of his friend's pleasure in life and of his own bafflement when first confronted with a Calder work. But suddenly, he said, he had found a way in. The mobiles were like the ever-shifting nature of human relationships; it was the spaces, the silences in his work that generated life.

Calder had found consolation and inspiration in the physical world around him. Appropriately, it was now that Miller and Inge published *In the Country*, the book that was a celebration of Roxbury and that part of Connecticut. Miller was aware that the values it implied and that were caught by Inge's camera were not only threatened but perhaps too seductive. Writing about his wife's photographs, he acknowledges the nostalgia of the image, capturing as it does the shadow cast by a past that seems to imply an assured simplicity against which the individual can only seem estranged, alienated, deracinated. The photographs, particularly those of a historically rooted world such as a New England township, 'speak of a symmetry of action and thought and a revolution based on empirical common sense'[13] that had been lost. Even those who made their living from the soil, of necessity kept an eye on the world beyond, which had its own rhythms and imperatives. Yet some new negotiation had been opened between the given and the possible as incomers arrived, with mixed motives, to try the business of living in an environment that seemed to resist the very pressures that now, in part, defined its parameters.

He and Inge were not alone in Roxbury for much of 1976. In the spring, they were joined by William Sloane Coffin Jr, the man with whom he had stood in anti-Vietnam War demonstrations and who had become a family friend. Having left Yale, and his wife, he came for a weekend but, Miller joked, stayed for six months, entertaining his hosts at the piano, playing classical music. Speaking at Miller's funeral in Roxbury nearly thirty years later, Coffin recalled this visit and in doing so offered a portrait of Miller on his own ground:

> That's really how I see Arthur best – in blue jeans and boots because, for all his being a giant of a man ... he was wonderfully down to earth, wonderful company ... I see him best at the house, in his studio, at the workbench, by the pond, always with Inge ...
>
> Mornings were for writing. In the afternoon he and I planted potatoes and tomatoes. Actually, I did most of the work while Arthur lectured me on Archimedean principles.[14]

The Archbishop's Ceiling did finally find both a producer and a director. Though the Watergate scandal was doubtless one source, it was also a product of his years as President of PEN, of his trips to Russia and Czechoslovakia, a result of observing the political, social and moral ambiguities into which he had been inducted as he came to understand something of the metaphysics, let alone the complexities, of a shadow world in which no one could afford to appear what they were.

In his 1969 visit to Czechoslovakia he had been struck by the surreal nature of what he observed. Outside the Russian Embassy he had passed the largest limousine he had ever seen, bigger than anything in America. It flew 'the red banner of revolution, of liberty, equality, and fraternity'. How, he asked, 'can realism embrace what are no longer paradoxes but irrelevances'? Sheer power, he suggested, 'tends to press the mind further and further from the surfaces of daytime reality in order to grasp the relationships that create such disorder'.[15] It was unsurprising to him that Václav Havel had reached beyond realism in his own plays. In such a society people had to monitor their behaviour, editing what they were saying so as to protect both themselves and those they might mention. It seemed to him, though, that a similar process was occurring in Western society, where there was a degree of self-censorship so that the truth was suppressed or distorted, sometimes for reasons of conscience. It was that process that fascinated him. The metaphor at the heart of his play, though, was stronger in a society in which the stakes were high and an ill-considered word could have serious consequences. In *The Archbishop's Ceiling* he was less concerned with reaching for a non-realistic style than with posing the problem of how the real can be identified when language and even thought itself have been infiltrated by power.

The play opened not in New York but Washington, at the Kennedy Center. It was not a happy production. The text was radically simplified. Ambiguity had been sandblasted away, subtleties eliminated in the name of clarity. Not the least surprising thing was that Miller had agreed to such changes. Later, in his autobiography, he would accuse himself of too ready a capitulation. It took publication of the original text, a regional American production and two British ones to establish the play's value.

The Archbishop's Ceiling, which opened on 30 April 1977 (for a run of thirty performances), though inspired by the situation in Eastern Europe, was also a response to the 'indefinition' Miller saw around him in the 1970s.[16] The sharpness of the 1960s, with their idealism, their stress on common goals had, he felt, given way to a sense of exhaustion. In the theatre, there was a retreat from the barricades into something approaching privatism. The predominant metaphor was that of illness: cancer, deafness, aphasia. Now that the retreat from Vietnam was finally effected – with the same linguistic legerdemain that had once sustained the war – there no longer seemed to be an issue, unless it was feminism, then still gathering momentum. Suddenly, politics were passé. With Nixon gone, there was no longer even anyone worth hating. With his immediate pardon, it was almost as if the past years could be wished away. As the returned soldiers discovered, they were the veterans of a non-existent war.

Nixon's tape-machines and hidden microphones, however, and Miller's personal experiences of surveillance in Central and Eastern Europe, had already introduced him to the potential exposed by the idea of a hidden audience. What was private had long since been made public, as psychiatrists' offices were burgled and Republican 'plumbers' attempted to discover supposed secrets from the Democratic Party – with the same enthusiasm, though not the same talent, as their counterparts in the Soviet Union bugged embassies, hotels, restaurants and private apartments. In fact, it transpired that Washington hotels and embassies were equally wired for sound. Miller explained *The Archbishop's Ceiling* in 1995:

> I wrote the play about the idea of the government, any government, listening to us. But more important than that to me was that this play is about a group of writers who socialized in the former home of the Archbishop of Prague. I did not identify Prague but it was quite obvious to anybody. It was now the home of a Czech writer and nobody was quite sure that he was not an agent of the government while, at the same time, he, himself, had been imprisoned ... for several years. Of course, that was no guarantee. You could be imprisoned and then come out and make a deal with the government, in order to get out of prison, and inform on your fellow writers. In fact, they used to bring a lot of girls there and have a fine old time, some of the writers. The scuttlebutt was that this place was bugged by the government, by the secret police, and nobody was ever sure. They still loved the whiskey, the girls, and so on, and they all went and fooled around there, but finally the government arrested, or threatened to arrest, their best writer. They all, even those who disliked him, had to admit that he was their one genius and in him the spirit of the country resided. So now it became a crisis, how to approach this writer who owned this apartment to try to get him to intervene with the government. It wasn't certain he could do that, but it seemed likely that he could.[17]

Beyond the problems involved in living a highly coded existence within an authoritarian system lay other issues. Thus, what Miller said of the situation in Czechoslovakia had implications that extended beyond the Iron Curtain. The questions proliferated:

> When are we talking to whoever we are talking to, and when are we talking to authority, whether it is the authority of the university, or the city administration ... or the actual government? So there were two listeners in every conversation: one was the person you were talking to, the other was some authority or another. So how do you wriggle through that maze and what is left of you, finally, when you have wriggled through it? Can you identify yourself any more? So the nature of human reality began to come into play; what it was, what it entailed, and whether, indeed, you could even speak of sincerity any more, since everybody had to engineer his speech in one way or

another, even with the best of motives. That was really what lay behind that play because I thought that, in a different way, it applied to the United States and probably everywhere else.[18]

Nonetheless, the trigger was undoubtedly his experience in communist Europe. Václav Havel, discovering a microphone in his chandelier, thoughtfully returned it to the police on the grounds that it was their property. On a later visit to Russia Miller was warned against naming a mutual friend, by means of a familiar gesture of the hand pointing ceilingwards. The question was, what effect did this have on the mind, the psyche and, ultimately, the soul given that, since the play took place in an old archbishop's palace, for millennia it had been assumed that we all exist under God's watchful eye.

In 1996 I interviewed Miller in the baroque splendour of a former archbishop's palace at Schloss Leopoldskron in Salzburg. The technicians from Austrian television fixed radio microphones on us and we withdrew to the library while the invited audience filed in. Having just been discussing his play *Broken Glass* (about Kristallnacht), we speculated whether that audience might not contain a fair quota of Nazis. Later, I was sent a tape of the interview with, at the beginning, a recording of our supposedly private conversation. The microphones had been live. We had successfully bugged ourselves. Schloss Leopoldskron, incidentally, had been occupied by the Germans during the war, religious power having given way to secular. It had also once been home to the director and actor Max Reinhardt, whose original name had been Goldmann. It was a building, in other words, that had seen a great deal of theatre of one kind or another. Austrian television were discreet enough, incidentally, not to transmit our incautious conversation.

For Miller, *The Archbishop's Ceiling* was less concerned with the politics of the situation than the ambiguities to which the very idea of covert surveillance gave birth, the impact on the sense of self, on relations with other people, on the very notion of the real. Those ambiguities themselves depended on the uncertainty of the characters, and through them of the audience, as to the existence or otherwise of the supposed hidden bugs. It was that uncertainty he was persuaded to abandon in the American production, by the director Arvin Brown and the producer Robert Whitehead, and with it went the functional ambiguities. 'They played it,' Miller later explained, 'as though the guy was guilty, beforehand.' It 'became a kind of political thing, which was never my intention'. He was told that it would be necessary to confirm whether or not the microphones were present. The audience, he was assured, 'will need to know'. 'Here in America,' he lamented, 'people in the theatre were not interested in this whole dilemma, or they did not understand it.'[19] The play never made it to New York.

When I was sitting with Miller in his studio in 1983, I asked what had happened to *The Archbishop's Ceiling*, which had been neither published nor produced since its initial production. He reached into his filing cabinet and handed me the text, saying, 'It didn't do any business.' As we talked I thumbed through the text and realized it was different from the one he had sent me some years earlier. It struck me as far less effective. Indeed, the changes seemed to me to be damaging. It was then that I asked him why the two texts were different, and he told me about the changes he had made. Would he be interested in publishing the original? I asked. He was but, surprisingly, no longer had a copy. At the same time we talked about his two one-act plays, produced in America under the title *Two by A.M.* I asked if he would be interested in publishing those but suggested that the title was uninspiring – hence my suggestion to rename them *Two-Way Mirror*, a suggestion which to my surprise he immediately accepted. I flew back to England and contacted his British publisher Nick Hern, then at Methuen (later he would establish his own imprint). We flew back, as I recall, in a matter of weeks if not days. In December 1983, Miller wrote in response to a letter from me:

> I am hastening to answer yours of the 18th because . . . it is a good letter with which I agree. I have only myself to blame, of course, but in the case of Archbishop anyway I was unable to penetrate with the theme. It was probably a question of our historical naiveté, and as a result I made more and more obvious – and hence unpersuasive – a process whose very force lies in its muteness and indirection. In fact, as you now see, the play is an outgrowth of my previous work quite as much as it is a comment on the 'East'. In short, I would want Methuen to publish this, the earlier version.[20]

I had suggested a few line revisions that I thought might help. In a handwritten PS he wrote: 'Your suggested line additions – Maybe I can consider them when I have the final copy in front of me. Can you bring one when you come? I don't have one handy but believe there is one in Austin [at the Harry Ransom Center of the University of Texas].' Just over a week later, he wrote again: 'The year hardly begun and I am already confused. I'm not sure what with the various versions of Archbishop that flew around just before production, that I have the same one you refer to in your good letter. Is it possible for . . . you to copy it and send it to me? I find myself thinking about the thing more and more lately.'[21]

Because it seemed to me that the response to these plays had been over-literal and he was still being described as a writer of realistic plays, I suggested that we should put Escher drawings on the cover. This is why the 1984 edition of *The Archbishop's Ceiling* features Escher's *Drawing Hands* (and *Two-Way Mirror*, his 1955 drawing *Rind*). It was this version of *The Archbishop's Ceiling* that opened at the Cleveland Playhouse in October 1984, at the Bristol Old Vic in 1985 and the Royal Shakespeare in 1986. In July 1984 Miller inscribed my copy: 'Now let's see what happens! – with thanks.' What happened was positive reviews.

The play opens with the arrival, in an unidentified Central European country, of a successful American writer, Adrian, who has written a novel based on the lives of those he now encounters. He comes, it seems, to seek some kind of validation, as in a sense Miller was seeking a similar validation, uncertain whether he could write about a country that keeps its secrets close to its chest. In a play about power, Miller was aware that the writer, too, possesses and seeks power. As Maya, herself a writer, observes, writers 'all write books condemning people who wish to be successful, and praised, who desire some power in life'.[22] There are, in fact, four writers in the play. Besides Adrian and Maya (the latter having seemingly traded in her integrity for success, while admiring the integrity of others) there is Marcus, a seeming apparatchik who nonetheless has spent six years in prison, and Sigmund, focus of state animus. Each has a different kind of power.

In the 1990s, at the request of the Authors' League, Miller would go to Washington to talk to Senators in support of the National Endowment for the Arts, then under attack. 'I was assigned the most reactionary right-wing Senators to talk to,' he later recalled. To his surprise, when he had finished, Senator Lugar of Indiana remarked: 'The best explication I have ever seen of the problem of the government and the suppression of literature and the arts, and so on, was a play called *The Archbishop's Ceiling*.' He apparently made no connection between the play and the man he was talking to. For Miller, he had responded to the play precisely because, as a politician, he was close to power, 'where you have to watch everything you say ... The idea of just talking to somebody out of the goodness of your heart is a very remote thing to these people.'[23]

The old archbishop's palace is a place of 'weight and power', in whose ceiling microphones may or may not be concealed. Once it was God who saw and heard all, now it is either nobody, or a functionary for whom what transpires becomes a form of theatre. The palace is in a state of disarray. Works of art are propped against its walls. The room in which the action takes place is scattered with seemingly random furniture. There is a casualness at odds with the formality of the building, not least because it is ruled over by Marcus, who is a kind of magus, a manipulator whose loyalties are uncertain. He has a freedom of action and movement that makes him suspect, but he also seems determined to use his obvious links with authority to defend his fellow artists, in particular Sigmund, who is seen as in some respects the conscience of the nation and who finds himself persecuted accordingly. The manuscript of his masterwork has just been stolen, presumably by state operatives. It is his only copy.

Sigmund appears to have been modelled on Havel who, like Miller, had suffered the loss of his passport, and was imprisoned in 1977 (for having been one of the initiators of Chapter 77), the year Miller's play opened. Nine years after its production, Havel explained his situation in a way that makes the link evident:

> One of the expressions of the various obsessive neuroses which I suffered from at that time (or perhaps still do) is one that is well known to every dissident: you live in fear for your manuscript. Until such time as the text which means so much to you is safely stowed somewhere, or distributed in several copies among other people, you live in a state of constant suspense and uncertainty – and as the years go by, surprisingly enough, this does not get easier but, on the contrary, the fear tends to grow into a pathological obsession. And if, at first, all you feared was the police search of your house or person, so that you hid your manuscript with friends every night, in time this fear becomes more universal – you begin to worry that they'll lock you up tomorrow, that you'll fall ill or die, that something indefinite is going to happen (and the more indefinite the danger you fear, the more advanced is your disease), all this making it impossible for your work to see the light of day ... Once the play is finished and in a safe place, they can do with me as they will; I am happy and feel that once again I have triumphed over the whole world. But as long as the papers are spread over my desk in an almost illegible manuscript, I tremble with apprehension. Not only for the play, you understand, but for myself, that is, for that piece of my identity which would be torn from me were I to lose the manuscript.[24]

The British actor John Shrapnel, who appeared as Sigmund in the 1986 production of the play by the Royal Shakespeare Company, described his own approach to the role: 'I was finding it useful to think about Václav Havel, then suffering under constraint, harassment, deprivation and periods of confinement.' Two years later he appeared in the same company's production of Havel's own play, *Temptation*: 'A videotape version of our production had been made, and the director Roger Michel and I decided to fly out to Prague with a smuggled copy to show to Havel. During conversations in his apartment (then the operations centre for Civic Forum) we talked about Arthur and I asked Havel if he had read *The Archbishop's Ceiling*. "Of course." He wanted to know about the production: which character had I played? "Sigmund, the writer." "Oh yes: that's me," he had replied.'

Havel, though, was not the only Czech writer to experience this fear of losing his work and thereby his sense of self. Ludvik Vakulik had made a critical speech at the 1967 Czechoslovak Writers Congress for which he was expelled from the Party. The following year during the Prague Spring, he was readmitted, and wrote his 'Two Thousand Words' manifesto criticizing the regime, only to be expelled again. As a result he would not be allowed to publish officially until 1989. In 1975 in an open letter to the Secretary General of the United Nations, Kurt Waldheim, himself not unacquainted with politically authoritarian systems, he recalled his experience of being arrested the previous year, having his passport withdrawn and his publications seized, including the manuscript of a book he had been working on for several years. He subsequently signed Charter 77 and was responsible for a samizdat series called *Padlock*. His 1977 article, 'A Cup of Coffee with My Interrogator', offered an ironic account of his conversation with a polite but baffled inquisitor, which made it clear that the two men occupied different realities.

In a piece for the *New York Times* in 1975 Miller had written that 'the secret police have been methodically entering writers' homes and confiscating manuscripts, works-in-progress, cleaning out their files. Some writers,' he added, 'accept the opportunity to make recanting statements on television, others commit a sort of suicide by simply writing to the leadership repeating their commitment to a country run by Czechs for Czechs.'[25] Amnesty, he noted, could not intervene because the writers were not jailed, merely 'castrated'.

In the splendour of the archbishop's palace it is clear that it had always been thought necessary to bend the knee to power. That is clearly no less true in the play. But the power of the state lies less in its certainties than in the doubt it seeds in citizens who can never be sure of the ground they stand on. How does art function in such a world?

Ivan Klima, as a participant in the Prague Spring of 1968, was blacklisted as a writer and had his passport seized. He hit back by organising readings in his apartment. Havel was one of those who read, as was Milan Kundera. Ludvik Vakulik brought along a writer who, apparently, had just been released after a year in prison. It turned out that he was an informer; he later gave the names of everybody present to the police.

Those gathered in Miller's archbishop's palace are in some sense all compromised. For Adrian these are his friends, but also raw material for his work. He is thus himself an eavesdropper. Maya, a fellow writer, has made compromises with her art and perhaps even compromised those with whom she has shared privacies not as private as they imagined, sex being another form of power. She, however, is dedicated to helping Sigmund, whom she admires. Marcus, meanwhile, politically astute, seems protective of Sigmund who has displaced him in public regard. Marcus points out that the authorities are more liberal than they were in the past, offering his own freedom as evidence. After all, he had been imprisoned by a former regime. Thus he presents himself as an intermediary, anxious to defend his fellow writer but anxious, too, not to disturb the equilibrium of those whose power might be if not benign then tolerable. What are his motives? It is impossible to say. As Sigmund remarks, theirs is a society in which everybody lies – indeed, in which lies provide a necessary protection and even the seeds of hope.

Paradoxically, Sigmund derives his significance precisely from the fact that his is a resistant voice. His real fear of exile, Maya points out to him, lies in the fact that once in America he will be no more than another refugee speaking broken English, drained of significance. In other words, his power as a writer derives in part from the repressiveness of the state against which he rebels. He speaks of the need for freedom while aware that freedom would diminish the significance of his words. These are, it seems, people locked together in some terrible embrace, fearing the very liberation they seek, as those with a hold on political power must be aware of its factitiousness so long as it relies on a system which they themselves know to be contingent. The samizdat copies of Klima's books were eagerly sought out in Czechoslovakia. When they first became available after the Velvet Revolution, they sold over a hundred thousand copies. Today, he sells no more than four thousand a year.

The Archbishop's Ceiling is an account of the degree to which performance has replaced being and the real has become problematic. What is ostensibly the story of the persecution of a writer in Eastern Europe becomes something more, for these are people who try to address one another in a suspect language, who can never be sure of the motives of others or, indeed, of their own. As Miller remarked, 'We're all impersonators in a way. We are all impersonating something, including ourselves ... We have all become actors.'[26] 'Our country,' Sigmund observes, 'is now a theatre, where no one is permitted to walk out, and everyone is obliged to applaud.'[27] All, he says, have become 'some sort of characters in a poem which they are writing',[28] 'they' being those who determine the nature of reality in the state, in any state. In *The Crucible*, it is worth remembering, the state had determined witches to be real and imprisoned those who thought otherwise.

The Archbishop's Ceiling is a play that not only captured the reality of the moment but, curiously, appears to have anticipated events. As it concludes, Sigmund is offered the chance to leave. He refuses. On 29 May 1979, Havel and fifteen others were arrested and charged with criminal subversion of the republic. Havel was being held in detention awaiting trial when a letter arrived from Joe Papp, at the instigation of Milos Forman, inviting him to become a dramaturge at the Public Theater in New York for a year. The authorities made it clear that if he accepted he would be released. He refused. According to Forman, 'Havel realized he was the model of moral courage to his fellow dissidents.' Havel himself explained:

> When I was in custody facing trial, it was at Joe Papp's initiative that I received an offer to go to the United States to study. That offer – although I did not take advantage of it and chose trial and prison instead – was of immense

political significance: our state was thus compelled to offer me the trip to the United States in exchange for not disgracing itself by bringing me to trial. That, in turn, gave me the opportunity to humiliate the totalitarian power by declining the offer.[29]

When communism fell, Havel found himself, as the new President, synonymous with the state against which he had rebelled. Did the ironies then end, the ambiguities of language, the suspect nature of power? Certainly, surveillance would become an increasingly familiar feature of modern life. In 2004, a former British Cabinet minister revealed that a British intelligence agency had bugged the office of the Secretary General of the United Nations as well as various meeting rooms in which members of the Security Council had discussed their attitudes to a resolution with respect to the then impending war on Iraq.

Miller's point is not that governments have a habit of invading privacy but that the very concept of privacy has been eroded, as individuals project themselves into the world, performing their lives as if performance were indeed a form of truth. 'Reality' TV proposes nothing less than that we derive our significance from being observed. The real fear is that nobody will be watching or listening, that we perform in an empty theatre where no one will grant us the grace of their attention (a fear that led Tennessee Williams to write his *Two Character Play*). The need for attention survives, for how else do we know we exist? As Miller remarked:

> We are all secretly talking to power, to the bugged ceilings of the mind, whether knowingly or not in the West; even unconsciously we had forgone the notion of a person totally free of deforming obeisances to power or shibboleth. It was more and more difficult to imagine in the last quarter of a century the naked selflessness of a free human being speaking with no acknowledged interest except his own truth.[30]

The 1977 product of *The Archbishop's Ceiling* at the Kennedy Center was a critical failure. Instead of reviewing it, Arvin Brown complained, the *New York Times* sent a news reporter who wrote about its mixed reviews in Washington – apparently confirming Miller's status as a writer whose future lay behind him. The production in Israel that same year of *All My Sons* may have set a record for the length of run because of its immediate relevance to the contemporary world: Yitzhak Rabin told Miller that its proposition that people made money out of war while others were giving their lives had obvious relevance to those in his own society who readily acknowledged its truth. In America, though, Miller seemed largely disregarded. He later remarked of the failure of *The Archbishop's Ceiling* and its later success in England: 'In an altogether or semi-subsidized theater you can do a play like *The Archbishop's Ceiling* because you don't have to attract a mass audience for two years in order to pay off the cost of it. In our theater, the Broadway theater, you're asking a man to invest his cash in a play which may get very good reviews but probably will not run more than ... six months. That's just not long enough any more.' Beyond that, for all that 'Americans bug everything and everybody for ever, it's not in the consciousness of people'. It was, anyway, he claimed, not essentially a social play: 'It's really a play about reality.'[31]

In March 1978 he began *The Love Drug*, a play rather than the earlier planned film, about the invention of a drug that fills people with love. He was also at work on his adaptation of Fania Fénelon's wartime memoir *Playing for Time* (a project commissioned by CBS television) and beginning *The Ride Down Mount Morgan* that would not surface as a completed play for another thirteen years. Intriguingly, he was also trying out ideas for what, twenty-four years later, would turn into *Resurrection Blues*. In this one month he was engaged in three works whose gestation would take decades. Five months later he was giving thought to what would become 'The Turpentine Still', a sixteen-thousand-word story that would be published posthumously (though in an edition dated 2004). *Death of a Salesman* may have been written quickly, but it is clear that others stayed in his mind for years until they found their moment.

Miller still found time, though, for his political commitments. In June 1978 he joined Kurt Vonnegut and Edward Albee in protesting against the Sharansky and Ginsburg trials in the Soviet Union. Natan Sharansky, who had spent time in solitary confinement and in 1973 been denied an exit visa to Israel on the grounds of national security, was arrested in March 1977 and in 1978 charged and convicted of treason and spying for the United States. He was sentenced to thirteen years' forced labour, spending nine of them in a Siberian labour camp. Alexander Ginsburg, a dissident, had already served two terms in prison when he was arrested again, then convicted of anti-Soviet agitation in 1978 and sentenced to eight years.

That same month Miller met another Soviet dissident, Aleksandr Solzhenitsyn, at a dinner hosted by Tom Whitney, a former correspondent for the *New York Times* and translator of Solzhenitsyn's work. It was a dinner attended by Miller's long-term friends Harrison Salisbury, the Pulitzer Prize-winning journalist who had spent five years in the Soviet Union after the Second World War, and the poet and human rights activist Rose Styron. The Russian writer spoke no English and little German, so that his remarks had to be translated. Earlier, Miller had been one of a number of writers who wrote a letter of protest at Solzhenitsyn's expulsion from the Writers' Union.

Solzhenitsyn had left the Soviet Union in 1974 and moved to Switzerland, before going to the United States where he settled on a fifty-one-acre estate in Vermont. The day before the dinner party he had delivered a speech at Harvard attacking American materialism. To Miller, the speech revealed a Russian love of autocracy and distrust of the messiness of democracy, whose weaknesses Miller knew well enough, granting its corruptions and occasional repressions even as he believed in its central principles. It was to be the most famous speech of Solzhenitsyn's long stay in America.

The Western world, he asserted, had lost courage. The law triumphed over justice, while greed pressed individuals and companies to sail as close to the legal wind as possible. Mediocrity, he declared, was the rule, with the vital individual and the imaginative statesman hemmed in by restrictions. For a man who had so recently been released from prison, his reference to a destructive and irresponsible freedom being given boundless space struck many in his audience as perverse. Crimes in America, he said, went unpunished, and were more rife than in the Soviet Union. Furthermore, the press struck him as cowardly, serving the interests of the marketplace rather than truth. Terrorists were lionized, while government secrets were thoughtlessly revealed. If the psychic disease of the twentieth century was superficiality, the press were the principal expression of this. Americans were assumed to have no interest in the rest of the world.

He was not, he hastily added, speaking in favour of socialism, having suffered from it. On the other hand he was not ready to endorse the West, which he regarded as spiritually exhausted. The harrowing experiences people had suffered in the Soviet Union, he said, had resulted in a stronger people, with a sense of transcendent values. In America there was what he called TV stupor and intolerable music, features of a vapid life. He recalled that a power cut in New York had resulted in looting. Civilization was wafer-thin. Most strikingly to someone like Miller, he accused the anti-war movement in America of being involved

> in the betrayal of Far Eastern nations, in a genocide and in the suffering today imposed on thirty million people there. Do those convinced pacifists hear the moans coming from there? Do they understand their responsibility today? ... The American intelligentsia lost its [nerve] and as a consequence thereof danger has come closer to the United States ... Your short-sighted politicians who signed the hasty Vietnam capitulation seemingly gave America a carefree breathing pause; however, a hundred Vietnams now loom over you.[32]

Beyond that he attacked what seemed to him to be the Enlightenment values America had embraced, which had no room for spirituality and placed the individual at the heart of experience. God had been overthrown in the name of a suspect humanism. In a sense, he insisted, communism and capitalism went hand in hand, and communism had thrived because of support from

Western intellectuals who remained perversely blind to its crimes.

This must all have seemed particularly offensive to Miller. He had been one of those intellectuals. He did place responsibility on the individual and eschewed the idea of God, except as a product of need. He had opposed the Vietnam War. At the dinner party the next day, however, nothing seems to have been said about the Harvard speech. Instead, Miller noted, the Soviet dissident was humorous and appeared relaxed, though he struck him as carrying more than the physical wounds of his imprisonment. In *The Archbishop's Ceiling* Miller had written of the potential fate of the writer who leaves his own country and is forced to inhabit an alien language, his particular force and energy dissipating with distance. Here, though, was one who for the moment seemed to have lost none of his edge. Having left his own country he had found another whose inadequacies and betrayals he felt compelled to address.

Solzhenitsyn's comments on Vietnam must have been especially objectionable, but it was now a decade since Miller had watched people being teargassed outside the Democratic Convention in Chicago and he was more than inclined to agree with the Soviet author's portrait of a society lacking in transcendence. He was also ready to acknowledge that America could justifiably be charged with corruption and moral malfeasance. In some respects, he conceded, it had not significantly improved since the Gilded Age. Nonetheless, he drafted a fourteen-page response to Solzhenitsyn's speech in which, while acknowledging the legitimacy of some of his comments about American society and, indeed, adding criticisms of his own about a culture whose educational system was broken, whose lakes were being polluted and whose railroads barely functioned, he challenged his basic assumption that the solution lay in Christian faith and the rejection of Enlightenment values. Religion, he noted, had led to brutal wars, while to reject the Enlightenment was to reject science, which might have the power to redeem.

He accepted Solzhenitsyn's suspicion of the masses, subject to fashion and occasional hysteria, but rejected his notion of an elite that alone had the wisdom to rule. Indeed, he suggested that the overthrow of Nixon was evidence of the resilience of the American system. As to the notion that the Cambodian genocide could be laid at the door of America's peace movement, this struck him as manifestly absurd. Beyond that, if America was as decadent as Solzhenitsyn suggested, how could its culture have left such a visible imprint on the world? Where the former saw evidence of decay, Miller saw a revivifying energy. It needed an attack like this, it seemed, for him to spring from his corner in defence of the society of which he himself had been so critical. In his draft reply, he sings America.

Reacting against Solzhenitsyn's distrust of democracy, he nonetheless acknowledged and sympathized with his puritanical distrust of materialism.

There was anyway something of the puritan in Miller himself. He was always careful with his money (his sister Joan preferred the word 'tight') – a habit laid down during the Depression – and with the exception of cars, which had always fascinated him, never indulged in conspicuous consumption. Even those cars – Mercedes – caused him a twinge of guilt, though he took pleasure in driving them along the twisting roads of rural New England, blue dashboard lights glowing in the night. As Joan remarked, 'automobiles were so much a part of his life. As a boy he was so proud of the Model T Ford that he had.' When he had his first success he was asked what he was going to do with all his money. His response, Joan recalled, was:

> I just want to be rich enough to be able to buy a car, a Model A Ford maybe, take it apart and not worry if I can't put it together again. To him, that was the ultimate in luxury. My other brother, Kermit, who was older than him and had had more years of privilege in growing up, was not like that at all. He wasn't a spendthrift but he always wore Brooks Brothers shirts or English clothes. He loved that kind of luxury. He was not constrained the way Arthur was. He would go into a store and admire things, but he wouldn't buy them. One time Arthur came to me with an old jacket. He knew that I sewed. He asked me to fix it for him. I said it wasn't my thing. I found somebody who could do it and he was so happy to be able to revive this tweed jacket which had already had its elbow replaced. He could make something last for ever. That was his way. I think he was fashioned by the Depression. So was I. I was always very cautious about how much I could spend. When I was about ten years old I starting baby-sitting in the basement of our house. I grew up with that kind of frugality, but not as extreme as Arthur's.[33]

Miller kept a suit for formal occasions, but never quite looked at home in it. It is true that over time he acquired a wide tract of land around his Connecticut home but he never saw this as an investment, beyond his vague idea of growing trees for sale. His apartment in Manhattan was modest. In his days with Marilyn Monroe he often found himself trying to restrain her expensive tastes. Though Inge always looked immaculate in designer clothes, many of these she acquired through her work as a photographer. They were given to her by designers. She was otherwise no more extravagant than her husband.

In August 1978, a month after publishing a story called 'The White Puppies' which appeared in the July issue of *Esquire* magazine, about a strange family in which the rich Jewish father threatens violence while his son behaves with increasing irrationality, he wrote a twenty-eight-page play called *Finishing the Picture* in which he revisited his painful days working on *The Misfits*. This was the play that would open in 2004, shortly before his death, and which by then would run to some eighty-two typescript pages. In 1978 the characters were already in place and bear the names they would in the play that would open at Chicago's Goodman Theatre. Much of the dialogue would remain too, despite the intervening twenty-six years between this draft and the final version (the last words are given to the same character, differing only slightly). Given that in essence the play was already in place, what made him hesitate to complete it is impossible to say, but his spirits were not high and he had been burned once before when making Marilyn the principal character in a play.

The following month he had discussions with Jim Conway, about another murder. A girl of fifteen had had the back of her head smashed in and the police had proved as inept as they had in the Reilly case. Later Conway would seek Miller's help with a third case, in which the integrity of the Connecticut State Police was again in question. This one concerned a man in prison for the murder of his father and mother-in-law in nearby Waterbury, on what seemed like dubious evidence following two trials, the first of which had resulted in a hung jury. A second possible suspect had supposedly confessed to the crime and subsequently committed suicide. Miller was torn between writing a piece for the *New York Times* or shaping the material into a novel or play. He began to sketch out dialogue and possible motivations.

He had also finished a television version of *Fame*, an expanded version of his earlier story and play. This featured Meyer Shine, a dramatist in negotiation with an Italian film director about adapting one of his plays. Unrecognized by some and pursued by others as he moves around New York, he finds it difficult to grasp what is real. Things are hardly any simpler when he flies to Rome, where a mysterious man who speaks no English gives him a lift. He assumes, incorrectly, that he is being kidnapped. Negotiations over the film quickly turn into farce as it becomes clear that the producer, played by José Ferrer, has little interest in the play as written and wants to star a jockey named Mona. A slight comedy, it was not well received. As John J. O'Connor pointed out in his *New York Times* review, it 'was at one time being written as a stage play' but was expanded only to make 'a rather insubstantial hour. The medium alone,' he added, 'cannot fatten anemic messages.'[34]

Though prospects brightened with an impressive audition for *Up from Paradise*, due to go into rehearsals in the New Year, Miller was once again depressed by what seemed to be his inability to follow through on new ideas. His public failures were matched by a series of stillborn projects that he filed away against the day when inspiration would return.

In October 1978, however, he published a short story in *Atlantic Monthly*. 'The 1928 Buick' looked back to 1930 and to the Brooklyn of Miller's youth. At the heart of the story is his old East 3rd Street home. 'The street had not changed, with its facing rows of small clapboard houses which cost seven thousand dollars when the thirties began. Third Street was a dead end that stopped at the wire fence of the Friends' School athletic field. Beyond it, past the diamond and the outfield and the bumpy tennis courts, lay the cemetery, but nobody thought about it being there.'[35] This is a precise description of the Miller home and its immediate environment.

The story features Max Sions who, unlike other people in the Depression-hit area, is flourishing. He is a little short but otherwise an attractive man, thoughtful of others, the centre of attention. His pride is his 1928 Buick car. He is also, it seems, immune to the general collapse of purpose and direction evident in an America suddenly cut adrift from its moorings. The narrator appears to be the young Miller. He certainly shares his age at the time and, as Miller once had, delivers rolls for a local baker from four to seven in the morning. He describes a woman who had tripped over a chamber pot on the stairs of the East Side tenement where she had once lived, precisely as Miller's own aunt had done. Directly and indirectly he is describing his own family.

The woman's daughter and Max are plainly courting. All seems well. Then the action moves forward seven years. The narrator has returned from college on a hot July weekend. Something, though, has changed. The bright Buick is now showing signs of rust. Max's marriage is equally in a state of disrepair. He still has his wealth, but something else has slipped through his hands. He climbs into another car – a new green Cadillac convertible – and drives off alone to the beach, leaving his wife and two children behind. That evening, he is brought back in another car by a hump-backed man in a bathing suit. Max's wife and mother watch the vehicle draw up at the kerb. The man is a doctor and explains that Max had collapsed with a heart attack. He is on the back seat, dead. The two women scream and attack the doctor, rejecting him again when he turns up at the funeral. The story ends as the narrator returns to college, leaving behind his 3rd Street life and a woman (Max's wife) who tends to get disturbed whenever a large car pulls into this street where, we are told, nothing ever happens.

At last Miller had managed to give fictional shape to an actual event from his college years. In July 1937 he had been finishing his junior year. This real-life incident had been one source for *The Man Who Had All the Luck* but the story itself had not made its way into that play, only the sense of arbitrariness it implied, an arbitrariness which continued to disturb him. He had repeatedly tried to find the best form in which to tell a story that had otherwise struck him as simply a bizarre incident. Here, he places the car at the centre (just as a car plays a central role in *The Man Who Had All the Luck*), its decay coming to stand as a correlative of the erosion of everything he had once thought fixed and permanent.

The self-doubts that frequently surface in Miller's private papers tend to send him, like Quentin in *After the Fall* or Mr Peters in *Mr Peters' Connections*, restlessly searching back and forth for a clue to his own present. His past is his sea anchor, but it is also where he looks for evidence of his failings. In 'The 1928 Buick' he is an observer, a stranger in what had so recently been his own home, whose deficiencies he now recognizes even as he writes about the collapse of a marriage that mirrors that of his own parents. Family embraces, the narrator admits, are now drained of affection. Home seems nothing more than a place to visit with mixed emotions, a place that is unchanging in its banality. This was indeed how Miller had felt about his family, and there is surely a sense in which he is indicting himself. The writer/observer is not innocent.

It was in 1978 that Miller and Inge found themselves in Brussels at the invitation of Jacques Huisman, head of the Belgian National Theatre, for a twenty-fifth-anniversary production of *The Crucible*. It brought back memories. It was Huisman who had directed the first French-language production, which Miller had been unable to see because of the State Department's refusal to issue a passport. He now ran into passport trouble again, though this time through his own fault. Travelling from Paris to Brussels, he managed to leave the essential document behind. Allowed through by an unusually benign official who, as it happened, recognized the playwright, he nonetheless found himself requesting a new passport from the Consul General of the US Embassy, who threw an impromptu reception in his honour.

The next day the passport was ready and when he went to collect it the staff burst into applause. Twenty-five years on, the world had changed. He still recalled going to the passport bureau, accompanied by the actor Montgomery Clift, only to be refused on the grounds that he was a security risk. But there were further ironies, beginning with the fact that the Consul General had himself been fired from the State Department during the McCarthy years and had had to sue to get his job back. The reason for his dismissal, he belatedly discovered, was that, unknown to him, he had once shared an apartment with a homosexual. This automatically made him suspect. The hearings officer who restored him to his position was a man who then went on to preside over the Embassy in Saigon, as American power there collapsed and helicopters landed on the roof. No wonder that when Miller published his autobiography in 1987 he called it *Timebends*. It was not only in his plays that past and present interacted ironically.

There was an echo of the past, too, in his meeting that spring with a Russian writers' delegation, one of a series between Russian and American writers that had been going on for a decade. He was asked to join the meeting by Harrison Salisbury when one of the American writers dropped out to have a tooth pulled.

The surreal nature of these occasions always made it difficult to penetrate the masks worn by those who attended and who, on the Soviet side, were under the surveillance of their fellow delegates. At an earlier meeting, in the late 1960s, Miller had been surprised when a Russian delegate, who had spoken forcefully about the freedom of Soviet writers in their own country, privately sent him a twenty-four by thirty-inch woodcut of Pasternak. Ten years on, at the Academy of Arts and Letters, along with John Updike, Kurt Vonnegut and William Styron, he now faced another delegation, led by Nikolai Fedorenko, the former UN Ambassador who, years before, had treated the Israeli delegate to the United Nations with contempt. Having signed many petitions protesting against the treatment of Soviet writers during the previous decade and seen his book *In Russia*, along with his plays, banned, Miller knew he would not be welcome to the Russians – and, indeed, he detected their hostility.

After a lunch characterized by coolness on the Russian side, Miller made a few, it seemed to him, anodyne remarks, confessing that he knew few of the Soviet delegation, a fact which suggested to him the need for more translations. In reply Fedorenko denounced him, suggesting that there were many writers present who were at least as famous as he. In the middle of Fedorenko's speech Kurt Vonnegut rose to his feet, swore, and left. Miller stayed, imagining what his own fate would have been had he been a Soviet writer, at the same time recalling his experience of living in a country in which he had been sentenced to a year's imprisonment for refusing to name a fellow writer and offer him up to the state machine. The judge at his contempt hearing, he subsequently learned, had expressed regret at having to sentence him. He doubted that Fedorenko would feel similar regret, though as an expert on Chinese art he should have had sympathy for a fellow artist.

China, as it happened, was on Miller's mind. In 1978 he and Inge finally travelled there, achieving what they had set out to do five years earlier. Their proposed itinerary was carefully contrived to appeal to the authorities. Along with visits to places of historical and cultural interest they listed possible trips to oil fields to see an example of China's industrial future, and to the People's Republic's most famous agricultural production brigade.

As was her usual practice, Inge had learned the language of the country she was about to visit. She worked on it daily for eight years and studied Chinese art and history at Yale University in nearby New Haven. Miller later remembered her working in the vegetable garden at Roxbury while a man's voice on a tape recorder recited Chinese lessons from the lettuce row. For Miller, China, like the Soviet Union, recalled early commitments. It was the China of the 1930s that stuck in his mind, a China that had been invaded by Japanese fascists. From Edgar Snow's *Red Star over China*, originally published in 1938, the year Miller had graduated from the University of Michigan, he had derived a picture of another Marxist country promising an enlightened revolution. For him, the book was 'the best single reportage I had read and surely among the most influential ever written' about what 'seemed at the time to promise a new stage of human development, a Marxist revolution whose leaders had a sense of humor, irony, and, in Zhou[Chou En-lai]'s case a cultivated sensibility one had never associated with their kind in the Soviet Union'.[36] It told an inside story, and told it by way of the lives of those who fought what would otherwise have seemed a remote and merely ideological battle in a country still largely a mystery in the West.

In the early 1950s Snow had been one of the group of some twenty writers, including Miller, who had gathered in the Greenwich Village apartment of Jack Goodman, a Simon & Schuster editor. Others included the novelist John Hersey, Jack Belden, another China specialist, and, occasionally, the photographer Robert Capa. They met together with the intention of writing articles that would challenge the new orthodoxy represented by HUAC. Snow was then an editor of the *Saturday Evening Post*. They were unsuccessful – none of them succeeded in placing any articles or striking any response from the media and, as they later discovered, an informer had been placed in their midst: Jack Goodman was summoned to Washington to appear before HUAC, where he was questioned about the meetings.

Miller's faith in Edgar Snow as a guide seems to have been misplaced. For Jung Chang and Jon Halliday, in their 2005 biography of Mao, he was a vain, sadistic, deceitful, manipulative mass murderer, responsible for the deaths of many millions, outdoing even Joseph Stalin. Snow's account, they argued, was thus false in almost every respect and dangerous in that it rallied people, inside and outside China, to Mao's cause – which was, ultimately, his lust for power. The Chang/Halliday book, though challenged by some, forced a re-evaluation not only of Mao but also of the man given privileged access to him, Edgar Snow, the man on whom Miller placed such reliance.

According to Chang and Halliday,

> Mao left nothing to chance, and dictated instructions on handling Snow's visit: 'Security, secrecy, warmth and red carpet.' The Politburo carefully coordinated answers to the questionnaire Snow had to submit beforehand. Mao offered Snow a mixture of valuable information and colossal falsification, which Snow swallowed in toto, calling Mao and the CCP leadership 'direct, frank, simple, undevious'. Mao covered up years of torture and murder ... and invented battles and heroism in the trek across China, astutely now titled 'the Long March' ... Mao took the added precaution of checking everything Snow wrote afterwards, and amending and rewriting parts ... *Red Star* was published in English in winter 1937–8, and played a big role in swaying

Western opinion in favour of Mao. The CCP organised its publication in Chinese ... *Red Star* – and the two books of edited excerpts – profoundly influenced radical youth in China. Many, like the Tibetan Communists, joined the Communists as a result of reading Snow.[37]

Snow, however, was only one of those seduced by Mao. The list of people willing to accept his version not only of history but even of contemporary conditions was long, including Britain's Lord Boyd-Orr, former chief of the UN's Food and Agriculture Organization, who in 1959 denied the reality of food shortages in China just as Field-Marshal Montgomery denied the 1961 famine. France's socialist leader François Mitterrand added his voice, as did Canadian Prime Minister Pierre Trudeau, who wrote a book with the inadvertently accurate title, *Two Innocents in China*.[38] Revelations about the Chinese manipulation of Snow, however, came decades after Miller's visit.

In preparing for the trip Miller also found a handy guide in the form of William Hinton's *Fanshen*, a study of the anti-feudal thrust of the communist revolution (subsequently dramatized by David Hare). Hinton had visited China in 1947 and been shocked by the corruption of the Kuomintang government, later following Mao's forces to their ultimate success. Back in America at the height of McCarthyism, Hinton found his notes on his trip taken from him by customs and sent to a Senate committee on internal security. Later, his passport was withdrawn. On his return from China, Miller read Hinton's *Hundred Days War*, which centred on the events that took place at Tsinghua University in Beijing, where factional fighting had proved particularly intense and only been resolved by the action of Beijing workers – an intervention which Hinton, somewhat remarkably, regarded as a triumph for 'Marxism-Leninism-Mao Tse-Tung thought'. The hyphens alone might be thought to carry a warning. Miller met Hinton in Beijing, and found him a man struggling to reconcile his idealistic faith in the Revolution with the evidence of its errors.

The Cultural Revolution ended only with the death of Mao on 9 September 1976 and the arrest on 11 October – on the orders of the new chairman of China's Communist Party, Hua Guofeng – of the Gang of Four, a name given to the Shanghai-based hard-core radicals led by Jiang Qing, Mao's wife, and including Wang Hongwen, Yao Wenyuan and Zhang Chungiao. They were all members of the Politburo when they were arrested and disgraced. By the end of 1978, Deng Xiaoping had effectively taken over power from Hua Guofeng.

Miller and Inge thus arrived in the country at a moment when people suddenly felt free to speak after decades of intimidation. The Gang of Four became a lightning rod for everything wrong with the country. Intellectuals began their first hesitant attempts to get their lives together. It would have been impossible to attempt the trip as recently as two years earlier. Now, not only could they visit, but it was possible for people to talk openly to foreigners.

Miller and Morath's book, *Chinese Encounters*, which emerged from this visit, was not to be offered as an account of the Cultural Revolution. It was, Miller explained, to be the witness of two people encountering the collapse of an orthodoxy 'at the very time when the faithful were emerging from the fallen temple with blinking eyes, trying to make out ordinary objects in the no longer charmed, unearthly light of ordinary days'.[39] In that sense it was an experience that they themselves had gone through in profoundly different ways, Miller as a man who had himself once drifted away from the fallen temple of Marxism, and his wife as one who had witnessed the end of barbarism as Nazi power collapsed.

Inge's photographs capture a sense of the landscape, the collision of old and new, with, on the one hand, objects from an imperial past and, on the other, shop window displays. The past which, at the level of rhetoric, had been abolished or transcended, in fact clearly infiltrated daily life. It was formally preserved in museums, which gathered together objects from a feudal period, but it persisted too in buildings scattered throughout the city and countryside that stood in contrast to a new uniformity.

There are few of her pictures in which the human figure is not present. The texture of daily life becomes as important as that of the artefacts against whose backdrop that life is lived. The ideology might resist nostalgia and require iconoclasm, a break with history and from old loyalties, but there was a counter-current at the level of individual lives; and what Miller learned from his visit, and especially from what he saw of the theatre, was, unsurprisingly, 'that human emotions, at least as expressed on stage, are universal'.[40] This was a theme he would develop in interviews over the coming years. Returning to China in 1984 to direct a production of *Death of a Salesman*, he would be reminded of fundamental cultural and social differences that led the play to be seen in a different way there, yet at the same time he registered the degree to which human relationships and emotions remained a constant despite what he called 'different etiquettes'.

As with *In Russia*, *Chinese Encounters* is a book that focuses on writers, actors and intellectuals, in this case newly liberated and eager to speak, captured in Inge's photographs in all their formality and intensity. But it is also a book in which individuals seem anxious to explain themselves to themselves as much as to their Western guests.

One of the greatest shocks came early, when Inge met actors and directors. All had served time in prison. One, Jin Shan, China's most famous film star and director, had lost his wife, murdered because of her popularity. Shan had known Jiang Qing, Mao's wife, in Shanghai, a past that Jiang was anxious to suppress by suppressing those who knew of it. It was precisely because she was a former actress herself that Jiang had given her attention to the theatre. Under the Gang of Four, whose evils provided the backdrop to virtually all discussions, there were only eight permitted plays, and each work was allowed 'Three Prominences': an agent of imperialism, a group of peasant heroes or Number Two Heroes, and a Number One Hero. The theatre, in other words, existed to create morality plays detached from the life of ordinary people. Miller quotes an article from *China Reconstructs* (a Chinese Communist Party publication) of August 1976, which defined the nature of this required gap between art and experience: 'Persist in the principle of creating characters in which the best and highest of the working class is portrayed, *unrestricted by real life and people*.'[41]

The difference between this trip and those Miller and his wife had undertaken to the Soviet Union, Czechoslovakia and Poland lay not only in the lack of surveillance but in the willingness, even the anxiety, of people to speak openly. Indeed, he came to suspect that these conversations were themselves part of the politics of the moment. He quickly realized his ignorance of the extent of the suffering of so many artists and intellectuals. Their lives had been suspended. In a world in which politics and art were intertwined, shifts in the power structure had had a direct impact on individual lives. This was a society in which, if Chou En-lai expressed his admiration for Beethoven, then Jiang Qing, whose marriage to Mao he had opposed, would ban the playing of his music. This chimed with Miller's conviction that behind the political, and driving an apparently volitionless history, lay the personal. But there was still, it seemed to him, a degree of denial on the part of those he met, as Mao was excepted from the criticism aimed at the Gang of Four, who for so long had patently operated with his approval.

When he spoke to Sol Adler, one of a number of old China hands driven out of America in the 1950s, and asked him about the extent to which Mao was believed to be aware of the excesses of the Cultural Revolution, he saw that it was painful, if not impossible, for him to reply: 'I wondered,' he said, 'whether this amnesia-like effect was also due to the common human inability to recall a lost enthusiasm. Nothing is more inexplicable than a vanished zeal. It's like a love-affair gone sour.' The 'redeemer Mao, and the revolution itself', meanwhile, had 'borne a fatal flaw into the world'.[42]

Meeting William Hinton, now owner of a farm back in Pennsylvania, Miller found someone unwilling to disavow his own country through admiration of another, but nonetheless retaining his faith in the integrity of the Cultural Revolution, however compromised it had been. In describing his views, however, Miller implicitly restated his own principles ascribing to Hinton precisely those beliefs that lie behind so much of his own work. The present, Miller insisted, 'is but the leading edge of a long and particular past whose failures, confirmations, and denials reach deeply into the personality and self-conception of each people ... Perhaps,' he suggested of Hinton, but again with relevance to his own convictions, 'he is the bearer of an unfamiliar kind of consciousness for whom the past is not a mistake to be denied and exorcised and thus left to repeat itself so insistently that it overwhelms the future.'[43]

1979 began with the completion of *Chinese Encounter*, and subsequently the casting for a new production of *The Price*, eleven years on from its initial staging. He was far from confident, acutely aware that he had little to show for the intervening years and fearing critical attack. Trying to break away from such depressing thoughts, he went to Haiti to research what he was now calling 'Corkish', his putative novel set on the island. Like much of his work, it was based on a real incident, and he travelled up into the pine forest where it had largely taken place. Meanwhile, he finished the script of *Up from Paradise*, the musical version of *The Creation of the World and Other Business*, and pressed on with a possible new play (the typescript runs to thirty-nine pages, though there is more than one version) with the provisional title 'Smoke'. Its theme was to be evasion but it also addresses something of his own feelings including his sense of failure.

In the opening scene Caroline is in bed, apparently suffering from the effects of drugs administered for an operation. Certainly she is not rational. The dark humour of the piece derives from her confusions and her occasional visions, in particular one of a nude woman playing a cello, in her mind blending a *Playboy* model with a musician at a funeral. The other characters are her husband and a nurse.

He is a Jewish writer called Del, preparing for a trip to China. His reputation has faded. The critics who once admired him are no longer around. In this unfinished play, Miller writes about a man who has difficulty finishing his work, instead reaching back to earlier material as though, he explains, he were sweeping his dust together. Del has embraced causes with what amounts to almost to a fatal irresponsibility. Throughout the 1930s and 40s he had always been expecting the system to collapse and hence had lived a temporary life. Now he is repelled by the vulgarity, the superficiality, of life in America and again looks for its collapse, if no longer in the name of anything as clear-cut as socialism. In one version of the play Del is told that there are certain people who become symbols on whom others rely. If they fail to respond, others will lack the will to rally to the cause. In his case, though, he may have given too much of himself, allowed his social expectations to erode his work.

After several attempts Miller abandoned the play, which mixes realism with fantasy. Perhaps it was simply too close to his own circumstances. After all, he had for a decade and a half thrown himself more directly into social and political issues, and this had coincided with a decline in his reputation as a writer. Was his activism the cause of what he thought of as his failure? On the other hand, he could not accept the idea of political and social disengagement, though it seemed to him that society was indeed changing, and not for the better. This, after all, was the 'me decade', so called by Tom Wolfe in 1976 as he surveyed an America that after thirty years of boom appeared to have turned its back on social and political issues in favour of a concern with the self.

Miller's work and his political activism, as we have seen, had been based on the idea of shared values, an assumption for which there was ever less evidence. Beyond that, his trip to China had sharpened a concern that keyed in not only to his own experience, as youthful utopianism had collapsed in the face of totalitarian cruelties and betrayals, but to a more general loss of purpose and direction. His early Marxism had offered him a glimpse of transcendence. With the collapse of that dream, what was left? The American dream of self-fulfilment and self-improvement had devolved, it seemed to him, not merely into a vapid materialism but a pointless solipsism. Literature itself was becoming self-reflexive.

In art, parody and absurdity seemed the prevailing modes, a postmodern irony the dominant style. For the fashionable critics, character and plot implied a factitious coherence, just as history was deconstructed into a house of mirrors. The author was dead. At the end of the century Miller's Mr Peters would lament the loss of a subject, the absence of a spine to experience, but that was already apparent as the 1970s edged towards the 80s. The various plays and novels he sketched out are concerned with failed ventures, individuals no longer secure either in their past or their present.

His interest in writing had originally been fired by his reading of the great Russian writers of the nineteenth century. There he had found a conception of the individual as part of history, an actor in a national drama. Then, novels and plays had engaged with social and moral issues. There was an existential drive to works that compelled precisely because their characters were both a product of and creators of their society. Such presumptions seemed no longer to prevail.

The election of Margaret Thatcher in 1979 and of Ronald Reagan in 1981 signalled a victory for a particular view of the political and moral economy. Both proposed a version of social action that turned on competing individuals regulated, if at all, only by the forces of a value-free market. Miller was not the only writer to be momentarily disoriented by a perceived moral vacuum at the heart of affairs. It was surely his sense of this collapse that led him to write *The American Clock*, as a reminder of a time when the need for shared values was at its most obvious. In particular, he had lost a sense of endings – he experienced increasing difficulty in finishing plays and stories – because he had lost a sense of beginnings. Some animating principle, however suspect, had disappeared. A history that had once been driven, in Europe, America and China, by a sense of revolutionary zeal was now no more than a series of events without a spine, the relations between states reducible to a violence threatened or withheld, an anarchy that entered the aesthetic world whose coherences were increasingly presented as illusory.

The China book recalled another sensitivity, a sense of guilt about the process of writing. He acknowledged the extent to which, as a writer, he was potentially an appropriator of other people's lives. It had been true of his plays and it was true of *Chinese Encounters*. It was evidently a momentary doubt because not long after this, when Jim Conway tried to interest him in a murder case involving a woman with multiple personalities, he noted down the details. This later became the basis for *Some Kind of Love Story*. Everything, it seemed, was available for cooption. Not untypically, his response to such thoughts was to sketch out a play, in this instance called 'Bernie', which would, he hoped, be a history of an American, the action moving from the 1920s, through the Depression and the war, in an effort to dramatize the individual's struggle to exist in the world. But after thirteen pages he broke off, not least because he was due in Paris, where he sat in on rehearsals of a Peter Brook production, watched by a group of deaf mutes aged between ten and fourteen. It was the kind of theatre he had grown to dislike, one seemingly concerned more with its own procedures than engaging with an audience.

In England, meanwhile, Michael Rudman had directed a highly successful revival of *Death of a Salesman* starring Warren Mitchell, at first glance an unlikely candidate for Willy Loman. Mitchell, whose own father was a travelling salesman, was known in Britain for his performance as Alf Garnett in the television show *Till Death Us Do Part* (American version, *All in the Family*). He first played Willy Loman with the West Australian Theatre Company in Perth, where he found himself fighting to keep the Requiem, which the director thought downbeat. Rudman's decision to cast him in the National Theatre production, in what he was thinking should be an all-Jewish production, was a bold one, since he was so associated in the public mind with his television persona. Miller agreed to Willy being portrayed as a Jewish character only provided that none of the accoutrements of the Jewish faith was on display. This might be a Jewish family, if it suited this particular production, but it was not to his mind a Jewish play. The production was a triumph.

1979 ended with a protest, signed by Miller and a host of other writers, members of the American PEN Center and the US Helsinki Watch Committee, against the detention of Václav Havel and ten other signatories of Charter 77. They were charged with subversion under Article 98 of the Czechoslovak penal code. On 22 October that year six of them, including

Havel, had been found guilty and sentenced. The letter, published in the *New York Review of Books*, called for the release of all eleven men and women and for the Czechoslovak government to honour its international commitments.

For the moment, though, it was the past rather than the present that commanded Miller's attention as he adapted Fania Fénelon's memoir *Playing for Time* for a television film. It is an episode in his life strangely absent from his autobiography, perhaps because it turned out to be in some respects an unpleasant experience, even though the end product proved impressive. It was certainly a project that once again took him back to the questions raised by the Holocaust, so central to his thinking.

In the book on which Miller was to base his screenplay, Fania Fénelon outlined her wartime experiences. In 1943 she was a cabaret singer in Paris and a member of the Resistance, for which she carried letters, arranged meetings and provided a safe house. She was also half Jewish and hence doubly vulnerable. When an informer betrayed her, she was arrested and taken to the Quai de Gesvres, where she was beaten until she offered her real name – Goldstein. She was immediately sent to Drancy prison, where she stayed for nine months before being shipped out to the women's camp at Auschwitz-Birkenau. Here she would have died, but for failing to join those around her who climbed into a truck marked with a red cross that carried them not to hospital, but the gas chambers. Even so, her reprieve would have been short-lived had she not been recognized and enrolled in a women's orchestra, following an audition in which, in a state of shock and exhaustion, she was required to sing an aria from *Madame Butterfly* to prove her ability.

Mere chance had saved her life, but to stay alive meant to close her mind to her surroundings, and at the same time to become complicit. This was the paradox within which she and her fellow musicians had to live if they were to survive. To survive was to harden your heart; to harden your heart was, in another sense, not to survive. Hope was essential, but hope was the source of irony. Their only subversive act was to infiltrate the work of Jewish composers into their repertoire. But always there was the risk that they would be sent to the gas chambers. Stripped of power, they could do nothing but struggle to please those whose approval was a kind of curse. Even worse, they had to play for the near corpses who stared at them as the orchestra was required to play for those being marched off to work, who would spit at them and call them 'Quitters, bitches, traitors!' As Fénelon remarks, 'I dared to look at them. I forced myself to. I had to remember, because later I would bear witness. This resolution was to harden and give me strength until the end.'[44]

The march music they played, the concerts they were obliged to offer, almost defy decoding. Contempt, irony, cruelty, sentimentality, pragmatism – all swirl around. The SS too, it seemed, required assurance that the world they were so assiduously deconstructing survived their depravity. Yet the music was redemptive. It was not merely a way of waiting out time. It was its own universe, with its own parameters, its own values, into which it was possible for the individual to retreat. Their sin was that they too, the musicians, could become happy for a moment inside the music.

Alma Rosé, the conductor, exercises an absolute authority over the members of the orchestra, even, according to Fénelon, striking them, forcing them to work when they are exhausted, because she serves a higher cause. Certainly, she wishes herself and her fellow musicians to survive, but she also serves an idea of professionalism, a sense of the legitimate demands of art. This is a long way from the authority exercised by the Germans, yet they too purport to serve a legitimate ideal: they, or some of them, fall back on a concept of professionalism to protect themselves. It is not a thought that Fénelon pursues, but the unease at what she and others did ebbs and flows through the text. Fénelon's response is to insist on the need to open one's eyes and stare into the heart of evil. Forgetting, erasing, become crimes in their own right, a subtle conspiracy with those who seek to imagine that aesthetics can ever substitute for ethical behaviour. This is the boundary line they must walk.

There are odd moments when an inexplicable reprieve is offered, when the musicians are allowed out of the camp into a world that was once normative but which now has become alien. They cry when they see buttercups and harebells. When they reach a pool some of them bathe. They pick flowers. They behave, as she says, like children on a Sunday walk. When, as they pass other prisoners, they are spat at, it seems not to matter. Outside, they pass a peasant, sickle in hand. It occurs to Fénelon that, should he later be asked what life must have been like for the prisoners, he would answer that they had been happy. 'That's what eye-witnessing is all about,' she says, in doing so casting a shadow of doubt over her own account: like Primo Levi, acknowledging that she sees through the eyes of memory. Yet this is an account that begins with a reunion thirty years later, and with Fénelon's assurance that '"it" thinks *for* me'.[45] In other words, the reunion is offered as a validation that the point of view given in the book is not Fénelon's alone, just as her insistence that 'it' thinks is an assurance that her time in the camps was so deeply etched, so vivid, so all-encompassing that, unlike the peasant's glimpse, her account is not based on a moment become a totality. It is a translation into words of experiences that words alone can barely communicate.

As the war closes in on Auschwitz-Birkenau, the women have a new fear. As witnesses, they are at risk. They can testify to a reality the Germans have reason to deny. Bombers swoop down, aiming, at last, for the gas chambers and crematoria that have been allowed to function for so long. Suddenly, it is 'Jews to the left, Aryans to the right', only this time the order is a prelude to an eastwards journey as they are carried away by a train, so much evidence being hurriedly removed.

After two days of travelling without water or facilities, they are offloaded by Wehrmacht soldiers. A thousand women move forward into a wood, as the chatter of machine guns echoes ahead of them. Once again, Aryan confronts Jew, guard challenges prisoner, man faces woman, and the overtones of that other tension are stressed by Fénelon as she speaks of the soldiers advancing with their guns, 'phalluses of death trained upon us'.[46]

She and others now crawled into a large, low-slung tent where she fell asleep, not knowing then, what she learned later, that only a matter of a few feet away from her in Bergen-Belsen, for that is where they were, lay the young Anne Frank in process of succumbing to illness and despair within such a short time of what would have been her release. There were no gas chambers here, simply phenol injected into the heart. Food was sometimes provided and sometimes not. They were rounded up for work at a nearby factory where cellophane was produced, as the men at Auschwitz had worked for I.G. Farbenindustrie: 'And let no one tell me that the bosses, the directors, the foremen, the workers who saw those pitiful gangs enter their workshops every morning didn't know of the existence of the camps and the way the deportees were treated.'[47]

In the last days, Fénelon contracts typhus and is suffering exhaustion when on 15 April 1945, four hours before they were all to have been shot to prevent them bearing witness, the British arrive and they are freed. She weighed only sixty-two pounds. Less than five feet in height, she looked like a broken doll. Nonetheless, she summoned up her remaining strength and sang the Marseillaise. A BBC correspondent heard her and placed a microphone in her hands. Back in London a cousin heard her voice and fainted. She had survived.

Fania Fénelon, for the Nazis prisoner 74862, resumed her career and retired in 1972. Thirty years to the day after her release from Bergen-Belsen, she began to write, with the assistance of Marcelle Routier. She had waited, she explained, because first 'I've had to live, to have the youth we never had ... After thirty years of silence during which I tried to forget the unforgettable, I saw that it was impossible. What I had to do was exorcise the orchestra.'[48] Her account was published in French in 1976 and in English the following year. *Playing for Time* was dedicated to the survivors of the Auschwitz-Birkenau extermination camp. She died six years later, of cancer.

It did not take Miller long to produce the screenplay, some four weeks in all. He responded to Fénelon's book partly because it addressed his often expressed anxiety about what seemed to be Jewish passivity in the face of what he feared Jews too readily accepted as their fate. He had always been troubled at what he took to be the lack of resistance by those in the camps.

Why had they not rebelled more than they did? Why did they climb on board the trains? Why did Jewish committees sometimes seem to collaborate in plans for their own extinction? For all his trip to Mauthausen and his work on *After the Fall* and *Incident at Vichy*, there still seemed to be a gap in comprehension. Here, nevertheless, was a book that explained something of the compromises necessary for survival, which showed that revolt could take many forms.

The challenge of the adaptation turned out to be the least of his problems. In August 1979 he was confronted with a major public row over the casting of Vanessa Redgrave to play the part of Fania Fénelon. Redgrave was known for her support of the Palestinian cause and had been described by one critic, albeit ironically, as 'La Pasionaria of the PLO'. In 1977 she had sold her house to fund *The Palestinian*, a documentary about the Palestinian Liberation Organization. When the following year she was nominated for an Oscar for her performance in *Julia*, based on Lillian Hellman's book *Pentimento*, a group of pro-Israelis campaigned against the award. When she received it, she proclaimed, 'I think you should be very proud that in the last few weeks you have stood firm and you have refused to be intimidated by the threats of a small bunch of Zionist hoodlums whose behaviour is an insult to the stature of Jews all over the world and to their great and heroic record of struggle against fascism and repression.'[49]

Miller had responded with enthusiasm to the original approach of the producer, Linda Yellin. On finishing the screenplay, he wrote to tell her that he was delighted to be involved in the project because he had long believed that the Holocaust constituted the single most important event in the twentieth century. The problem, though, he added, had always been to discover a way of handling it aesthetically, dramatically. In terms of the script he had chosen to focus on a limited number of figures while striving to give a sense of the orchestra as a group, even when that meant that individuals might have no more than a line or two. For all the difficulties, however, it seemed to him that the subject might have found its proper form.

Explaining the attraction of the project, Miller recalled that the first reports coming out of Europe in 1945 had kept him awake at night, and that the issue of anti-Semitism had never been far from his mind. The essence of *Playing for Time*, he said, was that Fania Fénelon's struggle to survive had shown that 'it was possible to exercise free will even in a concentration camp'. He did not 'want to write about victims'. The Holocaust 'was emblematic for Jews and for the human race; it revealed mankind at the abyss'.[50] But even in the face of the abyss, he was keen to insist, there was still choice. He wanted to celebrate the resistant spirit, and there were many Jews who joined him in this, anxious for evidence of heroes and martyrs. For Lawrence L. Langer, though, who gathered together Holocast testimonies, often survival had come at the price of the very humanity others were anxious to celebrate. It came at the cost of family and group loyalty and a subjugation of the qualities that might be thought to define the moral self. There were instances of sacrifice, of communal strength – Miller places one at the centre of *Incident at Vichy* and another in *Playing for Time* – but, Langer maintains, such survivors cannot be seen as emblems of the Holocaust. Miller, though, wished to see Fania Fénelon as just such a figure.

His enthusiasm for the project would drain away as Redgrave was attacked and he himself was denounced. He received a number of letters of protest, some from concentration camp survivors, both before and after transmission. He was also challenged with respect to details of his script. A letter from a former inmate of Auschwitz refuted the notion that any female SS commander would have played with a Jewish child, as happens in Miller's screenplay, or that Dr Mengele would have put flowers into the coffin of a dead Jewish woman, as Miller has him do. Anyone interrupting Mengele, as Miller has Fénelon do, would have been instantly killed. He had, she wrote, managed to put humanity into monsters.

Another, signing herself with her tattoo number, wrote to say that she would not watch the programme because of the anguish which he, a Jew, seemingly wished to revive. Some letters went to CBS, others to the *New York Times*, whose chairman, like Yellin and Miller, was Jewish. Yet another quoted from *Incident at Vichy* – 'I don't want your artistic purity, I want your responsibility' – to which Miller, drawing a line between the two parts of the sentence, added that the two were the same suggesting that the correspondent should wait to see the finished film. There were others, too. David Wolper, producer of *Roots*, intimated that he would cancel a project with CBS as a result of the casting.

Somewhat grudgingly, Miller issued a statement to the *New York Times* stating that nobody could play the part without generating sympathy for the Jews. In an echo of the past, here was a demand for the blacklisting of an actress and he could never agree to that, but he felt the pressure of what he called the Israeli patriots. As far as he was concerned Redgrave might be in thrall to a simplistic form of Marxism, but she was not anti-Semitic. She was also committed to the part. He noted that other actresses had declined a role that required them to shave their heads and lose weight. On 20 August, a *Sixty Minutes* programme was dedicated to the issue. For the moment, though, things calmed down, with Fénelon giving an inscribed copy of her book to the actress and she reciprocating with a signed copy of the script, a gesture perhaps reinforced by Redgrave's statement on *Sixty Minutes* that a fascist or anti-Semite should not be allowed to play the part and that she was assuredly neither. She added the reminder that Palestinians were also Semites.

CBS executives received death threats. There was a bomb scare at the production office. The Anti-Defamation League of B'nai B'rith and the American Jewish Congress complained, the former suggesting that the casting was 'an insult and an injury to the millions of victims of the Nazi Holocaust'.[51]

To Redgrave's support came Jane Fonda, no stranger to controversy herself, and John Schlesinger, who reminded people that he was himself half Jewish. Fellow members of the cast signed an open letter urging that Redgrave's personal views should not obscure a dynamic and honest piece of work, a slightly two-edged gesture of support, conceding, as it seemed to, a certain distaste for her politics.

The press, meanwhile, was largely supportive, seeing the casting of Redgrave as a civil liberties issue, though some chose to denigrate while ostensibly supporting her. Thus, John Pascal of *Newsday* maintained her right to perform while dismissing her as an 'icy harridan of no noticeable talent'. The *Chicago Sun-Times*, while objecting to the pressure groups working for her dismissal, highlighted her 'half-baked politics' and hoped that the role might educate her. The actor Alan Alda defended her artistic freedom while insisting that he found her political beliefs 'horrendous and atrocious ... reprehensible'. The Screen Actors' Guild underscored her right to speak out while deploring her views. Gilbert Cates, director of *I Never Sang for My Father*, said that he would not support her dismissal but he found her casting 'incredibly tasteless' and attested to the 'pain and discomfort' she would cause. Even Joseph Chaikin, who believed that one of the parts had been written with him in mind, wrote indicating that he would be unable to take part.

Writing to Linda Yellin on 5 September 1979, Fania Fénelon now raised four objections, three of them to do with the script. First, she insisted that the SS never referred to any of the women by name, only by number. Second, they neither applauded nor showed any evidence of pleasure in the orchestra's performances. Third, she felt that her sense of humour and the confidence that had enabled her to survive had been excised; and finally, she would never allow herself to be portrayed by Vanessa Redgrave. Her reason for dismissing Redgrave was that fanatics of any kind frightened her, whether Israelis or Palestinians, and, more pragmatically, it struck her as absurd that she, four feet nine inches tall and at the time a twenty-five-year-old who looked seventeen, was to be portrayed by someone of six feet two who looked forty. She had wanted Liza Minelli. Furthermore, the script seemed to her ignorant of the real conditions in the camp, details which she insisted were clear in her book. It was a bitter letter.

She also took particular exception to a scene in which it becomes evident that one of the women, Louise, has fallen in love with another, Maria (though the names differed in the script). The scene begins with the direction, 'Now their eyes meet, FANIA is surprised, curious. LOUISE is innocently fascinated, openly in love but totally unaware of it.' Both women, we are told, stare in silence at one another. 'Now MARIA tenuously reaches out her hand which LOUISE touches with her own.' Fénelon has scrawled down the edge of the script: 'All this is out, must not be shown in the film. In the contract it has been cut.' In the final published version the characters – now Michou and Laure – do not touch, though they are clearly drawn to one another, but the direction remains.[52] Miller retained the scene in his later play version while changing the names to Lotte and Helene. It is difficult to know why Fénelon objected. In her book, where the characters are called Marta and Irene, the scene is more extensive and the nature of the relationship is clear. As Fénelon observes, 'In Birkenau, one couldn't long remain ignorant of homosexuality – it was rife; it offered the women satisfaction for their fantasies, allayed their solitude, their sexual needs.'[53]

Charles Rensac, editor, co-publisher and copyright owner, wrote to Yellin on 11 September, assuming that Miller had known nothing of the agreement to delete the scene from British and American editions but underlining the fact that Louise in the film script (Marta in Fénelon's book, Laure in the film) was a real woman who would undoubtedly sue if the sequence was not removed. On 18 October Miller's lawyers were informed, and they in turn informed him.

On 9 October Miller had written to Robert Whitehead, who had inquired about Redgrave. Miller confirmed that she had insisted that she was not anti-Semitic but that she was opposed to Israel because, on Marxist grounds, she saw it as an extension of American imperialism. He added that in England no one took her politics seriously and that in a previous conversation with her about the British political situation he had found her incoherent and even delusionary. He had sympathy, he explained, for former camp inmates who had objections, but others he had little time for. None of those objecting, as far as he was aware, had themselves ever done anything to defend either Jews or civil liberties.

In another letter to Whitehead dated the next day he repeated some of these points and recalled his own dismissal from the juvenile delinquency film he had been commissioned to write by the New York Youth Board in 1955. The *World Telegram* had suggested he should be allowed to write it but that his name should be removed from the credits; this, it had said, was not blacklisting. Given this experience, Miller explained, reiterating his statement in the *New York Times*, he was not about to be involved in blacklisting anyone else. He noted that the man who had initiated the campaign against Redgrave, Dore Schary, had been the chairman of the Waldorf Hotel meeting of Hollywood producers in 1947 that had buckled before HUAC and agreed to drop those who refused to cooperate with the Committee. In fact Schary had not chaired the meeting: he was there to represent RKO and spoke against a blacklist, though he did sign the document they produced. The only objection to Redgrave's casting he took seriously, Miller said, was Fania Fénelon's. Certainly, he rejected the idea that to be against Israeli policies was to be anti-Semitic, not least because that was essentially his own position.

On 19 September 1980, twelve days before its scheduled transmission, a dozen actresses appearing in the film wrote a public letter expressing the hope that Jewish organizations and advertising agencies would back it. The letter pointed out that several of the signatories were Jewish and that they had been so committed to the project that, like Redgrave, they had allowed their heads to be shaved. It was too important, they declared, for anyone to seek to undermine it.

Miller himself had his own problems with the film, which struck him as under-funded. The actors refused to travel to Harrisburg, Pennsylvania, for filming, afraid of contamination from Three Mile Island where there had been a nuclear accident. At one time CBS considered closing the production down. It seemed to Miller that Redgrave's performance was mixed. In some scenes she was excellent while in others she seemed flat. However, he admired Max von Sydow, who was playing Dr Mengele. Later, Vanessa Redgrave gave her own account of shooting the film:

> To my mind, whatever the shortcomings of the film may have been, his script is the deepest insight into the horror of the Nazi mentality. There is a moment in one scene between the women when one girl asserts that Fascists cannot be thought of as human beings. The pianist replies, 'Don't you see? The whole problem is that they *are* human beings?' For me, this sentence reveals the quintessence of Arthur Miller's great spirit, as a man and as a playwright. Many crewmembers had accepted low wages because they wanted to work on this film. Our film extras, who had arduous days filming, drove in to the location from miles away, having taken part because they felt Arthur's script would explain the Nazi Holocaust and they deeply wanted to know. They were, I know, not disappointed as we had several discussions while we were waiting for lighting and camera set-ups ... I also remember that there were many organised campaigns from some Jewish organisations to get me off the film, or to get the State of Pennsylvania to deny CBS the permit to film there. I know that Arthur always said he felt that I was the best actress for the role he had written. I also know that the majority of Jews always resisted my being blacklisted, or denied a role, or being threatened in any way.[54]

For Redgrave, who had first seen Miller with Marilyn Monroe at a Sunday evening symposium held at the Royal Court Theatre (of which her husband Tony Richardson was an associate director) in 1956, when *The Crucible* had been the second play of its first season, the essence of *Playing for Time* lay in the fact that it 'showed us *how* Fascist ideology operates in and through human beings and just how difficult it is for human beings to struggle against being dehumanised'.[55] Later, she recalled the experience, noting something that no one else commented on:

> We rehearsed for two weeks and then filmed for five weeks in the barracks of an internment camp in Pennsylvania, where US citizens of foreign origin had been interned during World War Two. Arthur and his wife Inge, who photographed the production, were with us throughout the shoot. I believe I still have a Polaroid somewhere I took of Arthur in his cap, standing under the scaffold erected for the scene of a hanging, grinning at me. We had many discussions about the scenes, about the Holocaust, about the war.

Redgrave had just been offered the part of Mary Tyrone in O'Neill's *Long Day's Journey into Night* and was uncertain whether to accept. Miller told her, "'Well, I'd pay to see you in that.' His look and his words decided me, and he came to the first night the next spring.'[56]

The filming was a fraught affair, with Miller at one stage nearly taking over its direction from Joe Sargent. At the suggestion of Elia Kazan, he called Francis Ford Coppola for advice, and there was talk of finding finance for reshooting parts of the film. Sargent was replaced by Daniel Mann.

The film was transmitted on 30 September 1980. CBS found advertisers reluctant to buy time on a programme they presumed would be depressing and which featured a controversial actress. Commercial rates were a fraction of normal prices. As it transpired, both the film and Redgrave's performance were well received and, far from being silenced by Jewish attacks, in June Miller had signed a letter, with other American Jews, protesting against the expansion of West Bank settlements by the Begin government. However, this was not the end of his problems. After it was transmitted, to Miller's surprise Fania Fénelon again attacked it. Since in his view his script had been true to the book, within the constraints of film, he was baffled by her response. thinking that she might be suffering from survivor's guilt. For the moment he regretted having become involved in the venture, though he had warmed to Vanessa Redgrave who had, to his mind correctly, forced them to reshoot certain sequences. She was, he now realised, a consummate film actress. In the end she had the last word, winning an Emmy Award for her performance.

When he wrote the play version of *Playing for Time*, Miller raised issues that had first struck him at the Frankfurt trials. Expecting to see men and women who bore the marks of their evil, he was confronted instead with seemingly ordinary people. In *Playing for Time*, Fénelon and the other prisoners discuss whether the woman who has power over them can be described as beautiful when her actions are those of a brute. The scene exists in Fénelon's text, but there the author sees the issue as signifying nothing more than that evil does not obligingly clothe itself appropriately. For Miller, the issue is more fundamental and more disturbing, and chimes with the concerns of

After the Fall and *Incident at Vichy*: it is that she is human, flesh of our flesh, and not some alien breed that might enable us to console ourselves with her difference. 'Don't try to make her ugly ... she's beautiful and human. We are the same species. And that's what's so hopeless about this whole thing.'[57]

The play, as a final note tells us, was to be 'a demonstration, a quality that need in no way be disguised'.[58] It was, in other words, not to disguise its theatricality. The actors would change their clothes in full view of the audience as if a certain honesty of presentation was required in a play that offered itself as a potent truth. They were not required to shave their heads, openly donning bald wigs.

Years later, a number of challenges were mounted not only against Miller's version of *Playing for Time* but, more radically, against Fénelon's own account which was denounced by other members of the camp orchestra. She had, they claimed, placed herself at the centre of events, offered a false picture of the orchestra's leader Alma Rosé and of themselves. Neither the book, nor the film based on it, told the truth. What was offered as documentary testament was in fact no more than a self-serving fiction. Fénelon's account, it was suggested, also had something to do with its intended audience, a French public desperate to be told they had resisted. It is not hard to see Miller's enthusiastic embracing of the project as coloured by a similar desire to write not just about a survivor, but a survivor who could stand as evidence for his own faith in a resistant human spirit.

The most systematic dissent from Fénelon's version of events was contained in Richard Newman and Karen Kirtley's book *Alma Rosé: Vienna to Auschwitz*, but this would not appear until 2000. It detailed a whole series of errors, some dutifully replicated by Miller. Does this negate the value of Fénelon's memoir, and the film and play it prompted? In one sense it surely does, in so far as she offered it as an accurate account, underscoring the precision and completeness of her memories. She presented herself as a witness and in certain key respects proved fallible, serving other interests than those of the dead. The essential story, however, was true enough, and its filmic and stage presentation commanded an audience for whom this was, perhaps disturbingly, genuine news. There was still a remarkable ignorance of the Holocaust – hence the success, only two years earlier, of NBC's *Holocaust*, a nine-and-a-half-hour mini-series, dangerously close to soap opera, but which commanded an audience of a hundred and twenty million, then half the population of the United States. Miller's film and play were of a different order.

On 24 May 1980, Miller opened *The American Clock* at the Spoleto Festival. The play tells the story of the Baum (Miller) family and the unfolding crisis of an America discovering that its principles, its agencies – almost its *raison*

d'être – are suddenly challenged. Set in the 1930s, it creates a tapestry drama-
tizing the Depression, a time when, as he explained, the past seemed suddenly
wiped away and it was as if everything had to start again from the beginning.
As America moved from the 'me' decade of the 1970s into a decade of greed,
he laid before the American public a reminder that although the country
had previously experienced a boom, when the stock market had risen and
materialism had been seen as a virtue, it had ended with economic, social and
political collapse. The implication is clear. It could do so again.

In an article in *Esquire* in 1973 he had looked back to the thirties, a decade
that had done so much to shape him. 'It seems easy,' he suggested,

> to tell how it was to live in those years, but I have made several attempts to
> tell it and when I do try I know I cannot quite touch that mysterious
> underwater thing. A catastrophe of such magnitude cannot be delivered up
> by facts, for it was not merely facts whose impact one felt, not merely the
> changes in family and friends, but a sense that we were in the grip of a
> mystery deeper and broader and more interior than an economic disaster.
> The image I have of the Depression is of a blazing sun that never sets,
> burning down on a dazed, parched people, dust hanging over the streets, the
> furniture, the kitchen table. It wasn't only that so many high-class men,
> leaders, august personages, were turning out to be empty barrels – or common
> crooks, like the head of the Stock Exchange. It was that absolutely nothing
> one had believed was true, and the entire older generation was a horse's ass.[59]

The difficulty in writing the play, he confessed, had primarily to do with
discovering a form that could encompass both the life of an individual family
and that of a nation. The epic and the personal, the objective and the
subjective, seemed hard to integrate, not least because the solidarity presumed
to have been a product of common need had hardly characterized a country
in which the interests of the city and the country, producer and consumer,
had been seen as at odds.

The immediate inspiration for *The American Clock* came from his reading
of Studs Terkel's oral history of the Depression, *Hard Times*; but the book
served to take him back into his own past until, he said, there was very little
of Terkel left. What there are are scenes and passages that come out of his
first play, *No Villain*, written at the University of Michigan and now retrieved
to become part of a virtual cyclorama of American history fused with his
personal history. His sister Joan once remarked of Miller that he carried the
scars from that time in his memory, his nerves and his muscles, and that he
could not get rid of them. It was, he said, 'hard to know where my own family
situation left off and where society began ... It was all happening right there
in the living room.' What he wanted was to develop a subjective and personal
form that would engage a political and social dimension 'head on' and 'not

obliquely', as he felt he had done in his earlier work. He had, he explained, 'never written a play like this before ... It's in a kind of epic form I've never used, and more fluid in its structure ... The play is about the romance of our lives ... it's obsessed with time. There has to be this sense of astonishment about discovering the past.'[60]

In explaining his return to the 1930s, he repeated a conviction by now familiar. The past, it seemed to him, had become a foreign country. The present was severed from it by those who re-encountered its problems without understanding the history of those problems. He returned to a time when necessity had forced people to confront fundamental truths.

Miller was entirely capable of capturing the essence of his society in a single image – Willy Loman carrying the hopes of a culture as well as himself as he sets out, a hopeful pioneer. Plays, he would always insist, were essentially metaphors. In *The American Clock*, however, he set himself to create a diorama in an attempt to combine the personal with the epic, the story of Miller's own family and the story of America at a moment of crisis. As Ralph Waldo Emerson once observed, 'We are always coming up with the emphatic facts of history in our private experience and verifying them here ... in other words there is properly no history, only biography.' The list of characters runs to a minimum of forty-four and though many of these are doubled or trebled, even then it called for fifteen actors. In terms of the staging he looked for a sense of 'surrounding vastness ... as though the whole country were really the setting, even as the intimacy of certain scenes is provided for. The background can be sky, clouds, space itself, or an impression of the geography of the United States.'[61] The 1930s, he said, was 'his time', the time that shaped so many of his views, when he read the world awry but with a spontaneity that came from youth's encounter with it.

Studs Terkel's book had rapidly fallen away when he returned in his imagination to his own family, their lives disintegrating under the impact of a Depression that was deconstructing America. Into the play come all those arguments he recalled from his youth, the complaints about his paternal grandmother who took what she considered her due and offered nothing back; about the maternal grandfather, called here as his real-life counterpart was, 'the boarder', an arrogant King Lear demanding his due. Into it comes the pain of a fracturing marriage, of an immigrant dream turned sour. Lee Baum, narrator and character, and a patent version of the young Arthur Miller, is sent on his bicycle to pawn his mother's jewels, as Miller himself had been, and has that bicycle stolen as had happened to Miller's the day after withdrawing twelve dollars from the bank to pay for it, a bank which in fact, and here again in fiction, then closed its doors. Lee speaks of planting a fruit tree in the back yard of their Brooklyn home. The tree Miller planted as a teenager at the family's East 3rd Street house is still there today and blessed each year by its Jewish owners, not for its association with Miller, of which they knew nothing, but as an annual ritual. Lee, like Miller, learns that the family can no longer afford to send him to university. He lends his father a quarter for the subway in a scene that Miller replayed several times in published and unpublished works, and as such plainly the moment when the young Arthur had felt power shift between his father and himself. That same father then colludes with his son in getting on relief, as Miller's father had with him. Lee's mother, meanwhile, plays cards with her sisters in the heat of summer, just as Miller's own mother did, living from day to day in fear of debt collectors.

Perhaps bizarrely, the part of Rose (in real life, Augusta Miller) was played by Joan, for whom the portrait of her mother was not one she recognized. She later recalled:

> I was rehearsing one particular scene with the director and I worked on it until it was so real, it was palpable. I don't think I ever did better acting in my life ... Out of the shadows Arthur appears. I said did you see that? He said, yes, what were you doing? I said that's the way she was. He said, no she wasn't. I said yes, she was, Arthur, she was. He said, no, she wasn't anything like that. I said the event you are describing in the play was something that occurred when you were in college. You were miles away in Michigan and I was in Brooklyn and I remember this time you describe very clearly. I said she was a depressed woman. He said, no, she wasn't. I said she was worried that you wouldn't be able to go back to school. There was no money. She kept writing to you that Dad's business is doing wonderfully. Just go back to school. Everything is going to be great. And I was here watching this woman go to pieces and my dad's business had totally disappeared. He described this time in *The American Clock*. That's the thing that stunned me. So we talked about it for a while and I learned something. I learned that you can never play your mother. You have to play the author's mother. It was a relief to me. I didn't owe my mother anything by being true to her. I had to be true to the role, to the playwright's mother.[62]

That family, or that family re-imagined, had appeared in *After the Fall*, but now they move to centre stage, become exemplars. Society was cracking up and so were they, except that the young Arthur Miller/Lee Baum had felt immune, no more than an observer, not quite realizing the degree to which he had been internalizing a breach of faith that operated at both a private and a public level. It was F. Scott Fitzgerald who remarked that while, of course, 'all life is a process of breaking down ... the blows that do the dramatic side of the work – the big sudden blows that come, or seem to come, from outside – the ones you remember and blame things on ... don't show their effect all at once. There is another sort of blow that comes from within – that you don't feel until it's too late to do anything about it ... The first sort of breakage seems to happen quick – the second kind happens almost without your knowing it but is realized suddenly indeed.'[63] Miller lacked Fitzgerald's romantic self-regard evidenced in his essay 'The Crack Up', but, as ever, he was concerned to trace a connection between personal psychology and social trauma. It is as though, half a century on, he was still trying to understand the significance of a period in which he had watched a process without fully grasping its significance.

When he first began work on the play in 1970, having read Studs Terkel's book, there was nothing much happening to recall the 1930s – America seemed to be thriving. But by the time it was staged it seemed entirely possible that the past might indeed be repeating itself. When it opened in May 1980 at the Spoleto Festival in Charleston, South Carolina, America was in recession; the prime lending rate was at 21.5 per cent while the Ford Motor Corporation had suffered a record loss. By 1982 unemployment was soaring (at nearly 11 per cent), the economy was in the eighteenth month of recession and industrial output was at a thirty-four-year low. A third of the country's industrial capacity lay idle. Banks were in trouble, with more failures than in any year since 1938. By 1985 America had become a debtor nation. In October 1987 the stock market crashed. Miller had withdrawn from the market some months earlier, having learned a lesson from 1929.

The American Clock, though, was offered as something more than a prescient comment on the fragility of capitalism. It is a comment equally on the fault lines in private no less than in public life, even as Miller doubted that contemporary audiences would easily understand a time when reality itself seemed to dissolve, when the fixed points of social and family life had vanished.

Lee Baum is seen first in his fifties, greying hair, tweed jacket, a writer. His initial speech reflects comments frequently made by Miller in interviews and conversations. 'There have only,' he says, 'been two American disasters that were truly national. Not the first or second World Wars, Vietnam or even the Revolution. Only the Civil War and the Great Depression touched nearly everyone wherever they lived and whatever their social class.'[64] This was when a fear was born that had never entirely gone away, the thought that everything could disappear, that nothing was certain, that no one was in charge. For a Jew this could only reinforce a knowledge bred in the bone.

Arthur Robertson, a corporate leader who, we learn, made money during the Depression, interrupts the speech. He insists that such a collapse could never happen again. Robertson's remark, 'We've been tossing the whole country on to a crap table in a game where nobody is ever supposed to lose',[65] however, would be echoed twenty-eight years later when once again the stock market soared, housing prices seemed on an unstoppable upward trend and nobody, it was presumed, could lose – until, with the same suddenness as in 1929, they did. Bankers, Lee observed, were 'but pickpockets in a crowd of believers'. So they were again in 2008, when greed and fraud seemed synonymous and *The American Clock* was suddenly revealed as a great deal more than a portrait of a distant time.

The real victims, both Lee and Robertson agree, were the true believers, those who bought not only into a rising stock market but into an idea of America that turned on the inevitability and significance of success. And already Miller is braiding together the private and the public, as a family story enmeshes with that of other families, other individuals. So, as Lee, suddenly a boy again, at his mother's urging sings a popular song, a black shoeshine boy confesses to having a hundred thousand dollars in stock, even though he has only forty-five in cash. Robertson urges him to sell – but how could he do that when the market is rising and everyone is climbing aboard the train to tomorrow? America is on a high, speeding up as though every day some-one will run faster, fly faster. Change can only be for the better. Fantasy is taken for reality. But, as Robertson observes, this is a time when 'Nothing is real! ... if it was Monday and you wanted it to be Friday, and enough people could be made to believe it *was* Friday – then by God it was Friday!'[66] This is Miller's version of F. Scott Fitzgerald's observation that the snow of 1929 was not real snow. If you did not want it to be real snow you just paid some money and it went away.

The wider social world is constituted through a series of vignettes. When a man is dispossessed of his land and property by a bank, his fellow farmers hold deputies at bay and threaten to lynch a judge while it is sold for a dollar. The same man later becomes a hobo, presenting himself at the Baum door in search of food and work. A woman outlines the virtues of Marxism and union solidarity. Lee recounts the story of the General Motors strike in Flint, Michigan, which Miller had covered as a student reporter. The play ends as Robertson contemplates whether such a depression could ever happen again and whether Roosevelt had restored Americans' faith in their country.

Asked by an interviewer in September 1980 if he had not been wounded by the failure of other plays, Miller replied, 'I can't really say that I've been wounded to death – though maybe I should have been ... I've rejected the idea of gritting my teeth and suffering through these things ... There are times when you feel the whole weight of mankind is on your shoulders – and maybe it is; but now I just kind of throw the bread on the waters and wait for the fish to come up.'[67] They were not biting. The Charleston Festival version of the play, directed by Dan Sullivan, had been reasonably well received, but he made some changes to the text and the New York production, now directed by Vivian Matalon, had a different feel. It closed after ten days. It was a disaster. As the *New York Times* critic Frank Rich observed:

> Sometimes it seems there's just no justice in the world … when it opened at
> the Spoleto Festival in Charleston after New York previews [there were
> twelve of these], Arthur Miller's 'The American Clock' was a flawed but
> powerful play about the Depression of the 1930s. Mr Miller was in touch
> with his best themes again; he seemed on the verge of creating an epic, tragic
> statement about a family, caught in the midst of the collapse of the American
> dream. Last night, Mr Miller's drama arrived at the Biltmore with an exten-
> sively rewritten script, a new director and a partially new cast. The result is a
> tragedy of another sort. Upsetting as it seems, the once beautiful pieces of
> 'The American Clock' have been smashed almost beyond recognition … Mr
> Miller has tinkered with his play to the point of dismantling it.[68]

He praised Joan Copeland but thought William Atherton hopelessly miscast
as Lee, Miller's alter ego. *The American Clock*, he concluded, had unwound.
Miller's explanation for its abbreviated run was rather different. Although
within days it was playing to a half-full house its failure, he maintained, was
a result of the producer having no money to advertise it. In so far as it was
offered as a warning that the system could collapse again, that faith in the
market was misplaced and that human values should resist a bland materialism, it was anyway not a message that America was disposed to hear. (In
November 1980, Ronald Reagan was elected President, promising tax cuts
and an expansion of the military.) Speaking of the failed New York production,
Miller commented:

> As had happened more than once before, in the American production I had
> not had the luck to fall in with people sufficiently at ease with psychopolitical
> themes to set them in a theatrical style … I had described the play as a 'mural'
> of American society in the Depression crisis, but the very word *society* is death
> on Broadway and, as with *The Archbishop's Ceiling*, I had hopelessly given way
> and reshaped a play for what I had come to think of as the Frightened
> Theatre. In the end, as always, I would only blame myself, but I had felt
> despairingly alone then and was persuaded to personalize what should have
> been allowed its original epic impulse, its concentration on the collapse of a
> society.[69]

What was missing, then, was the epic sweep. He explained to Studs Terkel
in an interview conducted in the year of *The American Clock*'s first performance:

> There's an attempt here to do two things at the same time, which is the
> nature of a mural. Rivera's and Siqueiros's in Mexico are prime examples.
> Large renaissance paintings are in that order. When you look close at any
> face, it may turn out to be a real person's. When you step away you see the

whole pattern, the grand movement ... I don't care for a theatre that is absolutely personal and has no resonance beyond that ... I've attempted a play about more than just a family, about forces bigger than simply overheard voices in the dark. It's the story of the United States talking to itself.[70]

From Joan Copeland's point of view, 'the original version ... was the purest form the play ever had. That was what we did when it first previewed at the Harold Clurman Theater before opening at the Spoleto Festival in Charleston.' When it came back to Broadway 'he changed things in the play that did not help it so that the purity of the original production, and the tale it was telling, which was raw, became more of a family play'.

Though there is no reference to music in the text, in fact Miller called for songs of the period designed to underline the positive tone he was concerned to infiltrate into a story of collapse. The play, he asserted, did not end in despair, not least because he was alive to tell the story and himself remained hopeful. Its fate, however, proved rather less so, and he entered the 1980s as he had left the 70s, with a failed play. As his sister Joan remarked, 'The patina of his reputation was beginning to get dulled. A new kind of playwright was emerging. I think some people resented his longevity in the theater. I think he was very guarded against the sentimental and I think that some of his later plays were bloodless. The lifeblood of the characters was drained.'[71]

The American Clock had opened at the Biltmore Theatre on 20 November 1980, and closed on 30 November after twelve performances.

10

SALESMAN REDUX

A man lives not only his personal life as an individual but also consciously or unconsciously the life of his epoch and his contemporaries.

Thomas Mann, *The Magic Mountain*

Miller ended 1980 with the publication, in the December issue of *Esquire*, of *Elegy for a Lady*, still wondering whether it should form part of a double bill with *Some Kind of Love Story*, finished six months earlier. He also ended it with a broken right ankle, having fallen from a ladder in his barn, a double inconvenience since it meant he could not drive and would have to spend his forthcoming visit to Egypt in a plaster cast.

He spent two weeks in Egypt on a yacht provided by the top UN official, Sadruddin Aga Khan, struggling to see the sights while limping along with the help of crutches. William Styron, his travelling companion, later recalled:

> I remember Arthur settling back in an armchair on a luxurious boat cruising the Nile, exclaiming expansively, 'What is it that the working class is complaining about?' I realize that the laughter induced in me by the mock-plutocratic tone has an ambiguous quality owing to my knowledge of his working-class experience and allegiances. Likewise, an exquisitely American perception of the dynamics of class and power overlaid his response to the colossal Pharaonic effigies sculpted into the cliffs of the Valley of the Kings. They were created, Arthur observed, in precisely the same spirit as that which caused to be erected the various façades of the First National City Bank and bore the identical message for their beholders: 'We're in charge. Keep the hell out.'[1]

He continued his trip down the Nile, chancing the narrow landing plank with his crutches and struggling along behind the others in the party as they visited tombs and temples that seemed to him to be located in disappointingly remote places. On one occasion he had to ride a donkey through the loose sand. He looked in vain for any trace of the Jews whose exodus had been so much a part of his upbringing. It baffled him that an event that was in many ways pivotal to everything Jews believed, that was evidence of their taking their fate in their own hands, a memory of wandering the world on a promise, had disappeared so completely.

In Egypt he registered hostility towards the Jewish state, a feeling he understood since he himself found the Israeli position one that increasingly baffled him. Twenty years later, when that bafflement and, indeed, anger had intensified, he talked to me about his sense of his own Jewishness and his attitude towards Israel:

> To me ... there is an element of symbolism in Jewishness. In other words, when the Jews go down democracy usually goes with them. It almost never fails. I don't know of a regime that's hostile to Jews that is democratic. Ever. Including back in 1492. But the ambiguity is there. Ultimately, there's a suffocating quality to the whole thing. The other night I was at a Jewish Historical Society meeting, along with some other writers and a neuro-surgeon. He was talking about the rise of anti-Semitism in Europe and he asked me whether this reminded me of the 1930s. And I said, 'This is a different kind of anti-Semitism than Hitlerism. Then the Jew was seen almost as a carrier of disease. This, I think, is a reaction to Israel, its persecution of the Palestinians and occupation of Palestinian territory. This is a political thing.' I didn't know that they had anti-Semitism in Europe. I knew that there was some but suddenly it got significant. It corresponded with this dreadful policy of Sharon, being aggressive with other people instead of finding some way [forward]. It's not that I blame the Israelis only. I think the Palestinians have been just as stupid. This is idiocy from both sides ... And that's why this latent anti-Semitism may have arisen. I think that the Jews were understandably justified in trying to find a place where they would be safe. After all, they were nearly totally destroyed in those fine old civilizations. So I can understand that and support it. Where I get off the train is when they begin to assert their superiority in every direction ... That I find retrograde and stupid, and somebody's got to say that. I was reading James Joyce's letters again two weeks ago and it reminded me of my attitude toward the Jews. On the one hand, he adored Irishness. It was part of his bones. On the other hand, he hated Ireland to the point where he would have liked to drown them all. Not that I'd like to drown anybody but his ambivalence toward them made me laugh. It's like a family. There's a simi-larity, too, because it is small people who are struggling to assert some identity in the face of a world that could sneeze and wipe them out, and they have dispersed all over the world. It's a very parallel thing.[2]

To his surprise, in Egypt he met people who knew his work, the most unlikely of whom was a policeman who rode at full gallop on a brown Morgan horse to interview him for a police magazine that had published *The Price*, perhaps because a policeman is a central figure in that play. The policeman was a would-be writer who felt he had no subject, but under Miller's questioning he related the drama of a young woman whose throat was cut by her mother to purge the family reputation when she became pregnant. He was surprised to find that this seemed, to Miller, sufficiently interesting as a subject. He then rode off at such speed that he caused the donkey bearing their guide, a professor in his mid-seventies, to rear up and deposit him, unconscious, on the ground. This was little more than a sightseeing trip, but it resulted in a touching article for *Vogue* in which Miller described his friendship with another Egyptian guide called Saber with whom he forged a strong, if temporary, relationship.

In May 1981 he once again went travelling with William Styron, this time to François Mitterrand's inauguration in Paris. He and a group of other writers, none of them French – so as to avoid factionalism, thought William Styron – found themselves at the Arc de Triomphe. Styron recalled standing between Miller and Elie Wiesel, informally dressed in ties and jackets, as representatives of world socialism arrived, including Hortensia Allende, widow of the murdered President, accompanied by Pablo Neruda. 'All in all,' Styron noted, 'it was an extraordinary sight, this gathering of illuminaries and votaries of a cause which had been lost so often throughout European history.'[3]

After a celebratory lunch, Miller set off in a car with Styron, Wiesel and Carlos Fuentes. They were to join a triumphal walk, but the driver got lost and unloaded them into the middle of an enthusiastic crowd. Fuentes later recalled the occasion:

> There exists a photograph of some thousands of Parisians marching along the rue Soufflot towards the Panthéon on the day of the inauguration of the President of France, François Mitterrand, in May 1981. Among the crowds, a man taller than any of the others stands out. Those who know him can easily identify Arthur Miller, his head uncovered in the stormy afternoon, his raincoat flung over a shoulder, his spectacles firmly placed on that dignified profile so reminiscent of the monumental presidential sculptures of Mount Rushmore. Or as William Saroyan says, 'Arthur Miller is the Abraham Lincoln of North American Literature.'

For Fuentes, Miller had come to represent the best of America. 'Whenever my faith in the great North American nation began to crack,' he explained, 'it was enough to turn my gaze to Arthur Miller to renew it. He confronted Senator McCarthy ... He confronted Senators McCarran and Walter who withdrew his passport, as if the practice of criticism were an act of treason against the homeland.'[4]

The four writers struggled to penetrate the crowd, waving their formal invitations, only to be rescued by Melina Mercouri, who was accompanying Andreas Papandreou and whose fierce gesticulations finally won them free passage.

While he was in Paris, Miller also saw productions of two of his plays. Raf Vallone played Eddie Carbone in the highly successful French production of *A View from the Bridge* at the Théâtre Antoine, directed by Peter Brook (it ran for 550 performances). The translator, Marcel Aymé, whose French version of *The Crucible* had been so suspect, proposed changing the ending so that Eddie would survive. Brook countermanded it. Vallone had appeared in the film version (shot in both English and French), directed in 1961 by Sidney Lumet. Despite enthusiastic audiences, Miller was unimpressed by this production of *A View from the Bridge*, as he was also by one of *Incident at Vichy* at the Jewish Repertory Theatre.

It was a year for travelling. In July he went to Venezuela, finding there that mixture of wealth and poverty that would later be reflected in *Resurrection Blues*. The poor lived in slums and suffered from a range of diseases. The rich had expensive homes and private jets. It was a scene that would once have stirred his Marxist conscience. Now what depressed him was the sense of resignation, the acceptance of injustice. Castro might be held up by some as a model of resistance, but ideological battles seemed remote.

Back from South America in August 1981, under the provisional title 'Reno – '60', Miller began writing an account of his experience in Reno on the set of *The Misfits*. He recalled not only the heat – a hundred degrees – in which he had fallen asleep on the grass, but also the despondency he had felt, likening his mood to someone who tries to tie up a boat in the middle of a storm and feels the rope snatched from his grasp, aware that nothing is to be done. Even John Huston had fallen asleep from time to time when the cameras were rolling, or filmed a scene he had already shot. He writes of a conversation with Paula Strasberg and time spent awaiting the arrival of Lee Strasberg, who they hoped might persuade Marilyn to show up on set. The document runs to some nine pages before breaking off, and seems less a memoir than an attempt to shape a fiction. He tried again, though this time the real names are suppressed. Paula Strasberg becomes Flora Tishl, with Lee called Jerome, Huston, Dirk, and Marilyn, Kitty. At this stage it is still a story, though dialogue has begun to take over as it edges towards the form it would later take in his final play, *Finishing the Picture*, twenty-three years later.

In August, too, Miller's was one of many signatures on a letter to the *New York Review of Books* protesting against the shooting, by firing squad, of Saeed Sultanpour, one of Iran's leading poets and playwrights. He had been charged with trafficking in foreign currency. His death had caused many of the country's leading intellectuals to go into hiding. Sultanpour's had been one of a hundred signatures by writers and other intellectuals published in the *New York Review* in June of that year, critical of the Iranian government's suppression of human and democratic rights. Universities, libraries and museums had been closed and books destroyed. Sultanpour had served on the executive committee of the Writers' Association of Iran. It seemed likely that his death had been a result of his public protest rather than anything to do with currency. Miller and the others called on governments around the world to condemn the harassment and repression of Iranian intellectuals and to demand that the rulers of Iran should account for their violation of the right to cultural integrity and peaceful expression.

In terms of work, a concert version of *Up from Paradise*, Stanley Silverman's operatic arrangement of *The Creation of the World and Other Business*, was staged at the Whitney Museum as part of the 'Composers' Showcase'. This was the long-delayed New York premiere of the work first staged at the University of Michigan seven years earlier. As at Michigan, Miller was the narrator. The music, in eclectic styles, was written for piano, wind quintet and tape. Miller thought it a success but noted the *New York Times's* negative review. Written by the critic and composer Edward Rothstein, it was, in fact, not wholly negative but a thoughtful response, though he did think the singing 'rough' and the work characterized at times by an 'awkward weightiness'. For once, though, this was not a case of reviews determining whether a show ran or not, though if Miller had hoped that the concert version would lead to a full production he was disappointed. That would have to wait another two years. Meanwhile, news came from England of the success of Michael Blakemore's production of *All My Sons*, which had prompted excellent reviews, and Rosemary Harris's nomination for an Olivier Award as Best Actress for her portrayal of Kate Keller.

At home, and as the year ended, the Long Wharf Theater production of *A View from the Bridge*, directed by Arvin Brown and with Tony Lo Bianco (who himself came from Brooklyn) as Eddie Carbone, proved an equal success, quickly selling out and prompting a positive review from Mel Gussow in the *New York Times*, for whom it was 'an exemplary revival' confirming its status as 'a modern American classic'. The only flaw in the play, he suggested, was the intrusion of the narrator. Otherwise, he had nothing but praise which, for Miller, meant that a transfer to New York would be possible – though not, it turned out, for some time.

The new year, 1982, opened with eye trouble, as the previous one had with a broken ankle. On having his eyes checked Miller had been sent directly to hospital and had undergone a five-hour operation. The eye remained painful for several weeks. There was a tear in the retina and the operation involved removal of the eye, so that a silicone band could be put around it.

He now tried his hand at a novel about the gang violence he had witnessed in the 1950s. It went nowhere. He turned down an approach to write the screenplay for Malcolm Lowry's *Under the Volcano* and instead, in February 1982, wrote a nine-page play to be performed at an evening in support of Václav Havel: *The Havel Deal*. In this, a communist functionary, a writer turned diplomat, suggests a solution to the fact that imprisoned writers, journalists and professors seem to have become the source of difficulties between Czechoslovakia and the United States, stirred up, he asserts, by Zionists and émigrés. In particular he and those he represents have become disturbed by the campaign to free Václav Havel. He proposes that America should arrest half a dozen of its own writers to balance those held under arrest in his own country, who would then be sentenced to between two and four years in prison. Among those on the list are William Styron, John Cheever and ... Arthur Miller. In the course of the evening it turns out that the functionary has similar lists for other countries, including Heinrich Böll in Germany.

The man to whom the proposal is made is himself a scientist, and readily accedes to the notion that such figures are finally not of great importance to either government. But his wife, he fears, will object. At this moment she returns, and the man spills a sheaf of lists applying to other countries, including Switzerland. When the scientist objects that Switzerland is a neutral country and not part of Cold War politics, he is told that the Swiss list contains only two or three names, for whose imprisonment his country is willing to buy Swiss watches and, as an afterthought, cheese. A brief sketch, it is in tune with the satirical pieces he was now in the habit of sending to the *New York Times*. Though its front page bears the note 'Written for Václav Havel' and the date 21 February 1982, in the end he wrote another piece for the occasion.

When Miller had met Havel on his visit to Czechoslovakia the latter was preparing his first full-length play, *The Garden Party*, to be performed at the Theatre on the Balustrade. Miller had followed his subsequent fate with interest and alarm. When he was asked to contribute an original play for 'A Night for Václav Havel', which turned out to be a six-hour evening of plays by writers from around the world (with two new works – Miller's, and Samuel Beckett's *Catastrophe*), he finally submitted *I Think About You a Great Deal*. This features a writer who works at his desk, as another figure sits silently nearby. He is the Imprisoned One. The writer, plainly Miller, is going through his mail, which includes a number of appeals to support international causes. The appeals bring the Imprisoned One to mind, and he duly addresses the silent figure. He has received, he explains, appeals from Ban the Bomb, Save the Children, Amnesty International and a host of others. He is being asked to save Africa, the rain forest and animals.

I must say, though – [all this] does remind me of you. Your situation seems worse than all the others, though . . . I'm not sure why. Maybe it's the immense investment so many of us have made in socialism. That people who even call themselves socialists should imprison the imagination . . . That's really what it is, isn't it? – the war on the imagination. And maybe, too, because your prison is probably further west than Vienna. You are almost in range of the sound of our voices. You can almost hear us. I suppose. In effect. Whatever the reason, I really do think about you a great deal . . . I suppose we must raise it all to the moral level . . . In fact, it joins us together, in a way. In some indescribable way we are each other's continuation . . . you in that darkness where they claw and pound at your imagination, and I out here in this place where I think about you . . . a great deal. There will be another clump [of postal appeals] tomorrow. And the next day and the next. Imagine . . . if they stopped! Is that possible? Of course not. As long as mornings continue to arrive, the mail will bring these acts of goodness demanding to be done. And they will be done. Somehow. And so we hold your space open for you, dear friend.[5]

A note to the published version states: 'This monologue was written as an expression of solidarity with Václav Havel, for performance at the International Theatre Festival in Avignon on 21 July, 1982.'[6] In April 1983, six weeks after his release, when Havel heard of the Avignon celebration he wrote to Beckett describing

the shock I experienced during my time in prison when, on the occasion of one of her one-hour visits allowed four times a year, my wife told me in the presence of an obtuse warder that at Avignon there had taken place a night of solidarity with me, and that you had taken the opportunity to write, and to make public for the first time, your play *Catastrophe*. For a long time afterwards there accompanied me in prison a great joy and emotion which helped me to live on amidst all the dirt and baseness.[7]

In writing a play for Havel, Miller was reminded of the contrast between the writer's role in Eastern and Central Europe and that in America. There, the situation charged that role with significance. Havel was constantly followed. The police even built a guard hut in the field across from his house, pursuing him when he was taking his dog for a walk. The writer was a keeper of the truth and was recognized as such by those who harassed and imprisoned him. Illegal performances, samizdat publications, responded to a hunger for resistance, making the writer a focus of political hopes in a society in which everything was inspected for its political significance. In America, Miller could no longer convince himself that the writer was anything more than a licensed entertainer. Money ruled. A peremptory demand for success inhibited experiment. The writer was turned into a mendicant, ingratiating himself. And if he stood up to be counted he was no longer indicted, as in the 1950s he had been, but simply dismissed. His metaphors were decoded as realist observations with little purchase on contemporary reality.

For all his attacks on the Soviet Union, however, Miller was not ready to equate communism with fascism, though Susan Sontag did exactly that in a speech that stirred the kind of flurry of intellectual debate, not always on the highest level, which had earlier been prompted by Hannah Arendt.

In February a number of writers, including Gore Vidal, E.L. Doctorow and Kurt Vonnegut (who sang a song in Polish to the tune of 'Are You from Dixie?' that he had learned as a prisoner of war in Germany), had attended an evening of protest against martial law in Poland and in support of Solidarity at New York City's Town Hall. Carlos Fuentes, not present, sent a message urging people not to forget America's own interventions in El Salvador. For once, Miller was not there and therefore did not hear Sontag's intervention, a speech reprinted in the *Nation*, which stirred controversy both on the night and subsequently. He did prepare a response, but never published it.

Sontag offered a *mea culpa* that managed at the same time to be an accusation levelled at all those who had failed to condemn communism early enough. Those who read the *Reader's Digest*, she said, would have been better informed than readers of the *Nation* or the *New Statesman*. She now characterized the Polish as a 'fascist regime' – not, as it turned out, a slip of the tongue. People on the left, she asserted, for fear of giving comfort to what they would have called 'reactionary' forces, had 'told a lot of lies'. They had been reluctant to identify themselves as anti-communists because 'that was the slogan of the Right' and 'the justification of America's support of fascist dictatorships in Latin America and of the American war on Vietnam'. Only now did she realize that the principal lesson to be learned from the Polish events had been 'the failure of Communism, the utter villainy of the Communist system'.

Having identified fascism as the enemy, she and others had applied a double standard, seeking to distinguish Stalinism from communism, as many of those who had attacked Miller in the 1940s had done. In fact – and here she used a phrase that would raise hackles in the hall and, later, when the speech was published, unofficially in the *Soho News* (she sued for $50,000) and officially in the *Nation* – communism, she announced, '*is* fascism – successful fascism'. It was 'a variant, the most successful variant of fascism. Fascism with a human face.' The words 'radical' and 'progressive' had been compromised.

It was a curious speech to be making in 1982 and, certainly, to be making on this occasion. People lined up to respond, including Diana Trilling, who offered condescension rather than analysis. Welcoming Sontag 'into her new difficult life as an anti-Communist', she said that her remarks indicated 'that today, more than thirty years later, with Hungary and Czechoslovakia behind us, with the Twentieth Party Congress behind us, with the Cultural Revolution and the "boat people" and Laos and Cambodia behind us, with Daniel and Sinyavsky and Solzhenitsyn and Sakharov behind us, with Afghanistan behind us, it is still a shock to hear of an important defection from the ranks of intellectual sympathizers with Communism'.

The journalist Andrew Kopkind, who had sat in a North Vietnamese bomb shelter with Sontag, wondered how she could fail to distinguish between the criminality of some communist regimes and the struggle of the Vietnamese people. David Hollinger, professor of history at Miller's alma mater the University of Michigan, suggested that Sontag's were no more than 'the parochial and incautious after-dinner remarks'[8] of a New York intellectual belatedly released from a Popular Front mentality. Only Christopher Hitchens, in the *Nation*, came out in her support. Responding to these attacks, Sontag casually batted most of them aside, emphasizing that Solidarity had more to do with Catholicism than with democratic socialism, something she equally detected in the Soviet Union.

Outside the pages of the *Nation*, Mary McCarthy supported her, even while doubting whether calling the situation in Poland 'fascism' was likely to help anyone understand it. The ex-Marxist French philosopher Bernard-Henri Lévy remarked, 'American intellectuals have now understood that a government that locks up its detractors, that tortures its workers . . . and that pulls out of history's garbage can the old anti-Semitic arsenal is a fascist government. What do I think of this stunning discovery? Very simply, that it was about time.'[9]

Miller wrote a series of notes on Sontag's speech but forbore to shape them into an article. Soviet crimes, it seemed to him, required no balancing denunciations of American ones, although he himself had been active in attacking most of them and insisted that it remained necessary to do so. What he did recoil from was the equation of communism with fascism – not so much an ideology, he believed, as a system that served no purpose beyond the acquisition and demonstration of power. Communism drew on a humanistic and intellectual tradition, even as it systematically betrayed it. Fascism had no tradition beyond atavism. Had not André Malraux in 1937, in the context of the war in Spain that had never left Miller's mind, written of communism that 'we aim to preserve or create, not static and particular values, but humanist values – humanist because they are universal', the last being a word thrown at Miller by Mary McCarthy and others, code for a political faith that they saw infiltrating his plays, and not to their advantage. It seemed odd to him, though, that such issues were being rehearsed in 1982 when there were few with any illusions about the ideology to which he had once been committed. As so often before, however, he did not see himself joining in a debate conducted by the New York Intellectuals in their house magazines. For him, the key issue was no longer a matter of ideology. It was the need for nuclear disarmament.

Three months later he delivered a speech in front of three thousand people at the Beacon Theater. The meeting was hosted by the TV personality and composer Steve Allen. In 1959 Miller, along with Marilyn Monroe, Marlon Brando and Henry Fonda, had been one of the founders of Hollywood SANE (the Committee for a Sane Nuclear Policy that had been created two years earlier by Coretta Scott King, Albert Schweitzer and Benjamin Spock). In subsequent years he had continued to support a movement that grew in scale and influence. It was SANE that had organized the march on Washington in November 1965 which Miller had signed up to. In 1966 his friend William Sloane Coffin had become the chairman of SANE's 'Voter's Pledge Campaign', which urged Congressional candidates to support peace in Vietnam. SANE had endorsed Senator Eugene McCarthy for President and later lobbied to stop the bombing of Cambodia. Now, in election year, it stepped up its activities.

Following his speech at the Beacon Theater, in June, to co-incide with the opening of the United Nations special session on Disarmament, nearly a million Americans marched to Central Park protesting against the nuclear arms race, the largest political demonstration in American history up until that point. The immediate cause was the possible deployment of new US missiles to counter the threat of Soviet SS-20 missiles. So significant was it that ten years later the *Nation* marked its anniversary. In 1982, a resolution introduced into the Senate by senators Kennedy and Hatfield calling for a nuclear freeze with the Soviet Union on the testing, production and deployment of nuclear warheads and delivery systems was passed. The House of Representatives passed a similar resolution the following year. Miller continued to make appearances for SANE, which in 1983–4 would merge with the Nuclear Weapons Freeze Campaign. In 1987, William Sloane Coffin became President of SANE/FREEZE. I attended one of these meetings with Miller, chaired by the actor Tony Randall. Miller was there to present a prize. Pressed for time, he walked to the front of the room, presented the prize and walked out again. Randall shouted after him, 'Geez, I wish I was a genius.'

Miller's involvement with SANE did not, then, follow his commitment to the anti-Vietnam War movement: it fed into it. Though he had welcomed the nuclear attack on Japan at the time, he later accused himself of a moral myopia. For a man for whom guilt was in some way a motor force – guilt over his failure to fight in the Spanish Civil War and the Second World War, guilt over the advantage he took of his brother's loyalty to his parents, over two failed marriages, over his ideological naivety with respect to communism – here was another source of concern. His enthusiasm in 1945 was not easily forgotten or forgiven. As his play on the subject showed, in retrospect he blamed President Truman for refusing to allow a demonstration of the weapon on a non-civilian target. Now Miller wanted testing stopped and such weapons abolished.

As 1982 edged towards its end, Miller received a letter from Tennessee Williams. He had registered the failure of a series of Miller's plays and wrote to offer commiserations. While Miller appreciated the gesture, it had the contrary effect. As he explained, 'It was his lovely attempt to tell me the whole thing didn't matter ... and that he'd been through it a number of times. It bucked us both up, I guess. And it made me feel 140 years old.'[10] When Williams died, the obituaries stressed that same sense of failure, and once again reinforced Miller's feeling that his own career was equally on the slide.

Writing in 1949, Stephen Spender had distinguished between failure in Europe and failure in America, and there is something persuasive about his argument. Success, it seemed to him, had its own problems. One risk was that it 'may separate the writer physically and spiritually from the most fertile material of felt experience, which may well be associated with childhood and easy strivings'. Another was that audiences might praise the writer for qualities that were not those he or she saw as at the heart of their work. Yet another was that his writing might be lost in the context of a public reputation turning on his failed marriage. This comes close to some of Miller's own concerns. Faced with this kind of success, Spender suggested, writers often chose to retreat from the public gaze, as, indeed, Miller had done. As to failure:

> In Europe ... success and failure are comparative terms, particularly failure. One has the feeling that European failure is often a kind of secret success ... It is possible to envy Keats the position he enjoyed in Leigh Hunt's circle, or Gide his reputation when his publishers had sold only a few copies of 'Paludes', or Rilke when he commanded the attention of only a few princesses. But in America there are seldom these public failures who are private, superior successes. There is a lack, within a civilization which is changing and expanding so rapidly, of a sense that if one misses one's time, one will be discovered by another time. Failure, therefore, like success, has something definite and final about it. It creates a gulf which separates the unsuccessful writer from America.

Miller's fear was precisely that just as his early success had indeed risked compromising the sensibility that had given birth to it, so, now, he had missed his time, become detached from the culture on which he drew and which he wished to address. What is more remarkable, though, is the fact that even in moments of depression he seems always to have believed that the times would catch up with him, that he would be rediscovered. It was this that gave him an amazing resilience and perseverance. Nor was he wrong. Virtually every failed work, with the exception of *The Creation of the World and Other Business*, would find its audience. For the moment, though, his career was faltering even though there was a first hint of a forthcoming production that would prove a considerable success as Dustin Hoffman, who had previously indicated his desire to appear in a Miller play, agreed to play the part of Willy Loman. Miller duly visited him on the set of *Tootsie*, a Sydney Pollack film in which Hoffman appeared as an out-of-work and difficult actor who secures a part in a soap opera by dressing as a woman. Michael Rudman was approached to direct, with Robert Whitehead as producer. They all duly met up in an Italian restaurant on 57th Street and Lexington Avenue. Hoffman arrived in drag. Miller was impressed. According to Whitehead, 'It was an enthusiastic lunch … But then later it got drowned out in the trials and tribulations of "Tootsie". We never discussed it again and I assumed it was lost. A year and a half went by and Dustin surfaced and said, "Look, I'm still interested."'[11]

As September 1982 finished Miller began rehearsals of his two one-act plays – *Elegy for a Lady* and *Some Kind of Love Story* – at the Long Wharf Theater in New Haven, under the uninspiring title *2 by A.M.* He himself directed. He had hopes that they might transfer to New York, though as ever that would depend on an enthusiastic review in the *New York Times* and by now he had little confidence of this. For a writer who had always been irritated by the critics' tendency to see him as an incorrigible realist – an opinion based, he thought, on *All My Sons* – these plays were to be a reminder that he had always seen himself in a different light.

In a note to *Elegy for a Lady* (published with *Some Kind of Love Story* under its new title *Two-Way Mirror*) Miller speaks in a way he had not before. Of a play in which it appears a man contemplates the death of a woman he remarks:

> It isn't always clear exactly where one stands in psychic space when grief passes up through the body into the mind. To be at once the observer and observed is a split awareness that most people know; but what of the grieved-for stranger, the other who is 'not Me'? – Doesn't it sometimes seem as though he or she is not merely outside oneself but also within and seeing outward through one's own eyes at the same time that he or she is being seen? There is an anguish, based on desire impossible to realize, that is so unrequited, and therefore so intense, that it tends to fuse all people into one person in a so-to-speak spectral unity, a personification which seems to reflect and clarify these longings and may even reply to them when in the ordinary world of 'I' and 'You' they cannot even be spoken aloud. Nor is this really so

strange when one recalls how much of each of us is imagined by the other, how we create one another even as we speak and actually touch.[12]

The play begins with music as a man appears in a single beam of light. He is, we are told, staring ahead as though lost in thought. As the lights come up, it is revealed that he is in a boutique, though this is indicated by nothing more than a few objects scattered on a counter or seemingly suspended in space. When the lights are at full, the man moves into this space where, among the objects, a woman stands as though herself lost in thought. It is not clear which character summons the other into existence. What follows is a conversation in which the man is apparently looking for a present for a dying thirty-year old woman, except that it emerges that her death, seemingly of cancer, is presumed by the man on the basis of nothing more than hints that he might have misinterpreted. Indeed, as the conversation continues, the truth of the situation becomes less and less certain. Neither, it transpires, has mentioned the existence of the other to anybody else. They exist, in other words, only for themselves, and in speaking to the woman in the store, he is unable to verify anything he says.

We are not told the age of the man except that he remarks: 'someone my age ought to be past these feelings ... I go on as though there's all the time in the world.' Thirty, the age of the woman, he explains, is 'far back down the road'. In other words, the death he refers to could be that of the feelings which once vivified his existence. The Proprietress, for her part, seems more and more like the woman he describes. She has 'her colouring' and is 'just about her age'.[13] She says of herself that she is 'just that way' and laughs in exactly the same way as the woman he invokes. Is she, then, the woman or is she a memory from his past? He expresses surprise that 'You're seeing me ... That isn't right',[14] memory being a one-way process.

Is this Miller recalling the Marilyn he married when she was thirty and he eleven years older? Certainly, he confessed to still dreaming of her from time to time. 'She asked me once,' the man explains, 'Can you remember all the women you've had? because she couldn't remember all the men, she said.' She would 'never be demanding', she promises, as Marilyn had once promised Miller. He observes that 'there is some flow of indifference in her ... in some deepest part of you there has to be some contempt',[15] an accusation Miller had directed at Marilyn as at himself. And is there a shadow of his relationship with Marilyn when the Proprietress says to him, 'If you couldn't bring yourself to share her life, you can't expect to share her dying.' In response he asks, 'What is a friend who only wants the good news and the bright side? I love her. But I am forbidden to by my commitments, by my age ... What could she have seen in me?'[16] Perhaps meeting as they do in a dream state, 'we are as close now as we ever can come'.[17]

Suddenly, as he uses the word 'you' to her, when supposedly speaking of the absent woman, the Proprietress and the woman have become one. The play ends as the Proprietress becomes the woman who may or may not be dying, who may already have died, leaving only this trace. The lights begin to lower and the man strolls away as the woman vanishes into the darkness from which, it appears, he had summoned her.

The continuities with Miller's previous work are clear – in his concern with the past, with a self-conscious exploration of motives, betrayals and denials. In both of these short plays an older man is drawn to a younger woman; as had been true of *The Crucible*, *A View from the Bridge* and *After the Fall*. But the discontinuities are equally plain. As in the later *Mr Peters' Connections*, he steps into a dream world in which nothing is certain – not character, not action, not even language. For a man who had been suspicious of the indeterminacies of avant-garde theatre he is surprisingly drawn to its processes and deceptions of thought. For Willy Loman, memories were to be shuffled in search of the source of a failure he could not acknowledge. In *Elegy for a Lady* dreams offer an alternative world gifting resolutions unavailable in an existence in which history exerts implacable demands and the real is taken to stop at the boundaries of consciousness. In speaking of both this play and its companion piece Miller says, 'In the unreal is an agony both to be striven against and, at the same time, accepted as life's condition.'[18]

Some Kind of Love Story, inspired by Miller's work on the Reilly case and by another that his friend the private detective James Conway had sought to interest him in, does propose an external reality. A crime has been committed. A private detective seeks to solve it. A rational process will work itself out. A witness is to hand, ready, it seems, to collaborate, a model of social cohesion in the face of anarchy. And yet slowly this assurance begins to dissolve. The woman has multiple personalities and has a vested interest in deceit. The law is exposed as no more than a series of propositions without substance. Even the detective is unsure of his motives, alarmed at his inability to penetrate not simply the mystery of a crime but the nature of relationships. Every rule he believes to underpin reality is broken. There are, it seems, stories within stories.

The action takes place in the bedroom of the woman, Angela, who apparently has information relating to the crime being investigated by a detective, Tom O'Toole. A man has been in jail for five years. She has the evidence to exonerate him but hesitates to provide it, in part for fear and in part because it is the promise of revelations that brings O'Toole to her side, a man she loves and with whom she once had a relationship. She has contacts with the Mob, is a prostitute, her husband probably acting as pimp, but is genuinely in fear for her life, O'Toole finally realizes. His problem is that when the pressure builds up she reverts to one of a series of alternative personalities generated out of fragmentary memories and anxieties. He has begun to wonder, though, whether within her madness there may be truth.

There are discoveries. Angela has been sleeping with the principal players in what was a drug cartel, involving the police, in which she herself was a co-conspirator. She has letters revealing the complicity of the prosecutor. Words like 'law' and 'justice' no longer carry any force. As O'Toole remarks, 'Somewhere way upstream the corruption is poisoning the water and making us all a little crazy.' Angela reveals that the conspiracy reaches all the way to Washington. Whatever facts might be revealed, the reality of personal relationships, of a society supposedly rooted in agreed values, seems beyond the detective's reasoning power. He remarks, 'I've got to stop looking for some red tag that says "Real" on it ... If it's real for me then that's the last question I can ask.' How, he asks himself, 'did I get into this goddamn dream'?[19] Angela both conceals and reveals an apparent truth, never willing to give O'Toole the information he wants because what appears to be a crime story is, as the title suggests, a love story in which story itself is a key component. If she tells him everything she knows he will no longer have a motive for seeing her. But is the love she expresses real?

The *New York Times* review killed any idea of a transfer. Frank Rich chose to begin by recalling the 'failure' of *The American Clock*, two years earlier, referring to it as a 'sprawling work'. The two one-acts he characterized as 'worthy though unsuccessful'. The themes, he suggested, had been 'force-fed into characters and situations that are too thin to accommodate them'. Miller's beliefs, he added, 'always pour forth' but 'they do so at the cost of distorting the human dimensions of his dramas'. *Elegy for a Lady* he found 'hard to believe ... mostly because the writing is contrived', though he also thought Charles Cioffi miscast and Christine Lahti saddled with a 'hopeless task'. Turning to *Some Kind of Love Story*, he objected to the language and Miller's 'ill-fated attempt to snare the profane vernacular'. As to his skills as a director, Rich objected to what he called his 'sledgehammer staging'.[20]

For his part, Miller had enjoyed directing and now wished he had done more of it, as the only way to protect the integrity of his work. He admired the work of the actors, especially Christine Lahti. When the reviews came out, however, he was once again precipitated into a momentary depression. Play after play had failed. Now these poetic, allusive, ironic works were dismissed as if they had been failed attempts at realism. It would be another seven years before the plays found their audience and provoked positive reviews, and then they would be staged by England's Young Vic, under their revised title *Two-Way Mirror*.

1983 began with a production of *A View from the Bridge*, surprisingly the first time the full-length version had played on Broadway, twenty-seven years after its premiere in London and fourteen months after it had opened at New Haven's Long Wharf Theater. It had been successfully produced Off Broadway in 1966, starring Robert Duvall as Eddie Carbone, a role played in the new production by Tony Lo Bianco who, like Miller, had grown up only a few blocks from its Red Hook, Brooklyn, setting. Asked why New York saw less of his work than the rest of the world Miller offered a commercial answer, 'I keep them out of New York, unless there is a very unusual situation, a star who wants to do it or something like that. The New York reception tends to influence the reception of a play for six months or a year. If it's condemned ... it could hurt it.' The tone of the interview, conducted by Helen Dudar in the *New York Times*, was defensive. She reported: 'When he finishes a scene these days, he said, "I think that probably it will take 20 years to be understood for what it is ... Art is recognition in the face of resistance."' Only months after the rejection of his double bill, *Two by A.M.*, he was braced for another potential failure. As Dudar observed, 'Mr Miller has felt alienated from Broadway and its reviewers for years and serenely disdainful of much of the critical establishment which habitually trashes his work.' Indeed, the article begins with Miller's anecdote about an encounter with a woman at a limousine service desk: 'As he repeated his name ... the young woman eavesdropping from the next desk piped up, "Oh, that's the same name as the man who wrote that book." ... Mr Miller replied, "Yeah, that's me." The pair of them, no more than a year out of their teens, stared in stark disbelief. "Oh no, that's impossible," said the woman. "He's been dead for years."'[21]

In fact, *A View from the Bridge* received a positive review from Frank Rich in the *New York Times*, while Lo Bianco was nominated for a Tony and won an Outer Critics' Circle Award, though even now there were detractors. *Time* magazine's review, while praising Lo Bianco, described the play as 'a tabloid melodrama' and offered a somewhat curious reason for the fact that it seemed 'faded'. At least two things 'now vitiate the play's impact. In 1955, during the heyday of Freudian illumination ... Eddie's love for his niece possessed shock effect. Incest isn't what it used to be. Furthermore, one doubts whether the current flood of illegal [immigrants] cowers before an immigration official as if he had sounded a storm trooper's knock in the night.'[22]

But it was another early play that was on Miller's mind when in 1983 he went abroad again, this time with a definite project in mind. He returned to China, at the invitation of the China Federation of Literary and Arts Circles, to direct a production of *Death of a Salesman*. The initial plan was for him to stay for fifty days, Inge and Rebecca for two weeks, as the Federation's guest. He was the first foreign theatre director to work in the People's Republic. The production was to take place in the People's Art Theatre in Beijing, a city of three and a half million cyclists and at the time with only the most primitive of sanitation arrangements, struggling to move itself into the modern world. He went with some reluctance and considerable doubt, unsure to what extent a play rooted in American myths and values would make sense to a Chinese audience only recently emerged from the devastation of the Cultural Revolution and after thirty-four years of communism.

He returned to China partly, he revealed, out of curiosity but primarily because of his conviction, expressed to the actors when they first gathered for rehearsals, that 'at the deeper level where this play lives we are joined in a unity that is perhaps biological'. On meeting the cast he explained that his main motive in agreeing to the trip was 'to try to show that there is only one humanity'.[23]

The trip was not without its symbolism. For China it marked the end of a period of isolation; it was a conscious opening of doors. On his earlier visit he had been surprised that neither directors, playwrights nor actors knew anything of his work, so complete had been the barrier between the two societies. By the same token he knew nothing of them. Now he met a few theatre people who had begun to read Beckett and Albee in an attempt to get some sense of what had been going on in the theatre beyond China's borders. American novels were beginning to become available, including Heller's *Catch-22* and Bellow's *Humbold's Gift*. Meanwhile a new generation of play-wrights and directors was staging Chinese plays that would have been unacceptable only five years earlier.

On his earlier visit he had been shocked to discover that virtually all those he met had suffered. Almost without exception they had just returned from periods of imprisonment or 're-education'. Cao Yu, former head of the Beijing People's Art Theatre, had been demoted to the position of gatekeeper. Ying Ruocheng, director and playwright and later to appear as Willy Loman in a text he had himself translated, had been relegated to the rice fields. Ying's father, the principal of Beijing University, had left China for Taiwan at the time of the Revolution. Ying, however, then in his teens, decided to commit himself to what he saw as the new China, and returned. Both Cao and Ying had later visited the United States, in 1980, Ying appearing in a television production of Eugene O'Neill's *Marco Millions* (he would later appear as the prison warden in Bertolucci's film *The Last Emperor*).

With China now opening up, both wanted to stage foreign plays. In 1979 they had considered a production of *All My Sons* but changed their minds, preferring the stylistically challenging *Death of a Salesman*. In Shanghai a production of *The Crucible* had already introduced Miller's work to one Chinese audience, who saw in it a parable of their own situation during the Cultural Revolution, a time when, as in 1692 Salem, the young suddenly acquired absolute power. Not the least fascinating aspect of staging *Salesman* was the fact that the play dated back to the year in which China had been 'lost' to America. Thus Chinese ideas about America, familiarity with its styles, its cultural products, also dated to that moment. Consequently, the costume designer had no difficulty in creating authentic clothes for the actors, precisely because this was the last period in which they had had any familiarity with American fashions.

China was changing in ways that offered points of contact. Apartment houses were springing up here as they had in Willy's Brooklyn. The figure of the salesman had appeared, if not quite in the iconographic form of American myth, and this despite the fact that back in America Ying had denied their existence. Much, it turned out, had changed in a year. There was, however, no such thing as insurance in China, so that Willy's ace in the hole would not be fully understood. As Miller later remarked, however, '"Salesman" is about family and business, and the Chinese practically invented both.'[24]

In 1978 Ying had read *Salesman* to the company and they had decided that audiences would not be able to follow it. Five years on, the country had changed so profoundly, opening itself up to foreign investment and to the foreign media, that he now judged that, small matters of insurance aside, there would be an audience.

Miller suggested that he had a good deal riding on the production, though it is hard to understand why unless it was the chance of opening up the world's largest country to his work and, perhaps, the presence of a surprising number of foreign journalists, including the principal American television networks. He was accompanied on the visit not only by Inge, whose Chinese was once again proving a major asset, but also by Rebecca, now a student at Yale and not wholly unsympathetic to aspects of the Cultural Revolution. In that, she shared something even with the actors who had suffered as a result of its excesses. What they and she responded to was idealism, its commitment to questioning established ways of being.

While Miller rehearsed, battling with actors shaped by an entirely different theatrical tradition that stressed artifice, a declamatory theatre unsure how to handle an American play, Inge and Rebecca explored the city and the country. They took a three-day trip to Luoyang, where they climbed the seven thousand steps to the top of the sacred mountain, having suffered the privations of a supposedly luxury hotel whose luxuries did not run to heating their room in the freezing temperatures. When they returned and watched rehearsals, like Miller himself, they were moved to tears.

There remained certain cultural problems. For all Willy's sense of economic fragility, he seemed rich by Chinese standards. He had been earning a good wage; he ran a car; he owned a house. Why, then, should he be quite so desperate? In so far as China did have salesmen, they had historically been regarded as occupying the lowest social rung. So how was Willy to aspire to social acceptability, to be well liked, in such a disregarded profession? Miller was struggling daily with theatrical traditions and acting styles in an attempt to find some equivalent to the dilemmas that faced the Loman family. He was also confronted with the paucity of stage lighting, whose intensity, anyway, varied according to the time of day as the power demands of Beijing fluctuated.

The trip was simultaneously a journey into the text of his own play and into an evolving China. With Inge he took to cycling for hours at a time around Beijing when not struggling to find ways to turn his Chinese actors into plausible Americans. On the streets he saw a still largely peasant culture tentatively coming to terms with the beginnings of a market economy. In conversations he detected the bewilderment of those who had so recently emerged from the sufferings of the Cultural Revolution and were anxious to embrace the outside world.

In the end all the effort seems to have paid off. A new kind of theatre had been introduced into China and *Salesman* was not interpreted, as once it would have been, as merely an attack on American capitalism. The first-night audience, which included American diplomats following the performance in their own paperback copies, gave it a standing ovation. In later years it played throughout China and had a significant influence on younger Chinese writers. The interpretation placed on it, however, was not always what might have been expected. The Chinese have an expression, 'Everyone wants their son to be a dragon', to be a success. In a one-child-per-family country the relationship between parents and child can be intense and not without difficulties. It was perhaps that aspect of the play that brought about a shock of recognition. For them, Biff was failing to live up to his father's legitimate expectations. On the other hand, the personal dimension proved as powerful as in America, if somewhat unpredictably so. One woman came up to Inge in tears. Inge asked her if she was weeping because her father was like Willy Loman, to which she replied, 'No, my mother was like Willy Loman.'

While Miller and Inge were in China, there was an alarming development back in Connecticut. A fire broke out in their Roxbury home. Only Inge's mother was there at the time and it took a while for the fire brigade to arrive, alerted by a neighbour. By now Rebecca was back in the country and on 3 May at seven in the morning, Chinese time, she called her parents: 'A lot of it is okay. My room is pretty much gone, but yours is only sort of half. And the dining room is just smoked up, and the front parlor. But the living room is pretty much sort of disappeared, but the kitchen's okay.'[25] At the time, Miller later confessed, the news had barely registered. It was just four days before opening night in Beijing. Inge's primary concern was for her mother, but she was uninjured. There was nothing to be done. In fact, half the house had been destroyed.

When they got back ten days later they found the house partly boarded up and its contents mainly strewn over the lawn and in the garage. Inside, the ash was wet from the firemen's hoses. The rear veranda was full of piled-up clothes. The fire had burned through the dining-room floor so that it was possible to stare directly down into the cellar where the conflagration had started with a failed oil-burner cut-off valve. The hi-fi and television had melted in temperatures of 1800 degrees along with Miller's collection of 2,200 jazz records. The Picasso drawing, given to Inge by the artist when she photographed his sister and her family, was destroyed.

Upstairs, Miller and Inge found their bed turned on its end, the springs melted. Inge's designer clothes had seemingly evaporated. In the darkness he had to use a flashlight. The only object that seemed to have survived was a gold watch in a leather box. When he saw the house stripped down to its frame he spoke of the curious sense of seeing its skeleton emerge; it was a house that had been insulated with horse-hair and corncobs, built when Washington was fighting the French. He observed as he watched the men rip out the damaged floorboards, windows and trim, that in less than two weeks 'two centuries had been dropped onto the lawn'.[26] One builder suggested tearing everything down and starting again. It was not something, Miller suddenly realized, he could do. There was too much history invested in it, his own but also that of those who had lived there before. The rebuilding retained the house's colonial features but opened it up in a way that made it more useful. Not all the work was done with complete efficiency, however, as I can personally testify. Whoever installed the shower in the upstairs guest room managed to reverse the hot and cold taps, with interesting effects.

In October 1983 *Up from Paradise* was staged not on Broadway but at the hundred-seat Jewish Repertory Theater on part of the second floor of a community centre on 14th Street. Miller attended few rehearsals, his time taken up with auditions for the forthcoming production of *Death of a Salesman* with Dustin Hoffman as Willy Loman. In an article in the *New York Times*, a few days before *Up from Paradise* opened, Samuel G. Freedman described it as 'something of a rehabilitation campaign', *The Creation of the World and Other Business* – its source – having failed so comprehensively. Freedman quotes Miller as remarking: 'Like a lot of writers . . . it's these rejected babies that are very often closest to you. I open up the text of that play . . . sometimes and I think it's still got its charms. I felt, and I still do, that there was a way to do that play – a theatrically fascinating way. But we didn't achieve it.'[27]

The defensive tone was catching. One of the cast, Len Cariou, insisted: 'I would like people to look at the piece for what it is instead of saying, "Why hasn't he given us another 'Death of a Salesman'?" It's the same problem Tennessee Williams had. Artists go into other areas of their creative beings, and I think Arthur wants this play to be treated respectfully. Maybe that's why he decided, after the original play was treated so badly, to make it into a musical, so everyone would get another chance.' According to Frank Rich, writing days later, *Up from Paradise* was no better. 'The promised land,' he observed 'is still well out of reach.' Its only future lay with 'amateur church and synagogue groups'. The score had 'surprisingly little impact', while the show was 'clumsily' staged and none of the actors was 'in top form'.[28] For Miller, though, 'There's a lot of joy in this piece. No one's going to make any money on it. This isn't Broadway . . . The word "play" means "play", but when Broadway became too commercial you didn't get much play, did you? But I'm doing exactly that, playing, now. I reserve the right of my own exuberance.'[29]

In the New Year, news came of the death of Hedda Rosten (née Rowinski). She was the vivacious woman Miller had first met as an undergraduate back in Ann Arbor and thought for a moment might be worth the chase. In truth, she was drawn to him but went on to marry his friend and rival Norman Rosten (who would die in March 1995). Later the couple became confederate in his courting of Marilyn Monroe and over the years built a friendship with her, becoming beneficiaries of her will in which she left $5,000 for the education of their daughter Patricia. Hedda, like Miller, wrote for radio (in 1944 adapting a book by Florence Mary Fitch into a play called *One God*), as well as for television (*The Happy Housewife*, 1952). An inveterate smoker, and fifty years on from their first meeting, she had gone, and with her a fragment of his own past.

For all his work on his plays Arthur Miller still found time to write op-ed pieces on a range of topics and to join his voice with others protesting on behalf of a variety of causes. In March 1984, he fired off a piece to the *New York Times* attacking proposals for a period of prayer to start school days, an odd but not unprecedented proposal in an allegedly secular society. Three years into the Reagan presidency, to be renewed by a landslide victory that November, the forces of the Right seemed stronger than ever. He recalled his bewilderment as a child at being forced to recite the Oath of Allegiance every day. To him the oath and the prayer alike were simply devices to enforce patriotism, obedience and conformity; and, not without cause, he feared an increasing role for religion in America and elsewhere. 'What kinds of governments adore joining the authority of Deity with that of political institutions?' he asked. Answer: the 'Czars, Kaisers, the Francos and Mussolinis . . . People ought to ask themselves why such good men as Washington, Jefferson and the rest took such explicit steps to keep praying out of politics. It was to spare America the inevitable misuse of religiosity-by-government that had helped to fasten tyranny on Europe.'[30]

He also took time out to appear at St Peter's Church in New York City for an event organized by PEN and the Fund for Free Expression. The occasion was a protest against the US Immigration and Nationality Act, also known as the McCarran-Walter Act, which denied access to the United States under an 'ideological exclusion' provision. The Act was described by Miller as one of the pieces of garbage left behind by the sinking of the great scow of McCarthyism. And indeed, thirty years on from McCarthy there were still remnants of a time that had left its scars on him.

Along with other writers, including Susan Sontag, William Styron and John Irving, Miller read from the work of writers who had suffered from the Act. The list included Carlos Fuentes, Gabriel García Márquez, Pablo Neruda and Ángel Rama, a Uruguayan critic. In a later piece for PEN Miller quoted directly from Rama's interrogation. Having denied being a communist or affiliated with any pro-communist organization, he was asked why he had travelled to China, a question whose absurdity was likely to strike Miller, who had only just returned from there. Having admitted to being a socialist, Rama was asked whether that was not the same as being a communist. Then he was asked a question that took Miller back to his own appearance before HUAC. What, Rama was asked, had he ever done to show his opposition to world communism, and what organizations had he belonged to which actively opposed world communism? Desperately, he named Amnesty International, ironically an organization that had been critical of the very regimes that had exiled him in the first place. In Orwell's iconic year – 1984 – the inverted logic of ideologues retained its perverse integrity.

In October Miller joined Elizabeth Hardwick, Norman Mailer, Bernard Malamud, John Updike, Kurt Vonnegut and others in expressing concern for Alexandr Bogoslovski, a writer and archivist, who had been arrested in May and sentenced to three years in prison in July for violating the Russian criminal code. He was, they protested, innocent and ill. In 1987 he would publish an open letter to Mikhail Gorbachev welcoming the democratization of Soviet society, a process in which he could only participate if released and allowed to return to Moscow.

Having supervised the Chinese production of *Death of a Salesman*, Miller now turned his attention to a Broadway revival of the same work. Dustin Hoffman had first read *Salesman* at the age of sixteen when his brother gave him a copy of John Gassner's *The Best American Plays*. He had never read a play before – 'I had a kind of small breakdown for about two weeks after that. I would walk around just suddenly bursting into tears every once in a while.'[31] He had first met Miller when assistant stage manager of *A View from the Bridge*. Miller's memory of the meeting was of an adenoidal young man who Ulu Grosbard, then directing the Off Broadway production, predicted would one day play the part of Willy Loman. Miller was amazed, wondering 'how the poor fellow imagined himself a candidate for any kind of acting career'.[32] Nineteen years later, it was Miller who suggested that he play the part. What followed was a series of meetings between the two men, mostly in Roxbury. They sat on the grass and talked, or Hoffman would call to discuss aspects of the play. For Hoffman, Miller was his 'artistic father'.[33]

To Miller, Hoffman had a true actor's imagination. The lugubrious Lee J. Cobb, in the first production, had effectively played himself. Hoffman had to feel his way into the part. He was far closer to Miller's original idea, a small man, feisty yet baffled and broken, and to the playwright his was the most lucid performance he had seen – a judgement which, he remarked, he might have arrived at through having worked so closely with him and observing the processes whereby he had arrived at the portrait he presented. Michael Rudman, an American long resident in Britain, who had been responsible for the National Theatre production with Warren Mitchell as Willy Loman in 1979, directed the play. It was not at first an easy collaboration: Hoffman was suspicious of aspects of Rudman's approach.

Rudman had first read *Salesman* in an air-conditioned library in Harvard when he was a summer-school student there. He, too, had cried: 'I am glad to say that I never cried again over the play except twice. Once when John Shrapnel, playing [Willy's son] Biff at the Nottingham Playhouse, talked about going to "the U of Virginia", and once when Doreen Mantle did the "attention must be paid" speech at her audition in rehearsal room 4 at the National Theatre.'[34] Rudman worked on the play with Miller over a period of eight months, spending days at Roxbury, occasionally breaking off to watch the playwright teach Rebecca to parallel-park. The production was not without its tensions. Rudman later reminded Miller of his response when he made a facetious remark about Hoffman crying when John Malkovich missed a performance in Washington (where it was staged before moving to Broadway): 'You shouted at me as we were walking across the Watergate complex. You were, quite rightly, very protective of Dustin. So was I. I wanted to keep his crying to a minimum. "That's enough of your fucking jokes" was what you said.'[35]

The production nearly foundered over the tension between Rudman and Hoffman, whose styles were at odds. Rudman had been alternately abrasive and facetious, while Hoffman was sensitive to what he perceived as slights. There was a possibility that Rudman would pull out or that Hoffman would press for a replacement, even asking Miller to step in as director. A meeting was called by Robert Whitehead and the misunderstandings resolved. The production had become too important to all of them to allow it to collapse. Thereafter, they worked well together. Miller himself stood to make a considerable sum on the production, possibly a million dollars.

At various times in the five-week rehearsal period Miller despaired of John Malkovich (as Biff), who seemed unwilling to commit to a full-throated performance, and of Kate Reid, playing Linda, whom he even thought of replacing. The play opened in Chicago, with Miller stepping in when Rudman was temporarily absent.

In the end, the power of the production came from having cast Malkovich alongside Hoffman. For once this seemed like a battle of equals, as father and son contested both their futures, wrestling with one another, desperate to free themselves of guilt and yet acknowledging responsibility, surprised into recognizing as love what they had taken for contempt. The result was a startling moment of theatre as both men grasped one another in a prolonged embrace. As it happened, this reflected a tension between the two actors. As Malkovich told me in 2006,

> Dustin wanted me to do it a certain way, which I didn't wish to do. And did not do. And so probably underneath that relationship in a certain way was something very similar to the play. Why won't you conduct yourself like I'd like you to? Well, because I don't wish to and I'm not going to. That gave a kind of tension to that production which I think helped. So many times he'd say, 'Why can't you come over here, why couldn't you just come over here and say it?' And I would say, 'Because I'm not going to.' I don't have an ideal version of it in my head. My fight with him throughout was 'quit working so hard. Stop thinking, stop working, stop pushing. Just do it. You can do it in a coma. Just go do it.' In a certain way we couldn't have agreed on the colour of the sky or the colour of grass. And I actually thought at the time, and think still, that that's part of what gave that production such power.[36]

Before making his appearance, Hoffman would run up and down the iron staircase backstage so that he could appear looking exhausted. It was a preparation that Malkovich despaired of. One day, Hoffman had a cold which prevented his preparing in this way. When he came off, Malkovich remarked, 'You see, just act.' For Robert Falls, who would direct Brian Dennehy in the play in 1999, Hoffman's 'was the most radical Willy Loman I've seen. It was highly successful, really idiosyncratic, a completely original take, a very personal take.'[37]

When Malkovich accepted the part, he remembered, 'all my hipster friends were really not looking forward to it. It was this old fifties play and a lot of them were really shaken by it because the emotions were so raw ... To do it well you can't waltz around it. You can't finesse it. To do that play you have to go to the well every night.'[38] Attempting to explain its impact, he remarked, 'As Faulkner said, in, I think, 1949 [in fact, in his Nobel Prize acceptance speech in 1950], the young man or woman writing today has forgotten the problems of the human heart in conflict with itself which alone can make good writing because that alone is worth writing about, worth the agony and the sweat. And I think that very much defines what *Death of a Salesman* is about. It's about the human heart in conflict with itself.'[39]

The Broadway production was a critical and commercial success. The limited run sold out almost immediately. On opening night, following five curtain calls, Hoffman called for the author to take a bow. The theatre echoed to Miller's name, but he had already left.

After so much critical disdain he once again had a Broadway hit. The *New York Times* review, five days later, hailed the production as 'an exceptional ensemble effort'. Hoffman's Willy Loman 'becomes a harrowing American everyman', while Malkovich 'gives a performance of such spellbinding effect that he becomes the evening's anchor'. Kate Reid is 'miraculously convincing'. Even now, however, praise for the play was prefaced by the observation that 'its reputation has been clouded by the author's subsequent career'. Though acknowledging the play's flaws, Frank Rich described it as Miller's masterwork, written with 'a fierce, liberating urgency'. At its heart, he went on, is the relationship between Willy and his son, and with Hoffman and Malkovich Miller's play had found ideal actors to express their tortured relationship: 'When their performances meet in a great, blinding passion, we see the transcendent sum of two of the American theater's most lowly, yet enduring, parts.'[40]

Capitalized at $850,000 (CBS put up $600,000 and Whitehead, Miller and Hoffman the other $250,000), it did three hundred thousand dollars' worth of business in its first weekend. Indeed, it had already recouped the $850,000 while in Chicago and Washington. Miller and Hoffman between them received 45 per cent of the weekly profits and Whitehead 10 per cent. For the actor and playwright that meant $63,000 a week, $14,000 going to Whitehead. The production was more than a success: it was a financial bonanza.

For all its success, though, to Miller's annoyance the annual Tony Awards contained no nominations for the actors, though the production did receive one. Five weeks after the opening, a *New York Times* article noted that the 'slight only serves to reinforce the playwright's deep-seated skepticism about working in the commercial theater and the durability of his achievement. In a recent interview in his East Side apartment, he spoke of times when he considered "swearing off" playwriting altogether and noted, with an ironic laugh, that the rave notices received by "Salesman" must have succeeded in irking his long-time critics.' He was, clearly, well aware that this success was being achieved with a play first staged thirty-five years earlier (as the previous year's had been with a work first staged twenty-eight years before). Indeed, Michiko Kakutani now recalled that his career had 'traced a spectacularly uneven course' – *The American Clock* was seen as 'sadly abortive' and *2 by A.M.* as 'awkward and contrived'.

It is curious to note how often critics responded to a Miller success by recalling his failures – though he hardly needed reminding of the fact that success with *Salesman* served to highlight his subsequent difficult relationship with American critics and audiences. As he explained to Kakutani, 'I don't feel triumphant by any means ... I feel I've dealt with a lot of wasting circumstances as best I could, but I've had to waste my time defending my space ... Had there been a working theatre, it could have been or might have been otherwise. After all, I haven't had a continuing relationship with a director in 25 years, no real relationship with a critic – except with Harold Clurman in a way.' Clurman was a passionate, ironic and witty man, who had produced Miller's success and had then worked with him at Lincoln Center. Despite now having on his hands a hit 'of phenomenal proportions', Miller found it wrong 'for a show to be a hit' because to be so it had to sell out. The theatre 'is healthy when a play can run half or two-thirds full. When I came into the theatre, it was a rare thing that you went into a theatre and it was full. Now, if you've got four empty seats, unbought, you know your time has come.'

Miller was aware, as well he might be in view of his experience of the sixteen years that had elapsed since *The Price*, that 'It has to be the right season for [a particular] play, the right historical moment, the right tonality. And think of the chances of getting the right person – it depends on who's available, on whom the director may have seen or what dinner party he might have been at and heard of a certain person. This is why the theatre is so endlessly fascinating – because it's so accidental. It's so much like life.' The emergence of new writers, the change in social values, had left him feeling 'pretty lonely' because he 'could make no connection with the kind of theatre that we were creating, theatre which had no prophetic function'.[41]

Not everything, however, was straightforward at the Morosco Theater. On the morning after the notices appeared, Hoffman declared that he would not play matinées, the strain of eight performances a week being too much to expect.* His decision, though, was a blow since it was likely to lead to tickets being returned. The solution was to reduce the number of his performances to seven, rather than the six he had proposed, and increase the price of tickets (from a high of $37.50 on weekend nights to $42.50 for all performances) so as not to lose income, while extending the run to the end of June. The negotiation, however, caused tensions that would resurface several months later. Nor was this the end of the problems. As summer arrived in New York,

---

* British director Peter Hall recalled having lunch with the impresario Binkie Beaumont in which he complained that the National Theatre's repertory approach, which did not require eight performances a week, would be disastrous because 'Once an actor is allowed to play less than eight times a week, he will never want to play eight times a week.' Hall dismissed the idea, insisting that such a schedule was 'nineteenth-century and dreadful'. Certainly, Jason Robards had played Hickey in *The Iceman Cometh* only six times a week because the play's length would have meant paying overtime to the stage crew.

so Hoffman began to complain about the temperature in the theatre. He objected to the tardiness with which the air conditioner in his dressing room was installed and to the fact that a shower had scalded him. He then complained about the backstage temperature, which was accordingly lowered, leading to complaints from others that they were cold.

Then, when the play was due to move to the Broadhurst Theater for a limited additional run (the play had closed on 1 July and was due to reopen on 14 September), Robert Whitehead resigned, largely in a dispute over money, though the earlier negotiation over the number of Hoffman's performances was part of the problem. As Whitehead explained, 'The performance schedule created considerable confusion ... and I had to handle that confusion by long-distance telephone. And somewhere along the line my relationship with my colleagues became unhappy. I didn't realize how unhappy until I returned to New York.' According to Whitehead, 'Arthur wanted to renegotiate my deal ... I'm very hurt, naturally ... It's very damaging to an old friendship ... I feel extremely sad.'[42] There is no doubting the bitterness.

> Although Miller and Hoffman had the lion's share, Hoffman's lawyers got after me about giving up my connection, and Arthur went along with it. The greed. He was passive-aggressive. He wrote me a letter saying he regretted this terribly. He sort of indicated that it was Dustin who wanted to reduce the amount of money I was making. He didn't want to get involved in it, he said, but Dustin, who is a trashy character, couldn't have done it if Arthur hadn't gone along. The money was with Hoffman and Arthur went where the money is.[43]

Miller and Hoffman apparently felt that, with the transfer, Whitehead's share of the income should decrease since his workload was no longer so significant. According to a representative of Hoffman's company, Punch Productions, 'We were called by Arthur Miller's people and told he wanted to make a change ... And we said whatever he wanted was all right with us.' His lawyers confirmed this account, adding: 'It was a consensus kind of thing. I think Miller and Hoffman operate by consensus, and Hoffman tends to defer to Miller as the senior man of the theatre.' Whitehead's work in Australia, he added 'was a factor'. Somewhat gnomically, he added that some marriages lead to divorce and that Whitehead was doubtless pleased to be moving on. He was not. Miller refused to comment beyond saying that they would doubtless work together again in the future, which indeed they did. In fact, money had not been the only cause of the split.

Though Whitehead had seen the production through auditions, rehearsal and its out-of-town runs, in April and May he had gone to Australia to direct a production of *Medea* with his wife Zoë Caldwell – hence the long-distance phone calls. When he returned, he felt that he was about to be fired and so resigned, in the process losing his share of the profits from the televised version of the play, which had been CBS's motive for becoming involved in the first place. 'I felt there was no alternative,' Whitehead said. 'I felt neither of my colleagues wanted me in. Dustin didn't want to talk to me and Arthur wanted to renegotiate my deal. There were three votes and it was Dustin and Arthur against me. So I did better than that. I said, "I'll step down and let them have everything."'[44] Marvin A. Krauss, manager for many Broadway shows, took over Whitehead's role and *Salesman* closed on 18 November, after 158 performances, with Hoffman now giving six performances a week.

Both Miller and Hoffman wanted a permanent record of a production of which they were proud, but they also wanted it to be something more than a simple transposition from stage to screen. The television version was to be directed by Volker Schlöndorff, the French-educated German director whose best-known work had been the film version of *The Tin Drum* which had won the Palme d'Or at the Cannes Film Festival in 1979. In 1983 he had followed this with *War and Peace*. Hoffman and Miller had earlier considered Sidney Lumet, Steven Spielberg or Hugh Hudson. In the end Schlöndorff was recruited as a result of a misunderstanding on the part of Hoffman, who was under the impression that he was the director of *Mephisto*, a film he admired.

A television version had always been part of the deal, but its precise nature had been left unspecified. Miller had not liked the 1966 production, with Lee J. Cobb and Mildred Dunnock replaying their original stage roles. It had been videotaped in three days and he felt it never came to terms with the nature of the play. He wanted to get away from film and television's tendency towards realism. That was never how he had thought of *Salesman*, not least because he had in part been influenced by German Expressionism when he wrote it in 1948.

He observed to Don Shewey for an article in the *New York Times*, 'In the theater, while you recognized that you were looking at a house, it was a house in quotation marks ... On screen the quotation marks tend to be blotted out by the camera.' The problem, he said, for the new version, 'was to sustain at any cost the feeling you had in the theater that you were watching a real person, yes, but an intense condensation of his experience, not simply a realistic series of episodes. It isn't easy to do in the theater but it's twice as hard in film.' He welcomed Schlöndorff precisely because he 'understood that you could get to realism by a non-realistic technique ... I broached this problem with several American directors, and there was an eagerness to deal with it, but I got the feeling we were in strange territory for them. Volker, being a European, was used to this kind of talk.'

Schlöndorff spent two months watching the stage version. He was not interested in a conventional television production: 'I wanted to shoot it with a film camera in a film studio, to have a new set, and to do it with a mixture of reality and dream, a mixture of cinema and theatre. Don't treat it like a TV recording with three cameras criss-crossing, but do it properly, shot by shot.' This was a language likely to appeal to Miller and the decision was made to shoot it on film and to redesign it. It was to be made for $3 million and with a shooting schedule of twenty days, short for a film but long for television. The cast remained the same, except that Charles Durning was hired to play Charley. Alex North was flown in, expensively, to work on the music. Hoffman's own company filmed a documentary on the making of the production.

When he had staged the original Miller had been advised, he told me in an interview in 1994, to 'strip the memory sections' out because they got in the way of the plot. 'You could get it over with in an act-and-a half that way,' he was told. In the car on the way back from the Philadelphia try-out someone said of Willy's death, 'He didn't have to do that. There's a salesmen's union.' Miller had replied, 'Maybe he hadn't heard about that.' Now, forty years on, a CBS executive asked him if he could 'cut the art out'.

The film was shown first at a number of festivals including Toronto, Venice and Deauville, Miller and Inge flying to the last by Concorde, summoned by Hoffman. It finally aired on prime time (from 8 until 11 p.m.) in September 1985. On stage it had been seen by an estimated three hundred thousand people. Projections for the television version were for an audience of twenty-five million. Miller remarked: 'I never wrote this for the people that can afford $50 tickets. The people I wrote for can't afford to go to the theater.' On television, he hoped it would be for 'the guys in Brooklyn in a bar to watch'.[45]

Dan Sullivan's review in the *Los Angeles Times* was less than generous:

> Last Sunday's presentation of 'Death of a Salesman' on CBS was an honorable attempt to bring a great American play to the millions of Americans who don't go to the theater ... What it proved was that there's no choice but to see [such plays] in the theater. Uproot them from the stage and the power goes out of them ... the transplant didn't take. Not if you'd seen Hoffman and John Malkovich play 'Salesman' on Broadway. Not if you'd seen a good company tackle it on stage anywhere ... The TV 'Salesman' had neither the rhythm of film nor of the theater. It was a composite – an unconvincing attempt to photograph a metaphor in studio.[46]

Beyond that, Sullivan counted fifty commercials, which Miller deplored, including one for Velveeta, a processed cheese, in a play in which Willy Loman asks, 'How can they whip cheese?' John O'Connor, in the *New York Times*, thought the commercials 'arranged intelligently' and, more to the point, praised the production, from its design to all the individual performances. The film went on to win an Emmy for Art Direction, along with seven other nominations. Dustin Hoffman won a Golden Globe Award for his performance, while both Kate Reid and John Malkovich were nominated, as was the production, which won a Television Critics' Association Award.

Just down the street from the Broadhurst, in 1984, another production was staged, David Mamet's *Glengarry, Glen Ross*. While queues stretched round the block for *Salesman*, demand for tickets for the Mamet play, which had opened at the National Theatre in England, was disappointing. There were bets among some of the theatre reviewers that, despite the excellent notices, it would fold after a short run. When it won the Pulitzer Prize the queues began to form the next day.

Being an enthusiast for Mamet, I took Miller to see it. In retrospect it was not a wise thing to do. Here I was, taking the author of the classic American play about a salesman to see a play about salesmen being performed just down the street from his own. As we left I asked what he had thought of it. 'He's got a lot to learn,' he said, throwing the programme into a trashcan. Mamet, born two years before *Salesman*, was three years older than Miller had been at the time of that play's opening. Later that week Miller and Mamet met. Mamet was in need of a telephone and Miller took him to a store in the theatre district. On the way, the younger playwright, who had just seen *Salesman*, remarked like many before him that 'the characters in *Death of a Salesman* and *All My Sons* were reflections of my own family', that the relationship between Willy and Biff mirrored that between himself and his father. As he said later, 'We all stole the fountain pen – none of us won the football game – it was our story that we did not know until we heard it.'[47] Less than a decade later, Miller's enthusiasm for Mamet had grown, and with it a sense of the power of *Glengarry, Glen Ross*. It had, he now thought, bite.

Miller was now once again at the centre of attention, but there was plainly an ironic undertow to the celebration of his early work, and this seems to come through in an appreciation he wrote in 1984 of Tennessee Williams, who had died late the previous year. In a speech he gave before the American Academy – published, somewhat surprisingly, in *TV Guide* – he stressed not only his virtues as a writer but the fickleness of an American theatre that had deserted him from the 1960s onwards. It could only have been pride, he thought, that kept him writing after the professional theatre abandoned him.

His description of Williams's central theme comes remarkably close to being a description of his own. Indeed, he claimed it as the most pervasive in American literature. Williams wrote, Miller explained, about people 'who lose greatly in the very shadow of the mountain from whose peak they might have had a clear view of God'. He wrote of 'the romance of the lost yet sacred misfits, who exist in order to remind us of our trampled instincts, our forsaken tenderness, the holiness of the spirit of man'.[48] The first comment, accurate enough as a description of Williams's concerns, is surely also an apt description of the plight of Willy Loman, while his invoking of Williams's misfits is a reminder of his own celebration of them.

Miller chose the occasion of this encomium to reveal that only a few months before his death Williams had sent him a letter sympathizing with him about a play 'that had had some of the most uncomprehending reviews of my career'. The letter had suggested that both playwrights had 'lived to witness a chaos of the spirit, a deafness of ear and a blindness of eye, and that one carried on anyway'. Miller suggested, surely hearing an echo in his own life, that Williams had retained a worldwide audience, with hundreds of productions of his plays, 'but not on the Broadway that his presence had glorified'.[49] It is a telling remark: even with the spread of regional theatres and the growth of Off and Off Off Broadway, Miller still regarded Broadway as the true test of a play and in some way its final legitimation.

Speaking to Samuel Freedman for the *New York Times*, he expanded on his sense of the vulnerability of the American playwright. He recalled Eugene O'Neill's reputation in the late 1930s, even with someone like himself, then a budding playwright:

> I learned a lot from that . . . We don't always live long enough to see the tides coming in and out. But I've lived long enough to see them several times . . . In the late 30s and wartime, certainly among young writers and actors, O'Neill was dead. He was full of old-fashioned diction; he had no connection whatsoever to the whole development of the social theater. I didn't know what to make of him. He was as cold and icy as Aeschylus on first reading. No one did his productions. But I remember in 1947 . . . that when 'All My Sons' opened, down the street was playing 'The Iceman Cometh'. It was a failure. When I saw it there must have been 50 people in the whole theater. But I was overwhelmed by it. No one then would say 'Iceman' was anything but a relic. But now, to see it again become moving and meaningful, is a lesson.

It was a lesson not only about O'Neill. Artists, he asserted,

> are always the prey of sadists. People take vengeance on them. There's a great joy taken. That's not just O'Neill or Tennessee Williams, that's any great artist. The favorite artist is the one who commits a masterpiece and then dies in a gutter, the sooner the better. Who was it – Fitzgerald? – who said in American lives there are no second acts? You're supposed to submit to that . . . But if you refuse to submit . . . they can't get you. So I really go inch by inch. You follow your nose. You make what can be made in a day.[50]

In July when the run of *Salesman* was suspended, he went to England where his stock was already high and rising. In the next twenty years he would always be struck by the enthusiasm for his work there. He was embraced not as, in his own country, the author of past classics, but as a playwright who continued to produce works that bore on the moment. The British critics were never part of that political fight between the supposed Stalinists and the Trotskyites that had been so damaging to him at home. The British seemed to have a different perspective on theatre. They might argue about the extent of subsidy, but that there should be such was never in doubt. As a result, there were major repertory companies in London and beyond. The West End never had the power or centrality that Broadway had, nor was there an equivalent of the *New York Times* with its peremptory power to gift life to plays or close them down. Here, after all, there were four quality daily and four quality Sunday newspapers together with weekly publications, as well as BBC radio which regularly reviewed theatre. And here he found audiences for whom the theatre was precisely where one looked for comments on society; audiences who seemed to take a delight in language and who did not see him as a resolute realist. Even ticket prices, for the most part, were no bar.

In the coming years, works of his dismissed at home would find first-class productions as well as an enthusiastic reception in England. He sparked a similar response elsewhere in the world – productions of his plays proliferating in Germany, for example – but in England the National Theatre, the Royal Shakespeare Company, the Young Vic and the Bristol Old Vic would embrace his work in a way that his own country had not done for decades. Having complained for much of his life that he had not had a theatre, here, three and a half thousand miles from New York, he did.

Ostensibly he was in Britain for the publication of *Salesman in Beijing*. Following a platform performance at the National Theatre, where he read from the book and answered questions, the book-signing in the lobby had to be curtailed because the queue was so long that it was blocking entrance to the Olivier Theatre. From there he went to Cambridge for the British Council's Cambridge Seminar, which brought writers, academics, arts journalists and publishers from around the world to discuss literature. To his surprise and delight he was given £100 in cash, and immediately disappeared to a gentlemen's outfitters to buy a tweed coat and cap.

Later that year back in America, he noted the passing on 30 June, at seventy-nine, of Lillian Hellman. She died of a bronchial condition, weighing a mere eighty pounds. Miller had reached an age when friends and acquaintances began to disappear, leaving behind them that inevitable fading of reality that comes from the loss of witnesses to shared times. In this instance, it was a reminder of a past he and Hellman had shared to a greater degree than he was ready to admit, not least because he felt a personal distaste for her.

She had shared his commitment to the Republican cause in the Spanish

Civil War, helping to write Joris Ivens's film *The Spanish Earth*. She had been an enthusiast for the Soviet Union. For a while, Miller and she had shared an ideological position, except that where Miller, then at university, had chosen to ignore the Moscow trials, Hellman, ten years older, had signed a petition praising them and denouncing the idea that the USSR and totalitarian states were the same. Both, however, had managed to swallow the Hitler–Stalin Pact and maintain their Marxist beliefs into the Cold War era.

As a Marxist she had guilt, when success came her way. He had tried to address it in *The Man Who Had All the Luck*, and through his brief retreat to manual work at minimal wages after the success of *All My Sons*, reforging, he hoped, a link with the working class that in truth he had never had. She confessed that 'success caused a kind of guilt', while observing that 'I am suspicious of guilt in myself and in other people: it is usually a way of not thinking or announcing one's own fine sensibilities the better to be rid of them fast.'[51] Both had attended the notorious Waldorf Conference in 1949. There is a photograph of her at a session chaired by Miller in which a bespectacled Dmitri Shostakovich effectively denounced himself on Party orders. She has a half-smile. It is not entirely clear whether she is listening. Both had supported Henry Wallace in his third-party bid for the presidency. In a changed world, they both stood up against HUAC, she losing so much money that she took a half-day job under an assumed name in the grocery section of a department store. They had even shared a lawyer in Joseph Rauh Jr, and both had passport troubles, having to negotiate with the severe Mrs Shipley, head of the Passport Division of the State Department, she in 1952 and he in 1954.

At first Miller had tried to ingratiate himself with Shipley. It got him nowhere. Hellman had been more successful. Interestingly, Mrs Shipley had asked her if she thought the friendly witnesses had been telling the truth in their testimony, confirming that she herself doubted it. When, at the end of the meeting, and in contrast to Miller, Hellman was offered a passport, Rauh suggested that it was because 'one Puritan lady in power recognized another Puritan lady in trouble. Puritan ladies have to believe that other Puritan ladies don't lie'[52] – though it is hard to say what was puritan about the hard-drinking Hellman, who lived with her lover Dashiell Hammett. Miller had thought Shipley puritanical. It had never occurred to him to think Hellman likewise.

Both Hellman and Miller had been appalled by Elia Kazan's defence of his decision to inform, set out at length in an advertisement in the *New York Times*. She referred to it as 'pious shit'. They both denounced attacks on China experts, fired from the State Department because their analysis of events in China diverged from the official line. 'Truth,' she observed, 'made you a traitor as it often does in a time of scoundrels.' Miller would certainly have agreed with her statement that there were 'almost none who even now remind us that one of the reasons we know so little and guess so badly about China is that we lost the only men who knew what they were talking about'.[53] He would also have agreed with her attacks on *Partisan Review* and *Commentary*, which she accused of failing to come to the support of those harassed at home even as they protested at the treatment of dissidents abroad.

Miller, though, would have rebelled against the idea that he had so much in common with his fellow Jewish playwright. He had never really liked or perhaps even fully understood her. She had reportedly kept a book of news-paper cuttings about her stand against HUAC inside her front door to remind everyone of her heroic stance. She was, he thought, too self-regarding and, though the daughter of a salesman, too aristocratic in her manner. Miller had clung to his Marxist stance and his respect for the Soviet Union far longer than he should have done, but her loyalties outlived his. She had opposed the publication of Solzhenitsyn's work in 1969 and, according to Diana Trilling, pressed Little, Brown to cancel their contract with her husband Lionel Trilling because of his expressed support for Whittaker Chambers, who had supplied evidence against the patrician Alger Hiss when he was accused of espionage. In 1976, Hellman's publisher refused to publish Diana Trilling's book of essays unless unfavourable references to Hellman were deleted, although these were in response to Hellman's attack on her husband in her memoir *Scoundrel Time*. Trilling once said that anyone who attended his wife's parties was automatically banned from Hellman's.

Her politics struck Miller as those of a dilettante, what Tom Wolfe would later call 'radical chic'. He also suspected her of caring nothing for those who were victims of the faith she had once so loudly proclaimed. Had he, after all, not done his best to defend the victims of the Soviet system? Even the *New York Times* obituary deplored her failure to denounce the excesses of Stalinism. In truth, in *Scoundrel Time* she had said, 'Then and now, I feel betrayed by the nonsense I had believed', a remark that was partly about her faith in Stalin and the Soviet Union, but more about her naivety with respect to the New York Intellectuals who had attacked her no less than Miller: 'I had no right to think that American Intellectuals were people who would fight for anything if doing so would injure them ... Many of them found in the sins of Stalin's Communism – and there were plenty of sins and plenty that for a long time I mistakenly denied – the excuse to join those who should have been their hereditary enemies.'

She put their attitude down to their status as 'the children of timid immi-grants' who were 'energetic, intelligent, hardworking', and who 'often make it so good that they are determined to keep it at any cost', which was why they so easily abandoned their belief in freedom of speech and thought. They were welcomed by the Right because 'they wrote better English, had read more books, talked louder and with greater fluency'.[54] The philosopher Sidney

Hook, as Carol Brightman points out in *Writing Dangerously: Mary McCarthy and Her World*, was enraged at her glossing over the precise nature of Stalin's crimes and her own consequent complicity, while Alfred Kazin objected to her suggestion that the New York Intellectuals had failed to oppose Senator McCarthy. He found *Scoundrel Time* 'historically a fraud, artistically a put-up job and emotionally packed with meanness'.[55] Norman Podhoretz at *Commentary* lined up contributors to attack her. Her comments on immigrants sounded curious from someone herself of German-Jewish stock.

Seemingly taking pleasure in alienating friends and foes alike, she had a rancorous relationship with a number of people, especially Mary McCarthy, whom she was suing at the time of her death for $2.25 million for calling her a liar on *The Dick Cavett Show*. Carol Brightman reports a dinner party at which one of the guests, Eileen Simpson, once married to the poet John Berryman and now to a banker, was attacked by Hellman for mentioning McCarthy's name:

> Her host, Roger Strauss, had asked how Mary was doing in Paris, where Simpson had just been. Fine, everything's fine, she had replied, whereupon Hellman had pointed a finger at her and snapped, 'You! You were old enough, why didn't you talk to Mary? Why weren't you candid with her, why didn't you get her to see that her attitude was befuddled?' Simpson, astonished, had turned to see who Hellman was shouting at. 'She went on and on, and the table was paralysed ... I couldn't say, "I really don't know what you're talking about"'; but finally Roger Strauss said, 'Oh, Lillian, cut the crap, come off it', and that was the end of it. The event Hellman was fuming over was the Waldorf Conference, nearly twenty-five years before, where she had been a sponsor and McCarthy an insurgent.[56]

Hellman's reputation suffered a series of blows as doubts were cast on the accuracy and honesty of her work (in particular, *An Unfinished Woman* and *Julia*). A month before her death *Commentary* carried an acid article entitled '*Julia* and Other Fictions', in which it was claimed that she had appropriated another person's life for a work that she had claimed as autobiographically based.

Not that Miller had any reason to favour McCarthy, who had seen *Death of a Salesman* as 'enfeebled by its creator's insistence on universality', a fault she found too in *A View from the Bridge*, 'where the account of a waterfront killing that Miller read in a newspaper is accessorized with Greek architecture, "archetypes", and, from time to time, intoned passages of verse'. Throughout what she called his 'long practice as a realist', she asserted, 'There is not only a naïve searching for another dimension but an evident hatred of and contempt for reality' which was 'not good enough to make plays out of'.[57] The essay dated from 1961.

Such were the old battles brought to mind by the death of a woman who had been linked to Miller through their mutual loyalties and struggles. In the end, though, it is hard to believe he would have dissented from Hellman's analysis of the political world in which they had once lived, when the bright promises of communism coexisted with a stunning naivety and when a vision of the public good was oddly wedded to the ambitions of those dedicated to their own careers. As she said,

> Most of the Communists I had met had seemed to me people who wanted to make a better world; many of them were silly people and a few of them were genuine nuts ... The greatest mistake made by native Communists came from their imitation of Russians, a different breed with a totally different history. American Communists accepted Russian theory and practice with the enthusiasm of a lover whose mistress cannot complain because she speaks few words of his language; that may be the mistress many men dream about, but it is for bed and not for politics. Nor did they realize that as children of their time and place, they mixed idealism with the unattractive rules of the market place: gain, loss, fame.[58]

The fact is that Hellman behaved with considerable courage before HUAC when the stakes were rather higher than they would be in 1956 when Miller made his appearance. She was also the author of a number of powerful plays that earned their place in American theatrical history. Miller surely would have agreed with her statement about the anti-communist writers and intellectuals at whose hands he and others had suffered. Such people, she asserted, 'would have a right to say that I, and many like me, took too long to see what was going on in the Soviet Union. But whatever our mistakes, I do not believe we did our country any harm. And I think they did. They went to too many respectable conferences that turned out not to be under respectable auspices, contributed to and published too many CIA magazines. The step from such capers was straight into the Vietnam War and the days of Nixon.'[59]

She, like Miller, observed the capacity of Americans to forget. As she wrote in 1976, 'Mr Nixon brought with him a group of high powered operators who made [Roy] Cohn and [David] Schine [members of Joseph McCarthy's staff in the 1950s] look like cute little rascals from grammar school ... and one year after a presidential scandal of a magnitude still unknown, we have almost forgotten them, too. We are a people who do not want to keep too much of the past in our heads. It is considered unhealthy in America to remember mistakes, neurotic to think about them, psychotic to dwell upon them.'[60] The past, 'with its pleasures, its rewards, its foolishness, its punishments, is there for each of us forever, and it should be', because 'the then and now are one'. It would be hard to think of a more direct statement of Miller's own sense not only of the legitimate demands of the past but of its continuing presence, even if expressed here by a woman he instinctively distrusted.

In her final volume of memoirs, *Maybe* (1980), a telling title tellingly subtitled 'A Story', and perhaps responding to the accusations directed at her, Hellman comes as close to a confession as she was ever going to:

> It goes without saying that in their memoirs people should try to tell the truth as they see it or else what's the sense? Maybe time blurs or changes things for them. But you try anyway. In the three memoir books I wrote, I tried very hard for the truth. I did try ... In addition to the ordinary deceptions that you and others make in your life, time itself makes time fuzzy and meshes truth with half truth. But I can't seem to say it right. I'm paying the penalty, I think, of a childish belief in absolutes, perhaps an equally childish rejection of them all. I guess I want to say how inattentive I was – most of us, I guess – to the whole damned stew ... What I have written is the truth as I saw it ... but the truth as I saw it, of course, doesn't have much to do with the truth.[61]

She added, 'It's not easy. But not much is easy because as one grows older, one realizes how little one knows about any relationship, or even about oneself.'[62] For Miller, who was increasingly fascinated with the nature of reality, its shifting shape and form, but who was also just over a year away from his seventieth birthday and beginning to write his own autobiography, this was a useful reminder.

Ironically, at the time of her death he was also working on revisions of *The American Clock* which was precisely designed to recall the past, to remember mistakes as he returned to the 1930s, when the collapse of capitalism had seemed to clear the way for a more rational and just politics. The failure of that dream had led to the battles between those once committed to the cause, which continued for several decades and which had helped to poison responses to both Hellman's and Miller's work as well as generating his own suspicion of her. He responded to her death, therefore, less as the loss of a fellow playwright than as a reminder of his own equivocation and of commitments that had once made them confederates but which would later drive them apart.

For all Miller's sense of embattlement, his fears of a slipping talent, his difficulty in finishing projects, 1984 marked several significant productions. Just when *Death of a Salesman* was proving such a financial success, a revival of *After the Fall* opened at the small Off Broadway Playhouse 91 (located at 91st Street and with a capacity of 299 seats), starring Dianne Wiest and Frank Langella. Reviews were poor, but the production strengthened his faith in the play. In addition, *The Archbishop's Ceiling* opened in Cleveland, to a mixed response but with the promise of a British production the following year.

The year ended, though, with a dispute with the Wooster Group, an avant-garde theatre company spun out of Richard Schechner's Performance Group and directed by Elizabeth LeCompte. The Wooster Group, which operated at the Performing Garage in Soho, New York City (on Wooster Street), was an ensemble dedicated to creating new forms of theatrical expression, often incorporating film and video and constructing works from elements derived from classical and modern texts. It had already appropriated Thornton Wilder's *Our Town*, T.S. Eliot's *The Cocktail Party* and Eugene O'Neill's *Long Day's Journey into Night*. Now it closed in on *The Crucible*, a move to which Miller had been alerted the previous year.

The group had already run into trouble over the use of actors in blackface (in a production entitled *Route 1 & 9*), in consequence attracting charges of racism and losing state funding. *The Crucible*, of course, already had a black character, which seemed to justify a further exploration of race and stereotypes. As Elizabeth LeCompte remarked, 'I was so upset when people said you can't use blackface. I was hurt by that and driven to examine why that was. I found *The Crucible*, where Arthur Miller had written a black character. Well, if we can't play a black character, why can a white writer write a black character? That was one of the driving forces behind *L.S.D.*'[63] The play *L.S.D.* was described by the *Village Voice* as *The Crucible* on acid. It restaged the Salem witch-hunt as a day in the life of the House Un-American Activities Committee while reaching out to the drug culture of the 1960s, incorporating the figure of Timothy Leary. As described by Don Shewey in the *Village Voice*:

> The principals sit at microphones on a long, somehow sinister steel-gray table. Ron Vawter plays the witch-hunting Reverend Hale as a splenetic prosecuting attorney who exchanges double-time gobbledygook with court official Danforth, played by Matthew Hansell, an urchin who's 15 and looks 10. Spalding Gray's Reverend Parris with his underwater goggles and *Erasurehead* haircut looks exactly like the sort of preacher who would hide in the bushes for years on the chance that one day he might spy some naked girls dancing. And Kate Valk triumphantly impersonates the play's two maidservants in her notorious Aunt Jemima blackface from *Route 1 & 9*, hilarious and terrifying as the holy-rolling Tituba.[64]

Miller, Shewey thought, 'should feel honoured to be embraced by the avant-garde in his own lifetime and to see his work performed without the musty reverence that usually shrouds classics, in one of the few theatres in New York where something new and exciting is actually happening'.[65] He plainly did not know Arthur Miller.

The New York Times offered a rather more sober description:

> The Wooster Group borrows, bends and, in some cases, tries to trash dramatic works of the past ... As it turns out, the brief send-up of the Arthur Miller

play is the only evocative section of a random four-part evening at the Performing Garage ... This could be an odd though provocative basis for a freely interpretive production of 'The Crucible' ... However, as is often the case with this company, a concept seems locked in a developmental stage ... With a quasi-documentary collage technique, 'L.S.D.' is designed not only to link Salem and McCarthyism, but also to forge a bond among the Beat generation, the drug culture of the 60s and today's conservatism.[66]

The Wooster Group was not without its sensitivities. Comments by the *Village Voice* led it to ban reviewers from subsequent performances. Miller's response was equally abrupt. He was at an event at the Chelsea Hotel when he was approached by a cast member and invited to the show. To the surprise of the group, he turned up. As Kate Valk later explained, 'He came upstairs afterwards, and he seemed really bemused, like, who are these people and what are they doing? He didn't understand it.' With some degree of understatement, LeCompte remarked, 'I think he didn't get it – and that probably bothered him.'[67]

Not merely was Miller concerned to protect his property, the Wooster Group represented everything he disliked about avant-garde theatre. While it treated his work as found material, he commented wryly that in his view it had never been lost. On 9 November his lawyers issued a cease-and-desist order indicating that 'any and all performances or other uses of "L.S.D." constitute an infringing use of the valuable and protected copyright'. If the company did not cease, steps would be taken to close the show and perhaps seek damages. LeCompte admitted that Miller had already verbally refused to give rights to *The Crucible* at the end of 1983, when he had seen a rehearsal. 'Mr Miller said he enjoyed it,' LeCompte insisted while admitting that 'he said that he didn't want to give us the rights because it might inhibit a first-class production of the play'.[68] Indeed, a letter to that effect had been sent at the end of November 1983, as a result of which the section drawn from *The Crucible* had been cut from an original forty-five minutes to twenty, though without informing Miller. In the spring of 1984 she had invited him to rehearsals but he failed to respond. LeCompte took this to mean that she had his tacit approval.

She then tried to perform the *Crucible* segment in pantomime, but in the end closed the production at an estimated cost of $10,000 in expected box-office income, though not until she had telephoned Miller to tell him of her decision. To make up for it they substituted performances of Spalding Gray's *Swimming to Cambodia*. Miller responded by withdrawing the threat of legal action, saying, 'I don't want to harm them ... They were well-intentioned. It was just badly handled.'[69] The dispute ended in January 1985, when the company cancelled *L.S.D.* Miller later came to regret his action. In truth,

L.S.D. had never been a threat to future productions of *The Crucible* while for some his response was further evidence that he was out of touch with the young and what they took to be signs of innovation in the theatre.

That same year, though, a Royal Shakespeare Company production of *The Crucible* was staged in Central Europe, where it proved to have a continuing relevance in its original form. Directed by Nick Hamm, who would soon direct the same company's production of *The Archbishop's Ceiling*, and starring Alun Armstrong (later to play Willy Loman at the National), it went on a tour that took it to Poland, where martial law had just been lifted. These were the days of Solidarity. The group performed in Warsaw Technical College's Student Union and a film studio in Wroclaw. There were no seats – the audience was required to sit on the floor. To the company's surprise, the performance was attended by the British Ambassador and the Polish Minister of Culture, both of whom had to join the rest on the floor. Barry Kyle, a fellow director who worked with Nick Hamm, recalled the impact of the production:

> As Proctor was faced with the paper to sign his supposed confession, sudden tittering, whispering, laughter among the audience. A real drama was break-ing out amongst them. The tension intensified throughout the fourth act, and the play received an ovation. In the dressing rooms a British official, deeply excited by the show, told us that 'the stir' was because Solidarity actors, artists, directors had recently been asked to sign a paper disclaiming their Solidarity views, a condition to re-employment in state theatre and TV ... Seventeenth-century America was not just a metaphor for 50s America, but also Eastern Europe in the 1980s. *The Times* of London reviewed our performance as a political story.[70]

The Cannon Caucus Room is the grandest room built for the House of Representatives outside of the Capitol. It is ornate, elegant and classical, with Corinthian pilasters, decorative mouldings and four crystal chandeliers. It is where in 1956, Arthur Miller had been cited for contempt. In December 1984, he was there to receive the applause of a thousand dinner guests gathered to see him receive a Kennedy Center honor (established in 1978 to recognize members of the performing arts for their lifetime achievement). Ironically, perhaps, Elia Kazan had been so honoured the previous year. The ceremony was hosted by Walter Cronkite. Others receiving the award in 1984 alongside Miller were Lena Horne, Danny Kaye, Gian Carlo Menotti and Isaac Stern.

The day after the dinner there was a White House reception with President Reagan, followed by a performance at the Kennedy Center introducing the work of the honorees. Edward Albee delivered a speech in praise of Miller, while Karl Malden stepped in for Dustin Hoffman. Miller found himself revelling in the occasion. An Un-American in 1956, a man who had once refused an invitation to the White House, was now welcomed into the heart of the American establishment. If the phrase 'lifetime achievement' inevitably had a slightly menacing sound, it was also a relevant one, because Miller had just decided he would go ahead with a long-deferred project. He would write his autobiography.

He had been toying with the idea for a year and had even tried out a few passages. He was worried, though, that he would be mining precisely the material on which he had always relied for his work. A significant advance was offered, but he suspected that the publisher's interest was whetted by thoughts of revelations about Marilyn that he had no interest in offering. However, it presented a solution to the problem he was having in finishing other work. An autobiography lacks an ending, by definition.

In late 1984, Harold Pinter contacted Miller with the idea that they might both go to Turkey after hearing reports of the imprisonment and torture of writers there. Pinter had been approached by Mahmut Dikerdem, a former Turkish Ambassador to Jordan, Iran, Ghana and India and founding president of the Turkish Peace Association. Following the military takeover on 12 September 1980, he was arrested in 1982 and charged with disseminating communist propaganda. He was subsequently tried and imprisoned. This was familiar territory for Miller. He suggested that he and Pinter might go to Turkey under the auspices of International PEN, and they were duly briefed by Anne Burley, a researcher for Amnesty International who had herself visited Turkey in an attempt to discover details about those being imprisoned and tortured. In 2010 she recalled being offered several glasses of Chablis at Pinter's Holland Park home (as was Mahmut Dikerdem's son, who had been invited to meet the playwright). The encounter was not quite what she had expected: 'Harold Pinter was quite brusque and I nearly walked out on him ... he had asked me to tell him about human rights violations in Turkey and I was doing so but he kept on saying, "I know that. I know that." So I stood up and said, "Well, perhaps I haven't got anything to tell you." Miller was quite different, much more easy to talk to.'[71]

In March 1985 Miller and Pinter flew to Turkey. Now a key American ally and member of NATO, the country had been under military rule until 1983. Democracy had been restored but martial law remained in place. Large numbers of people had been arrested, and censorship imposed. There were more than fifteen thousand political prisoners. Amnesty International submitted a list of one hundred people assumed to have died in custody. The PEN visit was a gesture of support aimed at writers and political prisoners.

The visit did not start well for Pinter. One of his two suitcases failed to arrive and he had to borrow a pair of socks from Miller – 'Bloody good ones they were, too. Made to last.' They were met at the airport, with a Rolls-

Royce, by the writer and psychologist Gündüz Vassaf, head of Amnesty International in Turkey, and by the novelist Orhan Pamuk, not because he had political leanings but because he was fluent in English (in 2006, Pamuk would be awarded the Nobel Prize for Literature). Vassaf later recalled, '[Miller and Pinter] were like two schoolboys having a good time with each other ... They told lots of wonderful jokes, anecdotes. They did see the suffering but the two of them got on amazingly well. It was a wonderful friendship to be able to witness.'[72]

The major political figures they had wished to meet were either unavailable or unwilling to talk but, as Pamuk later recalled when giving the inaugural Arthur Miller Freedom to Write Memorial Lecture in 2006, they did visit struggling publishers and 'the dark and dusty headquarters of small magazines that were on the verge of shutting down; we went from house to house, and restaurant to restaurant, to meet with writers in trouble and their families'[73] They also attended the trial of a lawyer who had represented the Turkish Peace Association, a banned group, and a publisher whose brother had been beaten to death. Miller later recalled, 'He and his brother had been put in a van and, on their way to prison, had been struck repeatedly by four guards. He believed he had survived because he had been handcuffed with his arms in front of him, allowing him to use them to protect his head. His brother's hands were cuffed behind his back, so he was helpless. When they arrived at the jail, the guards pulled them out and kicked his brother as he lay on the ground until he stopped moving.'[74]

'We met dozens of writers,' Pinter noted. 'Those who had been tortured in prison were still trembling but they insisted on giving us a drink, pouring the shaking bottle into our glasses. One of the writers' wives was mute. She had fainted and lost her power of speech when she had seen her husband in prison. He was out now. His face was like a permanent tear. I don't mean tear as in tears, but tear as in being torn.'[75] Miller later remembered walking through the centre of Istanbul with a Turkish writer: 'We passed a very tall building, a twenty-five-storey skyscraper, and he said that was where all the torturing took place – up on some high floor. It was a building such as you would find on Park Avenue.' It was, Miller remarked, 'surrealistic'.[76] Vassaf was surprised and shocked when Miller suggested that torture might be in the Turkish nature, quite as if all recent Turkish coups had not been facilitated or sustained by the United States. He had simply not done his homework, Vassaf thought, while his blunt questions offended some. For Dikerdem, however, as his son later recalled, Pinter was 'like a knight. My father was an alpha person so that Pinter recognized a fellow alpha male. As for Miller, he was ... an alchemist of the soul.'[77]

The visit was important not only for Pinter and Miller but also for Pamuk; listening to the accounts of imprisonment and torture left him torn between a desire to retreat into his art and a temptation to become engaged. Miller and Pinter plainly came from a different world; there were aspects of Turkish society they did not understand. At the same time, they were all writers drawn together by a common cause. Pamuk later said, 'I clearly remember one image: at one end of a very long corridor in the Istanbul Hilton, my friend and I are whispering to each other with some agitation, while at the other end, Miller and Pinter are whispering in the shadows with the same dark intensity. This image remained engraved in my troubled mind, I think, because it illustrated the great distance between our complicated histories and theirs, while suggesting at the same time that a consoling solidarity among writers was possible.'[78]

A specially arranged dinner in a restaurant enabled the two visitors to meet more writers, discovering in the process a blend of socialism and nationalism for which they were not prepared. One reported having been tortured, but objected to American missile bases and the scale of the American military presence. Another seemed indignant that an American should feel free to criticize his country. Aziz Nesin, a poet and humorist, who had himself done battle with the military, spoke of the threat posed by the Soviet Union.

The visit culminated in a confrontation between Pinter and the American Ambassador, Robert Strausz-Hupé, at a dinner ostensibly in Miller's honour. It occurred the day after they had met the fiancée of a young theatre director, Ali Taygun, who had worked at Yale School of Drama, and the wife of a young painter Orhan Taylan. Both men were serving an eight-year prison sentence for membership of the Turkish Peace Association, a group that lobbied for nuclear disarmament. Speaking in 2010 Taygun's wife said: 'Harold Pinter was quite the opposite of Arthur Miller, who was quite cool ... he was very calm and speaks slowly and thinkingly, whereas Harold Pinter was a very exuberant character ... From the start Pinter was excited and completely in the mood of sympathizing with those in prison.' Orhan Taylan and Ali Taygun were later released, after three and a half years' imprisonment.

The Ambassador, who, Miller thought, resembled Lee Strasberg (not, in his mind, a favourable comparison), was a former campaign adviser to Barry Goldwater and a supporter of the Turkish regime. At first he responded apparently sympathetically to Miller's account of the previous evening's meeting but at dinner things began to unravel. Miller was sitting next to Erdal Inonu, leader of the Social Democratic opposition who, as a student in California, had seen *Death of a Salesman* in Los Angeles. Pinter, not renowned for his even temper, was quickly inflamed by an exchange he had with the American deputy head of mission Frank Trinka wearing tinted spectacles and a Turkish journalist, Nazli Ilicak.

Though a conservative, Ilicak had been briefly imprisoned by the military

junta and while in jail had discovered that electricity was used to torture
prisoners. But she was also a Turkish nationalist, and told Pinter that it was
for the Turks to solve Turkish problems and not for foreigners to lecture
them. In 2010 she revealed her thoughts at the time: '[Those foreigners] were
not in Turkey two or three years [before], when we were suffering from the
military coup. I had a reaction, a nationalist reaction towards somebody
interfering in Turkey's problems but [who was] not there when we needed
them ... Harold Pinter was upset because I was talking very frankly. At
that time [I] was thinking that it was the Cold War, that communism was
arriving in Turkey ... I didn't like them being in Turkey. I didn't think
that they were committed. It was a kind of Orientalism. They were just
looking for some material to write about.' She and others, she explained,
had to face the realities of the country while he, Pinter, was free to return
home and write a profitable play about it. Pinter, who at this point had
barely begun his hors d'oeuvres – Miller remembered that the first course
was soup – and had a history of exploding over much lesser issues, took
immediate offence: 'This is an insult and was meant to be an insult and
I throw it back in your face!'[79]

Cutting across the remark, the Ambassador proposed a toast to Miller,
who until then had been struck by his courtesy. He spoke of the developing
democracy in Turkey and, looking at Pinter, declared that disagreements were
evidence of freedom of speech. In his reply Miller drew a parallel between
what he had seen in Turkey and the situation in *The Crucible*, in which people
were imprisoned for what they were assumed to be thinking. Turkey, he
added, was a military dictatorship, merciless and brutal, and imprisoned its
own citizens for their views rather than their actions. For all the cultural
difference between nations, he declared, some principles were universal,
including the idea that democracy was incompatible with torture. He concluded: 'There isn't a Western lawyer who could come to this country and see
what is happening in these military courts who would not groan with despair.
The American part here ought to be the holding up of democratic norms, if
only as a goal, instead of justifying their destruction as the only defense
against chaos.'[80] In a twenty-minute speech, he called for America to distance
itself from the repressive policies of an ally that it seemed to feel the need to
support.

It is doubtful that Miller would have made this speech but for the argument
going on further down the table. It was a celebratory dinner, normally calling
for little more than anodyne exchanges. But the fuse was now lit. The reply
was offered by Erdal Inonu, a politician whose father had been both president
and prime minister. To Miller's surprise Inonu indicated his agreement with
the sentiments he had just expressed. No one rose to contest Miller's criticisms.
Nazli Ilicak declined the Ambassador's offer to respond.

However, when they retired to another room for coffee Pinter came face to face with the Ambassador, and tempers flared. Pinter shortly informed his fellow playwright that he had, he suspected, been asked to leave. The emollient Ambassador had suggested that Pinter should acknowledge the reality of the geopolitical situation. The Soviet Union, after all, was just across the border. There was room, he said, for many conflicting views – at which Pinter retorted that the only reality that interested him was that of having electric wires attached to one's genitals. The Ambassador took offence and the two writers left, forgetting, for the moment, that they had no means of transport. Pinter later recalled:

> The funny thing was that there was no car because we were at the Residence outside Istanbul. They had sent a car to bring us but they didn't provide one to take us back. Whereupon the French Ambassador suddenly came out. We told him we had no car and he said, 'I will give you a leeft.' And I said, 'What an Ambassador that is,' and he said, 'What a sheet!' He took us to the French Embassy and gave us a glass of champagne.[81]

As Miller said later: 'We decided we ought to form a team that would visit American embassies around the world.'[82] As to the Ambassador, 'He knew what was going on, but they wanted to prevent Turkey from going left. They didn't much care how that would happen.'[83]

At a concluding press conference the following day, held at the Journalists' Association, they both repeated their observations in the knowledge that none of their remarks would make their way into the Turkish press – and, indeed, that the press did receive instructions to limit its coverage of the occasion. Pinter explained to me what followed:

> We went to a lunch given by writers and at the lunch someone came up to us and said, 'The military have just issued a decree for your detention.' We finished our lunch and got into a car. The driver was a very reputable businessman and was against the authoritarian rule. He drove us to the airport but we didn't realise how nervous he was until we got there. There were armed soldiers. They let the car through but instead of going to Departures he went towards Arrivals. Then he stopped. He knew the airport well but was extremely tense. Then he started to reverse. We were looking back and could see one of the soldiers turn round with a gun, looking to see what was going on. He pointed his gun and I thought we were going to be blown up. But we got through and staggered through Departures. It was a very, very tense moment. We finally got on the plane and as we were sitting on the runway I said, 'Well, Arthur. We made it.' And he said, 'We haven't gone up yet.' We were expecting the door to open at any time. They were really making themselves extremely clear. They were saying 'Get out of here!'[84]

Some eighteen hundred people, including Mahmut Dikerdem, were released from Turkish prisons after Miller and Pinter's visit, though whether because of that visit is doubtful. Pinter did write a play based on the Turkish situation, called *Mountain Language* (a reference to the Turkish habit of calling Kurds 'Mountain People'), published in 1988. A twenty-five-minute work, it was staged that same year by the National Theatre in London. Pinter commented:

> One of the things I learnt while I was [in Turkey] was about the real plight of the Kurds: quite simply that they're not really allowed to exist at all and certainly not allowed to speak their language. For example, there's a publisher who wrote a history of the Kurds and was sent to prison for 36 years – for simply writing a history of the Kurds. When I got back from Turkey I wrote a few pages of *Mountain Language*, but I wasn't at all sure about it and put it away; in fact I nearly threw it away but my wife persuaded me not to. I did nothing for three years with it and then one day ... I picked it up and suddenly wrote it. The springboard was the Kurds, but this play is not about the Turks and the Kurds ... throughout history, many languages have been banned – the Irish have suffered, the Welsh have suffered and Urdu and the Estonians' language [have been] banned; the Basque language was banned.[85]

Speaking in 2010, Orhan Taylan described their visit:

> It was a great feeling of confidence, of people thinking very much like you existing around the world, and some of them courageous enough to come over to a country ruled by the military where they shoot people out on the streets. It [showed] great courage on their part, and the fact that they accepted to care for a country with those conditions. Just to show their solidarity for our position is a great feeling and this is how all intellectuals, all around the world, should be. They should be as brave as Pinter and Miller. We are grateful for their actions.[86]

In 1998, Miller and Pinter would be among the one hundred and fifty scholars and writers to sign an 'International Affirmation of the Armenian Genocide', which asserted that more than a million Armenians had been exterminated by the Turks in 1915, a genocide which the Turkish government continued to deny. The document denounced as morally and intellectually corrupt such a denial, and called upon everyone – scholars, politicians and the media – to refrain from using euphemistic terminology. Among the other signatories were Miller's friends Alfred Kazin, William Gass, William and Rose Styron, Derek Walcott and William Sloane Coffin, along with the man whose release from prison he had helped secure many years earlier – Wole Soyinka.

Writing twenty-one years after Miller and Pinter's visit, Orhan Pamuk remarked, 'The writers, thinkers, and journalists with whom we were meeting mostly defined themselves as leftists in those days, so it could be said that their troubles had much to do with the freedoms held dear by Western liberal democracies. Twenty years on, when I see half of these people ... now align themselves with a nationalism that is at odds with Westernization and democracy, I of course feel sad.'[87] His meeting with Pinter and Miller, however, had significantly changed him. 'In the ten years following their visit, a series of coincidences fed by good intentions, anger, guilt, and personal animosities, led to my making a series of statements on freedom of expression that bore no relation to my novels, and before long I had taken on a political persona far more powerful than I had ever intended' – more powerful because as a writer 'I know I cannot reduce my thoughts about life to a single voice and a single point of view', and because 'living as I do in a world where, in a very short time, someone who has been a victim of tyranny and oppression can suddenly become one of the oppressors, I know also that holding strong beliefs about the nature of things and people is itself a difficult enterprise'.

Holding strong beliefs did indeed prove difficult for Pamuk: legal moves were made against him when he spoke out against the Armenian genocide, a particularly sensitive subject in Turkey. But when he delivered the first Arthur Miller Memorial Lecture in 2006 his target was not the failings of the Turkish state but the United States, which he denounced in terms that echoed Pinter's:

> So let us now ask ourselves how 'reasonable' it is to denigrate cultures and religions, or, more to the point, to mercilessly bomb countries, in the name of democracy and freedom of thought. My part of the world is not more democratic after these killings. In the war against Iraq, the tyrannization and heartless murder of almost a hundred thousand people have brought neither peace nor democracy ... This savage, cruel war is the shame of America and the West. Organizations like PEN and writers like Harold Pinter and Arthur Miller are its pride.[88]

On returning from Turkey Miller wrote an article in which he expressed surprise that the Turkish Prime Minister, on a visit to Washington, could declare that there were no political prisoners in Turkey, adding, 'There is nothing farther away from Washington than the entire world.'[89] The article was accepted by the *New York Times*, only to be rejected three days later. He tried the *New Yorker*, which also turned it down. It finally appeared in the *Nation* in a cut-down version. Since he had had a number of short stories rejected at this time and was having difficulty placing the screenplay inspired by *Some Kind of Love Story* (*Almost Everybody Wins*), once again he felt momentarily depressed.

Perhaps this was the reason, along with his approaching seventieth birthday, that Miller chose this moment to write a short story (unpublished) called

'Constantine's Story', about a composer whose reputation has faded. Even the public that once eagerly awaited his next work have drifted away. Now, unaccountably, he decides to contact Vera, the wife he had divorced long before, a woman to whom he had once been attracted because of her judgemental nature and severity – a severity that had eventually come between them, together with a single affair in which he had been discovered. He had tried to make it up to this woman whose validation of his work he had once sought. He had even undergone analysis five days a week designed to mend their relationship. The story is that of Miller and his first wife Mary. Constantine and Vera meet one final time, as the Millers did not (except over a hospital bed when there was a scare over one of their children). Constantine was seeking absolution, not least, intriguingly, because Vera knows that he once lied before a grand jury. The meeting comes to nothing. He leaves. There is to be no neat ending, no forgiveness of her or of himself, no confirmation that there had once been love when he knew there had not.

It is a painful story and doubtless never meant for publication, not least because Miller uses the first name of the woman with whom he had an affair many decades earlier. As to his one-time wife, Constantine had gone in search of the young woman she had once been and found instead an old woman, as implacable as ever. The encounter is a reminder of Miller's own age. The story ends as Constantine buys a walking stick, afraid he may trip and fall as, long ago, he had in betraying the woman he did not love.

On 17 October 1985, Miller turned seventy. There was no temptation to slow down. The autobiography was edging forward. He continued sporadic work on *The Ride down Mount Morgan* and remained committed to PEN. In November he made another visit to the Soviet Union, for a three-day writers' conference in the Lithuanian capital Vilnius, entitled 'The Role of the Writer in Furthering Human Values'. With him went the novelists William Gaddis and William Gass, the playwright Charles Fuller, the poet Allen Ginsberg and his old friend and neighbour, former *New York Times* correspondent in the Soviet Union, Harrison Salisbury. The conference was part of a series sponsored by Dartmouth College and inaugurated under President Eisenhower. Norman Cousins, editor of the *Saturday Review* and a peace campaigner whose anti-nuclear views had been forged with the dropping of the atom bombs in 1945, led the occasion.

It was not a meeting of minds, the Soviet delegation reminding the Americans of their history of racism and the Americans, especially Miller, drawing attention to the Soviet treatment of dissidents. Ginsberg provided the cabaret, chanting his verses and playing what Louis Auchincloss, another participant, called 'a species of accordion'. Gaddis spoke of the small sales that writers of literature could expect in America, and when asked to suggest a topic for a future meeting proposed that poets and novelists should be separated so that the accordion could be heard only 'down a long corridor, through a closed door'.[90]

On his return, Gass wrote a piece for the *New York Times* describing the visit. Grouped around a U-shaped table, he reported, in a palace where Napoleon had reputedly stabled his horse, each writer in turn had been invited to talk about their work, 'a procedure,' Gass remarked, 'designed by the Soviet organizers to produce a maximum of flatulent vanity and eat up our hours without seriously touching on the topic (for two days we went from tick to tock in this fashion)'. At first, then, it was no more productive than many such meetings, with an excess of food and drink accompanied by vacuous remarks. Harrison Salisbury recalled the number of Jews who had fled persecution in Lithuania and discussed his new book on China, in which he compared the Long March with the siege of Stalingrad, his study of which had been banned in the Soviet Union since 1969.

Ginsberg spoke of homosexuality, not something his hosts were ready to hear about, and read a poem by one of the Vilnius group of Yiddish poets who had died in the Second World War. In response, the Soviet writers accused him of elevating the interests of the individual above those of society. Fuller's suggestion that it was time for black writers to escape the confines of race and speak for and to a general readership also failed to accord with Soviet ideas. The conference was beginning a less than elegant slide into mutual hostility, urged on by Mikhail Sagatelyan, a journalist, who launched an attack on sex and violence in America, a consequence, he suggested, of an excessive emphasis on individual freedom.

Miller, increasingly frustrated, now stepped forward declaring that America had been spared the hierarchies and subordinations of feudalism. It was a place where everyone was free to make money, rather than just a few. Some, he admitted, 'write pornography (an activity we deplore), and you have writers you have put in prison (an activity you refuse to acknowledge)'. Pornography was something of which he disapproved, but censorship was not a satisfactory solution.[91]

Nikolai Fedorenko, a former United Nations ambassador and Secretary of the Writers' Union, asked how it was possible to say that America was anti-feudalistic when it was responsible for the slave trade. Miller replied that it was the American legal system that was anti-feudalistic, to which Fedorenko responded by invoking American Indians. The gloves were now off. As Miller later explained,

> My turn came, and I looked at Harrison who had delivered a most wonderful speech about his youth, how he first got interested in Russia because he was brought up in Minnesota in a Jewish ghetto, with all the Russian Jews. Gass

talked about his upbringing. And what we're getting from the Russians is boilerplate. So I said, 'Look, I'm not going to talk about my life. It's clear to me now that there's not going to be candour. We're talking about our lives. You're talking about something I could have read in *Pravda* yesterday. So why should we come all this distance? I can't tell you guys apart. Every time we ask a question, you all give the same answers. So what's the point? If you're going to talk about the United States, I'm going to talk about Russia.

His comments on Russian writers carried little weight because, as they pointed out, he seemed to know little about them. This was true enough, but as it happened he had brought with him a dossier from PEN which he now presented as the press entered (half an hour before they were due), so that they heard him ask Fedorenko about the fate of a number of writers including the poet Irina Ratushinskaya, who had been in prison since 1982 for having poems published in the West without permission (she would not be released until 1986, shortly before the summit between Ronald Reagan and Gorbachev). It is almost certain that Miller knew nothing of her work. What was at stake was a principle. 'You want to talk about this woman?' he asked. 'Her crime is that she wrote some poetry that nobody liked. I had hoped that candour must break out some time. When? It'll be after I'm dead. But it will. And at that time there can be some kind of understanding between our two cultures.'[92]

The Soviet delegates, Gass reported, 'reacted very strongly to what they believed (not without reason) was a breach of promise'. Fedorenko declared that 'he resented the way the Americans were attempting to meddle in the internal affairs of the Soviet Union'.[93] The conference then adjourned for a display of folk dancing before the visiting writers moved on to Minsk, Moscow and Leningrad.

Whatever the mood of the conference, however, the Soviet Union was changing. Ginsberg may have been refused his request (subsequently reversed) to extend his visa, but at the Soviet Writers' Union's own conference Yevgeny Yevtushenko attacked censorship in a speech apparently sanctioned by Fedorenko. In March Mikhail Gorbachev had come to power and had already started work on opening up the system he had inherited and of which he had been a part. Shortly after the writers' conference he and Reagan met in Geneva and, if there was no breakthrough, there were the first signs of a possible understanding. Miller's attitude to Reagan had been largely negative, though he had warmed to him when he met him personally for the Kennedy Center honour. He despised his policies with respect to Latin America but began to feel that on the question of nuclear weapons, a subject dear to Miller's heart, they shared common ground. Though he was unaware of it at the time, the Lithuanian conference had set in train a process that would soon lead to a personal meeting with Gorbachev.

At the conference he met Chingiz Aitmatov, a novelist and playwright from Kyrgyzstan in Central Asia, on the border of China and Afghanistan, whose father had been executed in one of Stalin's purges for the sin of 'bourgeois nationalism'. In time, Aitmatov became the most decorated of Soviet writers. A winner of the Lenin Prize, he had benefited from the thaw under Khrushchev. He was not a dissident, remaining a loyal communist, but he did explore aspects of Soviet society that others shunned, including the treatment of those from his own region. His novel *A Day Lasts Longer Than a Century* had featured a people not unlike his own, effectively destroyed by a larger culture. Plainly not an apparatchik, he was supportive of Miller's remarks. His play *The Ascent of Mount Fugi*, Miller later recalled, had concerned a group of intellectuals brought face to face with their own betrayal of friends who had stood up to Stalinism. His was, though, it seemed at the time, an isolated voice. On the other hand, he was a member of the Congress of Soviets close to Gorbachev (still something of an enigma). Indeed, a member of the Supreme Soviet he left the conference in order to address a meeting of the Congress to be attended by Gorbachev himself.

A year later, in 1986, Miller received a letter inviting him to a meeting of writers, scientists, directors and musicians from the United States, Britain, various other European countries plus Cuba and Ethiopia. The group was to look forward to the end of the millennium and discuss what lay ahead. The invitation was backed by Aitmatov, who telephoned Miller from his home in Kyrgyzstan. Nobody would be under Party discipline, he asserted, and the discussions would be open and free. Miller decided to go, even though it would mean celebrating his seventy-first birthday away from his family, except Inge who was keen to accompany him because of the photographic opportunity it would offer.

They assembled in the mountain resort of Lake Issyk-kul in Kyrgyzstan. Among those in the United States party besides Miller and his wife were James Baldwin and his brother David, together with the futurologist Alvin Toffler and his wife. They were joined by the novelist Claude Simon from France, Peter Ustinov from Britain and the Turkish novelist Yashir Kemal.

The exchanges ranged widely – and without, Miller noted, the usual determination by communist writers to score ideological points or put their orthodoxy on record. Nor were these discussions primarily of literary matters. Topics included pollution, the accident at Chernobyl of April 1986, and unemployment. Miller spoke of the dated ideologies that ruled both the United States and the Soviet Union, and the Tofflers of the likely effects of technology. There was talk of the need for a free flow of information. They decided to widen their circle and meet again at some indefinite point.

As they were all preparing to leave, however, they received an unexpected invitation to meet Gorbachev in Moscow. The meeting, which lasted two and a half hours, took place in the surprisingly tasteful headquarters of the Communist Party of the Soviet Union, looking out over the rain-slicked surface of Red Square.

When Gorbachev entered along with translators he shook hands with Miller, telling him that he had seen or read all of his plays, seemingly unaware that those plays had in fact been banned in Russia for the previous sixteen years. The meeting began with a few remarks from Gorbachev, then a summary of the Issyk-kul discussions by Aitmatov, before each around the table contributed. For his part, Miller elaborated a familiar theme: the need for the artist to speak truth to power. He also recalled his Michigan anthropology professor who had always asked a new class to define the function of a hospital, a library and an army, only to fail all the students for not realizing that the observable first function of all organizations is to sustain themselves. The political point was not lost on Gorbachev, who now proceeded to outline something of his own philosophy. He called for intellectuals to concern themselves with politics and to keep the human being at the centre of consideration. In doing so he quoted from Lenin: 'There must be a priority given to the general interest of humanity, even above that of the proletariat.'[94]

Sensing the importance of the occasion, Miller began taking notes. Why, after all, had Gorbachev chosen to call this meeting if he did not want news of what he said to get back to the United States in particular? Now the Soviet leader began to address the political situation directly. He had, he explained, only recently returned from a summit meeting with Reagan, which had been widely seen as a failure. He insisted, however, that it had represented an advance, and he identified a series of possibilities blocked only by propaganda largely designed for internal purposes. For his part, he saw the Soviet Union as democratizing and becoming more open. His guiding principle, he said, was glasnost, or openness. A last reference to the poet Andrei Voznesensky particularly struck Miller, for only the previous week he had published a poem expressing his alarm that a wartime grave of Ukrainian Jews had been desecrated and gold fillings taken from the teeth of exhumed bodies. He took the mention of Voznesensky as a reassurance that anti-Semitism was no longer to be fostered in the new Soviet Union.

When he returned to the United States, Miller tried to publish his report of the meeting only to find a lack of interest. At the behest of Harrison Salisbury, a former editor of the *New York Times*, he prepared an article which Salisbury sent to his old newspaper, expecting a front-page story. This was the first news of the emergence of a liberal voice at the top of the Soviet system. The *Times* turned it down. He called the *Washington Post*, with the same effect. Despite repeated efforts, no one seemed interested. *Business Week* magazine agreed to an interview but, in Miller's view, the result was a distortion. Finally, he published an abbreviated account in *Newsweek:* fourteen pages of notes boiled down to one.

Why this reluctance? The conclusion he drew was: 'We have a party line in this country. The head of the Soviet Union's not supposed to be saying these things!'[95] It was another few months before news began to emerge of a fundamental shift in Soviet views, and when it did there were those who denounced Gorbachev. As ever, *Commentary*, under Norman Podhoretz, offered its pages to those who wished to attack all aspects of the Soviet Union. Natan Sharansky, who had spent nine years in Soviet prisons, saw Gorbachev as more dangerous than his predecessors and called for opposition to his policies. The magazine even regarded President Reagan as soft on communism.

When he published his autobiography the following year Miller included a brief account of his meeting with Gorbachev, and in doing so recalled how far he had come from that moment on a Brooklyn street in 1932 when a student had first introduced him to Marxist ideas, but though he recognized, as the newspaper editors had not, that something potentially profound was afoot, he had no more idea than anyone else that the world was just two years away from the collapse of the Soviet Union, the end of most Marxist states and the tearing-down of the Berlin Wall, leading to a unification of Germany that he was far from ready to embrace unreservedly.

In August 1986 Miller joined with fifty-three other writers and academics to express concern in the pages of the *New York Review of Books* at the growing number of arrests being made in Poland following the arrest of Zbigniew Bujak, the underground leader of Solidarity. In particular they called for the release of Zbigniew Lewicki, head of the American literature department at Warsaw University, whom many of the signatories knew, as did I. Writing to me in 2009, Lewicki described what had happened:

> I got arrested for aiding a fugitive. I was part of a group of sympathizers who helped members of the underground Solidarity executive committee avoid arrest for five years. We moved five people from place to place in Warsaw. I had been in the States so my name wasn't originally on anyone's list. Then they arrested two or three of the committee, along with me and my girlfriend. We were in pre-trial detention. We were released after four months as part of a general amnesty. I didn't regard myself as in any way a victim. I knew they would catch up with me. I was arrested in May and released in August. I don't think the letter in the *New York Review of Books*, of which I knew nothing at the time, had anything to do with it and I'm sure that Miller would have had no idea what I did. I was truly impressed with the names when I read the letter after release. What they were told about me to sign

the letter, I have no idea. I tried to write to the signatories later, via the *New York Review*, but I don't think the letter got through.[96]

In October Miller spent ten days in the bowels of the Royal Shakespeare Company's London base at the Barbican, attending the final days of rehearsal for *The Archbishop's Ceiling*. For John Shrapnel, Miller 'hadn't come with the notion that there was a single, inevitable direction for his play and our characters; all possibilities were open'. They had been worried about tampering with the text in any way, but Miller's response was: 'It worries you, cut it.' Mainly, Shrapnel explained, 'He opened this dense play up for us, steered us away from piousness, and pointed us to solutions which then seemed obvious.' There is a moment in the play when

> [the dissident writer Sigmund] asks his American friend whether he is carrying a gun, a question which jacks up the tension since it introduces the possibility of firearms into a claustrophobic domestic situation. Playing Sigmund, I was approaching the moment rather heavily and tending towards melodrama. Much better, Miller suggested, to make this query very natural, and almost playful. He described a situation when a man at an airport had asked him the same question, very calmly and pleasantly. The man had then revealed that he was armed: Miller was horrified. A simple tale, but lethal.[97]

For Nick Hamm, the director, 'the discussions about a given moment were often intense, mainly funny, but always ended with a line for the actors to follow ... If Arthur had been there from the start, that exploration, that process of "getting lost" in order to come out the other side, would not have happened. The actors had a reservoir of possibilities to present. They were as pleased as I was to have at last a basis from which selection could take place.'[98]

At the end of the play there is a speech in which Sigmund lists those writers with whom he has communicated during the period in which he has been harassed. It includes Heinrich Böll, André Malraux and Saul Bellow. During rehearsals, Miller seized the script: 'Hey, lemme see that.' The following day he added the names of Graham Greene and Samuel Beckett, saying, 'Can't leave those guys out.'

Just as *The Archbishop's Ceiling* would be rescued by two British productions, so *The American Clock* finally received an excellent production at England's National Theatre in 1986. Peter Wood, the director, placed a jazz band on stage – impossible in New York, given the economics of Broadway – and seized on the epic qualities. It succeeded where the American production had failed, in offering 'a unified concept of human beings, the intimate psychological side joined with the social-political'.[99] Wood had directed the British production of *Incident at Vichy*. Now he had the resources of the National Theatre at his disposal and the result was a play suffused with the music of the 1930s, which created a portrait of a society simultaneously under stress and discovering a new resistant strength.

Asked by Wood how he should approach the play, Miller told him that it 'should have the panache of vaudeville, a smiling and extrovert style, in itself an irony when the thematic question was whether America, like all civilizations, had a clock running on it, an approaching time of weakening and death'. Yet, at the end he wanted audiences to feel, 'along with the textures of a massive social and human tragedy, a renewed awareness of the American's improvisational strength, his almost subliminal faith that things can and must be made to work out. In a word, the feeling of the energy of a democracy. But the question of ultimate survival must remain hanging unanswered in the air.'[100]

Before we walked into the auditorium, Wood drew me aside and said that he had made some changes without consulting the author, particularly with respect to the music and the play's ending, and wondered whether he should tell him then or let him discover for himself. In the event there was no time. Miller gave every appearance of being mesmerized, and embraced Wood after the performance. It was, he said, exactly what he had hoped. He made no reference to the changes, which involved the use of additional music and images that projected the implications of the play forward. The production was quickly moved from the National's Cottesloe Theatre to the Olivier, nearly four times bigger, where it continued to play to full houses.

Its reviews were in sharp contrast to those that had greeted the American production. For Blake Morrison in the *Observer* it was an attack on revisionist Reaganite notions of the 1930s and, though its action pre-dated Reagan, Miller was inclined to make the same connection. To Morrison, it was 'gloomily funny'. For Francis King it was brilliantly directed and acted, the music not only entertaining but also searing in its effect. Martin Cropper in *The Times* was less sure that the various elements came together, while Michael Billington in the *Guardian* wondered whether the balance between the private and public worlds was quite right; but, like Miller himself, responded to a production that gave life even to cameo roles.

Miller was thrilled by his London visit. He later remarked, 'Here were two plays of mine that at home had been branded null and void, but the London theatres were packed ... It was significant that though the reviews had not been uniform at all, no one critic in Britain was powerful enough to lower the curtain on a show and keep it down.'[101] Shortly afterwards a third play would be added, an outstanding production, again at the National, and it too would transfer to the West End. *A View from the Bridge* with Michael Gambon as Eddie Carbone, directed by the British playwright Alan Ayckbourn, would turn out to be one of the finest productions of the play.

It is tempting to feel that the British success of *The American Clock* may have owed something to the fact that it was produced in 1986 when Margaret Thatcher was in power. The social and economic model that she promoted was one in which individuals were in competition with one another, and those excluded from the new economy were in effect surplus to requirements. For an audience that had had to make its way past the homeless sheltering among the concrete pillars of the National Theatre, this was by no means necessarily an acceptable model. What, after all, were they doing watching an Arthur Miller play if they believed, with her, that there was no such thing as society? Indeed, the theatre itself offered a model of a functioning society in which meaning was precisely a product of the interaction of individuals with the community of which they were a part.

Perhaps, Miller said in the autobiography that was soon to appear, 'interviewers would now stop asking what I had been doing through the seventies and start looking into whether a significant number of worthwhile American plays had been chewed up and spat out by that lethal combination of a single all-powerful newspaper and a visionless if not irresponsible theatre management, some sectors of which had, yes, profiteered to the point where the whole theatrical enterprise was gasping for air and near death while a handful of men grew very rich indeed'.[102] He seemed 'to have been "revived" when in fact I had only been invisible in my own land'.[103] He noted that in order to play the figure of Adrian in the RSC's production of *The Archbishop's Ceiling*, Roger Allam had given up the role of Javert in *Les Misérables*. Such a decision was, he thought, unthinkable in his own country. Beyond that, the problem was not that the American theatre had no room for great plays but that it had no room for good plays. Theatre was a hit-or-miss affair, a miss being anything that was not an acknowledged and profusely praised hit.

In Britain Miller's plays were performed at the country's major subsidized theatres and often transferred to a West End that might increasingly resemble Broadway but that could still make room for serious dramas. Reviews were not always unequivocally good but each play was accorded careful consideration. At the same time, he was overstating his case. In America he had not really noticed the changes going on as theatre spread across the country, with new buildings opening and companies being established, though he did acknowledge the importance of the Guthrie, which had opened earlier than many of the regional theatres, in 1963. He might try out in New Haven but New York was always the measure, and in New York business values prevailed. Time and again he would attribute the failure of a work to managerial meanness. His plays, he would complain, closed with full houses because they could not be sustained without investment and because critics were obtuse and followers of fashion. There was certainly some truth in this, as would become publicly clear when Patrick Stewart made a similar complaint from the stage of *The Ride down Mount Morgan*. However, Miller was hesitant to turn to regional theatre or Off Broadway, not only because he distrusted some of its products but also because it seemed a mark of failure, a decision to trade down.

Space would be found on Broadway for serious plays but only if they had been stress-tested elsewhere, possibly in the regional theatres but also in England. When he came to present his next full-length work, *The Ride down Mount Morgan*, Miller would choose to open in Britain, subsequently regretting his failure to do the same with *Broken Glass* in 1994. Nor was he the only American playwright to take this path. Richard Nelson's career was in large part built on the loyalty of the Royal Shakespeare Company, while David Mamet had opened *Glengarry, Glen Ross* at the National, as he would *The Cryptogram* in the West End, for essentially the same reason as Miller, its director Greg Mosher finding this a more receptive environment.

Rehearsals for two new one-act plays, directed by Mosher, began in late December that year. Miller had failed in America with *The Archbishop's Ceiling, The American Clock, The Creation of the World and Other Business* and *2 by A.M.* Now he opened these one-acts under the composite title *Danger: Memory!* at Lincoln Center, his first return there since *After the Fall* and *Incident at Vichy* over twenty years earlier.

The first play - *I Can't Remember Anything* – is set in the living room of a small wooden house on a country back road in what is plainly New England. The room reflects the personality of the man, Leo, who lives in it. The furniture is old, well worn, faded, as are his clothes. Though 'the time is now' everything about the place speaks of yesterday. Life, it seems, is elsewhere. He is joined by Leonora, a little out of breath, her American accent touched with what we are told is 'a European aristocratic coloration', an echo of another time and place. But whatever they once were defers to what they now are, two people linked by a missing third, her long-dead husband who had also been his friend. Their encounter, it soon emerges, is part of a routine. They live close to one another, but separate. She visits him to drink his liquor and share his food. The tide has seemingly gone out on their lives. They are Vladimir and Estragon waiting for the end, a mildly comic duo, sparring with one another and yet drawn together. As Leo remarks, 'I know something you could kill time with.'[104] Somehow the meaning they once sought has eluded them. 'I used to believe,' Leonora says, 'we were taught to believe – that everything has its purpose ... But what purpose have I got? I am totally useless, to myself, my children, my grandchildren, and the one or two people I suppose I can call my friends who aren't dead.' Against this, Leo pitches his pragmatism: 'My mother was the only atheist in Youngstown, Ohio; she never talked about things having purposes.'[105]

They are witnesses to one another's lives, confirmations of what is now fast fading. Memories, hers in particular, are beginning to thin. He is making preparations for death, writing the phone number of the nearby hospital in marker pen on a piece of cardboard. He wishes to leave his body to science, as if some kind of meaning can thereby be ascribed to life even in the losing of it. In fact, he shows a persistent optimism that contrasts with her more cynical pose. He recalls to her the days when she had been the centre of attention, playing the piano and the accordion; 'It's just a damn shame to forget all that,' he adds. For her, though, 'It's just some page in a book I once read.'[106] 'I *think* I remember something,' she says, 'but then I wonder if I just imagined it. My whole life seems imaginary.'[107]

Her son has sent her a package containing a record, but it seems to be the first communication they have had for three years. Enclosed is a brief note: 'P.S. Moira and I have decided to separate, you'll be glad to hear',[108] a sentence which simultaneously hints at the cause of their apparent estrangement and the attenuation of relationships.

Once Leo and Leonora had both been committed, she supporting the republican cause in Spain, he a communist, a faith to which he still clings, though with nothing now to give shape to such a commitment. Somewhere along the line purpose seems to have drained away. 'Everything is so awful,' Leonora insists. 'Truly this is not the same country.'[109] She is baffled by the fact that he still shows an interest in affairs, continues to read the newspaper 'that peddles the same vileness every day, the same brutality, the same lies'. Nothing, she insists, 'is "happening"! Excepting that it keeps getting worse and more brutal and more vile ... Why can't you just admit that it's all nothing? You know it's nothing ... This country is being ruined by greed and mendacity and narrow-minded ignorance, and you go right on thinking there is hope somewhere ... it's this goddamn hopefulness when there is no hope.' Against this, he offers nothing more than that life is its own justification: 'If you're wondering why you're alive ... maybe it's because you *are*, that's all, and that's the whole goddamn reason. Maybe you're so nervous because you keep looking for some other reason and there isn't any.'[110]

They meet on her birthday and the eve of what would have been her husband's. For Leo, Leonora's despair has its roots precisely in the loss of a man who had once given meaning to her life: 'Frederick was your life, and now there's nothing.'[111] Leonora has projected her sense of private loss out into the world. Yet at the same time there are moments when she speaks of the natural world with a lyricism that underscores Leo's more positive view. And though neither seems to acknowledge it, their relationship has served to construct the meaning whose absence Leonora deplores.

They put her son's record on and both dance to the samba, for a moment discovering in the music what they thought they had forgotten. She leaves, and he waits for her to telephone to confirm she has reached home safely. Only then can he go to bed – a small gesture, but confirmation of the feeling that brings them together every day, like Vladimir and Estragon; though where Beckett was prone to focus on what struck him as a cold irony Miller was interested in the small change of relationships and the fact of momentary epiphanies, of a resilient human nature. For all Leonora's seeming misanthropy and despite the hollow at the heart of her life as she wilfully suppresses what can only be the source of pain, they find meaning in one another's presence, consolation even in their arguments. If there is an elegiac tone it is because, beneath the confusions, the wilful refusals to recall, the apparent loss of coherence, dignity and purpose, is a solidarity born out of mutuality.

Perhaps beyond this, the echo of their names – Leo, Leonora – hints at an internal debate conducted by a writer who himself was now the wrong side of seventy, conscious of the disappearance of friends, lamenting the loss of something more than political commitment, and searching as much as his characters for some justification. His own alternation between depression and optimism, his sense of the collapse of values yet his revelling in the natural world, is here spun off into characters who, in spite of everything, reach for and achieve some kind of reconciliation.

In talking of the play to Mel Gussow, Miller related it to his own situation, his own awareness of death as no longer a distant prospect:

> When you're twenty-nine or thirty ... the idea is impossible. But I've had so many friends die. I know I can't do things now that I could do before. I was just out in the yard two days ago running a machine, which I had to walk behind. I never thought twice about it before. I had to pull it up a hill and I had to stand there and catch my breath and I thought, I would never have thought about this. I would have done it and then done something else. Now I have to stop and think, well, that's one. I feel good because I was able to do it at that moment. I guess it's some stupid kind of optimism, which overcomes what's left of the brain. There's no other adjustment to it that I can accept. You can get blue and discouraged.[112]

Like Leo, he confesses to spending time reading newspapers, looking for some kind of connection with the world.

I Can't Remember Anything was inspired by and was a celebration of two of his friends, the sculptor Alexander (Sandy) Calder, whose father had created the arch in Washington Square, and his wife Louisa (a great-niece of Henry James), neighbours from Roxbury, where they had lived since the Depression 'when small, bony farms still covered the landscape'. For Miller, Sandy had the spirit of a child; he had little interest in theorizing about his work or society. A decade older than Miller, the couple were a link to an earlier generation. He saw in them 'a bohemian acceptance, judging no one, curious about everything', though 'not far beneath the surface was a stubborn and somehow noble sense of responsibility for the country, a sure instinct for decency'.[113] In this and in their quality of 'unpretentious simplicity' they were at odds with the times. Their air of eccentricity, bolstered by an occasional glass of red wine, was itself a judgement on the material drive of the 1980s, that desire to subordinate the world in the name of some principle no longer easy to articulate. The play, Miller explained, was a belated gesture of love.

If *I Can't Remember Anything* turns on being unable to remember, *Clara* stages the drama of a man who has a vested interest in not remembering. As in *Some Kind of Love Story*, Miller turns here to the figure of a detective. A crime has occurred, in this case a murder. As the play begins a man is discovered lying on the floor of an apartment, but he is not the victim. Albert Kroll is in shock, having discovered the body of his daughter Clara in a pool of blood. The action of the play concerns the efforts of one Lieutenant Fine to question him in an attempt to identify the killer. At first, Kroll has difficulty grasping what has happened. He, like the audience, sees images of his dead daughter; his faculties appear scrambled. Slowly, however, the play does something more than unravel the details of a crime. By degrees, aspects of the lives of these two men are exposed, fragments of a past they have both chosen to suppress. Nor is it simply a matter of their respective psychologies. As in its companion piece, what is explored is a sense of a society itself adrift, detached from its own idealism.

Little by little Fine draws out the truth. During the war Kroll had served in a black transport company and had rescued a group of black troops about to be lynched in Alabama. This is a story that crops up several times in Miller's papers. Here it proves a crucial incident in that when Kroll's daughter learned of it, along with his exploits against the Japanese, it made her idolize him, which in turn led her to emulate what she took to be his idealism. She worked with ex-prisoners, and it slowly becomes apparent that one of them has committed the murder. Kroll finds himself unable to identify the man because of his own feeling of culpability, not least because his own life has been marked by a betrayal of that idealism. Of black Americans he says, 'I just about give up on these people … I used to have a lot of understanding. But I gave up on it.'[114]

Kroll now works for a company run by the mob, even as he congratulates himself on his liberal politics as chairman of the zoning board, widening access to property, thus opening it to the very people who put his daughter's life at risk. It is plainly Clara's Puerto Rican lover who killed her, but it takes Kroll the length of the play to bring his name to mind. He cannot accept it because his whole life seems to have laid the foundations for the murder. It is his own name he is protecting, rather than that of the killer. In effect, her life has been sacrificed to uphold views he himself no longer holds and a self that is no longer what he had represented it to be. The complications, however, go further than that. He had suspected his daughter of a lesbian relationship and had welcomed her affair with the ex-prisoner as evidence of her heterosexuality.

Nor is Kroll the only one who has abandoned idealism. The Jewish police lieutenant, too, has made his adjustments. Asked what he believes in, he replies, 'Greed and race. Believe it or not, I have never taken an illegitimate nickel, but if you ask what I trust to run the world, it's greed – and that secret little tingle you get when your own kind comes out ahead. The black for the black, and the white for the white. Gentile for Gentile and Jew for the Jew.' Held back in his career by prejudice, he explains his position: 'That day in 1945, remember? – when they first showed those pictures of the piles of bones? Remember that? The bulldozers pushing them into those trenches, the arms and legs sticking up? That's the day I was born again ... and I've never let myself forget it. – "Do it to them before they can do it to you. Period."'[115]

Kroll finally offers the name he has been forgetting or suppressing, but only when the two men have both laid their lives before each other – not for absolution, but to restore the order in which neither of them any longer believes. The police lieutenant has witnessed justice perverted on a personal and public level, yet is required to serve it. Tempted to retire, he continues because the alternative is to 'sit looking at the ocean somewhere, wondering where my life went'.[116] Kroll has discovered, and now acknowledges, his capacity for good and evil. The play ends with the man who had been prone at the beginning now standing 'erect and calm'. For Miller, here is an individual forced to face the collapse of values and his own culpability but who cannot finally bring himself to renounce those values, much as Miller himself. While acknowledging the consequences of his own misplaced idealism, he can no more bring himself to deny the spirit that had led him to embrace it than could the playwright who imagined him into existence.

Elements of the play remain unresolved. To Kroll, the lieutenant recalls someone he once knew with the same name, a man who, like Fine, is missing a toe from his left foot and, again like Fine, has lost a son to suicide. The issue is never referred to again. In a play that seems to be the working-out of a rational process, this element refuses incorporation.

The play works obliquely. The crime at its heart is not the one that has left a young woman dead or the one the detective investigates. Nor, in a drama seemingly concerned with exposing reality, does it work by realistic means. Not only does Kroll see his daughter dead but slides of her dead body appear while in another room a photographer records the crime scene. Her figure moves through the scene, sometimes silently, sometimes speaking, as memories momentarily assume concrete form. It is a play in which time becomes plastic and the past explodes into the present with such force that it leaves Kroll numb, unable fully to articulate, whether face to face with his own former self or with the daughter he has loved and lost.

In one sense what we are watching is the power of shock to transform the world, of trauma to reorder the sensibility. But beyond that, Miller seems to suggest that motives, identity, perception are more fluid than they appear, more subject to immediate necessities, as the past is re-edited and the present filtered of suspect information. Kroll's character is not static. It is a kaleidoscope of contending selves that appear coherent but are, in truth, fragmented. For Kroll, the many denials that have sustained that coherence break down under the impact of his daughter's violent death. He has betrayed more than her. He has betrayed his own youthful self. For Miller, the play 'ends in his affirmation; in her catastrophe he has rediscovered himself and glimpsed the tragic collapse of values that he finally cannot bring himself to renounce'.[117] If this is so, it is a tentative affirmation. He is left bereft, staring into space, proud of his daughter's conviction but aware of the price she paid for principles he has himself abandoned. 'Here's a man,' Miller says, 'who inadvertently taught his daughter to be a heroine. Inadvertently he reached his apotheosis through her.'[118]

For Miller, though, this was not a play about one man. He was 'bringing onto the stage a slice of our own historical experience over the past decades since World War II'.[119] In *After the Fall* he had spoken of the past being holy. Here, in two brief plays, he once again suggested the price paid for suppressing, denying or forgetting it. As his detective remarks, 'What you can't chase you'd better face or it'll start chasing you.'[120] History, the past, after all, is 'a bit like inhaling and exhaling',[121] and time is anyway inescapable.

During rehearsals he noted that the actors had 'a kind of depth that I think is marvellous. Kenny McMillan [who played Kroll] is extraordinary ... The emotional equipment of that man is unbelievable. And [James] Tolkan [Lieutenant Fine]. They're as good as there are.' Geraldine Fitzgerald (Leonora) he thought 'fantastic'. He had, he believed, assembled the ideal cast while aware that 'the next time around, I'll call on one of them and they'll say, oh, gee, I'm going to be nine years on television. The theatre's a fifth wheel. You've got to face that.' For all that he was anxious about the reviews, experience having prepared him for the worst.

Frank Rich in the *New York Times*, the only review that really mattered, did not disappoint. He found the plays 'gray ... resolutely resisting the efforts of a high-powered cast to inject drama'. The writing he found 'studied and ponderous'. He attacked the director, Gregory Mosher, for 'hokey atmospheric touches' which made the first of the double bill prompt 'cloying remembrances of "On Golden Pond"', while describing *Clara* as 'essentially a "Dragnet" episode, with middlebrow political ruminations substituted for suspense'. It became 'a bitter unenlightening Sunday-morning talk-show debate about the continuing validity of Great Society social policy'. References to the Vietnam War and the Holocaust served only to 'accentuate its pre-tensions'. The whole, he asserted, led to 'an evening in which the pontificator wins out over the playwright'.[122] Gordon Rogoff, in a *Village Voice* review entitled 'Treadmiller', said that 'Miller is continually presenting shadowy events that haven't quite happened with imagery that makes no sense'.[123] Miller observed that the protagonist of *Clara* 'was understood by no one but some of the so-called second-string critics, a few television critics, three British reviewers for London papers, and the audiences that continued to pack the Lincoln Center Mitzi Newhouse Theater despite the main critics' incomprehension of even the bare facts of the story'. [124]

These two plays, though, were not Miller's only bid for success in the theatre in 1987. The year had opened with what he regarded as the best production of *All My Sons* he had seen when PBS's *American Playhouse* presented a television version starring Joan Allen, Aidan Quinn and James Whitmore. More important to Miller, though, was Broadway's first revival of the same play, forty years on from its premiere. Directed by Arvin Brown, it opened at New Haven's Long Wharf Theater before moving to Boston, where it was well received. When it transferred to Broadway, however, Frank Rich's review in the *New York Times* offered a combination of faint praise and condescension. Recognizing its contemporary significance – it was a time when space-programme managers closed a blind eye to defects (the Challenger disaster had occurred the previous year) and Oliver North was shredding National Security Council documents relating to the Iran-Contra affair – he suggested that '*All My Sons* may be too topical for its own theatrical good . . . it's hard not to ask the weary, eternal question, "So what else is new?"' There was much to be praised in 'a play often catalogued as a post-war warhorse', apart from one crucial piece of miscasting, that of Joyce Ebert as Kate Keller. He admired the staging while lamenting the fact that it 'cannot camouflage Mr Miller's creaky, waiting-for-the-other-shoe-to-drop exposition . . . or bald symbols . . . or melodramatic plot twists'. The director, however, he conceded, 'does convince us that there was a playwright, along with the Odets-inspired pamphleteer, at work in this early effort'.[125] *All My Sons* had launched Miller's career as a playwright. On its return to Broadway it was not so much reviewed as patronized. It closed after thirty-one performances.

But Miller was ready to offer the American public something altogether different – something, moreover, that was ostensibly less vulnerable in that criticism could not close it down. His autobiography *Timebends: A Life*, already chosen as the Book of the Month selection (guaranteeing a sale of 100,000) and with *Life* magazine offering $50,000 for a single instalment, was published in September 1987. The advance was $750,000. Translations were already under way in ten languages. This was to be more than an account of his life. His major publication of the 1980s, it was also an attempt to move back into the cultural centre and to engage with the major events that had shaped not only his life but also his society.

CBS's *Sixty Minutes*, with Mike Wallace, covered the book, twice visiting Roxbury and then travelling to the University of Michigan though Miller regretted the emphasis on Marilyn, something for which he was braced but which he nonetheless found dispiriting. Copies of the book arrived in September. Unlike his plays, which for some time now had been seen by few and failed to make their way into print except in acting editions, it would be available to all. At last there was a feeling of excitement about something he had written. It was also a chance for him to answer the critics whose power he resented.

Before the reviews came out, he left for Europe. He and Inge queued for an hour and a half to get into East Berlin. Inge had a friend to see; he was anxious to get a sight of the East. The scene there brought back memories for both of them. Even four decades after the war he was still haunted by the fate of the Jews and still sufficiently fired by his hatred of fascism to take a perverted pleasure in the ruins that were still to be seen on this side of the wall. In some sense, all modern literature had been written in the shadow of this time, certainly much of his own. Here, fascism had had a shape, a form, a name and an immediate physical reality in which millions had collaborated.

Back in London, his spirits were now raised by the transfer to the West End of *A View from the Bridge*, directed by Alan Ayckbourn. Ayckbourn had been invited by Peter Hall to form his own company at the National Theatre and stage a play in each of its auditoria. Ayckbourn was something of a British institution. Based in Scarborough, he wrote and directed at least one play a year, which regularly made its way down to London.

Rehearsals for *A View from the Bridge* had begun with a viewing of Robert De Niro in *Raging Bull*, as the actors, with the help of the voice coach Joan Washington, struggled to arrive at plausible American accents (Gambon added *Mean Streets* and *The Godfather*). Paul Allen, himself a playwright, has described Ayckbourn's approach to the play and to the actors. Elizabeth Bell, who played Beatrice, was too thin and had to wear a bodysuit – Ayckbourn insisted she should wear it from an early stage in rehearsals. Gambon was given heavy docker's boots to help him find a way of moving that gave a sense of power to this man, Eddie Carbone, for whom physical strength would ultimately prove beside the point. Gambon refused to allow the dresser to wash his shirt every night, feeling that the dirt and sweat were a way into his character. So as not to break the tension with a scene change before the final confrontation, Ayckbourn asked Gambon whether he could find a way around it:

A couple of days later, Gambon came into the rehearsal room and played the scene leading up to it. At some level the brooding Eddie already knows his doom. Suddenly Gambon kicked the chairs off stage. With gathering violence he picked up the table and hurled it after the chairs. The furniture fell in a heap just short of Bell and Susan Sylvester as the girl, Catherine, who cowered in the face of this volcanic and completely unexpected explosion. Gambon turned back to Ayckbourn and enquired, 'Something like that?'[126]

When Eddie begins to cry on news that his niece will be moving out, Gambon initially did what other actors had done, turning away from the audience so that all that could be seen was his heaving shoulders. Ayckbourn asked him to face the audience. Gambon's response was: 'You bastard', but two days later, 'He just did it, and it just took my head off.'[127]

For the British playwright Christopher Hampton the production was 'one of the handful of revelatory evenings that reward the life-long theatre-goer' and left him 'profoundly shaken and exhilarated'.[128] Miller found Gambon compelling and was struck by the power and authenticity of the production – so much better, he thought, than its British debut in 1956 whose opening night he had attended with Marilyn Monroe.

The *Guardian*'s reviewer hailed it as 'a red letter night in a critic's life,' and the *Telegraph* found the production impeccable. For the *New Statesman* it was the finest since the National Theatre had opened on the South Bank. When it transferred to the West End *The Times* declared it one of the triumphs of Miller's seventh decade. *Punch* said it was hard to believe there could ever be a better production of the play, while the *Guardian*, reviewing it for a second time, found it one of the great productions of our time. Ayckbourn won Best Director in the Plays and Players awards, and Gambon won both the *Evening Standard* and Olivier Awards for Best Actor. With *The American Clock* at the Olivier and *The Archbishop's Ceiling* at the RSC, Miller now had three favourably reviewed productions in London, all of them 'originally either condemned or shrugged off in New York over the previous thirty years'. *The American Clock*, he noted, had been nominated for the Olivier Award for Best Play along with Peter Wood as Best Director. Earlier, David Thacker had been nominated for Outstanding Achievement for his direction of *An Enemy of the People*.

Asked why his work was so popular in Britain and so disregarded in America, Miller replied, 'I'm not embittered for the reason that I don't think this is some cabal against me . . . It's an old story that Americans obey criticism as if it were a public duty: I'm totally incidental to this process . . . The atmosphere [in Britain] is less hysterical so there's a creative relaxation in the way you approach the work.' In fact, in the past he *had* suspected a cabal, but it was also, he knew, a matter of money. In New York, he suggested again, it was not a matter of a play failing but of it failing to sell out: 'That's the same as saying if you have a shoe store selling shoes and you don't sell every shoe every day, you can't stay in business.'[129] He felt that his own was a country which, lacking any real awareness of continuity with the past, lacked, too, a true theatre culture. He pointed out, 'I have gone through years when my plays were being performed in half a dozen countries but not in New York.' In the Soviet Union *Incident at Vichy*, so long banned, was at that time in its fourth month.

Reviews of *Timebends* in Britain were nearly all positive, though not without a certain equivocation. True to form, and with more than a little personal animus given his own marriage to Mary Ure, John Osborne, in praising the book, drew from it the moral that 'few men should be encouraged to marry actresses, and playwrights should be forcibly prevented from such self-slaughter. Their touted vulnerability is no more than the poison of deadly ambition and Marilyn was the venomous All American Flower.'[130] He was not alone in dwelling on the book's remarks about a marriage now more than a quarter of a century in the past. Inge flourished a copy of *Der Spiegel*, saying, 'It's all Marilyn.'[131] The *Guardian* review was headlined, 'Life, Love and Marilyn', though the article itself ventured considerably beyond this.

Miller returned to America to reviews of *Timebends* which, provincial papers aside, he found disappointing (though he was relieved that Robert Brustein would not be among the reviewers). *Time* took issue with him for 'hoarding spiteful anecdotes', found the book 'woolly ... often muddled, even mawkish' and its structure 'odd and often frustrating'; and, in a sentence that confirmed his worst fears, insisted that 'Miller remains fascinating because he fulfilled an almost universal male daydream: he married Marilyn Monroe'.[132] He was, though, praised by Jeffrey Meyers in the *National Review*, whereas Alfred Kazin, a man whose judgement he usually respected, while largely welcoming the book spoke of his writing 'ponderously' in a work that was 'not a literary achievement in technique and style so much as a flowing – sometimes overflowing – *apologia pro vita sua*'.[133] He upbraided Miller for his failure to appreciate Samuel Beckett and for suggesting that his falling reputation was a function of reactionary critics.

The *New York Times* was largely enthusiastic, if with reservations. Despite 'certain weaknesses' which included a 'lame' title, 'inept usage' and a lack of any reference to Yves Montand, whose adulterous relationship with Marilyn had played its role in ending Miller's second marriage, Roger Shattuck found the book neither 'self-serving nor self-indulgent', though he did reiterate a criticism of *The Crucible* familiar from the attacks on it by the Non-Communist Left: 'What does not come out here or in Mr Miller's 1953 play about the Salem witch trials ... is that behind McCarthyism and the unscrupulous and publicity-seeking HUAC investigations lay not giggling girls and a widespread belief in witches but a genuine international conspiracy that threatened Europe at the time, even if it did not threaten the United States. Mr Miller has never been moved to write a play comparable to the novels "Nineteen Eighty-Four" or "Darkness at Noon".'[134]

For Miller this must have had a weary sound, given that he was being chastened for not producing work echoing that of writers he distrusted politically; but the *New York Times* offered him a more comfortable read than the reviews in *Vanity Fair*, his old enemy *Commentary* and the *New Republic*.

James Wolcott in *Vanity Fair* dismissed the book, observing: 'That Miller came to regard himself as a great thinker is one of life's terrible mis-understandings ... The honest Abe Lincoln of American letters, ministering from his marble throne to the ailing soul of the Republic. Since the success of *Death of a Salesman* he has been the travelling secretary of liberal humanism, a global delegate for peace and dialogue ... If only he could give piety a rest ... Arthur Miller's sermonettes come straight from the gassy void.'[135] But this was nothing compared to James Tuttleton's all-out attack in *Commentary*. Miller, he suggested, on the evidence of the book, was unwilling to con-template imperfections in his plays, preferring to blame audiences, actors, producers, directors, executive boards, newspaper critics and academics. He found *Timebends* full of what he called 'psychoanalytic palaver' which extended to his approach to politics: 'Are we seriously to believe,' Tuttleton asked, 'that our century's hoard of revolutionary Marxists, who have destroyed whole societies and murdered huge populations, have been merely the maladjusted products of Oedipal problems with Dad? Or that this explains the Marxist political motivations of guilt-ridden middle-class intellectuals like Miller?' The weakness of his recent work – *The Creation of the World and Other Business*, *The Archbishop's Ceiling*, *The American Clock* and *Danger: Memory!* – had left him 'wondering whether his appropriation of this Freudian structure of ideas might not have drained his powers as a playwright'.[136]

It was the response he had feared. It was as if his decision to write an account of his life had woken those hitherto content to let him slide into obscurity. The listing of his plays was a dismissal of nearly twenty years of his work, and the disinterring of political disputes a reminder of what, to his mind, had so damaged him.

The one aspect of the review that rings true is its stress on the degree to which Miller had embraced Freudian ideas. At times he seemed to have abandoned Marxism in favour of another master story, this one not primarily concerned with the material world but an internal drama in which the struggle for authority is rooted in the family rather than in class or in contending systems of power, and creativity is seen as a form of sublimation. In describing his own life and art he was inclined to speak of the return of the repressed (*All My Sons*), of denial (*A View from the Bridge*), patricide (*All My Sons*), fraternal battles (*The Price*), incest (*A View from the Bridge*). Whereas Marx had been blasted away by the fierce wind of revealed history, Freud approximated too closely to his own feelings of rivalry, his love–hate relationship with his parents (*After the Fall, The Price, The American Clock*), the ambivalent role of father–lover he had played with respect to Marilyn (*The Crucible, A View from the Bridge*). He had not, after all, walked out of analysis in the 1950s because he thought it invalid, but because it pressed too close to the sources of his art. In fact, that art, as perhaps his autobiography too, had been a form of psychoanalysis, *After the Fall* even seeming to take the form of a psychoanalytic session.

Later in the year, Miller reread *Oedipus* and saw there aspects of his own art. It is certainly striking that he used to speak of it in sexual terms. He referred to writing with his penis, of not being able to get it up for one of his plays, of writing at his truest when he wrote out of shame. In 1989 he had an idea for a story that would not be published until 2002, when it appeared in the *New Yorker*. 'The Bare Manuscript' concerns a writer who overcomes writer's block by writing on the naked body of a young woman, thereby getting his creative juices flowing again. At the time the story went nowhere, but it surely underscores something of Miller's attitude to writing and, indeed, to Freud.

If reading the *Commentary* review was painful, the *New Republic*'s was worse, and stands as one of the most direct assaults on Miller and his reputation in the guise of a review of his autobiography. It began with its cover, which featured a scowling Miller casting a distorted shadow of himself as failed salesman. That same cover promised an article 'on the pretensions of an American playwright'. The title of the review, by David Denby, a journalist and film critic, was 'All My Sins'. It began by identifying Miller as the author of *Death of a Salesman*, which Denby described as 'a doggedly sincere and affecting minor work'. *Timebends*, he said, 'sounds a note of personal disappointment verging on outright betrayal – and an accompanying note of unconscious priggishness'. It upbraids America for its failure to appreciate its author as it should. 'The clear implication of Miller's disgust,' Denby explains, 'is that America's declining interest in his later work is evidence of the country's increasing frivolousness and illiberalism.'

For Denby it was 'a proud, haughty, often wrathful book' by 'a man conscious of his position in the world and of others' dereliction in not recognizing it'. Structurally the book was 'unwieldy and blockish, a failure' and with 'an amorphous and sluggish feel to it', composed of 'glutinous sentences' that failed even to show a proper respect for logic, since 'the reader of an artist's autobiography naturally expects chronological order'. The writing was 'marred, and sometimes destroyed, by outbreaks of rueful, village-elder sagacity and didacticism', and was characterized by 'the dry workmanlike drone of his style'. His plays, Denby asserted, are written 'in the now-vanished Broadway genre of ethical melodrama' of which Lillian Hellman had been the other master. As to his portrait of Monroe, he had simply failed to realize that she 'was a great tease, and he something of a blockhead ... Miller was mating with the golden-haired dream, quite a treat for a Jewish boy', this man who 'hid the obvious Jewishness of the Lomans and other characters'.

It would be hard to imagine a more calculatedly offensive assault under the guise of criticism. Those who admired Miller, Denby explained, were assistant professors of drama for whom the stupidity of his moral assertions 'will never go out of fashion in the classroom, where "great questions" are always teachable. Miller is the perfect school playwrite.'[137]

The *New Republic* set aside five pages for this diatribe which, as no doubt it was meant to, shocked Miller, who wondered at its venom even as he had braced himself once again for rejection. The reaction of this and some other American critics to *Timebends* was the culmination of a hostility that he traced back to the 1950s but that had intensified from the 60s onwards and that prompted the very petulance about reviewers that several noted in his book. Two years later, he observed that a *New York Times* article about Grove Press featured a photograph showing thousands of unsold copies of *Timebends*. In the view some, Miller was out of step not only with the culture but with the innovations of European theatre and the radical experiments of Off and Off Off Broadway. But in considering what might appear Miller's paranoid response to certain American reviews of *Timebends* it is worth recalling that those same reviewers, whether casually or caustically, had rejected his work of the previous twenty and more years.

In 1964, in *Partisan Review*, Susan Sontag had commented on the 'intellectual weak-mindedness' of *After the Fall*, claiming that it was 'belabored, trite ... wretched'.[138] Writing in the *New Republic*, Stanley Kauffmann had found *Death of a Salesman* 'a flabby, occasionally false work',[139] and struggling to account for Miller's success suggested that it came from the fact that he 'supplies the illusion of depth and gives his audience a painlessly acquired feeling of superiority just by being present at his plays'.[140]

William Dean Howells once remarked that anyone can make an enemy – the problem is to keep him. This was a skill that Miller had evidently acquired with respect to Robert Brustein, who over several decades conducted a sustained critique amounting to a vendetta. For Brustein, Miller was evidence of 'consumer theater'. When the Long Wharf Theater embraced his work (along, Brustein scathingly noted, with that of Cole Porter), it was opting for 'domestic realism – plays in which people discuss their problems over hot meals', the kind of theatre likely to appeal to New Haven's middle class who

wished to be 'lulled by the sight of familiar lives on stage',[141] and this, incidentally, from an admirer of Chekhov, a writer who once remarked: 'A
play should be written in which people arrive, go away, have dinner . . . just eat
their dinner, and all the time their happiness is being established or their lives
being broken up.'[142] Chekhov, however, was in process of being reinvented.

In truth, only *All My Sons* could be said to sustain Brustein's model
of Miller, a play, incidentally, in which a surface happiness does conceal
fragmenting lives. But somehow the model, once established, became short-
hand for his entire career. What Brustein wanted was 'risky' theatre, the kind,
he admitted, that lost half its audience every night. He thus attacked *The
Price* for 'imperviousness to modern moods'[143] for being solemn rather than
serious and 'divorced from concerns that any modern audience can recognize
as its own'.[144]

For Brustein, Miller's talent was 'minor'. *After the Fall* was scandalous,
Incident at Vichy 'an old dray horse about to be melted down for glue'.[145] The
two plays were 'moribund in their style, ideas, and language'.[146] In retrospect,
even *Death of a Salesman* seemed unimportant to him, 'essentially a realistic
problem play, in which Willy's hallucinations have the quality of factual
flashbacks, since most of them are recalled accurately'.[147] For Richard Gilman,
Miller was 'a playwright whose dramatic imagination has always operated
within the most stringent limitations, a narrow realist, with a hopeless aspir-
ation to poetry, and a moralist with greatly inadequate equipment for the
projection of moral complexity'.[148] Only once, in *Death of a Salesman*, did his
powers prove commensurate with his theme, so that he was able to compose
'a flawed but representative image of an aspect of our experience. One other
time, in *The Crucible*, his deficient language achieved a transcendence through
its borrowing from history. And that is all, literally everything.'[149] *A View from
the Bridge* had been simply 'dismal'.

The true line of descent for Gilman was Strindberg, via Chekhov (as
precursor to Beckett) to Beckett himself, all of whom, he felt, reacted against
'the idea of stage characters as coherent, consistent, orderly; as simulacra of
our own presumably coherent existences; as substitute, enacted biographies'.
Along with this went a dismantling of plot. Audiences were no longer to be
taken on a journey from problem to solution, unmeaning to meaning.[150] For
Gilman, Ionesco described the true spirit of the theatre, dispensing as he did
with what was presented as a limited version of the real: 'It was as though
there were two levels of reality, the concrete reality, impoverished, empty,
limited, of those banal living men, moving and speaking upon the stage, and
the reality of the imagination.'[151]

For Herb Blau, writing a later decade, even Miller's success in England
could be accounted for by the enthusiasm of socialist directors whose engagement with him was 'in a simpler vein, the association of a more objective kind

of truth ... with the urgencies of social and political theater'.[152] Delmore Schwartz, admittedly in a state of decline and attacking everyone in sight from F.O. Matthiessen to Jacques Barzun, wrote in a review for *Commentary* of 'the retarded conscience of Arthur Miller, the ballplayer for whom Marilyn Monroe consented to be circumcised',[153] though this proved too much even for *Commentary*. As late as 1996, in a letter to Nathan Abrams, Leslie Fiedler, himself a former Trotskyite, described Miller as 'an overrated playwright, whose dramas are as devious as his public life'.[154] Like John Lahr, he accused him of 'turgid naturalism',[155] of focusing on 'psychological man' instead of 'turning toward the void – a gesture at once potentially liberating and fearful'.[156] John Simon, always inclined to see Miller as a simple realist, dismissed *Incident at Vichy* as striking 'most discriminating viewers as bundles of attitudes: mere posturings conforming to the current expectations of middlebrow theater-goers'.[157] Again, he proposed an opposition between theatregoers duped into enthusiasm for the ersatz, and discriminating viewers such, presumably, as himself who had the ability to see beyond mere pleasure to a failure of imagination.

Robert Lewis in his book *Slings and Arrows* offered a surely fanciful explanation for the hostility of Brustein and Simon. He recalled an occasion when Miller had been speaking to Yale undergraduates and sat in on a session in which Brustein was introducing Simon, who had come to address drama students later in the day:

> After a few minutes of John's lecture, Arthur uncurled himself, whispering, 'Come on, I can't listen to any more of this shit.' As we escaped through the rear door I noticed the eyes of both Simon and Brustein catching our precipitous departure. I have often tried to measure how much this incident contributed to the particular pleasure the two critics seem to experience when murdering everything Miller puts his hand to. One day, at Brustein's house, when Bob was making a case for the proposition that everything Miller ever wrote was dishonest, I asked, 'Including *Death of a Salesman*?' 'Yes,' said Bob. Even his wife took exception to that.[158]

Rather like *Death of a Salesman*, *Timebends* moves backwards and forwards in time. As Miller remarked, 'Memory is a shuttle ... I'm moving along the lines of a paradox to a point that illuminates them. Any time you start to tell an event, you end up moving backward as well as forward.'[159] It is a book that has its silences. Apart from the early accounts of his parents and their extended families, his own immediate family make only occasional and fleeting appearances. Inge does feature as clearly the single most important figure in his life, but for the most part he was anxious not to make Robert, Jane and Rebecca part of his narrative. Their lives were their own, as was Daniel's, whose absence would be invoked by those later shocked to learn of his existence.

For the first time, and inevitably, he lifted the curtain on his relationship with Marilyn Monroe, while afraid that it would be this part of his life that public and critics alike would be drawn to. Indeed, he found himself battling with his British publisher, Methuen, who wanted a photograph of Marilyn on the front of the jacket. There is very little in the way of self-justification, however, simply an attempt to explain to himself, as well as to the reader, the reasons for the failure of a relationship he had once thought would be liberating and fulfilling. He does allow access to certain intimacies – the miscarriages, the arguments, the drug-taking and the humiliations – but there are few accusations, except those directed at himself for his feeling of impotence in the face of needs he had felt would yield to his emotional and intellectual support.

It is in part a book about his misjudgements, political no less than social, but again there is no indication that he was tempted to go back and rewrite the history of his allegiances. His passions had at times, he conceded, been misdirected and naive. They figure as such in the book, but they remain commitments that emerged out of the times as well as out of his own momentary fervour. He makes no attempt to wish them away. Indifference, it seemed, was the real enemy.

It is also a book of some lyricism and much humour, one in which, for the most part, he withholds peremptory judgements. Kazan's act of betrayal is treated with a deal more circumspection and admiration than Kazan afforded him in his own autobiography. Ironically, it tells the story of a man whose life seems a triumph of the very American dream that his work treats with such suspicion. Yet there is no trace of triumphalism, perhaps partly because he acknowledged that he no longer had a tight hold on the American public.

Timebends ends on a celebratory note, but that celebration has to do with his contentment with his place in the social and natural world as much as with any artistic satisfaction. At the time it seemed some kind of final summary, by a man already in his seventies and presumed, therefore, to be at the end of his career. In fact, it turned out to be a provisional account in that ahead lay another seventeen years of plays.

There is, though, a paradox at the heart of the book. For one British critic,[160] it was the autobiography of a playwright born in the wrong country, and this would become something of a commonplace in discussions of his work throughout the late 1980s and the 1990s. Just how could a writer for whom the past presses closely upon the present, who sees art as a transforming mechanism, who distrusts the material, function in a country that treats all such propositions with suspicion? For what also emerges from the book is the portrait of a man, born in the USA, who found himself at odds with a number of its core myths.

His publicity tour for the book took him to Washington, Chicago, Los

Angeles, San Francisco, Boston and Toronto. There were large audiences at each venue, though it had yet to make it to the bestseller list, much to his publisher's alarm. He was particularly depressed when Elia Kazan's autobiography came out within a few months of his own.

Suddenly, here were two autobiographies conducting an implicit debate about the past, offering two contrasting views of private and public responsibility. And they were significantly different in approach as well as in their interpretation of the meaning of that past. Kazan's opening-up of his private life, his seeming willingness to talk about intimate relationships, was fundamentally at odds with Miller's reticence. For the playwright that life had fed directly into his art, which bore its impress, as though thereby purged of a self-justifying impulse. In his autobiography Miller preferred an oblique approach, always afraid of the public hunger for scandal. Kazan's book he found lacking in humility and in a sense of responsibility. In particular, Miller challenged his account of a period in which he had offered up other people supposedly in the name of truth, while knowing that they represented no threat – knowing, too, that their careers were potentially forfeit while his prospered.

The differing responses to *Timebends* in Europe and America seemed to him to have something to do with the fact that European readers had no difficulty in understanding how intelligent people could have been drawn to Marxism. In America the anti-communism of the 1950s had contaminated such a political commitment. Kazan's militant anti-communism thus appeared to him so much more in the national grain. Born again, free of guilt and identifying fellow sinners, he became a familiar American icon in a culture based on the idea of reinvention, of recovered innocence, redemption.

One other dimension of Kazan's autobiography struck Miller: his own role in Kazan's life. What is most notable is not only Miller's significance to Kazan but Kazan's significance to Miller. They are like two warring brothers. There is no doubting the mutual respect with which the relationship began nor the closeness of their friendship. The break was thus the more bitter. That they should then have come together again for the production of *After the Fall*, that Miller should have drawn Kazan's portrait in that play and that Kazan had accepted it, says something about their mutual need. This was a play, moreover, in which the woman they had shared (Kazan having had an affair with Marilyn Monroe) was a central character. It was as though they had agreed to dramatize aspects of their own lives, to stage a history over which they were in contention.

The more Miller read of Kazan's book, the more self-serving it seemed. His mood was not likely to have been improved by the *New York Times* review by Arthur Schlesinger, which praised it for its 'remarkable candour' and found it 'indispensible', the 'impassioned testament of an artist who has done his valiant best to tell the truth about himself', precisely what Miller believed it did not do. And if Miller had forgotten Schlesinger's past connection with Americans for Democratic Action, then he would have been reminded by his comments on Kazan's naming of names before HUAC: 'It remains hard for those who have never faced the dilemma to pass judgment. I see a tendency today to regard the American Communists as heroes. But was it so heroic to conspire in secret, deny cherished beliefs, take the Fifth instead of emulating the Bulgarian Communist Georgi Dimitrov in the Reichstag trial [in] boldly declaring convictions?'[161]

Miller was even more irritated when Norman Mailer, who had written a version of Kazan and his encounter with HUAC in *The Deer Park*, praised his autobiography for giving an honest judgement of himself and others, suggesting that it had the kind of human detail expected of a major novel. It also had positive reviews in the *Wall Street Journal* and the *New Republic*.

Herb Greer, writing in *Commentary*, found Kazan's stand before HUAC the correct one and his later equivocations about betraying friends mis-guided.[162] His qualms about exposing and hurting 'human beings' were, he thought, absurd given that he had been exposing 'the fans of a regime that had itself slaughtered tens of millions more "human beings" than the Nazis murdered during the Holocaust. By some insane twist of logic,' he added, 'his friends had placed loyalty to that regime above the elected authority of a democratic government.' Greer ends his review by suggesting that the old left banner was now being carried by the likes of Vanessa Redgrave and those who supported the ANC in Africa, presumably including the future president of that country, Nelson Mandela, who would be released sixteen months after this article appeared.

The *New Republic*, however, found Kazan 'as tortured and compelling as Whittaker Chambers', (a former communist who testified against Alger Hiss, a former State Department official accused of spying and convicted of perjury) and the book by turns 'shameless ... compulsive, tasteless ... the self-portrait of an incorrigible sensationalist, a manipulative scene-maker and self-pitying bastard such as might turn his own stomach'.[163] It would last, its reviewer added, 'as long as the twisting souls of show people are irresistible to us'.[164] One observation, in particular, would have registered with Miller: namely, when the reviewer noted that 'the allure of Kazan's *Life* and the lesson in his work have to do with the way the manners and morality of acting, and of presenting drama, have invaded public life. This is one of those books that may show later generations when and how soul turned into performance, and why America began to prefer accomplished acting to awkwardness and difficulty.' Here was a thesis that Miller embraced and would elaborate on in subsequent years. Beyond that, to

Miller Kazan's autobiography revealed a man who believed he could have everything and who revelled in the deceits he practised. Miller, indeed, was now writing a play called *The Ride down Mount Morgan*, in which the central character was based squarely on Kazan.

11

THE RIDE DOWN MOUNT MORGAN TO *BROKEN GLASS*

The poetic truth of life is that you can't have everything.¹*Arthur Miller*

M iller and Inge spent the New Year of 1988 in Grenada. It was just five years after President Reagan had sent troops into this British Commonwealth country under the pretext of defending American students then on the island. Operation Urgent Fury had involved over 7,000 US troops, who were opposed by 1,500 Grenadian soldiers. The urgent fury was felt by much of the rest of the world, including Margaret Thatcher, who had been assured by Ronald Reagan that no invasion was planned even as it was under way. In 1984 I was in a BBC studio on 5th Avenue, interviewing Miller about the Dustin Hoffman production of *Death of a Salesman*, when we were interrupted for what was supposedly an urgent news story: that more medals had been awarded for the Grenada 'campaign' than there had been troops involved. What Miller found in 1988 was general support for the invasion, leaving him in the awkward position of siding with Reagan.

In May that year he was back in Europe, travelling to Paris, Milan and Urbino, where he received an honorary degree, and then to London, where *Danger: Memory!* was running, with Betsy Blair as Leonora and Paul Rogers as Leo. Miller was not unduly impressed. The following month he was off to Chile to write a report for PEN. Together with William Styron he was there for press interviews, a week of lectures and conversations with students at the Catholic University. One evening they attended a dinner given by the Journalists' Association, many of whose members had spent time in prison. There came a point when Juan Pablo Cárdenas, editor-in-chief of the weekly news magazine *Análisis* (whose foreign-news editor, José Carrasco, had been kidnapped and killed two years earlier), rose to his feet to return to prison. Cárdenas, an opponent of Pinochet, had been detained on various occasions for insulting the military and in 1987 was sentenced to eighteen months (541 days) of night-time imprisonment. He was required to share a prison cell with common criminals every night from 10 until 7 the following morning.

The next day, Miller accompanied him to prison, where their photograph was taken, the picture appearing in the following day's newspaper. Pinochet was preparing for a plebiscite later that month which could extend his powers for a further eight years. Opposition was not welcomed.

Miller returned to America to prepare for his new film, *Almost Everybody Wins*, to be directed by Karel Reisz, who now in the heat of the summer flew in for discussions. Reisz had been one of the Jewish refugees rescued by Sir Nicholas Winton, the British stockbroker who in 1939 set up the Kindertransport that would save the lives of 669 Jewish children from Czechoslovakia, an event that would later inspire W.G. Sebald's book *Austerlitz*, which the German author would present to Miller and Inge shortly before his death. Reisz's parents had both died in Auschwitz. He had an impressive track record in the cinema. His films included Alan Sillitoe's *Saturday Night and Sunday Morning* and John Fowles's *The French Lieutenant's Woman*, the latter with a script by Harold Pinter. *Almost Everybody Wins* (renamed, at Reisz's insistence, *Everybody Wins* for the movie) would not prove a happy affair.

Plans were delayed for a while by a writers' strike, which Miller was unwittingly to break. Casting proved difficult (among the actors considered were Robert Duvall and Harrison Ford; Melanie Griffiths seemed for a while a possible for the female lead), while the script, inspired in part by *Some Kind of Love Story*, lacked that play's subtlety. Reisz, a heavy smoker, was on medication for a heart condition, a fact that Miller was later inclined to think contributed to the film's failure. The strike ended in August, after twenty-two weeks. The script was now sent to Robert De Niro.

On the political scene, President Bush and Michael Dukakis were contending the 1988 elections. Polls showed them neck and neck, but with a massive 37 per cent undecided. George Bush as Vice-President had been involved in the shipping of arms to Iran (even while parading his patriotism by campaigning for the presidency in a flag factory). He had been implicated in the accumulating debt and blind to environmental issues. Dukakis had belatedly declared himself a liberal (a word from which, both before and after, Democratic candidates would distance themselves and which Dukakis had shied away from for most of the campaign) and was opposed to the death penalty, but struck Miller as uninspiring. On 8 November, George Bush won forty of the fifty states with 426 to 112 electoral votes, the first sitting Vice-President to be elected to the presidency since Martin Van Buren in 1836. In 1968 and 1972 Miller had attended the Democratic Conventions and followed the campaign with interest. Now, and despite his distaste for Bush, the stakes no longer seemed as high as they had been when America was visibly tearing itself apart. A bland culture seemed to mirror a society drifting directionless, apparently as withdrawn from the world as he felt himself to be.

He was more concerned with defending writers abroad in his role as Vice-President of PEN (Susan Sontag was President). Accordingly, he now wrote to the President of South Korea, then on an official visit to the United States for a meeting with President Reagan, thanking him for the release of two writers but reminding him that others remained in prison. Democracy, Miller and his fellow PEN members wrote, 'cannot be successful without freedom of expression. As long as writers, journalists, and publishers suffer for having voiced their opinions, the Republic of Korea cannot claim to be part of the free world.'[2]

On the other hand he was acutely aware that in terms of his work his was not a voice that commanded much attention but this, he realized, was not a fate unique to himself as a book came into his hands that seemed in many ways to sum up his own feelings about the American theatre and the contempt in which he felt himself held by American critics. If there had been a caesura in his own career when he was seemingly at the height of his powers, then so too had there been in the career of another man alternately praised and denigrated in his own country and who had finally looked beyond its borders for real appreciation.

When Miller received a copy of the selected letters of Eugene O'Neill to review, he recognized the playwright's alienation from the American theatre as mirroring his own. In the 1930s, as a young student, he had thought O'Neill an anachronism, wholly at a tangent to the political commitment of the times. Now the O'Neill he chose to embrace was the anarchist, a man 'passionately involved in his time' who wrote excoriatingly of government conspiracies, 'secret betrayers of their own people', and of greedy capitalists 'so stupid they could not even see when their own greed began devouring itself'. The words are O'Neill's, selected for quotation by Miller. He noted O'Neill's conviction that there was no public for his work in America. In one of his letters, Miller observed, he had spoken of the American public as materialistic and cut off from its spiritual roots, a people for whom the theatre was only a place to go for a laugh or a tear, antipathetic to any tragic sense of life. O'Neill had been hardened to the possibility of failure because he wished to drag the American public where it manifestly did not want to go, and that was a feeling Miller shared.

More significant, however, are the passages from the 602-page book that Miller selected as highlighting O'Neill's views of the American theatre. 'I stand for the playwright's side of it in this theater,' he quotes O'Neill as saying to Kenneth Macgowan in 1926. 'What's the use of my trying to get ahead with new stuff until some theater can give that stuff the care and opportunity it must have in order to register its new significance?' This had, after all, been Miller's complaint from virtually the beginning of his career. His O'Neill was a man who had spoken out in favour of modern tragedy, who saw America's spiritual potential, but saw too its 'brass band materialism'. As Miller observes, 'There are remarks in these letters that one cannot read without a sort of forlorn delight in the unchangingness of the torture that a playwriting life affords.' How apt to himself, he plainly felt, was O'Neill's rejection of irrelevant criticism, especially when it dismissed him as a failed realist. 'When I first spoke to you of the play as a "last word on realism",' he quotes O'Neill as writing to the critic George Jean Nathan about H.L. Mencken's criticism of his play *Welded*, 'I meant something "really real", in the sense of being spiritually true, not meticulously life-like.'

Tellingly, Miller concludes his review by noting O'Neill's comments on the productions of *The Iceman Cometh* and *Long Day's Journey into Night:* 'I dread the idea of production,' O'Neill had said, 'because I know it will be done by people who have only one standard left, that of Broadway success . . . The big fact is that any production must be made on a plane, and in an atmosphere, to which neither I nor my work belongs in spirit . . . because there is no longer a theater of true integrity and courage and high purpose.'[3] Miller himself was still inclined to look for success on Broadway, but he increasingly felt that the conditions prevailing there were inimical to the kind of work he was writing.

O'Neill had been seen as at the peak of his powers in 1936, when he won the Nobel Prize. He had then ostensibly lapsed into a ten-year silence (writing but not releasing plays) and seen his reputation decline. Miller too, after his early awards, had seemingly lapsed into silence in 1955, returning after nine years to find the critics, in particular, now indifferent at best. O'Neill had seen the European theatre as his possible redemption. For Miller, as we have seen, it was essentially the same, though his depression was now lifted by news from England of the success of his adaptation of Ibsen's *An Enemy of the People*, which had opened on 13 October.

The issue of free speech, which he saw as a key dimension of that play, suddenly gained a new relevance when in February 1989, a fatwa was declared on Salman Rushdie following the publication of his novel *The Satanic Verses*. The seriousness of the threat would be underlined by the murder of Hitoshi Igarashi, his Japanese translator, and the stabbing of his Italian translator. Bookstores in Britain and America were firebombed, while six people died in riots in Pakistan and twelve in India. Asked to appear on television to denounce the fatwa, Miller initially declined, but in June found himself discussing it with his neighbour William Styron and two people from the subcontinent: Aslam Syed from Pakistan and Susham Bedi from India. It was a conversation that ranged over other issues, including the British government's banning of direct interviews with members of the IRA (bizarrely, they could be interviewed but their words had to be voiced by actors), the suppression by Israel of Palestinian writings, and the American government's denial of visas to Yassir Arafat and Ernesto Cardenal of Nicaragua. The fatwa, it seemed to him, was to be resisted precisely because it was part of a wider phenomenon. He noted in particular the courage of the Egyptian novelist Naguib Mahfouz, whose own work was suppressed but who supported Rushdie despite the risk to his own life.

Miller stated his position on the subject in the summer issue of the *Authors' Guild Bulletin*. 'The Iranian attempt to unwrite Salman Rushdie's book' was, he noted, 'a very old and common story in the history of censorship ... the curse upon Salman Rushdie, colourful and frightening as it may be ... is an expression of the terribly familiar tyrannical fury felt by insecure men in power a thousand times before in as many different places and under every religion. Indeed, it must be resisted precisely because it is not unique.'[4] Miller now wrote a speech for the United Nations, denouncing the imprisonment of writers and, just under a year before the fall of the Berlin Wall, predicted the disintegration of the Soviet empire in the face of rising demands from submerged nations. In New York, in a church near the UN, he chaired a reading of prisoners' letters by Toni Morrison, Susan Sontag and Norman Mailer.

A year after the fatwa Rushdie was still in hiding, and writers from around the world, Miller among them, signed a letter that appeared in newspapers from Colombia to Finland. This not merely denounced the fatwa and the death threats but took note of what the signatories described as acquiescence and complacency in the face of the affront. This letter followed another, signed by over a thousand writers, that had already appeared thirteen months earlier in sixty-two newspapers and journals in twenty-two countries. Now the demand was for everyone in a position of influence to end the persecution of Rushdie and his publishers.

There are certain years that stand out. In 1956 the Hungarians revolted and for a brief while looked as if they night throw off Soviet rule. At the same time the British, French and Israelis conspired to invade Egypt to protect their various interests. In 1968, the Tet Offensive signalled the beginning of the end of the Vietnam War. Martin Luther King and Robert Kennedy were assassinated, America's cities burned, and the Democratic Convention endorsed its nominee with fighting in the streets. Student revolts flared across Europe. In 1989, something more profound occurred. The postwar world changed. What had seemed unyielding gave way. What had appeared unassailable capitulated. In Russia, Mikhail Gorbachev had not only committed himself to glasnost and perestroika (restructuring), but had taken on the military. In June 1988 Gorbachev had said that to oppose freedom of choice was to place oneself in opposition to the objective force of history, and in case that seemed too gnomic he repeated it in clearer terms that December at the United Nations, declaring that freedom of choice was a universal principle to which there should be no exceptions.

To those in Eastern and Central Europe used to registering the smallest shifts in the political terrain, these were significant tremors indicating imminent change. In 1988 a series of strikes had broken out in Poland, and the banned trade union Solidarity and its leader Lech Walesa began to gain a purchase on the political system, achieving legal status in April. Before that, significantly, it had opened talks with the government. This led to elections in June 1989 which, for once, could not be rigged. Solidarity swept to power, secure in the knowledge that this time the Soviet Union would stand aside. In Hungary the government announced economic and political reforms along with an inquiry into the 1956 revolution. Imre Nagy, murdered by the Soviets, was to be reburied with full honours. Free elections were promised and by October 1989 communism was effectively dead in that country.

The Baltic republics saw protests on the streets until on 23 August 1989, the anniversary of the Hitler–Stalin Pact which had wiped them from the map, some two million people held hands in a line four hundred miles long from Vilnius to Tallin. It is estimated that this represented a quarter of the population of the republics.

On 19 January East Germany's leader Erich Honecker had declared that the Berlin Wall would stand for another fifty or a hundred years. At the beginning of February, as if to underline his point, a student was shot dead trying to climb it. It was only the latest of many such deaths, but it would prove the last. When municipal elections were revealed to have been fixed, there were protests. In October, large demonstrations took place in Leipzig but the militia refused to fire on them.

In China, only military intervention prevented radical change. Protests followed the death of Hu Yaobang in April. He had resigned from his post as Secretary General of the Communist Party in 1987 when his calls for reform and his attack on the excesses of Mao had made him vulnerable to Deng Xiaoping. He had been obliged to offer public self-criticism but remained an influential figure in the eyes of reformers. On 15 April 1989 Hu Yaobang died of a heart attack. In June, up to one hundred thousand demonstrators occupied Tiananmen Square in Beijing. They had a number of causes, one of which was their demand for his official exculpation. The revolt was reported around the world and finally the troops were sent in. On 4 June more than two and a half thousand pro-democracy students were killed (Chinese officials put the figure at three hundred). What had seemed to signal the birth of freedom was quickly aborted.

In response to a telephone call from a student at Berkeley, Miller wrote a piece for the New York Times, though the angle he took was a personal one.

He began by recalling his time in Beijing staging *Death of a Salesman* and the importance to that production of Ying Ruocheng, who had played Willy Loman. Ying, he noted, had returned from Taiwan while still in his teens and, though exiled to the countryside during the Cultural Revolution, had remained loyal. He was later appointed Vice-Minister of Culture, working with the novelist Wang Meng to open the country up. Following the events in Tiananmen Square, both men were required to declare their support for the government's action against the protesters. They refused, and were relieved of their jobs. Miller ended the article by announcing a forthcoming march on the Chinese Embassy in Washington and declaring the centrality of America in the democratizing of China: 'Without being especially aware of it, America has become a sort of light-bearer to the Chinese. This students' demonstration in the Capitol will be a protest, but it is implicitly a gesture as well of their confidence in America's support of the libertarian spirit that our nation has helped engender in China and its stubbornly dedicated younger generation. Surely all Americans – artists, students and teachers especially – will sympathize with them.'[5]

The Hungarians immediately condemned the Chinese action at Tiananmen Square. They opened a border crossing into Austria, and large numbers of East Germans fled. Other borders into fellow East European countries began to be porous. Honecker moved to close them. In November, a huge demonstration in Berlin demanded change. An ambiguous announcement by the East German propaganda secretary led many to believe that the Wall would be opened. As the result of a misunderstanding, on 9 November people were allowed through to the West, and the Wall was effectively down. Members of the secret police, the Stasi, were pursued and their headquarters sacked. In Prague that month, police attacked a student march commemorating a student leader who had been killed by the Nazis. As a result, the universities were occupied and crowds gathered. Within a week the 'Velvet Revolution' triumphed as the communist leaders resigned and Václav Havel and others gathered in a theatre to create a new political force – Civic Forum. On 25 November a huge crowd greeted Havel and the former leader Alexander Dubček. On 29 December 1989 Havel became President of Czechoslovakia.

That same month in Rumania police opened fire on a demonstration. On the orders of President Nicolae Ceausescu a counter-demonstration was ordered, but when the crowd gathered beneath his balcony they were anything but supportive – they booed him. He fled by helicopter but was captured, and on Christmas Day he and his wife were summarily executed. Across Eastern and Central Europe communist regimes collapsed. Richard Eyre later recalled the role of Ion Caramitru, actor and deputy director of the Bulandra Theatre Company in Bucharest:

He returned to Bucharest on the 13th of December. There were reports of unrest in Timoşoara on the 16th December, but no one in Bucharest knew what had happened. Ion had to go to Cluj, in the north, to give a talk. While he was there he heard rumours of a massacre in Timoşoara, flew back to Bucharest and found Ceausescu on the TV at the airport speaking to a large crowd. Suddenly the TV broadcast stopped. He left the airport but could barely drive his car for the crush of coaches filled with riot police heading for the centre. He joined the crowd and the square was surrounded by soldiers and Securitate. Ion was recognised by students and teenagers, who asked him to help them persuade people to join the opposition ... The next morning there were opposition slogans in office buildings, groups of people emerging all over the city. By ten o'clock it was known that the Commander of the Army had either committed suicide or had been executed. The soldiers embraced the people, and the Securitate began to fight. Hundreds of protesters were killed ... Finding himself in a group near the TV station, Ion suggested that they take it over. A General said to him, 'My army is at your disposal. Tell us where to go.' Heady stuff for an actor ... There was fierce fighting round the TV station but by the time Ion went in, the crowd parted for him and he found the TV station guarded by only one Securitate man, who was trembling too much even to raise his hand in salute.[6]

Two or three hours later Ion became one of the twelve-man executive committee that formed a provisional government. So in Czechoslovakia a playwright had risen to the presidency; in Rumania an actor, if briefly, joined a new government.

In November 1989, then, the Berlin Wall was down, communism had collapsed; East and Central European countries were emerging from decades of semi-isolation and repression. Countries wiped from the map by Stalin reappeared. Flags flew that had been hidden in attics; patriotic songs were recalled. A process that Gorbachev had started, and whose first steps Miller had noted, had had consequences no one had foreseen. People across the world celebrated. Miller himself was less sure.

In an article in the *New York Times Magazine* entitled 'Uneasy about the Germans: After the Wall' he asked, 'Do Germans accept responsibility for the crimes of the Nazi era? Is their repentance such that they can be trusted never to repeat the past?'[7] There was, though, he said, a deeper mystery that concerned the idea of nationhood in the German mind. Germany might now be democratic, but theirs was not a democracy of their own making. It had been imposed. Germany had a history of authoritarianism that went back to Frederick the Great and Bismarck and that continued under Hitler. Jews, he suggested, were not alone in being concerned as to whether the new state would consolidate democracy or whether older habits would prevail. He

quoted one of Inge's schoolfriends as saying, 'When we are in trouble we turn
to authority; orders and work make us happiest.'

Germany, he suspected, was a factitious country and would scarcely cease
to be such when it absorbed East Germany, which had simply passed from
one dictatorship to another, from the Nazis to the communists. The Holocaust
remained a fact that seemed to him to have been incompletely absorbed. In
order to make a new state in West Germany after the war, much had had to
be buried. Awareness of the past had to be sacrificed to a commitment to the
future. Somewhat oddly, part of his concern lay in the fact that no one
had shed their blood for this new postwar state, that it was a bureaucratic
convenience whose roots were shallow. Much German blood had, of course,
been shed, but not, he believed, in the name of democracy. Germans themselves had been uncertain that democracy would be maintained in the new
state. Now, in 1989, though he supported reunification he did so with considerable apprehension, insisting that 'no German should take umbrage at
the reminder that his nation in a previous incarnation showed that it had
aggressive impulses that brought death to forty million people ... it is necessary never to forget what nationalistic blood lust can come to'.[8] As his greeting
to a reunified Germany this falls some way short of the celebratory. He
acknowledged a natural German resentment at being tied so resolutely to a
past they wished to escape. The Holocaust, after all, might have been
unequalled in its lethal scale, in the shame it brought on those who perpetrated, facilitated or implicitly supported it, but Germany was not the only
country guilty of persecutions.

What was required, he argued, was not simple contrition but political
responsibility. 'What do I care if a Nazi says he's sorry?' he asked. He wanted
to be assured that democracy would now live not only in and through
institutions, but in the German heart: 'The world has a right to reproach and
criticize and make demands of Germans if and when they seem to revert to
bad habits.' Meanwhile, there was nothing to be done but hope for the best.
He now quoted from an unnamed German journalist who instanced the
democratization of German universities as evidence of change. However, he
then recorded her as saying: 'the problem with the German, the one great
weakness of his character, is his worship of loyalty. Loyalty! Loyalty! It's the
supreme virtue, the chain around his heart.' Miller claimed that an uncertainty
about the nature of German identity was widely shared by Germans themselves, across the classes and independent of political allegiance.

For all his insistence that he required no apology, his feeling that it would
in some way be an irrelevance, he returned repeatedly to the German sin that
required expiation. If Germany was to achieve 'a deep sense of identity, it will
have to be real, not slyly apologetic, an identity reflecting the evil past and
the present resurrection together'. He required 'good works', quite as if he

were a priest not yet ready to offer absolution. The past had to be confronted in order for Germans to become 'more real in their own eyes'. He quoted from his own play *Incident at Vichy*: 'It's not your guilt I want, it's your responsibility.'[9]

Given that he had spent decades working on behalf of those who had suffered at the hands of communist forces in Central and Eastern Europe, and felt guilt at his own protracted loyalty to a cause gone sour, that he should respond in quite this way and in this tone in the aftermath of the fall of the Wall seems at the least surprising. While the rest of the world shared in the German euphoria – albeit temporarily, given the practical difficulties still to be faced – he was drawn back to the past. In truth, his anti-fascism had been stronger than his Marxism, which always had something of Whitman's sense of the universal about it. Fascism had killed his university friend. His brother had had his life blighted by his wartime experiences. He himself had stood in a concentration camp and acknowledged the scar it had left on humanity. In the end, these forces were more powerful than the desire to join in a general satisfaction.

Unsurprisingly, the article won him no friends in Germany. It also perplexed many Americans, who were celebrating what seemed to them the final victory of their way of life, as communism, the enemy for much of the twentieth century and certainly since the war, finally conceded defeat, leaving America as the world's only superpower.

In Europe, the Federal Republic's democratic institutions were seen as having withstood assault from without, in the form of Soviet aggression, and within, by the murderous Baader Meinhof gang, while its democratic processes seemed exemplary. Those born in the year the war ended were forty-four when the Wall fell. Miller was seventy-four. His scepticism was perhaps partly a product of his age, and he was not alone in his views. In Germany itself Günter Grass expressed alarm. Auschwitz, he said, would weigh on the conscience of a unified state that he suspected would be doomed to failure. In 2009 the British government published hitherto secret documents which revealed that Margaret Thatcher had been deeply opposed to reunification. She recoiled at the news that the Bundestag had allegedly sung 'Deutschland Über Alles' to celebrate the fall of the Wall. At the same time François Mitterrand warned Thatcher that the Germans were 'bad' people and that a united Germany would be more powerful than the Third Reich.

Back in London at the end of the year, on a trip that also took him to Egypt, Spain and Germany, Miller saw the Young Vic production of his adaptation of Ibsen's *An Enemy of the People*, with Tom Wilkinson as Stockmann, which had now transferred to the West End. He also attended rehearsals of *Two-Way Mirror*, with Bob Peck and Helen Mirren. The director of both was

David Thacker. As Miller remarked to the critic Sheridan Morley at the time of this new production, the greatness of Ibsen's play lay in 'its everlasting topicality', in the fact that

> in dealing with the conflict between the established order and the truth, when the truth gets uncomfortable ... is it better to alert people to subway firetraps or rocket-launch weaknesses, or to cover them up, in the hope that the explosion may never come? Certainly we know the answer to that; but do politicians? It's obvious that pollution is now poisoning the world, that large parts of America are becoming uninhabitable, but we are still in conflict with indifference and economic imperatives. One hundred years after Ibsen, people still don't want the truth if that truth is inconvenient.[10]

Writing in his diary, Richard Eyre, head of the National Theatre, was less sure of the play: 'Tom Wilkinson very good as Stockmann, but the play promises much less than it delivers. I'd wanted to do it at the NT but David Thacker got there first. He's used Arthur Miller's version, which irons out many of Ibsen's ironies and turns Stockmann into a Milleresque hero.'[11]

Nonetheless, the production was a major success and it gave Miller particular satisfaction. It seemed to him that its story was more applicable to 'our nature-despoiling societies than to even turn-of-the-century capitalism', whose depravations seemed 'child's play compared to ... our atomic contamination and oil spills, to say nothing of our tainting of our food supply by carcinogenic chemicals'. Beyond the details of plot, here was a play about the crushing of the dissenting spirit by the majority, 'and the right and obligation of such a spirit to exist at all'.[12] At the time of its first staging, he recalled, he was so identified with the Left that it was assumed the play was in some sense a defence of the communists and its distrust of the commercial imperative further evidence of political bias. Now, it seemed to him, its metaphoric force had become more apparent, as people were ready to challenge those who attempted to silence dissent.

He wrote an article, published in July 1989 in *Index on Censorship*, in which he declared, 'I don't suppose anything has given me more gratification than the success of *An Enemy of the People* in its recent Young Vic production. I have made no secret of my early love for Ibsen's work, and now to have been responsible, along with some very fine young actors and a passionately perceptive director, for a new appreciation of one of his most central ideas, is something that puts a satisfying warmth in my belly.' Once again he emerged as an environmentalist, reading the play as in part a warning about the contamination of the natural world, recalling Thoreau, who also 'found in nature's ruin the metaphor of man's self-betrayal'. This was the Miller who lived in the countryside and at local meetings fought, with his fellow townsmen and women, against attempts to lay pipe lines and trail cables through the Connecticut hills, the Miller who was suspicious of nuclear power plants. He observed, 'It often does indeed take moral courage to stand against commercial and governmental bureaucracies that care nothing for the survival of the real world outside their offices.'[13]

The play's success in Britain seemed to him symptomatic of that difference between the two countries, already noted. In the British theatre politics had an organic place. In America, he thought, *An Enemy of the People* would have been seen as propagandistic and lacking in the resonance that had led to its transfer from a small subsidized theatre to the West End.

Miller's relationship with its director David Thacker was to prove a crucial one over the next several years. It had begun when Miller's agent alerted him to the success of his production of *The Crucible*. Thacker would subsequently stage many Miller plays at the Young Vic and elsewhere, including the British premiere of *Two-Way Mirror*, *The Last Yankee* and *Broken Glass*, the last performed at the National Theatre and then for BBC television. Thacker had contacted him as he began rehearsals for *An Enemy of the People*, anxious to make adjustments to some of the language and to reinstate speeches from Ibsen's original. To his surprise, Miller was happy with the changes. As he later explained in 1995,

> When David called me to discuss *An Enemy of the People* I was encouraged. He was right in the middle of the idea of the play. He understood it so well that I could trust him with these little shifts of stuff he wanted to do ... What I enjoy a lot about David's productions is that British actors like to speak. Many American actors do too, but some feel that the words are a kind of encumbrance to the emotional life of the work. There is a quality in New York now which is very defeating. There is an atmosphere that is quite hostile. One production after another has left Broadway and gone some place else because if that relationship is stifled you begin to feel you're in a fight rather than a song ... In London, there's a much more open-hearted kind of exchange between stage and audience ... I enjoy the youthful energy [David's] got. He's terrific.[14]

He was equally relaxed in rehearsals for *Two-Way Mirror*, as Thacker oversaw improvisations around the text of *Elegy for a Lady* and invited Miller to improvise the other end of the telephone conversation between the detective and a psychiatrist in its companion piece, *Some Kind of Love Story*. Miller took to taking a nap on a mattress on a dressing-room floor each afternoon. During rehearsals he was anxious to demystify, readily answering questions about the characters. He saw his function as offering 'short cuts', throwing light on what might otherwise seem murky to an actor desperate for specifics, more especially in plays such as these in which there is deliberate ambiguity at the level of both character and narrative.

In *Two-Way Mirror* Bob Peck (who was to die of cancer ten years later) and Helen Mirren had taken some time to find their way. Peck commented, 'We found it incredibly difficult to assimilate the lines. A couple of days before the show opened we were still breaking down at very short intervals in both plays.'[15] Miller took them through it, explaining that he had written *Elegy for a Lady* in two and a half days and never altered a word. It had, he said, come straight out of his subconscious. Nonetheless, as Peck admitted, 'Even when we were playing, for the first fortnight we had trouble with *Elegy for a Lady* and had to cover for each other at least once in each performance. What was good about the production was that we seemed to learn more as we went on so that at the end of six weeks we hadn't exhausted the plays at all.'

Two-Way Mirror was performed in the round and the only changes Miller made involved cutting some of the false exits in *Some Kind of Love Story*, as the detective threatens to leave the distraught woman who may hold the clue to his case. In production the company reversed the order of the two plays, at first every week and then every night – like Miller himself, never coming to any conclusion as to the natural order. Peck remarked, 'People who were in the business preferred *Elegy for a Lady*, I think because of its strong form and its simplicity, whereas the public seemed to like to have the security of the detective thriller form ... If we did *Elegy* first the audience was tuned into a non-realist element and looked for that in *Love Story*. Whereas if we were doing it the other way around they tended to look for some kind of realism. What [Miller is] looking for is a nuance of emotion; it's an emotional journey.'

In playing *Some Kind of Love Story*, in which Angela switches personalities, Peck said, 'We couldn't help thinking of someone like Marilyn Monroe. How do you shunt from one self to another without damaging yourself psychologically? I think Helen Mirren had something of this duality. Her public image is of someone sexually provocative. At the same time she has a classical background. It focuses back to her first major performance as Cleopatra – a classical play but a character who is sexually energised, almost juvenile.'[16] In fact, Miller had been aware of a case in which a woman did have multiple personalities, but in Marilyn he had watched a fragile woman whose role-playing hardly stopped when she was off screen.

Miller had always taken pleasure in British actors, largely because of their refusal to indulge in what he regarded as some of the more irritating habits of method acting, with its pull towards realism: 'The wonderful thing about these actors is that they can be pointing over there and you can say no, it's there, and they do it. With American actors it will take three days to get 'em off the ceiling.'[17] 'What is so good about English actors,' he went on, 'is that they are not afraid of the open expression of large emotions: Americans crochet and knit performances into a kind of naturalism, whereas here you get a lyrical heroism which I like. You still have a high level of serious work, whereas we have a theatre of television stars.'[18]

A young usher at the Young Vic, yet to go to drama school, seeing a woman still standing as *Two-Way Mirror* was about to begin, asked her to take her seat. 'I'm in the bloody play,' she replied. She was Helen Mirren. He was Joseph Fiennes, in 1995 to appear in the Bristol Old Vic's production of *A View from the Bridge* and later in *Shakespeare in Love*.

Two-Way Mirror was critically well received, as *An Enemy of the People* had been, *Variety* acknowledging that his popularity in Britain, where he was 'all the rage', contrasted with his reputation in America.

It was at this time that Miller began work on a story he was calling 'Distinction'. It touches on the question of his own Jewishness. Set in the postwar world though referring back to the 1930s, it concerns a man called Gellburg, who since his high school days had always dressed in black. One day his wife, letting her life slip away in pointless daily rituals, is struck by paralysis of her facial muscles, which then spreads to her leg. Gellburg seeks advice from a doctor, who passes his wife on to a psychiatrist. In the course of his examination he comes to the conclusion that Gellburg has been denying his Jewish identity – as is evidenced by his anxiety to point out that his name is Gellburg rather than Goldberg (the real name of one of Miller's cousins). It is, seemingly, a denial built on self-hatred. Gellburg is, in effect, anti-Semitic, even while being manifestly Jewish. His wife has finally decided to rebel against this patched-together man and her rebellion has taken the form of hysterical paralysis. The story breaks off. Beyond a suggestion that she might be sexually frustrated, that is all there is.

The key difference between this and what five years later became *Broken Glass* is that the situation of the Jews in Germany goes unmentioned. It is a private dilemma, to be privately resolved, though that resolution is not detailed in what is no more than a fragment. *Broken Glass* would be set in 1938 and invoke Kristallnacht; 'Distinction' looks back from the postwar world. Central, though, is the question of a man whose success is intimately connected with his distancing of himself from his Jewish identity – for Miller, always a problematic issue.

In June 1989 he returned from his trip to Norwich, England (where he had opened the Arthur Miller Centre at the University of East Anglia), in time to go to Norwich, Connecticut, in the south-eastern part of the state, where *Everybody Wins* (with a budget of $17 million) was being filmed. Except for his short anti-Vietnam War film, this was his first original screenplay in twenty-eight years.

With a largely British crew, this was partly shot in an old Thermos-flask factory. As the technicians contended with drizzle and low cloud, Miller, in blue denim, explained that it was 'an entertainment', a 'kind of a love story'.[19]

As he was to point out, it was not common practice for a screenwriter to be on the set, unless to make quick alterations to the dialogue; it was, he explained, like having a guilty conscience on the scene of the crime. The image was not altogether inappropriate with respect to a film that never quite found its style, and his introduction to the published text betrays his sense that screenwriting is a second-order activity. 'Without in the least belittling screenwriting,' he wrote, 'I would say that it does not require one to write very well.'[20] He expressed a familiar anxiety: 'Writing screenplays has its own formidable challenges, not the least of which is the capacity to bear the pleasure and the pain of being a member of the orchestra – in the first section, perhaps, but a member nonetheless – rather than the playwright-soloist or novelist virtuoso. The good part is that if the screenwriter gets less of the credit than he deserves, he may also get less of the blame, so it evens out in the end.'[21]

The part of the private investigator was played by Nick Nolte and that of Angela, the woman who may hold the key to a murder for which the wrong man may have been sentenced, by Debra Winger. None of those involved appears to have been too clear as to the nature of the film they were making. For the director, Karel Reisz, it was 'a comedy-melodrama with film-noir tensions ... a small-town thriller, with a comic and ironic mixture of story-telling'. For Debra Winger it was a 'psychological drama', a 'good-type story'; for Nick Nolte, 'a small town morality play'. There was, indeed, a tension between Reisz and Miller over interpretation.

For the actors, the film was different from their usual work. There was more dialogue. Nick Nolte found his part 'very challenging', while the script read 'more like a play', not perhaps intended as praise. Each scene, he said, was like a play, 'with a beginning, a middle and an end'. Scenes that might normally last a page were three pages long. Debra Winger suggested that the writer's words 'don't always roll off the tongue ... What we are doing and saying is secondary – all of these subtexts are the focal points.'[22]

When he saw the rough cut, Miller was far from pleased. Reisz, he thought, had distrusted its subtleties, and he told him so. 'In the course of production Angela's character lost its various personas and her fantastic quality and she ended up merely a terrified woman who dares not reveal what she knows about a frightful murder.'[23] Certainly, the end product was unimpressive. Vincent Canby, the *New York Times* reviewer, concurred. *Everybody Wins*, he observed, was 'a mess', even if an entertaining one put together by people of talent. It had continuity errors, 'as if more material was shot than could be used in the finished film', and made no narrative sense. 'By the film's end,' he noted, 'all common sense has fled.' It is hard to disagree. The problem began with the script, which Miller seemed to have abandoned rather than finished, and continued with unconvincing direction. The *Washington Post* disliked it twice. On 20 January 1990 Rita Kempley dismissed it as an 'enigmatic muddle', 'a mess akin to Norman Mailer's "Tough Girls Don't Dance" . . . "Everybody Wins",' she suggested, 'should have been titled "Death of a Playwright".'[24] Six days later, Desson Howe commented that Miller 'takes his sweet time getting into characters – at the cost of plot', while the audience 'just shakes its collective head'. When the film ended, 'there was a collective pause before a splutter of nervous laughter and bewildered mutterings'.[25]

In his introduction to the published version, in the guise of a theoretical discussion, Miller put a certain distance between himself and the film, deploying a language that suggested something approaching contempt for the process of film-making and his own marginal role. In *The Misfits* he had felt personally involved, working with a director he respected in what had seemed a genuinely collaborative way; his comments in this essay, generalized as they are, suggest a particular animus that came from making a film in which he had lost all confidence.

'A funny thing happens to screenplays on the way to the screen,' he observed. 'They become brittle.' The screenwriter 'misses the lines that were merely shadings of meaning'. And though he conceded the need to press forward with the action, what happened was that 'suggestion through words became rather more blatant indication through images'. It was not, he hastened to say, 'a gripe' but a general observation about the form. The problem, he explained, was that while a 'description in words tends to inflate, expand, and inflame the imagination, so that in the end the thing or person described is amplified into a larger-than-life figment . . . something photographed is lifted out of the imagination and becomes simply what it really is, or less'. Words, unable to imitate reality, must by their nature serve it up in metaphoric guise, but 'film gives us the appearance of reality directly'. Given that to Miller theatre was essentially about metaphor and that he had been anxious to deny the label of realist, this was not a neutral description. At the same time, the weakness of his script had derived precisely from his own willingness to abandon the subtleties of the original play, sacrificing them to plot.

In fact, his introduction to the screenplay, entitled 'On Screenwriting and Language', turns into a celebration of the power of theatre, despite the pleasure he had felt in the creation of *The Misfits* in which, whatever its reception, he had always taken a pride. Film, he pointed out, requires a writer's sense of form 'while inherently rejecting his word-love'. If he is lucky, the missing words might become visible on screen, but

> I think that the quality of the final work is rougher and cruder, more brutally telegraphic, than when it was action described in words . . . The word made flesh may *be* more and suggest less . . . [Among] real writers, screenwriting, when it is not regarded as a cousin of engineering, is seen as on a par with

clothing design; the product has no life of its own until it is occupied by the wearer. I am afraid that this, at least in my view, is truer than one would wish.

He conceded that there had been many more significant films than novels or plays in the previous twenty-five years, but the screenplay was invisible, used up in performance and, unlike the play, was never 'assimilated to literature as a respectable form apart from performance'. In theatre, everything serves the play, which is to say the writer. A screenplay 'is equivalent to the words in a cartoon balloon'. The screenwriter is anonymous. In film, the focus is on the actor, and the more authoritative he or she is the less important the author: 'In effect, the actor has eaten him.' Words exist to be eliminated. Under such conditions, 'no Shakespeare play would last more than an hour'.

Screenwriting, he claimed, was a 'thankless profession'. There 'cannot be a Eugene O'Neill of the movies ... Very good prose writers do not usually prosper as screenwriters. Faulkner, Fitzgerald, Tennessee Williams, and a long line of eminent others discovered that their brightest stylistic inventions were precisely what movies reject like excrescences.' The choice of words is telling. Even when he elaborates a theory of film – like David Mamet, relating it to dream – it is to suggest that thereby it reaches back 'to archaic stages of our evolution, to a period antedating our capacity to understand language, when we communicated in the primitive sign language of infancy'. By this stage, explanation and theorizing seem to have given way to something approaching contempt: 'Long before he can understand words, the infant is obviously moved by what he sees, made frightened or happy or curious or anxious by visual stimuli. After a few months of life he has all the mental capacities required to direct movies.' The brain, he declared, 'needn't work hard before a film; it can coast along in neutral. And perhaps this absence of effort simply makes one's appreciation that much shallower ... At the movies we decide nothing, our treasured infantile inertia is barely nudged', because the director, actors, lighting designer 'lay before us the pre-digested results'. In fact, film operates at a more primitive level even than dreams, since the latter, he concludes, 'contain ambiguity and mystery'. No wonder directors often 'disinvite' writers from the sets and locations, though not (he diplomatically adds in a bracket) this one.[26]

The language of this essay is hardly likely to have appealed to Reisz, and so tense did his relationship with the director become that he declined to contribute to a book to mark Miller's seventy-fifth birthday, his wife explaining that it would be awkward for him to take part.

Happily for Miller there were always new productions of his plays to look forward to. In July 1989, Michael Blakemore had arrived at Roxbury to discuss a forthcoming production of *After the Fall* at the National Theatre. His chief proposal was that Josette Simon, a black actress, should play the role of

Maggie. The idea at once appealed to Miller. Since Maggie is a singer it made sense for her to be black. It would require no changes to the text. He recalled that when George C. Scott had cast a black actor as Willy Loman's next-door neighbour he had objected because it made no sense, given the social reality of the period in which the work was set. On the other hand, he had seen the same play with an all-black cast and it had worked well. Furthermore, he had authorized productions of *A View from the Bridge* with Asian and black casts. He had come to feel that any ethnic casting was acceptable provided that it served the play. Blakemore's suggestion of a black actress seemed to Miller a way of liberating the play from the association with Marilyn Monroe that had so distorted its reception twenty-five years earlier.

In the New Year of 1990 Miller was back in England (on a trip paid for by an appearance on the *Clive James Show*) for the Young Vic's production of *The Price*, which he liked, but about which he had at first some reservations. For David Thacker, Miller's arrival provided something of a jolt:

> When we did a run-through in front of Arthur he was pretty impressed, but he made it clear within minutes that we were miles away. He did it in the kindest way – by telling the truth. He talked about the dialectical nature of the play: every argument is matched instantly by a counter-argument and then countered again. Each must be given equal weight and force ... For three days we went through the play five minutes at a time. It was like a master-class ... Miller complained of the final section that he couldn't hear the actors, there was no emotional range and they seemed to be doing the play for themselves, adding – the final indignity – 'I don't think anyone would listen to you.' I suppose by the time you reach his age there's no time to waste on bullshit. But he also said some deceptively simple things about acting. For instance, when you make long speeches, you must not assume that no one else is going to speak. Your acting must demand no other response than that they listen.[27]

His response to Thacker's decision to play without an interval was even more direct. 'By the way,' he asked, 'are you going to have an interval? – because I did have a pee before I came in, but by God I want another one.'[28]

For the actors Miller was a source of advice. Thus, when Marjorie Yates wondered if her character, Esther, was suffering from any illness Miller told her that she had an overactive thyroid, not mentioned in the text but the kind of back story that can be helpful for actors. The character, he added, could have been happy living alone – another key to the life of a disappointed woman. David Calder was told that his character had been a radical in the 1930s. As he said, 'There's a smell of it in the text. But it's so clear now. It saves weeks.'[29]

To the actor Alan MacNaughtan Miller said that his character, Gregory Solomon, was 'the kind of guy that if he fell off a ten-story building, he'd land on a marshmallow. He's a fantastic counterpoint because he's the man who discovered the simplest secret: that the secret of life is life itself. That's the truth the other characters have not yet understood.'[30] He could, however, be tart at times. After a successful first preview in which the audience response had been overwhelming, he approached Bob Peck, who was playing Walter, and said, 'Bob, I always knew you could do it and when you do it'll be great.' For Peck the play had a special relevance. Like his character Victor he had a brother who was a policeman who had assumed responsibility for their father while he became successful as an actor.

At a press conference at the Young Vic Miller explained that he liked 'small, unsuccessful theatres' because actors 'become less playful when there's a million dollars riding on them'.[31] In fact the Young Vic was highly successful, if in financial difficulties. Harold Pinter, asked why Miller was so well received in Britain but dismissed in America, replied in characteristic fashion. There was, he said, 'a general tendency ... to regard him as severely radical ... any man who actually shows an intelligent concern for his fellows, for the society in which he lives, even an intelligent *interest* in the society in which he lives, is, in America, *understandably* a communist.'[32]

The *Sunday Independent* critic Irving Wardle, in a significantly entitled article, called Miller the 'American Patron Saint of the English Stage', but Britain was not the only place where his plays were popular at this time. On a trip to Russia he had seen three in a single day: *Incident at Vichy* at noon, *The Price* in mid-afternoon and *After the Fall* in the evening.

In June he returned to England to see the Bristol Old Vic production of *The Man Who Had All the Luck*, directed by Paul Unwin, a joint production with the Young Vic where it now transferred, with Iain Glen in the title role. It was a revelation to its author. Suddenly, the play that had once been so precipitately dismissed had found its style and its moment. It was possible to see Miller's career in the theatre as having started not with the realistic *All My Sons* but with a fable that staged a debate about the extent of human freedom. As with the BBC's production of *The Golden Years*, this served to push back further the start of his career.

He was now once again working with Michael Blakemore on *After the Fall*, scheduled to open at the Olivier auditorium of the National Theatre; *The Crucible*, directed by Howard Davies, had opened in the Cottesloe, also at the National, three weeks earlier.

Working with the designer Hayden Griffin, Blakemore had created a striking set. They had devised it in idle time together in New York when, doodling on a piece of paper in a restaurant, Griffin had inducted Blakemore into the wonders of the Golden Mean (also known as the Golden Ratio), a spiral generated from a series of rectangles with the ratio of 1:1.618, of which the most obvious example is a sea shell. In the original Lincoln Center production Kazan had used different levels, as had the first British production. Miller recalled the set used in Franco Zeffirelli's, which from the auditorium had looked like the inside of a bellows camera. He recalled too a visit he had made to Epidaurus in Greece, where he had been shown a flight of stairs leading up to a cave shaped to resemble a vortex. The final set for the National was modelled on a computer.

After a run-through Miller found himself in tears, not least because this play told a private story about his relationship with his first wife no less than with Marilyn. Josette Simon, who played Maggie, later recalled her own response:

> I knew that this material – not uncommon to other Miller works – encompassed very personal issues for Arthur and I was bringing to life this character – Maggie – and in doing so treading on some deeply sensitive and painful aspects of his life. In America this part had commonly – obviously – been totally associated with Marilyn Monroe and the play [seen as] a supposed dissection of their relationship ... I always believed that the character stood up on its own and that ... Miller had drawn on his personal experience to build this character, but that it did not mean it was a straight exposé of Monroe. If I did not believe that the character was a construction and stood in its own right, then I could not have played it. Indeed, would not have wished to.[33]

Richard Eyre remembered Miller's response to the production:

> We watched a run of *After the Fall*. Michael Blakemore had directed it very well and Josette Simon was electric. I sat next to Arthur trying to avoid a feeling of prurient fascination. It's a very intimate and revealing play, very accurately observed, about the hateful vicious circle of love, disaffection, deceit and painful disentanglement. 'It's just like real life,' I said to Arthur jokingly. 'It sure is,' he said solemnly.[34]

When, on returning to New York, Miller was asked to write a foreword to a book celebrating forty years of Washington's Arena Stage (which, like the National, had produced nine of his plays) he opened by observing that he had just returned from London where three of his plays were being produced, including *The Man Who Had All the Luck*, which he had last seen forty-six years earlier. The reason for stressing this, he said, was because in Britain key companies were subsidized. At the same time it was in this piece that for the first time he publicly contemplated the possibility that American regional theatre, which over the years had grown almost by stealth, in fact constituted the national theatre for which he had always searched. What was missing in America, though, he argued, was not theatres but a sense of theatrical continuity and a certain level of performance and clarity of purpose.

It was a theme he would take up again in an article he wrote two years later for *American Theater* magazine. 'It seems clear, now in 1992,' he wrote, 'that we are at the end of something. Without indulging in overblown praise for theater in the '40s and '50s, I do think that on the whole theater had far greater importance then than it does now.' This was true for writers, who now had difficulty commanding a stage, but it was difficult too for actors. Theatre was no more than a training ground for Hollywood: 'When a young actor who was previously unknown makes an impression in a play and is offered TV or film work, he has gone before he has practically learned all his lines. A director I know ... had a big Off-Broadway (really near Broadway) hit recently in which the cast was replaced three times in a matter of months. The man kept directing the same play for a quarter of a year.' The money offered by theatre was too low, while 'the chances of being blasted out of the water by critics [were] immeasurably higher'. The waste of people was what bothered him – 'that and my own inconvenience, of course, when it is so bloody hard to find mature people for my own plays, old and new ... We don't have an American theater but only the shards of one, some of the broken pieces reflecting light, others covered with the dust where they have fallen ... The vision of a prideful theater, with art rather than cynical greed at its center, is still beyond the horizon.'[35]

Privately he now outlined a possible play to be called *Chaos* about the end of history, prompted in part by the collapse of the Soviet Union and in part by his own sense of decline, a theme underlined by its subtitle, *Memoir of a Broken Writer*. The play was to deal with certain key presumptions, the first of which would be what had once seemed the inevitable victory of socialism. Other headings were 'Women's Lib' and the assumption that it would lead to happier marriages, and 'Atheism' with its presumption that it would mark an end to superstition and blind obedience. Already, though, it was beginning to sound like an out-of-control PhD and he set it aside.

The Soviet Union, however, was not the only political issue on his mind. In November 1990 he was unsure how to respond to the planned US-led response to the Iraqi invasion of Kuwait. Was America about to launch yet another war? He put his name to a petition against such a war. He found Saddam Hussein repellent and as Scud missiles began to land in Israel felt indignant at the assault, and yet he was not clear what war would achieve beyond harming civilians. He started an article entitled 'This War', but never finished it. The war seemed to him to distract from the necessary business of making the larger peace. When it began in the New Year, at the urging of his old friend Joseph Rauh he joined the board of American Peace Now and signed a statement calling for a ceasefire.

In December, Miller was commission by the BBC to travel to South Africa to conduct a television interview with Nelson Mandela who had been released from detention in February. It was his first visit to the country.

On arrival, he was taken to a black township outside Cape Town, though a concrete wall concealed it from view. It was, he thought, an investment in denial: 'I have seen some of the most expensive homes across the road from a garbage dump where people are consigned to live. It's like a play where people are blind to what's around them.'[36] The fear, he felt, was tangible. The papers carried advertisements for razor wire to be used as home protection, while luxury houses had signs announcing 'Instant Armed Response'. He was instructed not to stop for traffic lights in certain areas. Communal violence was claiming lives. However, to a native New Yorker this seemed familiar enough – there had been nearly two thousand murders in New York City the previous year.

Miller's meeting with Mandela took place against a background of black factional fighting around Johannesburg in which seventy-one people had been killed. 'We're looking at this violence as being utterly terrible,' Miller remarked. 'But I think there are a lot of white people who think it's great.' Mandela had slept only two hours the night before their encounter. He had been trying to stop the violence. By the end of the week eight thousand would be homeless.

Mandela's elaborate home was situated in the middle of Soweto, and seemed to Miller designed for defensive purposes. The interview took place before the alienation between Mandela and his wife Winnie became apparent, in the period between her indictment for murder and the revelation of some of the more unsavoury aspects of her behaviour. He spent two and a half hours with Mandela and was impressed especially by his pragmatism. He was not an ideologist. On the other hand, he was up against entrenched forces that, though willing, of necessity, to change, were anxious not to lose touch with power. Employing an image that was familiar from *The Golden Years* and to which he would return in *Broken Glass*, Miller suggested that the situation was 'like a dream paralysis where you're reaching toward something and you simply can't extend your arm'.[37]

'I thought it remarkable,' Miller said in the BBC programme, edited down from a two-and-a-half-hour conversation, 'that he seemed to show no bitterness toward his tormentors. He seemed a man in a hurry to build a new society who had no time for rancour. Nelson Mandela is one of the very few liberated leaders who inspires hope rather than fear. It was this quality that intrigued me enough to wish to meet him and try to learn the roots of his

unique behaviour under such horrible circumstances.' He had wished to talk
to Mandela 'as a man who was formed, as we all are, by his inheritance and
his time ... my interest was in illuminating some of the personal forces that
shaped his character and his views'.[38]

Mandela took him back through his life. His parents, he explained, had
been illiterate, but his father was a chief and to that extent the focus of
attention in his village. He had four wives. The young Mandela was taught
that the aim in life was 'to be rich in cattle and sheep, and you should also be
rich in wives'. It was the English rather than the Afrikaners who had made
education available to Africans. Asked by Miller how he could separate his
views of people from their political position, he ascribed it in part to his
prison experience. 'It is assumed that every warden in a prison was a cruel
man who believed in persecuting black prisoners. As a general rule this was
the case. But amongst them were good men who did everything within the
policy and framework of the prison to make our condition as comfortable as
possible. Some of them would give us newspapers. Some of them are very
good friends ... That experience may have influenced me in that direction.
It is always important to make a distinction between general policy and the
people who carry out that policy because there are very good men among
them.'

To Miller, even given the threatened violence in South Africa, there seemed
genuine hope, though the fact that it depended on a single man underscored
the fragility of that hope, if also the power of the individual to intervene.
After the interview he was taken on safari, where for the first time he saw
lions in the wild. A lion would subsequently feature in *The Ride down Mount
Morgan*, even appearing on the poster.

In June 1991, Miller opened a new play in New York. *The Last Yankee* premiered
at the Off Broadway Ensemble Studio Theater (described by him as practically
a bedroom closet), as part of the Marathon Annual Festival of One-Act Plays.
It ran for fourteen performances. It was the briefest of works, consisting then
only of the first scene of what later became a longer play. He had read it to
an enthusiastic audience on the stage of the town meeting-house of Strafford,
Vermont, the heart of Yankee territory and home of his friend William Sloane
Coffin. Expanded into a two-act version, it was subsequently performed by
the Manhattan Theatre Club at City Center Stage on 5 January 1993, running
for sixty-four performances, and then in England at the Young Vic just over
two weeks later. The American production struck few sparks, whereas the
the British one was a considerable success.

In New York the play was directed by John Tillinger, who had also staged
After the Fall, An Enemy of the People (in the 1980s) and *The Price* in 1992. Born
in Iran and educated in England, Tillinger had originally been a Broadway

actor, appearing in *A Day in the Death of Joe Egg* in 1968 and *The Changing Room* in 1973, before turning director in the 1980s. Coincidentally, he lived in the same small town as Miller, though the two did not meet until the production of *After the Fall*.

Like so many of Miller's plays, *The Last Yankee* took its inspiration from life. The two male characters both had their real counterparts. I was driving with him through his home town once when he pointed at a nearby hill and said, 'The last Yankee lives over there.' When I asked what he would think of the portrait of himself, Miller said, 'Oh, he never goes to the theatre.' Later, word seems to have got through, and Miller met him again: '"I hear you wrote a play about me." I said, "Well, yes, sort of." He said, "Could I see it anywhere?" I said, "Well, no, it's not playing." He was such an interesting guy. He had a daughter who was driven nuts by his wife.' Frick, the other male character, 'was a guy in a hardware store, an unbelievable character. I had never met him. We just said hello, goodbye, when I went in to buy something. He began to talk about everything in a most negative way imaginable. It was just comical. He was angry about everything. It was like out of Molière. No introduction. He was on. He had got someone to listen to him. It turned out he was a very well-to-do businessman. Nothing worked. Everything was wrong. It was falling apart.'[39]

The play is set in a mental hospital where a number of women are being treated for depression, a subject on Miller's mind not least because his near-neighbour William Styron had been suffering from it for some years and he had visited him in such an institution. In 1990 Styron had published a book, *Darkness Visible*, in which he detailed his experience.

For Styron, it had begun in 1985 when he was in Paris. Suddenly overwhelmed by what was clearly clinical depression, he planned his own suicide. In *Darkness Visible* he listed the other writers who had chosen to end their own lives. Like Miller, he had been an enthusiast for Albert Camus, and though he had died in a car crash, given the reputation of Camus as a driver Styron was inclined to see this as a suicide. Styron had been friends with Romain Gary and his ex-wife Jean Seberg, both of whom had killed themselves, as had Abbie Hoffman who, like Styron and Miller, had attended the 1968 Democratic Convention: he had taken the equivalent of 150 phenobarbitals. To these Styron added the poet and critic Randall Jarrell, also dead in a traffic accident, but who he was sure had allowed a car to hit him; and Primo Levi, whose presumed suicide had seemed so paradoxical – a Holocaust survivor who apparently no longer wished to survive.

Styron looked for clues in his own work that might provide evidence of a pre-history to his condition:

[until] the onslaught of my own illness and its denouement, I never gave much thought to my work in terms of its connection with the subconscious ... But after I had returned to health and was able to reflect on the past in the light of my ordeal, I began to see clearly how depression had clung close to the outer edges of my life for many years. Suicide had been a persistent theme in my books – three of my major characters had killed themselves. In rereading, for the first time in years, sequences from my novels – passages where my heroines have lurched down pathways toward doom – I was stunned to perceive how accurately I had created the landscape of depression in the minds of these young women.[40]

Miller might have made a similar observation. *All My Sons, Death of a Salesman, The Crucible* and *A View from the Bridge* all effectively end with the suicide of the central character (John Proctor and Eddie Carbone offer themselves up to death). In the original novel version of *The Man Who Had All the Luck* the protagonist had also killed himself, while Lou in *After the Fall* was a suicide as, effectively, was a principal figure in *Incident at Vichy*, though in the case of the last, as of Proctor, it was closer to martyrdom. For Miller, this partly reflected an aspect of his desire to create modern tragedies, yet the consistency with which he was drawn to this device perhaps suggests something else.

Looking for the roots of his own condition, Styron tracked it to passing a 'hulking milestone of mortality' (he had turned sixty in 1985; Miller was seventy) and to 'a vague dissatisfaction with the way in which my work was going – the onset of inertia which has possessed me time and time again during my writing life, and had made me crabbed and discontented'.[41] He recalled his father's depression and his own inability to mourn his mother's death. Miller too had grown dissatisfied with his work and suffered moments of inertia. He equally acknowledged his inability for some time to mourn the death of his mother. He must have read his friend's book, therefore, with a sense of recognition.

Styron preferred the word 'melancholy' to 'depression', and now identified a different line of descent that included Hawthorne and Dostoevsky. In particular, he found lines in Dante that echoed his own condition:

> In the middle of the journey of our life
> I found myself in a dark wood,
> For I had lost the right path.

It was the last line of that section of the poem, however, that gave the justification of his book and the hope he had to offer:

> And so we came forth, and once again beheld the stars.[42]

Vanessa Redgrave as
Fania Fénelon in *Playing
for Time*, November 1980
(Elbie Lebrecht)

Bill Bolcom, Arnold Weinstein and Arthur
Miller at work in the Chelsea Hotel on
the opera based on *A View from the Bridge*
(Inge Morath/Magnum)

During the British Council Cambridge seminar in 1984 (from left to right): Christopher Bigsby, Malcolm Bradbury and Arthur Miller (Inge Morath/Magnum)

Peter Falk in the 1998 production of *Mr Peters' Connections* at the Signature Theater in New York (Susan Johann)

Arthur Miller takes a bow with Elizabeth Franz and Brian Dennehy on the first night of the fiftieth anniversary production of *Death of a Salesman*, 11 February 1999. (UPI)

1983 Beijing production of *Death of a Salesman*
(Inge Morath/Magnum)

Dustin Hoffman in the 1984 production of
Death of a Salesman at the Broadhurst Theater
(Inge Morath/Magnum)

Liam Neeson with Arthur
Miller on the opening night of
The Crucible at New York City
Virginia Theater, 7 March 2002
(UPI)

Production of *Resurrection Blues*,
Guthrie Theater, Minneapolis,
2002 (Carol Rosegg)

Stage reading of *Elegy for a Lady* with Laila
Robins and Bob Dishy at New York's National
Arts Club, 24 April 2003 (UPI)

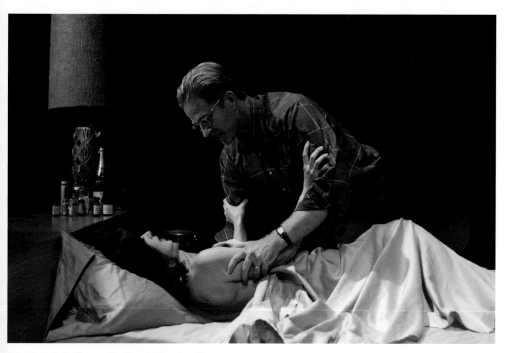

Matthew Modine as Paul and Heather Prete
as Kitty in *Finishing the Picture*, directed
by Robert Falls, at the Goodman Theater,
Chicago, in October 2004.

Arthur Miller and Agnes Barley at the 2004 PEN Literary
Gala (Patrick McMullan)

Arthur Miller on his 80th birthday at a gala
dinner held at the Arthur Miller Centre for
American Studies, the University of East Anglia.
(www.alanhowardphotography.co.uk)

In *Darkness Visible* Styron describes the moment he decided to take action and hospitalize himself. Listening to Brahms's *Alto Rhapsody*, he suddenly 'thought of all the joys the house had known ... the love and work'.[43] He emerged from the hospital because 'if the encouragement is dogged enough – and the support equally committed and passionate – the endangered one can nearly always be saved'.[44] In *The Last Yankee*, whose one-act version had been presented a year after the publication of Styron's book, Miller staged a play set in a mental institution in which, in the two-scene version, one woman, Patricia, if she is saved (and it is not certain) is redeemed by the dogged enthusiasm of her husband, while another finds in music a possible route to recovery.

The first scene takes place in a visiting room of what turns out to be a mental institution. Here we discover Leroy Hamilton, a casually but smartly dressed man in his late forties, who is quickly joined by Mr Frick, sixty, in a business suit and carrying a valise. He is plainly conscious of time and irritated at being kept waiting. It is not without significance that in the speech directions Miller identifies Leroy Hamilton by his first name and Frick by his second – an indication, perhaps, to actors and readers alike, of Miller's sympathies. Plainly, these are not two men who would normally come together outside of their professional roles: Leroy is a carpenter and Frick a supplier. They are here, it emerges, because they share a problem. And given the size of the institution, we take it that depression is something of a national disease.

Leroy's wife Patricia has been institutionalized before – indeed, she has suffered from her condition for many years. For Frick, though, this is something new, hard to reconcile with the comfortable lifestyle he and his wife share. Why, though, do such different men – Leroy none too well off, Frick, rich and vaguely racist ('Awful lot of coloured ... ain't there?'[45]) – come together at a state institution? At first, Leroy suggests that he is unable to afford the private facility eighty miles away, only to confess that his wife's sisters would have been willing to pay. He has resisted because 'I don't think it's a good place for her'. Frick initially suggests that it would cost 'fifty thousand dollars a year, plus tips' to put his wife there, but then claims that it is 'absolutely first class, much better than this place'.[46] He urges Leroy to take up the offer of his sisters-in-law. The 'plus tips' simultaneously suggests his social values and his gaucheness.

Frick is a man of contradictions: having denounced a workman for charging $27 an hour, he then praises Leroy when he reveals that he charges the same. But he is not alone in this. Leroy insists on the need for trust, having just confessed to not trusting a fellow workmate. Trust, indeed, is a central issue. It is what has eroded the connection between people in general, and what has eroded the relationships of these couples in particular.

Leroy is the last Yankee because he has qualities that are out of phase with the world he inhabits. A craftsman, he is independent and modest. He is in charge of his own fate, content with what he has and who he is. As we learn, he recognizes the restless desire of his wife to *become* – an American imperative – but regrets her inability to accept what is on offer, his love and that of her family. Frick condescends to Leroy, who is lacking, it seems to him, in ambition and drive while he himself restlessly moves from business to business, finding little time for the woman whose desperation he has hardly noticed. Leroy has lived with his wife's disappointment, her sense of having failed in some essential task to do with driving relentlessly on, succeeding, triumphing in a race in which he has no interest in competing. He merely persists, until she begins to acknowledge a value in persistence.

Perhaps there is an echo in this play of Miller's relationship with Marilyn, a woman he had married in the hope and expectation of redeeming her, not so much from depression, though she was familiar with that, as from the belief that her value was in some way related to her public success, from her need to win a competition of no real value. When he offered her the possibility of a life in the theatre he was not just shifting the ground of that competition, but suggesting that craft was its own reward, that art offered satisfactions of its own, as Leroy discovers and believes. Beyond that, Miller had hoped Marilyn would value the domestic world for which she said she yearned, just as Patricia in *The Last Yankee* edges towards an understanding that there are satisfactions that transcend the battle for prominence. Her brothers, we learn, surrendered their lives rather than live with the knowledge that they were like other people. The question is whether Patricia can live with that knowledge as Marilyn, in the end, could not.

The second scene expands the story beyond that of the two men. It is set, still, in the institution, in the bedroom Leroy's wife Patricia shares with a woman who lies on her bed, inert, throughout the rest of the play. It begins as Frick's wife Karen enters. She is in a worse state than Patricia, given as she is to non sequiturs, her mind seemingly wandering according to some associational logic. She is intimidated by her husband, acutely aware of his impatience. Patricia, by contrast, seems more secure, if still fragile. She reveals that she has succeeded in coming off the medication she has been taking for fifteen years. She came, she explains, from a golden family. One brother was the All New England Golf Tournament champion; the other came close to winning the pole vault at the Tokyo Olympics. But neither was content. Both men committed suicide. Their achievements fell short of their ambitions. The children of immigrants, they were raised on a dream that could never be realized. Patricia was dazzled by the same dream, and has been unable to live with her failure to achieve it. As a teenager she won a beauty pageant, but now 'I'm a torn-off rag of my old self. The pills took ten years off my face.'[47] Thinking that marriage might gift her what she was losing, she linked her fate to a man whose values were different, a man with no interest in competing with anyone but himself, a craftsman whose satisfaction comes from his work rather than its price. She says, 'We were all brought up expecting to be wonderful, and ... [I] just wasn't.' LeRoy asks, 'Is it ever going to be "wonderful"? Well – no, I guess this is pretty much it; although to me it's already wonderful.'[48] For him, family and the natural world are enough. Patricia has to decide whether it is for her too.

For her part, Karen has struggled to find something for herself in a marriage that seems to serve no one but her husband. In particular, she has learned to tap-dance and now, to Frick's embarrassment, asks him to sing so that she can dance in the bizarre costume she has asked him to bring. He does so and for a moment there is consonance between the two of them; even when the moment is broken it is clear that there is a connection, no matter how tenuous. He has built a special place for her to practise in the family home, and brings himself to perform with her when all his instincts would resist it. When Frick has left, Leroy, who has learned to play the banjo, accompanies Karen. The play ends as Patricia and Leroy leave, though whether Patricia will return to the institution is unclear. Karen stays behind, but even she seems to have established a contact with her husband that had seemed impossible before. Left where she was at the start of the second scene is the third woman, inert on her bed, apparently unredeemable. Which aspect of the play dominates depends on when the lights are lowered. Audiences want to applaud when Patricia and Leroy leave, seemingly reconciled, and on some nights at the Young Vic the lights would be lowered at this moment. On other nights, the lights would be left up and the audience discomfited as they watched the woman left behind, immobile.

In the American production, Miller agreed to omit the figure of the near-catatonic woman, which inevitably eliminated a key aspect of the play. For Tillinger, though, blame for the play's failure lay with the audience. 'What happened with *The Last Yankee* was that we were playing to a particularly stupid subscription audience – I called it a prescription audience because they were so old and out of it.'[49]

In the introduction with which he prefaced the play Miller addressed the question of realism, not least because of his irritation at being either praised or dismissed for what was seen as his success or otherwise in capturing the particular language of characters rooted in their environment. He noted the changing meaning ascribed to realism and traced his own commitment to a language that did something more than efficiently replicate everyday speech. What he was after in *The Last Yankee*, he explained, was

> to make real my sense of the life of such people, the kind of man swinging the hammer through a lifetime, the kind of woman waiting for her ship to

come in. And secondly, my view of their present confusion and, if you will, decay and possible recovery. They are bedrock, aspiring not to greatness but to other gratifications – a successful parenthood, decent children and a decent house and a decent car and an occasional nice evening with family or friends, and above all, of course, some financial security.[50]

That, he declared, was its subject matter. And what he was concerned to do was to work by indirection. The play was 'intended to be both close-up and wide, psychological and social, subjective and objective, but manifestly so. To be sure,' he conceded, 'there is a realistic tone' to the exchanges, 'people do indeed seem to talk this way, but an inch below is the thematic selectivity which drives the whole tale'. This had 'informed all the plays I have written. I have tried to make things seen in their social context and simultaneously felt as intimate testimony.'[51]

The language of *The Last Yankee* had, he thought, a surface realism, but its action was 'overtly stylized'. The ending was governed by a repression that was characteristic of his New England characters and which expressed his sense that the play's hope could only be tentative. The characters are 'the prey of the culture', subject to the imperatives of a competitive world that leaves them with a feeling of inadequacy, their private lives invaded not so much by social values as by social presumptions. There is a deliberately ritualistic rhythm to the insertion into conversations of references to money, success, wealth, poverty, the incantation of a culture. If *The Last Yankee* was to be seen as realism, 'it is of this kind, resulting from an intense selectivity which in turn is derived from the way these people live and feel'.

There is a counter-current to the tentative optimism that Miller stresses in his introduction, in which, significantly, he embraces Samuel Beckett, whom he had once rejected as expressing a dangerous absurdity. Now, he explains, 'I take it that in later years Beckett took pains to clarify this impression of human futility, emphasizing the struggle *against* inertia as his theme. In any case, however ridiculous so much of his dialogue exchanges are, the tenderness of feeling in his work is emphatically not that of the cynic or the mere ironist.'[52] The dominating theme of *Godot*, he observed, was 'stasis and the struggle to overcome humanity's endlessly repetitious paralysis before the need to act and change'.[53] He might just as well have been describing the theme of a number of his own plays, and indeed of *The Last Yankee*, in which the woman who remains on stage represents precisely the stasis against which Patricia and Karen, neither of whom felt able to leave their homes, rebel.

When the 1991 one-act version was staged at the Off Broadway 52nd Street Ensemble Studio Theater Mel Gussow greeted it as an unpretentious and observant new play. When the expanded version was presented two years later, Miller drafted an indignant letter to the *New York Times* protesting that it was not to be reviewed by the first-string reviewer, Frank Rich. That he should allow himself to appear to be begging for, or demanding, attention reveals his feeling of marginalization, though it is not clear that the letter was sent. When the review was published it was written not by Rich but Mel Gussow, who described the play as 'thinly written', one in which the actors were 'obliged to provide compensation'.[54] When it opened at the Young Vic in England the following week, Irving Wardle of the *Independent* called it '[Miller's] best play for a decade', finding the opening 'masterly'. The emotional logic he found 'devastating', confessing that he had been 'moved to tears'.[55] The *Times* reviewer noted that Miller was more honoured 'on this side of the pond' than on his own. As Miller commented, 'That play had a tremendous effect in England where it was marvellously produced. In fact ... it sold more tickets at the Young Vic than any play they had ever produced, and it ran eight months in the West End.'[56]

The part of Patricia was played by Zoë Wanamaker (later replaced by Margot Leicester, Thacker's wife), that of Leroy by Peter Davison and Karen by Helen Burns, who won two awards, including an Olivier for Best Supporting Actress. Wanamaker had earlier appeared in a production of *The Crucible*, which provoked a discussion with her father Sam Wanamaker, who had effectively been driven out of America by McCarthyism. He had appeared in Miller's early one-act play, *That They May Win*, which had proved popular with the radical theatre group Stage for Action back in the early 1940s, performing in factories and on shopfloors. He had refused to open a Washington production of *Joan of Lorraine*, starring Ingrid Bergman, until the theatre had been desegregated, and he was one of the Hollywood Ten who protested against the blacklist. Once in England, the family stayed, the American Embassy refusing to renew his passport when it ran out.

Asked at a press conference why it was women who were confined in the hospital, Miller replied that statistics showed that women were especially vulnerable, though it is hard not to notice that this figure of the mentally unstable woman had recurred in his work since his encounter with Marilyn Monroe. She makes her first appearance in *The Crucible* in the figure of Abigail, driven to destroy others and ultimately herself. She recurs in *After the Fall*, while even in *The Price* one of the women holds her world together only with the help of alcohol. In *Some Kind of Love Story*, *Broken Glass* and *Finishing the Picture* Miller offers portraits of a woman under stress. In a conversation with Robert Simonson of *Theatre Arts* magazine in 1993, Miller explained the wider context of *The Last Yankee*: 'Depression has become the major disease of a technological society. I think it has very much to do with raising expectations which can't possibly be fulfilled. But the main thing is that I think there are expectations of some kind of glory ... people have been sold on some kind of symphonic grandeur ... part of the ethos now ... is the idea that we all have infinite possibilities.' As far as Patricia is concerned, 'I think the play is about her accepting some of the realities she's been denying all along'.[57]

In 1991, on the back of so many successful productions in England and only four months after the opening of *After the Fall* (which, like *The Crucible*, was still running), Miller decided to open his new two-act play *The Ride down Mount Morgan* in London and not in New York (despite the successful Broadway production of *The Crucible*, with Martin Sheen and Michael York). He initially offered it to the National, but that theatre would not have been able to stage it for seven months. He chose, therefore, to open in the West End.

Miller had been writing the play for some years, wrestling with the central character, trying to establish some connection between the private drama that fascinated him and the wider sociopolitical context. It had begun as a portrait of Elia Kazan, even down to his appearance before HUAC (in the final version he has turned a business partner in for criminality rather than go to prison himself, an echo of *All My Sons*). Miller had been fascinated by Kazan's shift from social commitment to self-concern, as by his desire to live a double life: not, like the play's protagonist, Lyman Felt, in a bigamous marriage, but via a succession of relationships conducted while married to Molly. But Miller wanted to press beyond that. For him, Kazan − sexually voracious, manipulative, but with liberal principles − came to represent forces that he saw more widely in America as the self became a primary concern. There were, though, he recognized, aspects of himself in a man who had traded in one wife for another and had affairs.

After several days of rehearsals, problems seemed to be emerging: the principal one lay in the casting of the central character. The role of Lyman Felt requires someone who can walk a fine line between comedy and seriousness. Tom Conti, whom Miller had seen only in *Shirley Valentine*, had a reputation for playing light comedy. *The Ride dawn Mount Morgan* required something more than charm, and charm was what Conti seemed to have come to specialize in, though he had won a Tony twelve years earlier for his performance in *Whose Life Is It Anyway?*. As the premiere approached, so tensions rose, and there was talk of Conti stepping aside and of delaying the opening. Gemma Jones and Clare Higgins, who played Lyman's two wives, by contrast, seemed to have found the right tone quickly enough, in a play in which the level of reality of each scene is problematic.

The opening was deferred, but Conti stayed with the production. It received appreciative rather than outstanding reviews and ran for sixteen weeks. Later, when Miller met Conti in a New York bar, the actor apologized for never quite getting to grips with the part. Roy Hattersley, former deputy leader of the British Labour Party, recalled Conti telling him that he 'felt too young and too small for the part and found difficulty in making a hero out of a character who "whines and whinges his way through the first act". The play was obviously going wrong in rehearsals but he dared not say so.'[58]

For those who persisted in thinking of Miller as a realist, *The Ride down Mount Morgan* was something of a surprise. It begins with Lyman Felt, who has made his money in insurance and once proposed a policy to insure against bigamy ('great, especially for minority women'),[59] lying in a hospital bed. His head and body are covered with bandages, one leg is raised in a cast and one arm is at an odd angle. He wakes for a moment, speaks inconsequentially, then slips back into sleep before waking once more. His father enters wearing a panama hat, smoking a cigarette and carrying a cane. He drags a black cloth behind him, a hint of death. Close kin to Uncle Ben in *Death of a Salesman*, he offers advice to someone who is plainly Lyman as a young boy; time is layered here as in that earlier play, musical chords underscoring shifts of time and place. Lyman's problem, it quickly transpires, is that his two wives, to one of whom he is bigamously married, have rushed to see him on news that he had crashed while driving down an icy mountainside.

Hearing of their arrival, he slips out of his cast, the beds move away and the furniture of the hospital waiting-room is trucked on. Invisible, he listens as his first wife Theodora and his daughter Bessie talk anxiously. As he watches, he comments on them. It is a play, then, in which we see the characters in part through Lyman's eyes, while Lyman himself is prone to fantasize. He becomes the playwright. He was once, apparently, a writer, like Miller 'struggling to ... make something of my own that would last'.[60] Nobody, he insists, 'lusts after the immortal like a writer'.[61] 'Now what would they say next?'[62] he asks himself, seemingly precipitating the dialogue that follows. When his second wife enters he calls out, 'It can't happen! It mustn't!'[63] But it is never clear that this confrontation may not be precisely what he wished to precipitate, that he stages it in more ways than one.

Theodora is turning fifty, assured, not unduly upset. She has, Lyman tells us, an 'unadmitted greed for wealth'.[64] A one-time radical, she is now a super-patriot. Leah, twenty-four years younger than Lyman, is thirty with blond hair. She is Jewish, and as the play unfolds it becomes apparent that not only are the two women profoundly different from one another but that Lyman himself is a different man with each wife. With Leah, he flies his own planes; with Theo, he is afraid of flying. With Leah, he drives a sports car; with Theo, he is a nervous driver. It was his marriage to Leah that stilled his fear and liberated him. He plainly always contained both men. Where others would choose one path, he believed he could take both, revelling in the danger of doing so. Indeed, there comes a moment when he and Leah look through a window at Theo. He makes love to both women, one after the other, only blocks away from each other. He takes pleasure in his power, even as he convinces himself that he is making both women happy.

And in case this premise seems unbelievable, in 2009 it was revealed that a city tycoon in Britain maintained two households within blocks of one another, his mistress bearing him a child. He took both women, separately, on holiday to the same resort. The truth emerged only when he contested the amount of a divorce settlement. He had, he told a reporter, been 'an extremely good and caring husband. As far as I'm concerned, I have done nothing wrong. You get married men who have children with mistresses and pretend they never happened. That's disgraceful. I might be an old-fashioned male chauvinist but I believe men should look after all their children and the women they are involved with in a traditional way.'[65]

The play moves back and forward in time. At one moment Leah is talking to her lawyer Tom, a man himself in love with Theo; at the next, Lyman and Leah are in Reno nine years earlier, ostensibly for his divorce and their marriage. He is marrying her, he explains, because he can no longer 'go on faking emotions'.[66] Nor is he – though he is faking everything else, and this is his memory restaged at a moment of betrayal. We see him confess to Tom that he has considered divorce because he cannot face the idea of deception, that he wants 'to wear my own face on my face every day till I die', even as he is planning a bigamous marriage. A man who has established a major company and employed what he calls 'ghetto blacks', he evidently feels that by staying married to both women he is doing each a favour. He deploys, in other words, the language of liberal concern to cover his emotional rapacity. Aware that 'if you try to live according to your real desires, you have to end up looking like a shit', he believes he has found a way, and a language, to achieve his desires while convincing himself that everybody has what they want. 'Believe in your feelings,'[67] he says to Leah, a mantra of the 1980s – as is Leah's observation that 'he *wants* so much'.[68] Miller reminds us that the play is set in the Reagan years.

When Theo finally confronts Lyman, and Leah follows her in, he again steps out of the bed, leaving the bandaged figure behind. The light changes to 'an ethereal colourlessness . . . air devoid of pigment',[69] and he instructs the women to lie down. They instantly 'de-animate' and he directs their actions and, evidently, their words. A second later and he is on a park bench with Leah, then back in the hospital, the other characters slowly leaving the room before beginning to replay the scene.

In the second act Theo remembers a moment when Lyman stopped her from diving into the sea where a shark was circling, except that in memory she is no longer sure that his warning shout was anything more than a whisper. The scene is replayed three times as she tries out different scenarios. Likewise we now enter Lyman's dream as he summons up the two women, who appear on either side of him. They wear kitchen aprons and compete with one another in offering him culinary satisfaction. At this point, Lyman's father reappears and tries to smother him with the black cloth, expressive of the death he fears but with which he flirts.

Contemplating the lesson he believes he has learned, Lyman explains, in terms familiar from Miller's *The Creation of the World and Other Business*, 'A man can be faithful to himself or to other people – but not to both ... the first law of life is betrayal; why else did those other rabbis pick Cain and Abel to open the Bible? ... I can't worship self-denial ... it's just not true for me. We're all ego plus an occasional prayer.'[70] Marriage, he claims, is a product of nothing more than chance compounded with familiarity, while it is in the nature of men to contain contradictory needs: 'We're all the same,' he says. 'A man is a fourteen-room house – in the bedroom he's asleep with his intelligent wife, in the living room he's rolling around with some bare-ass girl, in the library he's paying his taxes, in the yard he's raising tomatoes, and in the cellar he's making a bomb to blow it all up'[71] He becomes an expression of his desires: 'What I wish I do.'[72] There is a truth in Leah's accusation, 'You are simply a craving.'[73]

There comes a moment, now reprised, in which Lyman restages the memory of a safari in Africa, during which he had faced down a lion – like Bellow's Henderson the Rain King believing that he is in touch with reality. In discussing the art of acting, Ian McKellen once remarked that while actors pretend to be someone they are not, 'lions don't, you know, a lion is a lion ... Human beings are for ever changing. Very good at lying, human beings.'[74] Lyman sees his duplicity as a form of truth, believing not only that he can have everything he wants but also that in doing so he will be making a gift to both of the women he embraces, who are the happier for their ignorance. This is the moment he loses his guilt.

But behind the bigamous marriage is a fundamental fear to which the marriages, the wild deceits, the restless energy are a response. The years are passing. Death, as symbolized by his father and the black cloth that threatens to smother him, provokes the kind of stasis Lyman feels impelled to resist: 'I could never stand still for death! Which you've got to do, by a certain age, or be ridiculous – you've got to stand there nobly and serene ... and let death run his tape about your arms and around your belly and up your crotch until he's got you fitted for that last black suit. And I can't, I won't ... So I am left wrestling with this anachronistic energy which ... God has charged me with and I will use it until the day the dirt is shovelled into my mouth. Life! Life! Fuck death and dying!'[75]

His plunge down the mountainside, on a road whose danger was known to him, was a case of 'dancing the high wire on the edge of the world ... finally risking everything to find myself'.[76] The word 'truth' comes easily to his lips, especially when he is betraying. Speaking of his son, he remarks, 'If I can teach him anything now it's to have the guts to be true to himself. That's all that matters.' When Leah asks, 'Even if he has to betray the whole world to do it?' this man who has thrived on deception, even deceiving himself into believing that others benefit from his lies, replies, 'Only the truth is sacred . . . To hold nothing back.'[77] What he denies is the power his deceptions have given him.

The play ends as everybody leaves except Lyman's black nurse, who earlier told him a story of her own family whose pleasure was to go ice fishing, when they would have inconsequential conversations as if they had all the time in the world, unobsessed by death, and showing no anxiety about the future. Lyman's own solution had been to chase life, to accrete power, to make himself the focus of other people's needs as also to satisfy his own. Now, in contemplating the nurse and her family, all he can feel is 'What a miracle everything is! Absolutely everything.' With a 'painful wonder and lingering in his face, his eyes wide, alive',[78] he begins to weep.

Just a week before the play's opening, on the eve of his birthday, Miller gave an account of the play to an audience at the University of East Anglia:

> Mount Morgan is a nonexistent mountain, or rather it exists in my mind, down which the main character drives in a heavy blizzard, in New York State, and crashes his car, ending up in a hospital. In effect, he falls into his life. He is married to two women at the same time, one unknown to the other. The point of the exercise is to investigate some of the qualities and meanings of truthfulness and deception. He is a man of high integrity but no values. He is a very typical figure in our world. He was probably always there but is especially evident now. It's a fluid play which moves in and out of his memory, a bit like *Death of a Salesman*. It's very idiotic, almost farcical at times, but it is riding over a tragic tide. It's an attempt to investigate the immensity of contradictions in the human animal and it also looks at man's limitless capacity for self-deception. He's terrible, but he works himself up from nothing to run a very socially responsible company. He has a lot of terrific qualities. He also has an immense appetite for life, for women. He's a Faustian character. Like our civilization he is capable of enormous construction and destruction. The play does not condemn him. It simply leaves him to one side of himself, trying to find himself.

Asked to elucidate his comment on Lyman, he added:

> Lyman is intent on expressing himself, on not suppressing his instinctual life, on living fully in every way possible. That is his integrity. He will confront the worst about himself and proceed from there. But the question is, what about other people? As he says, man can be faithful to himself or to other

people but not to both. And this is the dilemma of the play. The question of values would intercede in the normal course, but he manages to convince himself and, I suspect, some of the audience that there is a higher value, and that is the psychic survival of the individual. The play has no solution.

The play would undergo a number of revisions before it appeared on Broadway, seven years after its British premiere. In particular, the figure of the father would be removed. The last moments would also be changed. Whereas the original text ends with Lyman weeping, the 1998 version has him check his tears and insist that he has found himself at last, instructing himself to cheer up.

When rehearsals were well under way Miller retreated to Roxbury, but it was not long before he began receiving reports from England of dissension among the cast. One actress threatened to sue when she damaged her foot. Conti was indicating that he wanted to leave the production. There was a downturn in theatre bookings. Miller was not happy with the production or, indeed, completely with the play. Although at sixteen weeks it had run longer than it would have done at the National, and it compared more than favourably with anything he had achieved in America since *The Price*, it was not an entirely happy experience.

Four years later, Miller pointed out that the play had had successful productions in Germany and France but still, at that time, no American interest. It had been rejected both by the Manhattan Theatre Club and by a regional theatre – the Seattle Rep. He thought it might be a case of political correctness: the women in the play, he suspected, would be seen as too much the playthings of the male protagonist. They should both, by current standards, have instantly rejected him. 'One day,' he observed, 'somebody is going to do a production of it, and they will wonder why it was thought objectionable. However, life is long, but art is longer, and it will come around.'[79]

Towards the end of 1992, a year in which he had been presented with the National Arts Club Medal of Honor for literature, he finally published *Homely Girl*, a short story earlier rejected by the *New Yorker*, that he had now expanded into a novella. It was a story that took him back to the Depression, to the political loyalties of that time, and on to the disillusionment that followed. Prompted, perhaps, by a long-lasting recession – the Dow Jones had fallen 22.6 per cent in 1987 and the economic downturn lasted, on and off, until 1992, when the US unemployment rate reached a level that would not be seen again until 2009 – it recalled the austerity of that period. In many ways in *Homely Girl* he is revisiting his own past, a past he had shared with his first wife Mary; he also sums up his attitude to his own early commitments, invalidated to some extent by time but not to be denied. It is a story that has echoes of *The Man Who Had All the Luck* and of the forthcoming play *Broken Glass*, in that its central figure has to work her way towards an understanding of the fact that she is responsible for her own life and that finding meaning cannot be a project endlessly deferred.

Janice Sessions (the family's Jewish name was amended by Irish immigration inspectors, who found the original Russian unpronounceable) marries Sam Fink. She, like Miller, comes from an initially wealthy family at a time when 'to have been born to money was shameful, a guarantee of futility'. People her age, 'early twenties then, wanted to signify by doing good, attended emergency meetings a couple of times a week in downtown lofts ... to raise money for organizing the new National Maritime Union or ambulances for the Spanish Republicans'. Like Miller and Mary, Janice and Sam are drawn together as much by their politics as anything. She is plain, and the passion in their marriage is not sexual: they are united by their hatred of fascism.

The story goes back to the anti-Semitic New York world of the 1930s, when Upper East Side rallies baited Jews, and Janice, 'not particularly Semitic-looking ... feared the fear of the prey as she passed thick-necked men on 86th Street'.[80] The Depression itself, she sees with hindsight, had generated a sense of spiritual paralysis – 'Everybody kept waiting for it to lift and forgot how to live in the meantime.' She herself had waited 'to become someone else'. Sam, a committed communist, offers her this other identity and a means of purging her guilt. He 'brought her closer to the future and away from her nemesis, triviality, the bourgeois obsession with things'. Together, they have an impregnable sense of their own destiny, linked as it is to a vision of history that makes them its agents.

Art, to which she had been drawn for aesthetic reasons, must now be viewed only for its utility, its expression of class-consciousness. She marries Sam, as she imagines others marry, 'not out of overwhelming love but to find justification in one another'.[81] Their shared moral cause sanctifies their union. The cause of a distant Yugoslavia seems as relevant as her private life. When the Nazi–Soviet Pact challenges their position they subsist on denial, precisely as Miller and Mary had done, and when Germany invades the Soviet Union they feel the same sense of relief that they can become true Americans again.

The war, though, breaks their own pact. He goes to fight and she remains, discovering her sexuality (her relationship with Sam had never been satisfactory). When he returns she divorces him; his story of raping a German woman, which he somewhat implausibly narrates, providing the catalyst. Her life changes when she meets Charles, a blind man unaware of her homely looks, and finds fulfilment at last. In an echo of Miller's attitude towards his own early commitments he teaches her to be unashamed. 'You seem,' he says to her, 'to have a need to mock yourself as you were then. I don't think you should. A lot of the past is always embarrassing – if you have any sensitivity ... in some part of his beliefs every person is naive ... And memories of one's naivety are always painful. But so what? Would you rather have had no beliefs at all?'[82] Later, he says, 'Once you accept that you have chosen to be as you are ... then regret is not possible.' Janice's problem was that she did not feel that she had 'ever really made a choice in life'. Now she has come to reading the existentialists and admires the way Europeans 'liked talking about submerged connecting themes rather than mere disjointed events'.[83]

Homely Girl was initially published in a two-volume limited edition with drawings and photocollages by eighty-one-year-old Louise Bourgeois (who had come to the United States from France at the age of twenty-seven), and with a photograph of the author and the artist by Inge. Later, Miller himself would appear in a film version of the novella under the title *Eden*, directed by the Israeli director Amos Gitai. This transposed the story to Palestine in 1939. It is a confused and confusing film with little narrative coherence and only a tenuous connection with the story that inspired it. The characters are given to reading lengthy quotations from books. Long tracking shots slow the action for no apparent reason. Its primary interest lies in Miller's appearance as an actor, in scenes filmed in his barn at Roxbury. In one he says goodbye to his venal son, off to Palestine in search of profit. In another scene he is dying, his face gaunt and still.

Death, as it happens, was on Miller's mind. In November 1991, the musician Alex North had died. From a poor background, he had studied in Moscow from 1932 to 1935 and then composed for the Federal Theatre that had briefly employed Miller. North's music for *Death of a Salesman* remained Miller's favourite – he received an Academy Award nomination for the film version – and he went on to compose the music for many Hollywood films, including *A Streetcar Named Desire* – a saxophone solo proving sensual enough for the Legion of Decency to demand its removal as too 'carnal'. North also wrote the music for *The Misfits*. To the public, he was best known as the composer of the popular 'Unchained Melody', but he had fifteen Oscar nominations. Famously, his music for *2001: A Space Odyssey* was removed at the last moment. Like Miller, he had been shocked by Kazan's naming names, and refused to speak to him. He remained a radical, which was why, he once said, he so liked *Spartacus*, for which he had also composed the music.

Six months later another friend died, a man whom Miller had admired almost beyond any other, who had been important to him personally but who also represented Miller's own social and political point of view. Miller went to see him shortly before his death. When the following year a handwritten letter was sent to President Clinton proposing the posthumous award of the Congressional Medal of Freedom to Joseph L. Rauh Jr, one of the signatures was that of Arthur Miller.

To some extent they shared a background. Rauh, four years older than Miller, was the son of a Jewish immigrant father (in his case, from Germany) who had been in the garment industry. The family, like Mary Miller's, lived in Ohio. The father was conservative, the sons radical. But whereas the Millers lost their money during the Depression, the Rauhs held on to theirs, and Joseph was sent to Harvard, majoring in economics before entering the Harvard Law School from which he graduated first in his class. From there he went to Washington where he served as a law clerk to Justice Benjamin N. Cardozo, then in the same capacity to his old Harvard law professor, the liberal Felix Frankfurter, becoming one of Frankfurter's 'happy hot dogs'. Rauh had experienced the same anxieties as Miller as the Second World War approached: 'You have to realize that there was a lot of anti-Semitism in those days – Pelley's Silver Shirts, and Father Coughlin's Social Justice move-ment . . . Anti-Semitism resulted in part because many thought the Jews were trying to get us into the war. I plead guilty. I felt that Hitler was going to try to conquer the world, and the sooner we prepared for war and got into it, the safer this country would be.' Miller initially felt differently about the European war, but registered the same hostility towards himself as a Jew as well as the unwillingness of Jews to be seen above the parapet – hence the rejection by Jewish producers of his first Broadway play as 'too Jewish'. In Rauh's view, resistance to the war came largely from big business, which was unwilling to have its commerce interrupted. Once war came, Rauh signed up, as Miller had tried to do. 'I felt once war was declared – especially being Jewish – that I couldn't not go into the military.'

Where Miller would have been at odds with him was over his attack on the communist Left. The war over, on 4 January 1947 Rauh was one of the founders of Americans for Democratic Action (ADA), set up in opposition to the Progressive Citizens of America (PCA). As Rauh put it in an interview for the Harry S. Truman Library and Museum, he and others were concerned 'to separate the Commies from the liberals, and the anti-Wallace feeling on our side, from the anti-liberal feeling on the Wallace side'. There was no question but that in the PCA, of which, his FBI file noted, Miller was a sponsor, 'the Communists had control. Indeed, Wallace wrote a piece in 1950 flatly stating that he had not realized that the Communists had control of the group then. That was a real watershed in American liberalism.'

Miller had been a supporter of the progressive Henry Wallace. He and Rauh, though, had been at one in attacking the Smith Act, which had effectively outlawed membership of the Communist Party; but the ADA, in Rauh's words, 'was against disloyal people being in high positions even while believing that the accused should be allowed to face his accuser'. Yet Rauh had begun to establish a reputation as a supporter of individual rights. He defended those accused under Truman's loyalty programme. He involved himself in the civil rights movement, and in an echo of the debates that would take place before HUAC (including Miller's own hearings), insisted: 'You may advocate anything you want as long as you're not making clear and present advocacy of violence . . . But by God,' he had added, 'the Communists, they had nothing there. Where the Communists were a danger was on espionage and sabotage. Their goddamn performance over here – they couldn't overthrow your Aunt Tilley. They were wreckers, not doers.'[84] The ADA, in the end, equivocated; they were not willing, as Miller was, to say that the Smith Act should be repealed.

It was during his appearance before HUAC that Miller came to respect Rauh, who guided him through the hearing and the various stages of his appeals. Later, Rauh became the country's leading civil liberties lawyer. In the 1964 Democratic Convention he was an adviser to the Mississippi Freedom Democratic Party in its attempt to be seated at the convention in place of the all-white and racist delegation from Mississippi. Rauh lobbied on behalf of the Civil Rights Act of 1964 and the Voting Rights Act of 1965. Like Miller, he campaigned against the Vietnam War and was a supporter of Eugene McCarthy.

For Miller, Rauh was the epitome of decency, a man who throughout his life stood up for those oppressed by the state, who found themselves singled out because of their politics or race. He was never content, Miller noted, to stand on the sidelines, never considered the impact on his career of taking a public stance. Their differences over the PCA and the ADA were swiftly swept away. The letter to the President that Miller signed, along with twenty-four others including Edward Kennedy, John Kenneth Galbraith, Arthur Schlesinger and Roger Wilkins, spoke of a man who had devoted his life to the fulfilment of the Constitution's promise of equal justice and freedom for all. He was, the letter continued, a man who placed public interest above private gain. It noted his fight against McCarthyism and for union democracy, and his appearance before the Supreme Court on sixteen separate occasions. On 30 November 1993 President Clinton conferred the Medal of Freedom, posthumously, on Joseph L. Rauh Jr.

In late 1993, discussions continued over what was finally to be called *Broken Glass* (though Miller was still toying with other titles: *Gellburg's Time, Gellburg's Year, The Gellburg Time, Gellburg, The Glass Year, Year of Glass, The Glass Time, The Age of Glass, The Glass Age*). In America, attempts were made to sign Kate Nelligan, though Debra Winger, Meryl Streep and Stockard Channing were all considered for the part of Sylvia Gellburg, as Sam Waterston and Harvey Keitel were explored for Dr Hyman. They finally settled on Ron Rifkin to play the part of Phillip Gellburg with Amy Irving as his wife Sylvia and Ron Silver as Hyman.

According to Miller, the title *Broken Glass* was prompted by David Thacker. As he explained to me during rehearsals for the American production, 'I did that at the request of David. He said it's difficult to cast this play if you call it *Gellburg*. Besides, the title ought to spill over into its more general applications. And I thought this would open it up.' Thacker remembered receiving a phone call from Miller after their discussion in which the playwright himself first suggested the title *Breaking Glass*, later calling back to change it to *Broken Glass* when he discovered that there was a British film of that name, directed by Brian Gibson in 1980.

In England, it was agreed that the play would open at the National Theatre. All that remained to be debated was whether its premiere should be there or in New York. Miller's agent preferred the idea of a London premiere, but Robert Whitehead, supported by the director John Tillinger, was afraid that any poor reviews there would prejudice an American opening. The National had already agreed to bring the production forward from August. In the end it opened at the Long Wharf in March 1994, moving to Broadway in May, three months before its British premiere. The two productions provide a virtual case history of the perception of Miller in the two countries.

The Long Wharf is a producing theatre, with its own audience, but in this instance was effectively being used as a try-out venue, something strenuously denied when the *New York Times* ran an article on '"Broken Glass", the New Haven Tryout That Isn't.[85] Why, it asked, was Robert Whitehead the producer if the production was a Long Wharf show? The fact was, of course, that virtually nobody could open a play on Broadway. The old try-out venues that Miller had known – and *All My Sons* had previewed in more than one city – had largely gone. In fact, the Long Wharf, under Arvin Brown, had produced a number of Miller plays, but always, at least in Miller's mind, with the possibility of a Broadway transfer in mind. The *New York Times* noted that it was now twenty-two years since Miller had had a play on Broadway, its reviewer clearly forgetting *The American Clock*, though even this had opened all of fourteen years earlier.

Broken Glass is set in the last days of November 1938, in the immediate aftermath of Kristallnacht. The coordinated attack on Jews and their property that had taken place on the night of 9 November was presented as retaliation for the murder of Ernst vom Rath, a German official serving in the Paris Embassy. He was shot by Herschel Grynszpan, a seventeen-year-old whose parents were among the ten thousand Polish Jews who had moved to Germany and then been forcibly expelled. Grynszpan's target had been the Ambassador, but it was the Third Secretary who was sent out to see him and was shot. Arrested, Grynszpan said, 'Being a Jew is not a crime. I am not a dog. I have a right to live and the Jewish people have a right to exist on this earth. Wherever I have been I have been chased like an animal.'[86] He was still in prison when the Germans marched into Paris in June 1940. He was transferred to Sachsenhausen concentration camp. His fate is unknown, though a journalist subsequently reported that he had survived and changed his name.

In 1938 Grynszpan's action was used as a pretext for an assault on Jews. In a single night 1,350 synagogues were burned and over seven thousand Jewish businesses looted or destroyed. Kristallnacht derived its name from the smashing of plate-glass windows. It reportedly took Belgium's total plate-glass production to replace the breakages, while the Jews were charged a million Deutschmarks to pay for the damage. In addition, the government fined them $400,000,000, a fifth of their total wealth. It banned them from business, schools, cinemas and theatres ('sitting beside a Jew is a degradation of German art').[87] Of the seven hundred thousand Jews then living in Germany, thirty thousand were reported jailed. The issue of *Life* magazine that described these events also reported in its 'Newsfronts of the World' column that Queen Elizabeth of England had recently worn a hat with two birds on it and that an Anglo-Italian Treaty had been signed granting Britain's recognition of Italy's conquest of Ethiopia in return for British rights to Ethiopia's Lake Tana.

Broken Glass, on which Miller had been working for several years, opens with cello music specially written by William Bolcom. The action begins in a doctor's surgery as Phillip Gellburg, the Jewish head of the decidedly gentile Mortgage Department of Brooklyn Guarantee and Trust (the only Jew ever to work for the company), awaits the arrival of Dr Harry Hyman to discuss the sudden and baffling paralysis suffered by his wife Sylvia. Dressed in black except for a white shirt, Gellburg is described as an 'intense man in his late forties'. Hyman's 'lusty, energetic' wife Margaret, who in contrast to Gellburg has a powerful sense of humour, joins him. Like Patricia in *The Last Yankee*, she regrets her husband's lack of ambition and his social conscience, but has learned to live with it, as with his occasional infidelities.

She begins by confusing Gellburg's name. 'It's Gellburg, not Goldberg,' he insists. 'It's the only one in the phone book ... We're from Finland originally.'[88] Denial, it seems, lies at the heart of his character, just as, it transpires, it lies at the heart not only of the other characters but of a world in which German aggression provokes paralysis. Minutes later, Gellburg confesses that his parents in fact came from Poland or Russia. Perhaps there is a reference here to the 1930s family drama *The Rise of the Goldbergs*, written by Gertrude Berg, a popular radio and then television show which began life in 1929 when Miller was fourteen and ran until 1954. The scripts concerned an immigrant Jewish family's assimilation into American life. The parents speak with a heavy Yiddish accent while the children use standard American. One episode, on 3 April 1939, dealt with Kristallnacht.

Hyman is handsome and, a stage note tell us, a 'scientific idealist', an idealism implicit in his refusal to set up his practice in a wealthier area.[89] Asked by the cast why he would be dealing with what seems a psychological illness, Miller replied:

> In those days doctors, MDs, confronted psychological problems all the time. It was an age when you never thought of going to a mental doctor unless you were climbing up the wall. People had what we now think of as psychological problems but a GP in those days took on everything. I went to a doctor once. My back was killing me. I was about to leave on my first trip to Europe, on a ship. It was 1947. I couldn't move. I said, 'I can't straighten up.' 'Well, lie down,' he said, 'how about novocaine?' I said, 'What?' He said, 'You know, like a dentist uses. Let's try that.' Well, he shot me with novocaine and it cured the whole thing. I said, 'Did you ever do this before?' He said, 'No, but I've thought about it.' Doctors did everything.[90]

It is Dr Hyman who introduces the political context of the play. The Jewish stores, he says, have been smashed in Berlin. Old men have been forced to scrub the sidewalks with toothbrushes. Gellburg purports not to have been following the news while acknowledging that his wife Sylvia's sudden paralysis (she had lost the use of her legs nine days earlier) may have been connected with her distress at such events. Gellburg's response veers between a studied indifference – 'What can be done about such things? – and a desire to justify such actions: 'It's no excuse for what's happening over there, but German Jews can be pretty ... pushy.' The German Jews he mentions, however, are not in Berlin but New York: 'The German Jews won't take an ordinary good job ... And they can't even speak English.'[91] He seems oblivious to the fact that he is making a distinction that might seem to justify the treatment of Jews in Germany, desperate as he is to distance himself from his own Jewish identity. His subsequent attack on Roosevelt aligns him with the businessmen he serves, even as he regrets the publication of material from Germany that can only 'put some fancy new ideas into those anti-Semites walking around New York'.[92]

Gellburg oscillates between pride that his son Jerome is doing well in the Army, that he himself is the first Jew to be employed by a gentile company (as Miller had been, when he worked in the automobile parts warehouse to earn money for his university degree), the first Jew to set foot on his employer's luxury yacht – and his desire to deny his Jewishness. He sent his son into the Army because he 'wanted people to see a Jew doesn't have to be a lawyer or a doctor or a businessman'.[93] But at the same time, Sylvia observes, he 'never even wants to talk about being Jewish'.[94] He 'sounds sometimes like he doesn't like Jews'.[95] Meanwhile, he accepts the casual anti-Semitism of his employer who speaks of Jews as 'you people'. The humiliations of daily life, which he is seemingly powerless to address, are part of what unmans him.

In his own home, Gellburg has become something of a petty tyrant, prone to sudden acts of violence less because he wishes to exert his authority than because he fears he lacks precisely that. He subsists on denial, as, until now, has Sylvia, who has given up her own ambitions and simply acquiesced in her own irrelevance: 'I guess you just gradually give up and it closes over you like a grave.'[96] There comes a moment when Gellburg admits that he has regretted marrying a woman more intelligent than himself, a woman whose needs he can no longer satisfy. His sexual incapacity (he is impotent), it is suggested, is rooted in his denial but itself becomes the basis of a further alienation. He and Sylvia have not had intercourse for nearly twenty years (shortly after the birth of their only son), a source of frustration to her and humiliation to him. In conversation with Hyman he suggests that they have now made love, a desperate lie, it seems, as he struggles to deny that he might have any responsibility for her current condition.

Broken Glass begins when something in Sylvia breaks. In a way that at first she cannot understand, events in a distant country arc into her own life, as she recognizes the humiliations suffered by others, as she acknowledges a connection between the powerlessness of those whose photographs appear in the press and her own plight. Sylvia, like Miller's mother Augusta, surrendered her chance to go to college ('If I'd had a chance to go to college, I'd have had a whole different life')[97] and subordinated herself to a marriage that offered her nothing but wealth in return. 'I'm here,' she tells her husband, 'for my mother's sake, and Jerome's sake and everybody's sake except mine.'[98]

Miller had heard his parents argue, but divorce had never been a real possibility. People lived with their mistakes. Sylvia reveals that the idea of divorce has been in her mind but that she has simply settled into the new reality. Her paralysis now justifies her inaction, as it stands as an image for it. Miller remarked in rehearsal, 'It's as though something got settled. She's crippled now. There is nothing she can do.' When not following newspaper accounts of Kristallnacht, Sylvia spends her time reading a sprawling romantic novel of the time, *Anthony Adverse*, and listening to the singer Eddie Cantor on the radio. The journey of the play is the journey she takes back to herself. As Hyman comes to understand, what she wants above all else is to be free. Her paralysis gives her the wrong kind of freedom, liberating her from responsibility for daily duties but not from her sense of self-betrayal. Answering Amy Irving's questions about her character, Miller explained:

The image is one of suspended animation. It is as though [Sylvia] had something in her – which will be emphasized through the play – that she can't bring up. She can't give it birth. There's something alive in there that is trying to get out. The reason that Hyman is important to her is that she is being judged all the time, judged by her mother, judged by her rabbi who says 'You'll just have to go back there and be a wife.' No matter where she turns there'll be a judgement upon her. Hyman is the first one who's come into her life who manifestly isn't judging her.

Hyman, though, has his own denials. He finds it difficult to reconcile what is happening in Germany with his own experiences there, having studied in Heidelberg. 'German music and literature are some of the greatest in the world; it's impossible for those people to suddenly change into thugs like this.'[99] In rehearsals, Miller reminded the actors that Hyman 'had spent the best years of his life in Germany and his memories are very positive. In fact, in relation to the rest of Europe they were most positive. That's the place he liked the best. And to give that up is not easy. It wasn't easy for the Germans. It wasn't easy for a lot of people.' At the same time, he had studied in Germany because of the restrictions placed on Jews studying at American universities. There *is*, in other words, a connection between events in Germany and those in Brooklyn, much as so many of the characters are prone to deny it. 'When she talks about it,' Hyman remarks, 'it's not the other side of the world, it's on the next block.'[100]

Hyman is sensual, a life force. He has always been attractive to women and has had, we learn, a series of affairs. His wife believes that the reason he is drawn to Sylvia's case is not necessarily detached from her beauty. And though she represents an intellectual challenge he responds to her evident need in a way that would seem to blur the line between doctor and lover. 'What beautiful legs you have,' he tells her. 'You have a strong, beautiful body ... you're a very attractive woman. I haven't been this moved by a woman in a very long time.'[101] 'The depth of your flesh must be wonderful.' His method of delving into her mind is to say, 'I want you to imagine that we've made love. And now it's over and we are lying together.'[102] He even kisses her. The scene ends as she lies in bed, her legs spread apart. When he next sees her she has had her hair done and wears perfume. She suddenly kisses him.

This is a dimension of the play discussed during rehearsals. On the second day, Ron Silver (Hyman) offered his own understanding of the play, of Sylvia and of his relationship with her:

> The passivity of the people allowed them to be abused and violated and raped and destroyed and made nonexistent anymore. The horror of this was reflected in her private life by having a more personal Nazi in her life who made her into a passive, paralysed, fearful victim incapable of doing anything active on her own to change her position and save herself. Saving herself is getting laid, unfortunately not a good solution for me because I have my own demons and problems about sex.

Miller's response was: 'Everything you say is true. It's absolutely on the nose.' For Silver, however, Hyman's mixed motives were a problem. Miller's response was to add a line indicating that his affairs lay in the past ('There's been nobody for at least ten or twelve years ... more').[103] His sensuality, though, is an essential part of a play in which Gellburg's literal impotence is offered both as the root of his estrangement from Sylvia and as an image of the impotence of those who witnessed the events in Europe without intervening. The question was how to play scenes in which Hyman appears flirtatious. For Miller, confronting a woman who has effectively been told by her husband that she is unattractive and sexually irrelevant leads Hyman to deploy his own sexuality and Sylvia to respond to a man who, unlike Gellburg, is ready to listen to her. Since her sexual difficulties are part of her problem, she is forced to discuss them with a man who we know, as she does not, revels in his power over a women.

Miller noted, 'We should always sustain the idea that this is the first time she has ever been able to talk about this to anyone. So there is a freshness in her intent. It's not as if it's a twice-told tale. She would never talk about it to her sister Harriet. She can't talk about it to her mother because her mother loves Phillip. There's a freshness about her discovery of all this and a gratitude to him that he'll listen to her and spend time with her.' At the same time she feels the need to defend Phillip to Hyman: 'In her heart she has registered that Phillip has an anti-Semitic streak in him, but to this man who she hardly knows she both wants to say it and not say it.' As for Hyman, 'this is getting so fucking complicated now. He feels an abyss opening under him. He'd better get out of the reach of this woman that he is attracted to. She's defenceless to him ... very vulnerable. She is a great temptation to him.' When she has a dream of being attacked by her husband and tells Hyman of it, Miller indicates that 'the whole relating of that dream – I don't want to bludgeon this to death – but there's a wonder in it, the way it always is when you tell a dream. You get a certain ego satisfaction out of it. You wrote it. It's like a poem. It's come out of you. But the underlying thing is anxiety.'

By degrees Sylvia becomes more desperate. As Miller indicates in a stage direction, 'Everything is flying apart for her ... the focus is clearly far wider than this room. An unbearable anxiety.' Her private life is in crisis, but in Germany the unthinkable is happening: 'Why don't they run out of the country!' she cries. Under stress she tries to get to her feet, before collapsing, understanding now her collaboration in her own spiritual paralysis as Chekhov's Ranevskaya speaks of mislaying her life in *The Cherry Orchard*: 'What I did with my life! Out of ignorance ... A whole life. Gave it away like a couple of pennies – I took better care of my shoes.'[104] For Tillinger, 'If this Nazi thing had not happened, I think she would have gone to her grave accepting that this is the way she was supposed to have lived.' She had had to conceal her strength, something that she now begins to understand was the beginning of her self-denial. Where her husband had regretted his 'Jewish face', she now discovers her Jewish voice. 'How stupid it all is,' she remarks. 'You keep putting everything off like you're going to live a thousand years.' Phillip likewise says, 'I always thought there'd be time to get to the bottom of myself!' Following a sudden heart attack, he summons up memories of his Jewish upbringing: 'The street was full of pushcarts and men with long beards like a hundred years ago. It's funny. I felt so at home and happy there that day, a street full of Jews, one Moses after another.'[105] To grow up, though, was to encounter anti-Semitism.

'Why is it so hard to be a Jew,' Gellburg asks. 'Being a Jew is a full-time job.'[106] For Hyman, who had himself married outside the faith, Gellburg had 'tried to disappear into the goyim'. 'You hate yourself . . . I think you paralyse her with this "Jew, Jew, Jew" coming out of your mouth and at the same time it's coming out of the radio day and night?'[107] Finally, Gellburg begins to reclaim his Jewishness: 'They will never destroy us. When the last Jew dies the light of the world will go out.'[108] For the first time this solemn man, who dresses in black, in mourning for his life, is able to joke about his identity, amused at the idea that Chinese Jews do not look Jewish. It is at this moment that he collapses. In one of several American versions he 'falls back dead'; in the British one he 'falls back unconscious'. It is, of course, a crucial distinction, and it was around this moment that most discussions took place. As Amy Irving recalled, '[Arthur] did these rewrites and rewrites, up at the Long Wharf, because the ending wasn't working.'[109]

Speaking during rehearsals Miller remarked,

I don't want [Gellburg] to die. He's probably going to die later, although he might not. Besides, when a dead body's on stage everyone knows he's not dead. A fly comes down on his nose. Aside from that, I think it's much better that it be open. The play more truly comes to its conclusion and maybe he's still alive. It means [Sylvia's] prepared to go on with it. The whole dialectic is in motion, instead of stopped. They could end up together again. The thing need not be an ending. We've got it both ways. I don't know what would happen. I can't predict people. He could come out of this and she could say, 'I'm happy you're better but I can't stand it any more and I am going to leave.' She could also say, 'I think we understand each other somehow.' And suddenly he would know more now than he did at the beginning of the play about how she was and what she was going through. He would be a much more mature man than he was when he started. Given the conventions of the time you would have to lean toward it not being a divorce. People just didn't do it if they could avoid it but I'm not saying one way or the other. I really don't. First of all, these things can happen. People can go through these things and come out of it that way. The logic of it is possible. He may not be dead. The sense you would get is that it's ongoing. That's another reason he's not dead. That's not the issue, whether he lives or dies. The issue is their possible relationship, or not, on what has been gained or learned from all this, by him, by her, by everybody. That's the issue.

Phillip and Sylvia Gellburg were both based on real people. She, he said, was 'a very sweet, intelligent, energetic woman, who lived in my neighbourhood, who suddenly, and inexplicably, couldn't walk ... They had all kinds of doctors looking at her and nobody could figure it out. She went through her whole life and died, unable to walk.' Alongside that image was another, that of a man who always dressed in black, like Masha in Chekhov's *The Seagull*. There had been no connection between them. For decades they had been no more than random memories. Only with *Broken Glass* did their stories come together. Miller explained in an interview, 'I've known about that woman who lost the use of her legs and nobody could diagnose the reason for many years, since, I would say, 1940. I thought about writing it many times, but I could never find a way in.'[110]

Speaking to Ron Rifkin, who wanted to know the origin of Gellburg, Miller remarked,

> First of all there is no 'he' or 'him', not in the normal sense anyway. A dramatic character is actually a relationship first and foremost, a response to other 'characters' and to the theme and drift of events. I knew such a man many years ago, but what did I know? – that he always wore black even as a young guy. Go make a 'character' out of a suit. But the suit had suggestive implications, and the superior way he grinned, and what one knew was the terror behind the suit and the grin, and so on. So you begin to account for the terror, which is deeply disguised, and pretty soon 'he' is talking to his wife who, as it happens, has lost her ability to walk ... and so on. Actually, the initial image, the dramatic energy-source is the image of this woman, crippled without a mark on her, like most of us who show no marks. In her, it seemed to me, was the image of the world denying itself, its holy life, a life from which at first she is attempting to resign, but in the end it won't let her go. There is no 'he' or 'she' in the ordinary way we perceive individuals; there is a relationship-for-two.[111]

What kept him from writing the play for so long, he explained, was that he wished to bring together 'a public concern and a private neurosis' in an effort 'to find that juncture where they actually met'. He could have been talking about almost any of his plays, but in this case the connection seems more problematic. Indeed, in the end, it is precisely the problematic nature of the connection that drives the play. He had always felt that 'what we do privately has consequences. But since trying to trace that in concrete terms is almost impossible we are backed up into metaphor and analogy and poetry, which is the only way you handle it anyway.' In Salzburg in 1996, he said that he found he could write the play when, suddenly,

> it appeared to me to be a wonderful analogy for where we are now. We have all the equipment to understand everything and we can't move. There is Bosnia not far down the road from here. Everybody agrees that it is a catastrophe, but if my emotions are similar to others', I can't get onto that horse. I think, maybe, we've had too much catastrophe. If you put an electrode into any kind of an organism, after a while it doesn't react to it, and I think we've maybe been numbed by the brutality in our natures and something is telling us that the whole thing is hopeless, in a deeper way than we are willing to admit. That was one of the impulses to write the play.

Of the woman who lay at the heart of the play he said:

> She was one of the few people that I knew who, very early on, got excited about the Germans pursuing the Jews, three thousand miles away. And she was not a political woman. She read two or three newspapers a week, which was unusual for a woman in her position in those times, but there was no political ideology of any kind. It just reached across the ocean and stung her. And she became aware that this was a catastrophe that was bigger than anything anybody had ever known. That was at a time when most Jews (and certainly most non-Jews) were trying to hush-hush the whole Nazi thing, because they didn't want to draw attention to their situation in the United States ... for fear that it would awaken the same thing.[112]

As ever, Miller turned to the past not out of any antiquarian interest, out of a desire to write historical plays, but from a conviction that the past needed to be invoked in order to address the present. He wished to open a dialogue between two moments for the meaning that could flood through. Just as in the 1930s the world had stood by in the face of Nazi brutality and aggression, now in Africa the starving were left to their own resources, in Iraq the Marsh Arabs were gassed, in Europe there was a revival of right-wing groups, while in Yugoslavia there was a sudden explosion of 'ethnic cleansing'. Nor was the image at the centre of the play without its literal example. Speaking in the year of the play's first production he said,

> I only found out the other day ... that there was, in the 1930s especially, an unusual amount of physical paralysis among some Jews in America ... I never knew that. Just the other day there was an article in the paper about Cambodian women. After the Khmer Rouge got finished with them – and they supposedly murdered several million Cambodians in the most brutal

fashion – there was a lot of hysterical blindness among them. They can see but they seem not to register what they are seeing.

This, though, was information that came to him after completing his play. In terms of its 1930s setting, he was concerned with 'the terror which reached the United States in relation to the rise of fascism in Europe', a phenomenon that in retrospect he saw as having threatened order itself. Indeed, speaking of his Jewish background, he remarked: 'It probably supplied me, through my epidermis, because we were not an especially religious family, with the idea of order and disorder. I could smell from three thousand miles away that there was a tremor in the earth which was going to destroy that democracy and which was finally going to end up at my doorstep.'

It is that nexus that is explored in *Broken Glass*, a play in which he identifies himself with his Jewish characters, for 'that sense of being personally involved in something distant has been with me always, partly because, though we are very few people, it is miraculous that when a real reactionary regime begins, it goes after us very early on'.[113] 'To me one of the basic threats posed by the fascists was that here was a movement that was going to literally tear up all the underlying web of obligations that keeps society in place.'

Also, it was a play that took him back to a familiar place. It is set in Brooklyn, where Miller remembered people riding horses up and down the bridle paths alongside Ocean Parkway, as the doctor, Harry Hyman, does here. Miller remembered in particular the amazement at this sight shown by the fellow student he drove from Michigan to catch the boat to the Spanish Civil War, where he would lose his life. Hyman's home, Miller told the cast, would have been on 5th Street, as his own was on 3rd. 1938 was not only the year of Kristallnacht, it was also the year Miller graduated from Michigan and returned to the Brooklyn described here, still semirural, a place where the Depression, and the tension between his parents, were daily realities. As the play's director, John Tillinger, said, 'When he gave me this play he told me that it came from a dark side of himself and one that he didn't know and hadn't ever explored before.'

Rehearsals, which Tillinger later recalled as being 'tortured', began in late January when Miller and Inge returned from a stay in St Lucia with Derek Walcott. The contrast could hardly have been greater – the Connecticut hills were deep in snow. When I attended rehearsals with him he showed me how to slow a car on the ice-slicked road by nudging into the drifts beside the road.

Miller and his Jewish director assembled a Jewish cast for a Jewish play. Miller remarked, 'The great thing about this cast is that they really know the language. These two guys [Silver and Rifkin] speak the language better than

I do.' Rifkin, the son of immigrants, had been an orthodox Jew until he was thirty-two. In a *New York Times* interview he said that it remained important to him to be the best Jew he could, but 'there were periods in my own life when I wanted to be blond and I wanted to be a jock ... I don't have to study to be a Jew. I know it very well. I don't have to study what it means to be insecure or angry ... I went to a yeshiva [a rabbinical school] myself and I said to my parents that I wanted to go to a regular high school. I didn't want to wear the yarmulke all the time. One has episodes where you want to look like everyone else. But to spend your whole life like that, it's so shocking.' He recalled visiting a store in Glendale, California ('Glendale is notoriously right wing'), where there was a display of Nazi memorabilia: 'I started to speak Yiddish to my friend just to see how it would feel. And I thought, what must it have been like in 1938 in Germany? There I was, in Glendale, and I'm talking Yiddish and we're all getting frightened.'[114]

As a child, Amy Irving had watched two productions of *The Crucible* when her father Jules Irving (born Jules Israel) was director of New York's Repertory Company. In one of them her mother, the non-Jewish Priscilla Pointer, had a starring role. (Amy was the former wife of Steven Spielberg; she received a reported $92 million divorce settlement – a fact which got Miller into trouble when the *New Yorker* reported his comment, that 'She doesn't have a line on her face – that's what happens when you get ninety million dollars.'[115]) On the first day of rehearsals Amy described her view of her character, Sylvia:

> She's a multi-layered character with so many things going on inside you get stifled finding the journey from the beginning to the finding of the life force inside herself. She's on the edge. It's not just a part about a woman on the edge of hysteria. Other people say she looks as though she is enjoying it. There is a struggle to get past the passivity and take action. She's not going to lie down and be dead any more but at the beginning of the play she doesn't know that.

It was the first time Amy Irving had ever originated a role and she was conscious of looking too young for the part. She set herself to reading the books and newspapers of the time as well as *Timebends*, finding aspects of the author in the play: 'There's so much of him in this play ... There are glimpses of his mother ... the two men are very much a part of what he is.' She knew that in 1938 'you didn't talk about certain things. You don't deal with sexual problems openly. You do not communicate on a certain level. You do not embarrass your husband or expose family matters. There is a need to keep it under the table. You don't want to draw attention to yourself.' And what is true of Sylvia is doubly true of her husband, the Jew who is desperate not to draw attention to his Jewishness. Asked about this in rehearsals, Miller said:

It's a function of the minority, or people who feel they are. The Germans right now are loaded with this feeling that they are suspect, that they are in danger, not of physical annihilation, but that they are ashamed of being German. I was in Cambodia where the Vietnamese used to go around with this look because they were known as the Jews of Cambodia. They were the businessmen. And, indeed, two weeks after we left some 20,000 of them were slaughtered in one night by Cambodian people. It was a pogrom that never ended right through the night. The Mekong River was red with blood, and some of these families had been there for six generations. But that was it. Go to Africa, and it's the Indians who are the businessmen and better educated.

The central problem of the play, as Tillinger saw it, was that it is 'set in the late Thirties and makes assumptions about sexual relationships, psychiatry and even Jewish attitudes toward fellow Jews, which have all changed. The challenge is to get audiences to understand that, while not forgetting its contemporary force.' In that regard, Ron Silver questioned whether his character, a doctor who thinks of himself as a socialist, would really have been surprised by the events of Kristallnacht, or have expressed the naive confidence about the future that he does. Miller insisted that in fact few people in the thirties seemed to know or care, while many of those who did assumed that the situation could hardly get worse.

The following day, theatre staff located an original copy of *Life* magazine for 28 November 1938. Alongside photographs of wrecked shops and burning synagogues was a reassuring caption which noted that 'a hopeful sign was that for the first time large numbers of Germans seemed to be out of sympathy with the Nazis'. Two pages later it was reported that 'decent-hearted men and women all over the world went into churches to ask for help for the Jews from the God of all men of goodwill'. It is a statement at odds with the accompanying photograph of St George's Episcopal Church in Manhattan which shows, at best, a sparse congregation. 'See,' Miller remarked, 'that's the way it was. They did these things and nobody lifted a hand. It was amazing.'

Despite their shared Jewish background the cast found it difficult at first to feel their way back into the position of Jews in the 1930s, and on the first day of rehearsals, this led to a general discussion. John Tillinger explained:

> We wandered around the world, our tribe, and from every country we have been expelled, with very few exceptions. And the Jews in this country felt the same thing. They thought that at any time it could happen. That's why they said, 'Don't make waves.' It was a very real issue. It is hard for us to believe now but it was a very real issue, that a day would come that you live three hundred years in a country and then be told to get out the next day. It is inconceivable to us today, though I'm not sure it *is* inconceivable. The rise of

anti-Semitism is real. I was at a dinner the other night and somebody said, 'I've got a new car but everybody tells me it's very Jewish.' The woman said, 'Do you mean I have to get out my furs and pearls to get in it?' What do you do? Do you get up and leave?

The cast also explored the personal and political context of Kristallnacht. Tillinger explained that his own aunt and uncle had been sent to a concentration camp, while Miller recalled the immediate reality of Nazi Germany, in the course of his account pounding on the table around which they were all sitting:

In the center of Berlin there was and remains – it's a museum now – a prison. It's not very large. The Jews were not taken there, by and large. It was trade union leaders, communists or some of the very upper-class people who resented Hitler. And they have there meat hooks, a row about as big as that pipe there, about so far apart, where they hanged people. And you had an audience. They have a display of invitations which were sent out to people to witness these executions. The executions consisted of hanging these people. The room is about this size and they had about three rows of benches. One of the notes on the invitations says, 'If you cannot attend don't give this invitation to anyone else. This is for you, personally.' This is the center of Berlin. This is not Poland. These were trade union people, a lot of them. These trade unions continued to negotiate with the Nazi bosses. If we're talking about passivity, it boggles the fucking mind. This was not a secret. This is going on in the center of Berlin. These are not Jews. These are militant proletarian leaders. You tell me what the answer to that is. The power of this terror is so tremendous that it simply stops the heart. People go around with their jobs and a lot of them could have left, the trade union members, if they had had a little money. France was still there. We're dealing with an unfathomable thing, beyond passivity – authority, to which we are all subject. It's stunning when you go to that museum because, unlike Auschwitz, this was not in a secret place. This did not involve some stupid minority. These were all *echt* Germans and a lot of them were upper-class people, religious some of them. Some of them were disgusted with what they saw. Somebody informed on them and they came by and picked them up. But it had to have been known. They said, 'Well, they must have done something.' This is very important. It's a rational world. You don't pick up people in the street or at their work unless there's a good reason. So we have to respect the mystery here. That's what Sylvia is dealing with. It's this cloud of unknowing.

'In each of us,' Miller went on, 'whether we recognize it or not, is that same bloody ethnic nationalism. This is not coming from the moon. This is coming from us. And we have not come close to confronting this thing. All the patriotism and ethnic nationalism is knocking on the door, and it's as dangerous as ever it was.' In the words of a line from the play, 'Look in the mirror some time.'

In attempting to explain the political paralysis in the face of events in Europe, Miller recalled the German playwright Ferdinand Bruckner, who translated *Death of a Salesman* for the European premiere in Vienna: 'Bruckner was a German playwright, not Jewish. He came over here because he was an anti-fascist. He was not a leftie. He was basically a nationalist. He was anti-Hitler. And I sat with him in a room when the Russians started to move west. He was glued to the radio. He was waiting for the German revolt against Hitler. He said, "All these workers are armed." I looked at him and thought, he's crazy. How could he think that? This was late 1943 or early '44 and he's waiting for the German revolt.' He recalled sitting in a lecture at the University of Michigan: 'There was a professor, a great European expert, and in the question period somebody asked, "Do you think the Germans are going to go into Austria?", and he said that it was impossible. And when I came out of that class there was a kid selling papers on campus saying that the Germans had gone into Austria.'

After the first day's rehearsal, Miller drove back to Roxbury with Tillinger, and for an hour they went through the text making cuts, removing repetitions and redundancies. It was only when he heard actors read his words, Miller said, that he could get a clear sense of what might be missing. When he proposed cutting a stage direction that Tillinger particularly liked ('quietly, from the centre of his soul'), Miller commented: 'We could put that in another speech, for the same money.' He asked Tillinger to present the cuts to the cast – 'to avoid negotiations, especially with Ron Silver, who is a great lawyer'. At Tillinger's request, he wrote an additional two pages of dialogue between Dr Hyman and his wife at the end of the first scene, clarifying why she has stayed with him in spite of his philandering. Hyman is, we discover, a spinner of seductive stories, a man whose humour and imagination are an essential part of his character, in contrast to the dour Gellburg who suspects that jokes can only be at his own expense.

The main source of contention during rehearsals was the ending, and this continued to be a problem in previews and beyond. Although when David Thacker directed the London production he already had several versions of the text piled up in front of him, he requested an additional scene between the three women – Sylvia, her sister Harriet and Margaret Hyman. When Miller signed my copy on 3 August 1994 (it opened the following day) he wrote, 'Practically the final one. Now let history decide (what?!!).'

The ending changed considerably between the various drafts. In 1992, when the play was still called *Gellburg*, Phillip collapses on the floor. Hyman calls for an oxygen mask, but because he is busy giving artificial respiration cannot reach it. Sylvia rises from the wheelchair in which she is confined, walks the few steps to it and hands it to him. Phillip dies. The play ends with Hyman's ambiguous question to Sylvia: 'Do you have some feeling?' This remained the ending in the August 1993 version, now called *Broken Glass*. But by February 1994 the play ended as they await the arrival of an ambulance and Sylvia calls out, 'I'm all right! Can you hear me? I'm all right, Phillip! Can you hear me!' By April that year the ending was further modified, as Phillip dies at the moment Sylvia struggles to her feet. In a still later version it is unclear whether he is dead or not.

Addressing the British cast three months later, Miller observed that 'the play more truly comes to its conclusion when she's on her feet. It means she is prepared to go on with it and maybe he is alive.' The difficulty, of course, is to convey to the audience that Phillip is unconscious rather than dead. As it is, Sylvia stands, according to the stage directions, 'astounded, charged with hope yet with a certain inward-seeing alarm' before taking a faltering step towards her husband. In the British production she rose to her feet and stood with arms outstretched, paralysed this time by a sense of wonder, the connection with – and, incidentally, concern for – her husband momentarily broken. And though he was meant to be unconscious rather than dead, the difference proved impossible to communicate.

The ever-changing ending presented problems in New Haven. John Guare once said that when he was living in New Haven he never saw a play that was not broken and in process of repair, so that a certain amount of adjustment and fine-tuning was to be expected. What happened here was a mini-drama, as the opening was delayed while Miller reworked the text.

In an unprecedented move, at least as far as the Long Wharf Theater was concerned, reviewers were asked not to attend, or at least not to review on what had originally been scheduled as the opening night. It was not the only bad news the Long Wharf had to release. On Monday 7 March they were forced to announce the withdrawal of Al Pacino from a forthcoming pro-duction of *The Iceman Cometh*. On the Tuesday the critics were warned off; then on the Wednesday, supposedly the opening night, the ending was changed again. Word got out that the playwright had come up with fifteen new pages of text. This did little to ensure a respectful hearing. The play was scheduled to run for a little over three weeks before transferring to Broadway, where previews would start on 13 April, with the opening on the 24th. There was already speculation in the press as to whether Miller could break his 'new-play losing streak' on Broadway.

But even before then, things began to fall apart. Two Sunday performances were cancelled to allow Ron Silver to attend the Academy Awards ceremonies. The following week the Saturday evening show was cancelled. When Christopher Arnott of the *New Haven Advocate* commented on Silver's need to learn his lines, the actor blamed the backstage crew, and Arnott was approached to write a letter exculpating them. Miller thought Silver was playing the part like Al Pacino rather than a Jew. Then, two weeks before the Broadway previews were due to start, Silver withdrew, saying that things had not worked out. It was not the first time he had done this. In 1991 he withdrew from a production of David Hirson's *La Bête* because of 'irreconcilable interpretative differences'. A reliable regional theatre actor, Doug Stender, was drafted in as Hyman before David Dukes took over, performing during the last week with script in hand.

There was a feeling that a great deal was riding on this production. The effect of the delayed New Haven opening was not likely to help, even though out-of-town reviews were unlikely to be crucial. The *Hartford Courant* chose to attend the original opening night. Its headline was 'A Cracked Broken Glass'. The play, it concluded, 'needs patching'. The *New Haven Register* of 11 April found it intriguing but declared, 'Drama Splinters in Final Moments'. Returning later to see the revised ending, its reviewer announced: 'Revision Can't Completely Fix "Broken Glass".'

Some reviews appeared midway through the third week of March, others a week later. The subeditors' choices of headlines were not encouraging: '*Broken Glass:* Play Features Flat, Lifeless Direction and Uninspired Performances' (*Journal Enquirer*); 'Picking Up Broken Glass' (*Newport News*); 'Miller Play Reflects Major Flaws' (*Danbury News Times*); 'Broken Glass: Cracks Emerge in Miller Drama' (*Connecticut Post*); 'The Crippled Leading the Blind' (*New Haven Advocate*). On the other hand the *Record-Journal* of Meriden declared, "Broken Glass" Well Worth the Wait', while the *Providence Journal-Bulletin* found "Broken Glass" Is Sharp Stuff'. The *New Haven Jewish Ledger* soberly announced that the play was a valuable contribution to the literature of the Holocaust. The tone, however, was set by the headline of the *Providence Journal-Bulletin*: 'Arthur Miller Comeback'. He was, it seemed, at least in America, trying to retrieve a position that elsewhere in the world he had never lost.[116]

When the play reached New York, John Simon in the *New York Times Magazine*, in a review entitled 'Whose Paralysis Is It, Anyway?', greeted it with the words: 'Arthur Miller may be the world's most overrated playwright, but even he could not have served up the jagged shards of *Broken Glass* without some hidden agenda, some secret scenario under the banal plot and shoddy dialogue.' Miller, he asserted, was 'thrashing about desperately in search of a plot'.[117] The play had 'no legs'. The changes to the ending, which seemingly turned it from a patriarchal to a feminist work, revealed an arbitrariness that some found disturbing. William A. Henry III, in *Time*, was altogether more receptive but doubtful that it could survive. He found the play 'complex, full of arresting incident and grippingly played', but regretted that 'the bad news is that there is so little audience for serious work that its survival is, in the producer's words, "week to week".'[118] 'Alexis Greene in *Theater Week*, responded positively but wanted 'a warmer production, and rewrites'.[119]

Another British-based American critic, in the *Village Voice*, compared the play favourably with a popular revival of Priestley's *An Inspector Calls*, while others expressed the opposite preference. For the most part American critics showed little belief in *Broken Glass*. Jeremy Gerard in *Variety* had correctly forecast that, given a Broadway environment hostile to new play production, it would quickly fold there – though he regretted it, despite it seeming unfinished and histrionic. The days when adventurous audiences would be 'willing to take a chance on the minor work of a major playwright' had gone.[120] The reviewer of *USA Today* found the play impressive but thought the 'dramatic payoff' lacking in consequence. It was at times effortful, malformed and sluggish. For David Richards in the *New York Times Broken Glass* was 'all talk and fumbling confession . . . Ibsenism by the book'.[121] The characters were 'baldly utilitarian or expendable'. The play was dead from that moment.

In his review in the *New Republic* Robert Brustein addressed the question of Miller's contrasting reputation in Britain and America, implying that the British response was an endearing but essentially aberrant view. 'Arthur Miller didn't open *Broken Glass* in London,' he observed, 'but I'll bet he wishes he had.' While he 'may not be able to arouse much admiration for his new plays in this country . . . he's a living monument in England'. *Broken Glass*, he rightly suggested, 'may very well dazzle the critics and delight the public when it is eventually produced in London. Here it seems like just another spiral in a stumbling career.'

Nor was it simply a matter of Miller's new play. Brustein chose the occasion of his review to regret the playwright's declining reputation but stressed what seemed to him the 'plodding, pedestrian, predictable and . . . pompous' nature of his style, his 'moral preachments in lumbering prose'. His early reputation, he suggested, had been inflated and hence his apparent decline had been the more precipitate. Brustein ended with a partial explanation for the British enthusiasm for Miller's work by invoking Olivier's Old Vic production of *The Crucible* (a play, incidentally, that Brustein had denounced in an article called, 'Why American Drama Is Not Literature'), which 'gave that play a loftiness and magnitude it never enjoyed in its American incarnations, and it may well be that the reason the English so admire Miller is that they are able to produce him with the grandeur of Shakespearean tragedy rather than (as here) with the prosaic flatness of a sociological primer'.[122]

David Thacker, already preparing for rehearsals of the British production, flew out to see the penultimate performance and disliked what he saw. Sitting next to Miller, he braced himself to offer his opinion. After a ritual visit backstage, they climbed into a taxi. As they did so Thacker said, 'You know it's bad, don't you?', to which Miller replied, 'Yep.'

To a degree, Tillinger agreed. He had anyway never liked the three-quarter stage in New Haven and thought the play ill-suited to the proscenium arch at the Booth Theatre. To open in winter also struck him as a mistake. 'On the opening night performance of *Broken Glass*,' he recounted, 'Arthur and I were having a drink in a bar nearby. I told him that I was unhappy with my production of the play and felt I had failed him. Arthur replied, "Other than the original production of *Salesman*, none of my premieres were ever successful." And there were no recriminations on his part towards me. I told him I was certain *Broken Glass* would receive the approbation it deserved in London, whatever the production. "They like me over there," he said. "I don't understand why they don't like me in my own home town." At the time certain New York critics would not even review his plays.'[123]

For Thacker, it was not the text that was at fault. The production simply seemed to him not to have opened up the emotional truth of the play. In 2001 Miller told me: 'Partly it was the production. Amy Irving [as Sylvia] seemed to be tough when the fact is that the woman is very vulnerable. She did not seem vulnerable. She seemed angry at [Gellburg]. She should be angry at him but it is the anger of a vulnerable person and that wasn't there. So that the sympathy for her was missing.' As to the changed endings, he remarked, 'There is a curious question about the ending. The change was, basically, whether [Sylvia's] revived capacity to stand up was a victory over [Gellburg] or whether it was a discovery on her part, that she had the strength. That's a difficult thing, in view of the fact that he's dying. They did it well in England. They did it very beautifully.'

Nonetheless, audiences in New York *were* receptive. Amy Irving secured a Drama Desk nomination, and the play was nominated for a Tony. But this did not have the expected effect at the box office, and by late April the play was barely hanging on, just in profit but no more. Neither the play nor the actors won any awards, the Drama Desk Award going to Tony Kushner's *Angels in America: Perestroika*. Against his better judgement, Miller attended the ceremony, co-hosted by Amy Irving. The next day he was told that unless they could raise more money the show would have to close in a fortnight. It closed after seventy-three performances.

Miller entered a plea that the role of Sylvia in England should go to Margot Leicester, who had impressed him when she took over the role of Patricia in *The Last Yankee*. Henry Goodman played Phillip, and Ken Stott, Hyman. Joining the cast for rehearsals, Miller spoke of the wider context of the play and of the human capacity to stand aside while tragedy unfolds, to remain paralysed in the face of events. 'We've learned to suppress it, like Rwanda, with half a million down the sluice [in the course of three months from April 1994 a genocide was played out in Rwanda; Miller's figure is probably on the low side]. Why doesn't somebody do something about this?' As the play was rehearsed, shells were falling on Sarajevo. '[For Sylvia] it's this hopeless feeling of watching this thing happen, because they are her people.' At the same time he warned the cast, 'There's enough seriousness in this play. We don't have to do it every minute. Whenever there is a possibility of lightening it, do so, because it's more real. We can't stay serious all the time.' The cast impressed him. Speaking to Ken Stott, he said, 'I really believe you are a doctor. I'd send my friends to you. I'm not sure I would go, though.'

Henry Goodman commented:

> You can't avoid the lucidity of [Miller's] argument. He insists that we think about compassion, our moral responsibilities. As a person watching the play, you can't run away from the questions that the play makes you ask because, speaking as an actor, he makes you undergo certain experiences. Even on the simplest level you ask yourself, what would I do in that situation? Have I hidden those longings and needs and avoided them by taking decisions that repress them? With Miller, it is how you hang on to being a human and compassionate person when everything militates against it everywhere.'

'This play is largely about denial,'[124] Miller confirmed.

Three months after the American premiere, with one additional five-page scene and a further modified ending, the play opened at Britain's National Theatre. The director Richard Eyre attended the previews: 'The first preview of Broken Glass ... went well, the audience applauding long after the lights went up. The acting was excellent (Ken Stott, Henry Goodman, particularly), the play cumulatively good, but an awkward setting that forces clumsy scene changes where seamlessness is called for. For once, with a play of Miller's, the struggle is about the difficulty and the possibility of a woman taking control of her own life.'[125]

The reviews stood in sharp contrast to the American responses. In the Sunday Times John Peters welcomed it as a 'grand, harrowing play, deeply compassionate and darkly humorous', 'one of the great creations of the American theatre'. He thought that the National 'ought to be very proud of its great production'.[126] For Irving Wardle, in a review entitled 'Age Has Not Withered Him'[127] in the Independent on Sunday, it was characterized by a 'ferocious emotional energy'. Benedict Nightingale in The Times detected weaknesses, especially with respect to the figure of Dr Hyman, but found that the play's centre held and that in Gellburg 'you won't find a more sympathetic yet less sentimental piece of characterisation in London'. For Michael Billington in the Guardian, Miller had written a wise, humane, moving and complex humanistic play.

Broken Glass, Miller said in 1995, 'should never have been done on Broadway. I did not want it done on Broadway.' The idea of staging it at the Long Wharf was 'perfectly fine. That,' after all, 'was a non-commercial thing and [it] should have gone from there to a non-commercial theatre or an Off-Broadway theatre. The play did not belong competing with musicals, with *Cats*. It's not built for that.' Its relative failure in New York, he suggested, was 'not the play's fault. There is something wrong with the relationship of the theatre to its audience [there].'[128] Nonetheless, he persisted in thinking that he could 'beat the rap, beat the system'. When *Broken Glass* won the Olivier Award for Best Play of the Year in Britain, it was a week before news of this was reported in the *New York Times*, and then as an adjunct to a news story concerning an actor's denunciation of critics.

But Miller was not so carried away by his British success as to be unaware of what seemed to him to be the play's special relevance there: 'Part of the impulse behind the writing of *Broken Glass* was to open up the secret places of the heart where ethnicity snuggles, emitting its poisons and perfumes. The spectacular London reviews, incidentally, may in some way reflect the ventilation of some of the British reticence about this perplexing paradox which is very much alive in their hearts – their reverence for fairness as against a distaste for the foreigner, their respect for justice as against color prejudice and class privilege.'[129]

Asked why he chose this moment to write about this subject he replied:

Because we are living in a time when nothing has any relation to anything else and, just for my own sanity, I wanted to write about something that showed a relationship, even across the ocean; that 'A' led to 'B'. It is in relation to a culture that has severed all connections. We are now one individual and another individual ... The reigning philosophy is, 'You are on your own.' As Mrs Thatcher said, there is no society. That was breathtaking.

The image of paralysis at the heart of the play expressed a sense of power-lessness that art could perhaps address:

The idea of being paralysed in the face of overwhelming forces we do not understand is the mark of our time, maybe of all time. We are little ants climbing up and down a gigantic structure ... All we can see is the next ant ... I like to think it is art that can give us the structure, the vision, the big thing we are crawling up and down on. That was one of the impulses behind writing *Broken Glass*.[130]

12

ENDINGS

The creative act is mysterious, I suppose, because we dare not confront some of it. It's a fear of dying uselessly, in part, it's the wish to live more intensely.[1]

I think every artist of any seriousness at all, in some part of his brain, is dreaming that he's making something that might last, outlast his own life, whether he is conscious of it or not. That's why he's doing what he's doing.[2]

I don't pray, except in my work.[3]

Arthur Miller

In 1995 I travelled with a BBC producer, Julian May, to conduct a weekend of interviews with Arthur Miller on the back porch of his house. The interviews covered as much of his life and work as we could. We would break off from time to time. Inge cooked us a salmon for lunch that we ate at a table just beyond the back of the house, which looked out over the hills where he and Inge had planted thousands of trees thirty-three years earlier. When the programmes were transmitted it was possible to hear the songs of the birds as they laced in and out of the trees.

Julian was an amateur carpenter; he once built a boat in his living room that had necessitated removing the windows in order to extricate it. Miller had had a similar experience as a young man, and immediately took Julian to see his barn, where he was working on a bench. The conversation that followed, in which he spoke of his carpentry in terms that applied equally to his drama, became the basis of a programme. Julian later explained:

Arthur's seat was a solid, rather than elegant, bench made from blond timber that I did not recognise. 'Sassafras. Very easy to cut and light for a strong wood. It's like cherry to work . . . They use it for fence posts because it doesn't rot easily. This is for the porch, out in the open, so I thought I'd use it . . . I improvised the design, one thing led to another – a bit like improvising a play, to tell the truth ... something I enjoy doing.' Then Arthur pointed out a hefty piece of pale raw timber. It came from an apple tree, which had stood behind the Roxbury house since he had first moved there in 1956, and which was already old then. A swing for Rebecca ... was strung from it. But it had blown down the previous year. Arthur wanted to make something from it, could not decide what and was not to be rushed. 'I'm waiting for the moment. It hasn't arrived yet.' He ran his palm along the grain. 'It's waiting for the human hand to turn it into something useful, or beautiful. It's exciting to think of it like that. It's like the beginning of the world before it was shaped. It's like a blank piece of paper you could make into something boring or significant. That piece of wood is a challenge. If you want to accept it.'

Arthur had made a chair, too, using chestnut beams from a barn built before Independence. 'See, this little patch,' he said, jabbing a finger at a square that didn't match the rest of the surface. 'It's sunk into the other wood because it was splintering there ... This is called a Dutchman ... This is the breadboard design,' he said, pointing out how he had grooved a piece with the grain going in a different direction into the end of a board in the bedroom, to keep it from splaying in all directions ... 'I've always visualised things in concrete mass,' Arthur told me, as he picked up a weighty wooden bookend. 'Look at these. They're just chunks of wood. But they're beautiful. The wood is. I didn't try to fuss with it. And they hold the books real well. I get great satisfaction from creating something out of nothing.' As well as his bench, the dining table, the chairs, the shelves and bookends, Arthur Miller had built the bed on which he and Inge Morath slept all their married life. 'My wife, every time she goes to sleep, says, "I love this bed." Nothing's going to happen. It'll be there as long as anybody wants to use it ... There's something immortal in that bed.'[4]

That May a group of writers and actors attended a breakfast lobby to argue for continued Congressional support for the arts. The 104th Congress had been elected in the fall of 1994, with Newt Gingrich as Speaker of the House of Representatives. Here was a man who would target the National Endowment for the Arts for major cuts – indeed, who had announced that he wished to see both it and the National Endowment for the Humanities closed down. The NEA, he had protested in a *Washington Times* interview, was used by left-wingers to propagandize children against mainstream values; there was no right, he said, to coerce taxpayers to finance people 'doing weird things'.

In the course of the discussion, Gingrich invoked Miller as an example of a man who had been successful without the benefit of grants from the government. Miller was stung into responding. On 6 June, he wrote to Gingrich: on the contrary, he said, he had received such help at two crucial moments in his life – once as a student at the University of Michigan when the National Youth Administration had paid him to feed mice in a research laboratory, and once when he worked for the Federal Theatre. It was this, he argued, that had enabled him to launch his career, during which he, and others like himself, had paid enough taxes to finance the project. In the 1930s, he pointed out, 'the country was in crisis ... and the support of the arts by government was a vital gesture of mutuality between the American people and the artists, and helped sustain a faith in one another and the country's future.' He was against the kind of government funding available in totalitarian countries, but pointed to Britain as evidence of what subsidies could accomplish. He also reminded Gingrich that land-grant colleges (later to become state universities) had been established by the federal government as a condition of a state's admission to the Union, and that one of their functions had been to raise the cultural level of the country. 'We believe most in the reality of what is marketable,' Miller observed. 'This is a hallmark of commercial society and we glory in it. But there is often more enduring value in what is not marketable, or not immediately so.'5

Gingrich and the new Congress were unimpressed. In 1993 the budget of the NEA was $174,459,382. By 1996 it had been cut to $99,470,000. It had not fully recovered by 2009, when it stood at $155,000,000.

That July the investigative reporter Seymour Hersh (who broke the story of the My Lai massacre in 1968) asked Miller to confirm the authenticity of a document purporting to be an agreement between Marilyn Monroe and President Kennedy in which she undertook to remain silent about their affair in return for $600,000, which would be paid into a trust fund for her mother. Miller thought it possible, but while Marilyn's signature seemed genuine (a fact confirmed by handwriting analysts), he was sceptical. As it turned out, he was right to be. On the eve of the publication of Hersh's book *The Dark Side of Camelot* two years later, the documents were revealed as fraudulent. ABC News, which had bought the rights to the book, confessed that they were fakes and ran an edition of their regular programme *20/20* which exposed the fraud, their reporter Peter Jennings confronting the man thought to be responsible. There had, it seemed, been warning signs. When Hersh had shown the documents to Janet Des Rosiers Fontaine, a former secretary and mistress of Joseph Kennedy's whose signature was supposedly on the document, she had denied it was hers, that she had been in the hotel where it was signed or that she had ever met Marilyn. Hersh had dismissed her denials. Now he scrapped the relevant chapter.

In 1998 Lawrence Cusack III was charged with fraud, the court papers alleging that he had defrauded investors in letters and notes supposedly written by the Kennedys and Marilyn, to the extent of $7 million. Cusack's father had been a lawyer, and a supposed note from Kennedy had been written on his headed notepaper. Unfortunately it listed a zip code, and such codes were not introduced until two years later. The document had been typed on a machine with a self-correcting tape, not available until the 1970s. For Miller, the incident was yet further evidence of the obsessive interest in Marilyn that so dogged him. For many, it seemed, his significance lay less in his work than in his relationship with a woman now dead for thirty-six years.

The main business of 1995, though, was the filming of *The Crucible*. It had taken several years to get the project under way. At the time of its first production there had been no possibility of a commercial company undertaking it. There had been talk, though, of a television version (which Miller resisted when it was suggested that shooting would last no more than three weeks), and CBS and HBO had held the rights for many years. Finally, in 1990, those rights became available, and Miller's son Robert convinced his father that he could get it made if he would write the screenplay. He observed, 'Arthur had not had good experiences with films ... besides that, I had no track record as a producer. He had no reason to believe in me, but I kept pushing, and as I began to verbalize why I thought this could be a movie, he got more excited. I think this is the most cinematic of all his plays. It's less introspective and more linear than most of the others.'[6] Miller initially gave his son a six-month option, although: 'I was afraid that when I saw it on the screen, I'd want to flee the theatre. That's the way I felt with other films of my plays. This is the only time when what I imagined while writing showed up on the screen. And it would never have happened without Bob.'[7]

The main problem turned out to be that of finding a director. Miller was depressed by the number who turned the project down, taking this as further evidence of his own rejection. Kenneth Branagh was only one of a number who declined involvement. Finally, Twentieth Century Fox proposed the British director Nicholas Hytner, whose first film *The Madness of King George* had been released the previous year. Here was someone used to the theatre with whom Miller felt he could work, and whose film had dealt with a historical subject. Hytner went to Roxbury and the two of them did further work on the script, which had taken three months to write. The director expressed relief at Miller's willingness to make adjustments. It was, he felt, as if he were asking Shakespeare to a make changes to *King Lear*. To Miller's surprise, at no stage did Twentieth Century Fox intervene. The final film was thus precisely as he and Hytner wished it to be.

The cast was impressive. John Proctor was played by Daniel Day-Lewis, Judge Danforth by Paul Scofield, Abigail by Winona Rider and Elizabeth Proctor by Joan Allen. Salem was played by Hog Island in Ipswich Bay, twenty-five miles north of Boston, and, Hytner asserted, within sight of land once owned by the real John Proctor. An alternative name for Hog Island is Choate Island, named after the diplomat and lawyer Joseph Choate, who had himself been born in Salem. For reasons of cheapness, Hytner had been urged to film in Nova Scotia, but he wanted to shoot against the background of the sea – thereby underscoring the tenuous grasp the settlers had on the land but, more significantly, the paradise that would be lost. The instructions he gave to the director of photography, Andrew Dunn, and the production designer, Lilly Kilvert reflected this. Salem village itself had not been on the coast; the sea was a mile distant. For Hytner, though, moving the action to the very edge of the continent underlined the tension between 'the fate of a man's soul and the future of the whole community'.[8]

Shooting posed its own difficulties. Hog Island is an uninhabited 180-acre bird sanctuary consisting of pine forests, open land and salt marshes. There was no fresh water, which, along with food and construction equipment, had to be ferried in on barges manned by a squad of National Guardsmen, though the journey took not much more than five minutes. The water was not only for the cast and crew but also for the crops that would feature in the film – the people of Salem had been farmers. Joan Allen remembered watching as an apple tree was ferried in on a barge and a herb garden was planted. The island had one disadvantage. It was home to greenflies which meant that insect repellent had to be added to the list of products to be transported.

Slowly a village was built, leading down to the sea, and one of those constructing the buildings was Daniel Day-Lewis, who had already begun preparations for his role. During the summer of 1995 he had lived for a time on the mainland, working as a carpenter, before venturing on to the island. As he explained, 'It seemed that the important thing to do was some kind of physical work . . . So I spent some time on the island, because so much of the story of those people's lives was contained within the way they took possession of that land.'[9] Later, he would ride to the set on a brown horse rather than use one of the golf carts provided, and between shots he would whittle wood with an old knife, his intensity communicating itself to the other actors.

Clammers were paid $200 a day not to clam, while other local people were employed as extras or, as Hytner preferred to call them, villagers; many of them claimed to be descendants of the accused witches. Locals also played the children. The film had a budget of $25 million and was completed in fifty-six days. The interiors were shot in the nearby town of Beverly – the site of what had once been the parish of the play's Reverend Hale – while the production offices were located in a former mental institution.

At the end of August, Miller joined the cast for a read-through of the script, himself taking the parts of those actors who had yet to arrive. His son Robert spoke of his father's easy manner with those who worked on the set, several of whom had acted in the play in high school or college productions: 'He's more at ease talking about tractors and 2-by-4s than theatrical conquests.'[10]

For a man who had disliked all previous adaptations of his plays, Miller declared himself happy with the result. Little was lost in post-production. When the screenplay was published the following year he prefaced it with an essay called '*The Crucible* as Film'. Again he argued, at first, that film struck him as a second-order activity when compared to theatre, not least because theatre was 'a high-wire act' with 'no fifty-piece orchestras humming away from four walls of a movie theater to plaster over the cracks in the plot, not to mention actors' faces thirty feet high that can hold even the most wayward movie-goers' attention long after they have by any logic lost the claim to fictive existence'. In the theatre, language was central; in the cinema it was action. 'The play wants to tell, the movie to show.'[11] Adapting plays had always struck him as fruitless. Working on *The Crucible*, however, taught him otherwise.

Film, he now realized, offered the opportunity to open the action up, to move into the community of Salem. It became possible 'actually to show the girls out in the forest with Tituba in the wee hours'. He could also now present 'the wild beauty of the newly cultivated land bordered by the wild sea, and the utter disorder and chaos of the town meetings ... Now one could see the hysteria as it grew rather than for the most part reporting it only.' His problem was that he had always believed that film required language to be pared away, while *The Crucible* in particular was 'founded on words and scenes built on the kind of sculpted language which I feared now to disrupt'.[12] He credited Hytner with helping him to resolve the dilemma. He moved as much of the action outside as possible, making use of the Hog Island setting. The static nature of the play gave way to fluidity and its sexuality was foregrounded.

For Hytner, film made it easier to dramatize 'the inseparable link between chaos and personal trauma'; the community became a character; the camera was freed to roam through the village as news of events spread from house to house like a virus, and shots were intercut. That link between the private and the public, always central to Miller's work, became an aesthetic. He was struck by the topicality of a work that seemed to comment directly both on worldwide religious fundamentalism and on the orthodoxies to be found on college campuses. Miller remarked, 'Fundamentalism is happening internationally ... In Israel, they're rushing through the streets trying to stop traffic on the Sabbath. The absolutist passion is an undying feeling. The fanaticism of people attacking automobiles! The isolation that the Jews were forced into feeds that. In another age it was the Catholics. It ain't going to go away.'[13]

Among the changes made for the film, perhaps the most significant was to the ending. In the stage version Proctor dies off stage. In the film we see him hanged, as he and the other accused recite the Lord's Prayer, supposedly a proof that they are not witches. (When one George Burroughs did so in seventeenth-century New England, though the restive crowd were calmed by a speech by the Puritan minister Cotton Mather, the man was hanged anyway.) For Miller, this ending became 'one of the most persuasive moments of the film ... when you see that rope tighten around Proctor's neck. That is a message – the fact that he went down to the end and did not relent.'[14]

A powerful and compelling film, *The Crucible* (which was to win Miller an Oscar nomination) finished shooting in mid-November and was released in December 1996. In an article in the *Washington Post* Paula Span noted Miller's revelling in the fact that on its opening night it had been greeted with a ten-minute ovation; but she noted too that he had 'become one of those honored writers whose works are read and studied in their own country, but far more likely to be performed – to great acclaim – abroad'. This was 'one of the reasons Robert Miller wanted to put "The Crucible" on screen'. Most of his father's work, she quoted Robert as saying, 'is revered, up on a shelf, a masterpiece, a museum piece'. So, she added, 'he goes frequently to London, where one after another of his plays – including those dismissed or disparaged or unproduced in New York – have had successful runs'.[15]

James Houghton, artistic director of New York's Signature Theatre Company, then preparing to present a season of his plays, observed: 'There's a brutality [to America's treatment of its writers]. It's hit or miss – you hit and you're produced again, you miss and you're not.' Echoing his comments of the previous decades Miller confessed to feeling estranged, 'as most play-wrights do here [in New York]. There's a great deal more despair than anyone wants to talk about, because of this chaos, this production system that wastes so much talent.' Noting that works dismissed or disparaged or unproduced in New York had successful runs in Britain – *Death of a Salesman* was then running at the National – Span quotes Nicholas Hytner as saying of his British reception that 'All his plays are big events here ... People will listen.'[16]

Death of a Salesman was indeed a triumph at the National, though Richard Eyre was less sure about the play:

> The first preview ... directed by David Thacker, in the Lyttelton ... went well and was greeted with rapture, although the play is beginning to feel like a period piece, no longer a parable for our times, more about the destructive nature of dreams than the corrosive effect of capitalism. The plot seemed over-neat – Biff becoming a drop-out when he discovers his father with another woman – and the funeral scene seemed sentimental, but Alun Arm-strong and Marjorie Yates were luminously honest and thoughtful and unsen-sationally affecting.[17]

With the Signature Theatre's impending season of his plays, however, Edward Albee remarked, 'It's Arthur Miller time ... And high time,'[18] though the reception of *The Crucible* hardly indicated as much.

When the film was released, the *Washington Post*'s reviewer found it 'a period piece' with one-dimensional characters that 'could be subtitled "Blood-Crazed Teen Bimbos from Inner Space"'.[19] Other reviews were mixed. *Rolling Stone* found it 'a seductively exciting film that crackles with visual energy, passionate provocation and incendiary acting' despite 'some damaging cuts to the text' – an odd remark, given that it found Miller's screenplay 'a model of adventurous film adaptation'.[20] In the *Los Angeles Times* Kenneth Turan objected that despite the promise of its cast it was 'rife with screaming fits and wild-eyed rantings'. The film was 'too frantic to be involving'. Quoting from some of the original negative reviews in 1953, he observed that despite involving moments '"The Crucible" finally seems too schematic, more useful as an allegory than as drama, and possibly owing [its] undoubted popularity to its simplistic qualities as much as [to] its insights into group psychology.'[21] The *Cincinnati Enquirer* found it 'dull' despite outstanding performances. For Roger Ebert in the *Chicago Sun-Times,* 'the first scene in "The Crucible" strikes the first wrong note.' Showing overt sexuality in Puritan New England struck him as a mistake – at least in the play it had been kept off stage. He also found the ending unconvincing. What the film needed, he suggested, was 'less frenzy and more human nature'.[22] In the *New York Times*, though, Victor Navasky did not so much review it as offer a friendly account.

There was another significance to the filming of *The Crucible*. It was now that Daniel Day-Lewis and Rebecca Miller first met, though they had been in touch earlier when Rebecca had sent him a copy of the script that became her film *The Ballad of Jack and Rose*. He had turned it down, even though fascinated by it. Now they met, at Roxbury and then on set. Things moved fast. In October 1996 Daniel called his future father-in-law to tell him they planned to marry, which they did the following month in a ceremony presided over by William Sloane Coffin in a small Vermont church. Daniel's mother flew in for the ceremony, at which Jim Sheridan (who had directed Daniel in *My Left Foot* (1989) and *In the Name of the Father* (1993) and was about to direct him in *The Boxer*) was best man.

Rebecca, whose middle name is Augusta after her paternal grandmother, was born just a month before her father's forty-seventh birthday. As a child, she was conscious of her father's age and later revealed she had been afraid he might die. 'I think the thought of death, in particular men confronting death ... has always been touching to me and compelling.'[23] The daughter of a writer and a photographer, she was raised 'by artists to be an artist like tennis players raise their children to be tennis players'.[24] She told me in 2001:

> I always drew when I was a very little kid. I never had very much aptitude
> for math. I wanted to be a scientist. I wanted to be a botanist, a biologist,
> like my grandmother. I had a microscope. I liked to dissect things. I was

always doing litmus tests. I loved all that, but I didn't have the mathematical skills. But ... through high school I always thought of myself as someone who wrote as well as painted. I made the decision to start painting probably because of a teacher I had in high school, who was very encouraging. Then I emphasized that in college.

At high school she studied both *The Crucible* and *Death of a Salesman*; she appeared as Abigail, and wrote a paper on *Salesman*. 'My dad came to see me and said that he had never seen such a furious Abigail. I was very angry.'

When quite young, she went through a religious phase, and to her father's mystification and horror became a Catholic: 'We had some neighbours who were Catholic and my best friend was in that family and I would go with them to church.' It was Inge who convinced Miller to accept her decision. For several years she believed that Lucifer lived in the basement of the family home and she was eleven before she could bring herself to go down there. She has admitted to being terrified as a child that she might be kidnapped or murdered, a feeling that has not entirely left her. Though happy enough in rural Connecticut, she explained that she would have felt more secure in Manhattan. At the age of thirteen she arranged for her own baptism, turning to William Sloane Coffin to conduct the ceremony. Of her father's attitude she said:

He doesn't like religion. He thought that me becoming a Catholic was particularly odious. Of all things, a Catholic! But I was very serious about it for a long time, until I became a late teenager and my life took over. I never lost it, though. My first film, *Angela*, was about Catholicism, in a way about what a child absorbs of Catholicism. I was very drawn to it and I have never really lost some aspects of that. I've kept it with me. It's still in my work.

It is not hard to see this as an attempt to establish her own identity. Daughter of a Jewish father, she becomes a Catholic. Daughter of a writer and photographer, she becomes an artist. 'Maybe my decision not to write had to do with wanting space and freedom.'

Her father valued success – 'Absolutely. I don't think my father thinks that money is important, but he thinks that you ought to make something of yourself. I remember him telling me that you have to play the game. And I was definitely motivated to make them proud, especially my father. I went to Yale and was always good at stuff and always tried really hard. I was the little dog bringing back the bone, or the Frisbee that was thrown out. I was the good daughter, absolutely.' Growing up in a house where writers, actors, directors turned up for lunch, she remembered 'Robert Lowell and Bill Styron, and Vanessa Redgrave. The exotic was normal people. I was always drawn towards what I considered to be real people. I've continued to be.

That's who I am interested in. I find artists, with the exception of people I really love – obviously I am married to an artist – to be obsessed with themselves. Egomania. I am one. Being an artist is a kind of alienation. You are a watcher. It's just a curse, or a blessing, however you look at it.'

At Yale she majored in art, while taking courses in literature, including one in writing: 'I could have been a minor in literature but I decided not to do that. I took a number of academic courses. I was very interested in classical civilization, Greek and Aztec culture. I was very interested in ritual and the connection between literature and ritual. I had always been very interested in religion. I have always been interested in cosmologies, the ways in which we write ourselves through cosmologies.'

She travelled to Munich on a painting scholarship and then returned to New York, where she began to show her work in galleries. 'That was really all I did for years. I was a painter. It was really my life until I was twenty something. I showed in New York. I sold a lot of paintings. That was really my life.' Her works were, she explained, very opaque, dreamlike. Then there came a point when she decided to make short films, animating those dreams, and in 1985 shot a number of 16mm films, which she later incorporated into mixed-media presentations along with her sculptures. In 1987 she began acting, and in 1990 directed her first narrative film, *Florence*. 'I think a lot people around me thought I was lost, but I wasn't lost.' As a stage director she took on *After the Fall*, while as an actress she appeared in a series of films: *Regarding Henry, Consenting Adults, The Pickle* and *Mrs Parker and the Vicious Circle*. In theatre she worked with Peter Brook in the New York production of *The Cherry Orchard*. She made her debut as a film director with *Angela*, which won the Filmmaker's Trophy at the Sundance Film Festival in 1995. *Angela* concerns a ten-year-old girl who is obsessed by the idea of sin and is convinced that the Devil has moved into her basement.

For some time she had avoided the notion of screenwriting for fear of being seen to go head to head with her father, but she came to feel that films were essentially different from plays and that she thus had some kind of licence. Her father was shown the script of *Angela* only when it was nearing completion. Asked what she had learned from her parents she remarked that,

Film probably unifies the things that they gave me. My mother always took me to museums. I was continually seeing her seeing things. And seeing what she saw through photographs. Also she loved paintings very much and was hugely supportive of me as a painter. From my father I learned an enormous amount. I think my dad and I have a lot of similarities but also differences because my point of view is very much the female point of view. I am interested in women's lives and women in the world. But at the same time, I always had an ear for dialogue. The thing I learned most from him was the art of condensation. I was never intimidated but perhaps the reason I didn't choose to write [at first] had to do with wanting space and freedom.[25]

Speaking on the *Charlie Rose Show* in March 2005 she observed,

It is hard to say exactly how your parents have formed you, how to subtract them from whatever else will have given you what you are. I think that from both my parents I got a real work ethic, and I believe in what I do. I am happy to be telling stories. I think that there is something positive about constructing a bridge of empathy between a viewer and a character who they may not otherwise have understood or liked or wanted to give the time of day to. And I think my dad also had an optimistic view of storytelling. Technically, he loved condensation and a kind of utilitarian way of looking at words and language, that everything had to have a purpose. I remember once he stopped and was staring at this garbage truck and I said, 'Why are you doing that?' And he said, 'Isn't that beautiful?' It was the kind of garbage truck which takes the skip and everything fits in perfectly and he said, 'But everything fits, everything has a purpose.' In a more loose-limbed and very different fashion and style I have a similar aesthetic.[26]

She shared a taste for Russian literature with her father, but was also an admirer of F. Scott Fitzgerald. As to family relationships:

The Miller family were a little bit cool in a way with each other. There's a kind of distance. My parents are private. There's not a lot of sharing of emotions. I'm quite different from that. I've made myself be quite different. There's part of me that can cut off, but that's the way they are. They're just private. They don't talk about things. It's old-fashioned, partly, shyness, embarrassment. No scenes. That's what my father's family is like. My mother's mother was really quite hot. I used to sleep in her room. I think a lot of me comes out of my grandmother. But I don't really have a relationship with anyone in my family except my parents. And that's probably because there is a sense that we were different.

Later Rebecca would have a successful career as a short story writer and novelist, directing film versions of her work.

Daniel Day-Lewis was born in 1957, the son of Britain's Poet Laureate Cecil Day-Lewis (later C. Day-Lewis) who had been born in Ireland, son of a Protestant clergyman. Leaning towards communism in the 1930s, he removed the hyphen from his name, later restoring it. Daniel's mother was the actress Jill Balcon, daughter of Michael Balcon, head of Ealing Studios. Daniel grew up in Greenwich. Part Jewish, part Irish, and with what he characterized as a 'posh accent', he would adopt a working-class accent and demeanour every time he left home.

When sent away to a boarding school in Kent he was unhappy, but took to carpentry and acting. He appeared in Alan Paton's *Cry, the Beloved Country*, blacking up for the role. Before moving to another school he played a bit part in John Schlesinger's *Sunday, Bloody Sunday*, written by Penelope Gilliatt, for which he received £5. At Bedales school he continued to act, but on leaving considered a career in carpentry before joining the Bristol Old Vic Theatre School, where he slowly established himself as a star, though unhappy with aspects of the British theatre scene. It was his appearance in the film of Hanif Kureishi's *My Beautiful Laundrette*, directed by Stephen Frears, that brought him to public attention. He followed this with the film version of *A Room with a View* and Milan Kundera's *The Unbearable Lightness of Being*, a part that he later regretted, feeling that he had never quite grasped the essence of his character.

He performed a number of roles at the National Theatre until in 1989, playing the part of Hamlet, he suddenly walked off the stage. News reports insisted that the scene in which Hamlet speaks to his dead father had disturbed him. He himself put it down to simple exhaustion, as did the play's director, Richard Eyre: 'Dan's exhausted,' he wrote on 7 May 1989, 'stretched on the rack. If it weren't for his pride and his loyalty he'd be off tomorrow. He's completely lost heart. I couldn't tell him that I felt just the same. For him it's partly the subject matter – his father … but it's much more that he's deter-mined to investigate the truth of the part and he has to do it in a great barn with hopeless acoustics to 1,200 people who are craving spectacle. How *can* he reconcile this?'[27] It was the end of his stage career. Certainly it was in film that he now thrived, winning an Oscar for his performance in *My Left Foot*, a film based on the autobiography of Christy Brown, who suffered from cerebral palsy. This was followed by the impressive *The Last of the Mohicans* and the role of Newland Archer in Edith Wharton's *The Age of Innocence*, directed by Martin Scorsese. Later would come *The Gangs of New York*, *There Will Be Blood* and *Nine*.

Daniel had always admired American films, seeing Robert De Niro in *Taxi Driver* five or six times in its first week, though he was also an admirer of the socially conscious work of Ken Loach. America appealed, free, as it seemed, of the class-consciousness of Britain. Inevitably, he found himself in the public eye. He did not take kindly to being hounded, and so moved to Ireland buying a house at Castlekevin in the Wicklow Mountains. He was highly selective of the roles he played, never considering new proposals while working on another project. He turned down both *Schindler's List* and *The English Patient*. Once asked what he loved about acting, he replied, 'It's a game. It's a wonderful game. You don't know where the horizon is. You don't put fences around it. The possibilities are limitless, which is a fearful thing in some respects, but as you gather things towards you and try and nourish that little patch of ground and feel something growing, it's wonderful ... I enjoy the fact that it remains a mystery, even though that makes it always elusive.' For Rebecca, 'That is very much how I write. I write in a state of dark. I don't premeditate. I don't preconceive. I try to let things mature in an organic way. I give Daniel, the actor, something that's written but what is called an interpretative art is really an act of creation.'

When they married, Rebecca explained:

> I said to Daniel when I first met him that I don't think of you as an actor. He's not like any actor I've ever met. Daniel's not really an actor. He's some other creature. He's able to do it but he does it almost as though it were some other art. There's another dimension when he works. There's something magical about it. It's almost a spiritual thing to him. He's able to do that thing, which is acting, but he puts the same thing into making shoes or doing other things. Those things aren't just hobbies that he does. Those are real things. It's just that everybody sees that other thing so they all say he is an actor. But to me he is as much, potentially, a painter. He's a wonderful painter. So I did marry an actor, which is funny because I never went out with any actors.

In October 1995, when Miller and Inge returned to Britain to celebrate his eightieth birthday the *Observer* carried the headline: 'The Great Playwright Sticks in America's Craw, But Not Ours'.[28] It was a less than generous description, since in terms of his classic plays he remained as significant a figure as ever, and American PEN was already planning a celebration of his birthday in New York's Town Hall. In England, *Plain Girl* (issued in the US three years earlier as *Homely Girl*) was published, and a gala performance, sold out for months, was staged at the National Theatre. An on-stage interview with Miller was interspersed with scenes from his plays, performed by major figures from the British theatre, most of whom had appeared in his plays, including Rosemary Harris, Henry Goodman, Ken Stott, Joseph Fiennes, Josette Simon, Juliet Stevenson, Bernard Hill, John Shrapnel and Margot Leicester. The event was recorded for BBC television.

On his birthday, he travelled to Norwich and the Arthur Miller Centre at the University of East Anglia. Here he was to attend a gala dinner in the presence of actors, directors, reviewers and academics, some flying in from the United States and elsewhere in Europe. The dinner was also attended by members of Miller's family, including Inge's brother, flying in from Germany, and Miller's daughter Jane and her husband, arriving from the United States. The speakers were David Thacker and, still requiring heavy security at the time, Salman Rushdie. The evening concluded with fireworks, which led Miller, in his speech, to recall once watching fireworks in his youth when the barge carrying them exploded in the East River – a potentially disconcerting tale to tell, given that these birthday fireworks were being detonated outside the Sainbury Centre for Visual Arts, designed by Norman Foster with its thirty-foot-high glass walls and art collection worth many millions. The diners, given Rushdie's presence, were also aware of the possibility of explosions from something other than fireworks. From Norwich Miller moved on to Oxford University, where he was Cameron Mackintosh Visiting Professor of Drama, to receive an honorary degree.

Back in the United States, the fifteen-hundred-seat Town Hall was sold out for the PEN celebration of his birthday, consisting of speeches and readings by, among others, Edward Albee, John Guare, Carlos Fuentes and David Mamet, along with a brief extract from *The Crucible* performed by Sam Waterston and Dianne Wiest. Albee recalled attending a demonstration with Miller outside the Soviet Mission to the United Nations, which he saw as evidence of [Miller's] 'understanding, his comprehension of what it is to be a writer – always to the barricades'. David Mamet spoke of his ability to write drama 'informed by and always superior to the political'. John Guare praised his ability to 'get inside people's dreams', while Carlos Fuentes, whom Miller had first met at the PEN conference in New York in 1966, saw him as a 'Quixote of the American and world stage', adding caustically: 'I divide my time between Mexico and London . . . and one of the reasons I spend half my time in Britain is to get to see all of Arthur Miller's plays.'[29]

At the Sardi restaurant party that followed Miller swung a punch at Baird Jones, a young reporter from the *Daily News*, when he asked him if he still dreamed of Marilyn. Jones later recalled, 'He started to go after me. The closer he came, the faster I back-pedaled. Finally, about twenty feet from the table, he actually threw a punch, which hit me in the shoulder. He was a big guy with huge arms, and this man had a heck of a lot of power in that punch.'[30] The big guy was eighty years old. The reporter ran out on to West 44th Street.

May 1996 saw a one-off production of the enigmatic *Elegy for a Lady* as part of the Ensemble Studio Theater's festival of one-act plays, while *The Ride down Mount Morgan* finally arrived in America, opening at the Williamstown Theatre Festival. Directed by Scott Elliott, it starred F. Murray Abraham. It was scheduled for only a short run, but the reviews were positive. To Ben Brantley in the *New York Times* it offered 'a fascinating testament to one author's constancy of vision and his abiding willingness to experiment [in order] to put it over. In an age in which ethics and styles are changed like underwear, there is something reassuring about both the consistency and ferocity of this playwright.' It was, he noted, a comment on the Reagan years, if also a play in which 'the ontological doubts [Miller] expressed in "After the Fall" [were taken] to their most extreme conclusions'. The text, however, struck Brantley as 'at odds with the ominous urgency of Mr Elliott's sometimes disjunctive direction', while 'Mr Miller's fabled artisan's sense of construction isn't in evidence here'.[31] Nonetheless, regional theatre and Off Broadway had begun the business of putting Miller back at the centre of attention.

Miller's health had been deteriorating for some time. The sight in one eye had been failing, and he suffered from stenosis of the spine, which caused him considerable back pain. Stenosis is a narrowing of the spinal cord and loss of disc height that causes root pain and is often brought on by walking and relieved by rest. No wonder he could no longer walk more than a block. He underwent an operation to fuse two vertebrae, but the pain continued. Bone fragments remained around the spine, requiring injections along with daily tablets. He had a further eye operation. It took some time for his sight to improve, but within a month the last stitch was removed and he could read three more lines on the eye chart. This spurred him to tell me a joke. A Pole is shown an eye chart with its jumble of consonants. 'Can you read the bottom line?' the optometrist asks him. 'Read it?' he replies, 'I know the man.'

None of this, though, prevented him travelling abroad. In July 1997 he and Inge spent three weeks in Ireland and Spain. Inge was the subject of elaborate celebrations in Navalcán, which she had photographed many years before. A street was named after her and in later years a copy of the street sign was to be seen in her home in Roxbury, alongside a similar one given to her husband when West 49th Street was designated Arthur Miller Way (he objected that he was still not allowed to park there). They were accompanied on their visit to Spain by Derek Walcott who, like Miller, went on to lecture at the Escorial.

In 1997 the Signature Theatre put on a season of Miller plays. Though it is on 42nd Street, the theatre is located far from Broadway, between 9th and 10th Avenues. It was founded in 1991 by James Houghton and specializes in staging entire series devoted to the work of a single playwright, thus affording the admittedly small audiences – the theatre has only 160 seats – some sense of the shape of a writer's career though the choice in Miller's case, with one exception, favoured the later part of that career. The Miller season (1997–8) featured *The American Clock, I Can't Remember Anything, The Last Yankee, Mr Peters' Connections* and, interestingly, his old radio play *The Pussycat and the Expert Plumber Who Was a Man.*

The event was to open with *The American Clock*, in truth not well suited to a small theatre with limited resources. Even at Off Off Broadway rates, epic comes expensive. The *New York Times* review was what Miller had feared. Noting that he had returned to the stage in New York, 'which in recent years has tended to spurn a man it lionized in the first great decades of his career', Ben Brantley remarked that 'satisfying as it would be to report that this play now shimmers as a wrongly neglected jewel, that is not, alas, the case'. It was 'still an ungainly mechanism with only flickers of its author's fabled confrontational power'. Miller, he noted, had two personae, the spell-binding storyteller and 'the finger-wagging preacher ... here it's the preacher whose voice is by far the louder'. There was, though, something 'admirable and touching' about his insistence on saying 'what he believes is important to a largely unheeding audience'. As a piece of theatre, however, *The American Clock* was 'not something to rejoice over'.[32] Unsurprisingly, Miller found the condescension as unbearable as it had been predictable. Then in mid-November *A View from the Bridge* went into rehearsal at the Roundabout Theatre, even as he was attending casting sessions for a double bill of *The Last Yankee* and *I Can't Remember Anything*, with Joseph Chaikin directing. In early December Miller read the part of Howard in Wallace Shawn's *The Designated Mourner* in front of an audience of forty in a rehearsal room on East 4th Street.

He was also present at the first reading of *Mr Peters' Connections* (then called 'The Subject'), that was to star Peter Falk. Back in 1953, Falk had applied to join the CIA, an application rejected because he had once been a member of a left-wing union. He had gone on to a successful career as an actor, though this would be his return to the theatre after an absence of twenty-seven years, during which he had established his reputation as Lieutenant Columbo in the long-running television series. He was perhaps not a bad choice for a character who spends much of the play trying to puzzle out the mystery of his life, assembling the evidence, sifting through seemingly irrelevant details in an effort to understand.

A View from the Bridge at the Roundabout Theatre, with Anthony LaPaglia as Eddie Carbone and directed by Michael Mayer, opened shortly before Christmas 1997 to largely excellent reviews, though *Variety* dismissed it as miscast and badly acted. Ben Brantley in the *New York Times* called it 'first rate ... compelling' and distinctive, while suggesting that the device of making the lawyer character Alfieri 'a one-man Greek chorus' had never worked. It was, though, a reminder of 'what an utterly absorbing storyteller Mr Miller can be'.[33] Transfer to a larger theatre, however, seemed out of the question since it would cost half a million dollars. Certainly no theatre owners came to see it, much to Miller's disgust, if not surprise. The following June both the play and LaPaglia won Tony Awards. The production was cited, along with the film of *The Crucible*, when in May 1998 Miller received the first PEN/Laura Pels Foundation Award, bestowed on a master American dramatist.

Eight months on from its first review, *Variety* now praised the Roundabout production. In retrospect, LaPaglia was granted 'roiling depths' and the production had apparently metamorphosed from 'silly', a failed attempt to reinvigorate the play, to exuding 'theatrical vigor'. Both reviewers, though, dismissed the play itself. The first, Greg Evans, saw it as Greek tragedy by way of social realism, full of moralizing and speechy pretension; the second,

Charles Isherwood, described it as kitchen-sink drama tricked out with the trappings of tragedy. All the same, forty-three years on from its first appearance the play proved remarkably resilient and was to return in 1999, this time in the form of an opera in two acts, which would open at Chicago's Civic Opera House. Now *Variety* described the play as a work with a 'broad emotional canvas' and 'unusual intensity', which worked well 'with arias attached'.

The double bill of *The Last Yankee* and *I Can't Remember Anything*, however, with which Miller entered 1998, prompted a more equivocal response. To Ben Brantley in the *New York Times* both plays showed Miller in more reflective mood, 'something that has never been his strong suit'. The dialogue 'suggests a protracted series of acting exercises', while the plays displayed 'an oddly stilted and tentative air throughout that makes the production feel disjointed in ways that go beyond its thematic intentions'. The audience, he observed, 'spend most of the evening feeling like listless eavesdroppers'.[34] Two weeks later, in the same newspaper, Vincent Canby's brief review found the writing 'secure' and the central performances (Kate Meyer, Kevin Conroy and Peter Maloney in the first and Joseph Wiseman and Rebecca Schull in the second) 'true'. John Simon in *New York* magazine regarded *I Can't Remember Anything* as showing Miller 'at his soundest, working without grandiose aspirations', and *The Last Yankee* 'more pretentious and portentous . . . all Sociology crossed with Psychology, sprinkled with the facile feminism that reinforces male liberal complacency'.[35]

After nearly thirty years of poor reviews for his new plays in America, Miller was largely inured to the response of the New York papers and half inclined to think that the consignment of serious plays to small theatres (and they did not come much smaller than the Signature) was a reflection of America's rejection of serious drama from the time of O'Neill and Odets on though, curiously, he was forgetting his own and Williams's early triumphs. Nonetheless, there was good news when the Drama Desk Awards were announced. Three of the five productions nominated were by Miller – *All My Sons*, *A View from the Bridge* and *The American Clock*.

Mr Peters' Connections (a title finally urged on him by its Irish director Garry Hynes, previously Artistic Director of the Abbey Theatre in Dublin) opened at the Signature Theatre on 17 May 1998. The *New York Times* reviewer duly batted it back, not merely dismissing it but offering it as evidence of Miller's abandonment of the naturalism of his 1940s and 50s plays, whose revivals had reminded audiences simultaneously of his former achievements and his present failings. For Ben Brantley, the play 'can be a numbing experience'. Belatedly acknowledging that 'Mr Miller has never really been the hard-core realist he is often assumed to be', Brantley invoked 'the enduring vitality and relevance of this great playwright's more naturalistic plays', the better to denounce his 'recent exercises in abstraction [which] have an oddly old-fashioned feeling'. Miller had, it seems, become an avant-garde writer, only to discover that he had done so too late: *Mr Peters* was an 'example of the experimental, ruminative style the dramatist has adopted of late that is by no means his most effective'. The result was 'blunt and even clumsy'.[36]

As part of the Signature season, the play was only scheduled for a brief run. Even so, a brickbat from the *New York Times* could prove damaging when it came to the possibility of future productions. One outcome of the baffled response to the play was Miller's decision to offer the kind of explanation in the published version that he had seldom done before. Thus, he explained that Harry Peters, 'retired airline and military pilot and lecturer', is discovered in that 'suspended state of consciousness which can come upon a man taking a nap, when the mind, still close to consciousness and self-awareness, is freed to roam from real memories to conjectures, from trivialities to tragic insights, from terror of death to glorifying in being alive. The play, in short, is taking place inside Mr Peters' mind, or at least on its threshold, from where it is still possible to glance back toward daylight life or forward into the misty depths.' *Death of a Salesman*, of course, was to have taken place inside Willy Loman's mind, but where Willy searched back through his life for the moment when that life went wrong, Mr Peters looks for a governing principle that will make sense of the passing years. The play is 'the procession of Mr Peters' moods, each of them summoning up the next, all of them strung upon the line of his anxiety, his fear, if you will, that he has not found the center of energy – what he calls the subject – that will make his life cohere'.[37]

Miller introduces the characters: Cathy May, Peters' dead lover; her husband, not real, but the man to whom she might have been drawn; Calvin, Peters' long-dead brother; Charlotte, his wife; Peters' daughter Rose and her lover. The other character is Adele, a black bag lady who represents 'the to [Peters] incomprehensible black presence on the dim borders of his city life'.[38] The set is a place where, he explains, the living and the dead might meet. It is a form of limbo, a 'broken structure', an old abandoned nightclub in New York City, which over the years has had a series of other functions. Once it was a bank, with a sense of permanence and solidity, then a library, with its implications of stored knowledge, then a cafeteria. In 2009 Camilo José Vergara published *Harlem, 1970–2009*, in which he includes photographs of a street as it has appeared through the decades – the same store front morphing with the years, each generation moving on and through, leaving, it seems, little trace in a city in which change is a form of constancy. It is a city of ghosts. And it is that sense of things passing, of what once seemed permanent but has now transmuted, that disturbs Miller's central character. What is memory, when it can anchor itself to nothing secure, when all the fixed points have moved? What is a life whose trajectory once appeared so clear, when it seems to have led nowhere but to a general bafflement? What, he asks himself, was it all about, the striving, the passion? Where has the confidence gone that once stitched together a life in a country itself once so certain of its destiny?

Mr Peters' Connections is an old man's play, not in the sense of its author's diminishing powers but because it places at its centre a man who struggles to make sense of a long life, to detect the core of that life in the fragments of memory that crowd in upon him, in experiences now receding into an occluded past. Once there had been certainties. The world had seemed at his command. Family relationships, a profession, were all reassuringly in place, serving a confident self. There was a spine to existence. There was a political, social, psychological map in which to locate himself. He was the central figure in a story. Slowly, though, the fixed points have disappeared. Those whose existence once confirmed his own have gone. The deaths of family and friends have thinned his sense of reality.

The city itself has changed. What seemed permanent now appears merely contingent. The job that once gave him something more than status is now long since gone. He had been a pilot for Pan American until a new commercial imperative led to his dismissal; Pan American itself, once part of the fabric of America, is itself fading into the past. Indeed, it is not only Harry Peters who has lost his grasp on the world. The country, too, appears to have lost its definition for this is an end-of-century, end-of-millennium play staged at a time when summaries seemed called for, when what Henry Luce had called the American Century was edging towards its inconclusive end.

In some sense, clearly, Mr Peters is a version of Miller himself. Peters recalls a Polish maid who used to beat carpets on the roof, as the Millers' maid Sadie had done before the family lost their money. His characters invoke Miller's Brooklyn past. Once again, as in earlier plays, there are two brothers, friendly rivals as Miller and Kermit had been. Cathy May, whose underwear 'has been sold, stolen, or given away', may be a version of Norma-Jean: 'Ah yes. How proud of your body.'[39] 'Would it be a little less angry between us now?'[40] Peters asks, as Miller himself used to wonder of Marilyn, had she lived. Peters, like Miller, recalls his youthful enthusiasm for Russia and the conviction that during the war they were saving the world, confessing that 'next to nothing I have believed has turned out to be true'.[41] Miller shared his character's bewilderment at a world transformed.

What, character and author ask, has been the subject of his life, of history, of existence itself? What is the force that pulled together what Peters now fears may have been the merely random, what the connections that linked everything together? 'What I'm trying to ... to ... find my connection with,' he explains, 'is a ... what's the word ... *continuity* ... yes, with the past, perhaps ... in the hope of finding a ... yes, a subject.'[42] The fear is that he will collude with the forces that are slowly dismantling his world: 'In the end I'm afraid that one arrives at a sort of terminal indifference, and there is more suspense in the bowel movement than a Presidential election.'[43] Likewise, Miller admitted to having lost his own enthusiasm, noting his physical decline, as would he not who used to line up his tablets on the breakfast table alongside the cereal and the breakfast muffin? The play is also, though, a celebration of life: 'It's just that when you've flown into hundreds of glorious sunsets, you want them to go on for ever and ever ... and hold off the darkness.'[44] *Mr Peters' Connections* is Miller's attempt to do likewise. For him, at the age of eighty-three, Peters's cry, 'How terrible to go into that darkness alone',[45] had an immediate relevance.

Old passions have died, except that they still flare up in dreams, in memories edited to serve some need he can no longer recall. Has he been so many different people or is there a centre, after all? Those who were once so close to him – including members of his family – are now strangers, as others are dead leaving only a trace of their passing, though as Miller indicates there are those who never quite die, sometimes living more vividly in the mind than they did in actuality. What once seemed so vital, so definitional, are now no more than images. In a sense, Peters is doing what the theatre does. As Miller said, 'That is what its function is ... It's just to stop time. You stop time. That massive flow of images that floods every country, with no meaning, no definition – art stops it. Long enough for you to say, "Oh, that's what the hell it is!" It gives you a moment of recognition. But all you get is that moment.'[46]

At the beginning of the play all the characters appear, present in Mr Peters's memory, simply awaiting the moment to be summoned into view, into his consciousness. The piano plays 'September Song', with music by Kurt Weill and lyrics by Maxwell Anderson, which Miller had first heard in the year he left the University of Michigan, believing he could make his mark on Broadway. Its lyrics set the tone for a work written in the knowledge that time is running out and that somewhere back in the past something was lost, but might yet be redeemed. The play ends as Peters lays his memories to rest. The light, Miller tells us, begins to die as Peters's daughter Rose rests her head on his knee and he asks himself whether love might after all have been the subject for which he has been looking, rather as Willy Loman had once looked for meaning everywhere but in the love of the wife who believed in him as he could no longer believe in himself. The last stage direction is 'The lights fade out'.

But another light has been glimpsed in so far as Rose is pregnant. As it happens, Rebecca was pregnant as Miller finished writing the play and on 14 June she gave birth to a son, Ronan, in the Beth Israel Hospital. In the years to come his new grandchildren would become a source of genuine enthusiasm. If the Miller family were seldom demonstrative in their affections, he made an exception for Ronan and Cashel (born in 1998 and 2002, respectively).

1998 also marked the Public Theater production of *The Ride down Mount Morgan*, with Patrick Stewart, who explanined the history of his own involvement.

[The play] was sent to me by Sam Cohn, Arthur's agent, a couple of years before the Public Theater production … I remember opening this Arthur Miller play with real excitement. And I read it and I called Sam and I said, 'This isn't for me.' I was really disappointed. I feel slightly foolish because I can't tell what it was that made me pass on this play. I simply don't know because two years later, when Sam sent it to me again, I had a completely different reaction to it. I do know that when I read a play for the first time I wait for my feelings to be stirred in some way or another. It has to be something more than an intellectual experience and I suppose it didn't happen.

But when I read it a second time I said this can't be the same play. The director, who I had never heard of, flew out to California to see me. I still had real doubts about it, however. In some way I wasn't connecting with it. David Esbjornson [the play's director] came to my house mid-morning in LA and by some time after lunch it became clear to me that he had no intention of leaving until he had talked me into doing this play. He talked about the richness of the play in terms of its relationships and its emotions, and the terrific neediness of Lyman Felt and how here was a man with a terrific hunger who could never really be satisfied with what he had. That was something with which I could connect, because I had come to realize for several years that as an actor I had worked not just to put bread and butter on the table, as I once had, or because it was something that gave me a glamorous life, but because if I wasn't acting I didn't feel as though I was in the world. Lyman is an actor, but he takes what we do one stage further. There is a depth of self-deception in him, which in actors has to be the ability to convey an appearance of truth and reality to the audience. Lyman believes it. When he says things they are absolutely real. I felt it was a very active role. There were always needs that Lyman was expressing. I also found that the matter of his own belief in his love for these two women was something that I was certainly connecting with more strongly.

I finished the run on Broadway in order to go back to Los Angeles to get married for the second time to someone who I had known and been with for years and years. In fact friends, and my now wife, often teased me as to why I was planning to get married while fully absorbing myself in the life of

Lyman Felt. It was Dr Johnson who said, a man marrying for a second time is an example of the triumph of hope over experience. Arthur has been there and we talked about it at times.

The Ride down Mount Morgan finally arrived in New York seven years after its London opening. It ran for a month in the 299-seat Newman Auditorium of the Public Theater, but already Stewart was trying to arrange his schedule with a view to returning the following April. Reviews were mixed, but performances sold out. In the course of the run Stewart suffered mild concussion when he was struck by a piece of scaffolding that fell from the flies. 'I got hit on the head in the last performance at the Public Theater and I had to spend the night of the wrap party of the production in the emergency room of St Vincent's Hospital. I was there for hours. And I was talking to the staff, explaining the plot of the play, and they said, "It happens all the time. Lovers, husbands, children, this is where they meet."'[47]

Cut and revised, the play that on its first outing in London had seemed a comment on the age of Ronald Reagan with its casual assumption that everyone could have everything, now had a new edge, as the saga of President Clinton and his relationship with the intern Monica Lewinsky unfolded. On 17 August Clinton had finally confessed to the Grand Jury, while on 11 September the Special Prosecutor, Kenneth Starr, released his report, ten days before the Grand Jury testimony became publicly available. Here was a man who, like Miller's protagonist, plainly enjoyed the danger involved in his sexual encounters. His famous meetings with Lewinsky had taken place in the White House, where, presumably, the possibility of discovery added the same kind of frisson that Lyman feels in maintaining a double life. And Stewart played the role with much more sexual directness than Conti had done in the London production, or F. Murray Abraham in Williamstown. Lyman's political liberalism also matched Clinton's, his sense that political and social ethics were distinct from personal morality – something, incidentally, that Miller himself was inclined to believe, aware as he was of the sexual behaviour of so many presidents including, most significantly, Franklin D. Roosevelt, the president – his attitude to the Spanish Civil War notwithstanding – he most admired.

Miller's own defence of Clinton, incidentally, brought him into conflict with Christopher Hitchens, who published a tart book called *No One Left to Lie To: The Values of the Worst Family*, which reprinted an attack that had first appeared in the *Nation*. In October 1998 Miller had written an op-ed piece for the *New York Times* in which he suggested a parallel between the witchcraft hysteria in Salem in 1692 and what struck him as the moral and political hysteria surrounding Clinton. 'In both cases,' he said, 'there is a kind of relief in the unearthing of the culprit's hidden crimes.' There was also 'a parallel in the sexual element underlying each phenomenon'. Witch-hunts, he noted, were always prompted by women's sexuality, 'awakened by the superstud Devil'. Women's bodies had to be examined in detail. He professed to find something similar in the probings of Kenneth Starr and the media: 'I thought of this wonderful holy exercise when Congress went pawing through Kenneth Starr's fiercely exact report on the President's intimate meetings with Monica Lewinsky. I guess nothing changes all that much.' It was, Miller argued, 'Clinton's "imperious need of the female" that had unnerved'. Beyond that, he suggested that there was perhaps a racial element in that Toni Morrison had called Clinton the first black president. The animus against him, there-fore, might be traceable to that.[48] Hitchens now derided the parallel and characterized Miller as 'The Stupid One', dismissing his 'senescent musings' and 'asinine remarks', while suggesting that in Miller, 'the Left's hero of the 1950s, political correctness has achieved its own negation'.[49]

The parallel between Lyman and Clinton was not without plausibility. It was a play, Miller said, 'about a man who has got to have everything, including two wives at the same time, and a man who is really easy to condemn, and should be condemned. But he's a human being and he, for me, was the epitome of a kind of culture – the culture of appetite – which is what I think we have.'[50] *The Ride down Mount Morgan* would have only a limited run, but once again the *New York Times* review, by Ben Brantley, depressed him, especially since he took pride both in the rewritten play (this would be the text, he decided, to be published by Penguin) and in the production.

Brantley commented on the good luck that saw the play finally arrive on Broadway when it had a relevance it had lacked in the Williamstown Theatre Festival in 1996. At the same time, he insisted that it 'smells musty' and that it 'really brought nothing new to the table'. It felt too 'inevitable, pre-determined by theatrical convention'. While observing that the play had 'an elegiac dignity' and that Frances Conroy, who played Theodora, 'suggests that there can indeed be more to Miller's women than meets the eye', he thought that she 'deserves not just a better husband but a better play'.[51]

For Stewart, however, the closure of the Public Theater production signalled

unfinished business. There are some pieces of work where the experience I have had of doing them has simply not been enough. Some plays you have to be exposed to for longer. The three weeks at the Public were not enough and there were aspects of the production that neither David Esbjornson nor myself were happy with. It had been a difficult rehearsal period. We had lost our leading lady very close to opening. Frances Conroy came in and learnt the role over a weekend and was absolutely stupendous and was a Tony nominee. I simply knew there was more. There were areas we had not got into. The emotions of the play were not experienced deeply enough. We felt we had never really got it right at the end, so we left an audience somewhat unsatisfied. And that is where Arthur did the bulk of the work. He was rewriting during the last week at the Public. In preview I was on stage one afternoon, with a performance that night, going over yet another draft of the last speech. In fact, one night I read it on stage because I couldn't absorb all the little changes. So I drew a piece of paper out of my sleeve and I read it.[52]

For all the ambiguous response to *The Ride down Mount Morgan*, however, 1998 ended with some sense of satisfaction. Ahead lay a new production of *Death of a Salesman*, while talks were under way for a film version of his novel *Focus*, produced by his son Robert. Meanwhile, with Philip Roth, William Styron, Toni Morrison and others Miller agreed to sign a statement opposing Clinton's impeachment. The *New York Times* refused to publish it, their policy being not to publish letters with multiple signatures. It did, though, report a rally that December of artists and intellectuals at New York University, at which E.L. Doctorow was quoted as saying that the impeachment proceedings had all the legitimacy of a *coup d'état*. Not since the Vietnam War, William Styron remarked, had writers and artists been so vociferous. There was, the legal philosopher Ronald Dworkin remarked, a smell of brimstone in the air.

Miller flew to Chicago to see *Salesman* at the Goodman Theatre, where Robert Falls, formerly of Chicago's Off Loop Wisdom Bridge, directed. It starred Brian Dennehy and Elizabeth Franz as Willy and Linda Loman, and Kevin Anderson and Ted Koch as Biff and Happy. Mark Wendland's sets were perhaps not as challenging as those of Fran Thompson at London's National Theatre; nonetheless, with their abstract shapes, with turntables and rooms gliding in and out in pools of light, they opened up a space between this *Salesman* and Jo Mielziner's designs back in 1968–9. The music had a rawness that contrasted with Alex North's. Reviews were almost universally positive. For Richard Christiansen of the *Chicago Tribune* it was a brilliant revival and a landmark production. For the *Daily Herald*, the production revealed layers of meaning no previous version had exposed, and a grace, beauty and majesty unequalled by any other Goodman production. The *Northwest Herald* found it masterful. The *Wall Street Journal* thought it a play speaking as clearly to the current generation as it had plainly done to another, fifty years earlier.

The run was extended by three weeks. For his part, Miller was struck by a production that established the dreamlike quality he had been aiming at and that Jo Mielziner had achieved by lighting and the use of gauze curtaining. Brian Dennehy seemed to him to be still feeling his way, but he felt the play moving. Everything, though, would depend on the *New York Times* review. Without a positive response, a transfer to New York was implausible.

On 3 November Ben Brantley duly obliged. Dennehy and Franz were giving the performance of their careers, he wrote, and while Miller's reputation 'may have fluctuated in the succeeding years', *Salesman* remained a masterpiece, now re-imagined less as the naturalistic play some thought it to be than as a lyric poem, dreamlike and compelling. Dennehy's performance was 'stunningly disciplined' and Franz's 'superb'. He was no less impressed by the other actors. He had minor objections, but found that the production 'rejuvenates a familiar classic without ever betraying its soul'. The play 'seems only to grow larger with life'.[53] Though Miller resented the power of Brantley's paper, for once it was on his side and the transfer to New York was assured. It opened there fifty years to the day after its initial Broadway premiere, and it was this production of his best-known play that marked the beginning of the revival of Miller's fortunes in America.

Virtually the whole run was booked, with advance sales approaching two and a half million dollars. On the opening night, Miller was called on stage to take a bow, and afterwards there was a celebratory party at the Tavern on the Green at Central Park on West 67th Street. For once he could be confident of the *New York Times* review. As for Chicago, it was written by Brantley. Even here, though, in as enthusiastic a response as Miller could have wished for, there was a caveat: in art, Brantley remarked, 'greatness and perfection seldom keep close company, and the flaws of "Salesman" are apparent here: the contrived, detective-story-like exposition of why Biff resents Willy; the unfortunate moments of speechifying, especially in the final requiem scene, and the iconic presence of the fantasy figure of Willy's older brother, Ben'.[54] Nonetheless, it ran at the Eugene O'Neill Theatre for 274 performances, the longest run of any Miller play for over thirty years. It closed on 7 November 1999. Originally, it had been planned that Stacy Keach would take over from Dennehy after six months, but this never happened, though Dennehy did have to withdraw for a few days. As he explained:

> I had a little episode with my health. My blood pressure spiked and I went to the hospital. They gave me drugs and lowered my blood pressure. I was resting in the hospital, in a quiet room, when I heard a disturbance in the hallway. The door opened and there was this guy standing there, in a suit, with an attaché case, whom I had known twenty years before. I said, 'How are you?' through the tubes in my nose.
>
> He said, 'How are you feeling?'
>
> I said, 'Well, considering that I've got tubes up my nose and my arms I feel pretty good.'
>
> He said, 'I heard about it on the radio.'
>
> I said, 'Well, thank you, but I'm not supposed to have any visitors, but thank you for coming.'

He said, 'Yes, well, I just wanted to let you know about this great investment opportunity. This is probably not a good time to talk to you about it
but what I want to do is leave this stuff and when you get a chance, look at
the material and give me a call.'

Then he leaves and I turn to my wife and say, 'It's Willy Loman. The guy
is a sensational salesman!'[55]

Death of a Salesman would receive four Tony Awards (Best Revival, Best
Actor, Best Featured Actress and Best Director). Brian Dennehy also won a
Drama Desk Award, in a year in which three of the five nominees for best
revival were of Miller plays (*All My Sons* was the winner).

For Donald Lyons in the *New York Post* it was a 're-energizing and re-
imagining [of a] tidal wave of a play'.[56] Clive Barnes, writing in the same
paper three days later, saw *Salesman* as a watershed in drama, continually
pertinent, prompting a 'marvelously powerful rendering of Willy'. *Variety*
found Dennehy's Willy Shakespearean in scale. *USA Today* said it was *King
Lear* American style. The production was taped for television for transmission
in January 2000.

Before the New York opening of *Death of a Salesman* there had been another
reminder of the play, or at least of its original director, when on 7 January, by
a unanimous vote, the Academy of Motion Picture Arts and Sciences decided
to give Elia Kazan a lifetime achievement award. Old antagonisms, it seems,
were to be set aside, though at the annual Writers' Guild Awards dinner in
Beverly Hills it was revealed that screenwriters planned to publish advertisements asking members of the Academy to refrain from applauding. The
proposed text was to read: 'Do not stand or applaud Mr Kazan. Sit on your
hands. Let audiences around the world see that there are some in Hollywood,
some Americans, who do not support blacklisting, who do not support
informers.'[57] But forty years on, what so many had seen as a betrayal had
acquired a new context. Richard Cohen in the *Washington Post* said that
Kazan was to be honoured because no one any longer believed that the Soviet
cause had ever been a progressive one. Kazan's position had thus been just.
William Kristol's *Weekly Standard* noted that the award would rectify 'a long-
standing and bitter injustice' that had stood as a rebuke to the American Film
Institute, which had repeatedly refused to honour Kazan. An article in the
New York Times was headed, and not wholly ironically, 'Time Frees the
Hollywood One'.

In February Frank N. Stanton, a former president of CBS, was also given
a lifetime achievement award for his First Amendment work by the New
York chapter of the National Academy of Television Arts and Sciences. In
his time, he had faced down Richard Nixon when he sent armed process

servers to require him to turn over material from a programme called *The Selling of the Pentagon*, about the cost to the taxpayer of public relations efforts by the arms industry to sell arms to the US government. He had resisted attempts by the Teamsters Union to stop the showing of a documentary on Jimmy Hoffa, that organization's murdered president. He had also, however, overseen the network's blacklisting policies in the 1950s and 60s. 'Here,' Allan Sloane, a blacklisted writer, observed, 'was someone who had to make a choice between right and wrong, and he chose wrong.' But the climate was clearly changing. Sloane's remark that 'I don't believe in that kind of redemption,'[58] was plainly not shared by others. Miller read news of Stanton's award with indignation.

The reasons for hostility towards Kazan, Stephen Schwartz noted in the *Weekly Standard*, required 'sifting through the ruins of the intellectual Left for clues to the bizarre anxieties attached to the figure of the anti-Communist "informer"' – the label, derived, he maintained, from gangsters – 'which "liberals" had attached to Elia Kazan'.[59] His quotation marks are not without their significance. Why, he asked, as others had in the 1950s, had such people been vilified when they would not have been had they informed on Nazis? The blame, he suggested, lay with those such as Victor Navasky, publisher of the *Nation*, who had portrayed Kazan as a villain and Arthur Miller as a hero. The fact was, Schwartz went on, that evidence from secret files now showed that the KGB had targeted Hollywood. 'In the late '40s and early '50s,' he argued, 'many people, when called upon to choose between the House Committee and Stalin, chose the Committee. Today, belatedly, others may be starting to see the wisdom of that judgment.'[60]

There were, indeed, those who were arguing for a reassessment not merely of the 1950s but even of Senator Joe McCarthy. On 18 October 1998 Ethan Bronner had published an article in the *New York Times* entitled, 'Witching Hour: Rethinking McCarthyism, If Not McCarthy'.[61] It noted that the opening of the Soviet archives had led some to suggest that while McCarthy might have been a self-serving liar it did not follow that his search for communists and spies was without justification. Harvey Klein, a historian at Emory University, had pointed out that if FDR had died earlier, his Vice-President Henry Wallace (supported by Miller in the 1948 presidential election) would have become President with, in all probability, Laurence Duggan as Secretary of State and Harry Dexter White as Treasury Secretary. Wallace had been under communist influence, while both of the others, according to evidence drawn from the Venona files – the Venona Project was a US/UK intelligence operation that decrypted Soviet messages, until its existence was betrayed – were Soviet agents.

A few days later, however, the *New York Times* published an editorial declaring 'Beware the rehabilitation of Joseph McCarthy',[62] insisting that

McCarthy had been a lethal threat to American democracy and decency. It warned of the unreliability of intelligence documents, and while conceding that a number of traitors had now been identified, recalled the many who had had their lives and careers destroyed by McCarthy, whose activities had poisoned education, the arts and the press. Walter and Miriam Schneir followed this with an article in the *Nation* noting that *Time Magazine* had recently asked, 'Was McCarthy on the right track?' while Harvey Klehr had published his book *Venona*, which appeared to take the Venona papers as proven accounts, duly listing all those suspected of being agents or targeted as possible sources.

It was against this background that Kazan's award was announced. Some saw it as part of the rehabilitation not only of those who had willingly collaborated with HUAC and its Senate equivalent, but also of the process itself. The Left had simply got things wrong, and were unwilling even now to admit as much. Ronald Radosh, then a senior research associate at George Washington University, would attack Miller precisely along these lines. Radosh's parents had been members of the Communist Party of the USA. Like Miller's daughter Jane he had attended the Little Red Schoolhouse, a favourite of New York's communists. He had formally joined the Party in 1956. He became disillusioned only when, as a historian, he had researched the Rosenberg case. He later moved to the right, became a member of the Hudson Institute and wrote for *New Criterion*, the magazine that would attack Miller's reputation when he died. Radosh was careful, though, to dissociate McCarthyism from anti-communism. It was not a distinction made by all.

When he was approached for his response to the announcement of the Oscar, Miller refused to join those who denounced the award and who called for a boycott of the ceremony. He published a brief statement, significantly in Navasky's *Nation*, on 4 March 1999. It was reprinted by papers on the East and West Coasts. He began by endorsing the assertion of a militant blacklisted screenwriter, Dalton Trumbo, that in the 1950s struggle against government attempts 'to throttle the American left ... there were no heroes or villains, only victims', while acknowledging that this was a truth likely to be resisted by those whose careers had been destroyed. After outlining his own experience of blacklisting, which he was now ready to compare to Soviet practices, Miller added: 'My feelings toward that terrible era are unchanged, but at the same time history ought not to be rewritten; Elia Kazan did sufficient extraordinary work in theatre and film to merit its acknowledgment. Few of us are of a piece, as Trumbo seemed to be saying. Perhaps all one can hope for is to find in one's heart praise for what a man has done well and censure for where he has tragically failed.'[63] It was not absolution, but it was as close as Miller would come to forgiveness. Even Navasky conceded that, given his age and state of health and the fact that he had made a positive contribution to the film industry, Kazan should be honoured. When PBS made a documentary about the relationship between Kazan and Miller in 2003 it was called *Miller, Kazan, and the Blacklist: Not without Sin*. Earlier, at the instigation of fellow playwright A.R. Gurney, who also lived in Roxbury, the two had met for dinner at Gurney's house; these were two men he admired and who he felt should be reconciled.

Miller was not present in late March when Kazan received his award, having avoided the 250 demonstrators outside the Dorothy Chandler Pavilion at the Music Center of Los Angeles by using a side entrance rather than the red carpet down which assorted stars walked, to the flash of cameras. The award had been proposed by Karl Malden, who had worked with Kazan in *On the Waterfront*. He was introduced by Martin Scorsese and Robert De Niro. A full-page advertisement in *Variety*, however, accused Kazan of validating the blacklisting of thousands and damaging the motion picture industry. It was signed by several hundred, including Sean Penn, whose father had refused to name names and was blacklisted; by Ed Asner, whose drama series *Lou Grant* had been cancelled in 1982, seemingly for his support of the rebels in El Salvador who had fought against the Ronald Reagan-backed government and military; and by Theodore Bikel (like Miller, a delegate to the 1968 Democratic Convention). Norma Barzman, a blacklisted screenwriter who had fled America to avoid being called before the Committee, whose phone was tapped and whose movements while abroad were tracked by the FBI, observed that Kazan's lifetime achievement was the destruction of lives. Abraham Polonsky, who had been blacklisted and whose film about the blacklisting, *Guilty by Suspicion*, had its lead character – played, somewhat ironically given his role in presenting Kazan, by Robert De Niro – rewritten by the director Irwin Winkler as a liberal rather than a communist, hoped Kazan would be shot at the ceremony, thus livening up a boring occasion. He was, he said, designing a moveable headstone for himself so that his grave could be moved in the event that Kazan was buried in the same place. As it happens, he died later that year and did not have to share a cemetery with the man he despised.

In May 1999, Miller himself attracted controversy. He crossed a picket line in order to reach a PEN dinner, prompting a flurry of articles in the *New York Observer*, the *Daily News* and the *Village Voice*. PEN's American Center was scheduled to hold its annual black-tie fund-raising gala dinner at a Cipriani catering hall across the street from Grand Central Station. Six months earlier Harry Cipriani had taken over the management of the Rainbow Room at Rockefeller Plaza and dismissed two hundred and fifty union employees. The union picketed the restaurant. Two days before the dinner, Cipriani sued the union. At the catering halls, meanwhile, he had allegedly hired non-union labour, and the 22 per cent service fee, the *New York Times* reported, never reached the waiters; it was used to pay their wages instead.

The PEN gala was an essential part of the organization's fund-raising but many of its members came from a progressive background where the crossing of picket lines was unacceptable. In an article written for the *Village Voice*, Nat Hentoff, who had once served on a PEN committee but who had for many years been a union organizer, listed those who had refused to cross the lines. Paul Newman, he noted, had declined to attend the gala, as had Spalding Gray and Gay Talese. The *Nation* had cancelled its table. Those who crossed the line included Ron Silver (who had played in *Broken Glass*), Dan Rather, Oliver Stone, E.L. Doctorow and Miller, who was quoted as saying, 'It was more important for me to help PEN than worry about crossing a line. PEN helps writers over five continents. They have one fund-raising event each year, and this is it.' He confessed to feeling awkward about it, but it was a matter of priorities. PEN, and its concern with writers, remained a central commitment. Joanne Leedom-Ackerman, the Secretary of International PEN, later remarked on the fact that,

> in a letter to a Belgrade journalist whose friends and newspaper were under constant assault by the regime of Slobodan Milosevic in Yugoslavia, Miller recalled that it was the murder of writers and journalists that most affected him, since these were the eyes and ears of the people, and democracy depended on a well-informed citizenry. He felt particular sympathy for those who tried to function in the face of nationalism and tribalism in the Balkans, and insisted on the need for the writer to resist those who saw art as serving only political and partisan ends.[64]

Miller was equally concerned with the fate of the artist in his own country. Later in the year he was one of a hundred signatories of a petition by PEN members (including Cynthia Ozick and Mary Gordon) denouncing Mayor Giuliani's threat to shut down the Brooklyn Museum of Art because its *Sensation* exhibition (in fact a British exhibition put together by Charles Saatchi) included a painting by Chris Ofili called *The Virgin Mary* that was liberally adorned with elephant dung. To Miller's mind this was simply more evidence of the political threat to art as the millennium edged towards its end.

The production of *Salesman* was now attracting sales of $65,000 a day, and by mid-August the show was in profit. Plans for a London transfer were discussed, but the idea later foundered when Dennehy decided to direct a film instead, turning down the million dollars he would have received to tour and cross the Atlantic with Miller's play. Inge's career continued to flourish, with exhibitions and awards. In June 1999 she returned to the Vienna she had experienced immediately after the war, this time for a major retrospective of her work. One hundred and fifty of her photographs were hung in a white space a hundred and fifty feet long in the Kunsthalle. She was also there to receive the Gold Medal of the City of Vienna. Three days before his eighty-fourth birthday it was Miller's turn: he received the Gish Award in a ceremony presided over by E.L. Doctorow. He celebrated his birthday by buying himself a new scarlet Mercedes ($52,000) to go with his now fairly ancient one.

On 7 November *Death of a Salesman* finally closed. It was swiftly followed by a highly successful production of *The Price*, which moved from Williams-town (a second revival; the first was in 1992) to the 1,078-seat Royale Theater on Broadway. It opened to enthusiastic notices – though not, Miller observed, from his old *bête noire* the *New York Times*, which thought it 'unbalanced'.

Turning down an invitation to the White House, Miller saw in the mil-lennium in his own home with friends. *The Price* had survived the holiday break: it had made over half a million advance ticket sales and $185,000 in a single week. Even so, there were talks of the play closing. Another battle with producers was heaving into sight. Successful or not, it was falling below the stop-clause figures; and anyway, it turned out, the deal had been for a limited engagement. It was to be replaced by Michael Frayn's *Copenhagen*, a work that Miller admired. Another play was on the horizon, however. For the first time, he gave people a glimpse of *Resurrection Blues*, thinking of a possible small-scale production at the Public Theater. The Public rejected it.

In March 2000, Miller and Inge travelled to Cuba as part of a small group invited as 'cultural visitors'. The group included William Luers, former head of New York's Metropolitan Museum and Ambassador to Venezuela and Czechoslovakia, together with his human rights activist wife Wendy, plus William and Rose Styron, literary agent Morton Janklow and Patty Cisneros, organizer of a foundation to save Amazon culture. They were there to do no more than meet some writers, and in Miller's case the students of a theatre school: 'I met an acting class in the theatre school after they had shown me a beautifully modulated performance of a surreal student play in which a crucifixion suggests a symbolization of the HIV/AIDS anguish.' Miller and the others did meet a group of Cuban writers, an encounter of some mutual bafflement because neither side seemed to know quite what to say. They also visited a dissident author, Elizardo Sánchez, Cuba's best-known human rights activist who had spent eight and a half years in prison. Abandoning the government minibus in the hope of losing any security agents who might be following, they travelled by taxis: 'Knowing that his house was bugged, [Sánchez] felt free to say whatever he liked, since his positions were already well known. And if any of us had imagined the visit was secret, we were disabused by the friendly TV cameraman who photographed us out in the street as we left. So much for our taking taxis instead of the government bus.'

Havana struck Miller as having 'the beauty of a ruin returning to the sand, the mica, the gravel and trees from which it originated'. They stayed at the old Hotel Santa Isabel, and he wandered through the nearby streets trying to get a feel for a country so long out-of-bounds to Americans. To their surprise, they were invited to dinner with Fidel Castro in the Palace of the Revolution, with its black stone walls and chequered floors, where they were joined by Gabriel García Márquez, who Miller suspected had been responsible for the encounter. (Mexico's intelligence service, it was revealed in 2009, had spied on Márquez for decades, believing him to be a Cuban agent – apparently because he had given the publishing rights to his book *Chronicle of a Death Foretold* to Cuba's government.) On arrival, Inge was required to surrender her Leica camera, which was promptly dropped on the floor. Castro, dressed in a suit, joked with Miller about their respective ages, precisely calculating the gap between them in years, months and days. He also joked about their having disappeared for two hours that afternoon, a reminder that he knew of their visit to Sánchez.

Dining on shrimp and pork, they listened to Castro speak of the Russians, whom he now seemed to despise for recanting their core beliefs and specifically for failing to support his desire to spread the Cuban revolution throughout South America. The meal began at 9.30 and Castro stopped speaking at two in the morning, only when Miller indicated he was getting tired (Márquez, apparently, having dozed off already). Castro concluded the meeting, though not before plying everyone with the vitamin tablets that evidently kept him going. The next day, he caught up with the group in the countryside and questioned them about American literature. For Miller it was a strange occasion. Americans had been thrown out of Cuba because businessmen and the Mafia treated it as a place to make money, 'a bordello for Americans'. The blockade that followed was in Miller's view, 'at the behest, so it appeared, of a defeated class of exploiters who had never had a problem with the previous dictatorship'.[65] On the other hand, he had campaigned for those imprisoned by the regime that still stood for an unreconstructed version of the faith that Miller had once embraced and by which he felt he and others had been betrayed.

The Broadway production of *The Ride down Mount Morgan* at the Ambassador Theater, in which Patrick Stewart reprised his 1998 role, started well. The *New York Times* reviewer Bruce Weber responded positively. He found it an 'intelligent and savage satire ... the latest entry in the astonishing resurrection of Mr Miller's work on Broadway (and elsewhere) over the last two years'. He praised Stewart for his performance – 'he ... plays Lyman with the lustiness of a Mediterranean peasant and an ineffable energy for sucking the pleasure out of existence' – and Esbjornson for his direction.[66] The play, he felt, had found its moment.

It made headlines, though, for reasons other than its innate qualities. During matinée and evening curtain calls on 29 April, Patrick Stewart publicly berated the producers for stinting on the promotion budget and failing to advertise, in particular not posting excerpted reviews at the theatre. After the curtain call he stepped forward and addressed the somewhat startled audience: 'Arthur Miller and I no longer have confidence in our producers' commitment to this production, especially the Shubert Organization, or their willingness to promote and publicise it.' He added that he found the producers' attitude 'deeply puzzling, if for no other reason than this is an important play by America's most distinguished living playwright . . . Arthur and I feel frustrated and helpless.' Miller himself commented: 'Clearly the play has dropped through the memory hole . . . I haven't talked to management, but Patrick has, since he's there for every performance. Promises have been made repeatedly that were never kept. Patrick feels he was driven to this. I told him I agree with his statement.'[67] The audiences were smaller than had been hoped, and than Miller and Stewart thought they should be, and tickets had been discounted, many selling for 50 per cent of the regular top price of $80.

Stewart had informed Miller, Esbjornson and the cast of his intention but in a secret ballot the actors declined to join him on stage. The producers threatened to sue and demanded a public apology, to be delivered on stage. Stewart declared that he had no reason to comply. Other straight plays (he cited *The Real Thing* and *A Moon for the Misbegotten*), he pointed out, were being aggressively advertised. A promised advertisement in the Sunday issue of the *New York Times* had appeared in less than half of the copies, and quotations from the many positive reviews had not been posted outside the theatre. Gerald Schoenfeld, head of the Shubert Organization, then brought Stewart up before Actors' Equity, accusing him of unprofessional conduct by in effect adding material to the play (by which was meant his address to the audience), a breach of the rules. The producer claimed to have spent $600,000 on advertising, an estimate raised to a million a day later.

By turning to Equity, however, the producers were waiving their right to take other legal action. Stewart, meanwhile, had an added reason for his complaints: he had agreed to work for a reduced salary in exchange for a percentage of the show's profits.

Miller entirely supported him: 'They pretended they were going to advertise. At one time they even went so far as to say that the typesetter lost the type. It was absolutely insulting. He had to react. I thought it was terrific that he did that.'[68] Miller was at the time undergoing another eye operation and was unable to go to New York, but he signed an affidavit signifying his agreement with Stewart before his Equity hearing. Equity refused to reprimand him, but insisted he make an apology. The apology was read over the phone to Schoenfeld, who was still angry because Stewart was persisting with his complaints about the advertising budget. Equity rejected the apology as insufficiently contrite. Schoenfeld then issued a release to *Variety*, citing Stewart's contract forbidding him to make any public statement without the permission of the producer. Later, Stewart had second thoughts:

> I regret now, with hindsight, what I did. I should have found another way, a more effective way of voicing my dissatisfaction. Arthur was a rock. But I hope I have learned something from that experience. It was an impulsive act, and like most impulsive acts it gave momentary satisfaction. Both Arthur and I felt we had grievances, and yet there was another way. At the time my biggest regret was that it became a huge distraction. One of the reasons I did not continue the action was because I wanted to enjoy the end of the run and I could not have done. It also never occurred to me how it might appear: I was an English actor, standing on a Broadway stage, criticising the most powerful producing body on Broadway. It's all history and I hope to make good the damage that I did at that time. I feel there was a better way I could have handled it. I would like to find some peace with a couple of the individuals who were so offended, because I don't believe in such things lying there.[69]

The fact was that audiences had fallen off, and in an unsubsidized Broadway that could only spell a hastening closure, despite two Tony nominations.

On 4 June Stewart was a presenter at the Tony Awards. Nothing came of the nominations for *The Ride down Mount Morgan*. Two days later, a letter from Miller was published in the *New York Times*:

> Your report about the controversy between the actor Patrick Stewart and the producers of my play 'The Ride down Mount Morgan' ... says some have suggested that Mr Stewart's motive in speaking directly to the audience may have been the calculation that the publicity would enhance his Tony possibilities. How an actor could calculate that a conflict with his producers could somehow bring him closer to a Tony — which it obviously didn't — is one of those mysteries that this writer fails to wrap his mind around. I would think that the real question is what the circumstances were that drove a peaceable actor to such an extreme.[70]

In the end *The Ride down Mount Morgan* ran for 121 performances.[71] After the first six weeks it seldom managed much more than 50 per cent capacity, dropping to 36 per cent in the penultimate week. In that time, though, it was seen by nearly a hundred thousand people.

Shortly after it closed, Michael Douglas indicated his desire to make a film version with himself as Lyman, something that was potentially awkward, given Stewart's Broadway role and the fact that he himself had a production company. As Stewart explained:

Arthur and I and Sam Cohn had discussed the possibility of a film with me. When I got a call saying that Michael Douglas is really interested I thought about it for a couple of days. I was not comfortable thinking about it, but it became clear that there was much more chance of the film being made with Michael Douglas than with me. In fact, I knew it would be a long shot with me and my production company. And I also think that Michael Douglas is a terrific piece of casting for it. I said to Arthur, all right, here's the deal. I'll back off from this but I want to play the lawyer.

Such matters, however, were of little importance beside a worrying development with respect to Inge's health. She was showing a reduced platelet count. This could indicate any one of a number of conditions, from chronic stomach ulcers or renal failure to leukaemia or lupus, in which the body's immune system creates antibodies that attack its own organs. The condition carries a risk of haemorrhage. At the same time, a low count could be a result of a shortage of vitamin B12 that can be treated with folic acid. Alternatively, it could be idiopathic thrombocytopenia, medical-speak for a low platelet count of unknown cause. For the moment, it was a condition that required further exploration and monitoring.

In July, Miller flew to Toronto for the shooting of *Focus*, though he was feeling tired from Lyme disease, which he had picked up from ticks spread by deer on his Roxbury land. On the face of it, William H. Macy was an unlikely actor to play the lead, and said as much to the director, Neal Slavin: 'I told Neal I was all wrong for the role ... I said, "Anti-Semitism is a vicious thing, and I don't want to offend anyone by presuming to know what it feels like. Plus, I don't even look Jewish."' Initially, Miller felt much the same, but as Slavin remarked to Macy, 'That's why you're perfect. Intolerance has nothing to do with reality.' When Macy asked Mamet for his advice he replied, 'What's the matter with you ...? When Arthur Miller writes a novel, you jump to bring it to the screen.' Recalling criticism of himself by a journalist for failing to cast Jews in his 1991 film *Homicide*, he had said, 'Huh, interesting concept, casting by religion.'[72] Speaking in November 2001, the month the film opened, Macy saw an immediate relevance: 'Osama bin Laden teaches hatred, and so does Jerry Falwell, for blaming the attacks on homosexuals ... It's our collective responsibility to stand up and tell these people they're wrong. Just as Lawrence learns in "Focus", it is our fight. We are all responsible.'[73]

Then it was to London, where the National Theatre was having its biggest hit of the year with *All My Sons*; and on 20 July 2000 *Mr Peters' Connections*, directed by Michael Blakemore, opened at the Almeida Theatre, a 303-seat auditorium with a high reputation. Miller was impressed by both. He liked the set of *Sons* especially, a house with a real grass lawn in front and the audience on three sides. Reviews were positive and it went on to win four

Olivier Awards – for Best Director (Howard Davies), Best Actress (Julie Walters), Best Supporting Actor (Ben Daniels) and Best Set Design (William Dudley). *Mr Peters' Connections*, with John Cullum in the title role, fared less well: reviews were respectful rather than enthusiastic.

Miller returned to America, and to bad news about Inge's condition. A series of tests had led to a diagnosis of non-Hodgkin's lymphoma, a cancer of the lymphatic system. Lymphoma can occur anywhere but is usually to be noticed first in the lymph nodes. Cells start to divide before they are fully mature. This makes them unable to fight infection as normal white blood cells do. Abnormal, useless lymphocytes start to collect in the lymph nodes. Treatment is possible and the condition may disappear, though with some likelihood of recurrence. In Inge's case, nodes had already spread to her abdomen but it was diagnosed as a low-grade lymphoma – treatable, at least initially, by tablets, but as a means of controlling rather than curing the condition. For the moment, it seemed, nothing was called for beyond this regular medication. Nobody, however, takes such a diagnosis as anything but threatening, but Inge determined to carry on as usual, attending exhibitions of her work.

Miller was also feeling his age. His back remained painful and he had continuing eye trouble; another operation was performed in July. At the end of the month the stitches were removed in time for him to turn an ankle on the way to his barn – he fell twenty yards down the slope, a reminder that things were not quite as they had been. He no longer felt it was safe to use machinery.

Nevertheless, he and Inge flew to England for celebrations of his eighty-fifth birthday. He was to be given the freedom of the medieval city of Norwich. On the morning of the ceremony, to take place in the thirteenth-century Guildhall, I took them both for a walk around the grounds of the cathedral (whose foundation stone was laid in 1096). The Cathedral Close is striking for its serenity. Walking with a stoop, Arthur had to stop every hundred yards or so to ease the pain in his back, but was looking forward to the day's programme. Later that morning he crossed the road from his hotel to buy a newspaper, tripped on a paving stone and fell. A passing nurse called an ambulance, but when it came he refused to be taken to hospital, signing a release to that effect. Instead, with help from the ambulance driver he returned to the hotel and called me. Though it would not be confirmed until he returned to America, he had broken three ribs. Nonetheless, he went ahead with the day's events, which included speeches at the Guildhall, a public discussion at the Theatre Royal and a gala dinner at the University of East Anglia.

The next day the impact of the fall became apparent. His trip to Heathrow was to be by car rather than the scheduled train, and a wheelchair was arranged. When he arrived at JFK, to his relief, there was a man holding up a sign saying 'Miller'. He and Inge climbed into the car and were driven off. It was some time before they realized they were going in the wrong direction. The man had been meeting a different Miller. His own driver had been looking for a man of six feet two and a half inches, not one in a wheelchair. Back in Roxbury he found the pain too great to fly to Michigan, where a theatre was to be built bearing his name, so on 26 October he joined them instead by video link from his back porch.

In January 2001, having shot scenes for the film version of *Homely Girl* (to be called *Eden*) at his Roxbury home – John Huston's son was playing the part of the protagonist's son – Miller went to Chicago to see the opera version of *A View from the Bridge* staged at the Lyric Theatre, the country's third-largest opera company, behind the Metropolitan Opera in New York and the San Francisco Opera. The idea for the opera came partly from Bruno Bartoletti, the Lyric's former artistic director who had come across an Italian adaptation, and partly from the librettist Arnold Weinstein. Born in 1927 of British parents, Weinstein had grown up in Harlem and the Bronx and had lived, like Miller, at the Chelsea Hotel. He had known the composer William Bolcom for many years, first meeting him in Europe. In 1961 he had opened the play *Red Eye of Love* at the Living Theatre and worked with Bolcom on an operatic version of Frank Norris's novel *McTeague*. Now, the Pulitzer Prize-winning Bolcom, chairman of the composition department at the University of Michigan and composer of the music for *Broken Glass*, set out to write what he called 'grand opera Brooklynized'. Bolcom and Weinstein had played the last part of the opera to Arthur and Inge at the Chelsea Hotel one winter evening in 1998. Now it was to have a full production.

A View from the Bridge involved thirteen soloists, a chorus of forty-eight (in the operatic version Alfieri becomes its leader) and an orchestra consisting of seventy-five players. It cost $1.4 million and was scheduled for nine performances. The hope was that it would find a place in the American operatic canon, something of a long shot given that the most successful American opera, as judged by the number of performances, *Porgy and Bess*, dated back to 1935, while the most recent success was *Of Mice and Men* in 1970. Of *A View from the Bridge* the Lyric's general director William Mason said, 'Unless it receives exuberant admiration, it is unlikely to have a significant life beyond its run in Chicago. Even if it does, longevity is unlikely. Of the 125 works that had their world premieres in the United States in the 1990s, only about a dozen have been produced again.' Miller himself had no real expectations: it was 'kind of a lark ... What always manages to astound me is that all this work goes into something, and they're going to play it half a dozen or a dozen times and that's it ... It's an astounding devotion these people have for it. I just hope it goes to a thirteenth performance.'

Weinstein explained that it was not simply a case of setting the play to music. It needed to be re-imagined:

You're not just rendering it ... If that's all you do, the playwright loses. He loses his nuances of language and he doesn't have the fun of discovering anything new about the piece. That was the fun of working with Miller. He didn't see the point of doing the play set to music, like a long song cycle. I said to him, 'This play is strong enough to take a lot of kicking around, and I think it wants the exercise.' I ran through the thing like a mad dog, biting it up and then sticking in the mouthfuls where they would make an aria.

One of the most striking changes was the figure of Marco: 'I thought we needed to hear from Marco an explanation about how he got into this whole thing ... Plus, if you're going to have a good singer do Marco, you better have something for him to do other than eventually knife the guy at the end.' The result was an aria written in three days by Miller himself, 'A Ship Called Hunger', inspired, he said, by his 1947 trip to Italy during which he recalled seeing no fat people.

> To America I sailed on a ship called Hunger,
> Away from a country that starved my children,
> Away from the face of a woman grieving,
> I sailed away on a ship called Hunger.
>
> But America was life to me,
> America the smiling!
> America smiled for me,
> I worked in the rain and the heat of summer,
> I froze my fingers in the snows of winter,
> I love all the mornings, the smell of the sea
> And the smell of the docks and the sun on the water,
> Far from the land of the starving family,
> Far from the ship called Hunger.[74]

Miller remarked: 'I used to feel that the big drama was not in the lines but in the spaces between the lines ... even the greatest poet is always trying to express the inexpressible, and music comes closest as an art form to being able to do that. So the idea of a play being transformed into music is a very natural thing.'[75]

The opening night prompted a standing ovation. The 3,600-seat hall was sold out for every performance; a further thousand people were turned away. The production was widely and favourably reviewed. The *New York Times* reviewer Anthony Tommasini hailed it as an admirable and often affecting work that convincingly solves the problem of translating this play into an opera ... The production could not have been better ... The director, Frank Galati, has drawn memorable performances from the fine cast ... Where 'A View from the Bridge' ranks in the pantheon of opera is a boring question. Let history decide. For now we have a new work of integrity and skill that reached people and much deserves a hearing beyond the eight additional performances it will receive here.[76]

In fact it was performed three years later at the Metropolitan Opera and again five years after that at the Washington National Opera (in 2008, broadcast on National Public Radio). Following the Chicago opening Miller resolved to add further arias, but for the time being he had other commitments.

To Miller's dismay, George W. Bush was now President. The farce of the election being decided in the Supreme Court revealed, it seemed to him, the anti-democratic instincts of the Republican Party, which had been happy to demand that votes should not be counted. The election, in his view, had been given to Bush by Ralph Nader, whose votes in New Hampshire and Florida were enough to have tipped the outcome in favour of Gore. When counting was stopped, Bush had won Florida by 537 votes. Speaking in Prague in 2001 Miller remarked, 'We've just had an election ... And the man who won the election, lost. And the man who lost the election is the winner. And we are asking people to be rational about life ... We are now in the process of forgetting, trying to forget what has happened, which is that in the greatest democracy in the world a non-democratic election occurred.'[77]

Not long after Bush came to power, Miller had the opportunity to express his political misgivings at an event that took place at the very heart of political America when, in Washington, he delivered the Jefferson Lecture for the National Endowment for the Humanities in March 2001. It was a speech that effectively, and wittily, attacked politicians. In the audience were senators, congressmen and a Chief Justice. Before delivering it, Miller had received a call that he interpreted as a request to tone the text down, but as he said to me before leaving on the trip, 'I'm eighty-five and I don't care.' He had been invited by William Ferris, a Clinton appointee who had run into trouble when he asked Clinton to deliver the lecture in 1999, no serving politician having done so before. Miller was scarcely less controversial. He was to appear in the concert hall of the J. F. Kennedy Center, in front of an audience of nearly 2,500. Ferris was later removed by the Bush administration; in fact, the *National Review* called for his replacement in an article published on the day of Miller's lecture, which would itself be attacked by the same journal.

Miller's topic was the politician as actor. Ronald Reagan, he noted, frequently seemed incapable of distinguishing films he had seen from the actual

events in which he had participated. Now Miller pinpointed the 2000 elections as requiring all Americans to behave like actors, as they continued to
trumpet the virtues of American democracy to the world while an 'organized
mob of Republicans [was] banging threateningly on the door of a Florida
vote-counting office and howling for the officials inside to stop counting'.[78]
He described the election as a gift from the Supreme Court to the Republican
Party. 'I must confess,' he said, 'that as a playwright I would then be flummoxed
as to how to make plausible on the stage an organized stampede of partisans
yelling to stop the count and in the same breath accusing the other side of
trying to steal the election. I can't imagine an audience taking this for anything
but a satirical farce.' Politics, like the theatre, he went on, required strict form.
When that was ignored, the audience would legitimately feel 'cheated and
even mocked'.[79] The same had been true of the previous year's election in
which the Republican majority leader in the House of Representatives had
declared he would not attend the inauguration if Gore was elected.

Presidents, he suggested, were required to act whenever they appeared in
public. George Bush, once elected, had 'learned not to sneer quite so much,
and to cease furtively glancing to left and right when leading up to a punch
line, followed by a sharp nod to flash that he had successfully delivered it'.[80]
He had, in other words, been a bad actor who was trying to become a better
one. That he had been acting in the campaign was evident from the fact that
he 'made much of his interest in supporting education, child-protective
measures, as well as the environmental protections, but within days of his
administration's accession he moved to weaken one environmental protection
after another, his budget short-changed education and slashed the budget of
child-protection agencies.'[81]

Perhaps to balance this, he criticized Al Gore for his opportunism in
supporting the case of a Cuban boy, Elián González, the subject of a *cause
célèbre* during the elections when his father demanded his return to Cuba.
Both Gore and Bush, in order to win, had to present themselves as running
against the very Washington of which they were pure products. They had
thus been obliged to run against themselves. Bush was 'forced to impersonate
an outsider pitching against dependency on the federal government, whose
payroll ... had helped to feed two generations of his family'. There was,
Miller pointed out, a word for this: acting. Gore, for his part, had had to
disown 'Clinton the Unclean',[82] the genuine outsider, which 'took a monstrous
amount of acting', though there had been one moment in the debates when
truth was momentarily on display as Gore shook his head 'at some inanity
Bush had spoken'.[83]

Ronald Reagan had the virtue of appearing to believe what he said, no
matter if it defied logic, common sense or truth. Who else, Miller asked,
could have saluted a cemetery of Nazi dead with such apparent heartfelt

solemnity? Clinton, too, was a consummate actor, who did occasionally blush, 'but then again he was caught in an illicit sexual act, which is far more important than illegally shipping restricted weapons to foreign countries'.[84] For right-wing commentators, Miller compounded his offence by singling out only one politician for whom he had real respect. Unsurprisingly, given his own history, it was Franklin Roosevelt.

For all the humour of his Jefferson Lecture, it expressed a sense of bitterness. His praise for Clinton was the final irritant to those who regarded his whole speech as unacceptable. Clinton was, he said, 'our *Eulenspiegel*', a loveable prankster, Brer Rabbit, whereas George W. Bush had been mistakenly taken as running for the presidency of a fraternity, caught 'time after time fouling up his syntax'[85] until elected, at which point he had 'come close to sounding like a gunslinger in a Clint Eastwood film'.

According to George Will writing in the *Jewish World Review*, in the history of the Jefferson Lecture – delivered by such notables as Robert Penn Warren, Saul Bellow, C. Vann Woodward and Walker Percy – there had been remarkably few lapses from 'the generally exalted standards of the lectureship'. Miller's performance was an exception: 'never have those standards been as traduced as they were by Miller's political rant about the presidential election, the inadequacies of Ronald Reagan ... President Bush's public speaking.' The 'most embarrassing aspect', according to Will, 'was that Miller's self-absorption renders him immune to embarrassment. But, then, Ferris's NEH is similarly immune, making grants for a documentary film about the Miss America Pageant, for a feminist film on the historical significance of Cinderella and the like.'[86] The *National Review* described the lecture as 'appalling, a disgrace'.[87] Miller was aware that he might have placed Ferris's job at risk, but Ferris himself seemed certain of his support in Congress, at least from his own state of Mississippi. By December he was gone.

At home, Inge was responding to treatment. She had been travelling widely, seemingly confident that the lymphoma was now under control. Certainly, to speak to her on the phone was to hear reassurance about her prospects. Miller went back to work on *Resurrection Blues*, which he hoped would be directed by David Esbjornson. In Williamstown, Massachusetts, *The Man Who Had All the Luck* opened. It was its first American revival. Rejected by its initial reviewers, including the *New York Times* reviewer, it was now hailed by that same newspaper, which affected bafflement that it could once have been so easily dismissed. Noting Miller's 'resurgence in recent seasons', Bruce Weber found it bizarre that the play should apparently have been forgotten (he makes no reference to the Bristol Old Vic/Young Vic co-production). For him, it now became a comment on the fact that 'we are not a chosen people but a fortunate one'. The speeches were 'mythically charged', and hearing it in the theatre was like listening to 'an endangered bird'.[88]

Miller thus had the pleasure of seeing his one unalloyed failure embraced in America nearly sixty years after its first staging. Indeed, as he came to the end of 2001 he found himself rediscovered in his own country. A new play had been finished and another was on his computer. He was at work on speeches and articles. Where once he had relaxed with a game of tennis, though, he now chose a less energetic sport. He and Inge would walk down the road to his neighbour Frank McCourt's house to play a game of croquet. As the latter explained:

> My wife, Ellen ... organized a croquet tournament on our grass. (I suppose I should call it a lawn but it was too rough for that. A croquet purist would have sniffed.) We played in pairs, about eight of them. Arthur was teamed up with Ellen and Mia Farrow played with me. Mia and I were going strong and it looked as if we had a chance. As far as I know, Arthur had never played before but he went into the lead with a magnificent jump shot, one ball over another right there in the hoop. Mia and I still had a chance to at least pull even, but she blew a particularly easy shot. She looked apologetic and I asked what had happened. 'Oh, I was looking at Arthur and thinking how handsome he is.' His biographers, delving into obscure corners of Arthur's life, ought to know that the croquet champion of Tophet Road had his picture in the official magazine of the American Croquet Association (with my wife Ellen, of course).[89]

Miller was in Paris with Inge on 11 September 2001. They were there for a prize-giving ceremony in Versailles and television recordings for Inge's project *Border Spaces*, based on her visit to Slovenia. They were called by a friend and told to turn on CNN. Like the rest of the world they watched, unbelieving, as the twin towers of the World Trade Center fell. They took a second call. This one was from Regina Strassegger, who was working on the television film with Inge.

R.S.: Have you heard from Rebecca?

I.M.: No, the lines have been dead for hours. Hopefully Ronan didn't have to watch this disaster. He's tough. But this is a bit much.

R.S.: Under the circumstances we won't be seeing each other tomorrow ...

I.M.: Now that we're here there's anyway nothing we can do, let's stick to our plan. Arthur has cancelled his Versailles engagement, which likely won't please Chirac. But there's really nothing to celebrate now.

R.S.: Al Gore's in Vienna at the moment. He's trying to get back via Canada. He's issued no official statements as yet.

I.M.: Likely we'll have no alternative but to fly back via Canada too. At the moment we're doing all we can to contact Rebecca.[90]

Rebecca had been in Manhattan, and had seen events for herself. Later, Inge noted, 'Fortunately we now know that Rebecca and Ronan are safe. They really were on their way to the kindergarten at the time it was all happening. It must have been hell. The four-year-old seems to have taken the strain well. Rebecca is still beside herself.'

Miller later commented,

> I have no idea how to answer our grandson's countless questions. After all, I can't tell him that the process that ended in the past century with two hundred million war dead is possibly continuing. I feel personally assaulted, not as a Jew, but as a member of the human race. There are so many Muslims living in New York. Just recently a huge mosque was built on 96th Street in Manhattan. Through their attack these insane death-worshippers killed untold Muslims as well. I hope our President thinks of more than just violence, and I hope these events enable him to rise above himself.[91]

Miller responded to requests for interviews from the French press. He was as shocked as anyone, but alarmed, too, at the possibility of a military response. He prepared an article in which he argued that food rather than bombs should be dropped on Afghanistan. He could find no one who would publish it. The new national unity seemed to him to be fragile, and when on 6 November President George W. Bush announced that in the battle against terrorism 'you are either with us or against us', he was not the only one to see a link with *The Crucible*. His friend William Coffin, speaking in New Haven where Miller had first met him decades earlier, was already preaching against war.

In a BBC interview later in the year Miller denounced the attack on the twin towers as part of a war on humanity. 'The confrontation of a mass dying,' he observed, 'is a traumatic experience even for the dullest mind.' What he had witnessed in response was not, he insisted, hysteria. People had been drawn together, though he questioned whether this would be a long-term effect. He also, however, expressed concern at the establishment of military tribunals. 'The government now is taking advantage of it ... and using it as a way of increasing its power over civil rights ... I think people are prepared now ... to inquire as to why we are so hated in so many places ... It comes as a big surprise to a lot of people who have always accepted that American foreign policy was beneficent.'[92]

In June 1999, at an exhibition of her work in Vienna, Inge had been approached by Austrian television with a view to making a programme about southern Styria. Two years later it became a reality, when first in January and again in June and September she visited the country that bordered on her native Austria and where her mother's family had owned property. She remarked, 'I secretly long for that stretch of land along the border ... When someone asks me "Where are you from? Where do you feel at home?" then – apart from where I've lived so long in America – [the answer is] here in these vineyards, my childhood paradise. But the land across the border, about which my mother Titti told me so much, is also a part of it. Strange that I'm rediscovering these things now.'[93] She and her husband had spent some time with their friends Renate and Imo Moszkowicz on the border, and had strolled along a road that passed in and out of Austria and Slovenia, not an altogether safe thing to do, despite the thick fog. Now she recalled her time as a child here, gathering fossils laid down millennia before. The family had lost their Styrian land in 1918 when the Austro-Hungarian monarchy collapsed and Slovenia broke away from Austria. Between 1918 and 1919 fourteen thousand German-speakers were forced to leave and the border was redrawn. A language and a history had been lost, the language shunned as too provincial. The family was forced to leave almost everything behind. In a letter to Inge, her brother Werner, who had joined her in Styria, wrote, 'It was wonderful to relive memories together with you in the land of our family. We've not spent much time together since we were separated in 1941. Windischgrätz, so far away, known today as Slovenj Gradec, always held a particular fascination for me. When our mother Titti talked about it one always breathed the magic air of the Habsburg monarchy. No matter how unrealistic that might in fact have been.'[94] Inge's great-grandfather had once held office in Windischgrätz.

As Inge travelled the country, camera in hand, so other cameras followed her for the television film. Most pictures show her smiling and plainly enjoying her time there, as she explored the history of the country along with her family history. She was re-experiencing what she called the 'summer paradise of our childhood' and gathering evidence of a world that had slipped away; on the other hand she was reminded of the force that had destroyed that paradise. Her childhood friend Renate wrote to her recalling a particular moment in 1941: 'Our parents toasted Lower Styria ceremoniously. They talked about "coming home to the Empire". We were simply too dumb at the time to realize what had really happened. As you know, in invading Yugoslavia, still a kingdom then, the Nazis had opened up another war front ... we've never talked about your terrible time in Berlin.'[95]

Renate's father had been in the SS, and knew Goering and Himmler. After the war he fled to Argentina with his daughter, whose husband Imo, a film and theatre director, had survived Auschwitz while losing many of his family. Both Renate and Inge, then, had married Jews. Inge's grandfather had been a border surveyor for the Third Reich and her father a Nazi Party member. The past was full of ambiguities. What was intended as a journey of exploration was also, it seemed, a time to revisit old guilt. Inge herself had been a translator for the Nazi Foreign Ministry. One of the reasons she had learned other languages after the war was because, 'regardless of where I was working, I found that my language was the language of the enemy'.[96]

On 30 September she made her last visit to Slovenia. When she disembarked from the plane she complained of back pain that she thought a consequence of playing with her grandchild Ronan. Yoga, she felt sure, would put it right. It did not. The pain intensified. She felt 'pretty badly out of shape'. She thought it might be a trapped nerve and went to a clinic, but the doctor could see nothing wrong.

When she returned to America, she wrote to Regina Strassegger: 'At last I'm really on the mend. I'm on my feet again, doing yoga, driving. I still lack something of my old energy, but each day a bit comes back. Three more therapy sessions (chemo, unfortunately, as well), but I can begin work again mid-January – shooting the Broadway production of *The Crucible*.' After a few weeks the pain slackened and she seemed to gain strength, though suffered the hair loss that follows such treatment. Day by day, with regular injections, she appeared to improve. She could now walk with greater ease. It was at this point, on 14 December 2001, that I telephoned with news of the death of W.G. Sebald, killed in a car crash a few miles from his Norfolk home. They had met only twice, and then only briefly, but both Miller and Inge admired his work. When I spoke that day to Inge, she sounded weak.

Resurrection Blues was now in a final form. Miller sent me a copy with a handwritten note: 'Herewith the latest. We'll do it first at the Guthrie. Whitehead wants them to bring it to NY. David Esbjornson directing.' At the turn of the year Richard Eyre's production of *The Crucible*, with Liam Neeson, began rehearsals.

Then, in mid-January 2002, Inge began to deteriorate rapidly. She had never been a great eater, apparently subsisting on salads and a little fish, but now she barely ate at all, though the chemo, thankfully, was over. Her friend Honor Moore read poetry to her as she lay in some pain. Even now, Inge kept a camera behind the cushion where she lay, at one moment taking pictures of Honor, who later wrote a series of poems that recalled this time:

> ... Near eighty, photographing
> Styria, in Slovenia, the place her mother's
>
> family had always lived – *How are the pictures?*
> She collapsed on that trip. *From pain.* Yet continued
>
> photographing *Because it was important.* The proofs
> on her sickbed. Reaching for the pill bottle –
>
> *Darling, will you hand me those?* Lifting one leg
> to divert pain. *How are the pictures? Very*

> *interesting*, she said, though forthrightly
> modest. And we talked about what pain allows.

Another poem, 'Alive', recalls what in fact was a final encounter, in the Millers' New York apartment, and the relationship between husband and wife that was coming to its end:

> The last I saw her alive was in the apartment. Not the last time ever
> but the last time *alive* – that is, so we could have a conversation.
>
> *Oh darling, I'm not well*, quick exhale on the telephone. As always
> I dressed for her, but also grabbed poems. You should understand
>
> beneath the leap to a taxi, magenta raw silk, was a pull downward –
> in private I called it 'not a good feeling'. She was on the sofa, pale
>
> scarf around her head. I kissed her – nervous, self-consciousness
> I'd felt those years ago stumbling into the dusk with scissors.
>
> Her husband had to go out, and when I got there, was already
> putting on his tweed jacket, cap, standing, his back to us
>
> at the window. His face must have shown dread, which was why
> in addition to age, his hands were fumbling on the table
>
> as if he were blind. That was when I saw across her face
> such love for him it rose in me. *Do you have your keys, darling?*
>
> He turned, reluctant, and leaned to kiss her, delicate as a boy
> bowing at dancing school, and she, ignoring the pain,
>
> lifted herself toward him, all her beauty in the reach
> Strength still allowed. Door closing behind him . . . [97]

The last time Honor saw Inge was in hospital, giving her a chip of ice to place on her tongue when she was thirsty. That night, 29 January, Honor and the producer David Richenthal had joined Miller for dinner and he told them that the doctors had informed him that there was no hope of Inge's recovery, that she could die within twenty-four hours. The next day, in the middle of the morning, Inge died. Though she had been weak there had seemed every possibility of recovery when they spent the weekend in Roxbury. At the last minute, though, she had grown suddenly very much worse and they had driven back to the hospital in New York. Her husband was beside her at the moment of her death, this woman who had been his companion for forty years, a woman of high talent who had emerged from the chaos of war and won her way in the world, in the process rescuing him from confusion and despair. Rebecca had flown back from Europe, arriving just in time. Jane was to hand. Inge was not alone. Her family closed around her, but Miller found it hard to believe she had gone. Later that year he was looking at a photograph Inge had taken and told an interviewer:

> Two weeks after this photo was taken, Inge felt pain but thought it was a backache from fooling around with our grandchild. It was the cancer ... She had been treating it for a year and a half, and we thought we had it under control. She was doing chemotherapy and some sort of infusion, which worked up to a point. But then it exploded, which frequently happens with this sort of cancer. It just eats up the body. She stayed at home with me until the night before she died. I took her down to New York when I realized that we could not go on here. It just became impossible to deal with. We thought she was licking it, she was beating it. That is what we were told.[98]

The funeral, organized by Miller's two daughters, was held in the barn at their Roxbury home. Rebecca and Honor unpacked the flowers; Inge's assistant laid out photographs depicting Inge's life. William Coffin, the family friend of many decades, led the ceremony, while Francine du Plessix Gray spoke. In a poem called 'Music' Honor Moore captured the moment Inge's ashes were scattered on the pond where she had swum each morning, whenever weather permitted.

> Her husband leading us
> to the water
>
> even the black we wore was bright
> moving across blond grass
>
> afternoon unseasonable, warm
> darkness already present
>
> but also the feel of spring
> in weeks the first daffodils ...
>
> and when the moment comes
> the gesture is abrupt, ceremonial
>
> at the edge of the black water
> his great arm bending
>
> elbow rising in gray air
> he holds the wooden box
>
> he digs for ash as if for food
> (the hunger was sadness)

and then, the arm lifting, his hand
opened to the sky

and what she had burned to
rose, taking the light.[99]

Later, Miller discovered a black stone near the house and arranged to have
the name 'MILLER' inscribed on it. He stopped his car one day to show it
to me as it stood at the edge of a field, now an extension of the Roxbury
cemetery. He expected his own name to be inscribed along with hers, he said.
Later, her remaining ashes were buried alongside the stone in an urn made
by Tom Doyle, the sculptor husband of his daughter Jane. Miller read a poem.

In her will, dated 3 May 1984, she left her apartment on the rue de la
Chaise in Paris to Rebecca. Should her husband not survive her, Rebecca
would also inherit the house on Tophet Road, Roxbury, along with the forty
acres on which it stood.

In a letter to his brother-in-law, Werner Morath, Miller said, 'I'm still
astonished by the happiness that was ours for forty years. And what happiness!
I try to keep reminding myself of it, also how much she gave me. I can only
hope she experienced something similar regarding me. I think she did. She
was a courageous, fine woman. We were all blessed in being so close to her.'[100]
He tried to lose himself in work, attending the first three days of rehearsals
of *The Crucible*, directed by Richard Eyre with Liam Neeson as Proctor, and
finishing a story, 'The Performance' (to be published in the *New Yorker* that
April), but it was self-defeating. He had assumed he would die first and had
worried about her being on her own. Now he was alone.

Rehearsals took place in the building where two other British directors
were preparing productions: Nicholas Hytner, *The Sweet Smell of Success*, and
Trevor Nunn, *Oklahoma* – as Hytner observed, they were all creatures of
subsidized theatre. *The Crucible* arrived at a moment that both director and
playwright thought particularly timely. Miller remarked, 'The play is dealing
with the disintegration of a society. It's a play about paranoia and hysteria
and I imagine that people are reacting to it because they are feeling similar
things now, namely that an attack can come from anywhere, which is what
was happening in Salem, that they weren't quite sure why, that they weren't
sure what they would do or what they should do ... and here we have a
society that is scared, it's nervous.'[101] Richard Eyre recalled Miller remarking,
after the read-through, that this was a young man's play, that he couldn't write
this now.

On opening night Miller took the applause, proud once again of the play
but also empty because he no longer had someone with whom to share the
success. Ben Brantley in the *New York Times*, while praising Neeson and

Laura Linney, found the production 'unbalanced'. The supporting cast were 'exasperatingly uneven', and the play was 'an old warhorse'. It all meant little to Miller, who was left to return to Roxbury alone. In fact it was a fine production, finding a new relevance at a time when the White House was promoting a Manichean version of the world.

For the moment, Miller hesitated to remove Inge's possessions, though the photographs had to be gathered for what would become an archive. Once again, he turned to his work. There was a play to attend – *The Man Who Had All the Luck* was returning to Broadway for the first time in nearly six decades. The Roundabout production, at the American Airlines Theatre on West 42nd Street, directed by Scott Ellis and featuring Chris O'Donnell, was well received. As Bruce Weber noted in the *New York Times*, it followed a series of 'fine revivals' including *Death of a Salesman, The Price, A View from the Bridge, The Ride down Mount Morgan* and *The Crucible*. He now had two plays running on Broadway, even if *The Man Who Had All the Luck* was scheduled for a run of only seventy-seven performances, including previews (in the event, it was seen by 57,457 people). *The Crucible*, also on a limited run, ran for 120 performances. His American reputation was being restored.

On 26 April, Miller was in a theatre for another reason. A memorial service for Inge was held at the Mitzi Newhouse Theater at Lincoln Center. It was organized by Rebecca, but it was he who chose the Bach *Sarabande* and *Air on a G String*. Bob Dishy, who had appeared in *The Creation of the World and Other Business* and *The Price*, assumed responsibility for the music, which was played on the flute by Paula Robinson, with Romero Lubambo on guitar. Contributions were made by Honor Moore, the novelist Louis Auchincloss, the Magnum photographer Elliott Erwitt and the actress, and wife of Miller's long-term producer Robert Whitehead, Zoë Caldwell. Miller delivered a moving eulogy. He recalled Inge's habit of swimming in the pond at Roxbury, her pleasure in working in the garden and in cooking, but he recalled too her triumphs abroad, underlined by the flood of letters he had received. She was, he said, a survivor, and he instanced her wartime sufferings. Photographs of Inge were projected on a screen. A couple of weeks after they had become lovers, he said, she had confessed to him that she was a snob, but he had lived to discover that this meant she had a preference for the best. He spoke of her pleasure in Spain and the purity of her Spanish. She was, he said, a discreet woman who revealed only what she chose to and respected other people's privacies in her art no less than in her life. She had been the living centre of their home. He spoke of the difficult times in which she had been raised and of her determination to live each day to the full, while valuing people for who they were. She had a fear of violence, and a joy in life. She was, he said, noble.

That same month Miller published a piece in a women's beauty magazine called *Allure* in which he tried to capture something of Inge's attraction:

The most glamorous woman I ever met was certainly beautiful, although she would have thought other women far more so. Yet, everyone who knew her thought of her as glamorous, a living point of fascination who stirred so many of the emotions that move in people when confronting a star. There is no way to nail down her fascination but it may help to know that she read seven languages and was fluent in five; that she had travelled the world alone as a photographer, including what were then beautiful but forbidden places like bandit-ridden Persepolis where no law reached and the only place to sleep was in an ancient abandoned tomb. She was mother and grandmother, devoted wife and artist, a fabulous cook and a woman experienced in cultures and literatures as different as the French, German, English, Italian, Russian and Chinese.

In postwar France, as a novice, she sought out and photographed the worker priests who were living among the poorest Parisians and brought their unusual labours and the conditions of the poor to the country's attention. In Muslim lands she had worn the burnoose to penetrate women's quarters where no man could go; in the West she might show up in one of the Balenciaga gowns the designer had given her because she made them look so elegant, as well as because her Spanish was so pure and her courage so moving and her wit, as sharp as her love for Spain, was touching. [Her] glamour was largely the reflection of her values, her dynamic energy, and the unforgettable candor with which she dealt with people. In the sense that it was a glamour that expressed life-enhancing motives and accomplishments, it was worthy of the admiration it inspired. In short, it was real, her actual essence ... [102]

Though, during his oration, Miller had recalled Inge's struggle to survive in the chaos of war, he omitted any reference to the soldier who, she claimed, had saved her life. Afterwards, when I asked him why, he said that it was because he had never been entirely sure that the soldier existed. He thought it possible that Inge's mind had invented him in order to stay alive, having come to the verge of suicide.

Immediately after the ceremony, I joined Miller in a taxi. He was going to the auditions for *Resurrection Blues*, with David Esbjornson and Joe Dowling, Artistic Director of the Guthrie Theater in Minneapolis. At the time it struck me as odd; but he had done his mourning, and work was his antidote.

Life and death, however, continued to keep pace with each other. In June he presented a lifetime achievement award to a frail Robert Whitehead at the Tonys. Later, Terrence McNally protested at CBS's failure to televise the occasion – an omission all the more poignant when, two weeks later, Whitehead died. Born in Montreal, he had appeared as an actor on Broadway in 1936 before spending the war years as an ambulance driver. His doubts about working in the theatre were put to rest when he read an essay by Harold

Clurman which described the theatre as a conversation with society, equally Miller's conviction. After the war Whitehead became a producer and worked on plays by O'Neill, Wilder, Williams and Miller. According to Williams he looked like a riverboat gambler, but in truth he was more like an English gentleman. He collaborated with Miller on eight productions and was working on *Resurrection Blues* when he died.

And it was to rehearsals for the play that Miller now flew out to Minneapolis, where he had been provided with a house with its own swimming pool. David Esbjornson, the play's director, later recalled:

> It was difficult for Arthur to move forward. Obviously, [Inge's and Whitehead's] deaths had created an enormous vacuum in his life. It was essential that Arthur work and I think he understood that. Still, I was surprised that he could ... The play was still in an early form and under the circumstances many important aspects of the writing had not been attended to ... I was excited to be back in a rehearsal room with Arthur and grateful to be part of his healing process ... We had come to Minneapolis to escape the pressures of New York ... Arthur used every opportunity to say that.[103]

It was hot in Minneapolis, and after rehearsals he and the cast would resort to the pool. On 4 July they held a barbecue. Esbjornson described him 'up to his chest in the outdoor hot tub flanked by two beautiful women, a plastic cup of red wine in one hand and a sparkler in the other. He looked boyishly happy.'

Miller, though, was concerned about one aspect of the play, the raising of a cross on stage, in preparation for the crucifixion of a charismatic man who may or may not be the returned Christ: 'I don't know at this point what the ramifications might be. Some people may be filled with awe, others with resentment, amusement. I don't know what. But it's certainly going to count, because it's a great big cross, and it will be interesting to see what happens. But, then, it's built into that play. The sublime and the ridiculous are cheek by jowl.'[104] In 1992 he had written an op-ed piece for the *New York Times*, calling for public executions to entertain and educate the American public. In New York, these were to take place in Shea Stadium. Everyone would benefit, from the private companies charged with organizing them to the prisoners' families, who would receive payments. Capitalism and morality would thus triumph, although he conceded that the effect might quickly diminish, particularly since the evidence was that the murder rate tended to increase with the prevalence of executions.

This Swiftean parody was directed at the death penalty, which Miller opposed, but it was also an acknowledgement of the degree to which a new decadence was reflected in the public's apparent enthusiasm for pain and suffering, transmuted into entertainment. 'Reality television' presented psychological trauma, marital breakdown, medical horrors, car crashes, riots, in prime time. Military leaders offered press conferences in which it was possible to watch through a nose-cone camera as a missile closed in on an isolated individual whose death was then confirmed by an orgasmic snow of static. Reality, it seemed, existed in order to be reprocessed into a form of fiction until the dividing line became blurred, pain miraculously banished, death's sting withdrawn. No wonder that so many who saw the twin towers fall thought at first that they were watching a movie, so used were they to fact presented as fiction and fiction as fact.

In 2002, the year of *Resurrection Blues*, Dr Gunther von Hagens conducted a public autopsy and later presented an exhibition in which plasticized dead bodies were shown having sex. Nothing, it appeared, was impossible on television. The concept of good taste had long since been abandoned. When the truck bomber Timothy McVeigh was executed on 11 June 2001, bids came in offering to transmit it live on the Internet.

Resurrection Blues was in part a response to this. In an early draft, Miller has a character remark that there was 'no one left to call anything unreal'. After all, as another character observes, the Vietnam War was precipitated by an event (in which North Vietnamese boats supposedly fired on the destroyer USS *Maddox*) that probably never happened, while the funeral of disgraced President Richard Nixon was larger than that of Abraham Lincoln, quite as if he had never been forced to resign from the presidency. The play partly comes out of the same bewilderment Miller had expressed in *Mr Peters' Connections*. As Henri Schultz observes in *Resurrection Blues*, 'nothing seems to follow from anything else'.[105]

It was out of this swirl of ontological confusions that Miller wrote *Resurrection Blues* – that, and a sense of moral indignation and metaphysical irony. In part a satire, it is also a comment on post-revolutionary societies (of which America is one), on the caustic effects of ideology, on social inequity, as well as on the degradation of language, the casuistry of commerce and politics alike, and the need to construct a redemptive religion. It is also a comedy, mocking the values and rhetoric of Madison Avenue as well as the hypocrisies of the political world.

Resurrection Blues is set in an unnamed South American country, though Miller's visit to Colombia was plainly one source. A guerrilla war has been under way for thirty-eight years but now shows signs of slackening, though the President, General Felix Barriaux, has regularly to move house for security reasons. Recently, a leader has emerged. Some of his followers believe he may be the returned Christ. He is now under arrest and the General is planning his public crucifixion, selling the rights to an American advertising firm working for a pharmaceutical company. In an early draft this was Batten, Barton, Durstine & Osborn, for which Miller had worked in the 1940s when they were the producers for DuPont's *Cavalcade of America* radio series. Bruce

Barton had been famous for writing *The Man Nobody Knows* (1926), which suggested that Christ had been the world's greatest salesman. Miller changed the company's name in later drafts, presumably to avoid litigation.

Felix is confronted by his cousin, Henri, partly because his old radical allegiances give him a sense of solidarity with the poor. The country's infrastructure is falling apart. Having imported a grand piano, Henri cannot install it because the floor in his house would collapse, the foundations rotting away. The house, like the one in Tennessee Williams's play *A House Not Meant to Stand*, is an image of a society in collapse. Two per cent of the population, we are told, own 96 per cent of the wealth. In the United States – and the play is in many ways addressed to America – 1 per cent would own 42.2 per cent in 2004. Certainly, Miller frequently spoke of his disgust that America's wealth did not extend to the millions of poor lacking health care and who went to bed hungry, just as he rejected President Bush's tax cuts for the rich, even though he himself benefited.

Henri also finds himself disturbed because of the attempted suicide of his daughter who, like that of another father (in *Clara*, part of *Danger: Memory!*), had followed him into radical politics and now, in despair, throws herself through a window, as a result being confined to a wheelchair. There is another echo of *Clara* when Felix observes: 'Life is complicated but underneath the principle has never changed since the Romans – fuck them before they can fuck you.'[106] (*Clara*: 'Do it to them before they can do it to you.'[107])

Henri, who has now abandoned politics for philosophy, begs his cousin to stop the crucifixion, but the American advertising executive, Skip L. Cheeseboro, and his film crew are already on site. Though they are somewhat disturbed by what they are required to film, they seem ready to make the necessary compromises while at the same time attempting to keep the moral high ground. As Cheeseboro insists, 'I will not superimpose American mores on a dignified foreign people',[108] a line that always raised a laugh in the Guthrie production, following the Gulf War, the attack on Afghanistan and preparations for the Iraq War.

If the mysterious man *is* Christ, he returns to a world in which Satan offers not the dominion of the world as seen from a mountain top but that offered by a global television audience – tempting, at moments, even to the putative Redeemer. Sacrifice in the presence of a handful of people at Golgotha, after all, can hardly compare with that conducted via satellite. And this 'Christ' hesitates, as if unsure whether the bargain might not be worth accepting. After a while, even the poor he has come to serve begin to see the advantages to be wrung from their town being chosen as the site where the Son of God is killed, again.

This Christ figure, if such he is, has a disturbing habit of disappearing and reappearing, glowing brightly (rather like the Christlike figure in the 1999 film, *The Green Mile*), reportedly walking through walls. He also keeps changing his name. At one moment he is Jack Brown, at another Juan Manuel Francisco Federico Ortega de Oviedo. Then he is Charlie (a perverse echo, perhaps, of another would-be Christ, Charles Manson), Vladimir, Francisco or Herbie, an everyone but also someone uncertain as to his identity and purpose, if also eager to avoid the status of celebrity. In his earlier work, Miller had explored the human need to create God as an unchallengeable source of moral values. Here something similar seems to be happening. As Henri observes, 'My brain *demanded* an astonishment and I believe I proceeded to create one.' The chief threat posed by this new Christ, or pseudo-Christ, is that in a world in which people prefer fiction to reality '*he still feels everything*', a reverence for life that can only be threatening. 'Wherever we turned,' Henri says, 'our dead unfeeling shallowness would stare us in the face until we shrivelled up with shame.'[109] The message of the returned 'Christ', according to his disciple Stanley, is no more complex than 'Don't do bad things',[110] a challenge to those for whom he is a primary route to success and power.

Whatever the nature of this mysterious figure, lives are transformed. Henri's daughter Jeanine rises from her wheelchair, as Sylvia had done in *Broken Glass*. Emily Shapiro, the film's director, insists on visiting the poor and trying to change Felix. The play ends as the characters stare upwards, addressing an invisible figure – Felix and Skip appeal to him to stay and be crucified, to the greater glory of the dictatorship and Madison Avenue, and Stanley and Emily for him to leave. One by one they drift from the stage, Christ's second coming (and second crucifixion) deferred.

Resurrection Blues, though, is a comedy, from the opening exchange between Felix and Henri to his parody of a valueless Madison Avenue. Why, asks Felix, should anyone be offended by a man's crucifixion, when 'the son of a bitch is not even Jewish'?[111] The $75 million on offer for the television rights could, after all, 'provide funds for sewers so the better-off people wouldn't have to go up to the tops of the hills to build a house', while at the other end of the social spectrum it would be possible to 'send all our prostitutes to the dentist'.[112] His cousin ironically points out that the crucifixion would be interspersed with advertisements for relevant products, from underarm deodorants to treatments for athlete's foot – products which, as it happens, his own former company manufactured.

Those who arrive to film the crucifixion see the world in terms of the commercials they have shot. The world exists as a background to commerce, the real appropriated to serve the function of fiction. Nepal, thus, means 'the Ivory Soap shoot',[113] Kenya the Chevy Malibu, the Caucasus Head and Shoulders, the Himalayas Alka Seltzer, Chile, Efferdent. This is Nathanael West territory. Though Emily Shapiro, who previously refused to film the clubbing of baby seals, raises objections, this competes with her concerns for her cat and her own unintended pregnancy. Skip Cheeseboro rationalizes the shoot as a blow against capital punishment, while urging Emily to come on side because 'This is a door to possibly Hollywood.'[114] When she reminds him that Christ was crucified with a sign saying, 'The King of the Jews', he is horrified, fearing it will prejudice sales in Egypt and Pakistan: 'It's bad enough implying the son of God was Christian without making him Jewish.' Nor can the intended victim be given drugs or alcohol to dull the pain, for fear of the offence it might give in dry states – 'Kansas or whatever'.[115]

'I suppose in some ways, however unacknowledged and even perverse, the play touches on a kind of longing for deliverance from this bleak frustration in which all of us live, the promised *real* revolution and its apocalypse having died aborning after World War II and the victory over Fascism,'[116] Miller remarked. *Resurrection Blues* is a lament over lost and perverted idealism. Miller had seen Marxism corrupted in the direction of repression and violence, as he had witnessed the impact of a predatory capitalism. If Eastern Europe had suffered under the coercive impact of communism, South American countries had replicated those conditions with the help of the United States and in the name of free enterprise and foreign investment (an early reference to the CIA's role in this invented country was cut from the final text).

Miller's work echoes with regret at the loss of that human solidarity that had, to his mind, characterized not only the 1930s but the war that followed. Increasingly, as here, he laments the loss of a sense of transcendence. An atheist, he placed no hope in religion, whose destructive effects he had witnessed at home and abroad. As he remarked, 'I often think that the last remnants of religion have been flattened out. Some acid has been dropped on the thing and dissolved it. It's gone. If you pick up a nineteenth-century novel, whether it's Dostoevsky or a French or British novel, in the distance you hear the Bible somewhere, the spirit of the transcendent spirit. All we get now is the spirit of decay, the threat of dissolution, the feeling that this is imminent. It's on the horizon.'[117] Nonetheless, he registered the space once occupied by radical politics and religious faith, despairing of a system that offered only an endless cycle of production and consumption, that placed value on trivia, encouraged a retreat from painful truths in the name of nothing beyond self-regard. His bitterness is softened by his humour, but it is none the less felt. The dissolution of which he speaks is not likely, he implies, to be apocalyptic. Instead, it has to do with a slow leaching away of the spirit, a sense that nothing is of sufficient importance to command attention, or that everything is seen as of equal value with no ground for moral discrimination. Meanwhile, the rich flourish and the poor are disregarded, or are offered back their hopes in the form of distractions that mock their need for purpose and fulfilment.

Resurrection Blues does not so much end as drift away, like the characters. Perhaps it is a weakness. Perhaps it simply reproduces existence as Miller saw it, which would end not with a bang but a whimper. What was the bright light that apparently shone out of the mysterious figure, compelling, intangible, if not that desire for something not contained within the material world, in which we are told that satisfaction is to hand provided only that we do not try to strike through the pasteboard mask in search of something more profound?

Audience response was positive, but the *New York Times* was not. For Bruce Weber it was an 'indignant and disappointingly unpersuasive work'. The first twenty minutes were the best. Thereafter 'the play ... begins to disappoint', falling 'on the wrong side of cliché'. The humour was occasionally 'juvenile and truly beneath a playwright of Mr Miller's stature'. One character was 'poorly thought out', another 'sentimental'. 'Unfortunately,' he wrote, 'this play, which means to be acrid and even hip social satire, doesn't get there. Its most lingering effect is that of a serious finger wag, a respected elder's tone of disapproval.'[118] The *Chicago Tribune* complained that it failed to cohere, that it was 'rather stodgy' and played to Miller's polemical side. Even the local Minneapolis paper, while praising the script as the most challenging tackled by the Guthrie for many years, and welcoming its humour, found the production woefully uneven in tone, something the reviewer ascribed largely to the direction and the acting.

Miller was stung by the reviews, especially Weber's. Not only did it kill any chance of a transfer, but in all likelihood, it seemed to him, it would defer any further productions for some time – though in fact the East Coast premiere would take place a year later in Philadelphia. Eight years after its Minneapolis opening, however, the play had yet to reach New York. To Britain's *Daily Telegraph* Miller remarked:

These things need to be said, and I just decided to be the person who said them ... In no way do I regret the message of the play. If it sounds like despair, on some days it seems that way ... There is a problem with the way [the US] is run, with the values of our society ... It's not the country that rejects my play, it's some people in this country, and they are the ones who represent the ruling establishment I am criticizing ... In the Midwest, the audiences have been wonderful. They live in the real world. They know what is going on. Most of my plays have been rejected to start with. *The Crucible* was destroyed first time out. It was the same with *All My Sons*. Every other critic condemned it. Why? I rather imagine that it is because they are attuned to entertainment. That's part of the culture we are dealing with: entertainment for profit. When society and its ills are brought onto the stage, they don't know what to do about it. Until they see the aesthetic of the play, that it is not just a political tract, they are at a loss. And that takes time ... I will certainly try to bring *Resurrection* to Broadway, but will I find a producer willing to put it on? ... I have the name: but it costs so much to do anything in the theatre now. But we should take the risk. I still have faith in the American people. They will come to listen, and in the end the culture will get turned around, because they will turn it around.[119]

For the director, Esbjornson, there remained aspects of the play that needed working on, which was partly why it had opened in Minneapolis, but the American reaction, it seemed to him, was in part a rejection of its central thesis: 'We needed to test it in front of an audience for the feedback. Miller has experimented with "jumps" and discontinuity, shifts and changes, and some of it may need to be tidied up. No one's more willing to work on it than Miller ... that's among the qualities of a great playwright. But the problem is that the technical issues are not what the fuss is about. As Americans we're so invested in our value system that when someone takes a shot at it, we tend to be sensitive and reject them.'[120]

Michael Billington, writing in the *Guardian* newspaper, seems to have seen an entirely different play from American reviewers. The 'good news', he announced, 'is that the work is a funny, pertinent and sharp-toothed satire aimed at the materialist maladies of modern America.' It scored 'a number of topical bulls'-eyes'. He reported the Minneapolis audience as roaring with laughter, while insisting that the play 'says many necessary, urgent things'. ... They do Miller proud in Minneapolis, he added, but he, in turn, has given them a sparky, pugnacious play that proves that even in his 80s, he is still capable of taking the moral temperature of the nation. It also reminds us that within the supposedly solemn and sententious Miller there has always been a savage ironist.'[121]

This was not to be Miller's last play. As he lay by the pool in Minneapolis he was working on what would become his final work, *Finishing the Picture*, first begun twenty-four years earlier. Indeed, he had taken to looking back through his files for unfinished pieces, including two stories that would soon appear in magazines, 'Presence' and 'The Naked Manuscripts'.

In October 2002, Miller flew to Spain to receive the Prince of Asturias Award. These awards, established in 1981, are designed 'to promote scientific, cultural and humanistic values as a part of mankind's universal heritage' and are presented in Oviedo, capital of the principality of Asturias (the Prince is the heir to the Spanish throne). Those honoured alongside Miller were Woody Allen, Hans Magnus Enzensberger, Daniel Barenboim and Edward Said. Miller, who introduced and concluded his brief speech in Spanish, seized the occasion to recall the Spanish Civil War, saying that there had been no single event as powerful in the formation of his generation's awareness of the world. To many, he added, it was an initiation into the twentieth century. 'The Spanish agony,' he declared, 'has turned out to be classic, a model for many other democratic governments' overthrown by military forces, espousing a return to Christian values.' He recalled the death of his college friend, Ralph Neafus: 'For nearly four years, the first news we looked for in the morning papers was the news from the Spanish front. The word "Spain" in the 30s was explosive, the very emblem of resistance not only to the forced return of clerical feudalism in the world but also to the rule of unreason and the death of the mind. For many, even then, with the Nazis and Mussolini's troops in open support of Franco, this was the opening battle of the Second World War.' He recalled the bombing of civilians in Guernica. 'Spain came tragically to mind, or Chile, where Pinochet had overthrown another elected government.'[122] For the rest of the speech he stressed the importance of Spain to Inge, and the celebration of her and her work, particularly in Navalcán, which she had once photographed and to which she had returned in triumph.

The speech was an obvious provocation: the assembled dignitaries sat, some of them stony-faced, during his denunciation of the regime they had supported and the values they had espoused. The occasion was a reminder, as Miller said, of just how much Spain had meant to him, and perhaps of the guilt that his failure to fight in the Civil War had instilled in him.

Back in America, after a trip that involved a meeting with Henri Cartier-Bresson, he began a play about Inge, only to abandon it; and attended the operatic version of *A View from the Bridge* which, unlike *Resurrection Blues*, had made it to New York. It now had two new arias and Bolcom had made a number of minor changes. Anthony Tommasini, who had reviewed the Chicago production for the *New York Times*, found it 'dramatically assured and often haunting ... Brooklyn verismo'. Earlier weaknesses seemed to have been addressed. It was, he concluded, 'an involving and significant work'.[123]

For nearly a year now Arthur had been without Inge. His speech in Spain had been a way of celebrating her, while his meeting with Cartier-Bresson was a sharing of memories, though it is unclear if he understood the nature of the relationship he had once had with Inge. He had felt crushingly lonely. The truth was that he had never been without a woman in his life, and he missed the support, someone to share things with. Nor was he used to fending for himself. For all his practicality, he had never cooked his own meals. When she had gone off on her trips Inge always left his meals in the freezer. Now, his daughter arranged for a local woman to come in. When I visited him she arrived with a salmon for our lunch. Though he had plenty of acquaintances and professional colleagues, his contemporaries had been dying, so that he had few New York friends left. The Roxbury house, once so full of life, was now empty. He was also acutely aware of his growing frailty. His back remained a problem, and though he managed to work in the garden it was still painful, a reminder of what it would be like to try to function entirely on his own.

Then, in the late autumn of 2002, he met a thirty-two-year-old woman through the composer Michael Rohatyn, Rebecca's college friend who would go on to write the music for a number of her films. At a dinner party the young woman sat beside Miller. They seemed to have little in common, which was hardly surprising given the age discrepancy. She had little interest in theatre, and later admitted she had though he was dead. Her name was Agnes Barley. She quickly became a central figure in his life, to the extent that she would become a significant beneficiary in his will.

Agnes was born in Jacksonville, Florida, in 1970 when Miller was already fifty-five. She had left home at the age of fifteen and lived with her grand-parents. 'I had a very special relationship with my grandfather,' she explained. 'When I was very young, I used to sit by his bed when he was asleep and try to synchronize our breathing.'[124] She had studied at Parsons School of Design in New York City (now Parsons The New School for Design) before securing an MFA from the Academy of Fine Arts in Vienna. Like Inge, she spoke German. She then spent time at the Domaine de Kerguehennec, twenty kilo-metres north of the town of Vannes in France. Her work had been seen in various European exhibitions, but her career was very much in its early days.

Agnes arrived in New York City in 1998, where she worked as public relations director for Sigerson Morrison shoes. At the time she met Miller she had a part-time job in a stationery shop, painting in her Chinatown apartment at night – 'it was so small I didn't have enough room between the bed and the wall to turn my paper on a diagonal'.[125] Here she produced works that were not so much pictures as what Miller was later quoted as calling 'imagined captures of space' (though it is doubtful whether this phrase was Miller's): they were geometric shapes, each in a single colour, a tracery of lines. In offering a description for the Jen Bekman gallery on Spring Street in New York City's Lower East Side, she was faced with the usual difficulty of expressing in words what she was reaching for in terms of colour and shape. Her work, she said, attempts to 'crystallize harmony, to distil form into careful constructs of line that reveal an internal structure and its absence. These works on paper paint constellations that are self-contextualized and breathing. They are points in space or places isolated and unknown yet defined; con-structions that whisper of a horizon with both movement and stillness.'[126] It took Miller some time to appreciate the qualities of her work, and when he did it was perhaps partly, at least, an expression of his growing interest in the artist rather than the art.

Despite the age difference, their first meeting led to others. They began to visit galleries together, go to the cinema and theatre, meet for meals. Miller's sister Joan later remembered one such occasion:

> We were having dinner in a restaurant and there were about six people at the table. I saw these people talking together and he very surreptitiously almost touched her hand on the table. There was a sixteenth of an inch between their fingers. He just didn't feel free, I guess, to show that there was closeness there. But I thought to myself, those fingers are pretty close. Maybe there's something going on here. Of course, it had been going on for some while. Then, when she got in a taxi he said to her, 'Where's your place?' and she said, 'I'll just take this to such and such a place. Just drop me there.' He didn't seem to know where she lived so I thought maybe this was only the second or third time they had seen one another. But I think it was already burgeoning, at the very least.[127]

They were soon having dinner together most nights of the week. Looking back, Agnes explained, 'We talked about everything: our concepts of love, time, life. I think we spent six months together before I even admitted: God, I'm deeply in love with this person.'[128] Miller's own feelings for her appear to have deepened quickly, though he remained embarrassed on her behalf at being seen with a man who could have been her grandfather. Emotionally adrift, he turned to her for friendship if nothing else – and surely nothing else, he feared, was possible in the circumstances.

She introduced him to some of her friends, all younger. The difficulties were obvious, but neither seems to have wanted to end the relationship, while not sure where it was going. After a while, he took her to Roxbury and introduced her to his daughter Jane and her husband Tom. Miller appeared to be testing the waters. Indeed, he seemed anxious to tell people of his new relationship. Honor Moore recalled him taking her out to lunch and explaining that he had met someone, confessing that she was quite a bit younger than himself. Also over lunch, he told me and my BBC producer, without mentioning her name. There was something of the teenage lover about him, simultaneously exulting in a secret and anxious to share it.

By now he was to be seen more regularly with Agnes; she had begun to seem the centre around which his emotional life turned, though there were constant reminders of his age. He attended memorial services and noted the passing of those he had known – Katharine Hepburn, with whom he had played tennis, Hume Cronyn, who had featured as Willy Loman, Joseph Chaikin who directed several of his plays, Al Hirschfeld, who had drawn a caricature of Miller and whom Inge had photographed, George Plimpton, a friend and founder of the *Paris Review*. The world seemed to be closing down.

In August he travelled with Agnes to Prince Edward Isle where Rebecca was filming *The Ballad of Jack and Rose* with Daniel Day-Lewis. It was on his return that he had the first intimation that there might be something seriously wrong with his health: a cancerous growth was detected in his bladder, though one, he was told, that could be easily removed. It was, but quickly recurred. It was not this, though, that took him to hospital as an emergency case, but pneumonia. He had been more ill than he had realized – being sent straight to hospital from the doctor's surgery. Even a week after returning home he sounded disturbingly frail.

There is no doubting the impact Agnes had on Arthur Miller. They were now to be seen together at major events. In April 2004 they attended the PEN Literary Gala, honouring champions of free expression. There is a photograph of the couple, Miller looking slightly out of place beside his young companion. In September they attended the exhibition of her work staged at Jen Bekman's gallery. Bekman remarked of her, 'It's in no way a case of her hitting the jackpot. They are in love and it's a true romance. She is [as] astonished as anyone at the path her life has taken. I don't think she expected to fall in love but she genuinely did.'[129] Agnes herself remarked, 'I feel very lucky ... I feel just so fortunate ... I'm not naive to the fact that people are curious about us. I feel very lucky.'[130]

By now she had moved in with Miller at his Connecticut home, where she had prepared for her exhibition. Of their daily life at Roxbury she said, 'We wake up and have breakfast together ... Then we go into our respective studios to work. We usually meet for lunch and perhaps go for a little walk. Then I'll usually go back to my studio and paint some more.'[131]

When her New York debut exhibition opened (despite the rain, two hundred people turned up, including Miller's agent Sam Cohn and his neighbour Frank McCourt) it carried an endorsement from Miller, anxious to help her in every way he could. It is doubtful, though, whether she was helped much by the mannered contradictions of the collector Dini von Mueffling, who remarked that 'Barley's paintings are simultaneously familiar and utterly new. They are forms you cannot identify, but recognize. The deliberateness of her strokes contrasts with the freeform sensibility, creating worlds in which hard meets soft and absence meets presence. In her work you see memory; hers and yours.'[132] Asked about his relationship with Agnes in a *New York Times* interview, Miller said, 'I like the company of women ... Life is very boring without them. Women are livelier than men and more interested in people. Men get abstract with their ideas.' Asked why he had turned to a young woman for company when it would be easier to call on old friends, he replied, 'Not if they're dead ... Then it takes longer.'[133] On this occasion Agnes had driven him down from Roxbury to his one-bedroom East 68th Street apartment; she kissed him goodbye, leaving him to talk to an interviewer about the forthcoming *Finishing the Picture*.

If this relationship at first glance seemed discrepant, then another, equally unlikely, paired Miller with rap artist Mos Def. Laura Bush had organized a White House poetry reading but Sam Hamill, one of the invitees, had indicated that he intended to solicit anti-war poems and present them to her. In consequence, the event was cancelled. Hamill wrote an open letter saying: 'I believe the only legitimate response to such a morally bankrupt and unconscionable idea is to reconstitute a Poets Against the War movement like the one organized to speak out against the war in Vietnam,'[134] the organization to which Miller had contributed nearly forty years earlier. On 12 February 2003, the scheduled date of Mrs Bush's event, more than a hundred and sixty readings of poems 'Not Fit for the White House' were held across America. In New York it took place in the Avery Fisher Hall. The night was not ideal. There was a blizzard. Nonetheless, the hall was full. Miller prompted an enthusiastic response when he asked of the impending Iraq War, 'Why can't this wait for a month, or six months, or years, or long enough for Saddam Hussein to just die?'[135]

The following week, he published an article in the *New York Times* in which he attacked the Bush administration and lamented the failure of his own profession to address pertinent issues. 'Has the essence of America, its very nature,' he asked,

> changed from benign democracy to imperium? Why do such majorities across the water fear and despise this administration? Too much piety, triumphal arrogance? We are blasted by issues raised by an unprecedented American position at the top of the world. The meanings of words have changed; is it really a cause for unalloyed boasting that we can fight two wars at the same time, or is this to be lamented as the failure of America's creation: the United Nations and the system of collective security? One has to wonder sometimes if the art of giving things their right name is being surrendered. Ought our most public of arts reflect these confusions, or is it enough for Broadway to go right on sounding pretty much as it did sixty, seventy years ago?

The British theatre, he believed, had no difficulty in regarding social criticism as entertainment. By contrast, the American theatre showed little interest in engaging public issues: he observed, 'I can't think when the narrow-minded, the prejudiced, the stupid, the reactionary could have been outraged by something on the Broadway stage.' He looked back to *The Crucible* not only as a model but also as a harbinger. Just as when Judge Danforth had insisted that citizens were either with the court or against it, with no middle ground, he now heard 'a kind of Roman obedience and conformity echo in an attorney general, the highest legal officer of government, declaring that to oppose his ideas is to unpatriotically encourage terrorism, even as the American Bar Association warns that our vaunted legal rights and protections are being undermined by this kind of thinking.'[136]

When he received a call from the FBI at this time, he might have expected it to be in relation to his anti-war efforts. In fact, it was altogether more bizarre: his name had come up in connection with a kidnapping case. Four local men had set out to kidnap an assortment of wealthy people, starting with Edward S. Lampert, chairman of ESL Investments. He was released, but the FBI (involved because of the nature of the crime) had discovered Miller's name, along with others, amongst the empty pizza cartons, soda bottles, clothing and a portable radio abandoned by the kidnappers in the Days Inn motel in Hamden, Connecticut. Three were charged, while the fourth escaped. Miller was unmoved.

In April 2003 it was announced that he had been awarded the Jerusalem Prize, presented every two years for literary achievement in the field of freedom of the individual in society. Like several others offered the honour, he was uncertain whether to accept. His relationship with Israel had changed over the years. His 1998 poem celebrating the fiftieth anniversary of the establishment of the state of Israel had been decidedly ambiguous. As he wrote to me on 14 August that year, his poem was tough on both sides but would make not a spot of difference. On the one hand, he acknowledged Israel's response as a logical response to anti-Semitism:

> I quickly understand the Jewish dead,
> Know their shock at departing alone;
> See Jewish women at the blast
> Glancing back across the centuries
> As laughter of Goyim cracks the air;
> All this I see at the gunshot.

On the other hand, Jewish fundamentalists were no different from those of other religions, thus confirming his own resolute atheism:

> ... I salute the Jews,
> the Christians, the Muslims, Iranians,
> The Hindus – all their absolutists in our
> Dear world – and thank them for having
> Settled the question of whether god can
> possibly exist, and leaving me in peace.[137]

When he was interviewed by the *Jerusalem Post* he explained his attitude to the prize: 'I hesitated about it ... and then thought that to decline might make it appear that I think the Palestinians are totally right and the Israelis are totally wrong. ... So I thought that maybe a speech that mediates between the two positions, or the two attitudes, could be of use.' It might have been but it was not the speech he proceeded to write, as should have been apparent from his remark that 'I've thought for a long time that this kind of fierce nationalistic anger had to end in the self-destruction of Israel, just as it would anywhere else ... and that it would be disturbing to the country and the Jews if one just decided not to mention it'. He opposed Israel's settlement policy, he said, because it provoked unnecessary conflict, transforming a political issue into a military one: 'For every shot fired there's another shot coming the other way, and this can go on forever, which is what it seems to be doing.'[138]

He decided not to go to Jerusalem but to record his speech and, in tune with the directness of his Jefferson and Prince of Asturias lectures, to be frank about his views. The address was not well received, but then, neither had Susan Sontag's been when she had received the prize two years earlier. She had attacked Israel for its policy of collective punishment, for the disproportionate use of firepower against civilians, the demolition of homes and the building of settlements. She had been urged not to attend, a pressure that played its role in persuading her to go. A decade earlier, along with Miller and others, she had signed a letter (18 February 1991, in the *New York Times*) complaining at the continuing detention of the Palestinian activist Sari Nusseibeh, then professor of philosophy at Birzeit University. At the moment Sontag received the prize in 2001, moves were under way, she said, to shut down the administration and presidency of Al-Quds University, headed by Sari Nusseibeh. Following her speech, some left the hall. In contrast, Alexander Cockburn in the *Nation* criticized her for describing Mayor Olmert, who presented the prize, as 'a reasonable person' when he was 'one of the roughest of the Likud ultras', who had 'consistently pushed for the expropriation of Arab residency permits'.[139] Sontag's experience might well have played a role in Miller's decision to settle for a virtual presence in Jerusalem. His explanation to the organizers that he had other commitments was not, though, as disingenuous as it appeared – an exhibition of Inge's photographs was due to open forty-eight hours after the award. Nor was he attracted, as he might once have been, by a quick overseas trip.

He began his recorded speech by explaining why throughout his life he had strayed from his desk into the world of politics; why, in particular, he had worked for PEN in seeking to secure the freedom of imprisoned writers. It was because as a Jew he had been unable to forget the silence of the 1930s and 40s in the face of fascism, the apparent indifference in the face of threat. What might have seemed a platitude, however, was in fact a prelude to a denunciation of certain Israeli policies, even as he acknowledged his own distance from the daily realities of life in the region. He was, he declared, a believer in the two-state solution, but added: 'I have witnessed, initially with surprise and then with incredulity, what seemed a self-defeating policy.' The settlement policy 'appears to have changed the very nature of the Israeli state'. A new 'humanistic vision', he suggested, 'is necessary if the Jewish presence is to be seen as worth preserving. To put it perhaps too succinctly – without justice at its center, no state can endure as a representation of Jewish nature.'

He recalled his enthusiasm for the new state in 1948, his attendance at a celebratory dinner at the Waldorf Astoria, but it had simply not occurred to him that it would be a state like any other, 'defending its existence by all means thought necessary and even expanding its borders when possible'. Then, Israel had meant survival, idealism, dignity, peace. However – certainly since the assassination of Yitzhak Rabin – 'the settlement policy and the present leadership's apparent abandonment of Enlightenment values before the relentless suicide bombings and the fear they have engendered have backed the country away from its visionary character and with it the Waldorf prospect of a peaceful, progressive, normal society'. What was left, he concluded, was 'an armed and rather desperate society at odds with its neighbours and the world'. Israel, to him, had meant a triumph of justice; a balancing of the moral scales after the Holocaust, and as such had earned international regard. Now, under its present leaders, it seemed to be laying claim to a colonial tradition finally abandoned elsewhere, though he conceded that America under George W. Bush showed evidence of a similar attitude, dissipating the goodwill the country had earned at the time of 9:11.

Thomas Jefferson, he recalled, had written into the Declaration of Independence the phrase, 'in decent respect for the opinions of mankind'. Both countries, it seemed to him, had forgotten the force of that imperative. Jefferson had understood 'that no country can for long endure, whatever the urgency of its defences, with less than respect, let alone contempt, for the rest of mankind in its longing for justice and equity for all'. It was, he declared, 'time for Jewish leadership to reclaim its own history and to restore its immortal light to the world'.[140]

The recorded speech, played at the Jerusalem Book Fair, prompted an immediate response from Jerusalem's newly elected ultra-Orthodox mayor, Uri Lupolianski. Speaking in Hebrew, he described Miller as a playwright who had reached his peak fifty years earlier; Lupolianski denounced intellectuals who criticized Israel, especially from a distance, when the country was fighting for its existence. The Israeli novelist Aharon Appelfeld, who was on the prize jury, noted that the mayor was not a literary man. Another guest called the mayor's remarks, 'nationalistic garbage'.

In May 2003 Miller went to Washington to testify, along with fellow playwrights (Wendy Wasserstein, Marsha Norman, Stephen Sondheim), before the Edward Kennedy–Orin Hatch Committee. What was at issue was the Dramatists' Guild's petition to amend anti-trust laws to allow collective bargaining. Senator Hatch spelled out the problem. Everyone in theatre, it seemed, was permitted to engage in acting collectively to secure their rights, except playwrights. The Playwrights' Licensing Antitrust Initiative Act was designed to address this problem. Despite his poor health, Miller decided to attend, not to secure his own rights but to address the needs of young playwrights.

It was some time, he told the Committee, since he had testified before Congress. He had come because a failure to pass the legislation would leave young writers at a severe disadvantage, and this in turn would threaten the theatre, a place where it was possible to 'challenge social mores, ideology, beliefs, or simply entertain'.[141] In the end, he did not read his prepared statement, which would simply form part of the public record of the occasion, but instead described his early experience of being approached to write a play that would then be the property of the man who commissioned it. This, he explained, was why playwrights had had to protect themselves through the Dramatists' Guild, whose Bill of Rights laid down the right to receive royalties.

To the surprise of the assembled playwrights, they were joined by the producer Gerald Schoenfeld, chairman of the League of American Theaters and Producers, with whom Patrick Stewart had had his argument. The Shubert Organization, of which he also was chairman, owned twenty theatres. He was there, it turned out, not to support but to oppose the playwrights' case, arguing that they did not deserve an exemption from anti-trust legislation. In the event, the measure did not pass. When Miller died, Senator Hatch would introduce the playwright's speech into the record as part of his tribute.

As the year progressed, Miller worked on forthcoming productions. He auditioned for *Finishing the Picture*, which was to open at the Goodman Theatre in Chicago, and oversaw a new production of *After the Fall*, the first Broadway revival of his 1964 play, now set at an airport – appropriately, since it was produced by the Roundabout Theatre Company at the American Airlines Theatre on West 42nd Street.

Then, in the course of three weeks, two figures influential in his life died: Elia Kazan and Kermit Miller. Kazan, whom Miller had first seen as a student on his visits to the Group Theatre, died on 28 September 2003 at the age of ninety-four. He had directed Miller's two greatest successes, *All My Sons* and *Death of a Salesman*, and the two had become friends. Both sons of immigrants, both radicalized at university, they shared a sensibility – though Mary Miller, not without justification, always distrusted him, not least for his many affairs. He was, she feared, a dangerous model. Both men had entered analysis in an attempt to save their faltering marriages. They had also shared a lover, Marilyn Monroe. Just as Kazan himself constantly returned to that moment in 1952 when he had offered up the names of former Party members, sometimes justifying, sometimes castigating himself, so Miller, like a betrayed lover, never forgot his shock and dismay, frequently replaying it in the notes he wrote to himself.

Arthur's own brother Kermit, three years older than him, died on the playwright's eighty-eighth birthday. Kermit, always a moral lodestone, was the opposite of Kazan. He had sacrificed his own future for his younger brother, abandoning university and staying with the family through the Depression years. As Miller had begun to build his career, so Kermit, a genuine idealist, went to the war from which Miller had been exempt as a result of an old football injury. He returned partly broken by his experience. He commanded Miller's respect throughout his life. He was survived by his once radical and still politically alert wife Frances, who was to die of lung cancer nine months later.

Lonely and increasingly ill, Miller began to rely ever more on Agnes and, despite the fact that the play had been sketched out decades earlier, it would be tempting to see in the figure of Edna Meyer in the forthcoming *Finishing the Picture* a portrait of his new companion, though he would deny this as readily as he had the connection between Maggie and Marilyn in *After the Fall*. Edna is described as 'a petite, shy but determined woman in her forties'. Phillip Ochsner, the movie producer in *Finishing the Picture*, finds himself drawn to Edna, with whom he has a relationship. His explanation can surely stand as Miller's account of his own rejuvenation: 'You know, when my wife died I kind of cemented myself in a wall; you naturally assume you are supposed to be lonely to the end. But candidly I think I got more sensitive to everything. Maybe because death is constantly at your elbow once someone you care about disappears.'[142] Was this love or was it companionship? If it had originally been the latter, it was now plainly the former. Miller did not want to marry, indeed thought it an impossibility, but he could also not bear the thought of losing Agnes. She plainly restored his spirits though his new optimism was momentarily dulled by the disappointing reviews of *After the Fall*. Once again, Robert Brustein in the *New Republic* dismissed it, but the *New York Times* was equally negative. Ben Brantley called it a 'grievously misconceived revival [of] one man's cosmic yelp', 'one of the most guilt-choked plays ever written'. Peter Krause as Quentin, he suggested, 'delivers Quentin's ontological rants with, at best, the perplexed concentration of someone who is not mechanically inclined reading a car repair manual'.[143] Miller himself was less than convinced by Krause's performance, but this peremptory rejection was painful nonetheless. The play ran for ninety-three performances. Once again reviews were dominated by discussions of Marilyn, even though this time the actress wore red/brown hair rather than the blond wig of Barbara Loden. As the production closed, however, a new play with Marilyn at its heart prepared to open.

He was once again having trouble with his health as a cancerous growth returned; there were also worries about his heart. None of this, though, prevented him from going to Chicago to sit in on rehearsals for what would be his final play, with its apt title, *Finishing the Picture*. The director, Robert Falls, later recalled what it was like to work with Miller, offering a familiar parallel: 'He was simply and unpretentiously a writer, rolling up his sleeves and relishing his work, finding as much joy in crafting a play as he did in crafting furniture in his workshop in Connecticut. As we'd watch a rehearsal, he'd lean over to me and say, "Gee, that's a marvellous scene", or "Gee, that works well." And I'd see the tremendous satisfaction that comes simply from the act of creating something.'[144] The cast were warned against any mention of Marilyn, which created a certain air of unreality, until Miller himself began to invoke her. Heather Prete later recalled:

> In the show I played the role of Kitty. She is written as a drugged-out emotionally damaged movie star who can't seem to get up from her bed and to work on the set. Matthew [Modine] played my husband, Paul, the film's writer. His character struggles with trying to save Kitty from her troubled past and destructible present. In reality, Matthew and I were playing out the final days of Arthur Miller and Marilyn Monroe's marriage as they shot his film *The Misfits*. It was brutal and sad and bravely raw before the world. However, no one was ever to use Marilyn's name when addressing the character of Kitty. We were not to acknowledge that these people really existed beyond the boundaries of fiction. Just as is indicated in *After the Fall*, my hair was not to remain blonde. I wore a brown wig in production. We all watched videos of the making of *The Misfits* but were never able to speak of it in talks with Arthur ... sometimes it did feel like a contradiction to know who we were portraying and not publicly talk about it ... But it was not a contradiction. It read to me as pure uncompromised unapologetic strength ... Here was a man who almost always received negative reviews from his city's most important paper. Here was a man who had gone through a marriage that an often hungry, selfish public felt they had a right to know everything about and he simply said no and it floored me. It floored me to hear a hint of condescension in reviews that Arthur wasn't being 'truthful' enough about who Kitty and Paul were, but it was Arthur's right to refuse to participate in limiting his works to anything less than portraits of the universal man and woman, to make it less than it was. And no one in the cast broke the sanctity of the unspoken truth.[145]

Robert Falls confirmed: 'He certainly presented it to the cast and to me that this work is an act of imagination ... that we should not base it in any way ... on the people who were involved in the making of ... *The Misfits*. I think he has gone out of his way to avoid those connections, although he knows those connections are going to be made.'[146]

With *Finishing the Picture* Miller looked back forty-four years, though he had been sketching scenes from it for twenty-six of those years. It was set in 1960, the moment his marriage to Marilyn ended, but it was also about the price paid by both of them for the art that simultaneously drew them together and thrust them apart. Though the location is never mentioned, it is set in the city of lost dreams – Reno, divorce capital of America – in the Mapes Hotel where cast and crew had been accommodated. Here, a number of stories are coming to an end, but the play is a portrait of something more than a woman in psychological freefall who is being required to perform a work about redemption amidst the ashes of her life, in a place that has lost its innocence. In the distance fires are raging, as they had been during the shooting of *The Misfits*. These are all characters acquainted with trauma. On the television Kennedy and Nixon are debating the future of a country that the audience, though not the characters, know is soon to experience assassination and burning cities, at home and abroad. Beyond that, it is a play that explores the way in which power is deployed, in both private relationships and the public arena. As Miller explained in 2003, 'It's about the terrible impact of power on creativity.'[147]

Here, love breeds vulnerability as power shifts to the person who no longer feels its edge. A writer has the power to shape a narrative that may, as here, serve his own psychic needs. A movie star demonstrates her own power by forcing others to tolerate her suspect behaviour. The director has power to shape the finished product. The film studio can stop the picture at will, and here is tempted to do so. Art is not exempt, Miller seems concerned to say, from the conditions of its creation and consumption.

Finishing the Picture also afforded Miller the chance to draw a portrait of two people for whom he had long felt contempt and whose influence on, and power over, Marilyn he had thought deeply damaging: Lee and Paula Strasberg (here, Jerome and Flora Fassinger). He had always thought the Actors Studio dangerous, despite his own sister's involvement, and Strasberg a charlatan. He had watched what he saw as Paula's fawning attitude towards Marilyn, her manoeuvring for her own advantage, on the sets of *The Prince and the Showgirl* and *The Misfits*, and knew the contempt with which she was regarded by directors whose own power she challenged. Presenting herself as an intermediary between her husband and Marilyn, Paula Strasberg had disavowed responsibility for the star's behaviour while at the same time justifying it to the actress herself. In the play, as in reality, Jerome Fassinger/Lee Strasberg was summoned to help – but showed more concern about the lack of respect with which he perceived his wife, and by extension he himself, was being treated than at the plight of a damaged actress. Miller told me:

When I was still in Reno the idiot woman [Paula Strasberg] had brought a recording of some speech [Lee Strasberg] had made about [Eleonora] Duse [the Italian actress]. It was utterly empty . . . there was nothing. He was going to tell you that only he had the secret of Duse, but what was it? He never let on. And this thing went on for about an hour . . . They always had a New Year's party, where all the actors came. He was at the height of his fame. Marilyn didn't want to go until nearly midnight. It happened that only that day I had bought a book about Japanese drama, from Noh through to modern times, and had been reading it. We arrived there and everyone starts by sitting on the couch, eight or ten of the high-level actors sitting on the floor, literally at his feet. And what was he talking about? The history of Japanese drama. I thought, isn't that odd? So I sat down and listened and it was as though you were going to give the history of the United States starting with Andrew Jackson and then John Tyler and Washington and then Teddy Roosevelt and then Adams. It was a complete omelette. The whole thing was horseshit. And I thought, 'My God!' But he was secure in believing that none of the others knew anything about this.

In the play, Flora is dressed in the same black sack dress that Paula had worn and carries the same collection of watches, set to different time zones to remind her of the moment her husband's pupils were supposedly appearing on stages around the world. Jerome, when he arrives, wears the same cowboy boots as Lee had worn and is the same Svengali who feeds on the talent of the woman for whom he disavows any responsibility.

As the play opens, Phillip Ochsner, chairman of the aptly named Bedlam Pictures, has arrived to decide whether the film can continue, given the failure of its star, identified only as Kitty, to appear on set. With only days to go before completion, cast and crew are waiting to see whether it will be possible to shoot. It is five weeks over schedule and already four and a half million dollars over budget. Though Miller appears in the guise of the film's writer, Paul, there is also something of him in the person of Ochsner, born in Brooklyn, a one-time Marxist who suddenly finds his life reinvigorated through an affair with Edna Meyers, the star's secretary.

As those involved in the decision talk, they suddenly realize that Kitty is wandering the hotel in the nude (as Marilyn had done); her coach, Flora, has abandoned her to send flowers to 'Larry' Olivier (as Paula Strasberg had done). The audience hear Kitty's off-stage voice in a play in which she has only three speeches (in an early draft she was silent) and in which we infer her character and nature via the manner in which other people respond to her. She is hustled into Ochsner's bedroom as the fate of the production and, indeed, of its star, is discussed.

Each of the characters has a different take on Kitty. For the director,

Derek Clemson, 'She is a case of terminal disappointment. With herself, her husband, the movies, the United States, the world … she's been stepping on broken glass since she could walk. She is pure survival … She has ghosts sitting on her chest, ghosts of things she's done, or had been done to her.'[148] For Terry Case, the cinematographer in the play, 'You had a bird here who naturally sang. They started to teach her how to sing, and so naturally she can't sing anymore.'[149] For Ochsner, 'Any human life is a damaged apple – you just have to nibble around the spoiled spots and be thankful for the rest.'[150] To a degree these were all explanations of Marilyn, and Miller's attitude to her, and unsurprisingly it is Paul, Kitty's husband, who sums up his relationship with the fragile star, in words that Miller had previously used in interviews about his own failed marriage: 'We promised to cure the other of his life, but we turned out to be exactly what we were.'[151] She 'doesn't like me … And how could she? – I didn't save her. I didn't do the miracle I kind of promised. And she didn't save me, as she promised.'[152] Here, at the end of his life, Miller was reaching back and acknowledging a mutual failure. Since Kitty remains virtually silent and is glimpsed only occasionally, the playwright has to do her what justice he can.

In an echo of *The Last Yankee*, Paul declares that her problem is that 'She doesn't think she's wonderful anymore!'[153] The effect, of course, is that what appears her wilfulness becomes a product of her desire to be acknowledged. As Paul says, 'Her life has her by the throat. There is no way to reach into her that I know of. We're all a bit angry at her … but the key to this lock is probably love. Which she can't accept.'[154] In the play this is to be taken on trust. In life, it had seemingly been the truth about a woman who needed and demanded total commitment but who, when offered it, could not believe she was worthy of it.

The characters address Kitty but the audience cannot hear her replies, which they have to construct from what they do hear, just as they have also to summon the actress into being; she, for the most part, remains physically obscured as she was in life by the image that stood in her place, which she exploited and wrestled with. When Paul enters her bedroom she screams, as Marilyn had when Miller entered her room in Reno. He has become the focus for her anger and frustration, even as she speaks the lines he has written and Kitty's near-silence mimics that of the actress whose role is only to speak what others write.

Finishing the Picture, though, is not just a thinly disguised account of a climactic moment in Miller's life. Indeed, when I sent him a critical account of the play, stressing the biographical dimension, he sent me a swift rebuke complaining at the reductiveness of such an approach. He was right, of course. If the play were no more than that it would become simply a footnote to *Timebends*. The play has a context. When Miller sent me an early draft

I reminded him that the Kennedy–Nixon debates had been going on at the time and that he had watched them during the shooting of the film. I was fascinated when the next draft included them. Paul, in an echo of Miller's remarks in his Jefferson Lecture, observes, 'It's serious; the fate of the world could hang on this vaudeville. The whole thing has turned into vaudeville ... The presidency is a prize we give to the actor who does the best imitation of a president ... Jefferson was not a performer; Lincoln certainly wasn't.'[155]

Finishing the Picture, in part about the permeable membrane between life and art, leans out into society until performance becomes a central trope. A play about the crisis in the making of a film is also about the price paid by those who create art. As Derek, the director, remarks, 'It's not a business ... It's an art pretending to be a business ... the artist dies in his work, the businessman carries his work into the world. Like ants carrying off the rotting twigs of a fallen branch to feed other ants.'[156] Edna now reminds Kitty that 'writers can be a bit oblivious',[157] a withdrawal that is the necessary precondition for creativity but which is potentially corrosive of relationships. As to Kitty, her talent seems to require the very tension that destroys her. Just as the fire that rages in the distance and that threatens to close the production down may enable life to germinate as 'the heat opens up the seed', so Kitty (and Marilyn) creates not in spite of but because of the friction she creates.

Kitty finally agrees to be hospitalized, but the play does not end with her. It concludes as Edna, newly energized, takes out a mirror and rouge brush, plucking at her cheeks to bring colour into them. For her, at least, 'The sky's clear and bright.'[158] Miller, too, was feeling clear and bright, though he told Deborah Solomon in the *New York Times:* 'I feel like Eubie Blake ... He once said, "If I had known I was going to live this long, I would have taken better care of myself."'[159] On 10 October 2004, Miller sent me an email. Having noted that the project we had been working on, his diaries, was now ready to go to press (he subsequently decided to take these over himself), he added:

> Finishing the Picture has opened in Chicago and is a beautiful production. I have no way at the moment of knowing what the Times will make of it but my own feelings are very positive and I feel good about the whole thing. Resurrection Blues which I revised at length had a reading a few months ago with Bill Murray, Julia Louis-Dreyfus and Nathan Lane and was spectacularly received by an audience of about a hundred. All three of them have signed on to do the production which will get under way in spring. The director is Jerry Zaks, a farce and comedy director who is very successful here. The American production of Salesman opens in London in May with the director Robert Falls and I hope to be over for that. I've been having some health

problems but I can tell you about that when we next meet. I feel very well and expect to continue that way.

As ever, Miller awaited the reviews that would determine whether the play would transfer, as planned, to New York; and, as ever, there was only one newspaper that counted. Ben Brantley welcomed the new work as 'refreshingly free of the shrill self-justification and self-blame' of *After the Fall*, but was concerned at the 'less fleshed-out characters' and that the play's 'window on the past ... does not provide much in the way of illumination'. As to Monroe, there was 'little that is observed here that has not been brought up before, most notably in the coffee-table biographies by Norman Mailer and Gloria Steinem'. The review was not so much dismissive as patronizing. It concluded by invoking one of the songs in Rodgers and Hammerstein's *The Sound of Music* – 'When the nuns asked, "How do you solve a problem like Maria?" ... put it in a minor key, sex it up a little, stretch it two hours and substitute Kitty for Maria, and you've got "Finishing the Picture".'[160]

Chicago's Richard Christiansen, formerly of the *Chicago Tribune*, declared 'this new second-rank work ... neither a disaster nor a triumph', but noted that the *New York Times*'s 'unimpressive, dismissive review' meant that the producer, David Richenthal, 'must face the task of raising the money for the transfer of this new, flawed play to an unforgiving Broadway'.[161] Thus, Brantley's review had ensured that Arthur Miller's last play would not transfer to Broadway. *Death of a Salesman* did not open in London, as anticipated, the following year. The production of *Resurrection Blues* never took place.

Miller's health problems, meanwhile, intensified. He might have felt well, but he was incubating the cancer diagnosed earlier. When he fell ill in New York in December 2004 it was with a recurrence of pneumonia, but the more serious problem was draining his strength. When Nadine Gordimer's husband Reinhold died within weeks of Inge's death, Miller had written to her, 'to touch hands'. More recently he had agreed to the inclusion of one of his stories, 'Bulldog', in a collection she was putting together to raise awareness of the HIV-AID pandemic. In December he had been due to read his story at the book's launch, to be presided over by the Secretary-General of the United Nations, Kofi Annan. He now called to tell Gordimer that he was suffering from a second bout of pneumonia but that he also had cancer. On 22 December, David Amram received an email from Miller. Amram, who had composed the music for *After the Fall* and *Incident at Vichy*, was about to turn seventy-four. The email was to apologize for Miller's inability to turn up for his birthday party. He was 'a bit under the weather', he said. In fact, he was dying.

He and Agnes were now in his 68th Street apartment. He wanted to return to Roxbury, but his doctor advised against it. His sister Joan called and asked if she could visit. In 2008 she recalled the occasion:

I went over to his apartment and he came to the door in his pyjamas and said, 'I'm resting, so come into the bedroom.' So I went through and we talked for some while and then we went to the kitchen. But to get there you had to pass through the living room, and as I did so I saw a pair of high heels, stiletto-heeled, silver, tumbled on each other, and I didn't say anything. But then we had a cup of coffee and I asked him what his life was like – 'Do you go out? Do you have friends?' – because everyone was concerned about him being alone. So he said, 'Yeah, people come by.' And I said, 'I noticed as I came through the living room that there's a pair of silver slippers and they don't look your size and they're not your style.' And he said, 'Yes, I have a friend.' And that was the most he would say.

Then he got worse and had to go back into hospital and found out that he had this cancer. They had arranged to have the apartment painted so they knew they couldn't go back there. I said, 'Where are you going to go?' And he said, 'We don't know.' So I said, 'Why don't you stay at my place?' I came back the next day and he was sleeping. When Ages showed up he said, 'I've just been in a marvellous place. So bright I didn't know where I was. It was so real.' Then he went back to sleep. When he woke up again he said, 'I know where I was. I was in Joany's house.' So I said to Agnes, 'Well, I guess we know now where you are going to be staying.' And that's when they came to my apartment.

They both moved in. I gave them my bedroom. I don't think he would have lived as long as he did if it weren't for her. She was his nurse, his muse, everything good for him. And she was selfless. We shared a common wall between the bedroom he was in and where I was sleeping and I could hear him waking up at night and talking. And she would be rattling around the medicine chest. He had a real complicated regime of medication. You would have to have been a chemist to figure out what was needed, depending on what was provoking him at the time. I don't know how anybody could have lived through that. They were here for about six weeks.

When he first went to Joan's apartment he was still well enough to go to restaurants and receive people. Then things began to change, as Joan later recounted:

The thing that really stunned me one day. He was sitting in this room. He was lying on that couch just resting and we had a little music going . . . I was reading and he would just doze off for a few minutes. And then I suddenly see him get up and walk over to that desk where he had his computer. He walked slowly to the desk, sat down and worked for about twenty minutes. And then he got up and said 'I've finished the play' that he had been working on and he said, 'That's that. That's it.' . . . he knew that the end was near.[162]

Perhaps it was that knowledge that led him to propose to Agnes in December 2004,[163] though there was to be no deathbed marriage. It was a gesture of commitment. He felt a strong sense of responsibility towards her, a guilt at having involved her in a relationship that both knew could have no future. He wanted to protect her, assure her future, as it became evident that he was not going to recover. He chose this moment, 30 December, to rewrite his will, confirming the provision he had been planning to make since she had moved to Roxbury a year earlier. The New Year came and went. Sometimes he was able to do little more than lie in the living room, with his hands over his eyes. Finally, he decided that he wanted to go home, knowing it would be his last journey. His doctor agreed, there now being little reason not to.

Joan, who accompanied him to the ambulance, later recalled,

> He wanted to go back home. He knew he was on his way out. He wanted to go back to the house that he loved and the area that he loved. I remember, when the back door was open I reached in and couldn't quite reach him. He was sitting in a wheelchair facing me but I could only reach his knees. And I said, 'I'll be up there in two days. I can't come tomorrow.' I said, 'I love you', which I had never said, and he couldn't speak at that time but I knew he loved me too, and he mouthed the words. And then the door closed and they went off. And I never saw him again. He died the following day. It was where he wanted to be. He made it to there. He was back. We were closer then than we had ever been in our lives, since I was grown up. It was something special.

With Agnes sitting with him, the ambulance set off on its three-hour journey. It would take him past White Plains, New York, where he had married America's most famous actress almost fifty years earlier, and on into the wooded hills and winding roads of Connecticut, where once a journalist had died in an accident as she raced to Roxbury to cover the announcement of that marriage. Finally, the ambulance pulled on to the sloping drive of the house on Tophet Road, where he had lived with Inge until her death in 2002, and where he had written the film script of *The Misfits* and all of his plays since *After the Fall*. His family were waiting for him.

Once inside, he asked for a glass of cold water drawn from the well deep beneath the house. He was taken through to his downstairs study, where copies of his books, in different languages, were lined up in a bookcase. Robert described the moment: 'My father's foremost intent and hope was that he could get back home before he died, that he could drink a last sip of Roxbury water, breathe a last breath of Roxbury air. He had the biggest smile on his face when he arrived. He was very gracefully trying to let go, and coming home was the completion of it for him. He sort of scripted the last week or so of his life. It came out exactly as he would have written it.'[164]

Miller had signed a living will some years earlier, but there was no need to invoke it. He died at 9.17 p.m. on 10 February. His assistant Julia Bolus notified the press that the cause of death was heart failure. In fact arterio-sclerotic heart disease was a contributory factor. The main cause of death, as established by autopsy, was metastatic transitional cell cancer of the bladder. His daughter Jane registered the death. It was precisely fifty-six years to the day after the opening of *Death of a Salesman*. When the curtain fell on that performance, the audience sat in silence for what had seemed to Miller long minutes before the clapping began. Much the same would be true now: for many hours only the family knew that a life had ended. Once the news was out, the clapping began. The obituaries appeared, and the career of one of America's leading twentieth-century writers was celebrated in newspapers around the world.

Among those expressing regret at Arthur Miller's death was an organ-ization whose honorary chair persons included two former US presidents (Jimmy Carter and Bill Clinton), Senator Barack Obama, Simon Wiesenthal and Miep Gies (who had helped the Frank family and preserved Anne Frank's diary). It had been planning to present him, four months later, with the Anne Frank Human Rights Award, designed for an author whose work explored the ideas and ideals that had become synonymous with the young girl whose life had ended sixty years earlier in the desolation of Bergen-Belsen. In many ways it was an odd award because Anne Frank, who died shortly before her sixteenth birthday, had hardly begun to formulate her own response to a world whose cruelties she had yet to discover as she wrote the last passage in her diary. There is no doubt, however, that when Miller died many responded to him not simply as a major figure of world literature, but as a man who throughout his life had concerned himself with the fate, in his own country and around the world, of those threatened with state power. The organizers expressed themselves stunned and saddened.

A few years earlier he had joked about people's choice of burial place: 'I know a couple in Connecticut who had bought a grave, a space, in a particular small cemetery up in the country, because they liked the view. And it was serious. They wanted the good view. My grandfather asked to be buried in one of the cemeteries in Brooklyn, jam-packed, very crowded, and he asked that he not be buried on the aisle, because he didn't want people stepping over him to get to where they were going. He would rather be off in a corner somewhere

where nobody would be bothering him. What weird things we are.'[165] For himself, he wanted two things – to be buried in Roxbury and to be buried alongside Inge. He was. Just below the stone he had found, and which now bore the family name, were two rectangular memorial slabs, one of which was inscribed:

INGEBORG MORATH

MAY 29, 1923

JAN. 30, 2002

"BEAUTÉ MON BEAU DÉSIR"

The other bore the words,

ARTHUR MILLER

WRITER

1915–2005

'Beauté Mon Beau Désir' would seem to be a misquotation either from Baudelaire's *Les Fleurs du Mal* where a line reads, '*beauté dont mon désir*', or from Valéry Larbaud's story 'Beauté, mon beau souci', in a collection called *Amants, heureux amants* in which the narrator, in a monologue, invokes a perfect lover called Inga: 'Inga, when she loves, surpasses herself: she becomes the person loved, and there is, from this point on, a pact between them so narrow that nobody can hope to join himself to it. She is walled in by her love.'[166]

William Sloane Coffin Jr presided over a ceremony two weeks after Miller's death. He began with his version of a line from Edna St Vincent Millay: 'His absence is everywhere present' ('The presence of that absence is everywhere'). He remembered what Miller had said when Inge died: 'Arthur too would not wish to be held close by grief. And actually, I see him best when I grieve him least.' He recalled the opening night of the fiftieth-anniversary production of *Death of a Salesman:* 'In the whole theatre that night there were only two men without black ties – myself and Tom Doyle [Miller's son-in-law]. Before the curtain went up, I wandered over to ask Tom if he felt underdressed. "Yeah," he replied, "but look at Arthur" (at that moment charming Lauren Bacall); "No matter what he's wearing he looks as if he had gotten dressed in a hardware store."' And that, Coffin added, was how he remembered him, 'in blue jeans and boots. I see him best at the house, in his studio, at the workbench, by the pond, always with Inge.' Never, he said, in 'all changes of fortune and down to the gates of death, did I see a lifeless expression in his eyes'. He thanked Agnes for the care she had given him and concluded by insisting that, atheist or not, this Jew who had abandoned his faith seventy years earlier was nonetheless heading for glory, whether he believed it or not: 'In the hospital a few days before he died, I said to Arthur, "You may think you're headed for nowhere, but I'm better informed than you. There's a distinguished chair awaiting you. It's for God's favourite atheist. Your heavenly assignment will to keep Christians honest."'

On 9 May 2005 a memorial was held, fittingly enough at the Majestic Theatre in New York. Family and friends were joined by members of the public who had waited patiently in a line snaking along West 44th Street. Daniel Day-Lewis read from one of Miller's essays, and Estelle Parsons spoke Linda Loman's lines from the Epilogue to *Death of a Salesman*. Joan Copeland delivered a speech from *The American Clock*, playing the role of her long-dead mother. Robert read from his father's letter to the House Un-American Activities Committee, explaining why he would not name names, while Rebecca read one of her father's poems. Tributes were read out from Bill Clinton and George McGovern. Tony Kushner revealed that his own desire to be a playwright was born the night he saw his mother play the role of Linda Loman in a Louisiana community theatre. Edward Albee spoke in anger of the attacks Miller had suffered from the Right.

In Roxbury, there were those for whom Arthur Miller had been less a famous writer than a neighbour. A hundred people turned up at a memorial meeting, along with members of his family. His friend the playwright Tom Cole, who lived in the house where *Death of a Salesman* had been written, showed pictures of Miller, including one in which he was seen dancing at a bicentennial celebration, and another in which he was baiting Robert Whitehead's fishing rod as he was about to fish in the Miller pond (never overstocked). Miller, he pointed out, always had a preference for a woodsman shirt, faded jeans and an old work hat, and had spent some time trying to invent a bird feeder that could thwart the squirrels.

Rebecca recalled wanting a stereo for her birthday and getting one hand-made in wood by her father. Robert remembered people coming to their house to cook food when Hurricane Diane hit in 1955, a party that lasted for days. He remembered, too, the time when his father had repaired his mailbox on a cold spring day, so cold that he hammered the nail through his gloves and hand and, because he had dropped the hammer out of reach, had to wait for the mail lady to release him.

A neighbour described tennis matches in which she had partnered Miller against the actor Richard Widmark; Miller would play the net while she had to rush around hitting everything he missed. He was known for never bringing balls to the match, until one day he turned up with some he had retrieved from Widmark's rubbish bin. Widmark observed, 'You know, people can talk all they want about the genius of Arthur Miller, but we never paid attention to that ... He was just my best buddy down the road. We were just two country boys interested in tractors and mowers and the land.'[167] A.R. Gurney was one of those who had played tennis with Miller as had Dustin Hoffman).

He recalled an evening when Miller had sung 'Georgia on My Mind' as someone else played the piano, he never having mastered the instrument that had meant so much to his mother, who used to play tunes from the shows she had seen even during times when there was little money to spare.

A member of the local zoning committee remembered Miller's alarm at the decline of the native bluebird because of the use of pesticides, while another commented on his views on horseradishes and on his enthusiastic fight against a power company wanting to trail overhead wires through the town. One neighbour recalled taking a fish to the Miller house and being invited in to dine on it, while another remembered serving him at the family's farm stand and noting his respect for the land. He would visit the local drug store, another said, to buy the *New York Times*, sitting at the soda fountain talking to people and even helping children with their homework, although 'he couldn't spell for beans'. Jacqueline Dooley, a local woman who had once challenged Joseph McCarthy when on television he had asked if anyone could say that he had lied, remarked, 'That's why Arthur and I were so close … Just because he had progressive ideas and dared to challenge authority, they called him a communist. What he was was deeply devoted to moral responsibility and social justice. He also happened to be a great friend: no airs, no hidden agenda, just a real nice, down-to-earth guy.' According to First Selectman Barbara Henry he was 'unpretentious and always very approachable. He was a resident, a great tipper at the Roxbury Market, a taxpayer and a regular guy.'[168]

Later in the year a volume of reminiscences appeared in which eighty writers, directors, actors, publishers, friends, offered their memories of the man, from Václav Havel and Andrei Voznesensky whom he had supported in their battles against repression, to Patrick Stewart, Michael Gambon, Brian Dennehy, Vanessa Redgrave and Gene Wilder who had appeared in his plays. There were pieces by Harold Pinter and Tom Stoppard, John Guare, David Rabe and Carlos Fuentes. His friend and fellow writer Honor Moore recalled their last conversation: 'I remember him saying only two or three weeks before he died: "When life disappointed me, I always had my writing."'[169]

On 14 October, just short of what would have been his ninetieth birthday, a small ceremony took place at the University of Michigan. It was the groundbreaking for what would become the Arthur Miller Theatre. Sixty-seven years after he had left the university, waving goodbye to Mary Slattery, who would become his first wife, then riding back to New York with a salesman of saddles and riding equipment, a permanent memorial was being erected. It opened in March 2007 with a production of *Playing for Time*.

In March 2006 Agnes Barley, now travelling in India, said: 'I know that to many it must seem pretty strange a woman of my age wanting to go out with an old man, but he was the best companion I ever had. I had a short but amazing time with Arthur ... We got to know each other a lot better over time, to the point where it became romantic and I moved to be with him in Connecticut, where I had simply the happiest time ... Since the person I was in love with died, I have not really engaged with the outside world much. It has been a very hard year.'[170] Miller left Agnes his New York apartment. Five years later it was still his voice on the answer machine, announcing the number and inviting callers to leave a message.

One function of art is simultaneously to make a claim on immortality and to admit to the impossibility of doing this in the face of what George Steiner calls 'the affront of death'. The religion that Miller eschewed offered to resolve this tension. Religion abandoned, art stood alone. His art also registered another anxiety, one reflected in the desperate need of so many of his characters to leave a trace of themselves, to write their names across the heavens or, in Miller's case, to sign his name on the objects he made, whether plays or pieces of furniture. As Steiner says,

> The central conceit of the artist that the work shall outlast his own death, the existential truth that great literature, painting, architecture, music have survived their creators, are not accidental or self-regarding. It is the lucid intensity of its meeting with death that generates in aesthetic forms that statement of vitality, of life-presence, which distinguishes serious thought and feeling from the trivial and opportunistic ... [It is] within the compass of the arts that the metaphor of resurrection is given the edge of felt conjecture.'[171]

It is not simply that art, literature, music, survive the death of their creator, but that the spectator, reader, listener extend the text, detect resonances, translate it, become confederate in transforming fact into metaphor, prose into poetry. The identifications that were to lead so many to claim Willy Loman as a relative were an acknowledgement not merely that Miller had succeeded in bridging the gap between the real and its fictive presentation, but that this ageing salesman lived on through those who laid claim to his dilemmas.

There is a will on the part of audiences to reverse the flow from fiction back to its origins, as if themselves to authenticate characters presented as mere fictions. That active bargain was always part of Miller's appeal. Steiner contemplates the mystery whereby fictive creations can 'make ghostly so many of the women and men and empirical facts we come across "out there"'.[172] This is the sense in which Miller once remarked that he could never walk across Brooklyn Bridge without Hart Crane's poem, which celebrated it, coming to mind because 'it somehow defined the object being blessed more vividly than one's own eyes could'.[173] Art, in other words, can be more vibrantly alive, more present, than the reality it offers to engage. It is an uneasy truth.

Perhaps it is not really a truth at all. After all, Miller's characters may be as vivid as they are precisely because they are forever locked inside a single narrative, no matter how we extend and gloss that story as our own. But, fictive though they may be, they patently exist in the world, and have become part of the broader story that we choose to tell ourselves about the struggle to be in the world, and to leave it with what we choose to see as our integrity intact.

Miller was aware, though, that art could be seen as displacement, a spurious consolation. In *Resurrection Blues* a character remarks:

> I am convinced now, apart from getting fed, most human activity – sports, opera, TV, movies, dressing up, dressing down – or just going for a walk – has no other purpose than to deliver us into the realm of the imagination. The imagination is a great hall, where death, for example, turns into a painting, and a scream of pain becomes a song. The hall of the imagination is where we usually live; and this is all right except for one thing – to enter that hall one must leave one's real sorrow at the door and in its stead surround oneself with images and words and music that mimic anguish but are really drained of it.

It is a speech that is something more than a regret at a world in retreat from itself. It is also, surely, a confession of art's inadequacy – or, rather, of the gap which of necessity opens up between the truth of art and the truth of life, between the rhythm, rhyme, the ordered integrity of a poem or a play and the sharp and sometimes incommunicable immediacy of lived experience.

Yet language is what we have. It has to bear the burden of expressing the inexpressible, though that language, in theatre, may not wholly depend on words. It was Tennessee Williams who said that 'poetry doesn't have to be words ... In the theatre it can be situations, it can be silences.'[174] At the end of *Death of a Salesman* Willy Loman has surrendered to silence. The only sound is that of a single cello string, just as Chekhov in *The Cherry Orchard* calls for 'the sound of a breaking string, dying away, sad'. In that final moment, as the audience sits in silence, word and pain, perhaps, finally become one.

Arthur Miller died seventy years after he set out to recast the human drama into theatrical form. On the public stage he played the role of rebel, contesting the myths and values of a society towards which he was nonetheless drawn. Son of an immigrant father and a first-generation mother, he regretted the loss of transcendence in a national dream that proposed the inevitability of success and offered an account of history as little more than prelude to an enticing future. Yet he valued America's freedoms, celebrated its Enlightenment commitments. His grandparents had travelled across the Atlantic to escape persecution and embrace possibility. In doing so they made the compromises that seemed necessary to reinvent themselves, closing the door on their European past, as the golden door of America swung wide. For Miller, the past was not to be so easily denied, not least because those who had been left behind were claimed by a fate that reminded all that at least in myth the human story had begun with betrayal and violence.

Miller's early concern with tragedy can be seen as his attempt to find a secular equivalent of resurrection: his characters sacrifice themselves in order to sustain their integrity and leave a heritage of lives justified. In the case of Joe Keller, Willy Loman and Eddie Carbone, though, that is stained with self-deceit. The true resurrection lies in the life presence of Miller's fictions, in figures whose survival in art retrospectively redeems not simply them but the idea of inconsequential lives gifted immortality through the grace not of God but of a writer's attention. In Miller's case, towards the end of his career – in *Mr Peters' Connections*, *Resurrection Blues* and *Finishing the Picture* – he would express more directly his awareness of a slippage of meaning while at the same time implicitly dedicating himself to the pursuit of that meaning. What else, after all, was art for? He was a storyteller aware of the coercive nature of many of the political and religious narratives of the twentieth century but convinced, too, of the power of story to offer if not consolation then coherence.

Miller never disavowed his early passions, no matter how invalidated by experience they may have come to seem. Oscar Wilde remarked that a map of the world that does not include Utopia is not worth even glancing at. Youthful enthusiasms were not, Miller felt, to be denied, merely acknowledged for what they were. He lived long enough to see ideals compromised, political systems implode, promises broken, relationships collapse. He lived long enough to see his own reputation fade in a country in which people sometimes stared at tomorrow's sun, blinded, as Willy Loman had been, to the value of what they held in their hands. Miller wrote because he could not imagine doing otherwise. He invoked history because he believed we are all its children, responsible for and to it. He chose the theatre because it is there that people come together in their shared need to see experience given form. He wrote of flawed individuals and flawed societies, of the loss of a looked-for perfection, but also of consolation and redemption. In a society that dreamed of Eden he staged the lives of those who were the descendants of Cain as much as of Adam, not because betrayal and violence would prevail and not because he saw irony as the basis of the human situation, but because denial is ultimately damaging. In the words of the British playwright Dennis Potter:

> Our first allegiances are based upon Eden. The whole story of human culture is based upon the original sin. It's an inescapable fact of our mortality . . . It's the gap between our first perceptions of perfection and our later selves that

tries us ... If you feel merely nostalgia and contempt ... if you simply *mock*, then something has been killed inside you. If you feel remorse, regret, guilt ... well, that's better, but something has still been killed. If you feel a tension between the wish to preserve some of whatever idealism, whatever faith, whatever 'purity' you first perceived, and a rueful acknowledgement that a journey has been made away from that, and yet still preserve *some* of it, and more and more maybe, then that's human.[175]

NOTES

PREFACE

1. Charles Isherwood, 'A Playwright Whose Convictions Challenged Conventions', *New York Times*, 11 February 2005.
2. Arthur Miller, 'The Mad Inventor of Modern Drama', *New York Times*, 6 January 1985.

1 NEW BEGINNINGS

1. Ben McGrath, 'Vermont Postcard: The Light of Sunday', *New Yorker*, 1 December 2003, p. 39.
2. Robert A. Martin, ed., *The Theater Essays of Arthur Miller* (New York, 1978), p. 265.
3. Inge Morath, *The Road to Reno* (London, 2006), p. 43.
4. *Ibid.*, pp. 48, 54, 55.
5. *Ibid.*, p. 67.
6. *Ibid.*, p. 83.
7. *Ibid.*, p. 85.
8. Inge Morath, interview with the author, 25 May 2001.
9. Inge Morath, interview with the author, 2002.
10. Bosley Crowther, 'Screen: John Huston's *The Misfits*', *New York Times*, 2 February 1961.
11. Anon., 'New Picture', *Time*, 3 February 1961.

12. Barbara Gelb, 'Question: Am I My Brother's Keeper?', *New York Times*, 29 November 1964.
13. Anon., 'The Cops and the Comrades', *Time*, 3 August 1953.
14. Arthur Miller, *After the Fall* (Harmondsworth, 1965), pp. 31–2.
15. *Ibid.*, pp. 12–13.
16. *Ibid.*, p. 23.
17. Hunter Davies, 'Arthur Miller', *Sunday Times*, 23 January 1966.
18. *After the Fall*, p. 74.
19. Inge Morath, interview with the author, 2002.
20. C. Wright Mills, *The Sociological Imagination* (Harmondsworth, 1970; first published 1959), p. 9.
21. *Ibid.*, p. 10.
22. Quoted in Robert Boyers and Peggy Boyers, eds, *The Salmagundi Reader* (Bloomington, 1983), p. 160.
23. Robert A. Martin and Steven R. Centola, *The Theatre Essays of Arthur Miller*, revised and expanded (New York, 1996), p. 400.
24. *Ibid.*, pp. 400–1.
25. Wright Mills, *Sociological Imagination*, p. 24.
26. Philip Roth, 'Writing American Fiction', in Norman Podhoretz, ed., *The Commentary Reader: Two Decades of Articles and Stories* (New York, 1966), p. 598.

27. Daniel Bell, *The End of Ideology: On the Exhaustion of Political Ideas in the 1950s* (New York, 1962), p. 404.

28. Arthur Miller, *Presence* (New York, 2007), pp. 148–9.

29. *Ibid.*, p. 150.

30. *Ibid.*, p. 153.

31. *Arthur Miller in Conversation with Murray Briggs*, Ninth Annual Maynard Mack Lecture (New Haven, 2000), p. 5.

32. *Ibid.*, p. 9.

33. *Ibid.*, p. 10.

34. Miller, *Timebends* (1987), p. 512.

35. Willard Maas, 'Poetry and the Film: A Symposium', *Film Culture*, 29, 1963, pp. 55–63.

36. Arthur Miller, interview with the author, 2002.

37. Arthur Miller, *I Don't Need You Any More* (London, 1967), p. 156.

38. *Ibid.*, p. xii.

39. Inge Morath, interview with the author, 25 May 2001.

40. Dean Faulkner Wells, ed., *The Great American Writers' Cookbook* (Oxford, Miss., 1981), p. 66.

41. Lydia McClean, 'A Weekend with the Millers', *Vogue*, 15, March 1972, pp. 105ff.

42. Miller, 'The Power and the Glamour', *Allure*, April 2000, p. 123.

43. Inge Morath, interview with the author, 25 May 2001.

44. Arthur Miller, *Echoes Down the Corridor: Collected Essays 1944–2000*, ed. Steven R. Centola (New York, 2000), pp. 166–7.

45. Arthur Miller and Inge Morath, *In the Country* (New York, 1977), p. 45.

46. *Ibid.*, p. 23.

47. *Ibid.*, p. 100.

48. *Ibid.*, p. 7.

49. *Ibid.*, pp. 176, 184.

50. Inge Morath, 'About My Photographs', *Michigan Quarterly Review*, Fall 1998, p. 695.

51. Arthur Miller and Inge Morath, *Chinese Encounters* (New York, 1979), p. 112.

52. 'About My Photographs,' p. 696.

53. Arthur Miller, 'Introduction', *Portraits: Photographs by Inge Morath* (New York, 1986), p. 6, 90.

54. Interview with the author, 5 December 2009.

55. Harold Rosenberg, 'The Trial and Eichmann', *The Commentary Reader: Two Decades of Articles and Stories* (New York, 1966), p. 104.

56. Irving Howe, *A Margin of Hope* (London, 1983), pp. 258–9.

57. *Ibid.*, p. 248.

58. *Ibid.*, p. 271.

59. *Ibid.*, p. 249.

60. *Ibid.*, p. 281.

61. W. G. Sebald, *On the Natural History of Destruction* (London, 2003), p. 53.

62. Robert A. Martin, ed., *The Theatre Essays of Arthur Miller* (London, 1978), p. 256.

63. Martin Gottfried, *Arthur Miller: A Life* (London, 2003), p. 351.

64. *Ibid.*, p.351.

65. Arthur Miller, 'Challenge the Lincoln Center Board: Can or Will They Create Repertory?', *Dramatists' Guild Quarterly*, Summer 1971, vol. 8, section 2, pp. 1–2.

66. Miller, *Timebends* (1987), pp. 529–530.

67. Gottfried, *Arthur Miller: A Life*, p. 368.

68. Elia Kazan, *A Life* (New York, 1988), p. 493.

69. Miller, *After the Fall* (1965), pp. 43–4.
70. Kazan, *A Life*, p. 675.
71. *Ibid.*, p. 716.
72. *Ibid.*, p. 723.
73. *Ibid.*, p. 675.
74. *Ibid.*, p. 723.
75. Joan Copeland, interview with the author, 7 November 2008.
76. Miller, *Timebends* (1987), p. 527.
77. Mel Gussow, *Conversations with Arthur Miller* (London, 2002), p. 152.
78. Kazan, *A Life*, p. 708.
79. Interview with the author, 25 May 2001.
80. Gottfried, *Arthur Miller: A Life*, p. 364.
81. *Ibid.*, p. 32.
82. Kazan, *A Life*, p. 715.
83. Arthur Miller, 'Arthur Miller, Elia Kazan and the Blacklist: None without Sin', WNET New York, 3 September 2003.
84. Kazan, *A Life*, p. 717.
85. Gottfried, *Arthur Miller: A Life*, p. 365.
86. Miller, *Timebends* (1987), pp. 509–10.
87. Christopher Bigsby, *Writers in Conversation*, vol. 1 (Norwich, 2000), p. 13.
88. *Ibid.*, pp. 117–18.
89. Frances Stonor Saunders, *Who Paid the Piper: The CIA and the Cultural Cold War* (London, 1999), p. 345.
90. Miller, *Timebends* (1987), p. 510.
91. Gottfried, *Arthur Miller: A Life*, p. 368.
92. Quotations from *After the Fall*, pp. 11, 15, 25.
93. Gottfried, *Arthur Miller: A Life*, p. 536.
94. Albert Camus, *The Fall*, trans. Stuart Gilbert (Harmondsworth, 1963), pp. 26–7.
95. *Ibid.*, p. 10.
96. *Ibid.*, p. 60.
97. Christopher Bigsby, ed., *Arthur Miller and Company* (London, 1990), p. 140.
98. Camus, *The Fall*, p. 63.
99. *Ibid.*, p. 83.
100. Miller, *After the Fall* (1965), p. 42.
101. *Ibid.*, p. 11.
102. Miller, *Timebends* (1987), p. 523.
103. Bigsby, *Writers in Conversation*, p. 363.
104. Primo Levi, *The Drowned and the Saved* (London, 1991), p. 75.
105. Dorothy Knowles, *Armand Gatti in the Theatre: Wild Duck against the Wind* (London, 1989), p. 68.
106. Christopher Bigsby, *Arthur Miller: A Critical Study* (Cambridge, 2005), p. 475.
107. Charlotte Delbo, *None of Us Will Return* (New York, 1968), pp. 95–7.
108. *Ibid.*
109. *Ibid.*, p. 126.
110. *Ibid.*, p. 128.
111. Aharon Appelfeld, *The Immortal Bartfuss*, trans. Jeffrey M. Green (London, 1995), p. 57.
112. Aharon Appelfeld, *The Healer*, trans. Jeffrey M. Green (London, 1992), p. ii.
113. Arthur Miller, interview with the author, 26 May 2001.
114. Miller, *Timebends* (1987), pp. 526–7.
115. *Ibid.*, p. 47.
116. Gussow, *Conversations with Arthur Miller*, p. 93.
117. Miller, *After the Fall* (1965), p. 78.
118. *Ibid.*, p. 89.
119. *Ibid.*, p. 49.
120. *Ibid.*, p. 374.

121. *Ibid.*, p. 120.
122. Ron H. Feldman, *Hannah Arendt the Jew as Pariah: Jewish Identity and Politics in the Modern Age* (New York, 1978), p. 249.
123. Miller, *After the Fall* (1965), pp. 65–6.
124. Jerome Kohn, *Hannah Arendt: Essays in Understanding 1930–1954* (New York, 1994), pp. 131–2.
125. Miller, *After the Fall* (1965), p. 120.
126. *Ibid.*, p. 84.
127. W.J. Weatherby, *Conversations with Marilyn* (New York, 1992), p. 219.
128. Sheridan Morley and Graham Payn, eds, *The Noël Coward Diaries* (London, 1982), p. 558.
129. Susan Sontag, *Against Interpretation* (New York, 1966), pp. 285–7.
130. Harold Clurman, *All People Are Famous* (New York, 1974), p. 236.
131. *Ibid.*, p. 534.
132. Arthur Miller, 'With Respect for Her Agony – but with Love', *Life*, LVI, 7 February 1964, p. 66.
133. *Ibid.*, p. 66.
134. Robert Brustein, *Seasons of Discontent: Dramatic Opinions 1959–1965* (London, 1966), pp. 243–7.
135. Philip Rahv, *Literature and the Sixth Sense* (London, 1970), p. 385.
136. Richard Gilman, *Common and Uncommon Masks: Writings on Theater 1961–1970* (New York, 1972), pp. 152–4, 265.
137. Stanley Kauffmann, *Persons of the Drama: Theater Criticism and Comment* (New York, 1976), pp. 230–1.
138. Eric Bentley, *What Is Theatre?* (London, 1969), p. 399.
139. Gottfried, *Arthur Miller: A Life*, p. 371.
140. Oriana Fallaci, 'Apropos of *After the Fall*', *World Theatre*, January–February 1965, pp. 79–81.
141. Howard Taubman, 'A Cheer for Controversy', *New York Times*, 2 February 1964.
142. Letter from Laurence Olivier, in Arthur Miller's private papers.
143. Howe, *Margin of Hope*, p. 272.
144. Boyers and Boyers, *Salmagundi Reader*, p. 376.
145. Howe, *Margin of Hope*, p. 273.
146. Harold Rosenberg, 'The Trial and Eichmann', *Commentary*, November 1961, pp. 109–10.
147. Michael Ezra, 'The Eichmann Polemics: Hannah Arendt and Her Critics', *Democratiya*, 9, Summer 2007, p. 155.
148. Dwight Macdonald, 'Arguments', *Partisan Review*, 31 (1964), pp. 262–3.
149. *Ibid.*, p. 265.
150. *Ibid.*, p. 264.
151. Mary McCarthy, 'Arguments', *Partisan Review*, 31 (1964), p. 276.
152. Arthur Miller, interview with the author, 2001.
153. Gottfried, *Arthur Miller: A Life*, p. 376.
154. Miller, *Timebends* (1987), p. 524.
155. Shayla Swift, 'Lost Lessons: American Media Depictions of the Frankfurt Auschwitz Trial 1963–1965', digitalcommons.unl.edu/cgi/viewcontent.cgi?article=1005&context=historyrawley conference, accessed 27 December 2008.
156. Miller, *Timebends* (1987), p. 526.
157. Miller, *Echoes Down the Corridor* (2000), p. 63.

158. Interview with the author, 26 May 2001.

159. Miller, *Echoes Down the Corridor* (2000), p. 65.

160. Miller, *Timebends* (1987), p. 65.

161. Miller, *Echoes Down the Corridor* (2000), p. 64.

162. *Ibid.*, p. 64.

163. *Ibid.*, p. 65.

164. *Ibid.*, p. 67.

165. *Ibid.*, p. 68.

166. Miller, *Timebends* (1987), p. 540.

167. Chris Petit, 'A Game Concocted by the Criminally Insane', *Guardian*, 7 March 2009, Review section, p. 8 (but see Thomas Buergenthal, *A Lucky Child: A Memoir of Surviving Auschwitz as a Young Boy* (London, 2009).

168. Harold Clurman, 'Director's Notes: *Incident at Vichy*', *Tulane Drama Review*, vol. 9, Summer 1965, p. 70.

169. *Ibid.*, p. 80.

170. *Ibid.*, p. 82.

171. Miller, *Echoes Down the Corridor* (2000), p. 71.

172. Arthur Miller, 'Our Guilt for the World's Evil', *New York Times Magazine*, 3 January 1965, p. 10.

173. Miller, *Echoes Down the Corridor* (2000), pp. 70–1.

174. Miller, 'Our Guilt for the World's Evil' (1965), p. 10.

175. Miller, *Echoes Down the Corridor* (2000), pp. 70–1.

176. *Ibid.*, p. 74

177. *Ibid.*

178. *Ibid.*, p. 70

179. Brustein, *Seasons of Discontent*, p. 260.

180. Martin Gottfried, *Opening Nights: Theatre Criticism of the Sixties* (New York, 1969), p. 24.

181. *Ibid.*, p. 261.

182. Edward Isser, 'Arthur Miller and the Holocaust', *Essays in Theatre*, 10, ii, May 1992.

183. Leslie Epstein, 'The Unhappiness of Arthur Miller', *Tri-Quarterly*, Spring 1965, pp. 165–73.

184. Gilman, *Common and Uncommon Masks*, pp. 265–6.

185. Richard Gilman, *The Drama Is Coming Now: The Theater Criticism of Richard Gilman 1961–1991* (New York, 2005), pp. 107–9.

186. John Simon, *Singularities* (New York, 1975), p. 85.

187. John Lahr, *Up Against the Fourth Wall: Essays on Modern Theater* (New York, 1970), p. 102.

188. Philip Rahv, *Literature and the Sixth Sense* (London, 1970), pp. 387, 389.

189. Miller, Our Guilt for the World's Evil' (1965), p. 10.

190. *Ibid.*, p. 11.

191. *Ibid.*, p. 48.

192. Arthur Miller, 'On the Shooting of Robert Kennedy', *New York Times*, 8 June 1968.

193. Hannah Arendt and Peter Baehr, eds, *The Portable Hannah Arendt* (New York, 2000), p. 6.

194. Bruno Bettelheim, *Recollections and Reflections* (London, 1990), p. 249.

195. *Ibid.*, p. 258.

196. *Ibid.*, p. 253.

197. Arendt and Baehr, *Portable Hannah Arendt*, p. 376.

198. *Ibid.*, p. 260.

199. *Ibid.*, p. 271.

200. Miller, *Echoes Down the Corridor* (2000), p. 207.

201. 'After the Fall', *Time* magazine, 25 December 1964.

202. Interview with author.

2 PEN

1. Murray Briggs, *Arthur Miller in Conversation with Murray Briggs* (New Haven, 2000), p. 8.
2. Arthur Miller and Inge Morath, *In Russia* (New York, 1969), p. 15.
3. Arthur Miller, 'On Obliterating the Jews', *New Leader*, 16 March 1964, p. 7.
4. *Ibid.*, p. 8.
5. Gussow, *Conversations with Arthur Miller*, p. 81.
6. www.telegraph.co.uk/news/worldnews/1481260/Pentagon-planned-love-bomb.html
7. Robert Lowell, *Collected Prose*, ed. Robert Giroux (London, 1987), p. 371.
8. *Ibid.*, p. 367.
9. *Ibid.*, p. 281.
10. Lowell, *Collected Prose*, p. 270.
11. Arthur Miller, interview with the author, September 2001.
12. See Frances Stonor Saunders, *Who Paid the Piper: The CIA and the Cultural Cold War* (London, 1999), p. 365.
13. Edward Shils, 'Remembering the Congress for Cultural Freedom', *Encounter*, vol. 75, September 1990, pp. 55–6.
14. Miller, *Timebends* (1987), pp. 567–8.
15. Peter Coleman, *The Liberal Conspiracy: The Congress for Cultural Freedom and the Struggle for the Mind of Postwar Europe* (New York, 1989), p. 213.
16. *Ibid.*
17. Quoted in Alan M. Wald, *The Rise and Decline of the Anti-Stalinist Left from the 1930s to the 1980s* (Chapel Hill, 1987), p. 268.
18. Natalie Robins, *Alien Ink: The FBI's War on Freedom of Expression* (New York, 1992), p. 314.
19. Email from Keith Botsford to the author, 2002.
20. Ian Hamilton, *Robert Lowell* (London, 1983), p, 300.
21. Email from Keith Botsford to the author, 2002.
22. Saskia Hamilton, *The Letters of Robert Lowell* (London, 2005), p. 418.
23. For more on this see John Foot, 'The Secret Life of Ignazio Silone', *New Left Review*, 3, May–June 2000.
24. Saunders, *Who Paid the Piper*, pp. 362–3.
25. Carol Brightman, *Writing Dangerously: Mary McCarthy and Her World* (New York, 1992), p. 502.
26. *Ibid.*, p. 504.
27. Email from Keith Botsford to the author, 2002.
28. Saunders, *Who Paid the Piper*, p. 365.
29. *Ibid.*, p. 365.
30. Letter from David Carver to Arthur Miller, April 1965.
31. Letter from Keith Botsford to Arthur Miller, dated 23 April 1965.
32. Letter from Miguel Ángel Asturias, dated 12 June 1965.
33. Saunders, *Who Paid the Piper*, pp. 365–6.
34. Miller, *Timebends* (1987), pp. 573–4.
35. Miller, *Echoes Down the Corridor* (2000), p. 249.
36. Email to the author from Keith Botsford, 2002.
37. Miller, *Timebends* (1987), p. 578.

3 VIETNAM

1. Flyer in FBI file dated 30.11.65.
2. FBI file, dated 21 September 1965.
3. 'On Vietnam and the Dominican Republic', *Partisan Review*, 32, 3 (Summer 1965), p. 397.
4. Irving Howe, 'On Vietnam', *Partisan Review*, 32, 4 (Fall 1965), p. 627.
5. *Ibid.*, p. 627.
6. *Ibid.*, p. 642.
7. *New York Herald Tribune*, 27 September 1965.
8. Marguerite Higgins, 'On the Spot: Miller's Level of Ignorance', *Newsday*, 8 November 1965, p. 37.
9. Anon., 'Thanks without Enthusiasm', *Time*, 8 October 1965.
10. *New York Herald Tribune*, 28 September 1965, p. 20.
11. FBI memorandum dated 19 October 1965.
12. John Chamberlain, 'These Days: Arthur Miller's Position', *Washington Post*, 2 November 1965.
13. Letter from David Carver to Arthur Miller, 28 October 1965.
14. Interview with the author, September 2001.
15. *Ibid.*
16. Letter from David Carver, April 1966.
17. Arthur Miller, from letter to be sent to American writers.
18. Arthur Miller, 'The Writer as Independent Spirit', *Saturday Review*, 4 June 1966, pp. 16–17.
19. Saunders, *Who Paid the Piper*, p. 366.
20. Undated PEN memo in Arthur Miller's private papers.
21. Letter from Carlos Fuentes to Arthur Miller, July 1966.
22. See Russell Cobb, 'The Politics of Literary Prestige: Promoting the Latin American "Boom" in the pages of *Mundo Nuevo*'. *www.ncsu.edu/project/acontracorriente/spring–08/Cobb*, accessed 31 October 2009.
23. Saunders, *Who Paid the Piper*, p. 367.
24. Letter from Carlos Fuentes.
25. 'International P.E.N. Congress in New York', *Publishers' Weekly*, 18 July 1966.
26. Edward Shils, 'Remembering the Congress for Cultural Freedom', *Encounter*, vol. 75, September 1990, pp. 53–65.
27. Saunders, *Who Paid the Piper*, p. 401.
28. Arthur Miller, 'A Search for a Future', *Saturday Evening Post*, 13 August 1966, p. 70.

4 DANIEL

1. Inge Morath, interview with the author, 2001.
2. Arthur Miller, interview with the author, 26 May 2001.
3. Inge Morath, interview with the author, 25 May 2001.
4. Miller, *Timebends* (1987), p. 224.
5. Arthur Miller, interview with the author, 26 May 2001.
6. *Ibid.*
7. *Ibid.*
8. Miller, *After the Fall* (1965), p. 31.
9. *Ibid.*, p. 120.
10. *Guardian*, 4 October 2007, G2, p. 4.
11. *Ibid.*, p.4.
12. *Ibid.*, p. 6.

13. Charlotte Moore, 'The Throwaway Child', *Guardian*, Family section, 23 May 2009.
14. Suzanna Andrews, 'Arthur Miller's Missing Act', *Vanity Fair*, September 2007.
15. Arthur Miller, interview with the author, 26 May 2001.
16. Inge Morath, interview with the author, 25 May 2001.
17. Rebecca Miller, interview with the author, 26 May 2001.
18. Andrews, 'Arthur Miller's Missing Act'.
19. Andrew Billen, 'Arthur Miller: the Demonizing of My Father', *Times*, 25 July 2008. http://wom en.timesonline.co.uk/ tol/life_ and_style/women/article4392455 .ece
20. Andrews, 'Arthur Miller's Missing Act'. http://www.vanity fair.com/fame/ features/2007/09/ miller200709
21. Jason Zinoman, 'A New Stage for Arthur Miller's Most Private Drama of Fathers and Sons', *New York Times*, 30 August 2007.
22. Murray Briggs, *Arthur Miller in Conversation* (New Haven, 2000), p. 24.
23. Stephen Marino, 'A Conversation with Joan Copeland', *Arthur Miller Journal*, vol. 3, number 1, Spring 2008, pp. 64–5.

5 1968

1. Briggs, *Arthur Miller in Conversation*, p. 24.
2. Letter from Minerva Players to Arthur Miller, August 1967.
3. Miller, *Timebends* (1987), p. 583.
4. *Ibid.*, pp. 48–9.
5. Inge Morath and Arthur Miller, *Russian Journal 1965–1990* (London, 1991), p. 106.
6. Robert Giroux, ed., *Robert Lowell: Collected Prose* (London, 1987), pp. 119–21.
7. Interview with the author, 2001.
8. *Ibid.*
9. nobelprize.org/nobel_prizes/ literature/laureates/1987/brodsky- lecture-e.html, accessed 4 January 2009.
10. Interview with the author, 2001.
11. Inge Morath, *Portraits* (New York, 1986), p. 95.
12. Alfred Kazin, *New York Jew* (New York, 1978), p. 274.
13. Howard Fast, *The Naked God: The Writer and the Communist Party* (London, 1958), p. 105.
14. Kazin, *New York Jew*, p. 171.
15. Miller and Morath, *In Russia* (1969), p. 63.
16. *Ibid.*, p. 63.
17. *Ibid.*, p. 11.
18. *Ibid.*, p. 107.
19. Norman Mailer, letter dated 23 October 1967.
20. Miller, *Timebends* (1987), p. 542.
21. Miller, *Echoes Down the Corridor* (2002), pp. 297–8.
22. Arthur Miller, 'The Past and Its Power: Why I Wrote *The Price*', *New York Times*, 14 November 1999.
23. Joan Copeland, interview with the author, 7 November 2008.
24. Christopher Bigsby, *Arthur Miller and Company* (London, 1989), p. 151.
25. IBDB Internet Broadway Database.
26. 'The Price', *Time*, 16 February 1968.

27. Anon., 'Dramatic Drought', *Time*, 17 May 1968.

28. Clive Barnes, 'Arthur Miller's "The Price"', *New York Times*, 8 February 1968.

29. Martin Gottfried, *Opening Nights: Theater Criticism of the Sixties* (New York, 1969), pp. 101–3.

30. John Simon, *Singularities* (New York, 1975), p. 87.

31. Christopher Bigsby, *Remembering Arthur Miller* (London, 2005), p. 284.

32. Miller, *Timebends* (1987), pp. 510–11.

33. Peter Brook, *The Empty Space* (London, 1968), p. 49.

34. *Theatre 4* (New York, 1972), p. 97.

35. Miller, *Echoes Down the Corridor* (2000), pp. 130–1.

36. *Ibid.*, p. 132.

37. *Ibid.*, pp. 132–3.

38. *Ibid.*, p. 134.

39. *Ibid.*, pp. 137–8.

40. Resolution of the PEN-Zentrum Deutsche Demokratische Republik, dated March 1968, in Arthur Miller's private papers.

41. Letter from David Carver to Arthur Miller, 22 July 1968, in Arthur Miller's private papers.

42. Arthur Miller, 'Carta al Presidente de Mexico', *La Pajarita de Papel*, number 4, October–December 1968, p. 1.

43. Shils, 'Congress for Cultural Freedom', p. 63.

44. Gottfried, *Arthur Miller: A Life*, p. 383.

45. Lewis Chester, Godfrey Hodgson, Bruce Page, *An American Melodrama: The Presidential Campaign of 1968* (London, 1969), p. 4.

46. *Ibid.*, p. 137.

47. Burton Hersh, 'The Last Kennedy', in *Smiling through the Apocalypse: Esquire's History of the Sixties*, ed. Harold Hayes (New York, 1969), p. 127.

48. *Ibid.*, p. 57.

49. Mary McCarthy, *Hanoi* (London, 1968), p. 18.

50. Lowell, *Collected Prose*, p. 282.

51. *Ibid.*, p. 76.

52. *Ibid.*, p. 282.

53. *Ibid.*, p. 395.

54. Miller, *Timebends* (1989), p. 508.

55. *Ibid.*, p. 544.

56. 'The New Insurgency', *Nation*, 3 June 1968, vol. 206, p. 717.

57. Saskia Hamilton, ed., *The Letters of Robert Lowell* (London, 2005), p. 502.

58. Eugene McCarthy, *Up 'Til Now* (New York, 1987), p. 197.

59. Chester, Hodgson and Page, *An American Melodrama*, p. 349.

60. Arthur Miller, 'On the Shooting of Robert Kennedy', *New York Times*, 8 June 1968.

61. *Ibid.*

62. Chester, Hodgson and Page, *An American Melodrama*, p. 395.

63. *Ibid.*, p. 548.

64. Theodore H. White, *The Making of the President: 1972* (New York, 1973), p. 26.

65. Arthur Miller, 'The Delegate: A Story of a Political Man', unpublished, undated story in Arthur Miller's private papers.

66. Letter from Eugene J. McCarthy to Arthur Miller, 31 July 1968, in Arthur Miller's private papers.

67. Norman Mailer, *Miami and the Siege of Chicago* (New York, 1968), p. 28.

68. Joe Flaherty. "A Concurrence of Poets and One Who Stayed Home," *The Village Voice*, 22 August, 1968, vol XIII, no. 45. http://blogs.villagevoice.com/runningscared/archives/2010/05/george_plimpton.php, accessed 5 June 2010.

69. Miller, *Echoes Down the Corridor*, p. 77.

70. Christopher Bigsby, ed., *Writers in Conversation*, vol. 1 (Norwich, 2000), p. 366.

71. Miller, *Echoes Down the Corridor* (2000), p. 77.

72. Shirley Williams, *Climbing the Bookshelves* (London, 2009), pp. 183–4.

73. Miller, *Timebends* (1987), p. 545.

74. Chester, Hodgson and Page, *An American Melodrama*, p. 585.

75. Arthur Miller interview with the author, BBC, 1995.

76. Chester, Hodgson and Page, *An American Melodrama*, p. 583.

77. Mailer, *Miami*, p. 161.

78. Jean Genet, 'The Members of the Assembly', trans. Richard Seaver, in Harold Hayes, ed., *Smiling through the Apocalypse: Esquire's History of the Sixties* (New York, 1969), p. 163.

79. *Ibid.*, p. 36.

80. *Ibid.*, p. 168.

81. William Burroughs, 'The Coming of the Purple Better One', in *Smiling through the Apocalypse*, p. 168.

82. Chester, Hodgson and Page, *An American Melodrama*, p. 588.

83. Miller, *Echoes Down the Corridor* (2000), p. 82.

84. *Ibid.*, p. 83.

85. Chester, Hodgson and Page, *An American Melodrama*, p. 545.

86. *Ibid.*, p. 86.

87. Edward W. Knappman, *Presidential Election 1968* (New York, 1970), p. 210.

88. John W. Kirshon, *Chronicle of America* (Farnborough, 1995) p. 827.

89. Christopher Bigsby, ed., *Remembering Arthur Miller* (London, 2005), p. 282.

90. Rick Cech, 'Coffin, Miller Address Rally', *Yale Daily News*, 4 November 1968, p. 1.

6 CZECHOSLOVAKIA AND CAMBODIA

1. Matthew Roudané, *Conversations with Arthur Miller* (Jackson, 1987), p. 208.

2. Lewis Funke, 'Stars Help Arthur Miller Film TV Antiwar Allegory', *New York Times*, 17 November 1969.

3. Miller, *Timebends* (1987), p. 547.

4. Funke, 'Stars Help Arthur Miller'.

5. Arthur Miller, *The Reason Why*, directed by Paul Leaf, produced by Gino Giglio, was released in February 1970. The play text is located in the Harry Ransom Center of the University of Texas. See Joseph Kane, 'A Conversation with Eli Wallach', *Arthur Miller Journal*, 1, 2 (2006), pp. 53–64.

6. Miller, *Timebends* (1987), p. 553.

7. Arthur Miller, 'Are We Interested in Stopping the Killing?' *New York Times*, 8 June 1969, D 21.

8. 'A Letter to Anatoly Kuznetsov', *Time*, 5 December 1969.

9. Miller and Morath, *In the Country* (1977), p. 174.

10. Letter to the *New York Review of Books*, vol. II, number 12, 2 January 1969.

11. Bigsby, *Remembering Arthur Miller*, p. 93.

12. http://www.waggish.org/2003/04/07/the-guinea-pigs-ludvik-vaculik, accessed 3 February 2009.

13. Carol Rocamora, *Acts of Courage: Václav Havel's Life in the Theater* (Hanover, 2005), p. 109.

14. Arthur Miller, 'The Sin of Power', in *An Embarrassment of Tyrannies*, ed. W.L. Webb and Rose Bell (London, 1997), p. 76.

15. Miller, *Echoes Down the Corridor* (2000), p. 136.

16. *Ibid.*, p. 145.

17. Miller, 'The Sin of Power' (1997), p. 79.

18. Miller, *Timebends* (1987), pp. 517–18.

19. *Ibid.*, p. 518.

20. *Ibid.*, pp. 518–19.

21. The Phyllis Kind Gallery, *Edith Isaac-Rose: The Political Embroideries*. http://www.artworkshopintl.com/ blog/?p=163.

22. Telephone conversation with Edith Isaac-Rose, 12 December 2009.

23. Miller, *Timebends*, p. 520.

24. *Ibid.*, p. 520.

25. *Ibid.*, p. 520.

26. Arthur Miller, interview with the author, 2001.

27. Rebecca Miller, interview with the author, Roxbury, 2001.

28. Arthur Miller, interview with the author, 2001.

29. Bigsby, *Remembering Arthur Miller*, p. 281.

30. Miller, *Timebends* (1987), pp. 550–2.

31. Arthur Miller, 'Denial and Vietnam', (1987) in Miller's private papers.

32. *New York Times*, 1 May 1970. See also http://www.mekong.net/ cambodia/ nixon430.htm, accessed November 2009.

33. 'Nixon Puts "Bums" Label on Some College Radicals', *New York Times*, 2 May 1970.

34. Arthur Miller, 'The War between the Young and the Old, or Why Willy Loman Can't Understand What's Happening', *McCall's*, July 1970, p. 32.

35. 'Kerry's Testimony', *National Review Online*, 23 April 2004. http://www.national review.com/document/ kerry200404231047. asp

7 THE OBLONG BLUR

1. Bigsby, *Remembering Arthur Miller*, p. 282.

2. *Ibid.*, p. 283.

3. Rocamora, *Acts of Courage*, p. 107.

4. Robert A. Martin and Steven R. Centola, eds, *The Theater Essays of Arthur Miller* (New York, 1996), pp. 485–6.

5. Miller, *Timebends* (1987), p. 558.

6. *Ibid.*, p. 559.

7. William James, *Writings 1878–1899* (New York, 1992), pp. 486–7.

8. *Ibid.*, p. 599.

9. David Rosenberg, ed., *Genesis: Contemporary Writers on Our First Stories* (San Francisco, 1996), pp. 35–40.

10. Roudané, *Conversations with Arthur Miller*, p. 377.

11. Bigsby, *Remembering Arthur Miller*, pp. 71–2.

12. Roudané, *Conversations with Arthur Miller*, pp. 264–5.

13. Clive Barnes, 'Arthur Miller's Creation', *New York Times*, 1 December 1972.

14. Frank Rich, 'Stage: Miller's *Up from Paradise*', *New York Times*, 26 October 1983, C22.

15. Stanley Kauffmann, *Persons of the Drama: Theater Criticism and Comment* (New York, 1976), pp. 230–2.

16. *Ibid.*, p. 141.

17. *Ibid.*, p. 219.

18. *Ibid.*, pp. 142–4.

19. Arthur Miller, 'Willy Loman and "The Helpless Giant"', *Chicago Sun-Times*, 14 May 1972.

20. Miller, *Echoes Down the Corridor* (2000), p. 116.

21. *Ibid.*, p. 107.

22. Ernest R. May and Janet Fraser, *Campaign '72: The Managers Speak* (Cambridge, 1973), p. 146.

23. *Ibid.*, p. 151.

24. *Ibid.*, p. 168.

25. Miller, *Echoes Down the Corridor* (2000), p. 124.

26. *Ibid.*, p. 124.

27. *Ibid.*, pp. 116–17.

28. *Ibid.*, p. 118.

29. *Ibid.*, p. 132.

30. Arthur Miller et al., 'Soviet Inhumanity', *New York Review of Books*, 27 June 1974.

31. Miller, *Echoes Down the Corridor* (2000), p. 147.

8 PETER REILLY

1. Murray Briggs, *Arthur Miller in Conversation*, p. 10.

2. I am indebted to Joan Barthel's *A Death in Canaan* (New York, 1976) and to Donald S. Connery's *Guilty until Proven Innocent* (New York, 1977), for many of the details in what follows.

3. Barthol, *A Death in Canaan*, pp. 20–1.

4. *Ibid.*, p. 43.

5. *Ibid.*, pp. 48, 50.

6. *Ibid.*, p. 55.

7. *Ibid.*, pp. 58–9, 66.

8. *Ibid.*, p. 62.

9. *Ibid.*, p. 70.

10. *Ibid.*, pp. 78, 80.

11. *Ibid.*, p. 83.

12. *Ibid.*, pp. 98–9.

13. *Ibid.*, p. 109.

14. *Ibid.*, p. 115.

15. Connery, *Guilty until Proven Innocent*, p. 121.

16. *Ibid.*, p. 197.

17. *Ibid.*, p. 10.

18. *Ibid.*, p. 245.

19. *Ibid.*, pp. 277–8.

20. Miller, *Timebends* (1987), p. 557.

21. Connery, *Guilty until Proven Innocent*, p. 274.

22. Barthel, *A Death in Canaan*, p. 267.

23. Connery, *Guilty until Proven Innocent*, p. 274.

24. *Ibid.*, p. 291.

25. *Ibid.*, p. 291.

26. *Ibid.*, p. 293.

27. *Ibid.*, p. 289.

28. *Ibid.*, p. 322.

29. *Ibid.*, p. 323.

30. *Ibid.*, p. 294.

31. *Ibid.*, p. 347.

32. Miller, *Timebends* (1987), p. 556.

33. *Ibid.*, pp. 556–7.

9 *THE ARCHBISHOP'S CEILING*
TO *THE AMERICAN CLOCK*

1. Bigsby, *Remembering Arthur Miller*, p. 288.
2. Miller, *Timebends* (1987), p. 558.
3. Mel Gussow, 'Arthur Miller Returns to Genesis for First Musical', *New York Times*, 17 April 1974.
4. Arthur Miller, 'Sakharov, Détente and Liberty', *New York Times*, 5 July 1974.
5. Arthur Miller, 'Toward a New Foreign Policy', *Society*, March/April 1976, pp. 10–11, 15–16.
6. Arthur Miller, 'The Poosidin's Resignation', *Boston University Journal*, XXIV, 1976, p. 6.
7. *Ibid.*, p. 10.
8. *Ibid.*, pp. 12–13.
9. Miller, 'Toward a new Foreign Policy', pp. 10, 15–16.
10. Miller, 'The Sin of Power', Webb and Bell, *Index on Censorship*, May–June 1978, p. 3.
11. Bigsby, *Remembering Arthur Miller*, p. 287.
12. Brian Moynahan, '1989', *Sunday Times* magazine, 3 May 2009, p. 20.
13. Miller and Morath, *In the Country* (1977), p. 68.
14. Bigsby, *Remembering Arthur Miller*, p. 33.
15. Arthur Miller, 'A Kind of Despair', Webb and Bell, *Index on Censorship*, 6, 1981, p. 31.
16. Arthur Miller, Introduction, *The American Clock and The Archbishop's Ceiling* (New York, 1989), p. vii.
17. Bigsby, *Remembering Arthur Miller*, p. 286–7.
18. *Ibid.*
19. *Ibid.*, p. 287.
20. Letter to the author, dated 1983.
21. Letter to the author, 8 January 1984.
22. Arthur Miller, *Plays Three* (London, 1990), p. 97.
23. *Remembering Arthur Miller*, pp. 287–8.
24. Václav Havel, 'My Temptation', in Webb and Bell, p. 135.
25. Arthur Miller, 'The Prague Winter', *New York Times*, 16 July 1975, p. 37C.
26. Christopher Bigsby, *Arthur Miller and Company* (London, 1990), p. 163.
27. Miller, *Plays Three* (London, 1990), p. 155.
28. *Ibid.*, p. 143.
29. Rocamora, *Acts of Courage*, pp. 175–6.
30. Miller, *Timebends* (1987), p. 573.
31. Bigsby, *Arthur Miller and Company* (London, 1990, p. 164.
32. Alexandr Solzhenitsyn, 'A World Split Apart'. http://Columbia.edu/cu/Augustine/arch/solzhenitsyn/ harvard1978, accessed 23 February 2009.
33. Joan Copeland, interview with the author, November 2008.
34. John J. O'Connor, '"Fame", Comedy by Arthur Miller', *New York Times*, 30 November 1978.
35. Arthur Miller, 'The 1928 Buick', *Atlantic Monthly*, vol. 242, October 1976, p. 51.
36. Inge Morath and Arthur Miller, *Chinese Encounters* (New York, 1979), p. 8.
37. Jung Chang and Jon Halliday, *Mao: The Unknown Story* (London, 2007), pp. 234–5.
38. *Ibid.*, p. 561.

39. Morath and Miller, *Chinese Encounters*, p. 9.
40. *Ibid.*, p. 66.
41. *Ibid.*, p. 19.
42. *Ibid.*, p. 30.
43. *Ibid.*, p. 62.
44. Fania Fénelon, *Playing for Time*, trans. Judith Landry (Syracuse, 1997), p. 46.
45. *Ibid.*, p. ix.
46. *Ibid.*, p. 237.
47. *Ibid.*, p. 242.
48. *Ibid.*, p. ix.
49. Nicholas Wapshott, 'Tony Rehabilitates Vanessa Redgrave', *Times*, 10 June 2003.
50. James Atlas, 'The Creative Journey of Arthur Miller Leads Back to Broadway, and TV', *New York Times*, 28 September 1980.
51. Richard Corliss, 'Soloists in a Choir of Martyrs', *Time*, 29 September 1980, p. 43.
52. Arthur Miller, *Playing for Time* (New York, 1981), p. 94.
53. Fénelon, *Playing for Time*, p. 145.
54. Bigsby, *Remembering Arthur Miller*, p. 182.
55. Bigsby, *Miller and Company*, p. 150.
56. Bigsby, *Remembering Arthur Miller*, pp. 182–3.
57. Miller, *Playing for Time*, p. 62.
58. *Ibid.*, p. 91.
59. Arthur Miller, 'Miracles', *Esquire*, September 1973, p. 113.
60. Atlas, 'Creative Journey'.
61. Arthur Miller, *The American Clock* (London, 1983), p. 1.
62. Joan Copeland, interview with the author, 7 November 2008.
63. F, Scott Fitzgerald, *The Crack Up* (New York, 1945), p. 69.
64. *The American Clock*, p. 1.
65. Miller, *The American Clock* (1983), p. 9.
66. *Ibid.*, p. 10.
67. Atlas, 'Creative Journey'.
68. Frank Rich, 'Miller's "American Clock"', *New York Times*, 12 November 1980.
69. Miller, *Timebends* (1987), pp. 586–7.
70. Roudané, *Conversations with Arthur Miller*, pp. 313–14.
71. Jean Copeland, interview with the author.

10 *SALESMAN* REDUX

1. Bigsby, *Miller and Company*, p. 8.
2. Arthur Miller, interview with the author, 2002.
3. William Styron, *Havanas in Camelot* (New York, 2008), p. 83.
4. Bigsby, *Remembering Arthur Miller*, pp. 72–3.
5. Jan Vladislaw, ed., *Václav Havel: Living in Truth* (London, 1987), pp. 263–5.
6. *Ibid.*, p. 203.
7. 'Communism and the Left', *Nation*, 27 February 1982.
8. Anon., 'Seeing Red', *Time*, 15 March 1982.
9. Samuel G. Freedman, 'Miller Tries a New Form for an Old Play', *New York Times*, 23 October 1983.
10. Helen Dudar, 'A Modern Tragedy's Road to Maturity', *New York Times*, 25 March 1984.
11. Arthur Miller, *Two-Way Mirror* (London, 1984), np.
12. *Ibid.*, pp. 8–9.
13. *Ibid.*, p. 9.
14. *Ibid.*, pp. 17–18.
15. *Ibid.*, pp. 18–19.

16. *Ibid.*, p. 19.

17. *Ibid.*, np.

18. *Ibid.*, pp. 52–3.

19. Frank Rich, 'Stage: 2 by Arthur Miller; New Haven', *New York Times*, 10 November 1982.

20. Helen Dudar, 'New Life for an Arthur Miller Play', *New York Times*, 30 January 1983.

21. Anon., 'Blind Passion', *Time*, 14 February 1983.

22. Arthur Miller, *Salesman in Beijing* (London, 1984), p. 5.

23. Arthur Miller, 'Death in Tiananmen', *New York Times*, 10 September 1989.

24. Miller, *Echoes down the Corridor* (2000), p. 209.

25. *Ibid.*, p. 210.

26. Freedman, 'New Form for an Old Play'.

27. Frank Rich, 'Stage: Miller's "Up from Paradise"', *New York Times*, 26 October 1983.

28. Freedman, 'New Form for an Old Play'.

29. Arthur Miller, 'School Prayer: A Political Dirigible', *New York Times*, 12 March 1984.

30. Bigsby, *Miller and Company*, p. 70.

31. Miller, *Timebends* (1987), p. 373.

32. Bigsby, *Miller and Company*, p. 71.

33. Bigsby, *Remembering Arthur Miller*, p. 184.

34. *Ibid.*

35. *Playing the Salesman*, BBC Radio 4, 11 February 2006.

36. *Ibid.*

37. *Ibid.*

38. *Ibid.*

39. Frank Rich, 'Hoffman, "Death of a Salesman"', *New York Times*, 30 March 1984.

40. Michiko Kakutani, 'Arthur Miller: View of a Life', *New York Times*, 9 May 1984.

41. Samuel G. Freedman, '"Salesman" Collaborators Part Ways', *New York Times*, 15 August 1984.

42. Gottfried, *Arthur Miller: A Life*, p. 499.

43. Freedman, '"Salesman" Collaborators Part Ways'.

44. Don Shewey, 'TV's Custom-tailored "Salesman"', *New York Times*, 15 September 1985.

45. Dan Sullivan, '*Salesman* Shrunk in the Big Eye's Glare', *Los Angeles Times*, 22 September 1985.

46. Bigsby, *Miller and Company*, p. 64.

47. Miller, *Echoes Down the Corridor* (2000), p. 203.

48. *Ibid.*, p. 204.

49. Freedman, 'New Form for an Old Play'.

50. Lillian Hellman, *Three: An Unfinished Woman, Pentimento, Scoundrel Time* (London, 1979), p. 609.

51. *Ibid.*, p. 648.

52. *Ibid.*, p. 651.

53. *Ibid.*, pp. 606–7.

54. Brightman, *Writing Dangerously*, p. 607.

55. *Ibid.*, pp. 612–13.

56. Mary McCarthy, *A Bolt from the Blue and Other Essays* (New York, 2002), p. 72.

57. Hellman, *Three*, p. 656.

58. *Ibid.*, pp. 720–1.

59. *Ibid.*, p. 718.

60. Lillian Hellman, *Maybe* (Boston, 1980), pp. 50–1.

61. *Ibid.*, p. 11.

62. Jason Zinoman, 'Miller's Crossing', *Time Out*, 27 January–2 February 2005.

63. Don Shewey, 'The Devil in Liz LeCompte', December 1983. www.donshewey.com/theater_articles/wooster_group_lsd.html, accessed 4 April 2009.
64. *Ibid.*
65. Mel Gussow, 'Stage: Wooster Group', *New York Times*, 31 October 1984.
66. Zinoman, 'Miller's Crossing'.
67. Samuel G. Freedman, 'Miller's Fighting Group's Use of Segment From "Crucible"', 17 November 1984.
68. *Ibid.*
69. Bigsby, *Miller and Company*, p. 104.
70. Arthur Miller, 'Arthur Miller Speaks Out on the Election', *Literary Cavalcade*, November 1984, pp. 4–5.
71. *The Ambassador's Dinner*, BBC Radio 4, 10 April 2010.
72. *Ibid.*
73. Orhan Pamuk, 'Freedom to Write', *New York Review of Books*, 25 May 2006.
74. Miller, *Echoes Down the Corridor* (2000), p. 214.
75. Bigsby, *Miller and Company*, p. 4.
76. Mel Gussow, *Conversations with Miller* (London, 2002), p. 210.
77. *The Ambassador's Dinner*, BBC Radio 4, 10 April 2010.
78. *Ibid.*
79. *Echoes Down the Corridor.*, p. 216.
80. *Ibid.*, p. 217.
81. Interview with the author, in Bigsby, *Remembering Arthur Miller*, p. 171.
82. *Echoes Down the Corridor*, p. 218.
83. *Conversations with Miller*, p. 210.
84. Bigsby, *Remembering Arthur Miller*, pp. 171–2.
85. http://www/haroldpinter.org/politics/politics_kurds.shtml, accessed 21 December 2009 (excerpted from *Listener*, 27 October 1988).
86. *The Ambassador's Dinner*, BBC Radio 4, 10 April 2010.
87. Pamuk, 'Freedom to Write'.
88. *Ibid.*
89. Louis Auchincloss, 'Recognizing Gaddis', *New York Times*, 15 November 1987.
90. William H. Gass, 'East and West in Lithuania: Rising Tempers at a Writers' Meeting', *New York Times*, 2 February 1986.
91. Gussow, *Conversations with Arthur Miller*, p. 131.
92. *Ibid.*, p. 131.
93. Miller, *Timebends*, p. 563.
94. Bigsby, *Remembering Arthur Miller*, p. 294.
95. Email from Zbignieu Lewicki, 6 June 2009.
96. Bigsby, *Miller and Company*, p. 171.
97. *Ibid.*, p. 169.
98. *Ibid.*, p. 587.
99. Miller, *Timebends* (1987), p. 588.
100. *Ibid.*, p. 588.
101. *Ibid.*, p. 589.
102. *Ibid.*, p. 589.
103. Arthur Miller, *Danger: Memory!* (New York, 1986), p. 8.
104. *Ibid.*, p. 7.
105. *Ibid.*, p. 11.
106. *Ibid.*, p. 11.
107. *Ibid.*, p. 12.
108. *Ibid.*, p. 15.
109. *Ibid.*, p. 21.
110. *Ibid.*
111. Gussow, *Conversations with Arthur Miller*, p. 79.
112. Miller, *Timebends* (1987), p. 503.
113. Miller, *Danger Memory!* (1986), pp. 44, 51.

114. *Ibid.*, p. 52.

115. *Ibid.*, p. 362.

116. Miller, *Timebends* (1987), p. 591.

117. Gussow, *Conversations with Arthur Miller*, p. 133.

118. Miller, *Timebends* (1987), p. 49.

119. Miller, *Danger: Memory!* (1986), p. 30.

120. Nick Brown, 'Still Not Laid to Rest', *Sunday Times*, 8 November 1987.

121. Frank Rich, 'Arthur Miller's "Danger: Memory!"', *New York Times*, 9 February 1987.

122. Gordon Rogoff, 'Treadmiller', *Village Voice*, 17 February 1987, p. 99.

123. Miller, *Timebends* (1987), p. 591.

124. Frank Rich, 'Theatre: Richard Kiley in Miller's "All My Sons"', *New York Times*, 23 April 1987.

125. Paul Allen, *Alan Ayckbourn: Grinning at the Edge* (London, 2001), p. 225.

126. *Ibid.*, p. 226.

127. Bigsby, *Miller and Company*, p. 119.

128. Matt Wolf, 'Run of the Millers', *Observer*, 4 February 1990.

129. John Osborne, 'A Nice Guy Who Hasn't Finished Yet', *Spectator*, 5 December 1987.

130. John Mortimer, *Daily Telegraph*, 10 October 1987.

131. William A. Henry III, 'A Life of Fade-Outs and Fade-Ins', *Time*, 23 November 1987.

132. Alfred Kazin, 'Apologia pro Vita Sua', *New Yorker*, 14 December 1987.

133. Roger Shattuck, 'He Who Is Most Alone', *New York Times*, 8 November 1987.

134. James Wolcott, *Vanity Fair*, November 1987.

135. James W. Tuttleton, '"Timebends", by Arthur Miller', *Commentary*, March 1988.

136. David Denby, 'Arthur Miller, America's Connoisseur of Guilt: All My Sins', *New Republic*, pp. 30–4.

137. Susan Sontag, 'Going to the Theater and the Movies', *Partisan Review*, 33, Spring 1964, p. 285.

138. Stanley Kauffmann, *Persons of the Drama: Theater Criticism and Comment* (New York, 1976), p. 144.

139. *Ibid.*, p. 230.

140. Robert Brustein, *Making Scenes* (New York, 1981), p. 220.

141. Ronald Hingley, *Chekhov* (London, 1950), p. 233.

142. Robert Brustein, *The Third Theatre* (London, 1970), p. 105.

143. *Ibid.*, p. 106.

144. Robert Brustein, *Seasons of Discontent* (London, 1966), p. 259.

145. *Ibid.*, p. 19.

146. *Ibid.*, p. 242.

147. Richard Gilman, *Common and Uncommon Masks: Writings on Theater 1961–1970* (New York, 1971), p. 152.

148. *Ibid.*, p. 153.

149. Richard Gilman, *The Confusion of Realms* (New York, 1969), p. 221.

150. *Ibid.*, p. 225.

151. Herb Blau, *To All Appearances: Ideology and Performance* (London, 1992), p. 73.

152. James Atlas, *Delmore Schwartz: The Life of an American Poet* (New York, 1977), p. 361.

153. Nathan David Abrams, *Struggling for Freedom: Arthur Miller, the Commentary Community and the Cultural Cold War* (Birmingham, 1998) p. 276.

154. *Ibid.*, p. 102.

155. *Ibid.*, p. 259.
156. John Simon, *Singularities: Essays on the Theater 1964–1973* (New York, 1975), p. 85.
157. Robert Lewis, *Slings and Arrows: Theater in My Life* (New York, 1984), p. 347.
158. Shattuck, 'He Who Is Most Alone'.
159. Peter Accrete, 'A Serious Man of Plays', *Times*, 5 November 1987.
160. Arthur Schlesinger Jr, 'Behind That Anatolian Smile', *New York Times*, 1 May 1988.
161. Herb Greer, 'Theatrics', *Commentary*, October 1988.
162. David Thomson, 'The Scene Maker', *New Republic*, 9 May 1988, p. 34.
163. *Ibid.*, pp. 34–5.

11 THE RIDE DOWN MOUNT MORGAN TO BROKEN GLASS

1. Bigsby, *Remembering Arthur Miller*, p. 296.
2. Arthur Miller et al., 'In Korean Jails', *New York Review of Books*, vol. 35, number 18, 24 November 1988.
3. Arthur Miller, 'Selected Letters of Eugene O'Neill', *New York Times*, 6 November 1988. The letters were edited by Travis Bogard and Jackson R. Bryer (New Haven, 2008).
4. Arthur Miller, 'On Rushdie and Global Censorship', *Authors' Guild Bulletin*, Summer 1989, pp. 5–6.
5. Arthur Miller, 'Death in Tiananmen', *New York Times*, 10 September 1989.
6. Richard Eyre, *Utopia and Other Places: Memoir of a Young Director* (London, 1993), pp. 152–3.
7. Miller, *Echoes Down the Corridor* (2000), pp. 222–3.
8. *Ibid.*, p. 226.
9. *Ibid.*, pp. 228–9.
10. Sheridan Morley, 'Just a Lot of Show Business', *Times*, 11 January 1989.
11. Richard Eyre, *National Service: Diary of a Decade at the National Theatre* (London, 2003), p. 53.
12. Arthur Miller, 'The Worst Enemy of the People Is the Poisoner of the Mind', *Guardian*, 30 January 1989.
13. Miller, *Echoes Down the Corridor* (2000), pp. 220–1.
14. Georgina Brown, 'How We Met: David Thacker and Arthur Miller', *Independent*, 30 April 1995.
15. Bigsby, *Miller and Company*, p. 172.
16. *Ibid.*, p. 174.
17. Georgina Brown, 'How We Met'.
18. Morley, 'Just a Lot of Show Business'.
19. Kirk Johnson, 'Arthur Miller's Vision of Love Becomes a Movie', *New York Times*, 11 June 1989.
20. Arthur Miller, 'Preface: On Screenwriting and Language', *Everybody Wins* (London, 1990), p. xiii.
21. *Ibid.*, p. xiv.
22. Johnson, 'Miller's Vision of Love'.
23. Arthur Miller, *Plays Five* (London, 1995), p. 135.
24. Rita Kempley, 'Everybody Wins', *Washington Post*, 20 January 1990.
25. Desson Howe, '"Music Box" and "Everybody Wins"', *Washington Post*, 26 January 1990.

26. Miller, 'On Screenwriting and Language', in *Everybody Wins*, pp. v–xiv.

27. Bigsby, *Arthur Miller and Company*, pp. 161–2.

28. *Ibid.*, p. 158.

29. Heather Neill, 'Yours Precisely, Arthur Miller', *Times*, 1 February 1990. See also Bigsby, *Arthur Miller and Company*, pp. 161–2.

30. Bigsby, *Arthur Miller and Company, Ibid.*

31. Neill, *Ibid.*

32. Nigella Lawson, 'The All-American Outsider', *Sunday Times*, 28 January 1990, p. 3.

33. Bigsby, *Remembering Arthur Miller*, p. 189.

34. Eyre, *National Service*, p. 118.

35. Arthur Miller, 'Lost Horizon', *American Theater*, July–August 1992, p. 68.

36. Christopher S. Wren, 'For Arthur Miller, Denial is a Key to Apartheid', *New York Times*, 6 December 1990.

37. *Ibid.*

38. Arthur Miller, *Arena: Miller Meets Mandela*, BBC Television, recorded 3 December 1990, transmitted 18 January 1991.

39. Arthur Miller, interview with the author, 2002.

40. William Styron, *Darkness Visible: A Memoir of Madness* (New York, 1990), pp. 78–9.

41. *Ibid.*, p. 78.

42. *Ibid.*, p. 84.

43. *Ibid.*, p. 66.

44. *Ibid.*, p. 76.

45. Miller, *Plays Five* (1995), p. 4.

46. *Ibid.*, p. 8.

47. *Ibid.*, p. 16.

48. *Ibid.*, p. 33.

49. Interview with the author, Roxbury, 31 January 1994.

50. *Ibid.*, p. xii.

51. *Ibid.*, pp. xxiii–xxiv.

52. *Ibid.*, p. x.

53. *Ibid.*, p. xx.

54. Mel Gussow, 'Theater: Revised Last Yankee, Will focus on Wives', *New York Times*, 22 January 1993.

55. Irving Wardle, 'Miller Back with a Loser's Tale', *Independent*, 31 January 1993.

56. Interview with the author, Roxbury, 31 January 1994.

57. Robert Simonson, 'Values, Old and New: Arthur Miller and John Tillinger on *The Last Yankee*', *Theatre Week*, pp. 15–17.

58. *Remembering Arthur Miller*, p. 89.

59. Arthur Miller, *Plays Five* (London, 1995), p. 59.

60. *Ibid.*, p. 65.

61. *Ibid.*, p. 74.

62. *Ibid.*, p. 52.

63. *Ibid.*, p. 50.

64. *Ibid.*, p. 73.

65. *Daily Telegraph* reporter, *Daily Telegraph*, 12 May 2009, p. 17.

66. *Plays Five*, p. 58.

67. *Ibid.*, pp. 62–4.

68. *Ibid.*, p. 67.

69. *Ibid.*, p. 71.

70. *Ibid.*, p. 33.

71. *Ibid.*, p. 95.

72. *Ibid.*, p. 96.

73. *Ibid.*, p. 101.

74. Richard Eyre, *Talking Theatre: Interviews with Theatre People* (London, 2009), p. 53.

75. Miller, *Plays Five* (1995), p. 112.

76. *Ibid.*, p. 115.

77. *Ibid.*, p. 120.

78. *Ibid.*, p. 132.

79. Interview with the author, 1995.

80. Arthur Miller, *Homely Girl* (New York, 1995), pp. 6–7.
81. *Ibid.*, pp. 12–13.
82. *Ibid.*, p. 19.
83. *Ibid.*, pp. 30–1.
84. http://wvvw.trumanlibrary.org/oralhist/rauh.htm, accessed 1 May, 2009.
85. Alvin Klein, 'Theatre: "Broken Glass", the New Haven Tryout That Isn't', *New York Times*, 3 April 1994.
86. http://www.auschwitz.dk/Grynszpan.htm, accessed 7 May 2009.
87. 'For a Diplomat's Murder Nazi Germany Takes an Awful Revenge on Jews', *Life Magazine*, 28 November 1938, p. 13.
88. Arthur Miller, *Broken Glass* (London, 1994), pp. 1–2.
89. *Ibid.*, p. 3.
90. This and subsequent quotations are from recordings made during rehearsals for *Broken Glass*, 31 January and 1–2 February 1994.
91. Miller, *Broken Glass* (1994), pp. 5–6.
92. *Ibid.*, p. 10.
93. *Ibid.*, p. 19.
94. *Ibid.*, pp. 36–7.
95. *Ibid.*, p. 52.
96. *Ibid.*, p. 54.
97. *Ibid.*, p. 17.
98. *Ibid.*, p. 23.
99. *Ibid.*, p. 55.
100. *Ibid.*, p. 45.
101. *Ibid.*, p. 23.
102. *Ibid.*, pp. 36–7.
103. *Ibid.*, p. 45.
104. *Ibid.*, pp. 56, 59.
105. *Ibid.*, pp. 64, 66, 68.
106. *Ibid.*, p. 72.
107. *Ibid.*, pp. 73, 75.
108. *Ibid.*, pp. 69, 71, 70.
109. http://s3.amazonaws.com/americantheatrewing.org/media/downstage/mp3/Episode141.mp3, accessed 9 May 2009.
110. Arthur Miller, interview with the author.
111. Ron Rifkin, 'Arthur Miller', *Bomb Magazine*, 49, Fall 1994. http://www.bombsite.com/issues/49/articles/1821, accessed 5 November 2009.
112. Arthur Miller, interview on Austrian television, 1996.
113. *Ibid.*
114. Ron Rifkin, 'Arthur Miller'.
115. Richard Bernstein, 'Theater; Acting against Type: The Self-Hating Jew', *New York Times*, 24 April 1994, section 2, p. 6.
116. John Lahr, 'Talk of the Town: Miller's Tales', *New Yorker*, 11 April 1994, p. 35.
117. John Simon, 'Whose Paralysis Is It, Anyway?', *New York Magazine*, 9 May 1994, p. 80.
118. William A. Henry III, 'Sylvia Suffers', *Time*, 9 May 1994, p. 76.
119. Alexis Greene, 'Theater Review', *Theater Week*, 9–15 May 1994, p. 33.
120. Jeremy Gerard, 'Broken Glass', *Variety*, 25 April 1994, p. 128.
121. David Richards, 'Theater: Broken Glass; A Paralysis Points to Social and Political Ills', *New York Times*, 25 April 1994.
122. Robert Brustein, 'Separated by a Common Playwright', *New Republic*, 30 May 1994, p. 126.
123. Bigsby, *Remembering Arthur Miller*, p. 205.
124. Recordings from rehearsals of *Broken Glass*, July 1994.
125. Eyre, *National Service*, p. 258.

126. John Peter, 'A Raw Slice of Humanity', *Sunday Times*, 14 August 1994.

127. Irving Wardle, 'Age Has Not Withered Him', *Independent on Sunday*, 7 August 1994, p. 22.

128. Arthur Miller, interview with the author, 1995.

129. *Bomb Magazine*, 49, Fall 1994.

130. Bigsby, *Remembering Arthur Miller*, p. 298.

12 ENDINGS

1. Briggs, *Arthur Miller in Conversation*, p. 22.

2. Michael March, 'From Here to Eternity', Prague Writers' Festival, 2001. http://www.pwf.cz/en/archives/ interviews/335.html, accessed 5 November 2009.

3. James Carroll and Helen Epstein, 'Seeing Eye to Eye: Arthur Miller in Conversation', *Boston Review*, February 1989.

4. Bigsby, *Remembering Arthur Miller*, pp. 141–2.

5. Arthur Miller, 'To Newt on Art', in *The Best of the Nation*, ed. Victor Navasky and Katrina vanden Heuvel (New York, 2000), pp. 379–80.

6. Stephen Farber, 'Miller & Son', *New York Times*, 17 November 1996, SM 58.

7. *Ibid.*

8. Nicholas Hytner, 'Director's Foreword', in *The Crucible: A Screenplay by Arthur Miller* (London, 1996), p. xii.

9. Jeff Gordimer, 'Casting a Spell', http://www.ew.com/article/0295362,00.ktml, accessed 16 May 2009.

10. Paula Span, 'Miller's Dialogue with the World', *Washington Post*, 15 December 1996.

11. Arthur Miller, 'Author's Note: *The Crucible* as Film', in *The Crucible: A Screenplay* (London, 1996), p. vi.

12. *Ibid.*, p. vii.

13. Victor Navasky, 'The Crucible', *New York Times*, 8 September 1996.

14. *Ibid.*

15. Paula Span, 'Miller's Dialogue with the World', *Washington Post*, 15 December 1996.

16. *Ibid.*

17. Richard Eyre, *National Service* (London, 2003), pp. 368–9.

18. *Ibid.*, pp. 368–9.

19. Lloyd Rose, '"The Crucible": Guilt Tripping', *Washington Post*, 20 December 1996.

20. http://vvww.rollingstone.com/reviews/movie/5948849/review/59488, accessed 16 May 2009.

21. Kenneth Turan, '*The Crucible*: Hysteria Resides at Heart of Frantic "Crucible"', *Los Angeles Times*, 13 December 1996.

22. Roger Ebert, 'The Crucible', *Chicago Sun-Times*, 20 December 1996.

23. http://bigthink com/ideas/rebecca-miller-on-the-creative-life-and-death, accessed 17 May 2009.

24. *Ibid.*

25. Rebecca Miller, interview with the author, 2001.

26. 'An Hour with Actor Daniel Day Lewis and Director Rebecca Miller', *The Charlie Rose Show*, 22 March 2005.

27. Eyre, *National Service*, p. 72.

28. Michael Ratcliffe, 'The Great

Playwright Sticks in America's Craw, But Not Ours', *Observer* Review section, 15 October 1995, p. 7.

29. Peter Marks, 'Tribute to a Man of the Crucible', *New York Times*, 1 November 1995.

30. Gottfried, *Arthur Miller: A Life*, pp. 442–3.

31. Ben Brantley, 'Arthur the Fall, Still Feeling Pain After the Fall', *New York Times*, 25 July 1996.

32. Ben Brantley, 'Theater Review: Tarnished Dreams Hold Painful Lessons', *New York Times*, 20 October 1997.

33. Ben Brantley, 'Theater Review: Incestuous Longings on the Waterfront', *New York Times*, 15 December 1997.

34. Ben Brantley, 'Theater Review: They Converse But Do Not Speak to Each Other', *New York Times*, 12 January 1998.

35. John Simon, 'In Brief: "A Double Bill" at the Signature Theatre Company', *New York*, 19 January 1998.

36. Ben Brantley, 'Peter Falk: Search for Meaning', *New York Times*, 18 May 1998.

37. Arthur Miller, Preface, *Mr Peters' Connections* (London, 2000), pp. v–vi.

38. *Ibid.*, pp. v–vi.

39. Miller, *Mr Peters' Connections* (2000), p. 3.

40. *Ibid.*, p. 10.

41. *Ibid.*, p. 27.

42. *Ibid.*, p. 22.

43. *Ibid.*, p. 29.

44. *Ibid.*, p. 23.

45. *Ibid.*, p. 40.

46. Michael March, 'The End of Illusions', *Guardian*, 29 October 2001.

47. Patrick Stewart, interview with the author, 19 September 2001.

48. Arthur Miller, 'Op-Ed: Salem Revisited', *New York Times*, 15 October 1998.

49. Christopher Hitchens, *No One Left to Lie To: The Values of the Worst Family* (New York, 1999), pp. 47–8.

50. Briggs, *Arthur Miller in Conversation*, p. 11.

51. Ben Brantley, 'Sure, Devoted to His Wife: Question Is, Which One?', *New York Times*, 17 November 1998.

52. Patrick Stewart, interview with the author, 19 September 2001.

53. Ben Brantley, 'Critic's Notebook: A Dark New Production Illuminates "Salesman"', *New York Times*, 3 November 1998.

54. Ben Brantley, 'Theater Review: Attention Must Be Paid', *New York Times*, 11 February 1999.

55. Bigsby, *Remembering Arthur Miller*, p. 48.

56. Donald Lyons, 'Miller's *Death* Gets a New Life', *New York Post*, 11 February 1999.

57. Clive Barnes, '*Salesman* is Still a Seller', *New York Post*, 14 February 1999.

58. Bernard Weinraub, 'Kazan Honor Stirs Protest by Blacklist Survivors', *New York Times*, 23 February 1999.

59. Jeff Kisseloff, 'Another Award, Other Memories of McCarthyism', *New York Times*, 30 May 1999.

60. Stephen Schwartz, 'The Rehabilitation of Elia Kazan', *Weekly Standard*, vol. 4, issue 20, 8 February 1999.

61. Ethan Bronner, 'Witching Hour; Rethinking McCarthyism, If Not McCarthy', *New York Times*, 18 October 1998.

62. 'Revisionist McCarthyism', *New York Times*, 23 October 1998.

63. Arthur Miller, 'Kazan and the Bad Times', *Nation*, 4 March 1999.

64. Bigsby, *Remembering Arthur Miller*, p. 128.

65. Arthur Miller, 'My Dinner with Castro', *Guardian*, 24 January 2004.

66. Bruce Weber, 'Arthur Miller Takes a Poke at a Devil with 2 Lives', *New York Times*, 10 April 2000.

67. Robert D. McFadden, 'Patrick Stewart Denounces Show's Producers at Curtain Calls', *New York Times*, 1 May 2000.

68. Arthur Miller, interview with the author, 2001.

69. Patrick Stewart, interview with the author, 2001.

70. Arthur Miller, letter to *New York Times*, 6 June 2000.

71. IBDB Internet Broadway Database.

72. Naomi Pfefferman, 'Out of *Focus*', *Jewish Journal*, 1 November 2001.

73. *Ibid.*

74. Bruce Weber, 'Shooting for a Place in the Operatic Canon', *New York Times*, 4 August 1991, B1, B5.

75. www.pbs.org/newshour/bb/ entertainment/july-dec99/ opera_12-17.html, accessed 5 November 2009.

76. Anthony Tommasini, 'Music Unlocks a Play's Secrets', *New York Times*, 11 October 1999, B1, B5.

77. Michael March, 'From Here to Eternity', Prague Writers' Festival, 2001. http://pwf.cz/en/archives/ interviews/335.html, accessed 5 November 2009.

78. Arthur Miller, *On Politics and the Art of Acting* (New York, 2001), p. 64.

79. *Ibid.*, pp. 64, 67.

80. *Ibid.*, p. 10.

81. *Ibid.*, pp. 20–1.

82. *Ibid.*, p. 25.

83. *Ibid.*, p. 32.

84. *Ibid.*, p. 40.

85. *Ibid.*, p. 77.

86. George Will, 'Enduring Arthur Miller: Oh, the Humanities', *Jewish World View*, 10 April 2001.

87. Jay Nordlinger, 'Back to Plessy, Easter with Fidel, Miller's New Tale, &c.;, *National Review*, 22 April 2002.

88. Bruce Weber, 'Deflation of an Optimist, by a Young Writer', *New York Times*, 24 July 2001.

89. Bigsby, *Remembering Arthur Miller*, pp. 138–9.

90. Regina Strassegger, *Inge Morath: Last Journey* (Munich, 2003), p. 206.

91. *Ibid.*, p. 209.

92. David Lister, 'Arthur Miller Accuses Bush of Abusing and Curbing Civil Rights', *Independent*, 22 December 2001.

93. Strassegger and Miller, *Inge Morath: Last Journey*, p. 16.

94. *Ibid.*, p. 33.

95. *Ibid.*, p. 127.

96. *Ibid.*, p. 147.

97. Honor Moore, *Red Shoes* (New York, 2005), pp. 55, 60–1.

98. Liz Welch, 'What They Were Thinking', *New York Times*, 29 December 2001.

99. Moore, *Red Shoes*, pp. 74–5.

100. Strassegger and Miller, *Inge Morath: Last Journey*, p. 176.

101. *Charley Rose Show*, 7 March 2002. http://www.charlierose.com/view/interview/2651, accessed 26 December 2009.

102. Arthur Miller, 'The Power and the Glamour', *Allure*, April 2002, p. 123.

103. Bigsby, *Remembering Arthur Miller*, p. 62.

104. Interview with the author, May 2002.

105. Arthur Miller, *Resurrection Blues* (London, 2006), p. 8.

106. *Ibid.*, p. 8.

107. Miller, *Danger: Memory!* (1986), p. 60.

108. Miller, *Resurrection Blues* (2006), p. 33.

109. *Ibid.*, pp. 54–5.

110. *Ibid.*, p. 46.

111. *Ibid.*, p. 18.

112. *Ibid.*, p. 18.

113. *Ibid.*, p. 21.

114. *Ibid.*, p. 28.

115. *Ibid.*, pp. 37, 33.

116. Interview with the author, May 2002.

117. *Ibid.*

118. Bruce Weber, 'It's Gloves-Off Time for an Angry Arthur Miller', *New York Times*, 15 August 2002.

119. Charles Laurence, 'America's Nagging Conscience', *Daily Telegraph*, 25 August 2002.

120. *Ibid.*

121. Michael Billington, 'The Crucifixion Will Be Televised', *Guardian*, 21 August 2001.

122. http://fundacionprincipedeasturias.org/en/multimedia/17/, accessed 13 June 2009.

123. Anthony Tommasini, 'Musical Diversity for Arthur Miller's Fated Red Hook', *New York Times*, 7 December 2002.

124. Catherine Hong, 'Painted Love', *W Magazine*, December 2004, p. 182.

125. *Ibid.*

126. http://www.jenbekman.com/agnesbarley/agnesbarley_statement.html, accessed 14 June 2009.

127. Joan Copeland, interview with the author, 2008.

128. Hong, 'Painted Love'.

129. Anon., 'At 89, Arthur Miller Grows Old Romantically', *Daily Telegraph*, 11 December 2004.

130. Hong, 'Painted Love'.

131. *Ibid.*

132. Anon., 'Agnes Barley: "recent work."' http://www.jenbekman.com/agnesbarley_press.html

133. Deborah Solomon, 'Goodbye (Again), Norma Jean', *New York Times*, 19 September 2004.

134. Sam Hamill, Sally Anderson, John J. Simon, 'Unacknowledged Legislators: Poets Protest the War – Poetry Supplement', *Monthly Review*, April 2003.

135. Kelefa Sanneh, 'Ambiguity Is a Guest at a Readers' Evening', *New York Times*, 19 February 2003.

136. Arthur Miller, 'Looking for a Conscience', *New York Times*, 23 February 2003.

137. Arthur Miller, 'Waiting for the Teacher', *Harper's*, July 1998.

138. Allan C. Brownfeld, 'The Contradiction between Israeli

Power and the Human Jewish Tradition', *Washington Report on Middle Eastern Affairs*, October 2003, pp. 54–5.

139. Alexander Cockburn, 'What Sontag Said in Jerusalem', *Nation*, 4 June 2001.

140. Arthur Miller, 'My Israel, You Will Never Know Peace until you Rediscover Justice'. http://www.timesonline. co.uk/ tol/life_and_style/article1147506. ece, accessed 15 June 2009.

141. Testimony of Arthur Miller, United States Senate Committee on the Judiciary, 28 April 2004. http://judiciary.senate.gov/ hearings/testimony.cfm?id= 1160&wit_id=3348, accessed 15 June 2009.

142. Arthur Miller, *Plays Six* (London, 2009), p. 204.

143. Ben Brantley, 'One Guilt Trip, Plain, and Hold the Agony', *New York Times*, 30 July 2004.

144. Bigsby, *Remembering Arthur Miller*, p. 68.

145. *Ibid.*, p. 174.

146. Michael Kuchwara, 'Playwright Miller Creates a New Work', MSNBC Wire Service, 21 October 2004.

147. Arthur Miller, interview with the author, 2003.

148. Miller, *Plays Six* (2009), p. 216.

149. *Ibid.*, p. 227.

150. *Ibid.*, p. 244.

151. *Ibid.*, p. 230.

152. *Ibid.*, p. 261.

153. *Ibid.*, p. 226.

154. *Ibid.*, p. 224.

155. *Ibid.*, p. 220.

156. *Ibid.*, p. 257.

157. *Ibid.*, p. 239.

158. *Ibid.*, p. 263.

159. Solomon, 'Goodbye (Again), Norma Jean'.

160. Ben Brantley, 'Some Like It Hot, Some Like It Painted in Words', *New York Times*, 11 October 2004.

161. Richard Christiansen, 'Miller's Tale', *Guardian*, 30 October 2004.

162. Stephen Marino, 'A Conversation with Joan Copeland', *Arthur Miller Journal*, vol. 3, number 1, Spring 2008, pp. 61–2.

163. Confirmed by an email from Agnes Burley to the author on 28 December 2009.

164. Elizabeth Maker and Bruce Weber, 'Arthur Miller's Refuge among the Pines', *New York Times*, 20 February 2005.

165. Michael March, 'The End of Illusions', *Guardian*, 29 October 2001.

166. Melvin Friedman, 'Valéry Larbaud: The Two Traditions of Eros', *Yale French Studies*, no. 11 (1953), p. 97.

167. Maker and Weber, 'Arthur Miller's Refuge'.

168. John Addyman, 'Roxbury Honors Arthur Miller', *Voices*, 14 May 2005. http://www.zwire.com/site/ news.cfm?newsid=14523693& BRD=1380&PAG=461&dept − id=157525&r fi=6, accessed 20 June 2009.

169. Bigsby, *Remembering Arthur Miller*, p. 18.

170. Patrick Pringle, 'Indian Journey on Death of Her Man', *Calcutta Telegraph*, 30 March 2006.

171. George Steiner, *Grammars of Creation* (London, 2001), p. 141.

172. *Ibid.*, p. 142.

173. Miller, *Echoes Down the Corridor* (2000), p. 186.

174. Albert Devlin, *Conversations with Tennessee Williams* (London, 1986), p. 99.

175. Graham Fuller, ed., *Potter on Potter* (London, 1993), p. 46.

BIBLIOGRAPHY

Abrams, Nathan David, *Struggling for Freedom: Arthur Miller, the Commentary Community and the Cultural Cold War* (Birmingham 1998).

Accrete, Peter, 'A Serious Man of Plays', *The Times*, 5 November 1987.

Addyman, John, 'Roxbury Honors Arthur Miller', *Voices*, 14 May 2005. http://www.zwire.com/site/news.cfrn?newsid=14523693&BRD=1380&PAG=461&dept_id=157525&rfi=6, accessed 20 June 2009.

Allen, Paul, *Alan Ayckbourn: Grinning at the Edge* (London, 2001).

Andrews, Suzanna, 'Arthur Miller's Missing Act', *Vanity Fair*, September 2007. http://www.vanityfair.com/fame/features/2007/09/miller200709

Anon., Agnes Barley: http://www.jenbekman.com/agnesbarley_press.html

Anon., 'At 89, Arthur Miller Grows Old Romantically', *Daily Telegraph*, 11 December 2004.

Appelfeld, Aharon, *The Healer*, trans. Jeffrey M. Green (London, 1992).

——, *The Immortal Bartfuss*, trans. Jeffrey M. Green (London, 1995).

Arendt, Hannah and Baehr, Peter, *The Portable Hannah Arendt* (New York, 2000).

Atlas, James, *Delmore Schwartz: The Life of an American Poet* (New York, 1977).

——, 'The Creative Journey of Arthur Miller Leads Back to Broadway and TV', *New York Times*, 28 September 1980.

Auchincloss, Louis, 'Recognizing Gaddis', *New York Times*, 15 November 1987.

Barnes, Clive, 'Arthur Miller's "The Price"', *New York Times*, 8 February 1968.

——, 'Arthur Miller's Creation', *New York Times*, 1 December 1972.

——, '"Salesman" Is Still a Seller', *New York Post*, 14 February 1999.

Barthel, Joan, *A Death in Canaan* (New York, 1976).

Bell, Daniel, *The End of Ideology: On the Exhaustion of Political Ideas in the 1950s* (New York, 1962).

Bentley, Eric, *What Is Theatre?* (London, 1969).

Bernstein, Richard, 'Theater; Acting against Type: The Self-Hating Jew', *New York Times*, 24 April 1994, section 2, p. 6.

Bettelheim, Bruno, *Recollections and Reflections* (London, 1990).

Bigsby, Christopher, ed., *Arthur Miller and Company* (London, 1990).

——, ed., *Writers in Conversation* (Norwich, 2001).

——, *Remembering Arthur Miller* (London, 2005).

——, *Arthur Miller: A Critical Study* (Cambridge, 2005).

Billen, Andrew, 'Arthur Miller: the Demonizing of My Father', *Times*, 25 July 2008.

Billington, Michael, 'The Crucifixion Will Be Televised', *Guardian*, 21 August 2001.

Blau, Herb, *To All Appearances: Ideology and Performance* (London, 1992).

Bloom, Ken, *Broadway: An Encyclopedia* (New York, 2004).

Boyers, Robert and Peggy, eds, *The Salmagundi Reader* (Bloomington, 1983).

Brantley, Ben, 'Arthur Miller: Still Feeling Pain After the Fall', *New York Times*, 25 July 1996.

——, 'Theater Review: Tarnished Dreams Hold Painful Lessons', *New York Times*, 20 October 1997.

——, 'Theater Review: Incestuous Longings on the Waterfront', *New York Times*, 15 December 1997.

——, 'Theater Review: They Converse But Do Not Speak to Each Other', *New York Times*, 12 January 1998.

——, 'Sure, Devoted to His Wife: Question Is, Which One?', *New York Times*, 17 November 1998.

——, 'Peter Falk: Search for Meaning,' *New York Times*, 18 May 1998.

——, 'Critic's Notebook: A Dark New Production Illuminates "Salesman"', *New York Times*, 3 November 1998.

——, 'Theater Review: Attention Must Be Paid', *New York Times*, 11 February 1999.

——, 'One Guilt Trip, Plain, and Hold the Agony', *New York Times*, 30 July 2004.

——, 'Some Like It Hot, Some Like It Painted in Words', *New York Times*, 11 October 2004.

Briggs, Murray, *Arthur Miller in Conversation* (New Haven, 2000).

Brightman, Carol, *Writing Dangerously: Mary McCarthy and Her World* (New York, 1992).

Bronner, Ethan, 'Witching Hour; Rethinking McCarthyism, if Not McCarthy', *New York Times*, 18 October 1998.

Brook, Peter, *The Empty Space* (London, 1968).

Brown, Georgina, 'How We Met: David Thacker and Arthur Miller', *Independent*, 30 April 1995.

Brown, Nick, 'Still Not Laid to Rest', *Sunday Times*, 8 November 1987.

Brownfeld, Allan C., 'The Contradiction between Israeli Power and the Human Jewish Tradition', *Washington Report on Middle Eastern Affairs*, October 2003.

Brustein, Robert, *Seasons of Discontent: Dramatic Opinions 1959–1965* (London, 1966).

——, *The Third Theatre* (London, 1970).

——, *Making Scenes* (New York, 1981).

——, 'Separated by a Common Playwright', *New Republic*, 30 May 1994.

Burroughs, William, 'The Coming of the Purple Better One', in *Smiling through the Apocalypse: Esquire's History of the Sixties* (New York, 1970).

Camus, Albert, *The Fall*, trans. Stuart Gilbert (Harmondsworth, 1963).

Carroll, James and Epstein, Helen, 'Seeing Eye to Eye: Arthur Miller in Conversation', *Boston Review*, February 1989.

Cech, Rick, 'Coffin, Miller Address Rally', *Yale Daily News*, 4 November 1968.

Chamberlain, John, 'These Days: Arthur Miller's Position', *Washington Post*, 2 November 1965.

Chang, Jung and Halliday, Jon, *Mao: The Unknown Story* (London, 2007).

Chester, Lewis, Hodgson, Godfrey and Page, Bruce, *An American Melodrama: The Presidential Campaign of 1968* (London, 1969).

Christiansen, Richard, 'Miller's Tale', *Guardian*, 30 October 2004.

Clurman, Harold, 'Director's Notes: *Incident at Vichy*', *Tulane Drama Review*, vol. 9, Summer 1965.

——, *All People Are Famous* (New York, 1974).

Cobb, Russell, 'The Politics of Literary Prestige: Promoting the Latin American "Boom" in the pages of *Mundo Nuevo*'. www.ncsu.edu/project/acontracorriente/spring_08/Cobb, accessed 31 October 2009.

Cockburn, Alexander, 'What Sontag Said in Jerusalem', *Nation*, 4 June 2001.

Coleman, Peter, *The Liberal Conspiracy: The Congress for Cultural Freedom and the Struggle for the Mind of Postwar Europe* (New York, 1989).

Connery, Donald S., *Guilty until Proven Innocent* (New York, 1977).

Corliss, Richard, 'Soloists in a Choir of Martyrs', *Time*, 29 September 1980.

Crowther, Bosley, 'Screen: John Huston's *The Misfits*', *New York Times*, 2 February 1961.

Davies, Hunter, 'Arthur Miller', *Sunday Times*, 23 January 1966.

Delbo, Charlotte, *None of Us Will Return* (New York, 1968), pp. 95–7.

Denby, David, 'Arthur Miller, America's connoisseur of Guilt: All My Sins', *New Republic*, 8 February, 1988, pp. 30–4.

Devlin, Albert, ed., *Conversations with Tennessee Williams* (London, 1986).

Dudar, Helen, 'New Life for an Arthur Miller Play', *New York Times*, 30 January 1983.

——, 'A Modern Tragedy's Road to Maturity', *New York Times*, 25 March 1984.

Ebert, Roger, 'The Crucible', *Chicago Sun-Times*, 20 December 1996.

Epstein, Leslie, 'The Unhappiness of Arthur Miller', *Tri-Quarterly*, Spring 1965, pp. 165–73.

Eyre, Richard, *Utopia and Other Places: Memoir of a Young Director* (London, 1993).

——, *National Service: Diary of a Decade at the National Theatre* (London, 2003).

——, *Talking Theatre: Interviews with Theatre People* (London, 2009).

Ezra, Michael, 'The Eichmann Polemics: Hannah Arendt and Her Critics', *Democratiya*, 9, Summer 2007.

Fallaci, Oriana, 'Apropos of *After the Fall*', *World Theatre*, January–February 1965, pp. 79–81.

Farber, Stephen, 'Miller & Son', *New York Times*, 17 November 1996, SM 58.

Fast, Howard, *The Naked God: The Writer and the Communist Party* (London, 1958).

Faulkner Wells, Dean, ed., *The Great American Writers' Cookbook* (Oxford, Miss., 1981).

Fénelon, Fania, *Playing for Time*, trans. Judith Landry (Syracuse, 1997).

Fitzgerald, F. Scott, *The Crack Up* (New York, 1945).

Foot, John, 'The Secret Life of Ignazio Silone', *New Left Review*, 3, May–June 2000.

Freedman, Samuel G., 'Miller Tries a New Form for an Old Play', *New York Times*, 23 October 1983.

——, '"Salesman" Collaborators Part Ways', *New York Times*, 15 August 1984.

——, 'Miller's Fighting Group's Use of Segment from "Crucible"', 17 November 1984.

Funke, Lewis, 'Stars Help Arthur Miller Film TV Antiwar Allegory', *New York Times*, 17 November 1969.

Gass, William H., 'East and West in Lithuania: Rising Tempers at a Writers' Meeting', *New York Times*, 2 February 1986.

Gelb, Barbara, 'Question: Am I My Brother's Keeper?', *New York Times*, 29 November 1964.

Genet, Jean, 'The Members of the Assembly', trans. Richard Seaver, in Harold Hayes, ed., *Smiling through the Apocalypse: Esquire's History of the Sixties* (New York, 1969).

Gerard, Jeremy, 'Broken Glass', *Variety*, 25 April 1994.

Gilman, Richard, *The Confusion of Realms* (New York, 1969).

——, *Common and Uncommon Masks: Writings on Theater 1961–1970* (New York, 1972).

——, *The Drama Is Coming Now: The Theater Criticism of Richard Gilman 1961–1991* (New York, 2005).

Gordimer, Jeff, 'Casting a Spell', http://www.ew.com/article/0,,295362,00.ktml, accessed 16 May 2009.

Gottfried, Martin, *Opening Nights: Theater Criticism of the Sixties* (New York, 1969).

——, *Arthur Miller: A Life* (London, 2003).

Greene, Alexis, 'Theater Review', *Theater Week*, 9–15 May 1994.

Gussow, Mel, 'Arthur Miller Returns to Genesis for First Musical', *New York Times*, 17 April 1974.

——, 'Stage: Wooster Group', *New York Times*, 31 October 1984.

——, 'Theater: Revised "Last Yankee", Will Focus on Wives', *New York Times*, 22 January 1993.

——, *Conversations with Arthur Miller* (London, 2002).

Hamill, Sam, Anderson, Sally, Simon, John J., 'Unacknowledged Legislators: Poets Protest the War – Poetry Supplement', *Monthly Review*, April 2003.

Hamilton, Ian, *Robert Lowell* (London, 1983).

Hamilton, Saskia, ed., *The Letters of Robert Lowell* (London, 2005).

Havel, Václav, 'My Temptation', in *The Embarrassment of Tyrannies: 25 Years of Index on Censorship*, ed. Webb, W.L. and Bell, Rose (London, 1997).

Hayes, Harold, ed., *Smiling through the Apocalypse: Esquire's History of the Sixties* (New York, 1969).

Hellman, Lillian, *Three: An Unfinished Woman, Pentimento, Scoundrel Time* (London, 1979).

——, *Maybe* (Boston, 1980).

Henry III, William A., 'A Life of Fade-Outs and Fade-Ins', *Time*, 23 November 1987.

——, 'Sylvia Suffers', *Time*, 9 May 1994, p. 76.

Hersh, Burton, 'The Last Kennedy', in *Smiling through the Apocalypse: Esquire's History of the Sixties*, ed. Harold Hayes (New York, 1969).

Higgins, Marguerite, 'On the Spot: Miller's Level of Ignorance', *Newsday*, 8 November 1965, p. 37.

Hingley, Ronald, *Chekhov* (London, 1950).

Hitchens, Christopher, *No One Left to Lie To: The Values of the Worst Family* (New York, 1999).

Hong, Catherine, 'Painted Love', *W Magazine*, December 2004, p. 182.

Howe, Desson, '"Music Box"' and "Everybody Wins"', *Washington Post*, 26 January 1990.

Howe, Irving, 'On Vietnam', *Partisan Review*, 32, 4 (Fall 1965), p. 627.

——, *A Margin of Hope* (London, 1983).

Hytner, Nicholas, 'Director's Foreword', in *The Crucible: A Screenplay by Arthur Miller* (London, 1996).

Isser, Edward, 'Arthur Miller and the Holocaust', *Essays in Theatre*, 10, ii, May 1992.

James, William, *Writings 1878–1899* (New York, 1992).

Jaspers, Karl, *The Question of German Guilt*, trans. E.B. Ashton (New York, 2000).

Johnson, Kirk, 'Arthur Miller's Vision of Love Becomes a Movie', *New York Times*, 11 June 1989.

Kakutani, Michiko, 'Arthur Miller: View of a Life', *New York Times*, 9 May 1984.

Kauffmann, Stanley, *Persons of the Drama: Theater Criticism and Comment* (New York, 1976).

Kazan, Elia, *A Life* (New York, 1988).

Kazin, Alfred, *New York Jew* (New York, 1978).

——, 'Apologia pro Vita Sua', *New Yorker*, 14 December 1987.

Kempley, Rita, 'Everybody Wins', *Washington Post*, 20 January 1990.

Kerry, John, 'Kerry's Testimony', *National Review Online*, 23 April 2004. http://www.national review.com/document/kerry200404231047.asp

Kirshon, John W., *Chronicle of America* (Farnborough, 1995).

Kisseloff, Jeff, 'Another Award, Other Memories of McCarthyism', *New York Times*, 30 May 1999.

Klein, Alvin, 'Theatre: "Broken Glass", the New Haven Tryout That Isn't', *New York Times*, 3 April 1994.

Knappman, Edward W., *Presidential Election 1968* (New York, 1970).

Knowles, Dorothy, *Armand Gatti in the Theatre: Wild Duck against the Wind* (London, 1989).

Kuchwara, Michael, 'Playwright Miller Creates a New Work', MSNBC Wire Service, 21 October 2004.

Lahr, John, *Up Against the Fourth Wall: Essays on Modern Theater* (New York, 1970).

——, 'Talk of the Town: Miller's Tales', *New Yorker*, 11 April 1994.

——, 'Dead Souls', *New Yorker*, 9 May 1994.

Laurence, Charles, 'America's Nagging Conscience', *Daily Telegraph*, 25 August 2002.

Lawson, Nigella, 'The All-American Outsider', *Sunday Times*, 28 January 1990.

Levi, Primo and Rosenthal, R., *The Drowned and the Saved* (London, 1991).

Lewis, Robert, *Slings and Arrows: Theater in My Life* (New York, 1984).

Lister, David, 'Arthur Miller Accuses Bush of Abusing and Curbing Civil Rights', *Independent*, 22 December 2001.

Lowell, Robert, *Collected Prose*, ed. Robert Giroux (London, 1987), p. 371.

Lyons, Donald, 'Miller's *Death* Gets a New Life', *New York Post*, 11 February 1999.

Maas, Willard, *Film Culture*, 29, 1963, pp. 55–63.

Macdonald, Dwight, 'Arguments', *Partisan Review* 31 (1964), pp. 262–3.

Mailer, Norman, *Miami and the Siege of Chicago* (New York, 1968).

Maker, Elizabeth and Weber, Bruce, 'Arthur Miller's Refuge among the Pines', *New York Times*, 20 February 2005.

March, Michael, 'From Here to Eternity', Prague Writers' Festival, 2001. http://www.pwf cz/en/archives/interviews/335.html, accessed 5 November 2009.

——, 'The End of Illusions', *Guardian*, 29 October 2001.

Marks, Peter, 'Tribute to a Man of the Crucible', *New York Times*, 1 November 1995.

Martin, Robert A., ed., *The Theatre Essays of Arthur Miller* (London, 1978).

——, and Centola, Steven R., *The Theater Essays of Arthur Miller*, revised and expanded (New York, 1996).

May, Ernest R. and Fraser, Janet, *Campaign '72: The Managers Speak* (Cambridge, 1973).

McCarthy, Eugene, *Up 'Til Now* (New York, 1987).

McCarthy, Mary, 'Arguments', *Partisan Review* 31 (1964).

——, *Hanoi* (London, 1968).

——, *A Bolt from the Blue and Other Essays* (New York, 2002).

McClean, Lydia, 'A Weekend with the Millers', *Vogue*, 15, March 1972, pp. 105ff.

McFadden, Robert D., 'Patrick Stewart Denounces Show's Producers at Curtain Calls', *New York Times*, 1 May 2000.

McGrath, Ben, 'Vermont Postcard: The Light of Sunday', *New Yorker*, 1 December 2003, p. 39.

Mills, C. Wright, *The Sociological Imagination* (Harmondsworth, 1970; first published, 1959).

Moore, Charlotte, 'The Throwaway Child', *Guardian*, Family section, 23 May 2009.

Moore, Honor, *Red Shoes* (New York, 2005).

Morath, Inge and Miller, Arthur, *In Russia* (New York, 1969).

—— and Miller, Arthur, *In the Country* (New York, 1977).

—— and Miller, Arthur, *Chinese Encounters* (New York, 1979).

——, *Portraits* (New York, 1986).

——, and Miller, Arthur, *Russian Journal 1965–1990* (London, 1991).

——, 'About My Photographs', *Michigan Quarterly Review*, Fall 1998.

——, *The Road to Reno* (London, 2006).

——, Payn, Graham, eds, *The Noël Coward Diaries* (London, 1982).

Morley, Sheridan, 'Just a Lot of Show Business', *The Times*, 11 January 1989.

Moynahan, Brian, '1989', *Sunday Times* magazine, 3 May 2009, p. 20.

Navasky, Victor, 'The Crucible', *New York Times*, 8 September 1996.

Neill, Heather, 'Yours Precisely, Arthur Miller', *The Times*, 1 February 1990.

Nordlinger, Jay, 'Back to Plessy, Easter with Fidel, Miller's New Tale, &c', *National Review*, 22 April 2002.

O'Connor, John J., '"Fame", Comedy by Arthur Miller', *New York Times*, 30 November 1978.

Osborne, John, 'A Nice Guy Who Hasn't Finished Yet', *Spectator*, 5 December 1987.

Pamuk, Orhan, 'Freedom to Write', *New York Review of Books*, 25 May 2006.

Peter, John, 'A Raw Slice of Humanity', *Sunday Times*, 14 August 1994.

Petit, Chris, 'A Game Concocted by the Criminally Insane', *Guardian*, 7 March 2009, Review section, p. 8.

Pfefferman, Naomi, 'Out of *Focus*', *Jewish Journal*, 1 November 2001.

Pringle, Patrick, 'Indian Journey on Death of Her Man', *Telegraph*, Calcutta, 30 March 2006.

Rahv, Philip, *Literature and the Sixth Sense* (London, 1970).

Ratcliffe, Michael, 'The Great Playwright Sticks in America's Craw, But Not Ours', *Observer*, 15 October 1995, Review section, p. 7.

Rich, Frank, 'Miller's "American Clock"', *New York Times*, 12 November 1980.

——, 'Stage: 2 by Arthur Miller; New Haven', *New York Times*, 10 November 1982.

——, 'Stage: Miller's "Up from Paradise"', *New York Times*, 26 October 1983.

——, 'Hoffman, "Death of a Salesman"', *New York Times*, 30 March 1984.

——, 'Arthur Miller's "Danger: Memory!"', *New York Times*, 9 February 1987.

——, 'Theater: Richard Kiley in Miller's "All My Sons"', *New York Times*, 23 April 1987.

Richards, David, 'Theater: Broken Glass; A Paralysis Points to Social and Political Ills', *New York Times*, 25 April 1994.

Rifkin, Ron, 'Arthur Miller', *Bomb Magazine*, 49, Fall 1994.

Robins, Natalie, *Alien Ink: The FBI's War on Freedom of Expression* (New York, 1992).

Rocamora, Carol, *Acts of Courage: Václav Havel's Life in the Theater* (Hanover, 2005).

Rogoff, Gordon, 'Treadmiller', *Village Voice*, 17 February 1987, p. 99.

Rose, Charlie, 'An Hour with Actor Daniel Day Lewis and Director Rebecca Miller', *The Charlie Rose Show*, 22 March 2005.

Rose, Lloyd, '"The Crucible": Guilt Tripping', *Washington Post*, 20 December 1996.

Rosenberg, David, ed., *Genesis: Contemporary Writers on Our First Stories* (San Francisco, 1996).

Rosenberg, Harold, 'The Trial and Eichmann', in Norman Podhoretz, ed., *The Commentary Reader: Two Decades of Articles and Stories* (New York, 1966).

Roth, Philip, 'Writing American Fiction', in Norman Podhoretz, ed., *The Commentary Reader: Two Decades of Articles and Stories* (New York, 1966).

Roudané, Matthew, *Conversations with Arthur Miller* (Jackson, 1987).

Sanneh, Kelefa, 'Ambiguity Is a Guest at a Readers' Evening', *New York Times*, 19 February 2003.

Saunders, Frances Stonor, *Who Paid the Piper: The CIA and the Cultural Cold War* (London, 1999).

Schlesinger Jr, Arthur, 'Behind That Anatolian Smile', *New York Times*, 1 May 1988.

Schwartz, Stephen, 'The Rehabilitation of Elia Kazan', *Weekly Standard*, vol. 4, issue 20, 8 February 1999.

Sebald, W.G., *On the Natural History of Destruction* (London, 2003).

Shattuck, Roger, 'He Who Is Most Alone', *New York Times*, 8 November 1987.

Shewey, Don, 'The Devil in Liz LeCompte', December 1983. www.donshewey.com/theater_articles/wooster_group_lsd.html, accessed 4 April 2009.

——, 'TV's Custom-tailored "Salesman"', *New York Times*, 15 September 1985.

Shils, Edward, 'Remembering the Congress for Cultural Freedom', *Encounter*, vol. 75, September 1990, pp. 53–65.

Simon, John, *Singularities* (New York, 1975).

——, 'Whose Paralysis Is It, Anyway?', *New York Magazine*, 9 May 1994.

——, 'In Brief: "A Double Bill" at the Signature Theatre Company', *New York*, 19 January 1998.

Simonson, Robert, 'Values, Old and New: Arthur Miller and John Tillinger on *The Last Yankee*', *Theater Week*.

Solomon, Deborah, 'Goodbye (Again), Norma Jean', *New York Times*, 19 September 2004.

Solzhenitsyn, Alexandr, 'A World Split Apart', http://Columbia.edu/cu/Augustine/arch/solzenitsyn/harvard1978, accessed 23 February 2009.

Sontag, Susan, 'Going to the Theater and the Movies', *Partisan Review*, 33, Spring 1964.

——, *Against Interpretation* (New York, 1966), pp. 285–7.

Span, Paula, 'Miller's Dialogue with the World', *Washington Post*, 15 December 1996.

Steiner, George, *Grammars of Creation* (London, 2001).

Strassegger, Regina and Miller, Arthur, *Inge Morath: Last Journey* (Munich, 2003).

Styron, William, *Darkness Visible: A Memoir of Madness* (New York, 1990).

——, *Havanas in Camelot* (New York, 2008).

Sullivan, Dan, '*Salesman* Shrunk in the Big Eye's Glare', *Los Angeles Times*, 22 September 1985.

Swift, Shayla, 'Lost Lessons: American Media Depictions of the Frankfurt Auschwitz Trial 1963–1965'. digitalcommons.unl.edu/cgi/viewcontent.cgi?article=1005&context=historyrawleyconference, accessed 27 December 2008.

Taubman, Howard, 'A Cheer for Controversy', *New York Times*, 2 February 1964.

Thomson, David, 'The Scene Maker', *New Republic*, 9 May 1988.

Tommasini, Anthony, 'Music Unlocks a Play's Secrets', *New York Times*, 11 October 1999, B1, B5.

——, 'Musical Diversity for Arthur Miller's Fated Red Hook', *New York Times*, 7 December 2002.

Turan, Kenneth, '*The Crucible*: Hysteria Resides at Heart of Frantic "Crucible"', *Los Angeles Times*, 13 December 1996.

Tuttleton, James W., '"Timebends", by Arthur Miller', *Commentary*, March 1988.

Vladislaw, Jan, ed., *Václav Havel. Living in Truth* (London, 1987).

Voznesensky, Andrei, *Nostalgia for the Present* (Oxford, 1980), pp. 56–7.

Wald, Alan M., *The Rise and Decline of the Anti-Stalinist Left from the 1930s to the 1980s* (Chapel Hill, 1987).

Wapshott, Nicholas, 'Tony Rehabilitates Vanessa Redgrave', *The Times*, 10 June 2003.

Wardle, Irving, 'Miller Back with a Loser's Tale', *Independent*, 31 January 1993.

——, 'Age Has Not Withered Him', *Independent on Sunday*, 7 August 1994.

Weatherby, W.J., *Conversations with Marilyn* (New York, 1992).

Webb, W.L. and Bell, Rose (eds), *An Embarrassment of Tyrannies: 25 Years of the Index on Censorship* (London, 1997).

Weber, Bruce, 'Shooting for a Place in the Operatic Canon', *New York Times*, 4 August 1991, B1, B5.

—— 'Arthur Miller Takes a Poke at a Devil with 2 Lives', *New York Times*, 10 April 2000.

——, 'Deflation of an Optimist, by a Young Writer', *New York Times*, 24 July 2001.

——, 'It's Gloves-Off Time for an Angry Arthur Miller', *New York Times*, 15 August 2002.

Weiner, Tim, *Legacy of Ashes: The History of the CIA* (New York, 2007).

Weinraub, Bernard, 'Kazan Honor Stirs Protest by Blacklist Survivors', *New York Times*, 23 February 1999.

Welch, Liz, 'What They Were Thinking', *New York Times*, 29 December 2001.

White, Theodore H., *The Making of the President: 1972* (New York, 1973).

Will, George, 'Enduring Arthur Miller: Oh, the Humanities', *Jewish World View*, 10 April 2001.

Williams, Shirley, *Climbing the Bookshelves* (London, 2009).

Wolf, Matt, 'Run of the Millers', *Observer*, 4 February 1990.

Wren, Christopher S., 'For Arthur Miller, Denial is a Key to Apartheid', *New York Times*, 6 December 1990.

Zinoman, Jason, 'Miller's Crossing', *Time Out*, 27 January–2 February 2005.

——, 'A New Stage for Arthur Miller's Most Private Drama of Fathers and Sons', *New York Times*, 30 August 2007.

WORKS BY ARTHUR MILLER

'With Respect for Her Agony – but with Love', *Life*, LVI, 7 February 1964, p. 66.

'On Obliterating the Jews', *New Leader*, 16 March 1964, p. 7.

After the Fall (Harmondsworth, 1965).

'Our Guilt for the World's Evil', *New York Times Magazine*, 3 January 1965, p. 10.

'The Writer as Independent Spirit', *Saturday Review*, 4 June 1966, pp. 16–17.

I Don't Need You Any More (London, 1967).

'On the Shooting of Robert Kennedy', *New York Times*, 8 June 1968.

'Carta al Presidente de Mexico', *La Pajarita de Papel*, number 4, October–December 1968, p. 1.

with Inge Morath, *In Russia* (New York, 1969).

Letter to the *New York Review of Books*, vol. 11, number 12, 2 January 1969.

'Are We Interested in Stopping the Killing?', *New York Times*, 8 June 1969, D 21.

'The War between the Young and the Old, or Why Willy Loman Can't Understand What's Happening', *McCall's*, July 1970, p. 32.

The Reason Why, directed by Paul Leaf, produced by Gino Giglio, 1970.

'Will They Create Repertory?' *Dramatists' Guild Quarterly*, Summer 1971, vol. 8, section 2, pp. 1–2.

'Miracles', *Esquire*, September 1973, p. 113.

et al., 'Soviet Inhumanity', *New York Review of Books*, vol. 21, number 11, 27 June 1974.

'Sakharov, Détente and Liberty', *New York Times*, 5 July 1974.

'The Prague Winter', *New York Times*, 16 July 1975, p. 37C.

'Toward a New Foreign Policy', *Society*, March–April 1976, pp. 10–11, 15–16.

'The Poosidin's Resignation', *Boston University Journal*, XXIV, 1976.

'The 1928 Buick', *Atlantic Monthly*, vol. 242, October 1976, pp. 51ff.

and Inge Morath, *In the Country* (New York, 1977).

'The Sin of Power', in *An Embarrassment of Tyrannies: 25 Years of the Index on Censorship*, ed. W.L. Webb and Rose Bell (London, 1997), May–June 1978, p. 3.

and Inge Morath, *Chinese Encounters* (New York, 1979), p. 112.

'A Kind of Despair', in Webb and Bell, *Index on Censorship*, 6, 1981, p. 31.

Playing for Time (New York, 1981).

The American Clock (London, 1983).

Two-Way Mirror (London, 1984).

Salesman in Beijing (London, 1984).

'School Prayer: A Political Dirigible', *New York Times*, 12 March 1984.

'Arthur Miller Speaks Out on the Election', *Literary Cavalcade*, November 1984, pp. 4–5.

Danger: Memory! (New York, 1986).

Timebends (New York, 1987).

et al., 'In Korean Jails', *New York Review of Books*, vol. 35, number 18, 24 November 1988.

'Selected Letters of Eugene O'Neill', *New York Times*, 6 November 1988.

'On Rushdie and Global Censorship,' *Authors' Guild Bulletin*, Summer 1989, pp. 5–6.

'The Worst Enemy of the People Is the Poisoner of the Mind', *Guardian*, 30 January 1989.

The American Clock and The Archbishop's Ceiling (New York, 1989).

'Death in Tiananmen', *New York Times*, 10 September 1989.

et al., 'Celebrating Mencken', *New York Review of Books*, vol. 37, number 4, 15 March 1990.

Everybody Wins (London, 1990).

Plays Three (London, 1990).

Arena: Miller Meets Mandela, BBC Television, recorded 3 December 1990, transmitted 18 January 1991.

'Lost Horizon', *American Theater*, July–August 1992, p. 68.

Broken Glass (London, 1994).

Plays Five (London, 1995).

Homely Girl (New York, 1995).

The Crucible: A Screenplay (London, 1996).

'The Sin of Power', in *Embarrassment of Tyrannies: 25 Years of the Index on Censorship*, ed. W.L. Webb and Rose Bell (London, 1997).

'Waiting for the Teacher', *Harper's*, July 1998.

'Op-Ed: Salem Revisited', *New York Times*, 15 October 1998.

'The Past and Its Power: Why I Wrote *The Price*', *New York Times*, 14 November 1999.

'Kazan and the Bad Times', *Nation*, 4 March 1999.

'To Newt on Art', in *The Best of the Nation*, ed. Victor Navasky and Katrina vanden Heuvel (New York, 2000), pp. 379–80.

Mr Peters' Connections (London, 2000).

Arthur Miller in Conversation with Murray Briggs, Ninth Annual Maynard Mack Lecture (New Haven, 2000).

Echoes Down the Corridor: Collected Essays 1944–2000, ed. Steven R. Centola (New York, 2000).

Letter to the *New York Times*, 6 June 2000.

www.pbs.org/newshour/bb/entertainment/july-dec99/opera_ 12–17.html, accessed 5 November 2009.

On Politics and the Art of Acting (New York, 2001).

'The Power and the Glamor', *Allure*, April 2002, p. 123.

'My Israel, You Will Never Know Peace until You Rediscover Justice', *The Times*, 3 July 2003.

'Arthur Miller, Elia Kazan and the Blacklist: None without Sin', WNET New York, 3 September 2003.

'My Dinner with Castro', *Guardian*, 24 January 2004.

Testimony of Arthur Miller, United States Senate Committee on the Judiciary, 28 April 2004. http://judiciary.senate.gov/hearings/testimony.cfm?id=1160&wit_id=3348, accessed 15 June 2009.

Resurrection Blues (London, 2006).

Presence (New York, 2007).

Plays Six (London, 2009).

ACKNOWLEDGEMENTS

As with the first volume of this biography, primary acknowledgement must go to Arthur Miller for granting me access to all his papers and for conversations over many years, and to Inge Morath for allowing me to interview her and for her unstinting hospitality. I am particularly grateful to Arthur's sister Joan Copeland, to his son Robert and his daughter Rebecca. I am also grateful to all those who assisted me, including Honor Moore, Miller's able and helpful assistant Julia Bolus, and members of the Arthur Miller Society, especially Joseph Kane and Stephen Marino; to those who allowed me to reproduce their correspondence; and to International PEN for allowing me to quote from the letters of their General Secretary David Carver. I thank the Harry Ransom Center of the University of Texas and the Special Collections room of the University of Michigan, and the Arts and Humanities Board for their research leave grant.

I have drawn throughout on materials that Arthur Miller made available to me for two years before his papers were passed to the Harry Ransom Center. Where I refer to his private papers, these are now to be found in the care of those who administer that remarkable literary archive.

The author and publisher are grateful to Honor Moore for permission to reproduce her poems on pp. 482–3 and pp. 484–5 (© 2005 by Honor Moore). If we have been unable to locate copyright owners we shall be very happy to make acknowledgement in any subsequent edition.

INDEX